Eighty-fifth Annual Meeting of the

NATIONAL COMMUNICATION ASSOCIATION

Nov. 4 - 7, 1999
Chicago

Concurrent meetings with the:

American Alliance for Theatre and Education
American Association for Rhetoric of Science and Technology
American Debate Association
American Forensic Association
American Society for the History of Rhetoric
Association for Chinese Communication Studies
Association for Communication Administration
Association for Rhetoric and Communication in South Africa
Chinese Communication Association
Commission on American Parliamentary Practice
Cross Examination Debate Association
Delta Sigma Rho – Tau Kappa Alpha
International Listening Association
Kenneth Burke Society, NCA Branch
Korean American Communication Association
Lambda Pi Eta
National Federation Interscholastic Speech and Debate Association
National Forensic Association
Religious Speech Communication Association

National Communication Association
5105 Backlick Road, Bldg E
Annandale VA 22003
703-750-0533
www.natcom.org

Orlando L. Taylor
President

Raymie E. McKerrow
First Vice President

James L. Applegate
Second Vice President

James L. Gaudino
Executive Director

William F. Eadie
Associate Director

Sherwyn P. Morreale
Associate Director

Ann Nadjar
Publications Manager

Maureen Coleman
*Controller/Director
of Operations*

TABLE OF CONTENTS

Convention Information

Convention Theme 4

Registration and General Convention Information 5

Floor Plans: Chicago Hilton & Towers 8

Placement Center Information. 12

Acknowledgments. 13

Local Arrangements Committee 15

Association Information

NCA Presidents 16

NCA Officers, Staff, and Editors 17

NCA Legislative Council 17

NCA Administrative Committee 20

Officers of Affiliated Organizations Holding Concurrent Meetings 21

NCA Conventions 23

Program Listings

Events of General Convention Interest. 24

Preconvention Conferences 25

Seminar Series. 27

Short Courses 29

Business Meetings 34

Convention Schedule for Wednesday, Nov. 3 43

Convention Schedule for Thursday, Nov. 4 51

Convention Schedule for Friday, Nov. 5 131

Convention Schedule for Saturday, Nov. 6 223

Convention Schedule for Sunday, Nov. 7. 297

2000 Call

Call for Papers for 2000 Convention in Seattle 325

Indices

Index of Program Sponsors. 355

Index of Program Participants 359

Exhibitors Directory/Exhibit Hours 391

Index of Advertisers 393

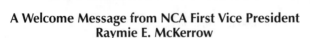

A Welcome Message from NCA First Vice President Raymie E. McKerrow

Dear Colleague:

I am writing on behalf of the program planners to invite you to Chicago for NCA's 85th Annual Convention. This is a "members convention" featuring programs the unit planners have deemed worthy of selection and presentation. I believe you will find their choices to be intellectually stimulating, at times provocative, and hopefully rewarding. Beyond sharing research ideas in formal programs, the convention also serves as a means to enhance your own network of friends and acquaintances, as you hear new ideas, meet new people, and begin plans for collaboration not envisioned prior to attending.

We return once again to the Chicago Hilton & Towers as the central convention hotel, with meetings also held in the adjacent Essex Inn, and in the Spertus Museum. Chicago promises to be a pleasant and pleasurable place to mix and mingle with friends. There will be a variety of extra-convention activities you may elect to participate in as well.

The convention theme, **Coloring Outside the Lines**, serves as a ready vehicle for many of the programs featured at this convention, as scholars recapture the sense of freedom enjoyed in our youth—when in the free play of our childhood, lines, borders and boundaries could be crossed with ease, and colors mixed in as creative a way as our imagination suggested—when the potentialities for what could be were less limited by rules, structures, discipline, and authority.

The new program series, "Challenging Boundaries," exemplifies this theme, as do several other programs scheduled across the convention. Three other programming changes also reflect the intent to promote this as the "members convention":

First, we created an opportunity at this convention for those wishing to participate in poster sessions to do so of their own free will.

Second, in lieu of using plenary sessions for keynote addresses, we have moved about a dozen or so *panel presentations* into each of the prime-time hours at 11 a.m. on Friday and Saturday; these panels represent a diverse set of disciplinary research issues and will give participants an opportunity to choose among a much smaller than normal set of programs (as other sessions will feature 30 or more).

Third, we have collapsed the Presidential Address and Awards Assembly into one late afternoon program session on Saturday — this will permit us to run a longer than normal program, and permit all attendees to participate.

I am very pleased to announce that this year's Arnold Lecturer will be Kathleen Hall Jamieson, Chair of the Annenberg School at the University of Pennsylvania. Prof. Jamieson has long been actively involved with political communication issues, both as a scholar and as a contributor on C-Span, NPR and the national networks.

Thanks for the programming efforts for this convention go to the unit planners, both for NCA units, as well as for all of the affiliate organizations whose members will attend and participate in this convention. There will be over 950 programs, along with more than 200 business meetings spread across the convention, from Pre-Conferences and Seminars on Wednesday, November 3, through the final program session ending at noon on Sunday, November 7.

Join us in Chicago for what promises to be a fulfilling, and perhaps even challenging time, as we, together, **color outside the lines**!

Sincerely,
Raymie E. McKerrow, NCA First Vice President

GENERAL INFORMATION
Registration

All members and guests are urged to register (or complete preregistration) as soon after arriving as possible. Admission to the meetings and to the Exhibit Hall will be by badge only. The NCA registration area, located on the lower level of the Chicago Hilton & Towers, will be open as follows:

ADVANCE REGISTRANTS CHECK-IN ONLY
Wednesday, November 3, 3:00-6:00 p.m.

REGULAR REGISTRATION
Wednesday, November 3, 6:00 p.m. to 8:00 p.m.

Thursday, November 4, 7:30 a.m. to 5:00 p.m.

Friday, November 5, 7:30 a.m. to 5:00 p.m.

Saturday, November 6, 7:30 a.m. to 5:00 p.m.

Sunday, November 7, 9:00 a.m. to 10:00 a.m.

Membership

Be sure to keep your membership current. Memberships that expire in October or before must be renewed before pre-registering. Mailing membership renewals early helps us to process them in a timely manner and avoids delays in registration. Registrations received before renewals, will be returned. If you have questions about your membership, we encourage you to call the National Office at 703-750-0533 before October 29. The National Office will be closed November 2 - 7, 1999.

Persons planning to use the Placement Center should also be sure to have memberships current. If you plan to join NCA and/or the Placement Service for the first time, do so early so that your file can be completed before the convention. Allow at least two months for that process. Call the National Office for membership forms if your department does not have a supply, or print the form from the NCA web site at www.natcom.org. Membership may also be paid on site at any registration counter.

Short Course Registration

Registration for short courses may be completed on site at a registration counter, beginning at 6:00 p.m. on Wednesday, November 3. Persons enrolling for short courses that begin Thursday morning are strongly urged to register or complete preregistration Wednesday evening. Thereafter, short course enrollment may be carried out during the regular registration hours listed above. Early registration is encouraged as short courses often fill during the preregistration period. Choose carefully. Short Course fees are not refundable unless the course is canceled.

Hospitality and Information

Do you want to know about local restaurants, sightseeing, and other things to do and places to see? If you need information about the hotel, the convention program, or help in locating rooms, visit the NCA Hospitality and Information Desk in the NCA Registration area, lower level Chicago Hilton & Towers. Volunteers from the Hospitality and Information Committee, familiar with Chicago, can answer questions about the city and will have brochures and maps available.

Tours and Theater Tickets

Preregistration is required to reserve theater tickets and tour spaces. Theater tickets will be available for pick-up at the NCA Hospitality Desk at the Chicago Hilton during posted registration hours. You must pick-up your theater tickets in person. Tickets will not be given to friends or family members. Tickets are not required for tours. Tour operators will have current rosters of those paid in full.

Transportation and Parking

American Airlines and US Airways are the official carriers for the Convention. To make reservations on American or US Airways, or for the lowest fares on all other airlines, call Conventions in America at 1-800-929-4242, and ask for Group #674. Or visit the Conventions in America website at www.scitravel.com. American can also be called direct at

1-800-433-1790; our Starfile number is #5309UH. Call US Airways direct at 1-800-334-8644, Goldfile #29621017. Taxi and limousine services are available from the airport. The Chicago Hilton does have limited parking facilities. Parking garages not affiliated with the hotel are located within walking distance, and prices vary.

Child Care

Parents interested in using the NCA child care center **must register their child with KiddieCorp. See** *Spectra* **for registration forms and details.** The one time fee of $80/per child covers unlimited use of the center. The center will be located in the Hilton and operate 7:30 a.m. - 7:30 p.m., November 3-6. On November 7, the center will operate 7:30 a.m. - 12:30 p.m.

Exhibits

Commercial and non-commercial exhibits will be located in the Northwest Exhibit Hall, lower level of the Chicago Hilton. Don't miss this opportunity to discover what's new in the discipline. A roster of exhibitors and exhibit hours appears elsewhere in this program. A convention badge is required to enter the Exhibit Hall.

Paper Distribution Center

Visit the paper distribution center in the Exhibit Hall. Details will appear in Spectra.

NCA Communication and Technology Center

Be sure to visit the Communication and Technology Center in the Exhibit Hall. The Center will be open during the posted exhibit hours.

Program Changes

Please consult the Program Supplement distributed at registration for information concerning program changes. Please note that the Convention Program lists programs and participants as of June 1, 1999; the Program Supplement lists changes in scheduling and participation after that date.

Hotels

The Chicago Hilton & Towers is the headquarters for the NCA Convention. The Hilton is at 720 S. Michigan Avenue. The general phone number is 312-922-4400. Additional guest rooms are held at the Essex Inn, 121 Eighth Street, 312-939-2800 and the Congress Plaza Hotel, 520 S. Michigan Avenue, 312-427-3800. Hotel guests may be reached by dialing the general hotel phone numbers. Be sure to make reservations early. Reservation information and rates may be found in the August issue of Spectra. Additional meeting rooms are located at the Essex Inn, second floor and the Spertus Institute of Jewish Studies, 618 S. Michigan Avenue, second and ninth floors.

MEETING ROOMS

CHICAGO HILTON & TOWERS

Lower Level
Northwest Exhibit Hall
Northeast Exhibit Hall

Lobby Level
Grand Traditions Room
Continental Ballroom A, B, C

Second Floor
Grand Ballroom
International Ballroom North
International Ballroom South
Normandie Lounge
Boulevard A, B, C

Third Floor
Waldorf
Astoria

Williford A, B, C
Marquette
Joliet
PDR1, PDR2, PDR3, PDR4, PDR5, PDR6, PDR7

Fourth Floor
Conference Rooms 4A, 4B, 4C, 4D, 4E, 4F, 4G, 4H, 4I, 4J, 4K, 4L, 4M, McCormick Board Room, Pullman Board Room

Fifth Floor
Conference Rooms 5A, 5B, 5C, 5D, 5E, 5F, 5G, 5H, 5I, 5J

Eight Floor
Lake Ontario
Lake Michigan
Lake Huron
Lake Erie

ESSEX INN

Second Floor
Essex Court
Windsor Court
Buckingham Court
Park East Walk

SPERTUS INSTITUTE

Second Floor
Cohn Room
Krensky Room
Auditorium

Ninth Floor
Rooms 902, 903, 904, 906, 907, 908

See Hotel Meeting Room Floor Plans on pages 8 - 11

Business Centers

Computer service, photocopies, secretarial support, and resources such as fax and data communications are available at prevailing prices in the Business Center on the lower level of the Hilton. Hours of operation are 8:00 a.m. – 11:00 p.m., seven days a week.

Fitness Centers

The Chicago Hilton Athletic Club is located on the eighth floor. The center offers the newest equipment in addition to a walking and jogging track as well as a full-size pool, jacuzzi, sauna and massage therapy. Open weekdays 5:30 a.m.-10:00 p.m. and weekends 7:00 a.m.–10:00p.m. There is a per visit fee for use of exercise equipment, however, use of the pool and sauna are complimentary to registered guests.

ERIC

Persons presenting convention papers are encouraged to submit two copies to the ERIC Clearinghouse on Reading and Communication Skills for possible inclusion in this important data bank system. Papers should be sent to ERIC/RCS, Indiana University, Smith Research Center, Suite 150, 2805 E. 10th St. Bloomington, IN 47405.

Convention Smoking Rules

In keeping with the spirit of the times, smoking is prohibited in any of the official convention sessions, including the business meetings. Program Chairs are instructed to strictly enforce this rule.

How to Use the Convention Program

Programs are listed by day and time. All poster sessions are scheduled Thursday, Friday and Saturday in the Exhibit Hall. Poster Sessions will run during posted Exhibit Hall hours. A complete poster session schedule can be found by day in the program.

If you have never attended an NCA convention - Be sure to attend the Newcomer's No-Host Welcome Reception and Orientation Thursday, November 4, 2:00-3:15 p.m. in the Normandie Lounge, Chicago Hilton.

If you wish to learn about and influence NCA and affiliated organizations - Be sure to attend business meetings, become active in the organization's work, and observe sessions of the Legislative Council in the Waldorf Room, Chicago Hilton.

If you would like to meet others and enjoy conversation with colleagues - Come to the No-Host Welcome Reception on Thursday, November 4, 6:30-8:00 in the International Ballroom North, Chicago Hilton.

If you're interested in convention-wide events - Be sure to attend the Carroll C. Arnold Lecture, the Awards Presentations, and Presidential Address. See events listed in this program under "Events of General Convention Interest."

If you want non-credit continuing professional education - Enroll in one or more of the Short Courses listed in this program.

If you want professional stimulation and exposure to new ideas – Attend programs, participate in the forum periods at the programs and talk to people in the halls, at the meetings, and at the social gatherings.

HOTEL FLOOR PLANS
Chicago Hilton & Towers

Lobby Level

Lobby Level, 2nd Floor

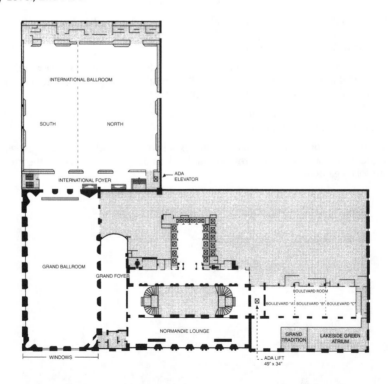

HOTEL FLOOR PLANS
Chicago Hilton & Towers

3rd Floor

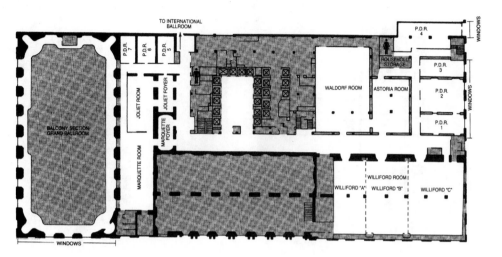

4th Floor

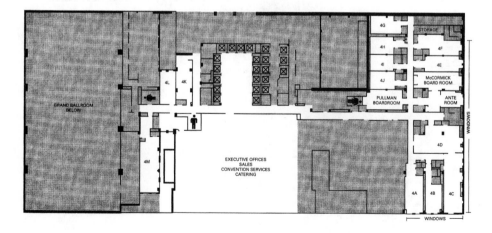

HOTEL FLOOR PLANS
Chicago Hilton & Towers

5th Floor

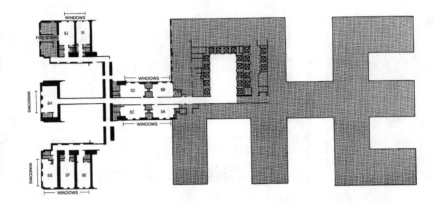

8th Floor

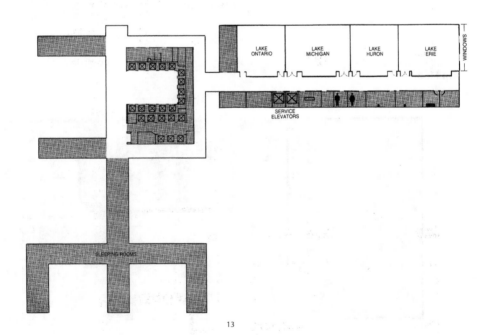

HOTEL FLOOR PLANS
Essex Inn

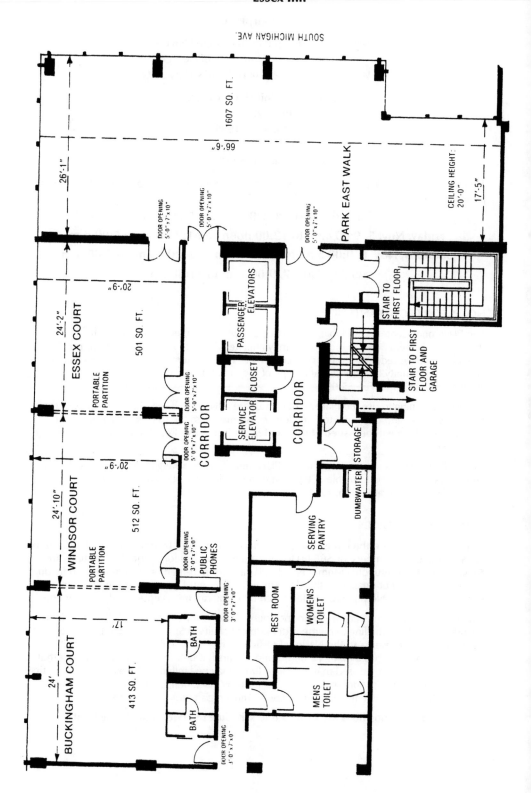

Convention Placement Center

Co-Chairpersons

Nina-Jo Moore, Appalachian State University
Dwight Freshley, University of Georgia
Walter Atkinson, Northern Illinois University

Northeast Exhibit Hall, Lower Level
Hilton & Towers
Nov. 4 - 7, 1999

HOURS

Thursday, Nov. 4, 9:00 a.m. to 12:00 noon, the Placement Center is open for registration of positions only.

Thursday, Nov. 4, 1:00 p.m. to 5:00 p.m.

Friday, Nov. 5, 9:00 a.m. to 12:00 noon and 1:00 p.m. to 5:00 p.m.

Saturday, Nov. 6, 9:00 a.m. to 12:00 noon and 1:00 p.m. to 5:00 p.m.

Sunday, Nov. 7, 9:00 a.m. to 11:00 a.m.

NOTES FOR REGISTRANTS

The Placement Center is available only to persons who hold membership in both NCA and the NCA Placement Service. Individuals may affiliate with both at the convention; prior affiliation is suggested. Prior to the convention, active Placement Service members will be given an opportunity to request that a copy of their confidential dossier be placed on file at the Placement Center. Fee $5.00.

Members planning to use the Placement Center are advised to bring multiple copies of their resume with them to distribute to interviewers. Admission to the Center is by Placement stamp only, **which will be issued at the Center**. All Placement Registrants must be registered for the convention.

Detailed instructions for registering in the Placement Center, arranging interviews with employers, etc., will be available at the Center beginning at 1:00 p.m. on Thursday; interviews will begin at 2:00 p.m.

NOTES FOR EMPLOYERS

Employers may list one-three positions at the Placement Center by paying a fee of $45.00 for NCA Institutional Members, or $65.00 for non-member institutions. Additional listings are $10.00 each for Institutional Members; $20.00 each for non-member institutions. Individual membership does not qualify for this discount. Payment must be made at the time the vacancies are listed. No purchase orders or credit cards can be accepted; only cash or checks.

Employers are to submit vacancy announcement(s) on the form(s) provided. (Forms will be included in an NCA mailing to member department chairs in September.) **Do not send vacancy announcements to the National Office.** They may be listed during the Position Registration Period, 9:00 a.m. to 12:00 noon on Thursday, or any other time thereafter that the Center is open. Be advised that interview times may be limited and are assigned on a first come, first served basis. Admission to the Center is by Placement stamp only, which will be issued at the Center. All employers/interviewers must register for the Convention.

Employers posting positions are expected to schedule interview time in the Center.

ACKNOWLEDGEMENTS

Raymie E. McKerrow, Ohio University
NCA First Vice President

Those listed below have made significant contributions to the NCA 1999 Convention. They have predominantly served as primary program planners, local arrangements committee chairs, and association-wide series coordinators. NCA appreciates all of the extraordinary services of those contributing to the success of the 1999 convention.

Alison F. Alexander	University of Georgia
Walter Atkinson	Northern Illinois University
Ann Bainbridge Frymier	Miami University
Barbara L. Baker	Central Missouri State University
Melissa Beall	University of Northern Iowa
Christina S. Beck	Ohio University
James Benjamin	University of Toledo
Catherine Blackburn	Brookdale Community College
Carole Blair	University of California, Davis
Deborah Borisoff	New York University
Frances Broderick	College of Mount Saint Vincent
Jerry Buley	Arizona State University
Judee Burgoon	University of Arizona
Gail Chryslee	University of South Alabama
Gina Collins Wesley	University of Wisconsin
Jim Crocker-Lakness	University of Cincinnati
Nelson A. DaCosta, Jr.	Elmhurst College
Treva Dayton	NFISDA
Cynthia Dewar	City College of San Francisco
Sue DeWine	Ohio University
Fran Dickson	University of Denver
Lynn M. Disbrow	Sinclair Community College
Veronica J. Duncan	University of Georgia
Deborah Eicher-Catt	Millersville University
Valerie A. Endress	University of Hartford
Donald Fishman	Boston College
Lawrence R. Frey	Loyola University, Chicago
Clark D. Germann	Metropolitan State College
Alan Gross	University of Minnesota
Diane Gruber	Arizona State University, West
Radha S. Hegde	Rutgers University
Judith Hendry	University of New Mexico
William Hill	University of North Carolina
Michelle A. Holling	Arizona State University, Main
Junhao Hong	SUNY Buffalo
Stephen K. Hunt	Southern Illinois University, Carbondale
Carol Jablonski	University of South Florida
Ronald L. Jackson	Penn State University
Mary L. Kahl	SUNY New Paltz
Lynda Lee Kaid	University of Oklahoma
Ruth Kay	Detroit Country Day School
Wade Kenny	University of Dayton
Karla Leeper	Baylor University
Greg Leichty	University of Louisville
Rebecca Lind	University of Illinois, Chicago
John Louis Lucaites	Indiana University
Casey M.K. Lum	William Paterson University
Patricia A. Lynott	Elmhurst College
Kristin L. Marshall	Clarion University
Judith Martin	Arizona State University
James C. McCroskey	West Virginia University

Mark L. McPhail	University of Utah
E.J. Min	Rhode Island College
Thomas Nakayama	Arizona State University
Brent Northup	Carroll College
Clark D. Olson	Arizona State University
Julie Patterson-Pratt	University of Minnesota, Morris
John L. Pauley	St. Mary's College
Eileen M. Perrigo	University of West Florida
Myrna Pietri	California State University, Los Angeles
Della Pollock	University of North Carolina
Nanette Potee	Northeastern Illinois University
Danna Prather	University of Iowa
Jim L. Query, Jr.	Loyola University, Chicago
Richard Quianthy	Broward Community College
Randy Richardson	Berry College
Randall G. Rogan	Wake Forest University
Philippe-Joseph Salazar	University of Cape Town
Warren Sandmann	Mankato State University
Pamela Shockley	University of Colorado, Colorado Springs
Raka Shome	University of California, Davis
John Smith	Ohio University
Ralph R. Smith	Southwest Missouri State University
Roger Smitter	North Central College
Morris Snively	Belleville East High School
Debbie Sonandre'	Tacoma Community College
Jim Tallmon	South Dakota State University
Glenda Treadaway	Appalachian State University
Kathleen Turner	Tulane University
Marsha L. Vanderford	University of South Florida
Richard West	University of Southern Maine
George Wharton	Curry College
Angie Williams	University of Wales, Cardiff
Kathleen Wong (Lau)	Arizona State University
Barbara Woods	Elmhurst College
Debra L. Wothington	University of Central Arkansas
Susan Zaeske	University of Wisconsin, Madison
Lori E. Zakel	Sinclair Community College

Special thanks go to Patricia Lynott, Chair, Local Arrangements Committee, her sub-committee chairs, and the numerous volunteers who have agreed to participate in making your visit to Chicago a pleasant and enjoyable one. As the chief planner, my efforts have been facilitated, supported, and as necessary, corrected, by the able assistance of Molly DeLaval-Hixson, my assistant in the School of Interpersonal Communication at Ohio University, and by the tireless efforts of Michelle Randall, Maureen Coleman, Ann Nadjar, Laura Haddon and Ellie Bruner at the National Office. I also wish to acknowledge the assistance, financial and otherwise, of the School of Interpersonal Communication, and the College of Communication, at Ohio University. Collectively, their support has made this a much easier and even enjoyable task.

Raymie E. McKerrow

LOCAL ARRANGEMENTS COMMITTEE

LOCAL ARRANGEMENTS COMMITTEE CHAIRPERSON
Patricia A. Lynott, Elmhurst College

HOSPITALITY & INFORMATION COMMITTEE CHAIRPERSON
Roger Smitter, North Central College

PLACEMENT SERVICE COMMITTEE CHAIRPERSON
Walter Atkinson, Northern Illinois University

PRESS & PROMOTION COMMITTEE CHAIRPERSON
Barbara Woods, Elmhurst College

REGISTRATION COMMITTEE CHAIRPERSON
Nelson A. Da Costa Jr., Elmhurst College

USHERS COMMITTEE CHAIRPERSON
Nanette Potee, Northeastern Illinois University

NCA Convention Calendar

2000
Seattle, November 8-12
Convention and Trade Center, Sheraton Seattle

2001
Atlanta, November 1-4
Atlanta Hilton & Atlanta Marriott Marquis

2002
New Orleans, November 21-24
New Orleans Sheraton, New Orleans Marriott

NCA Presidents

1915 J.M. O'Neill,* University of Wisconsin

1916 J.A. Winans, * Cornell University

1917 J.L. Lardner,* Northwestern University

1918 H.S. Woodward,* Western Reserve University

1919 H.S. Woodward,* Western Reserve University

1920 C.H. Woolbert,* University of Illinois

1921 A.M. Drummond,* Cornell University

1922 Glenn N. Merry,* University of Iowa

1923 Harry B. Gough,* Depauw University

1924 Wilber Jones Kay,* West Virginia University

1925 Ray K. Immel,* University of Southern California

1926 E.C. Mabie,* University of Iowa

1927 Andrew T. Weaver,* University of Wisconsin

1928 John P. Ryan,* Grinnell College

1929 F.M. Rarig,* University of Minnesota

1930 John Dolman,* Jr., University of Pennsylvania

1931 Clarence T. Simon,* Northwestern University

1932 Henrietta Prentiss,* Hunter College

1933 Lee Emerson Bassett,* Leland Stanford University

1934 H.L. Ewbank,* University of Wisconsin

1935 Arleigh B. Williamson,* New York University

1936 Maud May Babcock,* University of Utah

1937 Herbert A. Wichelns,* Cornell University

1938 J.T. Marshman,* Ohio Wesleyan University

1939 A. Craig Baird,* University of Iowa

1940 Alan H. Monroe,* Purdue University

1941 W. Hayes Yeager,* George Washington University

1941 Honorary President Thomas C. Trueblood,* University of Michigan

1942 Claude M. Wise,* Louisiana State University

1943 Robert West,* University of Wisconsin

1944 Bower Aly,* University of Missouri

1945 Joseph F. Smith,* University of Utah

1946 W. Norwood Brigance,* Wabash College

1947 Magdalene Kramer,* Columbia University

1948 Rupert Cortright,* Wayne State University

1949 J.H. McBurney,* Northwestern University

1950 Horace G. Rahskopf,* University of Washington

1951 Wilber Gilman,* Queens College

1952 Lionel Crocker,* Denison University

1953 H.P. Constans,* University of Florida

1954 Karl R. Wallace,* University of Illinois

1955 Thomas A. Rousse,* University of Texas

1956 Lester Thonssen,* College of The City of New York

1957 Loren Reid, University of Missouri

1958 Elise Hahn,* University of California

1959 John E. Dietrich,* Ohio State University

1960 Kenneth G. Hance,* Michigan State University

1961 Ralph G. Nichols, University of Minnesota

1962 Waldo W. Braden,* Louisiana State University

1963 Ernest J. Wrage,* Northwestern University

1964 Robert T. Oliver, Penn State University

1965 J. Jeffery Auer, Indiana University

1966 John W. Black,* Ohio State University

1967 Wayne C. Minnick, Florida State University

1968 Douglas Ehninger,* University of Iowa

1969 Marie Hochmuth Nichols,* University of Illinois

1970 Donald C. Bryant,* University of Iowa

1971 William S. Howell, University of Minnesota

1972 Theodore Clevenger,* Jr., Florida State University

1973 Robert C. Jeffrey, University of Texas

1974 Samuel L. Becker, University of Iowa

1975 Herman Cohen, Penn State University

1976 Lloyd F. Bitzer, University of Wisconsin

1977 Wallace A. Bacon, Northwestern University

1978 Jane Blankenship, University of Massachusetts, Amherst

1979 Ronald R. Allen, University of Wisconsin

1980 Malcolm O. Sillars, University of Utah

1981 Anita Taylor, George Mason University

1982 Frank E.X. Dance, University of Denver

1983 Kenneth E. Andersen, University of Illinois

1984 John Waite Bowers, University of Colorado

1985 Beverly Whitaker Long, University of North Carolina, Chapel Hill

1986 Wayne Brockriede,* California State University, Fullerton

Note: But for his untimely death, Donald Ecroyd, Temple University, would have succeeded to the presidency in 1986.

1986 Patti P. Gillespie, University of Maryland

1987 Patti P. Gillespie, University of Maryland

1988 Michael M. Osborn, Memphis State University

1989 Gustav W. Friedrich, University of Oklahoma

1990 Mark L. Knapp, University of Texas

1991 Dennis Gouran, Penn State University

1992 Dale Leathers,* University of Georgia

1993 David Zarefsky, Northwestern University

1994 Bruce E. Gronbeck, University of Iowa

1995 Sharon A. Ratliffe, Golden West College

1996 James W. Chesebro, Indiana State University

1997 Judith S. Trent, University of Cincinnati

1998 John A. Daly, University of Texas, Austin

1999 Orlando L. Taylor, Howard University

* Deceased

NATIONAL COMMUNICATION ASSOCIATION

Founded 1914
Incorporated 1950
1999 Officers and Staff

Orlando L. Taylor, *President*	Howard University
Raymie E. McKerrow, *First Vice President*	Ohio University
James L. Applegate, *Second Vice President*	University of Kentucky
James L. Gaudino, *Executive Director*	National Office
William F. Eadie, *Associate Director*	National Office
Sherwyn P. Morreale, *Associate Director*	National Office
Maureen Coleman, *Director of Operations*	National Office
Ann Nadjar, *Publications Manager*	National Office
Fred Barrett, *Publications Technician*	National Office
Eleanor Bruner, *ACA/Placement Administrative Assistant*	National Office
Laura Haddon, *Executive Assistant*	National Office
Alicia Jeffries, *Receptionist*	National Office
Michelle Randall, *Meeting Coordinator*	National Office
Kim Reichley, *Membership Clerk*	National Office
James Roberts, *Mail Clerk*	National Office
Linda Rouhani, *Administrative Assistant*	National Office
Omari Sanders, *Administrative Assistant*	National Office
Irene Wang, *Accountant*	National Office

Editors

Andrew King, *Quarterly Journal of Speech*	Louisiana State Univ
Michael J. Beatty, *Communication Monographs*	Univ of Missouri, St. Louis
Ruth Anne Clark, *Communication Education*	Univ of Illinois, Urbana-Champaign
James W. Chesebro, *Critical Studies in Mass Communication*	Indiana State Univ
Judith A. Hamera, *Text and Performance Quarterly*	California State Univ, LA
David R. Seibold, *Journal of Applied Communication Research*	Univ of California, Santa Barbara
Lawrence W. Hugenberg, *Communication Teacher*	Youngstown State Univ
Matthew W. Seeger, *Free Speech Yearbook*	Wayne State Univ
Mary Jane Collier, *International and Intercultural Communication Annual*	Univ of Denver
James L. Gaudino, *Spectra*	NCA National Office

Editors-elect

Joe Ayres, *Communication Education*	Washington State Univ
H. Dan O'Hair, *Journal of Applied Communication Research*	Univ of Oklahoma

1999 Legislative Council
Term of office expires in year indicated

Ames, Ina R., *Chair, Senior College/University Section*	Curry Col	2000
Anderson, Monica F., *Past Chair, Theatre Division*	Franciscan Univ	1999
Applegate, James L., *Second Vice President,*	Univ of Kentucky	2002
Aune, James A., *Chair, Rhetoric/Comm Theory Div*	Texas A & M Univ	2000
Bantz, Charles R., *Member, Finance Brd*	Arizona State Univ	2000
Beall, Melissa L., *Member at Large, 3 yr*	Univ of Northern Iowa	2000
Beatty, Michael J., *Editor, Communication Monographs*	Univ of Missouri, St Louis	2001
Benton, Carol L., *Chair, Gay/Lesbian/ Bisexual/Transsexual Studies*	Central Missouri State Univ	2000
Biesecker, Barbara A., *Past Chair, Critical/ Cultural Studies Div*	Univ of Iowa	1999

Booth-Butterfield, Steven, *Member at Large, 3 yr*	West Virginia Univ	1999
Bowman, Michael S., *Past Chair,*		
Performance Studies Div	Louisiana State Univ	1999
Buerkel-Rothfuss, Nancy, *Chair, Basic Course Div*	Central Michigan Univ	2000
Burggraf Torppa, Cynthia, *Past Chair,*	Torpa Psychological	
Family Comm Div	Counseling Services	1999
Burgoon, Judee K., *Chair, Publications Brd*	Univ of Arizona	2000
Carey, Colleen M., *Chair, Student Section*	Northwestern Univ	2000
Carlin, Diana B., *Chair, Political Comm Div*	Univ of Kansas	2000
Cegala, Donald J., *Chair, Health Comm Div*	Ohio State Univ	2000
Chesebro, James W., *Editor,*		
Critical Studies in Mass Communication	Indiana State Univ	2001
Clark, Ruth Anne, *Editor, Communication Education*	Univ of Illinois	1999
Collins, Mary E., *SSCA Representative*	Sam Houston State Univ	1999
Cronn-Mills, Daniel D., *Chair, Argumentation/*		
Forensics Div	Minnesota State Univ Mankato	2000
Daly, John A., *Immediate Past President*	Univ of Texas	1999
Daniel, Jack L., *Chair, Finance Brd*	Univ of Pittsburgh	1999
Darsey, James, *Selected LC, 3 yr*	Georgia State Univ	1999
Daughton, Suzanne M., *Past Chair,*		
Public Address Div	Southern Illinois Univ	1999
Davis, Wade S., *Past Chair, Student Section*	Univ of Iowa	1999
Drummond, Kent G., *Chair, Language/*		
Social Interaction Div	Univ of Wyoming	2000
Eadie, William F., *NCA Associate Director*	National Office	0000
Ellis, Carolyn S., *Chair, Ethnography Div*	Univ of South Florida	2000
Fitch, Kristine L., *Past Chair,*		
Language/Social Interaction Div	Univ of Iowa	1999
Fleuriet, Cathy A., *Past Chair, Basic Course Div*	Southwest Texas State Univ	1999
Floyd, Kory, *Selected LC, 3 yr*	Cleveland State Univ	2001
Frey, Lawrence R., *Past Chair, Applied Comm Div*	Univ of Memphis	1999
Gaudino, James L., *Executive Director, ex officio*	National Office	0000
Goodnight, G. Thomas, *Member at Large, 3 yr*	Northwestern Univ	2000
Goodnight, Lynn, *Past Chair, Elementary/*		
Secondary Section	Univ of Southern California	1999
Haefner, Margaret J., *Chair, Mass Comm Div*	Illinois State Univ	2000
Hamera, Judith A., *Editor,*		
Text and Performance Quarterly	California State Univ, LA	2000
Hariman, Robert, *Past Chair, Rhetorical/*		
Comm Theory Div	Drake Univ	1999
Harper, Anneliese M., *WSCA Prepresentative*	Scottsdale Community Col	2000
Hawkins, Katherine, *Past Chair,*		
Feminist/Women's Studies Div	Wichita State Univ	1999
Hefferin, Deborah, *SSCA Representative*	Broward Community Col	2001
Heineman, John R., *CSCA Representative*	Univ of Nebraska, Lincoln	2000
Ige, Dorothy W., *Member at Large, 3 yr*	Indiana Univ Northwest	1999
Jackson, Ronald L., *Member at Large, 3 yr*	Penn State Univ	2001
Jasko, Susan A., *SAC Representative*	California Univ of Pennsylvania	2001
Johnson, Deryl B., *Chair, Theatre Div*	Kutztown Univ	2000
Jordan-Jackson, Felecia F, *Selected LC, 3 yr*	Florida State Univ	2000
Jorgensen-Earp, Cheryl R, *Selected LC, 3 yr*	Lynchburg Col	1999
Kahl, Mary L., *Chair, Public Address Div*	SUNY, New Paltz	2000
Kern, Montague, *Past Chair, Political Comm Div*	Rutgers Univ	1999
Keyton, Joann, *Chair, Applied Comm Div*	Univ of Memphis	2000
King, Andrew A., *Editor, Quarterly Journal of Speech*	Louisiana State Univ	2001
Knapp, Mark L., *Past President,*		
Association for Comm Administration	Univ of Texas	1999

Krone, Kathleen J., *Past Chair,*		
Organizational Comm Div	Univ of Nebraska	1999
Larson, Mary S., *Past Chair, Mass Comm Div*	Northern Illinois Univ	1999
Le Poire, Beth A., *Member at Large, 3 yr*	Univ of California	2001
Lee, Wenshu, *Chair, Feminist/Women's Studies Div*	San Jose State Univ	2000
Leff, Michael, *Chair, Research Brd*	Northwestern Univ	2001
Leininger, Joan E., *Chair, Emeritus Section*	Oakland Comm Col	1999
Leland, Chris M., *Past Chair,*		
Argumentation/Forensics Div	Huntington Col	1999
Lerstrom, Alan C., *Past Chair,*		
Senior College/University Div	Luther Col	1999
Lum, Casey M. K., *Chair, International/*		
Intercultural Comm	William Paterson Univ	2000
Matthews, Donna, *SSCA Representative*	Hattiesburg MS	2000
McCorkle, Suzanne, *Member at Large, 3 yr*	Boise State Univ	2000
McDonald, Becky A., *Chair, Public Relations Div*	Ball State Univ	2000
McKenney, Janet K., *Past Chair,*		
Community College Section	Macomb Comm Col	1999
McKerrow, Raymie E., *First Vice President*	Ohio Univ	2001
Mongeau, Paul A., *Past Chair, Interpersonal Comm Div*	Miami Univ (Ohio)	1999
Moore, Linda, L., *Member, Finance Brd*	Wayne State Univ	2001
Morreale, Sherwyn P., *NCA Associate Director*	National Office	0000
Morris, Richard, *Past Chair, International/*		
Intercultural Comm	Northern Illinois Univ	1999
Nelson, Elizabeth J., *Member at Large, 3 yr*	Univ of Minnesota	1999
Nelson, Paul E., *Selected LC, 3 yr*	Ohio Univ	2001
Nicotera, Anne M., *Member at Large, 3 yr*	Howard Univ	2001
Parrott, Roxanne, *Past Chair, Health Comm Div*	Univ of Georgia	1999
Pearson, Judy C., *Chair, Educational Policies Brd*	Virginia Tech	1999
Pendell, Sue D., *WSCA Representative*	Colorado State Univ	2000
Pietri, Myrna, *Chair, Latino/a Studies Div*	California State Univ, L.A.	2000
Planalp, Sally, *Chair, Interpersonal Comm Div*	Univ of Montana	2000
Poole, Marshall S., *Chair, Group Comm Div*	Texas A&M Univ	2000
Robinson, Rena Y., *ECA Representative*	James Madison Univ	1999
Rodgers, R. Pierre, *Selected LC, 3 yr*	Morgan State Univ	2000
Rose, Nancy Oft, *WSCA Representative*	South Eugene HS	1999
Sabetta, Thomas J., *Chair, Community College Section*	Jefferson Comm Col	2000
Seibold, David R., *Editor,*		
Journal of Applied Communication Research	Univ of California	1999
Shields, Ronald E., *Chair,*		
Performance Studies Div	Bowling Green State Univ	2000
Slagle, Ray A., *Past Chair,*		
Gay/Lesbian/Bisexual/Transsexual Div	St Cloud State Univ	1999
Snively, Morris E., *Chair, Elementary/*		
Secondary Education Sec	Belleville East HS	2000
Socha, Thomas J., *Chair, Family Communication Div*	Old Dominion Univ	2000
Springston, Jeff K., *Past Chair, Public Relations Div*	Univ of Georgia	1999
Stohl, Cynthia, *Chair, Organizational Comm Div*	Purdue Univ	2000
Streiff, Jean A., *ECA Representative*	Oakland Catholic HS	2001
Taylor, Orlando L., *President*	Howard Univ	2000
Thibodeaux, Terry, *SSCA Representative*	Sam Houston State Univ	2002
Thomas, Douglas E., *Chair, Critical/*		
Cultural Comm Div	Univ of Southern California	2000
Turner, Lynn H., *CSCA Representative*	Marquette Univ	1999
Wallace, James D., *Chair, Training and*		
Development Div	Cameron Univ	2000
Weintraub, Sara C., *Chair, Instructional*		
Development Div	Bentley Col	2000

West, Richard L., *Past Chair, Instructional Development Div*	Univ of Southern Maine	1999
Willets, Nancy J., *ECA Representative*	Cape Cod Community Col	2001
Wong (Lau), Kathleen, *Chair, Asian/ Pacific American Studies*	Arizona State Univ	2000
Yep, Gust A., *Past Chair, Latino/a Comm Studies Div*	San Francisco State Univ	1999
Zakel, Lori C., *CSCA Representative*	Sinclair Community Col	2001

LC Members Without Vote

William F. Eadie, *Associate Director*	National Office
Sherwyn P. Morreale, *Associate Director*	National Office
James L. Gaudino, *Executive Director*	National Office

1999 Administrative Committee

Orlando L. Taylor, *President*	Howard Univ
Raymie E. McKerrow, *First Vice President*	Ohio Univ
James L. Applegate, *Second Vice President*	Univ of Kentucky
John A. Daly, *Immediate Past President*	Univ of Texas, Austin
Judy C. Pearson, *Chair, Educational Policies Brd*	Virginia Tech
Judee K. Burgoon, *Chair, Publications Brd*	Univ of Arizona
Michael Leff, *Chair, Research Brd*	Northwestern Univ
Jack L. Daniel, *Chair, Finance Brd*	Univ of Pittsburgh
Charles R. Bantz, *Finance Brd*	Arizona State Univ
Linda L. Moore, *Finance Brd*	Wayne State Univ
James L. Gaudino, *Executive Director*	National Office

OFFICERS OF AFFILIATED ORGANIZATIONS
Holding Concurrent Annual Meetings

American Alliance for Theatre and Education

Gretta Berghammer, President	AATE
Christy M. Taylor, Administrative Director	AATE
Janet Rubin, NCA Liaison	Saginaw Valley State University

American Association for Rhetoric of Science and Technology

Alan Gross, President	University of Minnesota
Joan Leach, President Elect	Imperial College of London

American Debate Association

Brett O'Donnell, President	Liberty University
Frank Harrison, Vice President	Trinity University

American Forensic Association

James F. Klumpp, President	University of Maryland
Karla K. Leeper, Vice President	Baylor University
James W. Pratt, Executive Secretary	University of Wisconsin

American Society for the History of Rhetoric

James M. Tallmon, President	South Dakota State University
Mari Lee Mifsud, Vice President	University of Richmond

Association for Chinese Communication Studies

Mary Fong, President	California State University, San Bernardino
Randy Kluver, Vice President	Oklahoma City University

Association for Communication Administration

Alison F. Alexander, President	University of Georgia

Association for Rhetoric and Communication in South Africa

Phillipe J. Salazar, President	University of Capetown
Yehoshua Gitay, Vice President	University of Capetown

Chinese Communication Association

Joseph Man Chan, President	Chinese University of Hong Kong
Shujen Wang, Vice President	Emerson College

Commission on American Parliamentary Practice

Donald Fishman, Chair	Boston College
Martha Haun, Vice Chair	University of Houston

Cross Examination Debate Association

Carrie Crenshaw, President	University of Alabama
Gina Lane, First Vice President	William Jewell College
Glenda J. Treadaway, Second Vice President	Appalachian State University
Greg Achten, Second Vice President Elect	Pepperdine University

Delta Sigma Rho-Tau Kappa Alpha

Frank Thompson, President   University of Alabama
Kellie W. Roberts, Vice President   University of Florida

International Listening Association

Charles Roberts, President   East Tennessee State University
Harvey Weiss, Vice President   Brooklyn Park, MN
Diana Corley Schnapp, Executive Director   Kansas City, Kansas

Kenneth Burke Society, NCA Branch

W. Lance Haynes, Chair   University of Missouri, Rolla
Bryan Crable, Vice Chair   Villanova University

Korean American Communication Association

Gwangjub Han, President   Howard University
Eungjun Min, Vice President   Rhode Island College

Lambda Pi Eta

Spiro Yulis, President   College of New Jersey
Sherwyn Morreale, Executive Director   NCA National Office

National Federation Interscholastic Speech and Debate Association

Treva Dayton, Liaison   NFISDA, Kansas City, MO

National Forensic Association

Larry Schnoor, President   Mankato, MN
Vicki Karns, Administrative Vice President   Suffolk University
Clark D. Olson, Professional Relations Vice President   Arizona State University

Religious Speech Communication Association

Kim S. Phipps, President   Messiah College
John Pauley, First Vice President   St. Mary's College
Kenneth Chase, Second Vice President   Wheaton College

NCA CONVENTIONS: 1915-2002

1915	Chicago	1959	Washington, D.C.
1916	New York City	1960	St. Louis
1917	Chicago	1961	New York City
1918	No Convention	1962	Cleveland
1919	Chicago	1963	Denver
1920	Cleveland	1964	Chicago
1921	Chicago	1965	New York City
1922	New York City	1966	Chicago
1923	Cincinnati	1967	Los Angeles
1924	Evanston	1968	Chicago
1925	New York City	1969	New York City
1926	Chicago	1970	New Orleans
1927	Cincinnati	1971	San Francisco
1928	Chicago	1972	Chicago
1929	New York City	1973	New York City
1930	Chicago	1974	Chicago
1931	Detroit	1975	Houston
1932	Los Angeles	1976	San Francisco
1933	New York City	1977	Washington, D.C.
1934	New Orleans	1978	Minneapolis
1935	Chicago	1979	San Antonio
1936	St. Louis	1980	New York City
1937	New York City	1981	Anaheim
1938	Cleveland	1982	Louisville
1939	Chicago	1983	Washington, D.C.
1940	Washington, D.C.	1984	Chicago
1941	Detroit	1985	Denver
1942	Chicago	1986	Chicago
1943	New York City	1987	Boston
1944	Chicago	1988	New Orleans
1945	Columbus	1989	San Francisco
1946	Chicago	1990	Chicago
1947	Salt Lake City	1991	Atlanta
1948	Washington, D.C.	1992	Chicago
1949	Chicago	1993	Miami
1950	New York City	1994	New Orleans
1951	Chicago	1995	San Antonio
1952	Cincinnati	1996	San Diego
1953	New York City	1997	Chicago
1954	Chicago	1998	New York City
1955	Los Angeles	1999	Chicago
1956	Chicago	2000	Seattle
1957	Boston	2001	Atlanta
1958	Chicago	2002	New Orleans

EVENTS OF GENERAL CONVENTION INTEREST
Challenging Boundaries Series

This series' programs are being held throughout the convention. Program formats will vary—paper presentations, scholar and scholarship exploration and investigation, idea exploration through interactive dialogue—but all speak directly to the spirit of the convention theme, *Coloring Outside the Lines*. Refer to the convention program for program titles and descriptions.

First Vice President Highlight Programs

Raymie McKerrow, NCA First Vice President and Primary Convention Planner has selected several programs of high quality and interesting content. These programs are "highlighted" on Friday and Saturday during the 11:00-12:15 p.m. time period. Refer to the convention program for program titles and descriptions

Wednesday, November 3

Legislative Council Meeting	12:30 – 4:45 p.m., Waldorf Room
2000 Convention Planning Committee Meeting	5:00 – 8:00 p.m., Marquette Room
Early Bird Welcome Reception	5:00 – 7:45 p.m., Normandie Lounge

Thursday, November 4

Poster Sessions	9:30 – 4:45 p.m., Northwest Exhibit Hall
Newcomers Orientation and Reception	2:00 – 3:15 p.m., Normandie Lounge
Carroll C. Arnold Lecture	5:00 – 6:15 p.m., International Ballroom South
No Host Welcome Reception	6:30 – 8:00 p.m., International Ballroom North
Pub Crawl: Jazz & Blues Chicago Style	6:30 – 11:00 p.m., Preregistration required

Friday, November 5

Poster Session	9:30 – 4:45 p.m., Northwest Exhibit Hall
Afternoon with the Arts: Eclectic Art Gallery Tour	1:30 – 5:00 p.m., Preregistration required
Chicago Highlights Tour & Dinner	6:00 – 11:00 p.m., Preregistration is required
Musical Performance by "Good Enough"	9:00 – 11:00 p.m., Lakeside Green

Saturday, November 6

Poster Sessions	9:30 – 3:45 p.m., Northwest Exhibit Hall
Museum of Contemporary Art Tour	12:30 – 2:00 p.m., Pregistration required
Lambda Pi Eta: How and Why to Start a Chapter	2:00 – 3:15 p.m., Joliet Room
Legislative Council Meeting	12:30 – 3:15 p.m., Waldorf Room
Presidential Address	5:00 – 6:15 p.m., International Ballroom North
NCA Awards Presentation	6:30 – 8:00 p.m., International Ballroom North
Blue Man Group's *Tubes*	10:00 p.m., Briar Street Theater, Preregistration required

Sunday, November 7

Legislative Council	8:00 – 9:15 a.m., Waldorf Room
2000 Convention Planning Committee Second Meeting	8:00 – 9:15 a.m., Joliet Room

Pre-Convention Conferences

Wednesday, November 3, 1999

Pre-registration is required for all pre-convention conferences.
Please see the August issue of *Spectra* for detailed information and registration forms.

Tenure and Promotion

Wednesday, November 3, 1999   8:30 a.m. – 6:00 p.m.

Boulevard A, Chicago Hilton & Towers   Fee: $60

Sponsors: Women's Caucus, Caucus on Gay and Lesbian Concerns, Black Caucus, Association for Communication Administration

Coloring Outside the Lines: Taking Risks in the Basic Course

Wednesday, November 3, 1999   8:00 a.m. – 5:00 p.m.

Continental Ballroom B, Chicago Hilton & Towers   Fee: $55

Sponsors: Basic Course Division, Harcourt Brace College Publishers

Public Relations Pedagogy: Topics in Teaching-Learning Strategies for Public Relations Education

Wednesday, November 3, 1999   8:30 a.m. – 6:30 p.m.

Continental Ballroom C, Chicago Hilton & Towers   Fee: $35

Sponsor: Public Relations Division

Teaming Beyond 2000: Technology Training for Creative Connections

Wednesday, November 3,1999   8:00 a.m. – 5:00 p.m.

Boulevard B, Chicago Hilton & Towers   Fee: $55

Sponsors: Training and Development Commission, Human Communication and Technology Commission

When the Corporation Meets the Classroom: Learning Communication Experientially

Wednesday, November 3, 1999   8:00 a.m. – 5:00 p.m.

Continental Ballroom A, Chicago Hilton & Towers   Fee: $60

Sponsor: Experiential Learning in Communication Commission

Studying Social Codes Through the Analysis of Language in Social Interaction

Wednesday, November 3, 1999   8:00 a.m. – 4:45 p.m.

Boulevard C, Chicago Hilton & Towers   Fee: $35

Sponsor: Language and Social Interaction Division

The State of Family Communication Education:
Building for the Future

Wednesday, November 3, 1999   8:00 a.m. – 5:00 p.m.

Williford A, Chicago Hilton & Towers   Fee: $30

Sponsor: Family Communication Division

All About Food and Conversation: An Ethnography Workshop on
Daily Consumption and Informal Dialogue

Wednesday, November 3, 1999   9:00 a.m. – 9:00 p.m.

Illinois Beach Resort and Conference Center   Fee: $90 + room

Sponsor: Ethnography Division

Building Community: Service-Learning
in the Communication Discipline

Wednesday, November 3   9:00 a.m. – 4:30 p.m.

Williford C, Chicago Hilton & Towers   Fee: $45

Sponsors: Second Vice President, American Association of Higher Education, Campus Compact

What Lines?: Interdisciplinarity and the
Rhetoric of Science and Technology

Wednesday, November 3, 1999   8:30 a.m. – 8:00 p.m.

Joliet Room, Chicago Hilton & Towers

Sponsor: American Association for the Rhetoric of Science and Technology
(Fees and registration taken by AARST)

From Medieval to Modern Rhetorics

Wednesday, November 3, 1999   8:00 a.m. – 5:00 p.m.

Newberry Library, Room 101

Sponsor: American Society for the History of Rhetoric
(Fees and registration taken by ASHR)

Seminar Series
Wednesday, Nov. 3, 1999
Hilton & Towers
Fourth & Fifth Floors

1. **Rethinking Structuration Theory in Communication**

    8:00 a.m. – 4:45 p.m.
    Conference Room 4A

Leader: Robert D. McPhee, Arizona State University

2. **Redrawing Communication Ethics: Emmanuel Levinas and the Call of the Other**

    8:00 a.m. – 4:45 p.m.
    Conference Room 4B

Leaders: Ronald C. Arnett, Duquesne University
          Michael J. Hyde, Wake Forest University
          Roy V. Wood, University of Denver

3. **The Fall of Communism and its Impact on Democratic Discourse: Ten Years After**

    8:00 a.m. – 4:45 p.m.
    Conference Room 4C

Leader: Noemi C. Marin, University of Maryland, College Park

4. **Color Us Queer: Communication and Alternative Relationships**

    8:00 a.m. – 4:45 p.m.
    Conference Room 4E

Leader: R. Jeffrey Ringer, St. Cloud State University

5. **Masculinity at the End of the Millennium**

    8:00 a.m. – 4:45 p.m.
    Conference Room 4F

Leaders: John M. Sloop, Vanderbilt University
          Thomas K. Nakayama, Arizona State University

6. **Twentieth Century First Ladies: Exploring the Intersections of Politics, Media, Theory, and Criticism**

    8:00 a.m. – 4:45 p.m.
    Conference Room 4G

Leaders: Lisa R. Barry, Albion College
          Mary L. Kahl, SUNY, New Paltz
          Anne F. Mattina, Stonehill College
          Beth Waggenspack, Virginia Tech University
          Molly M. Wertheimer, Penn State University, Hazleton

7. **Cold War Films 1945-1991**

    8:00 a.m. – 4:45 p.m.
    Conference Room 4H

Leaders: Bonnie S. Jefferson, Boston College
          Donald Fishman, Boston College

8. **Movements and Spheres: Challenging Us to Theorize Outside the Lines**

    8:00 a.m. – 4:45 p.m.
    Conference Room 4I

    Leaders: Valeria Fabj, Emerson College
    Catherine H. Palczewski, University of Northern Iowa

9. **British Public Address: Pages Yet to Colour**

    8:00 a.m. – 4:45 p.m.
    Conference Room 4J

    Leaders: James R. Andrews, Indiana University
    Sean O'Rourke, Vanderbilt University
    Barry C. Poyner, Truman State University

10. **Blurring the Boundaries: Bakhtin, Dialogue and Permeable Communication**

    8:00 a.m. – 4:45 p.m.
    Conference Room 4K

    Leader: V. Jeffrey Shires, Campbellsville University

11. **Intrapersonal Communication**

    8:00 a.m. – 4:45 p.m.
    Conference Room 4L

    Leaders: Leonard J. Shedletsky, University of Southern Maine
    Joan E. Aitken, University of Missouri, Kansas City

12. **Rhetoric and Psychiatry: Persuasion and Communication Issues**

    8:00 a.m. – 4:45 p.m.
    Conference Room 5E

    Leader: Richard E. Vatz, Towson University

13. **Creating a Collage: Communication and Culture in the Twenties**

    8:00 a.m. – 4:45 p.m.
    Conference Room 5F

    Leader: Kathleen J. Turner, Tulane University

14. **Interdisciplinary, Multi-Method Approaches to a Jewish Rhetorical Theory: Crossing the Boundaries**

    8:00 a.m. – 4:45 p.m.
    Conference Room 5G

    Leaders: Samuel M. Edelman, California State University, Chico
    Susan Kray, Indiana State University

15. **A Communication Approach to the HIV/AIDS Epidemic: Theory, Research, Practice, and Experience**

    8:00 a.m. – 4:45 p.m.
    Conference Room 5H

    Leaders: Gust A. Yep, San Francisco State University
    Thomas M. Steinfatt, University of Miami

Short Courses

Registration Information: Short Course registrants must be registered for the convention. The convention preregistration form should be used to designate the course(s) desired. You may enroll in as many courses as you wish, but be sure to include correct payment for each. The fee for each Short Course is listed with the description.

We encourage early preregistration. Courses are filled on a first come, first served basis. If your selected courses are filled at the time you preregister, you will be informed by mail. Preregistration will close September 24, 1999. **Do not attempt to preregister by mail after this date**. You may register on site at the convention as long as the courses are not filled.

Advance registrants will receive confirmation by mail. Check your confirmation letter carefully. Short Course fees are not refundable. Auditing of Short Courses is not permitted. Registrants will be verified at the door and during the class period. All Short Courses take place on the eighth floor of the Hilton.

THURSDAY, Nov. 4

8:00 – 10:45 a.m.   Lake Ontario
$50.00   **1   Teaching Communication Courses with Feature
                             Films**

Examples and strategies for using feature films to illustrate concepts and theories in a variety of communication courses—Interpersonal, Small Group, Gender, Intercultural, Persuasion, Theories. Presentations and discussions will demonstrate how feature films can be used in class sessions, assignments, and campus media centers. Handouts and bibliographies will be provided.

Staff: Ronald B. Adler, Santa Barbara City College; Russell F. Proctor II, Northern Kentucky University

8:00 – 10:45 a.m.   Lake Michigan
$50.00   **2   Teaching the College Course in the Rhetoric of
                             Twentieth Century First Ladies**

This short course will instruct participants in the development of a course that analyzes the rhetorical responses, communication strategies and activities of twentieth century first ladies. The course will address primary research in presidential libraries and effective integration of that material into the course. In addition, we will provide strategies that will help you turn your study of first ladies into publications.

Staff: Myra G. Gutin, Rider University; Leesa E. Tobin, Gerald R. Ford Library; Molly Meijer Wertheimer, Penn State University, Hazleton

8:00 – 10:45 a.m.   Lake Huron
$50.00   **3   Short Course for New Department Chairs**

During this short course, experienced administrators will provide insights into the challenges and opportunities that go with being a new department chair. The session is organized to promote interaction. Panelists will offer brief presentations on their area of specialty. Topics include getting organized; mission statements; personnel; students; budgets and finance; diversity and multiculturalism; and dealing with Deans.

Staff: Alison Alexander, University of Georgia; Bill Balthrop, University of North Carolina; Mark Knapp, University of Texas, Austin; Jarice Hanson, University of Massachusetts; David Zarefsky, Northwestern University; Jannette Dates, Howard University; Joe Foote, Southern Illinois University

8:00 – 10:45 a.m.   Lake Erie
$50.00   **4   Using Community Service in Communication
                             Courses**

Service-learning involves three aspects (1) taking course concepts into the field at the service-learning site to test their application, (2) using experience at the service site to raise questions about course content, and (3) systematically reflecting, in writing and discussion, on the experience of applying course content to a practical situation. Each participant is invited to bring a course outline that he or she would like to consider modifying for service-learning.

Staff: James Honeycutt, Louisiana State University; Richard Conville, University of Southern Mississippi; Tim Sellnow, North Dakota State University; Deanna Sellnow, North Dakota State University; Laurie McAdoo, North Dakota State University

12:30 – 3:15 p.m. Lake Ontario
$50.00 **5** **Teaching the College and University Course in Interviewing**

This course is designed for instructors who teach the college-level interviewing course or who include a unit on interviewing as part of a communication course. Axiomatic to our approach is that interviewing is an art as well as a skill that one can learn to use well. This course will offer a variety of lecture and content materials related to business, technological, and qualitative research interviews, including focus group interviews and computer-assisted interviews. Handouts will include example syllabi, course assignments, and a list of recent web sites for employment interview information. Use of videotaped interviews in the classroom will be demonstrated. Complimentary textbook provided to participants.

Staff: Roger N. Conaway, University of Texas, Tyler; Wallace V. Schmidt, Rollins College

12:30 – 3:15 p.m. Lake Michigan
$50.00 **6** **Teaching the Persuasion, Compliance Gaining, and/or Social Influence Course at the University Level**

This course is designed for instructors teaching or developing courses in persuasion, compliance-gaining, and/or social influence. The course covers instructional units, lecture materials, and readings, in addition to exercises and assignments designed to help students make sense of their learning experience. A packet of teaching materials will be distributed.

Staff: Robert H. Gass, California State University; John S. Seiter, Utah State University

12:30 – 3:15 p.m. Lake Huron
$50.00 **7** **Lectureless Learning: No More Talking Heads**

For faculty wanting step-by-step experience in integrating lectureless learning into their classes, this workshop offers a practical framework for experiencing non-lecture techniques which enhance verbal literacy and communication competency. Techniques will also be shared to enable faculty to share these perspectives with others and to design their own faculty development workshops for members of their departments and/or campus-wide use.

Staff: Allan Ward, University of Arkansas, Little Rock; Linda M. Pledger, University of Arkansas, Little Rock; Carol L. Thompson, University of Arkansas, Little Rock; Michael Kleine, University of Arkansas, Little Rock

12:30 – 3:15 p.m. Lake Erie
$50.00 **8** **Teaching the Adult Learner**

Now more than ever, adult students are returning to school after a long absence, or entering college for the first time. For college teachers and administrators interested in designing programs and courses aimed specifically at this new market of students, this course will explore the following topics: adult learning theory; adult learner characteristics; differences in learning styles; instructional strategies; and the adaptation of existing courses to a more non-traditional format (i.e. accelerated or workshop format).

Staff: Jeannette Kindred, Wayne State University; Elizabeth T. Tice, University of Phoenix

FRIDAY, Nov. 5

8:00 - 10:45 a.m.   Lake Ontario
$50.00   **9   Oral Communication Across the Curriculum:
                     Designing, Implementing, and Assessing a
                     University-Wide Program**

For college teachers and administrators interested in promoting oral communication across the curriculum, this course examines topics such as program design and implementation, internal and external support and funding, communication intensive courses across the curriculum, the communication laboratory, instructional materials including interactive multimedia instructional resources and development, accreditation issues, and program assessment methods.

Staff: Michael W. Cronin, Radford University; George L. Grice, Radford University

8:00 - 10:45 a.m.   Lake Michigan
$50.00   **10 Activity-Based Learning in the Small Group
                     Communication Classroom**

Activity-based learning is a teaching strategy that relies heavily on classroom exercises and activities designed to make course concepts and theories more accessible to undergraduate students. Classes using this technique are highly interactive and tend to be exciting and enjoyable. This short course will introduce communication instructors to some new classroom activities and rekindle their interest in some older ones, especially related to teaching small group communication.

Staff: Daivd R. Neumann, Rochester Institute of Technology; Keith B. Jenkins, Rochester Institute of Technology

8:00 - 10:45 a.m.   Lake Huron
$50.00   **11 Directing the Communication Internship
                     Program**

This will be a workshop for current and future directors of internship programs (departmental or college-wide, elective or required). Topics include eligibility requirements; appropriate placements; triangular and reciprocal relationships involving student, academic institution, and worksite; essential elements of the learning contract; and liability and risk management. The workshop format will be interactive and participants will receive handouts.

Staff: Karen M. Roloff, DePaul University; Eldra Rodriguez-Gilman, CBS News

8:00 - 10:45 a.m.   Lake Erie
$50.00   **12 Research Protocols for Usenet Applications**

Online Usenet forums provide a fertile field for research. However, research methodologies have failed to keep pace and traditional methods often are inappropriate in guiding researchers and protecting subjects. The focus of the workshop will be on guidelines for responsible research in news groups. Topics will include finding hard to reach populations, securing commitment, building trust, confidentiality and privacy issues, and more.

Staff: G. Jon Hall, University of Northern Iowa; Shing-Ling S. Chen, University of Northern Iowa

12:30 – 3:15 p.m.   Lake Ontario
$50.00   **13 Teaching the College Course in Leadership
                     Communication**

For teachers who are now or will be teaching a course in leadership. Topics include course organization, syllabus development, class activities, handouts, assignments, and interdisciplinary leadership minors and majors. Participants will receive a complimentary copy of *Leadership: A Communication Perspective* (3rd ed.).

Staff: Michael Z. Hackman, University of Colorado; Craig E. Johnson, George Fox University

12:30 – 3:15 p.m.   Lake Michigan
$50.00   **14 Your Speechfright: Teaching a Workshop or a
                    Module in a Basic Speech Course for High
                    Apprehensives**

For teachers and consultants who are interested in teaching a workshop or a unit/module in a
basic speech course for high apprehensives. Focus will be on organization, assignments, and
research-based interventions needed to form a creative, multidimensional approach.
Presented via interactive lecture, discussion, fun simulations, and practice. Textbook,
instructor's manual and materials will be provided.

Staff: Karen Kangas Dwyer, University of Nebraska, Omaha

12:30 – 3:15 p.m.   Lake Huron
$50.00   **15 Beyond the University, Into the Community:
                    Service-Learning in the Communication Course**

Service-learning provides students with the opportunity to develop skills and gain knowledge
through active participation in projects that meet community needs. Participants will gain the
skills needed to implement and assess service-learning projects, obtain ideas for a variety of
communication courses, and develop a plan for incorporating service-learning into their
courses.

Staff: Carolyn Lee Karmon, Washburn University; Russell Lowery-Hart, West Texas A&M
University; Carol Bruess, University of St. Thomas; Lori A. Byers, Spalding University; Laura L.
Shue, Ball State University

12:30 – 3:15 p.m.   Lake Erie
$50.00   **16 Teaching the College Course in Group
                    Communication**

For teachers interested in teaching the group communication course from an analytical or
process-oriented perspective. Participants will explore teaching assumptions through class
assignments designed to promote effective group interaction. Participants will receive a
complimentary text and instructor's manual.

Staff: Joann Keyton, University of Memphis

SATURDAY, Nov. 6

8:00 - 10:45 a.m.   Lake Ontario
$50.00   **17 Teaching Communication Courses with the
                    World Wide Web: Cognitive Technology**

This workshop is about using the Internet in teaching communication courses—Introduction
to Communication, Intrapersonal Communication, Internet for Educators, Multimedia,
Communication Education, CMC Research, and other classes. Participants will discuss uses of
the Internet from minimal limited use in a traditional classroom to full online use, including
using an online textbook. The workshop is intended for teachers who have never used the
Internet in their teaching or teachers who want to use a homepage-based course.

Staff: Leonard Shedletsky, University of Southern Maine; Howard Sypher, University of
Kansas; Melissa Beall, University of Northern Iowa; Joan E. Aitken, University of Missouri,
Kansas City

8:00 - 10:45 a.m.   Lake Michigan
$50.00   **18 Teaching Media Literacy in the Classroom**

This short course offers assistance in incorporating media literacy into media communication
courses. It will offer classroom tested instructional units, film/video resources, lecture
materials, readings, exercises, assignments, and classroom activities to help students make
sense of and analyze how media producers make and/or manipulate meaning. A packet of
materials will be distributed as well as a video tape of the film/video examples used in the
course and a copy of the video that the participants produce in the course. A familiarity with
Visual Literacy: Image, Mind, & Reality, (Messaris 1994), and *Media Literacy: Keys to*

Interpreting Media Messages, (Silverblatt) chapters 1-5, will prove useful.

Staff: Gary A. Noggle, Bethel College

8:00 - 10:45 a.m.   Lake Huron
$50.00   **19 How to Design a Course in Miscommunication**

This course will offer an overview of design specifications for a course in miscommunication and problematic talk. Instructors will place emphasis on strategies for active learning, acquisition of basic vocabulary and concept application, and will conduct a review of classic literature and techniques for generating conceptual outlines of crucial topics organized in sequential form. Participants will review case studies in protracted disagreement and mutual misunderstanding.

Staff: C. David Mortensen, University of Wisconsin, Madison

8:00 - 10:45 a.m.   Lake Erie
$50.00   **20 Innovative Approaches to ADR Courses**

This workshop provides training for instructors teaching many of the ADR specialty areas including negotiation, mediation, facilitation, arbitration, dispute systems design, and judicial processes. The course looks at how theory and practice must blend through the use of case studies, insights of prominent ADR professionals, simulations, and ADR models for the design of courses where both knowledge and skill are expected outcomes.

Staff: Michael Spangle, University of Denver; Myra Warren Isenhart, Denver University

12:30 – 3:15 p.m.   Lake Ontario
$50.00   **21 Incorporating Technology into the Intercultural Communication Course**

This course is intended for teachers who would like assistance in incorporating computer-based technologies into their intercultural communication course. The subject matter will focus on (1) how using computer technology can enhance the intercultural communication classroom, (2) how to incorporate technology into everyday lectures and activities, and (3) a hands-on visit to some World Wide Web sites that will enhance intercultural understanding. Supplements will be distributed.

Staff: Lisa A. Stefani, Grossmont College; Itsuo Shirono, Meikai University

12:30 – 3:15 p.m.   Lake Michigan
$50.00   **22 Racializing Communication: Teaching Interracial Communication on the Undergraduate and Graduate Levels**

This short course will serve as a spring board to learn how to implement/adapt a course in interracial communication to the respective needs of departments, university/colleges, and communities. The course will serve as a catalyst for a pedagogical tool that examines interracial communication as a communicative process distinct from intercultural communication. The course is designed to examine the evolution of culture to race and its effect on the development or avoidance of interpersonal relationships and improved race relations and communication. Participants will need to read *Brothers and Sisters* (Bebe Moore Campbell) prior to the conference.

Staff: Tina M. Harris, University of Georgia; Colleen Coleman, Bowling Green State University; Jennifer F. Wood, Bowling Green State University

Business Meetings

Listed by Program Sponsor

AAA

ADA BUSINESS MEETING
5:30-7:00 p.m.   Wednesday, Nov. 3   PDR 3   Third Floor   Hilton

AFA PROFESSIONAL DEVELOPMENT AND SUPPORT COMMITTEE
8:30-10:00 a.m.   Wednesday, Nov. 3   PDR 6   Third Floor   Hilton

AFA RESEARCH COMMITTEE
8:30-10:00 a.m.   Wednesday, Nov. 3   PDR 4   Third Floor   Hilton

AFA EDUCATIONAL DEVELOPMENT AND PRACTICES COMMITTEE
10:15-11:45 a.m.   Wednesday, Nov. 3   PDR 6   Third Floor   Hilton

AFA 50TH ANNIVERSARY COMMITTEE
10:15-11:45 a.m.   Wednesday, Nov. 3   PDR 1   Third Floor   Hilton

AFA FINANCE COMMITTEE
10:15-11:45 a.m.   Wednesday, Nov. 3   PDR 5   Third Floor   Hilton

AFA PUBLICATIONS COMMITTEE
10:15-11:45 a.m.   Wednesday, Nov. 3   PDR 4   Third Floor   Hilton

AFA NATIONAL COUNCIL
12:00-4:00 p.m.   Wednesday, Nov. 3   PDR 5   Third Floor   Hilton

AFA NIET COMMITTEE
12:00-4:00 p.m.   Wednesday, Nov. 3   PDR 1   Third Floor   Hilton

AFA NDT COMMITTEE
12:00-4:00 p.m.   Wednesday, Nov. 3   PDR 4   Third Floor   Hilton

AFA BUSINESS MEETING
4:00-5:30 p.m.   Wednesday, Nov. 3   PDR 2   Third Floor   Hilton

AFFIRMATIVE ACTION AND INTERCAUCUS COMMITTEE BUSINESS MEETING
1646   3:30 -4:45 p.m.   Thursday, Nov. 4 McCormick Brd Rm   Fourth Floor   Hilton

AFRICAN AMERICAN COMMUNICATION AND CULTURE DIVISION BUSINESS MEETING
2130   8:00 -9:15 a.m.   Friday, Nov. 5   PDR 5   Third Floor   Hilton

AFRICAN AMERICAN COMMUNICATION AND CULTURE DIVISION/BLACK CAUCUS BUSINESS MEETING
3633   3:30 -4:45 p.m.   Saturday, Nov. 6   Conf 4A   Fourth Floor   Hilton

AMERICAN ASSOCIATION FOR THE RHETORIC OF SCIENCE AND TECHNOLOGY BUSINESS MEETING
1632   3:30 -4:45 p.m.   Thursday, Nov. 4   PDR 7   Third Floor   Hilton

AMERICAN SOCIETY FOR THE HISTORY OF RHETORIC BUSINESS MEETING
1272   9:30 -10:45 a.m.   Thursday, Nov. 4   Rm 907   Ninth Floor   Spertus Institute

AMERICAN SOCIETY FOR THE HISTORY OF RHETORIC STEERING COMMITTEE MEETING
1372 11:00-12:15 p.m.   Thursday, Nov. 4   Rm 907   Ninth Floor   Spertus Institute

AMERICAN STUDIES COMMISSION BUSINESS MEETING
2546   2:00 -3:15 p.m.   Friday, Nov. 5   McCormick Brd Rm   Fourth Floor   Hilton

APPLIED COMMUNICATION DIVISION BUSINESS MEETING
3229 9:30 -10:45 a.m.   Saturday, Nov. 6   PDR 4   Third Floor   Hilton

ARGUMENTATION AND FORENSICS DIVISION BUSINESS MEETING
2231 9:30 -10:45 a.m.   Friday, Nov. 5   PDR 6   Third Floor   Hilton

ASIAN PACIFIC AMERICAN CAUCUS BUSINESS MEETING
2633   3:30 -4:45 p.m.   Friday, Nov. 5   Conf 4A   Fourth Floor   Hilton

ASIAN PACIFIC AMERICAN COMMUNICATION STUDIES DIVISION BUSINESS MEETING
2529   2:00 -3:15 p.m.   Friday, Nov. 5   PDR 4   Third Floor   Hilton

ASSOCIATION FOR CHINESE COMMUNICATION STUDIES BUSINESS MEETING
1631   3:30 -4:45 p.m.   Thursday, Nov. 4   PDR 6   Third Floor   Hilton

ASSOCIATION FOR COMMUNICATION ADMINISTRATION EXECUTIVE COMMITTEE MEETING
2541   2:00 -3:15 p.m.   Friday, Nov. 5   Conf 4I   Fourth Floor   Hilton

ASSOCIATION FOR COMMUNICATION ADMINISTRATION GENERAL BUSINESS MEETING
2641   3:30 -4:45 p.m.   Friday, Nov. 5   Conf 4I   Fourth Floor   Hilton

BBB

BASIC COURSE DIVISION BUSINESS MEETING
2530   2:00 -3:15 p.m.   Friday, Nov. 5   PDR 5   Third Floor   Hilton

BASIC COURSE DIVISION EXECUTIVE BOARD MEETING
2430 12:30-1:45 p.m.   Friday, Nov. 5   PDR 5   Third Floor   Hilton

BLACK CAUCUS BUSINESS MEETING
3136   8:00 -9:15 a.m.   Saturday, Nov. 6   Conf 4D   Fourth Floor   Hilton

CCC

CAUCUS ON DISABILITY ISSUES BUSINESS MEETING
1629   3:30 -4:45 p.m.   Thursday, Nov. 4   PDR 4   Third Floor   Hilton

CAUCUS ON GAY AND LESBIAN CONCERNS BUSINESS MEETING
3226 9:30 -10:45 a.m.   Saturday, Nov. 6   PDR 1   Third Floor   Hilton

CAUCUS ON GAY AND LESBIAN CONCERNS BUSINESS MEETING AND RECEPTION
2724   5:00 -7:45 p.m.   Friday, Nov. 5   Marquette Rm   Third Floor   Hilton

CENTRAL STATES COMMUNICATION ASSOCIATION BUSINESS MEETING
1630   3:30 -4:45 p.m.   Thursday, Nov. 4   PDR 5   Third Floor   Hilton

CENTRAL STATES COMMUNICATION ASSOCIATION BUSINESS MEETING
2622   3:30 -4:45 p.m.   Friday, Nov. 5   Williford B   Third Floor   Hilton

COMMISSION ON AMERICAN PARLIAMENTARY PRACTICE BUSINESS MEETING
3647   3:30 -4:45 p.m.   Saturday, Nov. 6   Pullman Board Rm   Fourth Floor   Hilton

COMMISSION ON COMMUNICATION AND AGING BUSINESS MEETING
2746   5:00 -6:15 p.m.   Friday, Nov. 5   McCormick Brd Rm   Fourth Floor   Hilton

COMMISSION ON COMMUNICATION AND LAW BUSINESS MEETING
2428 12:30-1:45 p.m.   Friday, Nov. 5   PDR 3   Third Floor   Hilton

COMMISSION ON COMMUNICATION IN THE FUTURE BUSINESS MEETING
3546   2:00 -3:15 p.m.   Saturday, Nov. 6   McCormick Brd Rm   Fourth Floor   Hilton

COMMUNICATION APPREHENSION AND AVOIDANCE COMMISSION BUSINESS MEETING
2126   8:00 -9:15 a.m.   Friday, Nov. 5   PDR 1   Third Floor   Hilton

COMMUNICATION ASSESSMENT COMMISSION BUSINESS MEETING
2131   8:00 -9:15 a.m.   Friday, Nov. 5   PDR 6   Third Floor   Hilton

COMMUNICATION ETHICS COMMISSION BUSINESS MEETING
2132   8:00 -9:15 a.m.   Friday, Nov. 5   PDR 7   Third Floor   Hilton

COMMUNICATION ETHICS COMMISSION BUSINESS MEETING
2730   5:00 -6:15 p.m.   Friday, Nov. 5   PDR 5   Third Floor   Hilton

COMMUNICATION NEEDS OF STUDENTS AT-RISK COMMISSION BUSINESS MEETING
2247   9:30 -10:45 a.m.   Friday, Nov. 5   Pullman Board Rm   Fourth Floor   Hilton

COMMUNITY COLLEGE SECTION BUSINESS MEETING
2028   7:00 -7:50 a.m.   Friday, Nov. 5   PDR 3   Third Floor   Hilton

COMMUNITY COLLEGE SECTION BUSINESS MEETING
3028   7:00 -7:50 a.m.   Saturday, Nov. 6   PDR 3   Third Floor   Hilton

COUNCIL OF FORENSICS ORGANIZATIONS
       2:00-3:45 p.m.   Wednesday, Nov. 3   PDR 1   Third Floor   Hilton

CRITICAL AND CULTURAL STUDIES DIVISION BUSINESS MEETING
3631   3:30 -4:45 p.m.   Saturday, Nov. 6   PDR 6   Third Floor   Hilton

CROSS EXAMINATION DEBATE ASSOCIATION BUSINESS MEETING
1627   3:30 -4:45 p.m.   Thursday, Nov. 4   PDR 2   Third Floor   Hilton

CROSS EXAMINATION DEBATE ASSOCIATION BUSINESS MEETING
2129   8:00 -9:15 a.m.   Friday, Nov. 5   PDR 4   Third Floor   Hilton

CROSS EXAMINATION DEBATE ASSOCIATION BUSINESS MEETING
3635   3:30 -4:45 p.m.   Saturday, Nov. 6   Conf 4C   Fourth Floor   Hilton

DDD

DELTA SIGMA RHO - TAU KAPPA ALPHA BUSINESS MEETING
2146   8:00 -9:15 a.m.   Friday, Nov. 5   McCormick Brd Rm   Fourth Floor   Hilton

DELTA SIGMA RHO - TAU KAPPA ALPHA BUSINESS MEETING
3247   9:30 -10:45 a.m.   Saturday, Nov. 6   Pullman Board Rm   Fourth Floor   Hilton

EEE

EASTERN COMMUNICATION ASSOCIATION EXECUTIVE COUNCIL MEETING
0746   5:00 -7:45 p.m.   Wednesday, Nov. 3   McCormick Brd Rm   Fourth Floor   Hilton

EASTERN COMMUNICATION ASSOCIATION EXECUTIVE COUNCIL MEETING
2230   9:30 -10:45 a.m.   Friday, Nov. 5   PDR 5   Third Floor   Hilton

EDUCATIONAL POLICIES BOARD BUSINESS MEETING
2742   5:00 -6:15 p.m.   Friday, Nov. 5   Conf 4J   Fourth Floor   Hilton

EDUCATIONAL POLICIES BOARD BUSINESS MEETING
3646   3:30 -4:45 p.m.   Saturday, Nov. 6   McCormick Brd Rm   Fourth Floor   Hilton

ELEMENTARY AND SECONDARY EDUCATION SECTION BUSINESS MEETING
2632   3:30 -4:45 p.m.   Friday, Nov. 5   PDR 7   Third Floor   Hilton

EMERITUS ADVISORY COUNCIL BUSINESS MEETING
1677   3:30 -4:45 p.m.   Thursday, Nov. 4   Imperial South   Hilton

EMERITUS/RETIRED MEMBERS SECTION BUSINESS MEETING
3156   8:00-9:15 a.m.   Saturday, Nov. 6   Conf 5I   Fifth Floor   Hilton

ENVIRONMENTAL COMMUNICATION COMMISSION BUSINESS MEETING
2427   12:30-1:45 p.m.   Friday, Nov. 5   PDR 2   Third Floor   Hilton

ENVIRONMENTAL COMMUNICATION COMMISSION BUSINESS MEETING
3032   7:00 -7:50 a.m.   Saturday, Nov. 6   PDR 7   Third Floor   Hilton

ETHNOGRAPHY DIVISION BUSINESS MEETING
2732   5:00 -6:15 p.m.   Friday, Nov. 5   PDR 7   Third Floor   Hilton

EXPERIENTIAL LEARNING IN COMMUNICATION COMMISSION BUSINESS MEETING
2046   7:00 -7:50 a.m.   Friday, Nov. 5   McCormick Brd Rm   Fourth Floor   Hilton

FFF

FAMILY COMMUNICATION DIVISION EXECUTIVE COMMITTEE MEETING
1126   8:00 -9:15 a.m.   Thursday, Nov. 4   PDR 1   Third Floor   Hilton

FAMILY COMMUNICATION DIVISION GENERAL BUSINESS MEETING
3628   3:30 -4:45 p.m.   Saturday, Nov. 6   PDR 3   Third Floor   Hilton

FEMINIST AND WOMEN'S STUDIES DIVISION AND WOMEN'S CAUCUS JOINT EXECUTIVE COUNCIL MEETING
1527   2:00 -3:15 p.m.   Thursday, Nov. 4   PDR 2   Third Floor   Hilton

FEMINIST AND WOMEN'S STUDIES DIVISION GENERAL BUSINESS MEETING
2533   2:00 -3:15 p.m.   Friday, Nov. 5   Conf 4A   Fourth Floor   Hilton

FREEDOM OF EXPRESSION DIVISION BUSINESS MEETING
2631   3:30 -4:45 p.m.   Friday, Nov. 5   PDR 6   Third Floor   Hilton

FORENSICS ORGANIZATIONS RECEPTION
     7:00 -10:00 p.m.   Wednesday, Nov. 3   PDR 2   Third Floor   Hilton

GGG

GAY/LESBIAN/BISEXUAL/TRANSGENDER COMMUNICATION STUDIES DIVISION BUSINESS MEETING
1628   3:30 -4:45 p.m.   Thursday, Nov. 4   PDR 3   Third Floor   Hilton

GROUP COMMUNICATION DIVISION BUSINESS MEETING
1528   3:30 -4:45 p.m.   Thursday, Nov. 4   PDR 3   Third Floor   Hilton

HHH

HEALTH COMMUNICATION DIVISION BUSINESS MEETING
3627   3:30 -4:45 p.m.   Saturday, Nov. 6   PDR 2   Third Floor   Hilton

HUMAN COMMUNICATIONS AND TECHNOLOGY COMMISSION BUSINESS MEETING
3131   8:00 -9:15 a.m.   Saturday, Nov. 6   PDR 6   Third Floor   Hilton

III

INSTRUCTIONAL DEVELOPMENT DIVISION BUSINESS MEETING
2626   3:30 -4:45 p.m.   Friday, Nov. 5   PDR 1   Third Floor   Hilton

INSTRUCTIONAL DEVELOPMENT DIVISION EXECUTIVE BOARD MEETING
2226   9:30 -10:45 a.m.   Friday, Nov. 5   PDR 1   Third Floor   Hilton

INTERNATIONAL AND INTERCULTURAL COMMUNICATION DIVISION BUSINESS MEETING
3127   8:00 -9:15 a.m.   Saturday, Nov. 6   PDR 2   Third Floor   Hilton

INTERNATIONAL FORENSICS ASSOCIATION BUSINESS MEETING
2547   2:00 -3:15 p.m.   Friday, Nov. 5   Pullman Board Rm   Fourth Floor   Hilton

INTERNATIONAL FORENSICS ASSOCIATION BUSINESS MEETING
2647   3:30 -4:45 p.m.   Friday, Nov. 5   Pullman Board Rm   Fourth Floor   Hilton

INTERPERSONAL COMMUNICATION DIVISION BUSINESS MEETING
3219   9:30 -10:45 a.m.   Saturday, Nov. 6   Astoria   Third Floor   Hilton

INTRAPERSONAL COMMUNICATION/SOCIAL COGNITION COMMISSION BUSINESS MEETING
3146   8:00 -9:15 a.m.   Saturday, Nov. 6   McCormick Brd Rm   Fourth Floor   Hilton

Bus Mtgs

KKK

KENNETH BURKE SOCIETY
3630   3:30 -4:45 p.m.   Saturday, Nov. 6   PDR 5   Third Floor   Hilton

KENNETH BURKE SOCIETY BUSINESS MEETING
3630   3:30 -4:45 p.m.   Saturday, Nov. 6   PDR 5   Third Floor   Hilton

LLL

LA RAZA CAUCUS AND LATINA/LATINO COMMUNICATION STUDIES DIVISION BUSINESS MEETING
3230 9:30 -10:45 a.m.   Saturday, Nov. 6   PDR 5   Third Floor   Hilton

LA RAZA CAUCUS AND LATINA/LATINO COMMUNICATION STUDIES DIVISION EXECUTIVE OFFICERS MEETING
2227 9:30 -10:45 a.m.   Friday, Nov. 5   PDR 2   Third Floor   Hilton

LAMBDA PI ETA BUSINESS MEETING
1157   8:00 -9:15 a.m.   Thursday, Nov. 4   Conf 5J   Fifth Floor   Hilton

LANGUAGE AND SOCIAL INTERACTION DIVISION BUSINESS MEETING
2128   8:00 -9:15 a.m.   Friday, Nov. 5   PDR 3   Third Floor   Hilton

MMM

MASS COMMUNICATION DIVISION BUSINESS MEETING AND RECEPTION
2727   5:00 -7:45 p.m.   Friday, Nov. 5   PDR 2   Third Floor   Hilton

NNN

NATIONAL DEBATE TOURNAMENT BOARD OF TRUSTEES
          8:30-10:00 a.m.   Wednesday, Nov. 3   PDR 5   Third Floor   Hilton

NATIONAL EDUCATION DEBATE ASSOCIATION BUSINESS MEETING
2232 9:30 -10:45 a.m.   Friday, Nov. 5   PDR 7   Third Floor   Hilton

NATIONAL FEDERATION INTERSCHOLASTIC SPEECH AND DEBATE ASSOCIATION BUSINESS MEETING
3147   8:00 -9:15 a.m.   Saturday, Nov. 6   Pullman Board Rm   Fourth Floor   Hilton

NATIONAL FORENSIC ASSOCIATION BUSINESS MEETING
3530   2:00 -3:15 p.m.   Saturday, Nov. 6   PDR 5   Third Floor   Hilton

NATIONAL FORENSIC ASSOCIATION EXECUTIVE COUNCIL MEETING
1635   3:30 -4:45 p.m.   Thursday, Nov. 4   Conf 4C   Fourth Floor   Hilton

NCA 1999 NOMINATING COMMITTEE BUSINESS
0815   6:30 -7:45 p.m.   Wednesday, Nov. 3   Boulevard B   Second Floor   Hilton

NCA 1999 NOMINATING COMMITTEE BUSINESS MEETING
2815   6:30 -7:45 p.m.   Friday, Nov. 5   Boulevard B   Second Floor   Hilton

NCA 2000 CONVENTION PLANNERS FIRST MEETING
0724   5:00 -8:00 p.m.   Wednesday, Nov. 3   Marquette   Third Floor   Hilton

NCA 2000 CONVENTION PLANNERS SECOND MEETING
4125   8:00 -9:15 a.m.   Sunday, Nov. 7   Joliet   Third Floor   Hilton

NCA 2000 NOMINATING COMMITTEE BUSINESS MEETING
4225 9:30 -10:45 a.m.   Sunday, Nov. 7   Joliet   Third Floor   Hilton

NCA AND AFFILIATE ORGANIZATIONS BUSINESS MEETING
2432 12:30-1:45 p.m.   Friday, Nov. 5   PDR 7   Third Floor   Hilton

NCA AND REGIONAL COMMUNICATION ASSOCIATION EXECUTIVE DIRECTORS BUSINESS MEETING
1404 12:30-1:45 p.m.   Thursday, Nov. 4   Grand Traditions   Lobby Level   Hilton

NCA AND STATE COMMUNICATION ASSOCIATION PRESIDENTS BUSINESS MEETING
2532   2:00 -3:15 p.m.   Friday, Nov. 5   PDR 7   Third Floor   Hilton

NCA COMMITTEE ON COMMITTEES BUSINESS MEETING
0946   8:00 -9:15 p.m.   Wednesday, Nov. 3   McCormick Brd Rm   Fourth Floor   Hilton

NCA COUNCIL ON PH.D. PROGRAMS BUSINESS MEETING
2178   8:00 -9:15 a.m.   Friday, Nov. 5   Conrad Suite   Hilton

NCA LEGISLATIVE COUNCIL BUSINESS MEETING
0418   12:30-4:45 p.m.   Wednesday, Nov. 3   Waldorf   Third Floor   Hilton

NCA LEGISLATIVE COUNCIL BUSINESS MEETING
3418   12:30-3:15 p.m.   Saturday, Nov. 6   Waldorf   Third Floor   Hilton

NCA LEGISLATIVE COUNCIL BUSINESS MEETING
4118   8:00 -9:15 a.m.   Sunday, Nov. 7   Waldorf   Third Floor   Hilton

NCA PAST PRESIDENTS BUSINESS MEETING AND LUNCHEON
2478   12:30-3:15 p.m.   Friday, Nov. 5   Conrad Suite   Hilton

NCA PUBLICATIONS BOARD BUSINESS MEETING
1347   11:00-12:15 p.m.   Thursday, Nov. 4   Pullman Board Rm   Fourth Floor   Hilton

NCA RESOLUTIONS COMMITTEE BUSINESS MEETING
1231   9:30 -10:45 a.m.   Thursday, Nov. 4   PDR 6   Third Floor   Hilton

NPDA BUSINESS MEETING
      2:00-3:45 p.m.   Wednesday, Nov. 3   PDR 3   Third Floor   Hilton

OOO

ORGANIZATIONAL COMMUNICATION DIVISION BUSINESS MEETING
2224   9:30 -10:45 a.m.   Friday, Nov. 5   Marquette   Third Floor   Hilton

PPP

PEACE AND CONFLICT COMMUNICATION COMMISSION BUSINESS MEETING
3447   12:30-1:45 p.m.   Saturday, Nov. 6   Pullman Board Rm   Fourth Floor   Hilton

PEACE AND CONFLICT COMMUNICATION COMMISSION BUSINESS MEETING
3547   2:00 -3:15 p.m.   Saturday, Nov. 6   Pullman Board Rm   Fourth Floor   Hilton

PERFORMANCE STUDIES DIVISION BUSINESS MEETING
2527   2:00 -3:15 p.m.   Friday, Nov. 5   PDR 2   Third Floor   Hilton

PHI RHO PI BUSINESS MEETING
2229   9:30 -10:45 a.m.   Friday, Nov. 5   PDR 4   Third Floor   Hilton

PI KAPPA DELTA BUSINESS MEETING
3634   3:30 -4:45 p.m.   Saturday, Nov. 6   Conf 4B   Fourth Floor   Hilton

PI KAPPA DELTA NATIONAL COUNCIL BUSINESS MEETING
1046   7:00 -9:15 a.m.   Thursday, Nov. 4   McCormick Brd Rm   Fourth Floor   Hilton

PI KAPPA DELTA NATIONAL COUNCIL BUSINESS MEETING
2047   7:00 -9:15 a.m.   Friday, Nov. 5   Pullman Board Rm   Fourth Floor   Hilton

POLITICAL COMMUNICATION DIVISION BUSINESS MEETING
1145   8:00 -9:15 a.m.   Thursday, Nov. 4   Conf 4M   Fourth Floor   Hilton

PUBLIC ADDRESS DIVISION BUSINESS MEETING
2429   12:30-1:45 p.m.   Friday, Nov. 5   PDR 4   Third Floor   Hilton

PUBLIC RELATIONS DIVISION BUSINESS MEETING
2426   12:30-1:45 p.m.   Friday, Nov. 5   PDR 1   Third Floor   Hilton

PUBLIC RELATIONS DIVISION BUSINESS MEETING
3637   3:30 -4:45 p.m.   Saturday, Nov. 6   Conf 4E   Fourth Floor   Hilton

PUBLICATIONS BOARD AND NCA EDITORS BUSINESS MEETING
1546　2:00 -3:15 p.m.　　Thursday, Nov. 4　McCormick Brd Rm　　Fourth Floor　　Hilton

RRR

RACIAL AND ETHNIC DIVERSITY ADVISORY COUNCIL MEETING
2246　9:30 -10:45 a.m.　　　Friday, Nov. 5　McCormick Brd Rm　　Fourth Floor　　Hilton

RELIGIOUS COMMUNICATION ASSOCIATION BUSINESS MEETING
2629　3:30 -4:45 p.m.　　　Friday, Nov. 5　　　　　　PDR 4　　Third Floor　　Hilton

RELIGIOUS COMMUNICATION ASSOCIATION BUSINESS MEETING
3636　3:30 -4:45 p.m.　　Saturday, Nov. 6　　　　　Conf 4D　　Fourth Floor　　Hilton

RESEARCH BOARD BUSINESS MEETING
1532　2:00 -3:15 p.m.　　Thursday, Nov. 4　　　　　PDR 7　　Third Floor　　Hilton

RHETORIC AND COMMUNICATION THEORY DIVISION BUSINESS MEETING
2729　5:00 -6:15 p.m.　　　Friday, Nov. 5　　　　　　PDR 4　　Third Floor　　Hilton

SSS

SEMIOTICS AND COMMUNICATION COMMISSION BUSINESS MEETING
2747　5:00 -6:15 p.m.　　　Friday, Nov. 5　Pullman Board Rm　　Fourth Floor　　Hilton

SENIOR COLLEGE AND UNIVERSITY SECTION GENERAL BUSINESS MEETING
2726　5:00 -6:15 p.m.　　　Friday, Nov. 5　　　　　　PDR 1　　Third Floor　　Hilton

SENIOR COLLEGE AND UNIVERSITY SECTION SMALL COLLEGE BUSINESS MEETING
1633　3:30 -4:45 p.m.　　Thursday, Nov. 4　　　　　Conf 4A　　Fourth Floor　　Hilton

SOCIETY FOR THE STUDY OF SYMBOLIC INTERACTION BUSINESS MEETING
3246　9:30 -10:45 a.m.　　Saturday, Nov. 6　McCormick Brd Rm　　Fourth Floor　　Hilton

SOUTHERN STATES COMMUNICATION ASSOCIATION EXECUTIVE COUNCIL MEETING
1647　3:30 -4:45 p.m.　　Thursday, Nov. 4　Pullman Board Rm　　Fourth Floor　　Hilton

SOUTHERN STATES COMMUNICATION ASSOCIATION EXECUTIVE COUNCIL MEETING
2646　3:30 -4:45 p.m.　　　Friday, Nov. 5　McCormick Brd Rm　　Fourth Floor　　Hilton

SOUTHERN STATES COMMUNICATION ASSOCIATION NOMINATING COMMITTEE
MEETING
2446　12:30-1:45 p.m.　　　Friday, Nov. 5　McCormick Brd Rm　　Fourth Floor　　Hilton

SPIRITUAL COMMUNICATION COMMISSION BUSINESS MEETING
2526　2:00 -3:15 p.m.　　　Friday, Nov. 5　　　　　　PDR 1　　Third Floor　　Hilton

STATES ADVISORY COUNCIL BUSINESS MEETING
3232　9:30 -10:45 a.m.　　Saturday, Nov. 6　　　　　PDR 7　　Third Floor　　Hilton

STUDENT SECTION BUSINESS MEETING
2528　2:00 -3:15 p.m.　　　Friday, Nov. 5　　　　　　PDR 3　　Third Floor　　Hilton

TTT

THEATRE DIVISION BUSINESS MEETING
2731　5:00 -6:15 p.m.　　　Friday, Nov. 5　　　　　　PDR 6　　Third Floor　　Hilton

THEATRE DIVISION BUSINESS MEETING
3130　8:00 -9:15 a.m.　　Saturday, Nov. 6　　　　　PDR 5　　Third Floor　　Hilton

TRAINING AND DEVELOPMENT DIVISION BUSINESS MEETING
1642　3:30 -4:45 p.m.　　Thursday, Nov. 4　　　　　Conf 4J　　Fourth Floor　　Hilton

VVV

VIRGINIA STATE COMMUNICATION ASSOCIATION BOARD MEETING
1346 11:00-12:15 p.m.　　Thursday, Nov. 4　McCormick Brd Rm　　Fourth Floor　　Hilton

VISUAL COMMUNICATION COMMISSION BUSINESS MEETING
3231 9:30 -10:45 a.m.   Saturday, Nov. 6   PDR 6   Third Floor   Hilton

WWW

WESTERN STATES COMMUNICATION ASSOCIATION BUSINESS MEETING
0859 6:30 -8:15 p.m.   Wednesday, Nov. 3   Lake Michigan   Eighth Floor   Hilton

WOMEN'S CAUCUS BUSINESS MEETING AND FRANCINE MERRITT AWARD RECEPTION
2725 5:00 -7:45 p.m.   Friday, Nov. 5   Joliet   Third Floor   Hilton

WORLD COMMUNICATION ASSOCIATION BUSINESS MEETING
2447 12:30-1:45 p.m.   Friday, Nov. 5   Pullman Board Rm   Fourth Floor   Hilton

Bus Mtgs

Congratulations

Orlando L. Taylor
**President, National Communication Association
1998-1999**

We're Proud of You!

The Graduate School
The School of Communications
Howard University

Wednesday,
November 3, 1999

8:00 a.m.

0106   8:00-5:00 p.m.   Continental BR A   Lobby Level   Chicago Hilton

PRECONFERENCE: WHEN THE CORPORATION MEETS THE CLASSROOM: LEARNING COMMUNICATION EXPERIENTIALLY

Sponsor: Experiential Learning in Communication Commission
Chair: Donald R. Martin, DePaul University

Panelists: Lillian Davis, IBM Corporation
Karen Inman, Ameritech Communication
Mark L. Knapp, University of Texas, Austin
Karen M. Roloff, DePaul University
Timothy L. Sellnow, North Dakota State University
Julia T. Wood, University of North Carolina, Chapel Hill
Dawn O. Braithwaite, University of Nebraska, Lincoln
Larry D. Browning, University of Texas, Austin
Roseanna G. Ross, St. Cloud State University
David Natharius, California State University, Fresno
Jef Dolan, Marymount University
Eileen M. Perrigo, University of West Florida
Shelly Hinck, Central Michigan University
Gregory H. Patton, University of Southern California

Advance registration required.

0107   8:00-5:00 p.m.   Continental BR B   Lobby Level   Chicago Hilton

PRECONFERENCE: COLORING OUTSIDE THE LINES: TAKING RISKS IN THE BASIC COURSE

Sponsor: Basic Course Division, Harcourt Brace College Publishers
Chair: Deanna D. Sellnow, North Dakota State University

Panelists: Lisa J. Goodnight, Purdue University, Calumet
Amy R. Slagell, Iowa State University
Lynn M. Harter, Moorhead State University
Paul D. Turman, University of Nebraska, Lincoln
Rebecca A. Litke, California State University, Northridge
Melissa L. Beall, University of Northern Iowa
Lynn M. Disbrow, Sinclair Community College
Brian D. Kline, Gainesville College
Nancy Buerkel-Rothfuss, Central Michigan University
Brian S. Titsworth, Moorhead State University
Robert R. Ulmer, University of Arkansas, Little Rock
William J. Seiler, University of Nebraska, Lincoln
Tamara Golish, Luther College
Bianca Grosche, North Dakota State University

Terry M. Perkins, Eastern Illinois University
Betty Jane Lawrence, Bradley University

Advance registration required.

0108   8:30-6:30 p.m.   Continental BR C   Lobby Level   Chicago Hilton

PRECONFERENCE: PUBLIC RELATIONS PEDAGOGY: TOPICS IN TEACHING-LEARNING STRATEGIES FOR PUBLIC RELATIONS EDUCATION

Sponsor: Public Relations Division
Chair: W. Timothy Coombs, Illinois State University

Advance registration required.

0114   8:30-6:00 p.m.   Boulevard A   Second Floor   Chicago Hilton

PRECONFERENCE ON TENURE AND PROMOTION

Sponsors: Women's Caucus
            Gay & Lesbian Concerns Caucus
            Black Caucus
            Association for Communication Administration
Chair: Lynne M. Webb, University of Memphis

Panelists: Marsha Houston, Tulane University
             E. Culpepper Clark, University of Alabama
             Brooke Quigley, University of Memphis
             John T. Masterson, Texas Lutheran University
             Nancy L. Harper, Grand Valley State University
             Barbara M. Montgomery, Millersville University
             John H. Nicholson, Angelo State University
             Mary Jane Collier, University of Denver
             Lois S. Self, Northern Illinois University
             Judith S. Trent, University of Cincinnati
             Richard R. Ranta, University of Memphis
             Don W. Stacks, University of Miami
             Tamara S. Bollis-Pecci, University of Denver
             Isaac E. Catt, Millersville University
             Catherine A. Collins, Willamette University
             Milan D. Meeske, University of Central Florida
             Nina-Jo Moore, Appalachian State University
             Jeanne S. Posner, Western Connecticut State University
             Sherri Smith, University of Alabama, Huntsville
             Katherine Hawkins, Wichita State University
             Michael R. Hemphill, University of Arkansas, Little Rock
             John I. Sisco, Southwest Missouri State University
             Robert M. Smith, University of Tennessee, Martin
             Anita Taylor, George Mason University
             Ronald L. Jackson, Penn State University
             Carl M. Cates, Valdosta State University
             Charles R. Bantz, Arizona State University
             Linda C. Lederman, Rutgers University
             Mittie J. A. Nimocks, University of Wisconsin, Platteville
             Fern L. Johnson, Clark University
             Kandi L. Walker, University of Denver
             Suzanne McCorkle, Boise State University
             Pamela J. Kalbfleisch, University of Wyoming
             William G. Christ, Trinity University
             Bill Balthrop, University of North Carolina
             Judy C. Pearson, Virginia Tech University
             Carol L. Thompson, University of Arkansas, Little Rock

Advance registration required.

0115   8:00-5:00 p.m.   Boulevard B   Second Floor   Chicago Hilton

PRECONFERENCE: TEAMING BEYOND 2000: TECHNOLOGY TRAINING FOR CREATIVE CONNECTIONS

Sponsors: Training and Development Division
        Human Communication and Technology Commission

Panelists: Karen R. Krupar, Metropolitan State College of Denver
        Mary Y. Mandeville, Oklahoma State University
        Clark Germann, Metropolitan State College of Denver
        Maurine C. Eckloff, University of Nebraska, Kearney
        Mark A. Aakhus, Rutgers University
        Mark E. Adkins, University of Arizona
        Paul Collins, Jordan-Webb, Chicago

Advance registration required.

0116   8:00-4:45 p.m.   Boulevard C   Second Floor   Chicago Hilton

PRECONFERENCE: STUDYING SOCIAL CODES THROUGH THE ANALYSIS OF LANGUAGE IN SOCIAL INTERACTION

Sponsor: Language and Social Interaction Division
Chairs: Gerry F. Philipsen, University of Washington
        Michaela R. Winchatz, Southern Illinois University

Panelists: Anita M. Pomerantz, Temple University
        D. Lawrence Wieder, University of Oklahoma
        Richard Buttny, Syracuse University
        Donal A. Carbaugh, University of Massachusetts, Amherst
        Kristine L. Fitch, University of Iowa
        Karen Tracy, University of Colorado
        Robert E. Sanders, SUNY, Albany

Advance registration required.

0121   8:00-5:00 p.m.   Williford A   Third Floor   Chicago Hilton

PRECONFERENCE: THE STATE OF FAMILY COMMUNICATION EDUCATION: BUILDING FOR THE FUTURE

Sponsor: Family Communication Division
Chair: Thomas J. Socha, Old Dominion University

Panelists: Kathleen M. Galvin, Northwestern University
        Roberta A. Davilla, University of Northern Iowa
        L. Edna Rogers, University of Utah
        Sandra Petronio, Arizona State University
        Fran Dickson, University of Denver
        Anita L. Vangelisti, University of Texas, Austin
        Lynne M. Webb, University of Memphis
        Dawn O. Braithwaite, University of Nebraska, Lincoln
        Arthur P. Bochner, University of South Florida
        Nancy Buerkel-Rothfuss, Central Michigan University
        Gail G. Whitchurch, Indiana University-Purdue University, Indianapolis
        Laurie Arliss, Ithaca College
        Lynn H. Turner, Marquette University
        Jennings Bryant, University of Alabama
        Beth J. Haslett, University of Delaware
        Rhunette C. Diggs, University of Louisville

Advance registration required.

Wednesday

| 0123 | 9:00-4:30 p.m. | Williford C | Third Floor | Chicago Hilton |

PRECONFERENCE: BUILDING COMMUNITY: SERVICE-LEARNING IN THE COMMUNICATION DISCIPLINE

Sponsor: NCA Second Vice President, American Association of Higher Education, Campus Compact
Chairs: James L. Applegate, University of Kentucky
Sherwyn P. Morreale, NCA National Office

Panelists: Edward Zlotkowski, American Association for Higher Education
John Saltmarsh, Campus Compact
David Droge, University of Puget Sound
Richard L. Conville, University of Southern Mississippi
Ruth A. Hulbert-Johnson, University of Colorado
Shirlee A. Levin, Charles County Community College

Advance registration required.

| 0125 | 8:30-8:00 p.m. | Joliet | Third Floor | Chicago Hilton |

PRECONFERENCE: WHAT LINES?: INTERDISCIPLINARITY AND THE RHETORIC OF SCIENCE AND TECHNOLOGY

Sponsor: American Association for Rhetoric of Science & Technology
Chair: Joan Leach, Imperial College of London

| 0132 | 8:00-4:45 p.m. | PDR 7 | Third Floor | Chicago Hilton |

1. RETHINKING STRUCTURATION THEORY IN COMMUNICATION

Sponsor: Seminar Series

| 0133 | 8:00-4:45 p.m. | Conf 4A | Fourth Floor | Chicago Hilton |

2. REDRAWING COMMUNICATION ETHICS: EMMANUEL LEVINAS AND THE CALL OF THE OTHER

Sponsor: Seminar Series

| 0134 | 8:00-4:45 p.m. | Conf 4B | Fourth Floor | Chicago Hilton |

3. THE FALL OF COMMUNISM AND ITS IMPACT ON DEMOCRATIC DISCOURSE: TEN YEARS AFTER

Sponsor: Seminar Series

| 0135 | 8:00-4:45 p.m. | Conf 4C | Fourth Floor | Chicago Hilton |

4. COLOR US QUEER: COMMUNICATION AND ALTERNATIVE RELATIONSHIPS

Sponsor: Seminar Series

| 0137 | 8:00-4:45 p.m. | Conf 4E | Fourth Floor | Chicago Hilton |

5. MASCULINITY AT THE END OF THE MILLENNIUM

Sponsor: Seminar Series

| 0138 | 8:00-4:45 p.m. | Conf 4F | Fourth Floor | Chicago Hilton |

6. TWENTIETH-CENTURY FIRST LADIES: EXPLORING THE INTERSECTIONS OF POLITICS, MEDIA, THEORY, AND CRITICISM

Sponsor: Seminar Series

| 0139 | 8:00-4:45 p.m. | Conf 4G | Fourth Floor | Chicago Hilton |

7. COLD WAR FILMS 1945-1991

Sponsor: Seminar Series

| 0140 | 8:00-4:45 p.m. | Conf 4H | Fourth Floor | Chicago Hilton |

8. MOVEMENTS AND SPHERES: CHALLENGING US TO THEORIZE OUTSIDE THE LINES

Sponsor: Seminar Series

| 0141 | 8:00-4:45 p.m. | Conf 4I | Fourth Floor | Chicago Hilton |

9. BRITISH PUBLIC ADDRESS: PAGES YET TO COLOUR

Sponsor: Seminar Series

| 0142 | 8:00-4:45 p.m. | Conf 4J | Fourth Floor | Chicago Hilton |

10. BLURRING THE BOUNDARIES: BAKHTIN, DIALOGUE AND PERMEABLE COMMUNICATION

Sponsor: Seminar Series

| 0143 | 8:00-4:45 p.m. | Conf 4K | Fourth Floor | Chicago Hilton |

11. INTRAPERSONAL COMMUNICATION

Sponsor: Seminar Series

| 0144 | 8:00-4:45 p.m. | Conf 4L | Fourth Floor | Chicago Hilton |

12. RHETORIC AND PSYCHIATRY: PERSUASION AND COMMUNICATION ISSUES

Sponsor: Seminar Series

| 0153 | 8:00-4:45 p.m. | Conf 5F | Fifth Floor | Chicago Hilton |

13. CREATING A COLLAGE: COMMUNICATION AND CULTURE IN THE TWENTIES

Sponsor: Seminar Series

| 0154 | 8:00-4:45 p.m. | Conf 5G | Fifth Floor | Chicago Hilton |

14. INTERDISCIPLINARY, MULTI-METHOD APPROACHES TO A JEWISH RHETORICAL THEORY: CROSSING THE BOUNDARIES

Sponsor: Seminar Series

| 0155 | 8:00-4:45 p.m. | Conf 5H | Fifth Floor | Chicago Hilton |

15. A COMMUNICATION APPROACH TO THE HIV/AIDS EPIDEMIC: THEORY, RESEARCH, PRACTICE, AND EXPERIENCE

Sponsor: Seminar Series

| 0178 | 8:00-5:00 p.m. | | | Off Site |

PRECONFERENCE: FROM MEDIEVAL TO MODERN RHETORICS

Sponsor: American Society for the History of Rhetoric
Chair: Mari Lee Mifsud, University of Richmond

| 0178 | 9:00-9:00 p.m. | | | Off Site |

PRECONFERENCE: ALL ABOUT FOOD AND CONVERSATION: AN ETHNOGRAPHY WORKSHOP ON DAILY CONSUMPTION AND INFORMAL DIALOGUE

Sponsor: Ethnography Division
Chairs: Ronald F. Wendt, University of South Dakota
Melanie B. Mills, Eastern Illinois University

Panelists: Nick L. Trujillo, California State University, Sacramento
Ronald F. Wendt, University of South Dakota
Melanie B. Mills, Eastern Illinois University
H.L. (Bud) Goodall, University of North Carolina, Greensboro
Patricia Geist, San Diego State University
Tami L. Spry, St. Cloud State University
Melissa W. Aleman, James Madison University
Nancy L. Anderson, Northwestern University
Martha A. Hagan, Whatcom Community College

Advance registration required.

12:30 p.m.

| 0418 | 12:30-4:45 p.m. | Waldorf | Third Floor | Chicago Hilton |

NCA LEGISLATIVE COUNCIL BUSINESS MEETING

Sponsor: NCA Legislative Council

5:00 p.m.

| 0713 | 5:00-7:45 p.m. | Normandie Lounge | Second Floor | Chicago Hilton |

EARLY BIRD NO-HOST WELCOME RECEPTION

Sponsor: National Communication Association

| 0724 | 5:00-8:00 p.m. | Marquette | Third Floor | Chicago Hilton |

NCA 2000 CONVENTION PLANNERS FIRST MEETING

Sponsor: 2000 NCA Convention Planners Committee

| 0746 | 5:00-7:45 p.m. | McCormick Board Rm | Fourth Floor | Chicago Hilton |

EASTERN COMMUNICATION ASSOCIATION EXECUTIVE COUNCIL MEETING

Sponsor: Eastern Communication Association

6:30 p.m.

| 0815 | 6:30-7:45 p.m. | Boulevard B | Second Floor | Chicago Hilton |

NCA 1999 NOMINATING COMMITTEE BUSINESS MEETING

Sponsor: 1999 NCA Nominating Committee

| 0859 | 6:30-8:15 p.m. | Lake Michigan | Eighth Floor | Chicago Hilton |

WESTERN STATES COMMUNICATION ASSOCIATION BUSINESS MEETING

Sponsor: Western States Communication Association

8:00 p.m.

| 0946 | 8:00-9:15 p.m. | McCormick Board Rm | Fourth Floor | Chicago Hilton |

NCA COMMITTEE ON COMMITTEES BUSINESS MEETING

Sponsor: NCA Committee on Committees

Wednesday

Colleagues of
THE SCHOOL OF
INTERPERSONAL COMMUNICATION
at
OHIO UNIVERSITY
congratulate
RAYMIE McKERROW, Ph.D.
on his election as
1999
First Vice President
of the
National Communication Association

Thursday,
November 4, 1999

7:00 a.m.

1046	7:00-9:15 a.m.	McCormick Board Rm	Fourth Floor	Chicago Hilton

PI KAPPA DELTA NATIONAL COUNCIL BUSINESS MEETING

Sponsor: Pi Kappa Delta

8:00 a.m.

1107	8:00-9:15 a.m.	Continental BR B	Lobby Level	Chicago Hilton

PERSPECTIVES OF COMPUTER-MEDIATED COMMUNICATION

Sponsor: Human Communication and Technology Commission
Chair: Kevin S. Trowbridge, Union University
  "Ambiguous Messages and Trust in Computer-Mediated Communication." Scott A.
    Chadwick, Iowa State University
  "A Design Schema for the Basic Course in CMC." Ken Williams, Marshall University
  "Managing Change: Balancing Technological Growth with Human Understanding."
    Heather M. McKissick, Lower Colorado River Authority
  "The Technologizing of Communication." Ulises A. Mejias, Ithaca College
  "Looking a Gift Horse in the Mouth: Corporate Sponsorship of Educational Multimedia."
    Chi-Feng Tsai, Saginaw Valley State University, Robert S. Drew, Saginaw Valley State
    University
  "The Journey of Narrative: The Story of Myst Across Two Mediums." Drew Davidson,
    University of Texas
  "Perspectives on the Spoken Word in the Age of Computers." Karen L. Lollar, University of
    Denver

Respondents: Bolanle A. Olaniran, Texas Tech University
             Kevin Howley, Northeastern University

1108	8:00-9:15 a.m.	Continental BR C	Lobby Level	Chicago Hilton

WOMEN COLORING OUTSIDE THE LINES: OUTLAWS, KANAKA AND CHICANA/LATINA SUBJECTS AND THE POLITICS OF DOMINATION AND RESISTANCE

Sponsor: Critical and Cultural Studies Division
Chair: Michelle A. Holling, California State University, Monterey Bay
  "Dancing Salsa and Chicana Latina Sexuality: Erotic Agency and the Feminist Politics of
    Mestizaje." Perlita R. Dicochea, Arizona State University
  "Empire, the Social Body, and Native Women." Rona T. Halualani, San Jose State
    University
  "Chicanas Exercising Agency: Resisting Ideological Positionings of Chicana Subjectivity."
    Michelle A. Holling, California State University, Monterey Bay
  "Outlaw Culture and 'Nutrolling Queens': The Politics of Domination and Resistance
    Among Women Prisoners." Dreama G. Moon, California State University, San Marcos

Respondent: Lisa A. Flores, University of Utah

1110   8:00-9:15 a.m.   Grand Ballroom   Second Floor   Chicago Hilton

REHEAR(S)ING THE FAMILIAR: QUOTATION IN THE EXPERIENCE OF OPERA

Sponsor: Performance Studies Division
Chair: Kay Ellen Capo, SUNY, Purchase
   "Callas as Quotation." Ronald E. Shields, Bowling Green State University
   "Blanching in the Glare of Realism: San Francisco Opera's *A Streetcar Named Desire*."
      Mary Agnes Doyle, Vox Humana Foundation
   "Gavryushka's Song Revisited, or Wordless Last Words." Paul C. Edwards, Northwestern
      University

Respondents: Kay Ellen Capo, SUNY, Purchase
             Leland Roloff, Northwestern University

1114   8:00-9:15 a.m.   Boulevard A   Second Floor   Chicago Hilton

CHILDREN AT THE CROSSROADS OF INTERSECTING MEDIA: POLICY AND RESEARCH FOR THE TWENTY-FIRST CENTURY

Sponsor: Mass Communication Division
Chair: Kelly L. Schmitt, University of Pennsylvania
   "Developmental Aspects of New Media." Ellen A. Wartella, University of Texas, Austin
   "Children's Responses to Television News." Barbara J. Wilson, University of California,
      Santa Barbara
   "The Changing Face of Children's Television." Emory H. Woodard, University of
      Pennsylvania
   "VCR Use and Children's Processing of 'Television'." Marie-Louise Mares, University of
      Wisconsin, Madison
   "The Family and the Internet: What Parents Think." Joseph G. Turow, University of
      Pennsylvania

Respondent: Amy B. Jordan, University of Pennsylvania

1115   8:00-9:15 a.m.   Boulevard B   Second Floor   Chicago Hilton

SUPPORTIVE COMMUNICATION I: COMPETITIVE PAPERS IN SOCIAL SUPPORT, SOCIALIZATION, AND CONFLICT IN GROUPS

Sponsors: Group Communication Division
             Interpersonal Communication Division
Chair: Kevin T. Wright, University of Oklahoma
   Help at Your Keyboard: Support Groups on the Internet. Stewart C. Alexander, University
      of Illinois, Urbana-Champaign, Jennifer L. Peterson, University of Illinois,
      Urbana-Champaign, Andrea B. Hollingshead, University of Illinois, Urbana-Champaign
   Small Group Socialization Scale: Development and Validity. Bruce L. Riddle, Kent State
      University, Carolyn M. Anderson, University of Akron, Matthew M. Martin, West Virginia
      University
   Language and Conflict in CMC Group Interaction: Powerful and Powerless Speech. Kevin
      J. Real, Texas A&M University, Monique L. Snowden, Texas A&M University, Marshall S.
      Poole, Texas A&M University

Respondent: Michele H. Jackson, University of Colorado, Boulder

---

1116   8:00-9:15 a.m.   Boulevard C   Second Floor   Chicago Hilton

JAPANESE APOLOGY ACROSS DISCIPLINES

Sponsor: International & Intercultural Communication Division
Chair: Naomi Sugimoto, Ferris State University
   "An Analysis of the 1987 Toshiba Apology for COCOM Violation." Takeshi Suzuki, Tsuda
      College

"Has Japan Done Enough to Apologize? The Former Japanese Prime Minister Murayama's Apology on August 15, 1995." Hiroku Okuda, Northwestern University
"Japanese and Australian Apology Styles Contrasted." Stephen M. Ryan, Eichi University, Naomi Sugimoto, Ferris State University
"The Status-Quo of Apology Research in Japan." Naomi Sugimoto, Ferris State University

Respondent: Roichi Okabe, Nanzan University

1118   8:00-9:15 a.m.   Waldorf   Third Floor   Chicago Hilton

STAYING CONNECTED, RESOLVING GUILT, AND CHANGING IMAGES: COLORING OUTSIDE THE TRADITIONAL LINES OF FATHERHOOD

Sponsor: Family Communication Division
Chair: Loren O. Murfield, Eastern College
   "Fathers Staying Connected: On the Outside Looking In." Deborah L. Whitt, Wayne State University, Ronald E. Whitt, Wayne State University
   "Images of Fatherhood Among the Urban Poor." Benson P. Fraser, Regent University, Adam Macchi, Regent University
   "Out, Out, Damn Spot: Non-Custodial Father's Efforts to Resolve Guilt by Coloring Outside the Lines of Traditional Fatherhood." Loren O. Murfield, Eastern College

Respondent: Bernard J. Brommel, Northeastern Illinois University

---

1119   8:00-9:15 a.m.   Astoria   Third Floor   Chicago Hilton

STRATEGIES OF AMERICAN FOREIGN POLICY RHETORIC

Sponsor: Public Address Division
Chair: Michael J. Hostetler, St. John's University
   "The Tragic Science: The Uses of Jimmy Carter in Foreign Policy Realism." Robert A. Kraig, University of Wisconsin, Madison
   "Talking 'Bout My Generation: George Bush Goes to War." Tracey Q. Lanicek, Penn State University
   "International Aid and the Role of the Nation-State: American Foreign Policy as Coercion." Matthew K. McGarrity, Indiana University

Respondent: J. Michael Hogan, Penn State University

1121   8:00-9:15 a.m.   Williford A   Third Floor   Chicago Hilton

ENCARTA AFRICANA AND THE RHETORIC OF HENRY LOUIS GATES, JR: FOMENTING DISCOURSE OR CONFUSION

Sponsor: African American Communication & Culture Commission
Chair: Melbourne S. Cummings, Howard University
   "An Afrocentric Critique of the Discourse of History." Molefi K. Asante, Temple University
   "DuBois' Dream and the Reality of Encarta Africana." Ray Winbush, Fisk University
   "The HBCU and the Encyclopedia of the African World." Virgie N. Harris, Fort Valley State University
   "The Role of Africa in the Discourse of the Encarta Africana." Cecil A. Blake, University of Nebraska, Lincoln

Respondent: Jack L. Daniel, University of Pittsburgh

1122   8:00-9:15 a.m.   Williford B   Third Floor   Chicago Hilton

COLLABORATIVE APPROACHES TO SUCCESS IN/OUTSIDE THE ACADEMY: AFRICAN AMERICAN COMMUNICATION PERSPECTIVES

Sponsor: Black Caucus
Chair: Mark P. Orbe, Western Michigan University
   "Collaboration: Surviving the Conflict." Karen E. Strother-Jordan, Oakland University, R. Rennae Elliott, Oakwood College

"The Value of Collaborative Research on Subjective Racialized Positioning: Studying the Face Strategies of [BLIND] European American Reviewers." Trina J. Wright, Howard University, Mark P. Orbe, Western Michigan University

"Showcasing a Piece of History: A Case Study of Collaborative Work to Build the First African American Heritage Museum in Iowa." Doris Y. Dartey, Mount Mercy College

"Diverse Traditions in Conflict Resolution and Peacemaking*." Mary Adams Trujillo, Northwestern University

"Aligning African American Communication Studies in Multidisciplinary Partnerships." Jeffrey L. Woodyard, Stetson University

*Student Debut Paper

1123   8:00-9:15 a.m.   Williford C   Third Floor   Chicago Hilton

WOMEN'S LIVES, IDENTITIES, AND RHETORICAL APPROPRIATIONS

Sponsor: Feminist and Women Studies Division
Chair: Catherine H. Palczewski, University of Northern Iowa
    "Ordinary Lives of Extraordinary Women: Female Participation in the American Anti-Slavery Movement." Anne F. Mattina, Stonehill College
    "'True Womanhood' and True Madness: The Sanity Trial of Mary Todd Lincoln." A. Cheree Carlson, Arizona State University
    "Faces of Scandal: Hillary Rodham Clinton and the Clinton Controversies." Karrin Vasby Anderson, Colorado State University
    "Standing in Solidarity: U.S. Jewish Women and the Israeli/Palestinian Conflict." Sandra J. Berkowitz, Wayne State University

Respondent: Barbara A. Biesecker, University of Iowa

1124   8:00-9:15 a.m.   Marquette   Third Floor   Chicago Hilton

CELEBRATING A PROBLEMATIC HERITAGE: A PERFORMANCE HONORING MAY IRWIN

Sponsor: Theatre Division
Chair: Marilyn A. Hetzel, Metropolitan State College of Denver

Panelists: Sharon Ammen, St. Mary of the Woods College
          M. Susan Anthony, University of Maryland, College Park
          Janice L. Dukes, St. Mary of the Woods College

Respondent: Patti P. Gillespie, University of Maryland

In July, 1999, Sharon Ammen was given a New York State Arts Grant to present a performance on the work of Vaudeville comedian and "coon-shouter" May Irwin. This panel features excerpts of that performance and a discussion on the problems of presenting materials of a controversial nature.

1125   8:00-9:15 a.m.   Joliet   Third Floor   Chicago Hilton

MASS COMMUNICATION: STORIES AND STRUCTURES

Sponsor: Student Section
    "Cultivation Analysis: Joining of Television, Theory and Film." Amy M. Tilton, Texas A&M University
    "Network Structure on TV Crime Dramas." Rebecca M. Chory, Michigan State University
    "Abortion and the New Rhetorical Style: An Analysis of the Arthur S. DeMoss Foundation Advertisements." Mary C. Johnson, University of Texas
    "Analysis of the Methods of Anti-Commercialism Present in *Pop-Up Video**." Carrie O'Brien, Saint Mary's College

Respondent: Brenton J. Malin, University of Iowa

*Debut Paper

| 1126 | 8:00-9:15 a.m. | PDR 1 | Third Floor | Chicago Hilton |

FAMILY COMMUNICATION DIVISION EXECUTIVE COMMITTEE MEETING

Sponsor: Family Communication Division

| 1128 | 8:00-9:15 a.m. | PDR 3 | Third Floor | Chicago Hilton |

COLORING OUTSIDE THE LINES: PRESENTING COMMUNICATION THEORY AND PRACTICE IN NON-TRADITIONAL CONTEXTS

Sponsor: Applied Communication Division
Chair: Ken Danielson, Messiah College
   "Theory That Works: Presenting Communication Theory to Community Audiences." Helen M. Sterk, Calvin College
   "Theory That Works: Public Speaking Outside the Communication Curriculum." James M. Sloat, Dickinson College
   "Theory That Works: Teaching Communication Skills to Ex-Offenders Through Mentoring." Donnel A. Brown, Step Out/Step Up Program, Harrisburg, PA, Ken Danielson, Messiah College
   "Theory That Works: Using Communication Principles to Give Hope to At-Risk Youth." Mark Frederick, Gordon College

Respondent: Dwayne D. Van Rheenen, Abilene Christian University

| 1129 | 8:00-9:15 a.m. | PDR 4 | Third Floor | Chicago Hilton |

CAN FREE EXPRESSION GO GLOBAL? OR CAN LOCAL REGULATION BECOME INTERNATIONAL

Sponsor: Freedom of Expression Commission
Chair: Susan J. Drucker, Hofstra University
   "Whose Law Is It Anyway?" Harvey Jassem, University of Hartford
   "The Changing Telecommunications Law Landscape: National Sovereignty and EU Law." Susan J. Drucker, Hofstra University, Gary Gumpert, Communication Landscapers
   "Misappropriation and Unfair Competition." Donald Fishman, Boston College
   "EU Regulations, Public Broadcasters and the Little Guys: Electric Minorities in the New Europe (?)." Donald R. Browne, University of Minnesota

| 1130 | 8:00-9:15 a.m. | PDR 5 | Third Floor | Chicago Hilton |

EXPLORING THE QUANDARY OF RISK

Sponsor: Communication Needs of Students at Risk Commission
Chair: Christie A. Logan, California State University, Northridge
   "Making Sense of Education: The Promises and Risks of Success and Failure." Deanna L. Fassett, Southern Illinois University, Carbondale
   "Erasing Color: Dysfunctional Bodies and School Norms." John T. Warren, Southern Illinois University, Carbondale
   "Disciplining Desire: Heterosexism and Control in the Classroom." Michael T. LeVan, Southern Illinois University, Carbondale
   "'At-Risk' in a Dyslexic Paradigm: Reconsiderations of Normality in Education." Keith C. Pounds, Southern Illinois University, Carbondale

Respondent: Jo Sprague, San Jose State University

| 1131 | 8:00-9:15 a.m. | PDR 6 | Third Floor | Chicago Hilton |

PLANNING THE COMMUNICATION DEPARTMENT IN A MARKET-BASED ENVIRONMENT

Sponsor: Association for Communication Administration
Chair: Jolene Koester, California State University, Sacramento

Thursday

Panelists: David Henry, University of Nevada, Las Vegas
A. Susan Owen, University of Puget Sound
David Ritchie, Portland State University

Departments are being asked to justify their budget claims in marketing terms, based on ability to recruit new students and deliver an educational "product" at an acceptable cost. In this panel, three communication administrators, each representing a different type of institution, will discuss the emerging market-based environment and consider how communication departments can effectively respond.

1133   8:00-9:15 a.m.   Conf 4A   Fourth Floor   Chicago Hilton

STEPPING INTO HOT WATER: THE ROLE OF INTERCULTURAL COMMUNICATION THEORY AND RESEARCH IN RESOLVING SOCIAL AND CULTURAL ISSUES

Sponsor: International & Intercultural Communication Division
Chair: Benjamin J. Broome, George Mason University
  "The Saudis are Coming!: Ascertaining the Community's Understanding of a Proposed
   Islamic Saudi Academy." William J. Starosta, Howard University
  "Please Translate for Me: Intercultural Communication During Natural Disasters." Dolores
   V. Tanno, California State University, San Bernardino
  "The Multinational Organization as a Laboratory for Cultural and Technological
   Innovation." Robert Shuter, Marquette University
  "Building Intercultural Interpersonal Alliances Among Middle Eastern and U.S. Young
   Women: Managing the Challenges and Keeping the Faith." Mary Jane Collier, University
   of Denver
  "Intercultural Communication Competence & Acculturation: Local, Regional, and Global
   Applications." Nemi C. Jain, Arizona State University

Respondent: Benjamin J. Broome, George Mason University

1134   8:00-9:15 a.m.   Conf 4B   Fourth Floor   Chicago Hilton

A THIRTY-YEAR RETROSPECTIVE ON THE POLITICAL COMMUNICATION OF ROBERT F. KENNEDY

Sponsor: Political Communication Division
Chair: J. Gregory Payne, Emerson College
  "The Politics of Social Passion: A Comparison of Robert and John Kennedy's Political
   Rhetoric." Vito N. Silvestri, Emerson College
  "Robert F. Kennedy's Impact on Contemporary Political Communication." J. Gregory
   Payne, Emerson College
  "Robert F. Kennedy's Existentialist Appeal in the 1968 Presidential Campaign." Grant C.
   Cos, Texas A&M University, Corpus Christi

Respondent: John M. Murphy, University of Georgia

1135   8:00-9:15 a.m.   Conf 4C   Fourth Floor   Chicago Hilton

CONSUMING SUBJECTS: RHETORICS OF CONSUMPTION AND THE SUBJECTS WHO WOULD RESIST THEM

Sponsor: Critical and Cultural Studies Division
Chair: Ronald Greene, University of Texas, Austin
  "The Millennium Bug as Counterhegemonic Millennial Dream, or Why Stocking Up at
   Lehman's Hardware Isn't Radical." Susan L. Biesecker-Mast, Bluffton College
  "The Road to Consumeropolis: The Mall of America as Idealized Commercial Space." Joan
   McAlister, University of Iowa
  "'. . .Because Stone Cold Says So': Wrestling Heroes, 'White Trash' and the Ethos of
   Death." Greg Spicer, California University of Pennsylvania

Respondent: Ronald Greene, University of Texas, Austin

1136   8:00-9:15 a.m.   Conf 4D   Fourth Floor   Chicago Hilton

STAGING THE FARM AT THE AMERICAN FOLKLIFE FESTIVAL: A JOINTLY TOLD TALE

Sponsor: Ethnography Division
Chair: Shing-Ling S. Chen, University of Northern Iowa

Panelists: Karmen Mehmen, Mehmen Busyhill Farm, Iowa
          Phyllis Carlin, University of Northern Iowa

1137   8:00-9:15 a.m.   Conf 4E   Fourth Floor   Chicago Hilton

BEYOND DOCTOR-PATIENT COMMUNICATION: THE ROLE OF FAMILY, FRIENDS, PEERS, AND SPOUSES ON HEALTH-RELATED OUTCOMES OF INDIVIDUALS WITH CHRONIC ILLNESS

Sponsor: Health Communication Division
Chair: Bruce L. Lambert, University of Illinois, Chicago
    "Communicative Dilemmas in the Aftermath of Myocardial Infarction." Daena J.
      Goldsmith, University of Illinois, Urbana-Champaign
    "Through Thick and Thin?: The Impact of Illness on Friendship." Virginia M. McDermott,
      University of Illinois, Urbana-Champaign
    "Familial Adjustment to Having a Chronically Ill Child." Kristen B. Leslie, University of
      Illinois, Urbana-Champaign
    "Peer Support in Chronic Illness." Dale E. Brashers, University of Illinois,
      Urbana-Champaign, Judith L. Neidig, Ohio State University, Jennifer L. Peterson,
      University of Illinois, Urbana-Champaign, Debbie Ng, University of Illinois,
      Urbana-Champaign

1139   8:00-9:15 a.m.   Conf 4G   Fourth Floor   Chicago Hilton

TRANSFORMING PROFESSIONAL IDENTITIES IN TURBULENT TIMES

Sponsor: Organizational Communication Division
Chair: H.L. (Bud) Goodall, University of North Carolina, Greensboro
    "Soul, Spirituality and the World of Work: Implications for Communication, Identity and
      Leadership in the New Organization." Bethany C. Goodier, University of South Florida
    "Transforming Organizational Identity Through Conversations for Possibility: Combining
      Media Studies and Ethnographic Approaches to Organizational Communication." Patrick
      O. Cannon, University of South Florida
    "Nursing Identities." Linda E. Laine-Timmerman, University of South Florida
    "Self and the Intern: Proposing a Triadic Model of Identity in Novels of Medical
      Residency." Ellisa J. Foster, University of South Florida
    "Researching Identity in Organizations: A Question of Methodology." Robert D. Kreisher,
      University of South Florida
Respondent: Alexandra G. Murphy, DePaul University

1141   8:00-9:15 a.m.   Conf 4I   Fourth Floor   Chicago Hilton

HOSPITALITY EQUALS PROFITABILITY: AN EXAMINATION OF PUBLIC RELATIONS' IMPACT ON THE TRAVEL/TOURISM INDUSTRY

Sponsor: Public Relations Division
Chair: Pamela G. Bourland-Davis, Georgia Southern University
    "Looking at Tourism Through a Multi-Dimensional Model of Public Relations." Don W.
      Stacks, University of Miami
    "Georgia Practitioners Build Relationships to Promote Cultural Tourism." Jackie Erney,
      Georgia Southern University
    "Being Hospitable to Internal Audiences: An Examination of Major Chain Hotels'
      Employee Relations Programs." Joseph P. Fall, Michigan State University

Thursday

"Success Stories in the Field: An Analysis of the Top State Tourism Promotional Campaigns." Lisa Fall, Michigan State University

---

1142   8:00-9:15 a.m.   Conf 4J   Fourth Floor   Chicago Hilton

CHANGING ROLES OF COMMUNICATION DEPARTMENTS: GENERAL EDUCATION REQUIREMENTS

Sponsor: Senior College & University Section
Chair: Hwei-Jen Yang, Clarion University
"Re-Designing the Introductory Communication Course for Inclusion in the Liberal Arts Core." Nessim J. Watson, Westfield State College
"To Re-Design, or Not to Re-Design for the Liberal Arts Core: That is the Real Question." Edwin J. Abar, Westfield State College
"Communication: The 'Core' of General Education in Liberal Arts Learning." Gerald Lee Ratliff, SUNY, Potsdam
"Teaching Research, Teaching Speech: The Communication Course and General Education." Mark D. Gellis, Kettering University

---

1143   8:00-9:15 a.m.   Conf 4K   Fourth Floor   Chicago Hilton

UNHEARD VOICES: SCRIPTWRITING FOR A COMMUNITY

Sponsor: Theatre Division
Chair: Renee Vincent, University of North Carolina, Wilmington
"Service-Learning: Script Development and the Community." Julie R. Patterson-Pratt, University of Minnesota, Morris
"Drama with a Difference: Redefining the Marriage of Town and Gown." John C. Countryman, Berry College
"Attention Must be Paid: Disclosing Monologues for the Working Poor in Cincinnati in 1999." Norma Jenckes, University of Cincinnati
"Telling the Untold Stories: The American Festivals Project." Ann Ellis, U.S. Naval Academy
"InterACT Teen-to-Teen Theatre." Mark J. Kelty, William Woods University
"Will You Take the Challenge?: Explorations of Race, Gender, and Identity Within One University Community." Cecelia Hayes, San Jose State University

Respondent: Renee Vincent, University of North Carolina, Wilmington

---

1144   8:00-9:15 a.m.   Conf 4L   Fourth Floor   Chicago Hilton

THE PLACE OF THE PASSIONS IN THE AGE OF REASON AND SCIENCE

Sponsor: American Society for the History of Rhetoric
Chair: Arthur E. Walzer, University of Minnesota
"Rhetoric, the Passions, Ethics, and Cartesian Epistemology." Dana Harrington, Syracuse University
"Passion Well Trained: Love in the Age of Reason." Daniel D. Gross, Montana State University
"Rhetorical Pathos in Risk Analysis." Carolyn R. Miller, North Carolina State University

---

1145   8:00-9:15 a.m.   Conf 4M   Fourth Floor   Chicago Hilton

POLITICAL COMMUNICATION DIVISION BUSINESS MEETING

Sponsor: Political Communication Division

1149   8:00-9:15 a.m.   Conf 5B   Fifth Floor   Chicago Hilton

COLORING OUTSIDE THE LINES WITH COURSE PHILOSOPHY: ALTERNATIVE FOUNDATIONS FOR THE BASIC COURSE

Sponsor: Basic Course Division
Chair: Michael S. Hanna, University of South Alabama

"Rethinking Our Approach to the Basic Course: Making Ethics the Foundation of
   Introduction to Public Speaking." Jon A. Hess, University of Missouri, Columbia
"COMMON SENSE in the Basic Public Speaking Course." Calvin L. Troup, Duquesne
   University
"Thinking Outside the Lines: The History of Ideas as a Foundation for the Basic Course."
   Amy Enderle, University of Missouri, Columbia
"Coloring Outside the Lines of Communication Requirement: Teaching a Course in
   Communication and Professional Civility to Physicians' Assistants." Ronald C. Arnett,
   Duquesne University, Janie M. Harden Fritz, Duquesne University

Respondent: Steven A. Beebe, Southwest Texas State University

---

1151   8:00-9:15 a.m.   Conf 5D   Fifth Floor   Chicago Hilton

COPING SKILLS FOR FAMILY CAREGIVERS WHO CARE FOR LOVED ONES WITH DEMENTIA: THE INTERSECTION OF INTERDISCIPLINARY METHODS AND RESEARCH GOALS

Sponsor: Communication and Aging Commission
Chair: Laura C. Prividera, Bowling Green State University
   "Confessions of a Quantitative Researcher: When Theoretical Perspectives and
      Predominant Methodologies Clash." Jennifer M. Kinney, Miami University
   "Confessions of a Qualitative Researcher: The Intersection of Interdisciplinary Methods
      and Research Goals." Lynda D. Dixon, Bowling Green State University
   "Communication Research in the Field: Interaction with Participants with Dementia." John
      Howard, Bowling Green State University
   "The Responsibility of a Caregiver: A Transcriber's View." Amy E. Capwell-Burns, Bowling
      Green State University

1152   8:00-9:15 a.m.   Conf 5E   Fifth Floor   Chicago Hilton

TOWARD A MORE ADEQUATE CONCEPTION OF PRESUMPTION

Sponsor: Rhetorical and Communication Theory Division
Chair: Jean Goodwin, Northwestern University
   "Presumptions In Medieval Legal Argumentation: Rhetoric and Dialectic in Disputations
      and Trials." Hanns J. Hohmann, San Jose State University
   "The Liberal and the Conservative Presumption Revisited." G. Thomas Goodnight,
      Northwestern University
   "Presumptive Reasoning as a Kind of Reasoning." Hans Vilhelm Hansen, Brock University
   "The Confusion at the Heart of Whatelian Ideas About Presumption." Fred J. Kauffeld,
      Edgewood College

1153   8:00-9:15 a.m.   Conf 5F   Fifth Floor   Chicago Hilton

FORENSICS AND SCHOLARSHIP: A RENEWED INTERCONNECTION

Sponsor: American Forensic Association
   "The Thin(ning) Gray Line: Stories from the Borderlands of Academia." David F. Breshears,
      University of Texas, Austin
   "Insulating Yourself from Opposing Argument: The Texas High School Debate Successionist
      Front Gets Romantic for Stagnation." Brian McBride, Northwestern University
   "Between and Beyond Academic Achievement: Debate as Micro-Citizenship." Kevin D.
      Kuswa, University of Texas, Austin
   "Academics as Resistance in Academic Debating." Joel D. Rollins, University of Texas
   "Reflections on an Old Idea: Praxis as a Way of Forging Scholarship and Debate." Joseph P.
      Zompetti, Mercer University

1154   8:00-9:15 a.m.   Conf 5G   Fifth Floor   Chicago Hilton

COLORING OUTSIDE THE LINES OF INSTRUCTIONAL COMMUNICATION

Sponsor: Instructional Development Division

Thursday

Chair: Sara C. Weintraub, Bentley College
  "Communicating (Within and About) Technology: The Case of TCOM 451/MCOM 551."
    Radhika Gajjala, Bowling Green State University, Melissa M. Spirek, Bowling Green State
    University
  "Henry David Thoreau: American Transcendentalism and the Implications for Rhetoric in
    American Education." Ronald P. Grapsy, Northern Kentucky University
  "The 'Other' TA: You Know, Graduate Teaching Assistants of Color (GTACs)." Katherine G.
    Hendrix, University of Memphis, Aparna S. Bulusu, University of Memphis, Orin G.
    Johnson, University of Memphis

Respondent: Sara C. Weintraub, Bentley College

1155	8:00-9:15 a.m.	Conf 5H	Fifth Floor	Chicago Hilton

AN EXPLORATION OF THE STATE OF DISABILITY AND FILM: PROBLEMS IN THE CURRENT METHODOLOGY AND DEFINITION OF DISABILITY AND FILM STUDIES

Sponsor: Caucus on Disability Issues

Presenters: Thomas B. Hoeksema, Calvin College
            Christopher R. Smit, University of Iowa

1157	8:00-9:15 a.m.	Conf 5J	Fifth Floor	Chicago Hilton

LAMBDA PI ETA BUSINESS MEETING

Sponsor: Lambda Pi Eta

1158	8:00-10:45 a.m.	Lake Ontario	Eighth Floor	Chicago Hilton

SHORT COURSE #1. TEACHING COMMUNICATION COURSES WITH FEATURE FILMS

Sponsor: Short Courses

Instructors: Ronald B. Adler, Santa Barbara City College
              Russell F. Proctor, Northern Kentucky University

Fee required. See complete Short Course descriptions elsewhere in the program.

1159	8:00-10:45 a.m.	Lake Michigan	Eighth Floor	Chicago Hilton

SHORT COURSE #2. TEACHING THE COLLEGE COURSE IN THE RHETORIC OF TWENTIETH-CENTURY FIRST LADIES

Sponsor: Short Courses

Instructors: Myra G. Gutin, Rider University
              Leesa E. Tobin, Gerald R. Ford Library
              Molly M. Wertheimer, Penn State University, Hazleton

Fee required. See complete Short Course descriptions elsewhere in the program.

1160	8:00-10:45 a.m.	Lake Huron	Eighth Floor	Chicago Hilton

SHORT COURSE #3. SHORT COURSE FOR NEW DEPARTMENT CHAIRS

Sponsor: Short Courses

Instructors: Alison Alexander, University of Georgia
              Bill Balthrop, University of North Carolina
              Mark L. Knapp, University of Texas, Austin
              Jarice Hanson, University of Massachusetts
              David Zarefsky, Northwestern University
              Jannette L. Dates, Howard University

Joe S. Foote, Southern Illinois University

Fee required. See complete Short Course descriptions elsewhere in the program.

| 1161 | 8:00-10:45 a.m. | Lake Erie | Eighth Floor | Chicago Hilton |

SHORT COURSE #4. USING COMMUNITY SERVICE IN COMMUNICATION COURSES

Sponsor: Short Courses

Instructors: James M. Honeycutt, Louisiana State University
Richard L. Conville, University of Southern Mississippi
Timothy L. Sellnow, North Dakota State University
Deanna D. Sellnow, North Dakota State University
Laura McAdoo, North Dakota State University

Fee required. See complete Short Course descriptions elsewhere in the program.

| 1162 | 8:00-9:15 a.m. | Essex Court | Second Floor | Essex Inn |

BLURRING THE LINES: CHALLENGES TO AND FROM A THEISTIC PERSPECTIVE OF COMMUNICATION THEORY

Sponsor: Religious Communication Association
Chair: Steven H. Kaminski, Trans America Small Business Capital
    "Liberation Theology: A Bold Challenge to the Communication Discipline." Nancy J. Eckstein, University of Nebraska, Lincoln
    "Relational Virtues Communication Paradigm." William O. Strom, Trinity Western University
    "Communication as Covenental." Mark A. Gring, Mississippi State University
    "Religion, Communicative Action, and Jurgen Habermas." Fred E. Fitch, University of Kentucky
    "Learning the Grammar of Faith: Transforming Experience Through Sunday School Talk." Jay R. Martinson, Olivet Nazarene University

Respondent: Steven H. Kaminski, Trans America Small Business Capital

---

| 1163 | 8:00-9:15 a.m. | Windsor Court | Second Floor | Essex Inn |

LINES AND BORDERS AND BOUNDARIES, OH MY: EXPERIMENTING WITH PERFORMANCE AND ETHNOGRAPHY

Sponsor: Ethnography Division
Chair: Leigh Anne Howard, Spalding University
    "Whose Story Is It Anyway? Ethical and Performance Dilemmas of Performing Personal Narratives by Members of a Group Home for Men with Mental Retardation." Sharon E. Croft, Capital University
    "Personal Awareness, Social Connection, Cultural Critique: Some Complicated Issues About the Performance of Ethnography." Leigh Anne Howard, Spalding University
    "Negotiating Blackness Down Under: Researching the Cafe of the Gate of Salvation Gospel Choir." E. Patrick Johnson, University of North Carolina, Chapel Hill
    "Touring Graceland: Power, Play and Performance in the Palace of the King—A Screenplay." Daniel W. Heaton, Capital University

---

| 1164 | 8:00-9:15 a.m. | Buckingham Court | Second Floor | Essex Inn |

THREE CASE STUDIES IN THE RHETORICS OF PRODUCTION AND SELF-CONSTRUCTION: OR, CHARACTER AND SPECTACLE IN AMERICAN STUDIES

Sponsor: American Studies Commission
Chair: Mary F. Keehner, Purdue University

Thursday

"Fanny Fern's 1855 *Ruth Hall* and the Rhetoric of Character as Nonsynchronous
   Contradiction." Stephen J. Hartnett, University of California, Berkeley
"Killing Culture: Twain's Spectacular Character and the Rhetoric of Reform." James B.
   Salazar, University of California, Berkeley
"Rat Man, Wolf Man, or Mad Man?: Reading the 1998 Psychoanalytic Profile of Mike
   Tyson as an Exercise in the Spectacular Rhetoric of Character." Jon D. Rutter, University
   of Texas, Austin

Respondent: Judith Yaross Lee, Ohio University

1166   8:00-9:15 a.m.   Cohn Rm   Second Floor   Spertus Institute

COMPLEX LITIGATION AND HINDSIGHT BIAS: EXPLORING ISSUES AND STRATEGIES TO REDUCE JURORS' RETROSPECTIVE ATTRIBUTIONS OF FAULT

Sponsor: Communication and Law Commission
Chair: Thomas D. Beisecker, University of Kansas

Panelists: Merrie Jo Stallard, Center for Trial Insights
            Joseph M. Price, Faegre & Benson, L.L.P.
            Debra L. Worthington, University of Central Arkansas

This panel examines the hindsight bias as it occurs generally in the courtroom context and
specifically in commercial litigation and medical mass-tort suits. Discussion will center on why
the traditional methods used to overcome hindsight bias are not appropriate in the courtroom
setting. In addition, the panel will propose techniques for reducing, and perhaps eliminating,
the hindsight bias and discuss methods of testing these techniques.

1169   8:00-9:15 a.m.   Rm 903   Ninth Floor   Spertus Institute

INTEGRATING AND ASSESSING EXPERIENTIAL LEARNING INTO COURSE CURRICULA: PERSPECTIVES FROM THREE COMMUNICATIVE CONTEXTS

Sponsor: Experiential Learning in Communication Commission
Chair: Dacia Charlesworth, Southeast Missouri State University
   "Integrating Asynchronous Communication in the Undergraduate Core:
      Computationalized Experiential Learning." William J. McKinney, Southeast Missouri
      State University
   "Competition and Critical Thinking: Debate as a Co-Curricular Experiential Activity."
      Jennifer L. Rigdon, Southern Illinois University, Carbondale
   "Conflict Workshops: Integrating Role Playing Activities into the Introductory Interpersonal
      Communication Course." Jackson B. Miller, Eastern Oregon University
   "Embodying Experiential Learning: Assessment of Performance-Based Activities Through
      Self-Report." Dacia Charlesworth, Southeast Missouri State University

---

1170   8:00-9:15 a.m.   Rm 904   Ninth Floor   Spertus Institute

COMMUNICATION AND GLOBALIZATION

Sponsor: Peace and Conflict Communication Commission
Chair: Noreen M. Schaefer-Faix, Defiance College
   "The Contours and Mind-Set of Globalization: Toward a Global Civic Society." Guo-Ming
      Chen, University of Rhode Island
   "The Dialogue on Freedom and Responsibility in the Process of Globalization." D. Ray
      Heisey, Kent State University
   "Globalization Through Communication: From Free Flow of Goods to Free Flow of
      Messages." Ringo Ma, SUNY, Fredonia
   "Chinese Bureaucracy Model in the Process of Globalization." Shuang Li, Heilongjiang
      University, China

Respondent: Jensen Chung, San Francisco State University

1172   8:00-9:15 a.m.   Rm 907   Ninth Floor   Spertus Institute

ON-CAMPUS DEBATE PROGRAMS: A PANEL DISCUSSION

Sponsor: Cross Examination Debate Association
Chair: Sue L. Wenzlaff, Duquesne University

Panelists: Elizabeth Dudash, Miami University
        Michael R. Berry, King's College
        Anand Rao, Clarion University
        Brett M. O'Donnell, Liberty University
        Sue L. Wenzlaff, Duquesne University

Respondent: Gordon R. Mitchell, University of Pittsburgh

Panelists will present information on the nature of their on-campus debate programs designed
to provide debate opportunities for a variety of students interested in debate. The respondent
will lead discussion with panelists and audience members on ideas for expanding these
opportunities.

9:30 a.m.

1206   9:30-10:45 a.m.   Continental BR A   Lobby Level   Chicago Hilton

MISCELLANEOUS TOPICS IN ETHNOGRAPHY

Sponsor: Ethnography Division
Chair: Amber E. Kinser, East Tennessee State University
    "Cyberethnography: Reading Each 'Other' On-Line." Radhika Gajjala, Bowling Green
        State University
    "Theoretical Roots of Ethnography of Communication: Austinian Speech Act Theory."
        David S. Worth, University of Oklahoma
    "Reflections on the Practice of Ethnography: Pages from a Field Notebook." Linda L.
        Lampl, Lampl/Herbert Consultants, Florida
    "Speaking of Work and Family: Spousal Collaboration in the Discursive Production of
        Self-Identity." Annis G. Golden, Rensselaer Polytechnic Institute

Respondent: Thomas R. Flynn, Slippery Rock University

1208   9:30-10:45 a.m.   Continental BR C   Lobby Level   Chicago Hilton

JUST WHAT IS TECHNOLOGY, AND SO WHAT IF IT'S NEW?

Sponsor: Critical and Cultural Studies Division
Chair: Steve Jones, University of Illinois, Chicago

Panelists: Bernardo Attias, California State University, Northridge
        Jody Berland, York University
        Gregory Elmer, University of Massachusetts, Amherst
        Jennifer D. Slack, Michigan Technological University
        Jonathan E. Sterne, University of Illinois, Urbana-Champaign
        Theodore G. Striphas, University of North Carolina, Chapel Hill

J. Macgregor Wise, Clemson University

1210   9:30-10:45 a.m.   Grand Ballroom   Second Floor   Chicago Hilton

COMPETITIVE PAPERS IN PERFORMANCE STUDIES

Sponsor: Performance Studies Division
Chair: Eric E. Peterson, University of Maine, Orono
    "Live and Mediated Performance: A Medi(t)ation." Marcy R. Chvasta, Southern Illinois
        University, Carbondale

Thursday

"The Haymarket Trial: A Performance of History and Forgetting." Susan S. Sattell, Northwestern University

"Biology as Performance: Female Bodybuilding Serves Queer Theory." Marla A. Morton-Brown, University of North Carolina, Charlotte

"Doing Whiteness: On the Performative Dimensions of Race." John T. Warren, Southern Illinois University, Carbondale

Respondent: Eric E. Peterson, University of Maine, Orono

1201   9:30-4:45 p.m.   Northwest Exhibit Hall   Lower Level   Chicago Hilton

NCA POSTER SESSION

Sponsor: Poster Session

1. "The 'Hill Women' Meet the 'Cyborg': A Queer Ecofeminist Literary Criticism of Sally Miller Gearhart's *The Wanderground*." Lincoln J. Houde, University of Utah
2. "Environmental Discourse: A Case Study." James C. Lundy, Doane College
3. "New Evangelical Talk Radio: Religious Radio Reformats Itself Again." Paul Creasman, Regent University
4. "Obeying the Great Commission: 'Going' to all Nations via Airwaves." Mike Farrell, University of Kentucky
5. "Testifications: Analysis of Meaning in CCM Radio Station Feedback." Stephen D. Perry, Illinois State University, Jennifer L. Tofanelli, Illinois State University
6. "Rhetorical Analysis of 700 Club Commercials." Andrew A. Klyukovski, University of Missouri, Columbia, John P. McHale, University of Missouri, Columbia
7. "Pastoral Burnout and Stress: An Analysis of the Causes of Burnout and Recommendations for Stress Prevention." Justin Geel, Point Loma Nazarene University, Jon Hall, Point Loma Nazarene University
8. "The Effectiveness of Women in Church Leadership Positions." Nathan Brisby, Point Loma Nazarene University, Tim Shubin, Point Loma Nazarene University
9. "Social Support in Religious Small Groups: Analysis of Small Group Leaders in Churches and Their Ability to Provide a Supportive Group Atmosphere." Brittany Keeling, Point Loma Nazarene University
10. "Understanding the Phenomenon of 'Church Hopping' Through Analysis of Congregational Satisfaction." Jennifer Burgess, Point Loma Nazarene University, Nicola Koch, Point Loma Nazarene University
11. "Christianese: The Language of Common Thought in the Christian Music Industry." David N. Graham, Point Loma Nazarene University
12. "The Women Designers of the Provincetown Players: Tilting at a Sexual Barrier in Theatre Practice." Cheryl Black, University of South Carolina
13. "'Will You Remember?': Female Lyricists in the American Musical Theatre from 1866 to 1943." Korey Rothman Bradley, University of Maryland, College Park
14. "Challenging the Backlash: The Women Producers of Broadway." Brett Ashley Crawford, University of Maryland, College Park
15. "Aristotelian Autobiographical Angst: Reflections on Peter Pan, Playwriting, and Performance Art." Theresa M. Carilli, Purdue University, Calumet
16. "What Shape Am I In?: Rhetorical Dimensions of Solo Performance." Jill Taft-Kaufman, Central Michigan University
17. "Family History, Narrative, and Redemption: Staging Community in Larry Wilwode's *Beyond the Bedroom Wall*." Robert J. Hubbard, Calvin College
18. "Imagining Text/Contextualizing Image: Improvisation, Theatricality, and Coincidence in Collective Creations of Robert Lepage." James Bunzli, Central Michigan University
19. "Gesture This: Dramatic Aesthetics in Theory and Practice." Arion Alston, Central Michigan University
20. "Artifacts as Text: Visual Storytelling of Angels in Popular Culture." Valerie R. Swarts, Slippery Rock University
21. "The Illinois Cantilever Sky City: A Consideration of Architecture as Visual, Contextual, and Physical Communication." Scott J. Berman, California State University, Northridge
22. "Determining Metaphor in Graphical User Interfaces." Neil F. Randall, University of Waterloo, Canada, Isabel Pedersen, University of Waterloo, Canada
23. "Sticking It To You: Pinning Down the Historical and Contemporary Visual Symbolism of the Twelve Most Common Body Piercings." Chrys Kahn-Egan, Longwood College

24. "Involving Students in a Community Needs Assessment Project: Putting Skills to Work." Judith A. Kolb, Penn State University, William J. Rothwell, Penn State University
25. "Perceptions of Gender and Power: Influencing Communication in Conflict Management." Mary C. Banwart, Western Kentucky University
26. "Existence and Prevalence of Hate Speech Policies in the Fortune 500 Companies." Sabrena R. Parton, Kennesaw State University, Jeffrey F. Anderson, Kennesaw State University
27. "To Speak or Not to Speak—That is the Question." Elizabeth A. Tuleja, University of Pennsylvania
28. "The Future of Literacy." Lori C. Ramos, William Paterson University
29. "An Examination of Factors Influencing Non-Native U.S. Student Perceptions of Native and Non-Native U.S. Teacher Effectiveness." Linda L. McCroskey, California Polytechnic State University, San Luis Obispo
30. "Neo-Expressionism as an Explication of Semiotic Rupture in Beyond Therapy." Marian Zeilinski, Mercer University

---

1214   9:30-10:45 a.m.   Boulevard A   Second Floor   Chicago Hilton

BREAKING TRADITIONS: CONNECTIONS BETWEEN COMMUNICATION THEORIES AND PRACTICE AS APPLIED TO CHILD SEXUAL ABUSE (A MULTI-MEDIATED FORUM)

Sponsor: Challenging Boundaries Series

Panelists: John Chetro-Szivos, University of Massachusetts, Amherst
Janice Haynes, University of Massachusetts, Amherst
Eric L. Morgan, University of Massachusetts, Amherst
Cynthia A. Suopis, University of Massachusetts, Amherst

1215   9:30-10:45 a.m.   Boulevard B   Second Floor   Chicago Hilton

NEW DIRECTIONS IN GROUP COMMUNICATION: EXPLORING NEW GROUP COMMUNICATION CONTEXTS

Sponsor: Group Communication Division
Chair: Lawrence R. Frey, University of Memphis
   "A Bona Fide Perspective for the Future of Groups: Understanding Collaborating Groups." Cynthia Stohl, Purdue University, Kasey L. Walker, Purdue University
   "Communication in Top Management Teams." Theodore E. Zorn, University of Waikato, New Zealand, George Tompson, University of Waikato, New Zealand
   "Cross-National Small Group Research: Prospects and Promises." Robert Shuter, Marquette University
   "Technology as Task: Rethinking the Role of Communication Modality in the Definition of Group Work and Performance." Edward A. Mabry, University of Wisconsin, Milwaukee

Respondent: Lawrence R. Frey, University of Memphis

1216   9:30-10:45 a.m.   Boulevard C   Second Floor   Chicago Hilton

ISSUES ON GLOBAL COMMUNICATION

Sponsor: International & Intercultural Communication Division
Chair: Xiaosui Xiao, Hong Kong Baptist University
   "Global Communication Competency: A Demand of the Twenty-First Century." Guo-Ming Chen, University of Rhode Island
   "Negotiating the Cultural Definition of Power in Global Context." Lin-Mei Huang, Shih Hsin University, Taiwan
   "The Discursive Construction of Global Listserve Ethics." Leda M. Cooks, University of Massachusetts, Amherst
   "The Impact of Globalization on Global Culture." Rueyling Chuang, St. John's University/College of St. Benedict

Respondent: William J. Starosta, Howard University

Thursday

1219   9:30-10:45 a.m.   Astoria   Third Floor   Chicago Hilton

RECONSTRUCTING WOMAN'S RIGHTS, WOMEN'S ROLES

Sponsor: Public Address Division
Chair: Amy R. Slagell, Iowa State University
   "A Discourse in Search of a Rhetor: Intertextuality in the Development of Nineteenth
      Century Woman's Rights Argument." Lynne Derbyshire, University of Rhode Island
   "Critiquing Patriarchal Images of Female Beauty: Elizabeth Cady Stanton and the
      Redefinition of Femininity." Lisa S. Strange, Eastern Illinois University
   "Virginia Woolf's 'Professions for Women' and the Women's Movement." Jill M. Carleton,
      University of Texas, Austin

Respondent: Bonnie J. Dow, University of Georgia

1222   9:30-10:45 a.m.   Williford B   Third Floor   Chicago Hilton

IDENTITY, CULTURE, AND POLITICS: NATIONALISM AND ITS RHETORICAL EXPRESSIONS

Sponsor: Political Communication Division
Chair: Robert L. Strain, Saint Louis University
   "Devolution or Divorce?: Stating the Case for Scotland's Political Future." Innes W. R.
      Mitchell, St. Edward's University
   "To the End of the Line: Extremist Symbolic Trajectories in Israeli Discourse." Robert C.
      Rowland, University of Kansas
   "Reformulating Lost Nationalism: Political Discourse as a Consensus Narrative of Brazilian
      Culture." Alice R. Araujo, Mary Baldwin College
   "We the People?: Nationalism and National Identity in American Political Cinema." Robert
      L. Strain, Saint Louis University

1223   9:30-10:45 a.m.   Williford C   Third Floor   Chicago Hilton

SOURCES OF THE FEMINIST ENERGY: YOUNG FEMINISTS AND THEIR MENTORS CHANGING THE FACE OF FEMINISM

Sponsor: Feminist and Women Studies Division
Chair: Gabrielle Prisco, University of Alabama

Panelists: Brenda J. Allen, University of Colorado, Boulder
           Karen L. Ashcraft, University of Utah
           Patrice M. Buzzanell, Northern Illinois University
           Carrie Crenshaw, University of Alabama
           Mary F. Hoffman, University of Kansas
           Nancy A. Riffe, University of Alabama
           Gregory J. Shepherd, University of Kansas
           Sherianne Shuler, University of Alabama
           Julia T. Wood, University of North Carolina, Chapel Hill

---

1224   9:30-10:45 a.m.   Marquette   Third Floor   Chicago Hilton

STUDENT DEBUT PAPERS

Sponsor: Theatre Division
Chair: Michele A. Pagen, California University of Pennsylvania
   "The Gilded Destroyer: Chinese Theatre's Survival and Growth Amid the Khans." Amanda
      Petefish, University of Minnesota, Morris
   "Murder in the Mise-en-Scene: An Experiment in Theatrical Deconstruction." David C.
      Burke, Bob Jones University
   "Anatomy of a Murderess: Performing Race/Performing Selves." Hsiu-chen Lin Classon,
      Northwestern University

Respondents: Sharon Ammen, St. Mary of the Woods College

Deryl B. Johnson, Kutztown University

1225   **9:30-10:45 a.m.**   Joliet   Third Floor   Chicago Hilton

ANALYZING ORGANIZATIONAL CULTURE: SEVERAL EMPIRICAL APPROACHES

Sponsor: Student Section
Chair: Sonia Zamanou-Erickson, Southern Illinois University, Edwardsville
  "Precious Vision: An Empirical Study of the Organizational Culture of the Precious Moments Complex." Wendy Cook-Mucci, Southern Illinois University, Edwardsville
  "Explaining Organizational Culture: A Case Study in a Day Care Setting." Robyn Lauman, Southern Illinois University, Edwardsville
  "Taking the Corporate Pulse: An Established Company Takes a Turn for the Better." Susan C. Miles, Southern Illinois University, Edwardsville
  "Advances to Integrate Academic Affairs with Student Affairs: A Case Study of a Student Center." Vicki L. Nolle, Southern Illinois University, Edwardsville

Respondent: Sonia Zamanou-Erickson, Southern Illinois University, Edwardsville

---

1226   **9:30-10:45 a.m.**   PDR 1   Third Floor   Chicago Hilton

THEATRE AND CLASSROOM PRACTICES FOR TEACHING ABOUT THE HOLOCAUST

Sponsor: American Alliance for Theatre and Education
Chair: Krin B. Perry, Southwest Texas State University
  "Insights, Ideas, Resources, and Rationales for Teaching About the Holocaust in the Classroom and on the Stage." Janet E. Rubin, Saginaw Valley State University

---

1227   **9:30-10:45 a.m.**   PDR 2   Third Floor   Chicago Hilton

STRATEGIES FOR EXPLAINING AND PREVENTING ALCOHOL ABUSE IN COLLEGE-AGED STUDENTS AND ADOLESCENTS

Sponsor: Health Communication Division
Chair: Michael J. Cody, University of Southern California
  "Constructions from Within the Collegiate Drinking Culture: An Analysis of Fraternity Drinking Stories." Thomas A. Workman, University of Nebraska
  "Issues of Validity in Self-Reports of Alcohol Consumption in a College Student Sample." Kevin J. Real, Texas A&M University
  "Attempting to Change College Students' Risky Behaviors: The Role of Personal Relevance and Behavioral Intention." Alicia A. Marshall, Texas A&M University
  "Conferring Resistance to Peer Pressure Among Adolescents: Using the Inoculation Paradigm to Discourage Alcohol Use." Linda C. Godbold, East Carolina University

Respondent: Michael J. Cody, University of Southern California

---

1228   **9:30-10:45 a.m.**   PDR 3   Third Floor   Chicago Hilton

THE NEW LEADERS: WILL THEY STAY INSIDE THE LINES?

Sponsor: Applied Communication Division
Chair: Pamela L. Stepp, Cornell University
  "The Study of Leadership and Communication Behaviors Exhibited by Hispanic Women in a Social Action Organization." Ashley J. Bennington, University of Texas, Austin
  "No, the Sky has to be Blue: What's Said to Corporate Women About Why Things Can't Change." Bren O. Murphy, Loyola University, Chicago
  "Women College and University Presidents Perceive Communication as Most Important in Necessary Competencies for the Presidency." Pamela L. Stepp, Cornell University
  "Leadership in the Twenty-First Century: Convergent Trends Affecting the Increasing Influence of Women." Patricia Witherspoon, University of Texas, Austin

Respondent: Elizabeth J. Natalle, University of North Carolina, Greensboro

Thursday

1229   9:30-10:45 a.m.   PDR 4   Third Floor   Chicago Hilton

THE MOST IMPORTANT FREE-SPEECH DECISION OF THE UNITED STATES SUPREME COURT IN THE TWENTIETH CENTURY

Sponsor: Freedom of Expression Commission
Chair: Lea J. Parker, Northern Arizona University
  "Whitney v. California." Juliet L. Dee, University of Delaware
  "West Virginia State Board of Education v. Barnette." Warren G. Sandmann, Minnesota
    State University, Mankato
  "New York Times v. Sullivan." Nicholas F. Burnett, California State University, Sacramento
  "Brandenburg v. Ohio." Richard A. Parker, Northern Arizona University
  "Cohen v. California." Susan J. Balter-Reitz, DePauw University
  "Miller v. California." Joseph S. Tuman, San Francisco State University
  "Hustler Magazine v. Falwell." Edward C. Brewer, Liberty University
  "Texas v. Johnson." Daniel H. Corum, University of Puget Sound
  "ACLU v. Reno." Douglas M. Fraleigh, California State University, Fresno

---

1230   9:30-10:45 a.m.   PDR 5   Third Floor   Chicago Hilton

CYBER-EDUCATION IN COMMUNICATION

Sponsor: Table Talk Series
Chair: Pixy Ferris, William Paterson University

Panelists: Sue Barnes, Fordham University
        Margaret Cassidy, Adelphi University
        Pixy Ferris, William Paterson University
        Peter L. Haratonik, New York University
        W. Lance Haynes, University of Missouri, Rolla
        Ron L. Jacobson, Fordham University
        Jessica S. Leonard, Missouri Western State College
        Maureen C. Minielli, Saint Joseph's College
        Sharon B. Porter, Northern Arizona University
        Lance A. Strate, Fordham University
        Paul A. Soukup, Santa Clara University
        Shannon L. Roper, Rutgers University

Panelists provide diverse perspectives on the potential for cyber-education in the field of communication, with a focus on educators' roles and responsibilities.

1231   9:30-10:45 a.m.   PDR 6   Third Floor   Chicago Hilton

NCA RESOLUTIONS COMMITTEE BUSINESS MEETING

Sponsor: NCA Resolutions Committee

1232   9:30-10:45 a.m.   PDR 7   Third Floor   Chicago Hilton

COLORING OUTSIDE THE LINES: REINVENTING INDIVIDUAL EVENTS

Sponsor: Argumentation and Forensics Division

Panelists: Scott G. Dickmeyer, Concordia College, Minnesota
        Larry Schnoor, Communication Links
        Kellie W. Roberts, University of Florida
        Daniel D. Cronn-Mills, Minnesota State University, Mankato
        Jeffrey D. Brand, North Dakota State University
        Carol Wightman, Cornell College, Iowa

The panel explores both how forensics is stabilized, and ways to reinvent forensics for the next decade. Dickmeyer and Schnoor examine issues of stability and potential stagnation in forensics. The other panelists explore forensics outside the traditional lines, addressing: If you could reinvent forensics any way you want, what would it look like; e.g., replace the traditional 11 events, and what events would you have instead? Would you change the traditional structure?

1233   9:30-10:45 a.m.   Conf 4A   Fourth Floor   Chicago Hilton

MEDIA GLOBALIZATION: CULTURAL IMPERIALISM RELIVED OR SOCIO-POLITICAL RENAISSANCE?

Sponsor: International & Intercultural Communication Division
Chair: Yahya R. Kamalipour, Purdue University, Calumet
   "Cultural Bane or Sociological Boon?: Impact of Satellite and Western Technology
      Programming in India." Kuldip Rampal, Central Missouri State University
   "The CNN Effect: Questioning Foreign Policy on/and/for Television." M. Mehdi Semati,
      Michigan Technological University
   "The Global Social Structural Shift: Supra-National Corporations and Their Impact on
      Nation State." Joel Thierstein, Baylor University
   "The Spanish Digital War." Richard M. Maxwell, Queens College, CUNY
   "Women in Magazine Advertising: Domination of Western Beauty in Thailand." Gee
      Ekachai, Southern Illinois University, Anucha Thirakanont, Southern Illinois University

Respondent: Richard A. Gershon, Western Michigan University

1234   9:30-10:45 a.m.   Conf 4B   Fourth Floor   Chicago Hilton

UNDERSTANDING THE EVOLUTION OF BLAXPLOITATION FILMS IN THE U.S.

Sponsor: African American Communication & Culture Commission
Chair: Tina M. Harris, University of Georgia
   "Sidney Poitier's Playing the Saint: Racial Identity, Assimilation, and the Birth of
      Blaxploitation Films*." Kelly A. Dorgan, University of Georgia
   "From *Coffy* to *Foxy Brown*: Pam Grier as Both Black Feminist and Queen of Blaxploitation
      Films." Sonja M. Brown, University of Georgia
   "Freddie's Dead, but the Damage Lives On: Black Male Stereotypes in 1970s
      Blaxploitation Films." Patrick L. Sterns, Bowling Green State University
   "What's Being Transmitted: Blaxploitation Movies in American Society." Jennifer F. Wood,
      Bowling Green State University

*Student Debut Paper

1235   9:30-10:45 a.m.   Conf 4C   Fourth Floor   Chicago Hilton

TEACHING AND LEARNING: TRENDS AND CONCERNS

Sponsor: Senior College & University Section
Chair: Myrna Foster-Kuehn, Clarion University
   "Effects of Communication Competence, Communication Satisfaction, and Social Support
      on Uncertainty Reduction for Graduate Research/Teaching Assistants." Mary Kathleen
      Hacker, Texas Christian University, Joyce L. Allman, Texas Christian University
   "Identifying Current and Future Trends in Communication Programs in the Mid-Atlantic
      Region: A Progress Report." Susan A. Jasko, California University of Pennsylvania, Dencil
      K. Backus, California University of Pennsylvania
   "Reflections from the Classroom on the Effects of Computer-Assisted Instruction on the
      Teaching-Learning Process." M. Carla Schenone-Stevens, St. Ambrose University

---

1236   9:30-10:45 a.m.   Conf 4D   Fourth Floor   Chicago Hilton

CLINTOONS: HUMOR OUTSIDE THE LINES

Sponsor: Media Forum Series

Panelists: Robert L. Content, Trinity College, Washington, D.C.
            W. Bradford Mello, Trinity College, Washington, D.C.

Thursday

1237   9:30-10:45 a.m.   Conf 4E   Fourth Floor   Chicago Hilton

COMPETITIVE PAPERS IN EVALUATING MODELS AND ASSUMPTIONS OF VIEWER RECEPTION AND RESPONSE

Sponsor: Mass Communication Division
Chair: David D. Knapp, Front Range Community College
   "A Meta-Analysis of Exposure Effects of Gangsta Style Rap: Situating Real World Scenarios
      and Methodological Issues in Research." Mark J. Jones, Ohio University, Krishna P.
      Kandath, Ohio University
   "A Synthesis of Media Studies Approaches." Tessa M. Pfafman, Indiana University-Purdue
      University, Fort Wayne
   "Re-evaluating Reception: Myths, Criticisms and Suggestions for Further Convergence."
      Yariv Tsfati, University of Pennsylvania

Respondent: Shing-Ling S. Chen, University of Northern Iowa

1238   9:30-10:45 a.m.   Conf 4F   Fourth Floor   Chicago Hilton

CHALLENGES AND PITFALLS FACING APPLIED COMMUNICATION SCHOLARS: AN EXAMINATION ACROSS KEY DOMAINS OF INQUIRY AND PRACTICE

Sponsor: Applied Communication Division
Chair: Sunwolf, Santa Clara University
   "Reducing Equivocality in the Millennium: Helping Organizational Communication
      Scholars Meet Key Tests." Gary L. Kreps, Hofstra University
   "Trials and Tribulations of the Millennium: Helping Communication Consultants Negotiate
      Adversity." Sue DeWine, Ohio University
   "Translating Barriers into Opportunities During the Millennium: Helping Group
      Communication Scholars Rise Above Theoretical Obstacles." Kathleen M. Propp,
      Northern Illinois University
   "Methodological Dilemmas Posed by the Millennium: Helping Health Communication
      Scholars Develop Population-Specific Research." Sandra L. Ragan, University of
      Oklahoma

1239   9:30-10:45 a.m.   Conf 4G   Fourth Floor   Chicago Hilton

THE INTERNET AND PEDAGOGY

Sponsor: Commission on Communication in the Future
Chair: Howard E. Sypher, University of Kansas
   "Planning an On-Line Course." Sally K. Murphy, California State University, Hayward
   "What You Need to Know About Teaching on the Internet." Melissa L. Beall, University of
      Northern Iowa
   "Teaching an Intrapersonal Communication Course Collaboratively." Joan E. Aitken,
      University of Missouri, Kansas City, Leonard J. Shedletsky, University of Southern Maine
   "Teaching Interpersonal Senior Seminar Partly with the Internet." Dudley D. Cahn, SUNY,
      New Paltz
   "Teaching an Interdisciplinary Core Curriculum Course: The Internet." Henry C. Amoroso,
      University of Southern Maine

Respondent: Anita Taylor, George Mason University

1241   9:30-10:45 a.m.   Conf 4I   Fourth Floor   Chicago Hilton

CIVIC PUBLIC RELATIONS: ENLARGING THE ROLE OF THE PUBLIC INTEREST IN PUBLIC RELATIONS

Sponsor: Public Relations Division
Chair: Greg Leichty, University of Louisville

Panelists: Debra A. Kernisky, Northern Michigan University

Margaret EM Pavlich, Northern Arizona University
Patricia A. Chantrill, Northern Arizona University
Calvin L. Troup, Duquesne University
Lois Kirkpatrick, Fairfax County, VA
Michael Dillon, Duquesne University

The audience will join the panelists for an open discussion, following the panel presentations.

1242   9:30-10:45 a.m.   Conf 4J   Fourth Floor   Chicago Hilton

USING COMMUNICATION THEORY TO ASSESS THE EFFECTIVENESS OF CAMPUS COUNSELING SERVICES

Sponsor: Senior College & University Section
Chair: Pamela A. Hayward, Lake Superior State University
  "Using Symbolic Convergence Theory to Assess Administrators' Rhetorical Visions for Student Counseling Services." Jay R. Martinson, Olivet Nazarene University, Jeanette Martinson, Pathways Psychological Services
  "Senders, Receivers, Channels, and Feedback: Using Information Systems Theory to Assess the Process of Student Counseling Services." Jennifer Schultz, Olivet Nazarene University
  "Telling the Stories of Counseling Experiences: Using Narrative Paradigm Theory to Assess Experiences and Values of Students Toward Student Counseling Services." Shannon Wheeler, Olivet Nazarene University
  "Encounters, Frames, and the Self on Stage: Using Goffman's Theory of Self-Presentation as Dramatization to Assess Student Counseling Services." Michael Johnson, Olivet Nazarene University
  "Using Symbolic Convergence Theory to Assess Students' Rhetorical Visions and Fantasy Themes Held Toward Campus Counseling Services." Bethany Heidel, Olivet Nazarene University
  "Too Much Semantic Noise! A Critique of Symbolic Convergence Theory and of Its Usefulness in Assessing Campus Counseling Services." Matthew D. Mund, Olivet Nazarene University, Amy Tallman, Olivet Nazarene University

Respondent: Donald C. Shields, University of Missouri

1243   9:30-10:45 a.m.   Conf 4K   Fourth Floor   Chicago Hilton

BUILDING BRIDGES: DEVELOPING RELATIONSHIPS ON THE CAMPUS AND IN THE PROFESSIONAL PUBLIC RELATIONS COMMUNITY

Sponsor: Public Relations Division
Chair: Bonita Dostal Neff, Valparaiso University
  "Beyond the Classroom: How to Develop and Build Relationships Between the PR Professional and the PR Student." Rise J. Samra, Barry University
  "Building Bridges to Broadcast Faculty: Partnering to Develop PSAs." Charles A. Lubbers, Kansas State University
  "Reaching Out: PR in the Programs of Others." John A. Madsen, Buena Vista University

---

1244   9:30-10:45 a.m.   Conf 4L   Fourth Floor   Chicago Hilton

REVISITING GENRE THEORY IN THE CONTEXT OF POSTMODERNITY: PUBLIC SPACE, PUBLIC MEMORY AND COMMUNICATION PEDAGOGY

Sponsor: Rhetorical and Communication Theory Division
Chair: Carolyn R. Miller, North Carolina State University
  "Public Art and Its Generic Travails: From Heroic Statues to Tilting Arcs." Margaret R. LaWare, Iowa State University
  "Genre as Social Action: Civil Rights Memorials, Public Memory and Postmodernity." Victoria J. Gallagher, North Carolina State University
  "Becoming 'Disciplined' in Talk and Text: Genre as Social Action Across the Curriculum." Chris Anson, University of Minnesota, Deanna P. Dannels, University of Utah

Respondent: Carolyn R. Miller, North Carolina State University

---

1245   9:30-10:45 a.m.   Conf 4M   Fourth Floor   Chicago Hilton

ORGANIZATIONAL COMMUNICATION AND CHANGE: MEANING CREATION, IDENTITY AND STAKEHOLDERS

Sponsor: Organizational Communication Division
Chair: Rachel Pokora, Nebraska Wesleyan University
  "Exploring Meaning Creation: Use of Metaphorical Analysis to Investigate Organizational Change." Christine M. Fischer, Eastern Michigan University
  "Organizational Change as Contested Identity." Brian Sandine, University of Colorado, Boulder
  "Communication, Identification, and Change: A Case Study of a Major Cultural Institution." Debra Zindler, University of Wisconsin, Milwaukee, Mike Allen, University of Wisconsin, Milwaukee, Nancy A. Burrell, University of Wisconsin, Milwaukee, Renee A. Meyers, University of Wisconsin, Milwaukee
  "Communication with the Multiple Stakeholders of Nonprofit Organizations: Change Implementers' Communicative Approaches and Topics of Talk." Laurie K. Lewis, University of Texas, Austin, Stephanie A. Hamel, University of Texas, Austin, Brian K. Richardson, University of Texas, Austin

Respondent: Susan Hafen, University of Wisconsin, Eau Claire

1249   9:30-10:45 a.m.   Conf 5B   Fifth Floor   Chicago Hilton

COLORING OUTSIDE THE LINES: HOW INTERNET COMMUNICATION VIOLATES THEORY AND PRACTICE IN THE BASIC COURSE

Sponsor: Basic Course Division
Chair: Pamela L. Gray, Central Michigan University
  "Emoticons, Flaming and Other Computer Stuff as Substitutes for Nonverbal Channels." Rick A. Buerkel, Central Michigan University
  "Rule-Breaking in Cyberspace Relationships: Netiquette vs. Interpersonal Competence." Nancy Buerkel-Rothfuss, Central Michigan University
  "Levels of Interpersonal Relationships: Cyber-Intimacy Without Having Ever Met." Pamela L. Gray, Central Michigan University

---

1251   9:30-10:45 a.m.   Conf 5D   Fifth Floor   Chicago Hilton

COLORING OUTSIDE THE LINES: ADVOCATING AND WORKING TOWARD WOMEN'S IMPROVED STATUS FROM INSIDE THE ACADEMY

Sponsor: Women's Caucus
Chair: Rosanne L. Hartman, SUNY, Geneseo
  "Integrating the Adult Learner into the Traditional Classroom." S. Diane McFarland, D'Youville College
  "Mentoring the Adult Learner to Expand Outside the Lines." Stan Klimowicz, McMaster University, Canada
  "Women Faculty Members and Older Female Students: A Case for Assisted Mentorships." Alice L. Crume, SUNY, Brockport
  "Gender and the Effect It Has on the Rehabilitation Relationships for the Returning Student." Sheila J. Sullivan, Mississippi State University
  "Expectations in the Academy: Identifying and Meeting Normative Roles." Erica Scharrer, SUNY, Geneseo
  "Women Mentoring Women Faculty: Going Outside the Traditional Structure." Rosanne L. Hartman, SUNY, Geneseo

---

1252   9:30-10:45 a.m.   Conf 5E   Fifth Floor   Chicago Hilton

COLORING OUTSIDE THE LINES: NEW FRONTIERS IN RESEARCH METHODS

Sponsor: Rhetorical and Communication Theory Division

Chair: Mary Jane Collier, University of Denver
  "Turning Me Inside/Out: The Prismatic Nature of Auto-Ethnography." Teresa A. Werner, University of Denver
  "Boundaries of Situated Interaction: Triangulated Interviewing Formats and the Natural Occurrence of Phenomena Under Study." David E. Weber, University of Denver
  "Confessions of Experience and Lessons Learned: A Journey Toward a Dialogical Research Praxis." Chris N. Poulos, University of Denver, Jennifer A. Thompson, University of Denver

Respondent: Lenore Langsdorf, Southern Illinois University, Carbondale

---

1254   9:30-10:45 a.m.   Conf 5G   Fifth Floor   Chicago Hilton

REFLECTIONS OF TEACHING ASSISTANTS: APPLYING INSTRUCTIONAL COMMUNICATION THEORY TO THE CLASSROOM

Sponsor: Instructional Development Division
Chair: Karla K. Jensen, Texas Tech University
  "Exploring How the Study of Instructional Theory Influences Teaching Assistants' Classroom Experiences." Karen A. Anderson, University of Kansas
  "Nonverbal Immediacy in the Classroom: Making Better Teachers." Derek C. Clapp, Texas Tech University
  "Reflections of Immediacy in the Classroom: An Examination of the Theory Put to Use." Chad Edwards, University of Kansas
  "The Power of Immediacy and the Clarity Research and their Pedagogical Implications: A Personal Testimony." Shawn T. Wahl, University of Nebraska, Lincoln

---

1255   9:30-10:45 a.m.   Conf 5H   Fifth Floor   Chicago Hilton

KEY VARIABLES WHEN EXAMINING PUBLIC SPEAKING ANXIETY

Sponsor: Communication Apprehension & Avoidance Commission
Chair: Debbie M. Ayres-Sonandre, Tacoma Community College
  "Personality Type As Indicator of Speech Anxiety." Jodi L. Hallsten, University of North Dakota
  "Examining Communication Apprehension and Its Relationship with Key Classroom Variables: Mass Lectures versus Self-Contained Formats of the Basic Communication Course." Janet Hester, Hopkinsville School System, Timothy S. Todd, Murray State University, Stephen A. Cox, Murray State University

---

1257   9:30-10:45 a.m.   Conf 5J   Fifth Floor   Chicago Hilton

ADDITIONAL COLORING OUTSIDE THE LINES

Sponsor: Lambda Pi Eta
Chair: Felicia R. Walker, Howard University
  "The Evolution of the Black Television Family in the Past 25 Years." Jasaun Buckner, Howard University
  "Think. Plan. Be Safe. A Rhetorical Analysis of the Perceived Safety in a Small Western City." Stacia Colby, University of Colorado, Boulder, Kathryn Dunkelberger, University of Colorado, Boulder, Jessica Oldham, University of Colorado, Boulder
  "Content Analysis of the Portrayal of Working Women in American Collegiate Magazines." Catherine Preisinger, Towson University
  "The Citadel, Coloring Outside the Lines: A Woman Challenges the Boundaries." Jennifer Barnett, Cameron University
  "Limited Effects Paradigm, Klapper's Phenomenistic Theory." Jessica Chesley Gammon, George Mason University

---

1262   9:30-10:45 a.m.   Essex Court   Second Floor   Essex Inn

REPRESENTATION OF THE CHRISTIAN EXPERIENCE IN HOLLYWOOD FILM

Sponsor: Religious Communication Association

Chair: Bohn D. Lattin, University of Portland
"It's Not Just a Job, It's a Calling: The Redemption of Soldiering as Religious Vocation in *Saving Private Ryan*." Marc T. Newman, Palomar College
"The Collar on Camera: A Rhetorical History of the Image of Clergy Presented in Hollywood Films." Robert M. McManus, Regent University, John D. Keeler, Regent University
"The Humiliation of the Faith: Representation and Evangelical Christianity in *The Apostle*." Mark Allan Steiner, Loyola University, Chicago

Respondent: Quentin J. Schultze, Calvin College

1263	9:30-10:45 a.m.	Windsor Court	Second Floor	Essex Inn

ETHNOGRAPHY AS SPIRITUAL PRACTICE: WHEN COLORING MAKES THE LINES DISAPPEAR

Sponsor: Ethnography Division
Chair: M. Cristina Gonzalez, Arizona State University

Panelists: Kirsten J. Broadfoot, University of Colorado, Boulder
Patricia Geist, San Diego State University
H.L. (Bud) Goodall, University of North Carolina, Greensboro
Robert L. Krizek, Saint Louis University
Michelle A. Miller, Penn State University

1264	9:30-10:45 a.m.	Buckingham Court	Second Floor	Essex Inn

DE-FAMILIARIZING STRANGERS IN THE POSTMODERN WORLD: PART I

Sponsor: Semiotics and Communication Commission
Chair: Isaac E. Catt, Millersville University
"Communicating Disability as Existential Practice and Semiotic Rupture." Tom Craig, Brock University, Canada
"Semiotic Irony in Familial Intimacy." Deborah L. Eicher-Catt, Penn State University, Wilkes-Barre
"Strangers in the Classroom." Maureen Connolly, Brock University, Canada
"The Illusion of Intimacy and the Disappearance of Public Space." Frank J. Macke, Mercer University

1265	9:30-10:45 a.m.	Park East Walk	Second Floor	Essex Inn

SEPARATED BY CONDITIONS OF OUR OWN MAKING: SOUNDING BURKE THROUGH MCLUHAN

Sponsor: Kenneth Burke Society, NCA Branch
"Alphabetic Typography and the Literate Condition: Defining the Modern." Corey Anton, Grand Valley State University
"Constitution: A Paper Lion in an Electronic Jingle." Wade R. Kenny, University of Dayton
"Watching Together as Being-Together: Identities, Communities, and the Global Village." Bryan Crable, Villanova University
"Rotten with Perfection: Reflections on the Natural, the Spiritual, and the Technological." Susan B. Mackey-Kallis, Villanova University

1266	9:30-10:45 a.m.	Cohn Rm	Second Floor	Spertus Institute

TRACING RHETORICAL PATHS IN COMMUNICATION AND LAW

Sponsor: Communication and Law Commission
Chair: Terence S. Morrow, Gustavus Adolphus College
"Encryption Policy: A Frame Analysis." Rita Zajacz, Indiana University
"Rhetoric's Renaissance: Delineating the Twin Trajectories of Modern Jurisprudence*." Geoffrey D. Klinger, University of Utah
"Doubts About Reasonable Doubt: Tracing the American Criminal Jury's Standard of Certainty." Mark J. Stoda, Arizona State University

Respondent: Terence S. Morrow, Gustavus Adolphus College

*Top Paper—Rhetorical Method

1269   9:30-10:45 a.m.   Rm 903   Ninth Floor   Spertus Institute

INSIDE OUT: CHANGING THE BOUNDARIES OF THE TRADITIONAL CLASSROOM

Sponsor: Experiential Learning in Communication Commission
Chair: Gay Lumsden, Kean University
   "When Business is the Business of the Classroom." Michael V. Pearson, West Chester
      University
   "Community Conversations: Young Minds Engaging Old Hearts." Eileen M. Berens,
      Villanova University
   "Real Family Communication for Real Families." Cynthia Burggraf Torppa, Torppa
      Psychological & Counseling Services
   "More Than Just Examples: Weaving Consulting and Teaching Together in the
      Organizational Communication Course." Anita K. Foeman, West Chester University
   "Taking Talk to the Streets with Peer Education." Teresa A. Nance, Villanova University

Respondent: Donald L. Lumsden, Kean University

1270   9:30-10:45 a.m.   Rm 904   Ninth Floor   Spertus Institute

THE ROLE OF CONFLICT RESOLUTION IN VIETNAM'S MODERNIZATION: THE APPLICATION OF PRINCIPLED NEGOTIATION IN VIETNAM BUSINESS

Sponsor: Peace and Conflict Communication Commission
Chair: Sherick A. Hughes, Wake Forest University

Panelists: Bruce C. McKinney, James Madison University
        Rex M. Fuller, James Madison University
        William D. Kimsey, James Madison University

Panelists will discuss their experience in working with Vietnamese professors, business, and
government leaders during training of principled negotiation in Virginia and Vietnam.

1272   9:30-10:45 a.m.   Rm 907   Ninth Floor   Spertus Institute

AMERICAN SOCIETY FOR THE HISTORY OF RHETORIC BUSINESS MEETING

Sponsor: American Society for the History of Rhetoric

11:00 a.m.

1306   11:00-12:15 p.m.   Continental BR A   Lobby Level   Chicago Hilton

COMPETITIVE PAPERS IN IMPLICATIONS OF ELECTRONIC MEDIA ON COMMUNITIES AND DEMOCRACIES

Sponsor: Mass Communication Division
Chair: Andrea D. Mitnick, Kutztown University
   "'I'm Not a Scientist, But. . .': Television News and the Reification of Expert Authority."
      Geoffrey Baym, University of Utah
   "Digital (Post)Colonial Communities." Radhika Gajjala, Bowling Green State University
   "Community and Performance: Getting the Whole Town Talking." Glenda R. Balas,
      DePauw University

Respondent: Judith M. Thorpe, University of Wisconsin, Oshkosh

Thursday

| 1308 | 11:00-12:15 p.m. | Continental BR C | Lobby Level | Chicago Hilton |

LABOR, COMMUNICATION, AND CAPITALISM

Sponsor: Critical and Cultural Studies Division
Chair: Robert McChesney, University of Illinois
  "Retheorizing Resistance: The Crisis of Capitalism, Class Struggle and Mass Media." Deepa
    Kumar, University of Pittsburgh
  "Eating Our Words: Coercion and Communication in Labor Movement." Dana L. Cloud,
    University of Texas, Austin
  "The Canadian Labor 'Beat': The Origins and Decline of a Journalism Specialty." Gene
    Costain, University of Iowa
  "The Proletariatization of Professional Class and New Media Technologies." Frederick
    Wasser, University of Pittsburgh

Respondent: Robert McChesney, University of Illinois

| 1310 | 11:00-12:15 p.m. | Grand Ballroom | Second Floor | Chicago Hilton |

QUESTIONS OF TRAVEL: ELIZABETH BISHOP IN PERFORMANCE

Sponsor: Performance Studies Division
Chair: Beverly W. Long, University of North Carolina, Chapel Hill
  "Listening to Miss Elizabeth." Paul H. Gray, University of Texas, Austin
  "Sestina." Leland Roloff, Northwestern University
  "A Verse 'In Action': Performing the Verbal Contours of Elizabeth Bishop's 'The Moose'."
    Matthew J. Spangler, Trinity College, Dublin
  "Elizabeth Bishop's Poetry in Performance." Sharon Eisner, University of Texas, Austin
  "An American in Ouro Preto." Margaret O'Connor, University of North Carolina, Chapel
    Hill
  "Crusoe In England." Paul Ferguson, University of North Carolina, Chapel Hill

Respondent: M. Heather Carver, University of Texas, Austin

| 1314 | 11:00-12:15 p.m. | Boulevard A | Second Floor | Chicago Hilton |

CHALLENGING BOUNDARIES: CUSTOMER SERVICE PROVIDERS AS BOUNDARY SPANNERS IN ORGANIZATIONAL AND INTERPERSONAL DOMAINS

Sponsor: Challenging Boundaries Series
Chair: Wendy Z. Ford, Western Michigan University

Panelists: Mara B. Adelman, Seattle University
          Wendy Z. Ford, Western Michigan University
          Clive Muir, Cornell University

This program will encourage dialogue about customer service providers as important
boundary spanners in our personal and professional lives. The session will begin with brief
presentations from panelists who have been "coloring outside the lines" of traditional
emphases in organizational and interpersonal domains. The presentations will be followed by
an interactive discussion among panelists and audience members to explore implications and
priorities for research, education, training, and practice in customer service contexts. The
panelists will provide information packets and other materials that may be helpful in
constructing research programs, developing undergraduate and graduate courses, designing
corporate training programs, and creating customer service policies with a communication
focus. Participants are encouraged to come prepared to share their own ideas and resources
in a highly interactive format.

| 1315 | 11:00-12:15 p.m. | Boulevard B | Second Floor | Chicago Hilton |

TOP FOUR PAPERS IN FAMILY COMMUNICATION

Sponsor: Family Communication Division

Chair: Fran Dickson, University of Denver
"Family Privacy Dilemmas: A Communication Boundary Management Perspective."
Sandra Petronio, Arizona State University, Susanne Jones, Arizona State University, Mary
Clair Morr, Arizona State University
"Becoming a Family: Developmental Processes Represented in Blended Family Discourse."
Dawn O. Braithwaite, University of Nebraska, Lincoln, Nancy J. Eckstein, University of
Nebraska, Lincoln, Tamara Golish, Luther College, Loreen N. Olson, University of
Minnesota, Morris, Jack E. Sargent, Kean University, Charles E. Soukup, University of
Nebraska, Lincoln, Paul D. Turman, University of Nebraska, Lincoln, Aysel Morin,
University of Nebraska, Lincoln
"Nonverbal Involvement, Expressiveness, and Pleasantness as Predicted by Parental and
Partner Attachment Style." Beth A. Le Poire, University of California, Santa Barbara,
Carolyn A. Shepard, University of California, Santa Barbara, Ashley P. Duggan, University
of California, Santa Barbara
"Does Communication Mediate the Association Between Personality and Marital
Satisfaction? Intrapersonal and Interpersonal Explanations of How Personality Matters in
Marriage." John P. Caughlin, University of Nebraska, Lincoln, Ted L. Huston, University
of Texas, Austin, Renate M. Houts, Kent State University

Respondent: Nancy Buerkel-Rothfuss, Central Michigan University

---

1316   11:00-12:15 p.m.   Boulevard C   Second Floor   Chicago Hilton

QUANTITATIVE APPROACHES TO INTERCULTURAL COMMUNICATION

Sponsor: International & Intercultural Communication Division
Chair: Gary B. Wilson, Hong Kong Baptist University
"A Comparison of the Nonverbal Communication Patterns Between the People of the U.S.
and Turkey: A Quantitative Analysis." Aparna S. Bulusu, University of Memphis
"Testing a New Measure of Culture: The Mainstream American Scale." Aaron C. Cargile,
California State University
"Testing a Measure of Intercultural Perspective Taking in a Community Engaged in
International Exchange." Barbara J. Kappler, University of Minnesota

Respondent: Nagesh Rao, Ohio University

1318   11:00-12:15 p.m.   Waldorf   Third Floor   Chicago Hilton

COLORING OUTSIDE THE LINES: QUALITATIVE RESEARCH ON
UNDERSTUDIED RELATIONSHIPS

Sponsor: Family Communication Division
Chair: Dawn Weber, Central Michigan University
"Communication in the Family System of Single Mothers by Choice." Karin E. McBride,
Central Michigan University
"The Influence of Culture on the Conflict of Black/White Interracial Couples." Derrick
Rosenoir, Central Michigan University
"When the Choice is Made for Her: A Study of Indian Arranged Marriages." Devika
Chawla, Central Michigan University
"Grandparent-Grandchild Relationships: Connecting Through Storytelling." Amy S.
Drenth, Central Michigan University

Respondent: Janet Yerby, Central Michigan University

1319   11:00-12:15 p.m.   Astoria   Third Floor   Chicago Hilton

REBELLION AND REBUILDING: CRISIS RHETORIC IN THE U.S., JAMAICA,
AND SOUTH AFRICA

Sponsor: Public Address Division
Chair: William D. Harpine, University of Akron
"'Put the Foot Down Firmly': Forgotten Speeches of Abraham Lincoln." Robert S. Brown,
Ashland University

Thursday

"Thomas Carlyle, George William Gordon, and the Colonial Discourse Surrounding the Governor Eyre Controversy." Marouf Hasian, University of Utah
"The Weakening of Nelson Mandela's Rhetoric: An Exploratory Use of Diction 4.0." Theodore F. Sheckels, Randolph-Macon College

Respondent: Roderick P. Hart, University of Texas, Austin

1321   11:00-12:15 p.m.   Williford A   Third Floor   Chicago Hilton

COMMUNICATING DIASPORICALLY

Sponsor: African American Communication & Culture Commission
Chair: Myron M. Beasley, Ohio University
    "Moroccan Men and Mesmerizing Behaviors: Male to Male Interpersonal Relationships in North Africa." Myron M. Beasley, Ohio University
    "'Wuz Up Star'?: Hip Hop Music as the Mode of Communication Between African American Women and African Men." Tia L. Smith, Ohio University
    "Jamaican and African American Women in Conflict: An Intercultural Analysis of the Social, Political, and Economic Underpinnings." Shawn Townes, Ohio University

Respondent: Trevellya Ford-Ahmed, West Virginia State College

---

1322   11:00-12:15 p.m.   Williford B   Third Floor   Chicago Hilton

PSYCHOLOGICAL PERSUASION: POLITICAL NARRATIVES, PUBLIC IMAGES, AND MILITARY DOCTRINES

Sponsor: Political Communication Division
Chair: Rita Kirk Whillock, Southern Methodist University
    "Military Psychological Doctrine and Persuasive Theory." Dennis White, Arkansas State University
    "The Impact of Visual Evidence on Public Assessment of Veracity." David E. Whillock, Texas Christian University
    "Seeing is Believing: The Effectiveness of Stories, Ads, and Images." David Slayden, University of Colorado, Boulder
    "Dangerous Comment: Truth Telling in Times of War." Rita Kirk Whillock, Southern Methodist University

---

1323   11:00-12:15 p.m.   Williford C   Third Floor   Chicago Hilton

WOMEN, MUSIC AND SURVIVAL

Sponsor: Feminist and Women Studies Division
Chair: Cynthia M. Lont, George Mason University
    "A Musical Lifeline: Women's Appropriation of Artists' Music." Ann M. Savage, Butler University
    "Sistah MC: African American Female Influence on Rap." Liz Lane-Johnson, Regent University
    "Spice Persuasion: A Rhetorical Analysis of the Spice Girls." Rebekah Farrugia, Wayne State University

Respondents: Alan D. Stewart, Rutgers University
             Cynthia M. Lont, George Mason University

1324   11:00-12:15 p.m.   Marquette   Third Floor   Chicago Hilton

PERFORMANCE ETHNOGRAPHIES: PROCESS AND PRESENTATION

Sponsor: Theatre Division
Chair: Robert D. Hostetter, North Park University
    "'The People Keep Comin': A Dialogical Performance." Eileen C. Cherry, DePaul University
    "The Palestinian 'Catastrophe': An Intercultural Performance." Robert D. Hostetter, North Park University

Respondent: Deryl B. Johnson, Kutztown University

The staging of a children's play, performed by Metro Theatre Company of St. Louis (on video), and Palestinian narratives of the "catastrophe" of 1948, performed by North Park University students.

1325   11:00-12:15 p.m.   Joliet   Third Floor   Chicago Hilton

ELECTRONIC COMMUNICATION

Sponsor: Student Section
   "Internet Use Motivations, Patterns and Their Interactions." Hong-Sik Yu, University of
      Alabama
   "Flamethrowers, Slashers, and Witches: Gendered Communication in a Virtual
      Community." Steven S. Vrooman, Arizona State University
   "H4cklng For G1r13z: A Neo-Aristotelian Criticism of the New York Times Web Site."
      Nathan Pitzer, DePauw University

Respondent: Thomas W. Benson, Penn State University

1326   11:00-12:15 p.m.   PDR 1   Third Floor   Chicago Hilton

LISTENING EDUCATION IN THE TWENTY-FIRST CENTURY

Sponsor: International Listening Association
Chair: Charles Roberts, East Tennessee State University
   "Listening: (Re)considering Its Role in Communication Theory and Research." Kelby K.
      Halone, Clemson University
   "Listening: Its Role in the Twenty-First Century." Sheila C. Bentley, Bentley Consulting
   "Listening Pedagogy." Andrew D. Wolvin, University of Maryland, Carolyn G. Coakley,
      University of Maryland
   "Listening Assessment." Robert N. Bostrom, University of Kentucky

---

1327   11:00-12:15 p.m.   PDR 2   Third Floor   Chicago Hilton

POSTPARTUM POLITICS: THE PERFORMANCE AND RHETORIC OF PARENTING

Sponsor: Performance Studies Division
Chair: Helen M. Sterk, Calvin College
   "One Contraction at a Time: Instinct, Endurance, and the Performance of Parenting."
      Joanne R. Gilbert, Alma College
   "Performing Motherhood: The 'How-To' Books To Do What We're ('Supposed To Be')
      Doing." Cindy J. Kistenberg, University of Houston, Downtown, Charla L. Markham
      Shaw, University of Texas, Arlington
   "The Year the Department Got Pregnant: Politicizing Family Values." Elyse L. Pineau,
      Southern Illinois University, Carbondale
   "Shapeshifting and the Performance of Motherhood." Heidi M. Rose, Villanova University

---

1328   11:00-12:15 p.m.   PDR 3   Third Floor   Chicago Hilton

APPLIED COMMUNICATION SCHOLARS CONFRONT GENDER ISSUES, TRANSACTIONS, AND HEALTH PROMOTION: EMPIRICAL PROMISES AND PERILS

Sponsor: Applied Communication Division
Chair: Alice L. Crume, SUNY, Brockport
   "A Woman's Worst Enemy? Standpoint Theory and Gender Relations Theory in the
      Examination of Gender Issues in Organizational Communication." Ann Lowry, College of
      St. Catherine
   "Role Status Expectancy and Gendered Transactions: Sociological Gender and Perceptions
      of Conflict." Debbie S. Dougherty, University of Nebraska, Lincoln, Steven M. Sommer,
      University of Nebraska, Lincoln
   "'Getting Squished' on Talk TV: The Potential Efficacy of a Daytime Talk Show in
      Encouraging Mammogram Use." Sandra M. Fortier, Penn State University

Thursday

Respondent: Mary Ann Danielson, Creighton University

1329   11:00-12:15 p.m.   PDR 4   Third Floor   Chicago Hilton

FREEDOM OF EXPRESSION IN RELIGION

Sponsor: Freedom of Expression Commission
Chair: Daniel D. Cronn-Mills, Minnesota State University, Mankato
   "Preaching to the People: The Voice of Women Religious in the Roman Catholic Church."
      Mary F. Hoffman, University of Kansas
   "The Limits of Freedom of Speech: Dissent in the Catholic Church." Kathleen M.
      Edelmayer, Albion College
   "Freedom of Expression at a Catholic University, or 'Don't Mention Women Priests'."
      Kirstin J. Cronn-Mills, Minnesota State University, Mankato
   "Jehovah's Witnesses and Their Contribution to the First Amendment." Daniel D.
      Cronn-Mills, Minnesota State University, Mankato

1330   11:00-12:15 p.m.   PDR 5   Third Floor   Chicago Hilton

THE PROBLEM OF COLLEGE DRINKING: HOW CAN COMMUNICATION BE A PART OF THE SOLUTION?

Sponsor: Table Talk Series
Chair: Robert D. Kully, California State University, Los Angeles

Panelists: Linda C. Lederman, Rutgers University
            Lea P. Stewart, Rutgers University
            Thomas A. Workman, University of Nebraska, Lincoln
            Nancy L. Harper, Grand Valley State University

This program is relevant to all educators and students who are interested in and concerned about the serious problems of dangerous drinking on college campuses today. Following brief presentations, the audience will interact and participate with the presenters.

1331   11:00-12:15 p.m.   PDR 6   Third Floor   Chicago Hilton

MY THREE THORNIEST ADMINISTRATIVE CHALLENGES AND HOW I SOLVED THEM

Sponsor: Association for Communication Administration
Chair: William G. Christ, Trinity University

Panelists: Lou D. Tillson, Murray State University
            Jannette L. Dates, Howard University
            Jennings Bryant, University of Alabama
            Mark L. Knapp, University of Texas, Austin
            Alison Alexander, University of Georgia

1332   11:00-12:15 p.m.   PDR 7   Third Floor   Chicago Hilton

AFTER-DINNER SPEECHES ON AFTER-DINNER SPEAKING: MAKING SERIOUS POINTS ABOUT ADS THROUGH THE USE OF HUMOR

Sponsor: Argumentation and Forensics Division
Chair: Vicki L. Karns, Suffolk University
   "Problems in After-Dinner Speaking: Ranting into the New Millennium." Randolph
      Richardson, Berry College
   "Everything I Need to Know About ADS I Learned from Eric Cartman." B. Keith Murphy,
      Fort Valley State University
   "Funny, but not HA HA Funny: The Evolving Criteria of Contest After-Dinner Speaking."
      Blaine M. Hall, Florida College
   "Post-Dinner Speaking." David Lindrum, Purdue University

"Oh, Now That's Really Funny." Kim Roe, Illinois State University, Rick Roe, Northwestern University

---

1333   11:00-12:15 p.m.   Conf 4A   Fourth Floor   Chicago Hilton

SURRENDERING TO THE VULNERABILITY: DISCOVERING SOMETHING NEW FROM SOMETHING KNEW

Sponsor: Ethnography Division
Chair: Patricia Geist, San Diego State University
   "Imagining Beyond Vision, Text, and Authority: Speaking the Moments of Creation." Gregory N. Brookes, San Diego State University
   "Revealing Ourselves: The Language of Life Changes and Survivorship." Jennifer Ott, San Diego State University
   "To Speak the Unspeakable: Forgiving the Death of a Loved One." Deborah Hicks, San Diego State University
   "Surviving Abuse: Re-Covering Life Through Language." Maggie Z. Miller, San Diego State University

Respondents: Carolyn S. Ellis, University of South Florida
              Barbara F. Sharf, Texas A&M University

1334   11:00-12:15 p.m.   Conf 4B   Fourth Floor   Chicago Hilton

COLORING OUTSIDE THE LINES: NEW PARADIGMS IN INDEPENDENT AFRICAN AMERICAN FILM

Sponsor: African American Communication & Culture Commission
Chair: Carolyn A. Stroman, Howard University
   "100 Years of Black Independent Film: Patterns of Production." S. Torriano Berry, Howard University
   "Charles Burnett: Film Auteur?" Bishetta D. Merritt, Howard University
   "Representations of Religion in Black Film." Paula W. Matabane, Howard University

Respondent: Vickey Saunders, Howard University

The panelists will discuss patterns of production in black independent film that generate new and old stereotypical paradigms of African American life and culture. Film clips will be shown.

1335   11:00-12:15 p.m.   Conf 4C   Fourth Floor   Chicago Hilton

VISUOLOGIES: IDEOLOGIES AND MYTHOLOGIES OF MANIPULATED IMAGES

Sponsor: Visual Communication Commission
Chair: Henry P. Krips, University of Pittsburgh
   "Staging an Ideal Body: Visual Manipulation of the Masses under Fascism and Communism." Vanda Rakova, University of Pittsburgh
   "*Myra, Myra* on the Wall, Who's the Scariest of Them All?: Complicating Images of a Child Murderer." Jennifer Friedlander, University of Pittsburgh
   "The Mythic Image: Uses of Computer Enhanced Imagery in Advertising." Michelle Silva, University of Pittsburgh

Respondent: Henry P. Krips, University of Pittsburgh

1336   11:00-12:15 p.m.   Conf 4D   Fourth Floor   Chicago Hilton

MEDIA-MEDIATED AIDS

Sponsor: NCA First Vice President
Chair: Linda K. Fuller, Worcester State College

"Visualizing 'Gay Cancer': Two Decades of Network Coverage of AIDS." Steven Konick, Linfield College

"AIDS-Related Conversations in Thailand: Mass Media and Interpersonal Communication." Yoshimi Nishino, Inter-American Bank, Washington, DC

"Planning HIV/AIDS Education and Prevention Media Messages for Asian Americans." Gust A. Yep, San Francisco State University

"Differences in Print Media Coverage of AIDS and Lyme Disease." Uriel Kitron, University of Illinois

"AIDSFILMS: Motion Picture Depictions of the HIV/AIDS Pandemic." Linda K. Fuller, Worcester State College

"A Longitudinal Study of Newspaper Type and Community Location as Influences on AIDS Coverage." Marshel D. Rossow, Mankato State University

Respondent: Gary L. Kreps, Hofstra University

1337   11:00-12:15 p.m.   Conf 4E   Fourth Floor   Chicago Hilton

RESEARCH 'OUTSIDE THE LINES' OF HEALTH COMMUNICATION: CULTURAL STUDIES OF HEALTH AND ILLNESS

Sponsor: Health Communication Division
Chair: Eileen B. Ray, Cleveland State University
    "Barbie, the Culture of Thinness, and the Health of Young Girls: A Discursive Analysis." Linda Baughman, Allegheny College
    "Infertile Bodies, Infertile Minds: Responsibility, Rights, and Regulation Within Infertility Discourse." Sara Connell, University of Illinois, Urbana-Champaign
    "Ophelia, Health Communication, and the Politics of Discourse." Maria Mastronardi, University of Illinois, Chicago
    "A Technological Dis-ease: Scientific Discourses, Mass Media, and the 'Truths' About 'Computer Addiction'." Lori K. Reed, University of Illinois, Urbana-Champaign

Respondent: Lawrence Grossberg, University of North Carolina, Chapel Hill

---

1338   11:00-12:15 p.m.   Conf 4F   Fourth Floor   Chicago Hilton

TALES FROM THE CLASSROOM: A VIDEO PRESENTATION OF PROFESSORS TELLING CLASSROOM STORIES

Sponsor: Media Forum Series

Panelists: Daniel M. Dunn, Purdue University, Calumet
           Theresa M. Carilli, Purdue University, Calumet
           Marybeth O'Connor, Purdue University, Calumet

1339   11:00-12:15 p.m.   Conf 4G   Fourth Floor   Chicago Hilton

DIFFERENCE MATTERS IN ORGANIZATIONAL COMMUNICATION: A ROUNDTABLE DISCUSSION

Sponsor: Organizational Communication Division
Chairs: Brenda J. Allen, University of Colorado, Boulder
        Karen L. Ashcraft, University of Utah

Panelists: Rosita D. Albert, University of Minnesota
           Robin P. Clair, Purdue University
           Diane S. Grimes, Syracuse University
           Bryan C. Taylor, University of Colorado, Boulder
           George E. Cheney, University of Montana
           Alberto Gonzalez, Bowling Green State University
           Dennis K. Mumby, Purdue University
           Angela C. Trethewey, Arizona State University
           Karen L. Dace, University of Utah

1340　　11:00-12:15 p.m.　　　　　　Conf 4H　　　Fourth Floor　　Chicago Hilton

USING THEORETICAL COLORS TO PAINT PRAGMATIC PICTURES: FIVE WORKSHOP SKETCHES

Sponsor:　Training and Development Division
Chair:　Judith A. Rolls, University College of Cape Breton
　　"Using Martin Buber's I/Thou Relationship to Enhance Client Sensitivity: A Workshop for Health Care Workers." Judith A. Rolls, University College of Cape Breton
　　"Communicating Our Way to Gender Equity: A Workshop for Elementary School Teachers." Terilyn Goins-Phillips, Christopher Newport University
　　"'I Thought I Heard You Say. . .' A Listening Workshop." Susan S. Vargo, Indiana University
　　"Outside the Box of Words: Using Nonverbal Communication to Foster Team-Building and Perceptual Sensitivity." N. Carlotta Parr, Central Connecticut State University
　　"Getting Good Answers Means Asking Good Questions: Applications for Interviewers, Facilitators, and Teachers." Janet MacLennan, Ohio University

Respondent:　Sue DeWine, Ohio University

This program is designed to provide trainers with workshop templates and materials that can be adapted to their training needs.

1341　　11:00-12:15 p.m.　　　　　　Conf 4I　　　Fourth Floor　　Chicago Hilton

COLORING OUTSIDE THE LINES: FUNDRAISING ISSUES AS SEEN BY ACADEMICS AND PRACTITIONERS

Sponsor:　Public Relations Division
Chair:　William L. Gillespie, Georgetown University
　　"Grant Writing: An Essential Building Block for Public Relations." Bonita Dostal Neff, Valparaiso University
　　"Using the Internet in Fundraising for Nonprofits." Gayle M. Pohl, University of Northern Iowa
　　"Generating Funds: A Strategic Approach for Development." Dee Vandeventer, Mathis, Earnest & Vandeventer
　　"Funding a National Public Radio Network: A Strategy in Support of a Liberal Arts Curriculum." William L. Gillespie, Georgetown University
　　"Soliciting Corporate Sponsorships: From an Agency Viewpoint." Joanne Wzontek, Moore Stickney Associates

1342　　11:00-12:15 p.m.　　　　　　Conf 4J　　　Fourth Floor　　Chicago Hilton

ASSESSMENT AND ACCREDITATION ISSUES: PREPARING AND EVALUATING

Sponsor:　Senior College & University Section
Chair:　Jacqueline Schmidt, John Carroll University
　　"Assessing the Institution: The National Accreditation Perspective." Joseph B. Miller, John Carroll University
　　"Assessing the Discipline-Specific Department: The National Discipline Accreditation Perspective." Joe S. Foote, Southern Illinois University
　　"Assessing the Department: The Department Perspective." Alan C. Lerstrom, Luther College
　　"Assessing the Course: The Department Perspective." Donald E. Rice, Concordia College

1343　　11:00-12:15 p.m.　　　　　　Conf 4K　　　Fourth Floor　　Chicago Hilton

RELATIONAL MAINTENANCE BEHAVIORS IN DIVERSE INTERPERSONAL CONTEXTS

Sponsor:　Interpersonal Communication Division
Chair:　Laura L. Stafford, Ohio State University

Thursday

"Relational Dependency, Self-Esteem, Equity and Perceptions of Partner's Maintenance Behaviors." Laura L. Stafford, Ohio State University, Ben J. Perry, Ohio State University, Caroline T. Rankin, Ohio State University

"Satisfaction, Commitment, Trust, and Expectations in the Maintenance of Long-Distance versus Geographically-Close Relationships." Marianne Dainton, La Salle University, Heather L. Kilmer, La Salle University

"Coordinating the Doctor-Patient 'Dance': An Application of Coordinated Management of Meaning in Maintaining the Doctor-Patient Relationship." Rebecca W. Tardy, University of Louisville

"We Pray to Her As 'Our Mother' and Not As Mary: An Examination of the Creation and Maintenance of Relationships with Our Lady of Guadelupe." Robert G. Westerfelhaus, University of Houston, Downtown, Rafael Obregon, Penn State University, Arvind Singhal, Ohio University

"An Afrocentric Lens on Interpersonal Communication: One of the Missing Tools." Laura K. Dorsey, Howard University

"But a 'Real' Friend Wouldn't Treat Me That Way!: An Examination of Negative Strategies Employed to Maintain Friendship." James Nix, Ohio University

This hybrid session will begin with 5-minute previews of each of the works, followed by opportunities to circulate and meet with the authors in poster format.

1344   11:00-12:15 p.m.   Conf 4L   Fourth Floor   Chicago Hilton

DEBATING TO LEARN: THE EDUCATIONAL FOUNDATIONS FOR THE DEBATE EXPERIENCE

Sponsor: National Federation Interscholastic Speech & Debate Association
Chair: Stefan A. Bauschard, Cathedral Preparatory School
    "From Argumentation to Argumentativeness and Back Again: Metaphoric Restoration of Civil-ization." Roy J. Schwartzman, University of South Carolina
    "Topoi and Contemporary Argumentation." Joseph P. Zompetti, Mercer University
    "Taking Notes Seriously: Assessing a Positive Relationship Between Flowing and Taking Notes in the Classroom." Michael R. Berry, King's College

Respondents: Barbara Stone, Imagination Group
              Joel D. Rollins, University of Texas

1345   11:00-12:15 p.m.   Conf 4M   Fourth Floor   Chicago Hilton

TOP 3 PAPERS IN HEALTH COMMUNICATION

Sponsor: Health Communication Division
Chair: Marsha L. Vanderford, University of South Florida
    "Perceived Self-Efficacy and Women's Use of Cancer Screening Tests*." Nichole L. Egbert, University of Georgia, Roxanne Parrott, University of Georgia
    "Adolescent Reactance and Anti-Smoking Campaigns: A Theoretical Approach*." Joseph R. Grandpre, University of Arizona, Claude H. Miller, University of Arizona, Eusebio M. Alvaro, University of Arizona, John R. Hall, University of Arizona, Michael Burgoon, University of Arizona
    "The Effects of Communication Skills Training on Patients' Participation During Medical Interviews." Donald J. Cegala, Ohio State University, Leola McClure, Ohio State University, Terese M. Marinelli, Ohio State University, Douglas M. Post, Ohio State University

Respondent: Teresa L. Thompson, University of Dayton

*Top Paper

1346   11:00-12:15 p.m.   McCormick Board Rm   Fourth Floor   Chicago Hilton

VIRGINIA STATE COMMUNICATION ASSOCIATION BOARD MEETING

Sponsor: Virginia Association of Communication Arts and Sciences

1347   11:00-12:15 p.m.   Pullman Board Rm   Fourth Floor   Chicago Hilton

NCA PUBLICATIONS BOARD BUSINESS MEETING

Sponsor: Publications Board

1351   11:00-12:15 p.m.   Conf 5D   Fifth Floor   Chicago Hilton

LEARNING IN THE CLASSROOM: THE EDUCATIONAL INFLUENCE OF SHIRLEY WILLIHNGANZ

Sponsor: Teachers on Teaching
Chair: Joy L. Hart, University of Louisville

Panelists: Joy L. Hart, University of Louisville
Charles A. Willard, University of Louisville
Chris L. Nix, University of Louisville
Shirley C. Willihnganz, University of Louisville

With a teaching career spanning over 20 years, Professor Willihnganz has influenced scores of students. This panel will explore the effect that she has had upon others, from an administrator, to a colleague to a graduate student.

1352   11:00-12:15 p.m.   Conf 5E   Fifth Floor   Chicago Hilton

CHALLENGING BOUNDARIES IN THE HISTORY OF RHETORIC

Sponsor: Rhetorical and Communication Theory Division
Chair: James A. Aune, Texas A&M University
"Exploring a Chinese Rhetoric in Liu Xie's *Wen Xin Diao Long*." Todd L. Sandel, University of Illinois, Urbana-Champaign
"American Africanism: Changing the Face of Rhetorical Inquiry." Shannon R. Davis, University of Colorado, Boulder
"The Reconstitutive Rhetoric of St. Augustine." M. Todd Bates, University of Texas, Arlington
"George Whitefield's Rhetorical Art: Neo-Sophism in the Great Awakening." Jerome D. Mahaffey, University of Memphis

1354   11:00-12:15 p.m.   Conf 5G   Fifth Floor   Chicago Hilton

COMPETITIVE PAPERS IN GROUP COMMUNICATION: DECISION-MAKING GROUP INTERACTION

Sponsor: Group Communication Division
Chair: G.Scott Sintay, Purdue University
"Decision Logics: A Decisional-Content Theory of Group Decision-Making." Jane Macoubrie, North Carolina State University
"Extending the Functional Perspective into the Twenty-First Century: Studies of Task Contingency Variables." Randy Y. Hirokawa, University of Iowa
"Motivation Losses in Decision-Making Groups." David D. Henningsen, Miami University, Michael G. Cruz, University of Wisconsin, Madison, Mary Lynn M. Williams, University of Wisconsin, Madison

Respondent: Joann Keyton, University of Memphis

1355   11:00-12:15 p.m.   Conf 5H   Fifth Floor   Chicago Hilton

COMPETITIVE PAPERS ON GAY/LESBIAN POLITICS AND CULTURE

Sponsor: Gay/Lesbian Transgender Communication Studies Division
Chair: Phillip A. Voight, Gustavus Adolphus College
"Whose Choice Is It Anyway?" Robert A. Brookey, Stonehill College

"United Kingdom's Equal Age of Consent Movement: Towards a Theory in Movement Personification." Jason S. Wrench, Texas Tech University

"Naming, Blaming and Claiming in Public Disputes: The 1998 Maine Referendum on Civil Rights Protection for Gay Men and Lesbians." Carolyn M. Wiethoff, Ohio State University

"Abominable Biblical *Knowledge*: Negotiating the Contested Rhetorical Space of Gay Christianity." Andrea R. Gregg, Penn State University

"The American Catholic Bishops' Letter, 'Always Our Children': Lesbians and Gays as Family." Jeffrey Nelson, Kent State University, Trumbull

---

| 1356 | 11:00-12:15 p.m. | Conf 5I | Fifth Floor | Chicago Hilton |

ON TEXTS AND MEDIA

Sponsor: Intrapersonal Communication/Social Cognition Commission
Chair: Michael T. Stephenson, University of Kentucky
    "The Effects of Different Computer Text Formats on Readers' Recall Based on Individual Working Memory Capacity." Moon Jeong Lee, University of Florida
    "Expressing Media Preferences: The Person Perception Consequences of Endorsing Different Genres of Movies and Music." Stephanie L. Sargent, Virginia Tech University, James B. Weaver, Virginia Tech University, Dolf Zillmann, University of Alabama
    "A Few More Effects and Defects of Electronic Mail: On the Spontaneous Social Positioning of Mohawk E-mail Users." Robert C. MacDougall, SUNY, Albany
    " 'Is it a Boy or a Girl?' " An Analysis of Anonymity and Gender in On-Line Interactions." Kathryn C. Maguire, University of Texas, Austin

Respondent: Alan D. DeSantis, University of Kentucky

| 1357 | 11:00-12:15 p.m. | Conf 5J | Fifth Floor | Chicago Hilton |

CREATIVE WORLDS IN COMMUNITY COLLEGE EDUCATION

Sponsors: Emeritus/Retired Members Section
        Community College Section
Chair: Joan E. Leininger, Oakland Community College
    "The Future of Communication Studies: High Touch, Low Tech." Isa N. Engleberg, Prince George's Community College
    "High Touch in Distance Education: Maintaining a Learner Focus." David L. Bodary, Sinclair Community College
    "High Touch/High Tech: Using Computers in the Community College Classroom." Sonya Hopkins, Del Mar Community College, Sarah L. Mohundro, Del Mar Community College

---

| 1359 | 11:00-12:15 p.m. | Lake Michigan | Eighth Floor | Chicago Hilton |

ASIAN AMERICAN USAGE OF THE INTERNET: COMPARATIVE AND DIFFERING PERSPECTIVE

Sponsors: Asian/Pacific American Caucus
        Asian Pacific American Communication Studies Division
Chair: Todd Imahori, Seinan Gakuin University, Japan
    "Nature of Network Interaction: Tracing Its Revolution." Vandana Pednekar-Magal, Bowling Green State University
    "A Comparative Time-Based Perspective of Internet Usage by Asian American Faculty in a Midwestern State University in the USA." Sundeep R. Muppidi, Bowling Green State University
    "Graduate Students and Their Information Literacy Skills: A Study of the Differences in the Comfort Level Between International and American Graduate Students at a Midwestern University in the U.S." Sanjanthi Velu, Bowling Green State University, Jane Rosser, Bowling Green State University, Melody Bennett, Bowling Green State University, Xuelun Liang, Bowling Green State University

Respondent: Srinivas R. Melkote, Bowling Green State University

| 1361 | 11:00-12:15 p.m. | Lake Erie | Eighth Floor | Chicago Hilton |

REPRESENTATION AND RECONSTRUCTION OF LATINOS IN MASS COMMUNICATION

Sponsor: Latina/Latino Communication Studies Division
Chair: Juandalynn L. Taylor, University of Texas, Austin
   "Making Latino News: Language, Race, Class." America Rodriguez, University of Texas, Austin
   "The Poetics of Cinematic Stereotyping." Charles Ramirez Berg, University of Texas, Austin
   "Latinos and the Media: A Selective Research Agenda for the Twenty-First Century." Federico Subervi, University of Texas, Austin

Respondent: Fernando P. Delgado, Arizona State University West

| 1362 | 11:00-12:15 p.m. | Essex Court | Second Floor | Essex Inn |

BOB DYLAN: FOUR VIEWS OF FAITH

Sponsor: Religious Communication Association
Chair: Kimberly A. Kennedy, College of Wooster
   "Street Legal Dylan's Pre-Christian Period." V. Jeffrey Shires, Campbellsville University
   "Slow Train Coming: A Metaphorical Analysis." Joseph R. Blaney, Northwest Missouri State University
   "A Simple Twist of Faith: Bob Dylan's Infidels and Rhetorical Perspectives." Brett A. Miller, Southwest Baptist University
   "Jokerman: Bob Dylan's Metaphors of Space, Time, and Eternity." Joe A. Munshaw, Southern Illinois University, Edwardsville

Respondent: William D. Romanowski, Calvin College

| 1363 | 11:00-12:15 p.m. | Windsor Court | Second Floor | Essex Inn |

DE/CONSTRUCTED IDENTITIES IN AUTOBIOGRAPHICAL PERFORMANCE

Sponsor: Ethnography Division
Chair: Teri L. Varner, University of Texas, Austin
   "Perusing/Pursuing the Pale: Whiteness/in Black and White." Becky K. Becker, Truman State University
   "Am I A. . . ?" Teri L. Varner, University of Texas, Austin
   "Mothers and Sons: Reproducing Our Identities." Melissa Hohauser-Thatcher, Eastern Michigan University

Respondent: Annette Martin, Eastern Michigan University

| 1364 | 11:00-12:15 p.m. | Buckingham Court | Second Floor | Essex Inn |

A SYMPOSIUM IN CELEBRATION OF 125 YEARS OF THE "CHAUTAUQUA PLATFORM"

Sponsor: American Studies Commission
Chair: Jane Elmes-Crahall, Wilkes University
   "William Jennings Bryan Under the Tent: Addressing Rural America." Paul H. Boase, Ohio University
   "Two Distinctive Voices Arguing For Equality: Susan B. Anthony and Helen Keller at Chautauqua." Jane Elmes-Crahall, Wilkes University
   "Jane Addams of Hull-House: A Rhetoric of Social Ethics." Angela G. Ray, University of Minnesota
   "The Chautauqua Platform of the 60's: A Forum for the Free Discussion of Divisive Ideas?" John W. Gareis, University of Pittsburgh
   "The Voices Behind the Heroic Legends: Charles Lindbergh and Amelia Earhart at Chautauqua." Bradford L. Kinney, Wilkes University

Respondent: Nancy N. Roos, Chautauqua Institution

Thursday

This program incorporates several examples of performance oratory and, in the spirit of Chautauqua, allows time for audience questions and reflections.

| 1365 | 11:00-12:15 p.m. | Park East Walk | Second Floor | Essex Inn |

PARLIAMENTARY PROCEDURE, POLITICAL RULES, AND THE CLINTON IMPEACHMENT TRIAL

Sponsor: Commission on American Parlimentary Practice
Chair: Bonnie S. Jefferson, Boston College

Panelists: Don M. Boileau, George Mason University
David L. Vancil, Colorado State University
Matthew J. Streb, Indiana University
Joan E. Horrigan, Framingham State College
Carol Rowe, Waveland Press
Darla Anderson, University of La Verne
Donald Fishman, Boston College

This roundtable discussion focuses upon parliamentary procedure, political ruling-making, and the 1999 impeachment trial of President Clinton. It examines the parliamentary procedures adopted by the Senate, historical guidelines available for handling a presidential impeachment trial, and the extent to which the trial proceedings were inconsistent with the rules of due process available to defendants in a criminal or civil trial.

| 1369 | 11:00-12:15 p.m. | Rm 903 | Ninth Floor | Spertus Institute |

CRITICAL QUALITY CONTROL ISSUES IN REQUIRED INTERNSHIP PROGRAMS

Sponsor: Experiential Learning in Communication Commission
Chair: Karen M. Roloff, DePaul University

Panelists: Jef Dolan, Marymount University
Marjorie C. Feinstein, College of Saint Elizabeth
Carol Montgomery, DePaul University
Karen M. Roloff, DePaul University

Topics for this roundtable discussion among panelists and audience members will include quality of supervision given numbers of students, evaluation and assessment, grades or pass/fail, GPA requirement, ethical and legal issues.

| 1370 | 11:00-12:15 p.m. | Rm 904 | Ninth Floor | Spertus Institute |

PUBLISHING OR PERISHING: SOME PRACTICAL ADVICE

Sponsor: Association for Chinese Communication Studies
Chair: Mei-ling Wang, University of the Sciences, Pennsylvania

Panelists: L. John Martin, University of Maryland
Randy Kluver, Oklahoma City University
Xing (Lucy) Lu, DePaul University
Shaorong Huang, University of Cincinnati

| 1372 | 11:00-12:15 p.m. | Rm 907 | Ninth Floor | Spertus Institute |

AMERICAN SOCIETY FOR THE HISTORY OF RHETORIC STEERING COMMITTEE MEETING

Sponsor: American Society for the History of Rhetoric

12:30 p.m.

1404   12:30-1:45 p.m.   Grand Traditions   Lobby Level   Chicago Hilton

NCA AND REGIONAL COMMUNICATION ASSOCIATION EXECUTIVE DIRECTORS BUSINESS MEETING

Sponsor: National Communication Association

1406   12:30-1:45 p.m.   Continental BR A   Lobby Level   Chicago Hilton

COMPETITIVE PAPERS IN STUDIES OF NEWS: NATIONAL, INTERNATIONAL, AND COMMUNITY IMPLICATIONS

Sponsor: Mass Communication Division
Chair: Pamela S. Marsh, College of New Jersey
   "Global Agenda-Setting: Limiting the Effects of the International Information System."
      Rebecca A. Carrier, California State Polytechnic University, Pomona
   "Exposure to Western Television and Acceptance of Western Values by Chinese College
      Students: A Path Analytic Examination of a Cognitive-Functional Model of Media
      Socialization." Kenneth D. Day, University of the Pacific, Stockton, Qingwen Dong,
      University of the Pacific, Stockton
   "The Louise Woodward 'British Nanny' Trial: Nationwide Newspaper Coverage of the
      Eappens, A Community Stakeholder Approach." John C. Pollock, College of New Jersey,
      Melanie J. Ryan, College of New Jersey, Ralph Citarella, College of New Jersey, Heather
      Morris, College of New Jersey, Spiro G. Yulis, College of New Jersey
   "The Language of Community: City Characteristics and Nationwide Newspaper Coverage
      of Bilingual Education." Andre Sebastian Guerrero, College of New Jersey, Lisa A.
      Sparaco, College of New Jersey, Dawn Scuorzo, College of New Jersey
Respondent: Robert H. Gobetz, University of Indianapolis

1407   12:30-1:45 p.m.   Continental BR B   Lobby Level   Chicago Hilton

DEATH NARRATIVES: REDEFINING THE BOUNDARIES OF LIVED EXPERIENCE

Sponsor: Language and Social Interaction Division
Chair: Kathleen C. Haspel, University of Denver
   "'The Day Our Baby Died': How Families Use Narratives to Cope with Sudden Infant
      Death." Kimberly A. Kennedy, College of Wooster
   "Grandpa Died the Other Day, or What am I Supposed to Do Now?: A Phenomenology of
      'Life After Death'." Chris N. Poulos, University of Denver
   "Inside/Out: Understanding the Incomprehensible via Narrative." Teresa A. Werner,
      University of Denver
Respondent: Kathleen C. Haspel, University of Denver

1408   12:30-1:45 p.m.   Continental BR C   Lobby Level   Chicago Hilton

MOBILIZING GENDER: SPACE AND THE PLACES THAT GENDER GOES

Sponsor: Critical and Cultural Studies Division
Chair: Darrin K. Hicks, University of Denver
   "(She's) on the Road Again: The Spatial Articulation of Gender in Popular Music." Tony L.
      Kirschner, Western Maryland College
   "From Station Wagons to 'Glorified Grocery Getters': Emasculating Mobility and
      Domesticating Drivers in the Age of Suburbanization." Jeremy Packer, University of
      Illinois, Urbana-Champaign
   "Refusing to be a Victim: Personal Security Technology and Fears of Urban Space." Carrie
      Rentschler, University of Illinois

Thursday

"Taking It to the Streets: Spatial Tactics in the 1911 California Suffrage Campaign." Jessica Sewell, University of California, Berkeley

Respondent: Darrin K. Hicks, University of Denver

1410   12:30-1:45 p.m.   Grand Ballroom   Second Floor   Chicago Hilton

THE AMBASSADORS ENCOUNTER CONTEMPORARY THEORY

Sponsor: Performance Studies Division
Chair: Michael S. Bowman, Louisiana State University

Panelists: John D. Anderson, Emerson College
          Mary Agnes Doyle, Vox Humana Foundation
          Mindy E. Fenske, Louisiana State University
          Terry Galloway, Independent Artist
          Donna M. Nudd, Florida State University
          Craig S. Gingrich-Philbrook, Southern Illinois University, Carbondale
          Mary Frances HopKins, Louisiana State University
          Olateju S. Omolodun, University of North Carolina, Chapel Hill
          Mary S. Strine, University of Utah

Featuring short performances of excerpts from Henry James' Novel, *The Ambassadors*, this panel will address implications of different critical-theoretical perspectives on the novel in performance.

1414   12:30-1:45 p.m.   Boulevard A   Second Floor   Chicago Hilton

"HELP! HOW CAN I BE A MORE CREATIVE INSTRUCTOR?:" CHALLENGING BOUNDARIES BY REDEFINING THE TRADITIONAL COMMUNICATION CLASSROOM

Sponsor: Challenging Boundaries Series
Chairs: Russell D. Lowery-Hart, West Texas A&M University
        Candice E. Thomas-Maddox, Ohio University

Panelists: Mary L. Brown, University of Arizona
          Carol J. Bruess, University of St. Thomas
          Lori A. Byers, Spalding University
          Sonya Hopkins, Del Mar Community College
          Kristina M. Langseth, Minnesota State College & University
          Jennifer Thompson Issac, Normandale Community College

Higher Education is facing a silent crisis. Students and Administration are demanding more creative instructional methods from instructors. Through experiential learning activities, project-based learning, service-learning initiatives, creative course assignments and grading procedures, and increased student responsibility, the communication discipline can redefine higher education instruction as it is presently realized. In this session, panelists and participants will share successful ideas on how to redefine the communication classroom. Participants are encouraged to bring a syllabus for a class or classes they teach that needs "transforming." Through an interactive dialogue, participants will receive suggestions on how to redefine instructional approaches to each course.

1416   12:30-1:45 p.m.   Boulevard C   Second Floor   Chicago Hilton

CULTURAL VALUES, DIFFERENCES AND INFLUENCES: APPLICATIONS AND ANALYSES

Sponsor: International & Intercultural Communication Division
Chair: Wenshan Jia, Truman State University
    "Cultural Values in Everyday Talk." Yumiko Yokochi, University of New Mexico, Bradford J. Hall, University of New Mexico
    "Different Eyes, Different Worlds: Interpretation of the Clinton and Lewinsky News Story." Jing Yin, University of New Mexico

"Cross-Cultural Perspectives on Social Influence: Review, Critique, and Suggestions for Future Research." Hee Sun Park, University of California, Santa Barbara

Respondent: Barbara J. Kappler, University of Minnesota

1418	12:30-1:45 p.m.	Waldorf	Third Floor	Chicago Hilton

EMOTIONAL EXPRESSIONS AND FAMILY COMMUNICATION FUNCTIONALITY

Sponsor: Family Communication Division
Chair: Sherilyn R. Marrow-Ferguson, University of Northern Colorado
   "Emotional Conveyance Between Siblings Following Parental Deaths." Barbara C. Mattingley, University of Northern Colorado, Sherilyn R. Marrow-Ferguson, University of Northern Colorado
   "The Pendulum of Emotion in the Midst of Transition: Midlife Women's Expression of the Reconstitution of Self Within the Family." Tamara S. Bollis-Pecci, University of Denver
   "The Expression of Emotion in Later-Life Married Men." Fran Dickson, University of Denver, Kandi L. Walker, University of Denver
   "Alexithymia and Satisfactory Spousal Relationships." Paul L. Yelsma, Western Michigan University

---

1419	12:30-1:45 p.m.	Astoria	Third Floor	Chicago Hilton

APPROPRIATING, DEBATING, AND CONTESTING RELIGIOUS CONVENTIONS AND CONCEPTS: WOMEN RHETORS IN EARLY REFORM EFFORTS

Sponsor: Public Address Division
Chair: James M. Farrell, University of New Hampshire
   "The Esther Image in the Rhetoric of Women Abolitionists." Susan M. Zaeske, University of Wisconsin, Madison
   "Angelina Grimke and Catherine Beecher: Moral Agency and the Limits of Social Reform." Stephen H. Browne, Penn State University
   "Labor's Irreverent Prophet: The Agitative Ministry of Mary Harris 'Mother' Jones." Mari Boor Tonn, University of New Hampshire

Respondent: James Darsey, Georgia State University

1421	12:30-1:45 p.m.	Williford A	Third Floor	Chicago Hilton

COMPETITIVE SPIRITS: AFRICAN AMERICAN SPORTS APOLOGIA

Sponsor: African American Communication & Culture Commission
Chair: Gray Matthews, University of Memphis
   "Rage and Repentance: Mike Tyson's Public Apology." R. Pierre Rodgers, Morgan State University, Lisa A. Harris, Kent State University
   "Towards Clarification: Reggie White and the Perception of Ethnic Stereotyping." Bernard J. Armada, University of St. Thomas
   "'I've Been Vilified': Justification and Apology in Latrell Sprewell's Public Statement." Grant C. Cos, Texas A&M University, Corpus Christi
   "The Stuff Legends Are Made Of: The Re-Invention of Muhammad Ali." Enrique D. Rigsby, Texas A&M University

Respondent: Mark B. White, Baylor University

1422	12:30-1:45 p.m.	Williford B	Third Floor	Chicago Hilton

POLITICAL COMMUNICATION AND PUBLIC POLICY

Sponsor: Political Communication Division
Chair: Lori M. McKinnon, University of Alabama
   "Narrative, the Rhetoric of Possibility, and Public Policy." Enid Sefcovic, Florida Atlantic University

Thursday

"Expert Control or 'Linguistic Possession': Lawmaker Questioning Styles in Contemporary Health Hearings." Kent J. Polk, University of Texas, Austin
"Partisan Rhetorical Styles: Democrats and Republicans on Welfare Reform." Sharon E. Jarvis, University of Texas, Austin

---

1423   12:30-1:45 p.m.   Williford C   Third Floor   Chicago Hilton

PINK MARKETS: THE GENDERED CONSTRUCTION OF INDUSTRIAL PRACTICES

Sponsor: Feminist and Women Studies Division
Chair: Angharad N. Valdivia, University of Illinois, Urbana-Champaign
"Born to Shop: Teenage Women and the Marketplace in the Postwar U.S." Angela R. Record, University of Illinois, Urbana-Champaign
"En-Gendering the Market: Women, the Family, and Personal Computers." Lori K. Reed, University of Illinois, Urbana-Champaign
"What a Riot! How the Market Shapes and Constrains a Feminist Aesthetic." Ellen Riordan, University of Oregon
"Private Spaces, Public Exhibitions: Gender and the Legal Definition of Home Entertainment." Lea Anne Sullivan, University of Illinois, Urbana-Champaign

Respondent: Angharad N. Valdivia, University of Illinois, Urbana-Champaign

---

1424   12:30-1:45 p.m.   Marquette   Third Floor   Chicago Hilton

A NEW BEGINNING FOR A CHERISHED TRADITION: AUDIENCE AND CAST RESPONSES TO AN ALL-FEMALE *TWELFTH NIGHT*

Sponsor: Theatre Division
Chair: Janice L. Dukes, St. Mary of the Woods College

Panelists: Sharon Ammen, St. Mary of the Woods College
Student Performers, St. Mary of the Woods College

This panel includes short performances of excerpts from the Fall 1999 all-female production of *Twelfth Night*. Survey results of audience reaction will be distributed and panelists will share their experiences and hold an open discussion of the event.

1425   12:30-1:45 p.m.   Joliet   Third Floor   Chicago Hilton

IS THIS OUR CALLING?: JOHN RODDEN'S "FIELD OF DREAMS" REVISITED

Sponsor: Student Section

Panelists: Kevin D. Kuswa, University of Texas, Austin
Jon D. Rutter, University of Texas, Austin
Brian S. Shapiro, University of Texas, Austin
Charles W. Wells, University of Texas, Austin

Respondent: Philip C. Wander, San Jose State University

1426   12:30-1:45 p.m.   PDR 1   Third Floor   Chicago Hilton

THE BASIC COMMUNICATION COURSE IN THE TWENTY-FIRST CENTURY

Sponsor: Educational Policies Board
Chair: Lori E. Zakel, Sinclair Community College
"The Basic Course as General Education." Isa N. Engleberg, Prince George's Community College
"The Basic Course in the Secondary School." Trudy L. Hanson, West Texas A&M University
"The Basic Course in the Post-Secondary Institution." Lawrence W. Hugenberg, Youngstown State University

Respondent: Cathy A. Fleuriet, Southwest Texas State University

| 1427 | 12:30-1:45 p.m. | PDR 2 | Third Floor | Chicago Hilton |

COLLABORATIVE BREAKTHROUGHS IN PERSONAL NARRATIVE RESEARCH

Sponsor: Performance Studies Division
Chairs: Sheron J. Dailey, Indiana State University
     Scott Carlin, University of Northern Iowa
    "From Silence to Siren: A Tale of Political Correctness." Lesa Lockford, Centenary College
    "Deep Talk Through Personal Narrative." Kristin B. Valentine, Arizona State University
    "Upon Reflection: Stories I'd Still Tell." Cathryn A. Baldner, Luther College
    "Unraveling the Story and Sharing the Yarn as Personal Narrative Ethnographers." Phyllis
      Carlin, University of Northern Iowa
    "Seeing Person as Persona: The Ghosts of Personal Narrative." Tami L. Spry, St. Cloud State
      University

| 1428 | 12:30-1:45 p.m. | PDR 3 | Third Floor | Chicago Hilton |

TOP THREE PAPERS IN GROUP COMMUNICATION

Sponsor: Group Communication Division
Chair: Lawrence R. Frey, University of Memphis
    "Communication Technology Use and Key Outcomes in Groups: A Comparison of Site
      and Virtual Teams." Craig R. Scott, University of Texas, Austin, Volker Frank, University
      of Texas, Austin, Karen M. Wolff, University of Texas, Austin, Charlotte A. Sullivan,
      University of Texas, Austin, Barbara Forster, University of Texas, Austin
    "Exploring Argumentative Competence in Group Decision-Making Interactions." Tara
      Wachtel, Hatch Staffing Services, Renee A. Meyers, University of Wisconsin, Milwaukee,
      Dale E. Brashers, University of Illinois, Urbana-Champaign
    "Telling Tales in Jury Deliberations: Jurors' Use of Fictionalized and Factually-Based
      Storytelling in Argument." Sunwolf, Santa Clara University

Respondent: Marshall S. Poole, Texas A&M University

| 1429 | 12:30-1:45 p.m. | PDR 4 | Third Floor | Chicago Hilton |

A FUNDAMENTAL RIGHT TO FREE SPEECH: IS THE FIRST AMENDMENT NECESSARY BUT NOT SUFFICIENT?

Sponsor: Freedom of Expression Commission
Chair: Stanley Morris, Attorney-at-Law
    "Muting and Silencing of Change Agents: Case Studies of American Women in the
      Twentieth Century." Susan Mallon Ross, SUNY, Potsdam
    "Abdication or Reconstruction: The Future of On-Line Speech." Brian M. O'Connell,
      Central Connecticut State University
    "The Role of Silencing Mechanisms in the Self-Regulation of Virtual Communities: Lessons
      from an Adult-Oriented Web Site." Thomas R. Flynn, Slippery Rock University, Chrissy
      L. Gallagher, Slippery Rock University

Respondent: Robert M. Fischbach, Central Connecticut State University

| 1430 | 12:30-1:45 p.m. | PDR 5 | Third Floor | Chicago Hilton |

A CLASSROOM WHERE NO ONE IS SILENCED: CREATING A SAFE PLACE FOR STUDENT SELF-DISCLOSURE

Sponsor: Table Talk Series
Chair: Marybeth G. Callison, Georgia State University

Panelists: Marybeth G. Callison, Georgia State University
      Kole Kleeman, University of Central Oklahoma
      Francine M. Mindel, Monmouth University
      Eddie Myers, Louisiana State University
      Kristi A. Schaller, Georgia State University

Thursday

Panelists will facilitate a discussion with the audience on classroom self-disclosure. Discussion will focus on appropriate or "safe" classroom environments, or those in which students feel comfortable self-disclosing without fear of negative reprisal. Among the questions to be considered: "Is the classroom a safe place to raise dissenting voices?" "Are instructors open to viewpoints other than their own?" "Should an instructor be responsible for encouraging student self-disclosure?" and "How do students feel about classrooms as places for safe disclosure?"

1431   12:30-1:45 p.m.   PDR 6   Third Floor   Chicago Hilton

HIGHER EDUCATION ADMINISTRATION: ADMINISTRATIVE CONCERNS AND INSTITUTIONAL IMPERATIVES

Sponsor: Association for Communication Administration
Chair: Judy C. Pearson, Virginia Tech University

Panelists: Janis F. Andersen, San Diego State University
          Judy C. Pearson, Virginia Tech University
          James Fletcher, University of Georgia
          Ellen A. Wartella, University of Texas, Austin
          Sarah N. Denman, Marshall University

Upper-level college and university administrators have diverse pressures from internal and external sources, ranging from state legislators, to alums, to current faculty and students, and to associations of their peers. How do these diverse pressures translate into administrative concerns and institutional imperatives? What are the current issues that are being discussed by upper-level administrators, and how will this ultimately influence departments? High ranking administrators tell all.

1432   12:30-1:45 p.m.   PDR 7   Third Floor   Chicago Hilton

PUBLIC DEBATE: HEGEMONY IS NEGATIVELY AFFECTING INDIVIDUAL EVENTS COMPETITION

Sponsor: Argumentation and Forensics Division
Moderator: Larry Schnoor, Comunication Links

Affirmative: Thomas A. Workman, University of Nebraska, Lincoln
            Christina R. Foust, University of Nebraska, Lincoln

Negative: Karen R. Piercy, University of Wisconsin, Eau Claire
            Daniel L. Smith, Bradley University

The argument that hegemony is empowered by judges who only reward the elitist style and by contestants who are unwilling to sacrifice competitive success by deviating from the norm is advanced and refuted by four forensics educators who have all been involved in large, small and growing programs throughout their careers. An opportunity will be given to the audience to add to the debate through questions and comments.

1433   12:30-1:45 p.m.   Conf 4A   Fourth Floor   Chicago Hilton

THE LEARNER LOCUS IN TRADITIONAL AND VIRTUAL CLASSROOMS

Sponsor: Experiential Learning in Communication Commission
Chair: Denise Ann Vrchota, Iowa State University
     "Learner-Centered Classrooms: Helping Students Color Outside the Lines of Traditional Education." Carol Fulton, Iowa State University, Barb Licklider, Iowa State University
     "The Learner-Centered Communication Classroom: Helping Students Color Outside the Lines in Communication Classes." Denise Ann Vrchota, Iowa State University
     "Learner-Centered Pedagogy: Applications for Service-Learning." Elizabeth R. Lamoureux, Buena Vista University
     "Web Spaces: Geography for Experiential Learning." Tracy C. Russo, University of Kansas
     "Experiential Learning on the Web: Are We Using the Web to Color Outside the Lines?" Scott A. Chadwick, Iowa State University

1434   12:30-1:45 p.m.   Conf 4B   Fourth Floor   Chicago Hilton

TEACHING ETHNOGRAPHY IN THE UNDERGRADUATE COMMUNICATION COURSE

Sponsor: Ethnography Division
Chair: Martha A. Hagan, Whatcom Community College
   "Experiencing Organizational Culture as Student Ethnographers." Charlotte G. Burke, Bob Jones University
   "Bringing the Outside In: Ethnography in/beyond the Classroom." Patricia J. Sotirin, Michigan Technological University
   "Ethnography: A Model for Understanding Theory-Building." John S. Dahlberg, Canisius College
   "Teaching the Undergraduate Course on Ethnographic Methods." Don C. Govang, Lincoln University
   "Extending the Margins of Expression: Ethnography in the Classroom." Martha A. Hagan, Whatcom Community College

1435   12:30-1:45 p.m.   Conf 4C   Fourth Floor   Chicago Hilton

FILM ISSUES: REPRESENTATIONS OF REALITY IN A DREAM WORLD

Sponsor: Visual Communication Commission
Chair: Alice E. Hall, University of Pennsylvania
   "Communicating the Experience of the Impossible in 2001: An Analysis of the Role of Editing Conventions in Viewers' Comprehension of Film." Alice E. Hall, University of Pennsylvania
   "Competing Visions of Emma: How Landscape Alters an Adaptation." Kathi L. Pauley, Calvin College
   "Christian Metz and Rhetorical Criticism." Robert E. Terrill, Indiana University
   "Frankenstein 1970: The Visual Recasting of Nazism as Monster." Caroline Joan S. Picart, University of Wisconsin, Eau Claire

Respondent: Richard L. Ward, University of South Alabama

1436   12:30-1:45 p.m.   Conf 4D   Fourth Floor   Chicago Hilton

DEALING WITH HIV, SMOKING, UNDISCLOSED MEDICAL PROBLEMS, AND CANCER IN AND THROUGH INTERACTION

Sponsor: Language and Social Interaction Division
Chair: Anita M. Pomerantz, Temple University
   "The Patient's Request as a Progressively Realized Project: A Case Study." Virginia Teas Gill, Illinois State University, Tim R. Halkowski, University of Wisconsin, Felicia Roberts, Purdue University
   "Nicotine Narratives: Some Functions of Smokers' Stories in Primary Care Visits." Tim R. Halkowski, University of Wisconsin
   "Closing Primary-Care Consultations and Generating Undisclosed Medical Problems." Jeffrey D. Robinson, University of California, Los Angeles
   "Managing Optimism in Talk About Cancer." Wayne A. Beach, San Diego State University

1437   12:30-1:45 p.m.   Conf 4E   Fourth Floor   Chicago Hilton

USING AN INTEGRATED BEHAVIORAL MODEL TO PREDICT CONDOM USE IN DIVERSE POPULATIONS: IMPLICATIONS FOR DEVELOPING MEDIA INTERVENTIONS

Sponsor: Health Communication Division
Chair: Martin Fishbein, University of Pennsylvania

Thursday

"Understanding Condom Use Behavior: A Theoretical and Methodological Overview of Project SAFER." Ina Von Haeften, University of Pennsylvania, Danuta Kasprzyk, Battelle Center for Public Health Research and Evaluation, Daniel Montano, Battelle Center for Public Health Research and Evaluation, Martin Fishbein, University of Pennsylvania

"Factors Influencing Condom Use Behavior for Vaginal Sex with Regular and Casual Partners Among Injecting Drug Users." Kate M. Kenski, University of Pennsylvania, Jane E. Appleyard, University of Pennsylvania

"Factors Influencing Condom Use Behavior for Vaginal Sex with Partners and Clients Among Male and Female Commercial Sex Workers." Brenda L. Johnson, University of Pennsylvania, Yariv Tsfati, University of Pennsylvania

"Factors Influencing Condom Use Behavior for Anal Sex with Regular and Casual Partners Among Men Who Have Sex with Men." Marina Levina, University of Pennsylvania, Gustavo Dantas, University of Pennsylvania

"Implications for Developing Media Interventions." Jane E. Appleyard, University of Pennsylvania

Respondents: Danuta Kasprzyk, Battelle Center for Public Health Research and Evaluation
Daniel Montano, Battelle Center for Public Health Research and Evaluation

---

1438   12:30-1:45 p.m.   Conf 4F   Fourth Floor   Chicago Hilton

OPENINGS AND TRANSITIONS IN TELEVISION

Sponsor: Media Forum Series

Panelist: Gary L. Thompson, Saginaw Valley State University

1439   12:30-1:45 p.m.   Conf 4G   Fourth Floor   Chicago Hilton

ON TRANSNATIONALISM

Sponsor: Spotlight on Scholarship

Moderator: Briankle G. Chang, University of Massachusetts, Amherst

Participants: Shujen Wang, Emerson College
Anandam P. Kavoori, University of Georgia
Kent A. Ono, University of California, Davis
Briankle G. Chang, University of Massachusetts, Amherst

This panel will address issues surrounding transnationalism as they bear upon the discipline of communication. In so doing, it will problematize the very concept of globalization, to nurture dialogues sensitive to concrete difference/diversity.

1440   12:30-1:45 p.m.   Conf 4H   Fourth Floor   Chicago Hilton

TRAINING MODELS AND METHODS

Sponsor: Training and Development Division

"Training High Technology Specialists to Communicate Effectively to Nonspecialist Audiences Within the Organization." Frederick W. Isaacson, San Francisco State University

"A Communication Systems Approach to Leadership and Evaluation in a Police Department." John Chetro-Szivos, University of Massachusetts, Amherst, Vernon E. Cronen, University of Massachusetts, Amherst

"Creating Growth Rather Than Problems in the Workplace." Shawn Worthy, Metropolitan State College of Denver, Madison Holloway, Metropolitan State College of Denver, Dawn Coney, Metropolitan State College, Denver

---

1441   12:30-1:45 p.m.   Conf 4I   Fourth Floor   Chicago Hilton

PUBLIC RELATIONS AND COMMUNITY BUILDING

Sponsor: Public Relations Division

Chair: Diane F. Witmer, California State University, Fullerton
"Media Relations in Bosnia: A Role for Public Relations in Building Civil Society." Maureen
Taylor, Rutgers University
"A Transformationalist Look at the Role of Public Relations in Developing a Collectivist
Ethic of Corporate Social Responsibility*." Virginia T. Rodino, University of Maryland
"Public Relations and Cultural Aesthetics: Promoting Health." Jeff K. Springston, University
of Georgia, Victoria L. Champion, Indiana University
"Divided We Stand: The Cultural Tribes of Public Relations." Greg Leichty, University of
Louisville

Respondent: Nilanjana Bardhan, Southern Illinois University, Carbondale

*Student Paper

1442	12:30-1:45 p.m.	Conf 4J	Fourth Floor	Chicago Hilton

COLORING OUTSIDE THE LINES: COMMUNICATION, DIVERSITY, AND THE SMALL COLLEGE CURRICULUM

Sponsor: Senior College & University Section
Chair: Craig E. Johnson, George Fox University
"Serendipity and the Discovery of Diversity in a College Curriculum." Solomon W.
Obotetukudo, Clarion University
"Using Performance to Foster Understanding: Developing a Course in Performing
Multicultural Literature." Alfred Golden, Linfield College
"'Aren't We All the Same'?: Emphasizing Diversity in the Interpersonal Course to a
Seemingly Non-Diverse Population of a Small University." Sam C. Mathies, Pacific
University
"Communication, Diversity and the Core Curriculum: Imperatives for Moving Beyond
Disciplinary Boundaries." Brenda D. Marshall, Linfield College

Respondent: Dennis R. Waller, Northwest Nazarene College

1443	12:30-1:45 p.m.	Conf 4K	Fourth Floor	Chicago Hilton

MOVING OUTSIDE THE LINES: ADVANCES AND CHALLENGES OF COMMUNITY-BASED INTERPERSONAL COMMUNICATION RESEARCH

Sponsor: Interpersonal Communication Division
Chair: Dawn O. Braithwaite, University of Nebraska, Lincoln
"Considering the Parameters of Community-Based Research and Service." Dawn O.
Braithwaite, University of Nebraska, Lincoln
"An Initial Test of Inconsistent Nurturing as Control Theory: How Partners of Drug Abusers
Assist Their Partners' Sobriety." Beth A. Le Poire, University of California, Santa Barbara
"Taking Scholarship into the Field: Case Studies of Single Mothers in College." Richard L.
Conville, University of Southern Mississippi
"Lessons Learned from a Wellness Initiative in a Low-Income Area." Paul Arntson,
Northwestern University, Jackie Reed, Westside Health Authority, Chicago

Respondents: Kenneth N. Cissna, University of South Florida
William F. Eadie, NCA National Office
H. Dan O'Hair, University of Oklahoma

1444	12:30-1:45 p.m.	Conf 4L	Fourth Floor	Chicago Hilton

EXPANDING THE LINES OF SPEECH AND DEBATE COACH TRAINING

Sponsor: National Federation Interscholastic Speech & Debate Association
Chair: Sue L. Wenzlaff, Duquesne University
"Speech Certification: What Does the Future Hold?" Lynn Goodnight, University of
Southern California
"Inner City Debate Teacher Training: The Barbara Jordan Program." James Dutcher,
Duquesne University

Thursday

"Summer Debate Workshop Teacher Training Programs." John Lawson, Birmingham
Groves High School, Michigan
"Mentoring and the College Course in Coaching and Director Forensics." Sue L. Wenzlaff,
Duquesne University

1445   12:30-1:45 p.m.   Conf 4M   Fourth Floor   Chicago Hilton

METAPHORS AND MEANING: A LOOK AT SOCIAL SUPPORT,
PERFORMANCES, AND STRATEGIC CHANGE

Sponsor: Organizational Communication Division
Chair: Michael A. Gross, Arizona State University
    "Stress and Social Support: A Metaphor Analysis." Gordon L. Forward, Point Loma
    Nazarene University
    "Smith's Root-Metaphors Revisited: Implications for Organizational Communication."
    Pamela J. Zaug, Arizona State University
    "Coordinated Management of Meaning: A Method to Align Corporate Culture with
    Strategic Change." Carolyn M. Wiethoff, Ohio State University
    "The Organizational Performance of Air Travel." Alexandra G. Murphy, DePaul University

Respondent: Patricia M. Sias, Washington State University

1449   12:30-1:45 p.m.   Conf 5B   Fifth Floor   Chicago Hilton

RESOURCES AND STRATEGIES FOR MENTORING GRADUATE TEACHING
ASSISTANTS IN THE BASIC COURSE PROGRAM

Sponsor: Basic Course Division
Chair: Edward A. Hinck, Central Michigan University
    "The Teaching Mentor Program from the Perspective of a First Year Graduate Teaching
    Assistant." Kara Cole, Central Michigan University
    "Reflecting on the Mentor Process: Looking into Two Different Mirrors." Scott A. Loftis,
    Central Michigan University
    "Undergraduate and Graduate Mentorships: Relationships of Transition and Change." Kim
    Smith, Central Michigan University
    "Description and Assessment of a Teaching Mentor Program for Graduate Teaching
    Assistants." Janet Yerby, Central Michigan University, Bradford A. Hart, Central Michigan
    University

Respondent: Pamela L. Gray, Central Michigan University

1451   12:30-1:45 p.m.   Conf 5D   Fifth Floor   Chicago Hilton

RE-MEMBERING MYTH AND SPIRIT IN A POSTMODERN WORLD: PART II

Sponsor: Spiritual Communication Commission
Chair: Anne Pym, California State University, Hayward

Panelists: Tony L. Arduini, Southern Illinois University
        Lisa R. Barry, Albion College
        James W. Crocker-Lakness, University of Cincinnati
        Christopher Johnstone, Penn State University
        Susan B. Mackey-Kallis, Villanova University
        Michael McGuire, Independent Scholar
        Trudy A. Milburn, Baruch College
        John S. Nelson, University of Iowa
        Roy J. Schwartzman, University of South Carolina

1452   12:30-1:45 p.m.   Conf 5E   Fifth Floor   Chicago Hilton

LEGAL REELISM: LAW IN POPULAR CULTURE

Sponsor: Rhetorical and Communication Theory Division
Chair: Marouf Hasian, University of Utah

"Play in the System: Lawyer as Trickster in *A Time to Kill* and *My Cousin Vinnie*." William F. Lewis, Drake University

"Bankruptcy as Resistance." Irwin A. Mallin, Indiana University

"Outlaw Judgment: An Intermediate Theory of a Symbolic Mode." James P. McDaniel, Indiana University

---

1453   12:30-1:45 p.m.   Conf 5F   Fifth Floor   Chicago Hilton

COLORING OUTSIDE OF THE LINES: ARTICULATING ENVIRONMENTAL JUSTICE RHETORICS IN NEW CONTEXTS

Sponsor: Environmental Communication Commission

Chair: Stephen P. Depoe, University of Cincinnati

"Brownfields of Dreams: Environmental Justice, Urban Revitalization, and 'Environment' in the Inner City." John W. Delicath, Allegheny College

"Migrant Farmworkers in the U.S.: The Rhetoric of Citizenship and the Environmental Justice Movement." Phaedra C. Pezzullo, University of North Carolina, Chapel Hill

"Meeting in a Redwood: The Convergence of Wilderness and Environmental Justice." Kevin M. Deluca, Penn State University

Respondent: Giovanna Di Chiro, Allegheny College

1454   12:30-1:45 p.m.   Conf 5G   Fifth Floor   Chicago Hilton

BECOMING BRICOLEURS: COLLAGES OF CLASSROOM INSTRUCTIONAL STUDIES AND POPULAR CULTURE

Sponsor: Instructional Development Division

Chair: Katherine G. Hendrix, University of Memphis

"Reflections of an International Graduate Teaching Assistant In Communication." Aparna S. Bulusu, University of Memphis

"Inclusion, Trust, and Self-Disclosure in Social Relationships on On-Line Chat." Valerie Howell, University of Memphis

"Considering Teaching Effectiveness from the Vantage Point of an African American Professor." Orin G. Johnson, University of Memphis

"Learning About Romance from Watching Soap Operas: A Preliminary Case Analysis of 'What' and 'How' Viewers Learn." Marceline E. Thompson, University of Memphis

Respondent: Sandra L. Herndon, Ithaca College

1455   12:30-1:45 p.m.   Conf 5H   Fifth Floor   Chicago Hilton

COMMUNICATION AND PEOPLE WITH DISABILITIES: RESEARCH ON BLINDNESS, WELLNESS, AND OTHER CULTURES

Sponsor: Caucus on Disability Issues

Chair: Audra L. Colvert, Towson University

"'Can You See What I'm Saying?': An Examination of the Relationship Between Visual Impairment and Gestures." Melissa J. Frame, University of South Florida

"Promoting Wellness Through Narrative." Cecilia L. Abbey, University of Missouri

"People with Disabilities in Asia and Africa: A Cross-Cultural Study." Miho Iwakuma, University of Oklahoma, Jon F. Nussbaum, Penn State University

---

1456   12:30-1:45 p.m.   Conf 5I   Fifth Floor   Chicago Hilton

COMPETITIVE PAPERS IN COMMUNICATION ASSESSMENT

Sponsor: Commission on Communication Assessment

Chair: Robert F. Edmunds, Marshall University

"Assessing Orality and Literacy in Electronic Communication." Sharmila Pixy, William Paterson University

"Department Level Assessment." Susan R. Hatfield, Winona State University

"The Intercultural Development Inventory: A Measure of Intercultural Sensitivity." Mitchell R. Hammer, American University, Milton J. Bennett, Intercultural Communication Institute

"Evaluating Communication Competence: A Comparison of Majors and Non-Majors." Joann Keyton, University of Memphis, Dudley Strawn, University of Memphis

---

1457   12:30-1:45 p.m.   Conf 5J   Fifth Floor   Chicago Hilton

FIVE THEORISTS FOR TWENTY-FIRST CENTURY ETHICS

Sponsor: Communication Ethics Commission
Chair: Sharon L. Bracci, University of North Carolina, Greensboro
"Charles Taylor's Practical Reason." Peggy Bowers, Saint Louis University
"Interactive Universalism in Seyla Benhabib." Sharon L. Bracci, University of North Carolina, Greensboro
"The Social Ethics of Agnes Heller." Clifford G. Christians, University of Illinois
"Foucault's Ethics." Martha D. Cooper, Northern Illinois University
"The Other Ethics of Emmanuel Levinas." Jeffrey W. Murray, University of Pittsburgh

Respondent: Josina M. Makau, California State University, Monterey Bay

---

1458   12:30-3:15 p.m.   Lake Ontario   Eighth Floor   Chicago Hilton

SHORT COURSE #5. TEACHING THE COLLEGE AND UNIVERSITY COURSE IN INTERVIEWING

Sponsor: Short Courses

Instructors: Roger N. Conaway, University of Texas, Tyler
Wallace V. Schmidt, Rollins College

Fee required. See complete Short Course descriptions elsewhere in the program.

1459   12:30-3:15 p.m.   Lake Michigan   Eighth Floor   Chicago Hilton

SHORT COURSE #6. TEACHING THE PERSUASION, COMPLIANCE GAINING, AND/OR SOCIAL INFLUENCE COURSE AT THE UNIVERSITY LEVEL

Sponsor: Short Courses

Instructors: Robert H. Gass, California State University
John S. Seiter, Utah State University

Fee required. See complete Short Course descriptions elsewhere in the program.

1460   12:30-3:15 p.m.   Lake Huron   Eighth Floor   Chicago Hilton

SHORT COURSE #7. LECTURELESS LEARNING: NO MORE TALKING HEADS

Sponsor: Short Courses

Instructors: Allan L. Ward, University of Arkansas, Little Rock
Linda M. Pledger, University of Arkansas, Little Rock
Carol L. Thompson, University of Arkansas, Little Rock
Michael Kleine, University of Arkansas, Little Rock

Fee required. See complete Short Course descriptions elsewhere in the program.

1461   12:30-3:15 p.m.   Lake Erie   Eighth Floor   Chicago Hilton

SHORT COURSE #8. TEACHING TO THE ADULT LEARNER

Sponsor: Short Courses

Instructors: Jeannette W. Kindred, Wayne State University
Elizabeth T. Tice, University of Phoenix

Fee required. See complete Short Course description elsewhere in the program.

1462   12:30-1:45 p.m.   Essex Court   Second Floor   Essex Inn

EXPLORING CONFLICTING IDENTIFICATIONS IN RELIGIOUS CONTEXTS

Sponsor: Religious Communication Association
Chair: Marcia K. Everett, Malone College
   "A Loyal Sisterhood? Negotiating Conflicting Identifications in a Benedictine Community."
     Mary F. Hoffman, University of Kansas
   "Mormon Women in Transition: Traversing the Boundaries of Patriarchy, Feminism, and
     Hegemony." Jennifer M. Huss, Claremont Graduate School
   "Using the Bible: The Family Amendment to the Southern Baptist Confession." Benjamin
     B. Coulter, Wayne State University

Respondent: Debra-Lynn Sequeira, Seattle Pacific University

1463   12:30-1:45 p.m.   Windsor Court   Second Floor   Essex Inn

OUTSIDE THE LINES OF THE RESEARCHER/SUBJECT RELATIONSHIP: RESPECTING THE MULTICULTURAL 'OTHER' IN ETHNOGRAPHIC RESEARCH

Sponsor: Ethnography Division
Chair: Dolores V. Tanno, California State University, San Bernardino
   "Listen to Reason and Other Reasons to Listen." William K. Rawlins, Purdue University
   "'The Other' as Tool in Social Interaction: Communication When Viewed Through a
     Spiritual Lens." M. Cristina Gonzalez, Arizona State University
   "Speaking Within a Parallax of Discourses: Approaching Verisimilitude of Voice by
     Involving the 'Other' in Ethnographic Projects." Marifran Mattson, Purdue University
   "Being Questioned and Asking Questions." Christina W. Stage, Arizona State University
   "Interpretation and Respect: The Role of 'Other' in Research." Robin P. Clair, Purdue
     University

Respondent: Dolores V. Tanno, California State University, San Bernardino

---

1464   12:30-1:45 p.m.   Buckingham Court   Second Floor   Essex Inn

THE SEMIOTICS OF CINEMA AND TELEVISION

Sponsor: Semiotics and Communication Commission
Chair: Elliot I. Gaines, Ashland University
   "Whatever Happened to Dante?: Some Thoughts on the Construction of Masculinity in
     the Classical Hollywood Film." Mary E. Hurley, San Joaquin Delta College
   "Mirroring Medusa: Counterveillance in *Shooting Back*." Jieun Rhee, Boston University
   "A Rhetorical Analysis of Masculine Symbols of Elmo: The Gender-Neutral Doll." Nina M.
     Reich, California State University, Long Beach

Respondent: James C. Lundy, Doane College

1466   12:30-1:45 p.m.   Cohn Rm   Second Floor   Spertus Institute

MAPPING THE RHETORIC OF TECHNOLOGY

Sponsor: American Association for Rhetoric of Science & Technology
Chair: Gordon R. Mitchell, University of Pittsburgh
   "Demystifying the 'Brave New World of Digital Education': An Analysis of the Rhetoric that
     Promotes Virtual Universities." Michelle L. Rodino, University of Pittsburgh
   "Vampire Projects, Patent Claims, and Disappearing Primitives: Genetic Research and the
     Guaymi Indians of Panama." Kelly A. Gates, University of Illinois, Urbana-Champaign
   "Mission Transfer: The Changing Role of Technology Transfer in the Mission of the National
     Laboratories." Karen M. Taylor, University of Pittsburgh
   "Science in the National Interest: The Rhetoric of Technology Policy." Timothy M.
     O'Donnell, University of Pittsburgh

Thursday

Respondent: Herbert W. Simons, Temple University

1469   12:30-1:45 p.m.   Rm 903   Ninth Floor   Spertus Institute

LEARNING FROM THE PAST

Sponsor: Pi Kappa Delta
Chair: Joel L. Hefling, South Dakota State University
   "Been There, Done That." Todd T. Holm, Ohio University
   "Untitled." E. Sue Weber, University of Minnesota, Minneapolis
   "I've Seen This Before 6/60." Cami M. Sanderson, Ohio University
   "I Just Found This Great Selection." Joel L. Hefling, South Dakota State University

Respondent: Jerry L. Miller, Ohio University

1470   12:30-1:45 p.m.   Rm 904   Ninth Floor   Spertus Institute

PEACE AND CONFLICT COMMUNICATION IN THE UNITED STATES AND VIETNAM

Sponsor: Peace and Conflict Communication Commission
Chair: Myrna Foster-Kuehn, Clarion University
   "The Vietnamese Executive Study Tour: Establishing Peaceful Relations Between
    Vietnamese and American Businessmen and Scholars." Rex M. Fuller, James Madison
    University
   "Vietnam Joint-Venture Negotiations: Doi Moi and the Importance of Win-Win Strategies."
    William D. Kimsey, James Madison University
   "Preferred Conflict Management Message Styles of American and Vietnamese College
    Students." Bruce C. McKinney, James Madison University

1472   12:30-1:45 p.m.   Rm 907   Ninth Floor   Spertus Institute

TAKING SPEECH SERIOUSLY: HEIDEGGER ON RHETORIC AND BEING

Sponsor: American Society for the History of Rhetoric
Chair: Michael J. Hyde, Wake Forest University
   "Messages as Possibilities: On the Constitutive Power of Rhetoric." Lenore Langsdorf,
    Southern Illinois University, Carbondale
   "The 'Rhetoric of Philosophy': A Reading of Heidegger's Lectures on Plato's *Sophist* and
    Aristotle's *Rhetoric*." Allen M. Scult, Drake University
   "The Ontologizing of Prudence: Phronesis, *Mitsein* and Speaking-Together in Heidegger's
    Thought." Susan Zickmund, University of Iowa

Respondent: Michael J. Hyde, Wake Forest University

2:00 p.m.

1506   2:00-3:15 p.m.   Continental BR A   Lobby Level   Chicago Hilton

COMPETITIVE PAPERS IN RESEARCH IN MEDIA EFFECTS: PRIMING, COGNITION, AND INFLUENCE

Sponsor: Mass Communication Division
Chair: Marina B. Krcmar, University of Connecticut
   "Media Priming: A Meta-Analysis." David R. Roskos-Ewoldsen, University of Alabama,
    Mark R. Klinger, University of Alabama, Beverly Roskos-Ewoldsen, University of Alabama
   "Psychological Processes and Cognitive Mechanisms in the Cultivation Effect." Lisa M.
    Schroeder, Kent State University, Tuscarawas
   "Investigating the Effects of Sexual Advertising Appeals on Consumer Responses." Tom
    Reichert, University of North Texas, Eusebio M. Alvaro, University of Arizona

"Role and Influence of Communication Modality in the Process of Resistance to Persuasion." Michael Pfau, University of Wisconsin, Madison, R. Lance Holbert, University of Wisconsin, Madison, Stephen J. Zubric, University of Wisconsin, Madison, Nilofer H. Pasha, University of Wisconsin, Madison, Wei-Kuo Lin, University of Wisconsin, Madison

Respondent: Alan M. Rubin, Kent State University

| 1507 | 2:00-3:15 p.m. | Continental BR B | Lobby Level | Chicago Hilton |

IDENTITY CONSTRUCTIONS AND PEDAGOGICAL ENCOUNTERS IN CYBERSPACE

Sponsor: Human Communication and Technology Commission
Chair: Marwan M. Kraidy, University of North Dakota
    "Why Communication Educators Should Examine Public Discourse About Education." Laura B. Lengel, American International University, London
    "Virtual Constructions: Identities in On-Line Environments." Marwan M. Kraidy, University of North Dakota
    "Parabolic Antennas on Adobe Houses: An Ethnographic Account of the Use of New Communication Technologies in Four Mexican Families." Raul E. Gonzalez-Pinto, ITESM Campus Queretaro, Mexico
    "Irrepressible Gender: An Ethnography of Internet Exchange in the Classroom." Priya Kapoor, Portland State University

Respondent: Patrick D. Murphy, Southern Illinois University, Edwardsville

---

| 1508 | 2:00-3:15 p.m. | Continental BR C | Lobby Level | Chicago Hilton |

"STEPPING OUT OF BOUNDS": SPORT, CONSUMPTION AND THE (GLOBAL) PUBLIC SPHERE

Sponsor: Critical and Cultural Studies Division
Chair: Shawn Miklaucic, University of Illinois, Urbana-Champaign
    "Consuming Cures: *The Race for the Cure* and the Politics of Breast Cancer Fundraising." Samantha King, University of Illinois, Urbana-Champaign
    "Modifying the Sign: Globalization and Sport." Toby Miller, New York University
    "A Sporting Gesture? Rupert Murdoch and Manchester (dis)United." Craig Robertson, University of Illinois, Urbana-Champaign
    "Soccer and Suburban Spatial Practices." David L. Andrews, University of Memphis

Respondent: James Hay, University of Illinois, Urbana-Champaign

---

| 1510 | 2:00-3:15 p.m. | Grand Ballroom | Second Floor | Chicago Hilton |

RETRIEVING THE TWENTIETH CENTURY: FAMILY NARRATIVES AND PUBLIC HISTORY

Sponsor: Performance Studies Division
Chair: Elizabeth C. Fine, Virginia Tech University
    "Memere Stories: Reproducing the Franco American Family." Kristin M. Langellier, University of Maine, Orono
    "From Pearl Harbor to the Rhine: Mapping My Father's War." Kay Ellen Capo, SUNY, Purchase
    "'Winter Hearts': Recreating the Emotional History of North Dakota." Lynn C. Miller, University of Texas, Austin
    "The Personal as Political: Palestinian Narratives of the 1948 Catastrophe." Robert D. Hostetter, North Park University

Respondents: Elizabeth C. Fine, Virginia Tech University
                    Elyse L. Pineau, Southern Illinois University, Carbondale

---

1513   2:00-3:15 p.m.   Normandie Lounge   Second Floor   Chicago Hilton

NEWCOMERS WELCOME AND ORIENTATION

Sponsor: National Communication Association
Chair: Jef Dolan, Marymount University

Panelists: James L. Gaudino, NCA National Office
           Orlando L. Taylor, Howard University
           Raymie E. McKerrow, Ohio University
           James L. Applegate, University of Kentucky

If this is your first convention, please attend this session. The NCA host committee, chaired by Jef Dolan, NCA officers, and National Office staff will be available to answer questions. Informal presentations will include information about how to become active in the Association.

1514   2:00-3:15 p.m.   Boulevard A   Second Floor   Chicago Hilton

NEGOTIATING NEIGHBORHOOD BOUNDARIES: CHALLENGING THE PUBLIC/PRIVATE DICHOTOMY

Sponsor: Challenging Boundaries Series
Chair: Kirsten Isgro, SUNY, Plattsburgh

Panelists: Kirsten Isgro, SUNY, Plattsburgh
           Margaret R. LaWare, Iowa State University
           Andrew E. Rudd, Bowling Green State University
           Lori A. Walters-Kramer, SUNY, Plattsburgh

This performance-oriented and interactive program addresses boundary challenges by focusing on texts created about and within suburban neighborhoods, playgrounds and garage sales.

1516   2:00-3:15 p.m.   Boulevard C   Second Floor   Chicago Hilton

TEACHING AND LEARNING IN INTERCULTURAL CONTEXTS: THEORY AND PRACTICE

Sponsor: International & Intercultural Communication Division
Chair: Mary Fong, California State University, San Bernardino
    "Immediacy and Its Relationship to Teacher Effectiveness: A Cross-Cultural Examination of Six Cultures." Alexia S. Jazayeri, Arizona State University
    "College Students' Conflict Management Styles in Collectivist and Individualistic Cultures." Jung-Soo Yi, Wright State University
    "Reframing the Teaching of Intercultural Communication Theory: Ethnography of a Com 463 Class." S. Lily Mendoza, Arizona State University

Respondent: Jolanta A. Drzewiecka, Washington State University

---

1518   2:00-3:15 p.m.   Waldorf   Third Floor   Chicago Hilton

COMMUNICATION, RACE, AND FAMILY: OLD PROBLEMS AND NEW DIRECTIONS

Sponsor: Family Communication Division
Chair: Thomas J. Socha, Old Dominion University
    "Family Communication, Race, and Young Black Children." Jack L. Daniel, University of Pittsburgh
    "Family Communication, Race, and Young White Children." Roberta A. Davilla, University of Northern Iowa

"Family Communication, Race, and Adolescents." Rhunette C. Diggs, University of Louisville

"Marital Communication and Race." Marianne Dainton, La Salle University

"Family Communication, Education and Race." Thomas J. Socha, Old Dominion University, Jennifer E. Beigle, University of North Carolina, Greensboro

---

| 1519 | 2:00-3:15 p.m. | Astoria | Third Floor | Chicago Hilton |

SPEAKING OUTSIDE THE LINES: THE RHETORIC OF SOCIAL CHANGE

Sponsor: Public Address Division

Chair: Heidi E. Hamilton, Augustana College

"Custom, Community, and Citizenship: The Immigrant Press as a Vehicle for Social Change." Linda C. Brigance, SUNY, Fredonia

"Pistol Packing Mamas: Public Arguments for Women in the Military." Heidi E. Hamilton, Augustana College

"Moving from the Personal to the Political: The Rhetorical Evolution of PFLAG." Anne F. Eisenberg, University of North Texas

"Speaking for the Animals: The Competing Discourse of Animal Welfare versus Animal Rights." Barbara E. Willard, Colorado State University

Respondent: Bruce E. Gronbeck, University of Iowa

| 1521 | 2:00-3:15 p.m. | Williford A | Third Floor | Chicago Hilton |

PERSUASION, ADS AND AFRICAN AMERICANS: DON'T BE FOOLED BY THE PRETTY PACKAGE

Sponsor: African American Communication & Culture Commission

Chair: Carlos D. Morrison, Clark Atlanta University

"A Critical Analysis of Hair-Care Advertisements Directed Towards African American Females*." Celnisha Dangerfield, Clark Atlanta University

"Like Stealing Candy from a Baby: Stereotypical Advertising and the Black Consumer*." Ryan Coates, Clark Atlanta University

"'The Image in the Ad': An Analysis of Images of Masculinity and Femininity in the Schlitz Malt Liquor Bull Advertisement." Akilah Palmer, Clark Atlanta University

"Just 'Ad' TV: An Analysis and Evaluation of African Americans in Today's Television Commercials*." Tiffany Brown, Clark Atlanta University

Respondent: Ronald L. Jackson, Penn State University

*Student Debut Paper

| 1522 | 2:00-3:15 p.m. | Williford B | Third Floor | Chicago Hilton |

POLITICAL COMMUNICATION AND INTERNATIONAL CONCERNS

Sponsor: Political Communication Division

Chair: Mike D. Chanslor, Truman State University

"The Catalytic Role of Television in the Romanian Revolution of 1989." John P. McHale, University of Missouri, Columbia

"Lack of Lateral Discourse: Geoffrey Howe's Resignation Speech as a Rhetorical Critique of Margaret Thatcher's European Policy Communication." Tomas P. Klvana, University of Southern Maine

"The Demonic Redeemer Figure in Political Myth: A Case Study of Vladamir Zhirnovsky." Jason Edwards, North Dakota State University

"Silence, Sound, and Fury: The Discourses of Australian Cultural Politics." Tracey Q. Lanicek, Penn State University

"Jimmy Carter and Martin Buber in Virtual Reality: The Camp David Peace Accords as Dialogue." Lowell Harris, University of South Florida

---

1523   2:00-3:15 p.m.   Williford C   Third Floor   Chicago Hilton

MEDIA MAPPINGS OF WOMEN

Sponsor: Feminist and Women Studies Division
Chair: Paige P. Edley, Bowling Green State University
   "Spotlighting Women Scientists in the Press: Tokenism in Science Journalism." Orly
      Shachar, Iona College
   "Feminist Intentions and Feminist Inventions: Representation and the Women's
      International News Gathering Service." E. Sue Weber, University of Minnesota,
      Minneapolis
   "Like Sheep For Slaughter: Hegemony and Body Image Awareness in Two Women's
      Magazines." Kristen E. Hoerl, University of Texas, Austin
   "What's New In Women's Magazines?. . . Not Much." Susan Walsh, Southern Oregon
      University
   "The 'Death' of History, Subjectivity, and. . .Feminism?: The Rhetorical Narrative of a *Time*
      Cover." Courtney W. Bailey, Indiana University

1524   2:00-3:15 p.m.   Marquette   Third Floor   Chicago Hilton

WHERE ARE THE LINES?: INTEGRATING THE ARTS ON CAMPUSES AND IN THE COMMUNITY

Sponsor: Theatre Division
Chair: Roberta L. Crisson, Kutztown University
   "Creating an Interdisciplinary Major: The Related Arts Program at Kutztown University."
      Deryl B. Johnson, Kutztown University
   "Creating an Arts Minor for Non-Arts Major: The Integrated Arts Program at Northwestern
      University." Carol S. Stern, Northwestern University
   "Using Storytelling Across the Curriculum: A Teaching Circle." Laura Facciponti, University
      of North Carolina, Asheville
   "Stories on South Hill: College Students and Fourth Graders Learning from Each Other."
      Bruce Henderson, Ithaca College

1525   2:00-3:15 p.m.   Joliet   Third Floor   Chicago Hilton

EXAMINING "OTHER" - SEX, RACE, AND SEXUALITY

Sponsor: Student Section
   "Analysis of Research Methods Used in the Study of Sex and Gender as They Relate to
      Communication." Michelle J. Mattrey, Penn State University
   "Breaking the Silence: A Feminist Rhetorical Criticism of Tori Amos' Lyrics." Kristan Poirot,
      Southern Illinois University
   "In the Balance: Lesbigay Politics in Adapting *Serving in Silence*." Alisha A. Lenning,
      University of Texas, Austin

Respondent: Thomas K. Nakayama, Arizona State University

1526   2:00-3:15 p.m.   PDR 1   Third Floor   Chicago Hilton

REFLECTIONS AND OPPORTUNITIES "AFTER" FORENSICS

Sponsor: International Forensic Association
Chair: Barbara S. Baron, Brookdale Community College
   "Life After Forensics at the Community College." Catherine M. Blackburn, Brookdale
      Community College
   "Moving On When Everything You Have Done Since High School Has Involved Forensics."
      Richard A. Knight, Arkansas Tech University
   "Evolving from Directing Forensics to Administration of the University." Jack L. Rhodes,
      Miami University
   "The Role of the Former DOF at Large Research Institutions." Robert A. Vartabedian,
      Western Carolina University

"Liberal Arts Enhancement from a Former DOF's Toolbox." Catherine H. Zizik, Seton Hall
    University
"Shifting from Forensics to Research." Hal W. Bochin, California State University, Fresno

---

| 1527 | 2:00-3:15 p.m. | PDR 2 | Third Floor | Chicago Hilton |

FEMINIST AND WOMEN'S STUDIES DIVISION AND WOMEN'S CAUCUS JOINT EXECUTIVE COUNCIL MEETING

Sponsors: Feminist and Women Studies Division
            Women's Caucus

| 1528 | 2:00-3:15 p.m. | PDR 3 | Third Floor | Chicago Hilton |

GROUP COMMUNICATION DIVISION BUSINESS MEETING

Sponsor: Group Communication Division

| 1529 | 2:00-3:15 p.m. | PDR 4 | Third Floor | Chicago Hilton |

GAY/LESBIAN/BISEXUAL/TRANSGENDER/STRAIGHT ALLIANCE: BUILDING COMMUNITIES ON CAMPUS

Sponsor: Gay & Lesbian Concerns Caucus
Chair: Trung T. Tieu, University of Wisconsin, Milwaukee

Panelists: Carol L. Benton, Central Missouri State University
            Billy W. Catchings, University of Indianapolis
            John R. Heineman, Lincoln High School, Nebraska

Sponsors of Gay/Lesbian/Bisexual/Transgendered/Straight Alliance groups will lead a
roundtable discussion on the challenges and successes of their organizations on campus. The
audience is invited to bring questions, stories, activities, and concerns to share with others at
the panel.

| 1530 | 2:00-3:15 p.m. | PDR 5 | Third Floor | Chicago Hilton |

SHOULD LISTENING BE PART OF THE COMMUNICATION DISCIPLINE?

Sponsor: Table Talk Series
Chair: Michael W. Purdy, Governors State University

Panelists: Kathy Thompson, Alverno College
            Andrew D. Wolvin, University of Maryland
            Charles Roberts, East Tennessee State University
            Margaret Fitch-Hauser, Auburn University
            Judi Brownell, Cornell University
            Philip Emmert, James Madison University

This panel examines the extent to which the study of listening conforms to and/or deviates
from communication discourse; it explores current training trends, research methods and
theoretical and metatheoretical discourses related to listening.

| 1532 | 2:00-3:15 p.m. | PDR 7 | Third Floor | Chicago Hilton |

RESEARCH BOARD BUSINESS MEETING

Sponsor: Research Board

| 1533 | 2:00-3:15 p.m. | Conf 4A | Fourth Floor | Chicago Hilton |

COMMUNICATION AND DIVORCE: TALK IN, ABOUT, AND SURROUNDING DIVORCE

Sponsor: Family Communication Division

Thursday

Chair: Nancy Buerkel-Rothfuss, Central Michigan University
"Sibling Stories of Parental Divorce: Implications for the Post-Divorce Sibling Relationship."
Jennifer L. Baker, University of Texas, Austin
"Communication Consistency and Relational Satisfaction: Examining the Non-Custodial
Father-Child Relationship Pre- and Post-Divorce." Heather M. Osterman, University of
Texas, Austin
"Becoming Divorced: A Process Model of How Divorcing Couples Reveal and Conceal the
Status of Their Relationship." Jeff S. Cook, University of Nebraska, Lincoln
"Adult Children of Divorce: Communication of Parental Divorce in Intimate Relationships."
Katheryn E. Carpenter, University of Texas, Austin

Respondent: Kathleen M. Galvin, Northwestern University

| 1534 | 2:00-3:15 p.m. | Conf 4B | Fourth Floor | Chicago Hilton |

AMERICAN BIBLE SOCIETY NEW MEDIA TRANSLATIONS

Sponsor: Religious Communication Association
Chair: Paul A. Soukup, Santa Clara University
"Semiotics, Visual Media, and Translating the Biblical Text." Robert Hodgson Jr., American
Bible Society Research Center for Scripture and Media
"A Holy Critique: Examining Visual Translations of the Bible." Terrence R. Lindvall, Regent
University
"Translation and Communication: Lessons Learned." Paul A. Soukup, Santa Clara
University

| 1535 | 2:00-3:15 p.m. | Conf 4C | Fourth Floor | Chicago Hilton |

ON LINES (OF FLIGHT): DELEUZOGUATTARIAN ANIMATIONS OF COMMUNICATION

Sponsor: Critical and Cultural Studies Division
Chair: J. Macgregor Wise, Clemson University
"Representations of Breastfeeding: Suckling Up to the Body Without Organs." Patricia J.
Sotirin, Michigan Technological University
"Beginning, Again, in the Middle: Communication and the Environment." Jennifer D.
Slack, Michigan Technological University
"Mapping the Communication of Student/Teacher Relationships: Beyond Sexual
Harassment." Christa Albrecht-Crane, Michigan Technological University
"The Drug War Assemblage: Outside the Lines of a Critical Rhetoric." Gordon Coonfield,
Michigan Technological University
"International Communication: State, Space and Flow." M. Mehdi Semati, Michigan
Technological University

Respondent: J. Macgregor Wise, Clemson University

| 1536 | 2:00-3:15 p.m. | Conf 4D | Fourth Floor | Chicago Hilton |

GROWING POINTS IN CONVERSATION ANALYSIS: QUESTIONING PRESIDENTS ADVERSARIALLY, DISPENSING WITH WORDS, AND SPEAKING BADLY OF OTHERS

Sponsor: Language and Social Interaction Division
Chair: Jeffrey D. Robinson, University of California, Los Angeles
"The Evolution of Questioning in Presidential Press Conferences." Steven E. Clayman,
University of California, Los Angeles, John C. Heritage, University of California, Los
Angeles
"On Dispensability." Emanual Schegloff, University of California, Los Angeles
"The Collaborative Construction of Delicate Formulations: Negotiating the
Authorship/Ownership of Unkind Words." Gene H. Lerner, University of California,
Santa Barbara

1537   2:00-3:15 p.m.   **Conf 4E**   **Fourth Floor**   **Chicago Hilton**

SEXUAL HEALTH, SAFE SEX, AND DISCLOSURE

Sponsor: Health Communication Division
Chair: Christina S. Beck, Ohio University
   "Overcoming Truth-Telling as an Obstacle to Initiating Safer Sex: Collaborative
      Construction of Deception in Pre-HIV Test Counseling Sessions." Marifran Mattson,
      Purdue University, Felicia Roberts, Purdue University
   "Women's Self-Disclosure About Sexually Transmitted Infections: Benefits and Barriers."
      Kelly A. Dorgan, University of Georgia
   "Women, Menopause, and (Ms.)Information: A Phenomenological Approach to
      Climacteric." Merry C. Buchanan, University of Oklahoma, Melinda M. Morris,
      University of Oklahoma, Sandra L. Ragan, University of Oklahoma
   "Applying Rhetorical Theory to Public Health and Mass Communication Research." Emily J.
      Plec, University of Utah
   "To Test or Not to Test: Considering and Impact of HIV Testing and Counseling on the
      Health Beliefs and Sexual Behaviors of College Students." Marifran Mattson, Purdue
      University

1538   2:00-3:15 p.m.   **Conf 4F**   **Fourth Floor**   **Chicago Hilton**

LEISURE-TIME ACTIVISM: THE MUSEUM AS NONDISCURSIVE RHETORICAL FORM

Sponsor: Media Forum Series
   "A Confrontation with the Past: Interactive Exhibits and the Rhetorical Use of Space at the
      National Civil Rights Museum." Bernard J. Armada, University of St. Thomas

---

1539   2:00-3:15 p.m.   **Conf 4G**   **Fourth Floor**   **Chicago Hilton**

WORKING TOGETHER: ROLES, INNOVATION, NETWORKS, AND SOCIAL INFLUENCES

Sponsor: Organizational Communication Division
Chair: Pamela S. Shockley-Zalabak, University of Colorado, Colorado Springs
   "Uncovering the Micro-Macro Link: An Examination of Communication Network
      Relationships, Teamwork Dimensions, and Performance Among Multi-University Project
      Teams." Alex M. Susskind, Cornell University, Denney G. Rutherford, Washington State
      University, Ali A. Poorani, University of Delaware
   "Intergroup Transmission of Organizational Cultures Through Social Influence: Effects of
      In-Group Communication." Shinobu Suzuki, Hokkaido University
   "Groups at Work: The Effects of Attitudes and Socialization on Commitment and
      Satisfaction with Workplace and Jobs." Carolyn M. Anderson, University of Akron,
      Matthew M. Martin, West Virginia University, Bruce L. Riddle, Kent State University
   "Explorations in Organizational Role Negotiation and Innovation: A Conceptual
      Approach." Eric B. Meiners, Michigan State University

Respondent: Robin P. Clair, Purdue University

1540   2:00-3:15 p.m.   **Conf 4H**   **Fourth Floor**   **Chicago Hilton**

DECISION-MAKING AND PROBLEM-SOLVING IN THE NEW MILLENNIUM: A TRAINER'S PARADISE OR A TRAINER'S TRAP

Sponsor: Training and Development Division

Panelists: Clark Germann, Metropolitan State College of Denver
         Karen R. Krupar, Metropolitan State College of Denver
         Mary Y. Mandeville, Oklahoma State University
         Maurine C. Eckloff, University of Nebraska, Kearney
         David C. Schrader, Oklahoma State University

What does the new millennium hold for practitioners of training and development? How will new concepts such as "just in time training" and "distributed intelligence" affect the craft? What are the pros and cons of "training at a distance?" Panel members will discuss these and other topics and look at the opportunities and risks that may be forthcoming.

1541	2:00-3:15 p.m.	Conf 4I	Fourth Floor	Chicago Hilton

COMPETITIVE PAPERS IN PUBLIC RELATIONS

Sponsor: Public Relations Division
Chair: Gayle M. Pohl, University of Northern Iowa
  "Searching for Dominant PR Voices: A Preliminary Investigation." Laura A. Terlip, University of Northern Iowa, Tricia L. Hansen-Horn, University of Northern Iowa
  "Crisis Communication in Racial Issues: The Case of Lubbock, Texas and Hampton University." David E. Williams, Texas Tech University, Bolanle A. Olaniran, Texas Tech University
  "The Changing Dynamics of New Technologies and Media Relations." Janice M. Barrett, Boston University, Elizabeth R. Alcock, Babson College
  "The Impact of Management-Employee Relations and Communication Exchanges on Nurses' Job Satisfaction, and Nurses' Near-Term versus Long-Term Retention Plans." Gary R. Heald, Florida State University, Matthew K. Girton, Florida State University, Natliya V. Kazanskaya, Florida State University

Respondent: Bonita Dostal Neff, Valparaiso University

1542	2:00-3:15 p.m.	Conf 4J	Fourth Floor	Chicago Hilton

TEACHING WITH NARRATIVE

Sponsor: Senior College & University Section
Chair: Ina R. Ames, Curry College
  "A Narrative Approach to the Capstone Course." George C. Wharton, Curry College
  "A Narrative Approach to Interpersonal and Family Communication." Craig E. Johnson, George Fox University, Clella I. Jaffe, George Fox University
  "The Role of Personal Narrative in Teaching and Learning." Pamela C. Miller, DePauw University
  "Narrative in Cyberspace: Using the Internet to Tell the Story." Miriam L. Zimmerman, College of Notre Dame
  "Enhancing the Communication Curriculum Through the Use of Narrative." Ina R. Ames, Curry College

1543	2:00-3:15 p.m.	Conf 4K	Fourth Floor	Chicago Hilton

ADOLESCENT VERBAL AGGRESSIVENESS AND ARGUMENTATIVENESS

Sponsor: Interpersonal Communication Division
Chair: Sandi W. Smith, Michigan State University
  "Predictors of Verbally Aggressive Communication in Adolescence." Charles K. Atkin, Michigan State University, Sandi W. Smith, Michigan State University, Anthony J. Roberto, Michigan Public Health Institute, Okemos
  "Adolescents' Impressions of Media and Interpersonal Aggression: Insights Gained from Focus Groups." Kelly Morrison, Michigan State University, Betty H. LaFrance, Wake Forest University, Francisco Villarruel, Michigan State University
  "The Relationship of Topic and Target to Argumentativeness and Verbal Aggressiveness in Adolescent Populations." Anthony J. Roberto, Michigan Public Health Institute, Okemos
  "Assessing Aggressive Communication in Adolescents: Problems and Alternatives." Andrew S. Rancer, University of Akron, Theodore A. Avtgis, St. John's University, Roberta L. Kosberg, Curry College

---

1545 **2:00-3:15 p.m.** Conf 4M Fourth Floor Chicago Hilton

APOLOGIAE, PICTURES, DECEPTION, AND KNOWLEDGE CONSTRUCTION: EXPLORING THE MEANINGS OF ORGANIZATIONAL COMMUNICATION

Sponsor: Organizational Communication Division
Chair: Glynis C. Hiebner, Central Connecticut State University
  "The Integration of Three Perspectives of Organizational Deception: A Typology of Deceptive Messages." Anne P. Hubbell, Michigan State University
  "Archetypal Metaphors: Advocating Through Pictures." Mary C. Banwart, Western Kentucky University
  "Organizational Communication as Palimpsest: What Lies Beneath the Inscription of Organizational Reality?" Monique L. Snowden, Texas A&M University
  "Invoking Lists in Organizational Apologiae." Jennifer Thackaberry, University of Colorado, Boulder

Respondent: Renee Houston, Rutgers University

1546 **2:00-3:15 p.m.** McCormick Board Rm Fourth Floor Chicago Hilton

PUBLICATIONS BOARD AND NCA EDITORS BUSINESS MEETING

Sponsor: Publications Board

1549 **2:00-3:15 p.m.** Conf 5B Fifth Floor Chicago Hilton

STUDYING CLASSROOM VARIABLES IN THE BASIC COURSE

Sponsor: Basic Course Division
Chair: Terry M. Perkins, Eastern Illinois University
  "Examining the Relationship Between Student Motivation, Teacher Credibility, Teacher Immediacy, and Communication Apprehension in Mass-Lecture and Self-Contained Formats of the Basic Communication Course." Stephen A. Cox, Murray State University, Timothy S. Todd, Murray State University
  "The Relationship Between Critical Thinking and Student Argumentativeness, Verbal Aggressiveness, and Locus of Control in the Basic Communication Course." Donna R. Pawlowski, Creighton University, Mary Ann Danielson, Creighton University, Scott A. Myers, Creighton University
  "Behavioral Learning in the Basic Course: The Effect of Different Delivery Formats." Susan J. Messman, Penn State University, Jennifer Jones-Corley, Penn State University, Kristan Falkowski, Penn State University

Respondent: Marybeth G. Callison, Georgia State University

1551 **2:00-3:15 p.m.** Conf 5D Fifth Floor Chicago Hilton

NON-FAMILIAL RELATIONSHIP DEVELOPMENT ACROSS THE LIFESPAN

Sponsor: Communication and Aging Commission
Chair: Jaye L. Shaner, Georgia State University
  "Elderly Patient-Provider Communication: A Meta-Analytic Review for Theoretical Interpretation." Barbara M. Gayle, University of Portland, Elayne J. Shapiro, University of Portland, Joanna M. Kaakinen, University of Portland
  "You Should Get Yourself a Boyfriend: The Communication Code of Romance in a Retirement Community." Melissa W. Aleman, James Madison University
  "Relationship Development Revisited: Communication in Friendship Constellations over the Life-Span." Brian R. Patterson, West Virginia University, Stephani Hewitt, West Virginia University, Karen Swart, West Virginia University

Respondent: Jon F. Nussbaum, Penn State University

1552   2:00-3:15 p.m.   Conf 5E   Fifth Floor   Chicago Hilton

WALTER BENJAMIN AND THE MAGIC OF LANGUAGE

Sponsor: Rhetorical and Communication Theory Division
Chair: Edward Schiappa, University of Minnesota, Twin Cities
   "Locating Benjamin's Notion of Form Alongside His Contemporaries." David Beard,
      University of Minnesota, Twin Cities
   "Benjamin's Magic." Joshua Gunn, University of Minnesota, Twin Cities
   "The Spellwriter: Walter Benjamin As Producer." Christopher N. Swift, University of
      Minnesota, Twin Cities

Respondent: Thomas B. Farrell, Northwestern University

1553   2:00-3:15 p.m.   Conf 5F   Fifth Floor   Chicago Hilton

UNFORESEEN IMPACTS OF THE INFORMATION AGE

Sponsor: Commission on Communication in the Future
Chair: Steven C. Rockwell, University of South Alabama
   "Making the Invisible Visible: Using Eye-Tracking Research to See how Viewers Process
      Visual Information in Cyberspace." Sheree Josephson, Weber State University
   "Achieving Universal Access to Internet Services in Rural America: Adoption Patterns of
      First-Time Rural Subscribers to a Free Public-Access Internet Service." Steven C.
      Rockwell, University of South Alabama, Loy A. Singleton, University of Alabama
   "The Internet, the Workplace, and Privacy: An Analysis of Employee Privacy Issues at the
      Workplace." Denise Weiss, University of South Alabama
   "The Gap Between Practice and Reality: A Need for Competence in Visual
      Communication in the Information Age." Gail J. Chryslee, University of South Alabama

Respondent: Jennings Bryant, University of Alabama

1554   2:00-3:15 p.m.   Conf 5G   Fifth Floor   Chicago Hilton

PASSAGES OF TEACHING

Sponsor: Instructional Development Division
Chair: Mary E. Bozik, University of Northern Iowa

Panelists: Mary M. Roberts, Pittsburg State University
            Robert M. Smith, University of Tennessee, Martin
            Pamela J. Cooper, Northwestern University
            Mary E. Bozik, University of Northern Iowa
            Jerry D. Feezel, Kent State University

Panelists will share a "passage" in their careers which will serve as trigger scripts for audience
participation. The session will be an exploration of the stages of entering the profession,
getting recognized, assuming leadership roles, and maturing in the profession.

1555   2:00-3:15 p.m.   Conf 5H   Fifth Floor   Chicago Hilton

PERFORMING OUTSIDE THE CIRCLE: SPECTATING, SPECT(ACTING), AND
PERFORMING DRAG

Sponsor: Gay/Lesbian Transgender Communication Studies Division
Chair: E. Patrick Johnson, University of North Carolina, Chapel Hill
   "Drag Droppings (Or the Making of a Woman)." Bryant K. Alexander, California State
      University, Los Angeles
   "All My Seams Are Visible or Confessions of a Real-Life, Psuedo-Drag Alter Persona."
      Daniel W. Heaton, Capital University
   "I Enjoy Being a Grrrl: Performing as Queer Bisexual Femme." Elizabeth J. Whitney,
      University of Utah
   "Hey, Miss Thing! Get Off MY Runway!: Drag and the Performance of Stylized Feminity."
      E. Patrick Johnson, University of North Carolina, Chapel Hill

"Welcome to My Queerdom: The Birth of a Diva and Cool Pose Revisited." D. Nebi Hilliard, Southern Illinois University

Respondent: Bryant K. Alexander, California State University, Los Angeles

This roundtable discussion examines the implications of performing drag, as well as viewing drag performance in light of performance, gender, feminist, and queer theory. Each panelist will speak from a specific "site" of drag performance based upon her/his personal experience of spectating and performing (or not) drag.

1556　　2:00-3:15 p.m.　　　　　　　Conf 5I　　　Fifth Floor　　Chicago Hilton

COMMUNICATION ASSESSMENT APPLICATIONS IN ORGANIZATIONAL COMMUNICATION: FROM THE CLASSROOM TO THE WORKPLACE

Sponsor: Commission on Communication Assessment
Chair: W. Timothy Coombs, Illinois State University
　　"Course and Curriculum Embedded Assessment for Organizational Communication Programs: Design Issues, Options, and the Protocol Process." Robert C. Chandler, Pepperdine University
　　"Interpersonal Communication in Organizations: Insights from the CCA (Communication Competency Assessment)." Michelle Shumate, Pepperdine Unversity, Hollie Packman, Communication Development Associates
　　"Overview of Assessment Strategies and Methods of Assessing Communication in Organizations." Dean C. Kazoleas, Illinois State University, Robert C. Chandler, Pepperdine University
　　"Assessment of Communication Role Behavior in Organizations." Vincent Hazleton, Radford University, Bill Kennan, Radford University
　　"Academic Departmental Assessment: Academic Accountability or Just Another Attempt to Herd Squirrel?" Joseph J. Cardot, Abilene Christian University

Respondent: Jeffrey D. Hobbs, Abilene Christian University

1557　　2:00-3:15 p.m.　　　　　　　Conf 5J　　　Fifth Floor　　Chicago Hilton

ISSUES AND ANSWERS: SUCCESSFUL PROMOTION AND TENURE FOR COMMUNITY COLLEGE FACULTY

Sponsor: Community College Section
Chair: John D. Reffue, Hillsborough Community College

Panelists: Bonnie L. Clark, St. Petersburg Junior College
　　　　　Joseph H. Rust, Rend Lake College
　　　　　Raymond C. Puchot, El Paso Community College
　　　　　Bradley W. Reel, Sinclair Community College

1562　　2:00-3:15 p.m.　　　　　　　Essex Court　　Second Floor　　　Essex Inn

ENGAGING AUDIENCES: RHETORICAL STRATEGIES FROM HISTORIC SOCIAL AND RELIGIOUS REFORM MOVEMENTS

Sponsor: Religious Communication Association
Chair: Kathleen J. Turner, Tulane University
　　"Modeling Ministry: The Emerging Apostolic Ethos of Martin Luther." Neil R. Leroux, University of Minnesota, Morris
　　"Transcendence and Transformation: Campbell Number Two and the Letter from Lunenberg." Peter A. Verkruyse, Kentucky Christian College
　　"Marching to the Promised Land: The Exodus Narrative in the Rhetoric of Martin Luther King, Jr.." Gary S. Selby, George Washington University

Respondent: Carol J. Jablonski, University of South Florida

Thursday

1563   2:00-3:15 p.m.   Windsor Court   Second Floor   Essex Inn

ETHNOGRAPHIC ANALYSES OF POLITICS AND PERFORMANCE

Sponsor: Ethnography Division
Chair: Robert G. Westerfelhaus, University of Houston, Downtown
"Illusions, Fantasies, Dreams, and Reflections: An Autoethnography of Abuse." Penny A. Phillips, University of South Florida
"Performing Culture Through Embodied Rhetoric: Dancing 'Where the Buffalo Roam'." Marilyn E. Bordwell, Allegheny College
"Relating in the Limelight: Karaoke as Pathway to Public Life." Robert S. Drew, Saginaw Valley State University
"Women Who Act and Speak Ditzy: A Critical Ethnography of Disempowering Discursive Practices." Ronald F. Wendt, University of South Dakota

Respondent: Bryan C. Taylor, University of Colorado, Boulder

1564   2:00-3:15 p.m.   Buckingham Court   Second Floor   Essex Inn

COMMUNICATING BASEBALL

Sponsor: American Studies Commission
Chair: Gary Gumpert, Communication Landscapers
"From Ebbets Field to Oriole Park at Camden Yard, or, Baseball Stadium as Communicator." Gary Gumpert, Communication Landscapers, Susan J. Drucker, Hofstra University
"Hot-Stove League Talk." Arthur D. Jensen, Syracuse University, Richard Buttny, Syracuse University
"Women's Ways of Playing." Susan Mallon Ross, SUNY, Potsdam
"Curves, Cockfights, and Communication." Jack A. Barwind, Syracuse University

Respondent: Stephen P. Depoe, University of Cincinnati

1565   2:00-3:15 p.m.   Park East Walk   Second Floor   Essex Inn

CHAOS: BURKE AND THE PARADOX OF TWENTY-FIRST CENTURY POLITICS

Sponsor: Kenneth Burke Society, NCA Branch
Chair: Bernard L. Brock, Wayne State University
"The Body Politic: Jesse Ventura and the Drama of Third Party Rhetoric." Richard D. Pineda, Wayne State University
"Values or Facts: The Impeachment Debate as a Struggle to Define American Morality." Robert B. Brito, Wayne State University
"A Paradoxical View of the Religious Right." Christopher D. Salinas, Wayne State University
"The Incongruity of Presidential Performance Satisfaction and Mistrust: It's Not 'Just the Economy. . .'." Robyn E. Parker, Wayne State University

Respondent: Tony J. Palmeri, University of Wisconsin, Oshkosh

Through the use of rhetorical inquiry and criticism, this panel will address questions of rhetorical importance, language creation and application, symbolic notions in political rhetoric, and apply these findings to contemporary society. In keeping with the conference theme, these papers will convey a break from traditional notions of political rhetoric and will point to the significance of this break for politics in the new century.

1566   2:00-3:15 p.m.   Cohn Rm   Second Floor   Spertus Institute

THREE APPROACHES TO THE RHETORIC OF TECHNOLOGY

Sponsor: American Association for Rhetoric of Science & Technology
Chair: Doreen Starke-Meyerring, University of Minnesota
"The 'Information Society': Discourses, Fetishes, and Discontents." Gerald Sussman, Portland State University
"Toward a Feminist Rhetoric of Technology." Amy Koerber, University of Minnesota

"Credibility and Evidence in the Digital Age: WWW Sites as Virtual Arguments." Mike T. Hubler, University of Georgia

---

1569   2:00-3:15 p.m.   Rm 903   Ninth Floor   Spertus Institute

COLORING OUTSIDE THE LINES: BRINGING EXPERIENTIAL LEARNING OUT OF THE CLASSROOM AND INTO THE COMMUNITY

Sponsor: Experiential Learning in Communication Commission
Chair: Edwin J. Abar, Westfield State College
   "The Externship: From the Classroom to the Newsroom." Ralph R. Donald, Southern Illinois University, Edwardsville
   "Student Literacy Corps: The Bridge Between the College and the Community." Nancy J. Hoar, Western New England College
   "'Coloring Outside the Lines': A Tale of Two Pros." Edwin J. Abar, Westfield State College

---

1570   2:00-3:15 p.m.   Rm 904   Ninth Floor   Spertus Institute

A COMPARATIVE PERSPECTIVE ON CHINESE COMMUNICATION PATTERNS AND MAINSTREAM AMERICAN COMMUNICATION PATTERNS

Sponsor: Association for Chinese Communication Studies
Chair: Michael H. Prosser, Rochester Institute of Technology
   "A Comparison of the Chinese View of Emotions and the Social Constructionist View of Emotions in the Contemporary West." Wenshan Jia, Truman State University
   "How Culture Influences Communication in the U.S. and China." D. Ray Heisey, Kent State University
   "Chinese Communication in Demystifying Perceptions of the U.S." Lu Liu, London School of Economics

Respondent: Chung Ying Cheng, University of Hawaii, Manoa

1572   2:00-3:15 p.m.   Rm 907   Ninth Floor   Spertus Institute

KRITIKS: THE STATE OF THE ART

Sponsor: Cross Examination Debate Association
Chair: Maxwell Schnurer, University of Pittsburgh
   "Critical Erasure: Permutations of Kritiks and the Deconstruction of Knowledge." Kevin J. Ayotte, University of Pittsburgh
   "Kritikal Praxis Revisited: Revenge of the Particular Intellectual." David F. Breshears, University of Texas, Austin
   "Critiquing Aesthetically: Theoretical Intersections with Policy." Marcy L. Halpin, University of Pittsburgh
   "Enacting Kritiking Through Permutations: Texts That Protect and Texts That Produce." Brian Lain, University of Iowa
   "(Per)formative Contradictions: Misunderstanding and the Importance of Action." Joseph P. Zompetti, Mercer University
   "Critiquing Debate: Unsettling the Settlers." Maxwell Schnurer, University of Pittsburgh

Respondent: Pat J. Gehrke, Penn State University

1578   2:00-4:45 p.m.   Off Site

WHAT'S NEW ABOUT NEW MEDIA?

Sponsor: Mass Communication Division
Chair: Rebecca A. Lind, University of Illinois, Chicago

Panelists: Noshir S. Contractor, University of Illinois, Urbana-Champaign
         James T. Costigan, University of Illinois
         Margaret J. Haefner, Illinois State University
         Steve Jones, University of Illinois
         Norman J. Medoff, Northern Arizona University

This event is co-sponsored by the Mass Communication Division and the Department of Communication at the University of Illinois Chicago, where the program will be held. The event is planned as a roundtable discussion and public forum, followed by a reception at the Jane Addams Hull House Museum at the University of Illinois at Chicago. Bus transportation will be provided and will depart the Chicago Hilton at 1:30 p.m. and return at 5:10 p.m.

3:30 p.m.

1606   3:30-4:45 p.m.   Continental BR A   Lobby Level   Chicago Hilton

THE ROLE OF PERSUASION IN CONTEMPORARY MEDIA EFFECTS

Sponsor: Mass Communication Division
Chair: Michael Pfau, University of Wisconsin, Madison
  "Forensic Journalism and the Attribution of Blame." David J. Dutwin, University of Pennsylvania
  "Which Words Count: An Examination of the Effect of Persuasive Appeal Typologies in Voter Mobilization." J. Kanan Sawyer, University of Washington
  "Too Close for Comfort: Persuasion and the Pitfalls of Cognitive Psychology." Lilach Nir, University of Pennsylvania
  "Second Order Agenda-Setting: A Model of Persuasion." Kate M. Kenski, University of Pennsylvania

Respondent: Robin L. Nabi, University of Arizona

1607   3:30-4:45 p.m.   Continental BR B   Lobby Level   Chicago Hilton

TECHNOLOGY, COMMUNITY, AND IDENTITY: HOW INDIVIDUALS AND COMMUNITIES ARE SHAPED BY TECHNOLOGY

Sponsor: Health Communication Division
Chair: Dale E. Brashers, University of Illinois, Urbana-Champaign
  "Segmented Response to Innovation: Telemedicine Technology in Rural America." Robert Thomas, Georgetown University, Jeanine W. Turner, Georgetown University, Michelle Gailiun, Ohio State University
  "Battle of the Sexes: A Comparison of Men and Women with Breast Cancer in an On-Line Support Group." Jennifer L. Peterson, University of Illinois, Urbana-Champaign
  "'You Know, Who's the Thinnest?': Countering Surveillance and Creating Safety in an On-Line Eating Disorder Support Group." Mary K. Walstrom, University of Illinois, Urbana-Champaign
  "Why Is It that Nobody Responds to the 'Abuse' Posts?: How Group Norms and Rules in an On-Line Depression Group Provide a Safe Place for Discussing Depression." Stewart C. Alexander, University of Illinois, Urbana-Champaign

1608   3:30-4:45 p.m.   Continental BR C   Lobby Level   Chicago Hilton

SEX, TEXT, AND THE POLITICS OF CULTURE

Sponsor: Critical and Cultural Studies Division
Chair: Elfriede Fursich, Boston College
  "A Rhetoric of the Gay Male Body." Davin A. Grindstaff, Penn State University
  "The Death of a Cyborgoddess: Star Trek: First Contact and Postmodern Anxiety." Steven S. Vrooman, Arizona State University
  "Masculinist Criticism: A Transformational Approach to Critique 'Outside the Lines' of Patriarchal Structures." Joel O. Iverson, North Dakota State University, David Airne, University of Missouri, Columbia
  "The Discursive (Re)Production of Social Problems: The Case of Child Sexual Abuse." Jennifer L. Coburn-Engquist, University of Denver

---

1610   3:30-4:45 p.m.   Grand Ballroom   Second Floor   Chicago Hilton

PERFORMANCE AS POWER

Sponsor: Performance Studies Division
Chair: Kirk W. Fuoss, St. Lawrence University
  "'Don't Sit in this Chair!': Performance and Academic Power." Ronald E. Shields, Bowling
      Green State University
  "Performance and Comic Inversion: The Andrew Jackson Bash." Donna M. Nudd, Florida
      State University, Kristina L. Schriver, California State University, Chico
  "'Awful but Cheerful': Consolations of Textual Power." Paul C. Edwards, Northwestern
      University
  "Performance as Political and Cultural Action." Robert L. Ivie, Indiana University
  "Movie Machismo: The Politics of the Hollywood Action Hero." Leah Lowe, Miami
      University, Ohio
  "Performance and the Communication of Organizational Authority." Drew Kent, Advocate
      Health Care, Chicago
  "Performance as a Way of Learning." Pamela J. Cooper, Northwestern University
  "Performance as Power in Community Self-Fashioning." Nathan P. Stucky, Southern Illinois
      University, Carbondale

1614   3:30-4:45 p.m.   Boulevard A   Second Floor   Chicago Hilton

BEYOND THE BOUNDARIES: FACILITATING CRITICAL THINKING IN THE
COMMUNICATION CLASSROOM

Sponsor: Challenging Boundaries Series
  "Learning by Praxis: Applying Critical Thinking to Rhetorical Criticism." Timothy J. Brown,
      Buffalo State College
  "Teaching Outside the Lines: Promoting Critical Thinking in the Interpersonal
      Communication Course." Lori A. Byers, Spalding University
  "'I Think They Should Do This': The Use of Case Studies as Critical Thinking Exercises in
      Computer-Mediated and Face-to-Face Courses." Carolyn L. Karmon, Washburn
      University
  "Reading Between the Lines of Conflict and Gender: Critical Thinking in the
      Communication Classroom." Jill Rhea, University of North Texas
  "Stepping Out of Bounds: Creating Transformative Intellectuals Through the Intercultural
      Communication Course." Laura L. Shue, Ball State University

---

1615   3:30-4:45 p.m.   Boulevard B   Second Floor   Chicago Hilton

COMPETITIVE PAPERS IN GROUP COMMUNICATION: INVESTIGATIONS OF
INFORMATION AND TIME IN GROUPS

Sponsor: Group Communication Division
Chair: Craig R. Scott, University of Texas, Austin
  "A Test and Theoretical Extension of the Information Sampling Model." Laura E. Drake,
      Northern Illinois University, Franklin J. Boster, Michigan State University, Sally
      Blomstrom, Financial Engineering Associates, Inc.
  "An Investigation of Involvement, Interaction Goal, and Identification in an
      Information-Sharing Experiment." Mary Lynn M. Williams, University of Wisconsin,
      Madison, Michael G. Cruz, University of Wisconsin, Madison, David D. Henningsen,
      Miami University, Joshua H. Morrill, University of Wisconsin, Madison
  "A Test of the Dimensionality of Time: Implications for Group Communication Research."
      Dawna I. Ballard, University of California, Santa Barbara, David R. Seibold, University of
      California, Santa Barbara

Respondent: Steven R. Corman, Arizona State University

1616   3:30-4:45 p.m.   Boulevard C   Second Floor   Chicago Hilton

HARD QUESTIONS—FEW ANSWERS: ISSUES IN NON-TRADITIONAL CASTING

Sponsor: Theatre Division
Chair: Michele A. Pagen, California University of Pennsylvania

Panelists: Julie R. Patterson-Pratt, University of Minnesota, Morris
Gail S. Medford, Bowie State University
Frank Mundy, South Carolina State University
Marilyn A. Hetzel, Metropolitan State College of Denver
Laura Facciponti, University of North Carolina, Asheville
Gerald Lee Ratliff, SUNY, Potsdam
Lisa Wolford, Bowling Green State University

Is color/gender/disability blind casting the way to go? Panelists will share experiences and discuss potential means for the inclusion of all people who wish to be in educational theatrical productions.

1618   3:30-4:45 p.m.   Waldorf   Third Floor   Chicago Hilton

ALL IN THE CULTURAL FAMILY: COMMUNICATION STRATEGIES AND INTERACTIONS WITHIN AFRICAN AMERICAN, GERMAN, JAPANESE, AND UNDOCUMENTED MEXICAN FAMILIES

Sponsor: Family Communication Division
Chair: Anita L. Vangelisti, University of Texas, Austin
"The Effects of Family Cohesion and Adaptability on Communication, Taboo Topics, and Satisfaction in African American Families." Donna R. Pawlowski, Creighton University, Scott A. Myers, Creighton University
"Family, Friends, and Foes: Undocumented Mexicans Whisper Secrets About Their Changed Family." Chad S. Thilborger, Saint Louis University
"The Role of Culture in Parent-Child Discipline Interactions and Research." Diane T. Prusank, University of Hartford
"Face and Facework in Conflicts with Parents and Siblings: A Cross-Cultural Comparison of Germans, Japanese, Mexicans, and U.S. Americans." John G. Oetzel, University of New Mexico, Stella Ting-Toomey, California State University, Fullerton, Martha I. Chew, University of New Mexico

---

1619   3:30-4:45 p.m.   Astoria   Third Floor   Chicago Hilton

DEBUT PAPERS IN PUBLIC ADDRESS

Sponsor: Public Address Division
Chair: Julia A. Haynes, Rowan College
"I Want to Be Your BJ Queen: Rock, Feminine Desire, and Phallocentrism." Jon Leon Torn, Northwestern University
"Clinton's Rhetoric of Affirmative Action: A Study in Political Myth." Olga A. Sotomayor, Southwest Texas State University
"The Quest for Authentic Diva-nity: A Rhetorical Analysis of the Videos of Shania Twain." Keith E. Nainby, Southern Illinois University

Respondent: Shawn J. Parry-Giles, University of Maryland

1621   3:30-4:45 p.m.   Williford A   Third Floor   Chicago Hilton

AFRICAN SOJOURNS: NEGOTIATING IDENTITY IN THE MOTHERLAND

Sponsor: African American Communication & Culture Commission
Chair: Melbourne S. Cummings, Howard University
"'I Have the Women at Heart': A First-Time Sojourner's Encounters with South African Women." Marsha Houston, Tulane University

"The Discourse of Dislocation: The Construction of an African Self in Nigeria." Joni L.
  Jones, University of Texas, Austin
"A Visitation from the Foremothers: Recovering African Women's Voices in Senegal." Olga
  I. Davis, Arizona State University
"'Go Straight': Negotiating Gender and Sexuality in Ghana." E. Patrick Johnson, University
  of North Carolina, Chapel Hill

1623   3:30-4:45 p.m.   Williford C   Third Floor   Chicago Hilton

THE SITE, TEXT AND TRANSFORMATION OF VIOLENCE AGAINST WOMEN

Sponsor: Feminist and Women Studies Division
Chair: Sandra L. Herndon, Ithaca College
  "'Whose History? Whose Comfort?': Entertainment as Public Memory and En-Gendered
    Ideology in Contemporary Japan." Kaori Koite, Northern Illinois University, Lois S. Self,
    Northern Illinois University
  "Victim Character and Rape Reform in Prime-Time Rape Episodes." Lisa M. Cuklanz,
    Boston College
  "Robbie McCauley and *Sally's Rape*: Testimony, Witnessing, and Dialogue." Carolyn Lea,
    Bowling Green State University
  "Survival Narratives: A Feminist Analysis of Abused Women's Stories of Disengagement."
    Loreen N. Olson, University of Minnesota, Morris

Respondent: Susan L. Biesecker-Mast, Bluffton College

1624   3:30-4:45 p.m.   Marquette   Third Floor   Chicago Hilton

SPEAKING WHAT WE SENSE AND SENSING WHAT WE SPEAK: EXPLICATING THE COMPLEXITIES OF BLACK COMMUNICATION OF SELF

Sponsor: Black Caucus
Chair: Doris Y. Dartey, Mount Mercy College
  "If You're Light, You're Still Right; If You're Black, Get Back: Color Consciousness and
    Perception Among African Americans." Katrina E. Bell, Northeastern Illinois University
  "Perceptual Differences and the Interpretation of Lived Experience." Karen E.
    Strother-Jordan, Oakland University
  "'You're not from here are you?': Perceptual Differences in Black Talk Across the Accent
    Divide." Doris Y. Dartey, Mount Mercy College
  "'Through Heaven's Eyes': African American Women's Accounts of Communicating Self in
    Corporate Contexts." Jeanne L. Porter, North Park University
  "Stigma of Singleness: A Study of Self-Perceptions of Single Black Women." R. Rennae
    Elliott, Oakwood College

1625   3:30-4:45 p.m.   Joliet   Third Floor   Chicago Hilton

COMPETITIVE PAPERS IN INTERPERSONAL AND GROUP COMMUNICATION

Sponsor: Student Section
  "Is Mom to Blame?: The Role of Mother-Daughter Communication in Body Image
    Development and Maintenance." Kerrie M. Smyres, Arizona State University
  "Resiliency Development: Importance of the Significant Other." Minuen A. Odom
  "Finding Strength Through Talk: The Relationship Between Stress Disclosure and Personal
    Resilience." Susanne Jones, Arizona State University
  "Parental Modeling and the Development of Communication Apprehension in Elementary
    School Children: A Latino Perspective." Paul Schrodt, University of North Texas, C. C.
    Carter, University of North Texas, Tara Tate, University of North Texas

Respondent: Randy Y. Hirokawa, University of Iowa

Thursday

1626	3:30-4:45 p.m.	PDR 1	Third Floor	Chicago Hilton

THE FUNDAMENTAL TOPOI OF RELATIONAL COMMUNICATION: A PANEL DISCUSSION IN HONOR OF JUDEE BURGOON AND JEROLD HALE, THE 1998 WOOLBERT RESEARCH AWARD RECIPIENTS

Sponsor: Research Board
Chair: Michael Leff, Northwestern University

Panelists: David B. Buller, AMC Cancer Research Center
L. Edna Rogers, University of Utah
Beth A. Le Poire, University of California, Santa Barbara
Mark L. Knapp, University of Texas, Austin

Respondents: Judee K. Burgoon, University of Arizona
Jerold L. Hale, University of Georgia

Panelists will comment on the way in which this article published in *Communication Monographs* in 1984, has had an impact on them and on the discipline.

1627	3:30-4:45 p.m.	PDR 2	Third Floor	Chicago Hilton

CROSS EXAMINATION DEBATE ASSOCIATION BUSINESS MEETING

Sponsor: Cross Examination Debate Association

1628	3:30-4:45 p.m.	PDR 3	Third Floor	Chicago Hilton

GAY/LESBIAN/BISEXUAL/TRANSGENDER COMMUNICATION STUDIES DIVISION BUSINESS MEETING

Sponsor: Gay/Lesbian Transgender Communication Studies Division

1629	3:30-4:45 p.m.	PDR 4	Third Floor	Chicago Hilton

CAUCUS ON DISABILITY ISSUES BUSINESS MEETING

Sponsor: Caucus on Disability Issues

1630	3:30-4:45 p.m.	PDR 5	Third Floor	Chicago Hilton

CENTRAL STATES COMMUNICATION ASSOCIATION BUSINESS MEETING

Sponsor: Central States Communication Association

1631	3:30-4:45 p.m.	PDR 6	Third Floor	Chicago Hilton

ASSOCIATION FOR CHINESE COMMUNICATION STUDIES BUSINESS MEETING

Sponsor: Association for Chinese Communication Studies

1632	3:30-4:45 p.m.	PDR 7	Third Floor	Chicago Hilton

AMERICAN ASSOCIATION FOR THE RHETORIC OF SCIENCE AND TECHNOLOGY BUSINESS MEETING

Sponsor: American Association for Rhetoric of Science & Technology

---

1633   3:30-4:45 p.m.   Conf 4A   Fourth Floor   Chicago Hilton

SENIOR COLLEGE AND UNIVERSITY SECTION SMALL COLLEGE BUSINESS MEETING

Sponsor: Senior College & University Section

1634   3:30-4:45 p.m.   Conf 4B   Fourth Floor   Chicago Hilton

SOMEONE IS LISTENING: CELEBRATING THE TEACHER AS LISTENER WITH ANDREW D. WOLVIN

Sponsor: Teachers on Teaching
Chair: John A. Daly, University of Texas, Austin

Panelists: John A. Daly, University of Texas, Austin
            Andrew D. Wolvin, University of Maryland

The effectiveness of Professor Wolvin's teaching is as memorable as the effectiveness of his research on listening. This panel will be devoted to listening to the words, ideas, and strategies of a pioneer, both in the classroom and in the research.

1635   3:30-4:45 p.m.   Conf 4C   Fourth Floor   Chicago Hilton

NATIONAL FORENSIC ASSOCIATION EXECUTIVE COUNCIL MEETING

Sponsor: National Forensic Association

1636   3:30-4:45 p.m.   Conf 4D   Fourth Floor   Chicago Hilton

THE LEGACY OF ROBERT HOPPER: A CELEBRATION AND MEMORIAL

Sponsor: Language and Social Interaction Division
Chair: Sandra L. Ragan, University of Oklahoma
    "Excavating the Taken-for-Granted: Studies in Language and Social Interaction. A Festschrift in Honor of Robert Hopper." Phillip J. Glenn, Southern Illinois University, Carbondale, Curtis D. LeBaron, University of Colorado, Boulder, Jenny S. Mandelbaum, Rutgers University
    "Talk at Play: A Collection of Robert Hopper's Publications." Phillip J. Glenn, Southern Illinois University, Carbondale
    "Lay Diagnosis: A Special Edition of TEXT." Wayne A. Beach, San Diego State University

Robert Hopper passed away in December, 1998. The panel presents updates on his intellectual legacy. Attendees are invited to bring memories, stories, photos, poems, and songs to celebrate his rich personal legacy at the conclusion of the panel.

1638   3:30-4:45 p.m.   Conf 4F   Fourth Floor   Chicago Hilton

VISUAL COMMUNICATION OF ACTIVISM, RESISTANCE, AND OPPRESSION

Sponsor: Visual Communication Commission
Chair: Michelle Moreau, University of South Alabama
    "Purposive Propaganda: Toward a Definition of the Relationship Between Art and Activism." Julie D. Phillips, Purdue University
    "Visual Rhetoric, T.V., and Cultural Studies: The Aesthetics of Nonviolent Resistance." Ellen W. Gorsevski, Washington State University
    "The Presence of Segregation: An Exploration into the Visual Artifacts of Segregation and Oppression." Angela Koponen, University of Northern Colorado, Lini Allen, University of Northern Colorado

Respondent: Marla R. Kanengieter, St. Cloud State University

1639   3:30-4:45 p.m.   Conf 4G   Fourth Floor   Chicago Hilton

HOMESTEADING ON THE TECHNOLOGY FRONTIER: MAKING DISTANCE EDUCATION WORK

Sponsor: Human Communication and Technology Commission
Chair: Michael J. Charron, Concordia University, Minnesota
"Exploring Frontiers in Distance Education: Coordinating Delivery. . . by the Seat of Your Pants." Joel Schuessler, Concordia University, Minnesota
"Exploring Frontiers in Distance Education: The On-Line Public Speaking Course." Tasha L. Van Horn, Citrus College
"Exploring Frontiers in Distance Education: Designing, Implementing, and Reflecting upon a Compressed Video Distance Education Course." Basma Ibrahim DeVries, Concordia University
"Exploring Frontiers in Distance Education: Students' Perspectives of Ethical On-Line Communication." Lori J. Charron, Concordia University, Minnesota, Marilyn E. Fuss-Reineck, Concordia University, Minnesota

Respondent: Mary E. Bozik, University of Northern Iowa

1640   3:30-4:45 p.m.   Conf 4H   Fourth Floor   Chicago Hilton

BUILDING HUMAN CAPACITY TO USE TECHNOLOGY IN TEACHING

Sponsor: Senior College & University Section
Chair: Cassandra L. Book, Michigan State University
"Motivating Faculty to Integrate Technology in College Courses: A Dean's Perspective." Carole Ames, Michigan State University
"Teach Guides: Providing Expert Assistance for Faculty and Students." Yong Zhao, Michigan State University
"Implementing Technology Requirements for Teacher Candidates and Graduate Teaching Assistants." Scott Turner, Michigan State University
"eWeb: An Integrated Web-Based Learning Environment." Yong Zhao, Michigan State University

---

1641   3:30-4:45 p.m.   Conf 4I   Fourth Floor   Chicago Hilton

THEORETICAL ISSUES IN PUBLIC RELATIONS

Sponsor: Public Relations Division
Chair: Dan P. Millar, Indiana State University
"Using Customer Complaint Letters for Strategic Planning." Glynis C. Hiebner, Central Connecticut State University
"Litigation Public Relations: Problems and Limits." Dirk C. Gibson, University of New Mexico, Mariposa Padilla, University of New Mexico
"Examining Public Relations Within the Framework of the Resource-Based Theory: A Synthesized Model*." Lisa Fall, Michigan State University
"When Public Relations Becomes Government Relations." Michael L. Kent, SUNY, Fredonia, Maureen Taylor, Rutgers University

Respondent: Cynthia E. King, California State University, Fullerton

*Debut Paper

1642   3:30-4:45 p.m.   Conf 4J   Fourth Floor   Chicago Hilton

TRAINING AND DEVELOPMENT DIVISION BUSINESS MEETING

Sponsor: Training and Development Division

1643   3:30-4:45 p.m.   Conf 4K   Fourth Floor   Chicago Hilton

GOING OUTSIDE THE CLASSROOM LINES, INTO THE WORLD, AND BRINGING THE WORLD'S COLOR INTO THE CLASSROOM

Sponsor: Experiential Learning in Communication Commission
Chair: Barbara Blackstone, Slippery Rock University
  "Combining Experiential and Service Learning in a Public Relations Capstone Course."
    Mark Banks, Slippery Rock University
  "Service Learning Project Videos in Small Group Communication Classes." Priscilla A.
    Schneider, California University of Pennsylvania
  "Action Plans Rising from the Cross-Cultural Adaptability Inventory (CCAI)." Barbara
    Blackstone, Slippery Rock University
  "Structured Learning with the CCAI's (Cross-Cultural Adaptability Inventory) *Cultural
    Passport to Anywhere*." Colleen E. Kelley, Consultant, La Jolla, California

---

1645   3:30-4:45 p.m.   Conf 4M   Fourth Floor   Chicago Hilton

PARADOX, RESISTANCE, OPPRESSION, EMOTION: EXPERIENCING ORGANIZATIONAL COMMUNICATION

Sponsor: Organizational Communication Division
Chair: Diane S. Grimes, Syracuse University
  "Jumping Out of the Frying Pan: Tracing Paradox, Resistance/\Oppression, and Meanings of
    Work in the Discourse of Midwives." Paaige K. Turner, Saint Louis University
  "Fooling Each Other or Fooling Ourselves? Toward a Postmodern Understanding of
    Emotion Labor." Sarah J. Tracy, University of Colorado, Boulder
  "Emotional Intelligence as Organizational Communication: An Examination of the
    Construct." Debbie S. Dougherty, University of Nebraska, Lincoln, Kathleen J. Krone,
    University of Nebraska, Lincoln
  "Organizational Entry (Employment) Experiences of At-Risk Youth: A Taxonomic Analysis."
    Mary Ann Danielson, Creighton University
Respondent: Anne M. Nicotera, Howard University

1646   3:30-4:45 p.m.   McCormick Board Rm   Fourth Floor   Chicago Hilton

AFFIRMATIVE ACTION AND INTERCAUCUS COMMITTEE BUSINESS MEETING

Sponsor: Affirmative Action and Intercaucus Committee

1647   3:30-4:45 p.m.   Pullman Board Rm   Fourth Floor   Chicago Hilton

SOUTHERN STATES COMMUNICATION ASSOCIATION EXECUTIVE COUNCIL MEETING

Sponsor: Southern States Communication Association

1649   3:30-4:45 p.m.   Conf 5B   Fifth Floor   Chicago Hilton

CREATIVE AND PEDAGOGICALLY SOUND WAYS TO DELIVER THE BASIC COURSE TO GREATER NUMBERS OF STUDENTS

Sponsor: Basic Course Division
Chair: Edward A. Schwarz, Prairie State College

Panelists: Donald K. Orban, University of Florida
         Susan R. Emel, Baker University
         L. Glen Williams, Southeast Missouri State University
         Karla K. Jensen, Texas Tech University

Panelists will explore a variety of creative ways to reach more students with fewer resources.

Thursday

1651   3:30-4:45 p.m.   Conf 5D   Fifth Floor   Chicago Hilton

MAKING IT ACROSS THE LINES: FEMALE GRAD STUDENTS AT (PREDOMINANTLY MALE) RESEARCH I INSTITUTIONS

Sponsor: Women's Caucus
Chair: Lynne M. Webb, University of Memphis

Panelists: Danna E. Prather, University of Iowa
            Joan Faber-McAlister, University of Iowa
            Suzanne W. Chapman, University of Iowa
            Vesta T. Silva, University of Iowa

This discussion seeks to address questions and co-create strategies for success in programs traditionally dominated by men, which continue to lack female faculty as role models. Using the University of Iowa as an example, we will discuss political implications and conflicts within Research I graduate programs. With the help of attendees, we will discuss ways of making spaces for women graduate students in such programs.

1652   3:30-4:45 p.m.   Conf 5E   Fifth Floor   Chicago Hilton

SPACE, PLACE AND MEMORY IN RHETORICAL PRAXIS

Sponsor: Rhetorical and Communication Theory Division
Chair: James Jasinski, University of Puget Sound
    "Place and Community: An Integrative Rhetorical Perspective." Gray Matthews, University of Memphis
    "Neighbors and Their Properties: Space and Discipline in Community Planning." Jennifer Thackaberry, University of Colorado, Boulder
    "Diagnosing a School Board's Interactional Trouble." Karen Tracy, University of Colorado, Heidi L. Muller, University of Colorado, Boulder
    "A Rhetoric for Memory and Space." Shannon Skarphol Kaml, University of Minnesota

---

1653   3:30-4:45 p.m.   Conf 5F   Fifth Floor   Chicago Hilton

POLITICAL DISADVANTAGES ASSASSINATED? A CONTEMPORARY ARGUMENT DISCUSSION

Sponsor: American Forensic Association
Chair: Richard D. Pineda, Wayne State University
    "Political Disadvantages: A Tool for the Study of American Politics." Benjamin B. Coulter, Wayne State University
    "Fiat and Political Arguments: Reassessing the Unspoken Dynamic." Ryan W. Galloway, University of Georgia
    "Comparing the Implications of the Political Disadvantage Against the Implications of the Affirmative in Policy Debating: A Critical Perspective on the Relationships Between Impacts." Christopher D. Salinas, Wayne State University
    "Political Disadvantages: Their Role and Function in Modern Debate." Ron Stevenson, Wayne State University

---

1654   3:30-4:45 p.m.   Conf 5G   Fifth Floor   Chicago Hilton

HUMOR, CULTURE, ETHNOCENTRISM AND THEIR LINKAGES IN THE CLASSROOM

Sponsor: Instructional Development Division
Chair: Elizabeth E. Graham, Ohio University
    "Student Perceptions of Teacher Humor Use in Relationship to Learning and Motivation: Examining Appropriate and Inappropriate Teacher Humor." Ann B. Frymier, Miami University, Melissa B. Wanzer, Canisius College

"Taking Humor Across Cultural Lines: An Analysis of the Use and Impact of Humor in U.S. and Thai Classrooms." Krisda Tanchisak, Bangkok University, Candice E. Thomas-Maddox, Ohio University

"Ethnocentrism and Student Perceptions of Teacher Communication." Rikki D. Amos, West Virginia University, James C. McCroskey, West Virginia University

Respondent: Elizabeth E. Graham, Ohio University

1655	3:30-4:45 p.m.	Conf 5H	Fifth Floor	Chicago Hilton

COMMUNICATION APPREHENSION IN UNIVERSITY INSTRUCTORS

Sponsor: Communication Apprehension & Avoidance Commission
Chair: K. David Roach, Texas Tech University
"Instructor CA Across Campus: A Dean's Perspective." Jerry L. Allen, University of New Haven
"Department Strategies of Managing Instructor/TA CA: When Good Teachers Don't Talk." Virginia P. Richmond, West Virginia University
"Communication Apprehension in Foreign Instructors." K. David Roach, Texas Tech University, Bolanle A. Olaniran, Texas Tech University
"Apprehensive Instructors: When Lectureholics Won't Let Students Talk." Kathleen M. Long, West Virginia Wesleyan College, Shirley D. Fortney, West Virginia Wesleyan College, Danette E. Ifert, West Virginia Wesleyan College

1656	3:30-4:45 p.m.	Conf 5I	Fifth Floor	Chicago Hilton

APPROACHES TO MESSAGES AND MESSAGE EXPECTATION

Sponsor: Intrapersonal Communication/Social Cognition Commission
Chair: Michael T. Stephenson, University of Kentucky
"Everyday Listening Expectations in Relational Communication: A Grounded Theoretical Model." Kelby K. Halone, Clemson University, Loretta L. Pecchioni, Louisiana State University
"Using Two-Sided Refutational Messages to Prevent the Boomerang Effect." M. Chad McBride, Texas Christian University, Melissa J. Young, Texas Christian University
"What Makes Anti-Marijuana PSAs Persuasive: Message Sensation Value and Involvement as Determinants of Multi-Modal Message Processing." Michael T. Stephenson, University of Kentucky, Philip C. Palmgreen, University of Kentucky
"In Search of Communicative Unity of Fragmented Meanings: An Explication of the Concept of Implicit Cognitive Processing." Shannon S. Dyer, Northwestern University

Respondent: Susan E. Morgan, University of Kentucky

1657	3:30-4:45 p.m.	Conf 5J	Fifth Floor	Chicago Hilton

SYMBOLIC INTERACTION AND COMMUNICATION: THE CONTRIBUTIONS OF DAVID MAINES' WORKS IN INTERDISCIPLINARY INQUIRY

Sponsor: Society for the Study of Symbolic Interaction
Chair: Arthur P. Bochner, University of South Florida
"The Idea of Structure and Communication in David Maines' Work." Bruce E. Gronbeck, University of Iowa
"The Maines-Stream: A Pragmatist Perspective on Social Organization and Policy Production." Peter M. Hall, University of Missouri, Columbia
"Framing Norms: The Culture of Expectations and Explanations." Gary Alan Fine, Northwestern University
"Telling Stories of David R. Maines: An Admiring Friend's Sampler." William K. Rawlins, Purdue University

Respondent: David R. Maines, Oakland University

Thursday

1659   3:30-4:45 p.m.   Lake Michigan   Eighth Floor   Chicago Hilton

FULFILLING THE DIASPORA: STUDIES IN MEMORY MAKING, PERFORMANCE, AND FILM

Sponsors: Asian/Pacific American Caucus
          Asian Pacific American Communication Studies Division
Chair: Kathleen Wong (Lau), Arizona State University
    "The FDR Memorial, National Identity, and the Interment Memory: Reflections of Public
    Cultures, Public Spaces, Public Spheres." Gordon W. Nakagawa, California State
    University, Northridge
    "Desi/Videshi: Reading the Text(s) of 'India Night'." Anandam P. Kavoori, University of
    Georgia, Kalyani Chadha, University of Maryland
    "Translating Masculinities? Gender, Genre, and Cultural Politics in John Woo's and Ang
    Lee's Films." Shujen Wang, Emerson College
    "Transmutation of Asian/American Masculinity: Chow Yun-Fat and the White Male
    Hyper-Masculine Mode." Kathleen Wong (Lau), Arizona State University
    "Le Pas Au-Dela' in Movie Talk." Briankle G. Chang, University of Massachusetts, Amherst

---

1660   3:30-4:45 p.m.   Lake Huron   Eighth Floor   Chicago Hilton

ISSUES IN FREEDOM OF EXPRESSION

Sponsor: Freedom of Expression Commission
Chair: James A. Schnell, Ohio Dominican College
    "Governing New Religious Movements: Persecution and the Protection of Pluralism."
    Kevin J. Cummings, Denver University, William V. Faux, Denver University
    "Beijing 1989: 'Here and Now at the Square!' A Student Democracy Movement Rhetoric
    of Emancipation from Official Discursive Constraints." Tomas P. Klvana, University of
    Southern Maine
    "Postscript 1968: A Contextual Reading." Tom Duncanson, Fair Street Communication

Respondent: Juliet L. Dee, University of Delaware

1661   3:30-4:45 p.m.   Lake Erie   Eighth Floor   Chicago Hilton

REACHING THE LATINO/A COMMUNITY: HEALTH PROMOTION, DIFFUSION OF INFORMATION, AND TARGET MARKETING

Sponsor: La Raza Caucus
Chair: Matthew Eastin, Michigan State University
    "Developing Campaign Messages to Promote Hearing Screening: Targeting the Latino/a
    Community." Janet K. McKeon Lillie, Michigan State University
    "Responses to the Television Program Ratings Among Latina and Caucasian Mothers of
    Young Children." Lynn A. Rampoldi-Hnilo, Michigan State University, Bradley S.
    Greenberg, Michigan State University
    "Target Marketing of Alcohol Billboards and the Impact on Mexican Americans." Dana E.
    Mastro, Michigan State University

Respondent: Alicia A. Marshall, Texas A&M University

1662   3:30-4:45 p.m.   Essex Court   Second Floor   Essex Inn

AT PLAY IN THE FIELDS OF THE LORD: COMMUNICATION IDENTITIES IN THE LOCAL CHURCH

Sponsor: Religious Communication Association
Chair: Gordon L. Forward, Point Loma Nazarene University
    "Conceptualizing the Pastoral Role: Why the Church Views Leadership as a Dichotomous
    Variable and What Should Be Done About It." Gordon L. Forward, Point Loma
    Nazarene University

"Communicating Clergy Identity: The Relationship Between Immediacy Behavior and Perceptions of Pastoral Leadership." Melissa B. Gentzkow, Point Loma Nazarene University

"Cyberspace Community in the Church: Analyzing Identity Through Local Church Web Sites." Randall E. King, Point Loma Nazarene University, Konrad W. Hack, Point Loma Nazarene University

"Communication, Gender and the Pulpit: When Principals Clash with Principalities." Lewis E. Rutledge, Point Loma Nazarene University

---

1663   3:30-4:45 p.m.   Windsor Court   Second Floor   Essex Inn

ETHNOGRAPHY AND MEDIATED COMMUNICATION

Sponsor: Ethnography Division
Chair: John S. Dahlberg, Canisius College
"Objectively Speaking: Reports from the Documentary Field." Teresa G. Bergman, University of California, Davis
"Ethnographic Research Issues in Studying Global Virtual Organizations." Angeli R. Diaz, Purdue University
"Re-Viewing Ethnography: Media Audiences, Cultural Studies, and the Limitations of Knowledge." Elana H. Levine, University of Wisconsin, Madison

Respondent: Robert S. Drew, Saginaw Valley State University

1664   3:30-4:45 p.m.   Buckingham Court   Second Floor   Essex Inn

POSTMODERN SELF: NORMALITY, MALADY, AND RESTORATION

Sponsor: Semiotics and Communication Commission
Chair: Alan C. Harris, California State University, Northridge
"Re-Writing the Self." Joseph V. Gemin, University of Wisconsin, Oshkosh
"Clinton's Search for Symbolic Redemption." Zachary M. White, Purdue University
"Weaving the Web of Meaning: How Meaning Construction Originates in the Minds of College Freshmen." Mark Lipton, New York University

Respondent: Isaac E. Catt, Millersville University

1665   3:30-4:45 p.m.   Park East Walk   Second Floor   Essex Inn

KENNETH BURKE SOCIETY: COMPETITIVE PAPERS

Sponsor: Kenneth Burke Society, NCA Branch
Chair: Richard H. Thames, Duquesne University
"The Ambiguity of Terms: An Ecological/Environmental Perspective on Kenneth Burke's Theory of Naturalism and Rhetoric." Susan S. Sattell, Northwestern University
"Embarrassments of Empire: The Post-Colonial Kenneth Burke." Brent A. Whitmore, University of Minnesota
"The Militia Movement: Comedy or Tragedy?" Sarah E. Mahan-Hays, Ohio University Eastern

Respondent: Elvera B. Berry, Roberts Wesleyan College

1669   3:30-4:45 p.m.   Rm 903   Ninth Floor   Spertus Institute

CHALLENGING TRADITIONS: CHANGING THE FACE OF INTERCOLLEGIATE FORENSICS

Sponsor: Pi Kappa Delta
Chair: Tracy R. Frederick, Southwestern College
"A Road Less Traveled: Going Local." Robert Greenstreet, East Central University
"Great Gains in the Great Plains: The Value of Forensic Conferences." Jeffery J. Gentry, Southwestern Oklahoma State University
"Making a Difference: Making it Special." Tracy R. Frederick, Southwestern College
"Crossing the Lines: A Student Perspective." Ryan E. Kane, Southwestern College

---

1670   3:30-4:45 p.m.   Rm 904   Ninth Floor   Spertus Institute

COLLABORATIVE INITIATIVES AND PUBLIC DISCOURSE FOR MORAL CONFLICTS

Sponsor: Peace and Conflict Communication Commission
Chair: Bryan C. Taylor, University of Colorado, Boulder
   "Choosing Sides?: Implications of the Unusual Alliances Formed Surrounding the Yellowstone Wolf Reintroduction Debate." Alison P. Peticolas, University of Denver
   "Building Community on Campus: Moral Conflicts and Institutional Commitments." Jennifer L. Simpson, University of Colorado, Boulder
   "Constructing Norms for Performance of Sexual Identities: Moral Conflict Among Rocky Mountain Women." Elenie E. Opffer, University of Colorado, Boulder
   "Taking Control of Our Destiny: Communication, Ethics, and Collaboration in Community Decision Making." Spoma Jovanovic-Mattson, University of Denver

Respondent: Bryan C. Taylor, University of Colorado, Boulder

1672   3:30-4:45 p.m.   Rm 907   Ninth Floor   Spertus Institute

TOURNAMENT FORMAT, FORENSICS PEDAGOGY AND QUALITY OF LIFE: IS IT TIME FOR A CHANGE?

Sponsor: Cross Examination Debate Association
Chair: Kelly M. McDonald, Western Washington University

Panelists: Scott Deatherage, Northwestern University
        Kristin C. Dybvig, Cornell University
        Jeffrey W. Jarman, Wichita State University
        Kelly M. McDonald, Western Washington University
        Joel D. Rollins, University of Texas
        Ross Smith, Wake Forest University

Discussion will focus on the rationale for tournament formats and the tensions arising between the formats and the programmatic and competitive benefits realized by each.

1677   3:30-4:45 p.m.   Imperial South   Chicago Hilton

EMERITUS ADVISORY COUNCIL BUSINESS MEETING AND RECEPTION

Sponsor: National Communication Association

5:00 p.m.

1712   5:00-6:15 p.m.   Int'l Ballroom South   Second Floor   Chicago Hilton

CARROLL C. ARNOLD LECTURE

Sponsor: National Communication Association
Chair: Raymie E. McKerrow, Ohio University

"Civility and Its Discontents: Lessons Learned Studying Decorum in the U.S. House of Representatives." Kathleen Hall Jamieson, University of Pennsylvania

6:30 p.m.

1811   6:30-8:00 p.m.   Int'l Ballroom North   Second Floor   Chicago Hilton

NO-HOST WELCOME RECEPTION

Sponsor: National Communication Association

All attendees are invited to this reception sponsored by Allyn & Bacon and NCA.

8:00 p.m.

1910   8:00-9:15 p.m.   Grand Ballroom   Second Floor   Chicago Hilton

JUANITA'S ART OF HAIR FASHI'N J2K: COLORING (AND PERMING) OUTSIDE THE LINES OR VIRAL PERFORMANCE IN THE PRE-MILLENNIAL SALON—A SURVIVAL(IST) GUIDE

Sponsor: Theatre Division
Chair: Kelly S. Taylor, University of North Texas

Panelist: Daniel W. Heaton, Capital University

This interactive performance, a "sequel" to Juanita's '92, '93, '95, and '96 performances, finds postmodern hair/art theorist Juanita emerging from retirement and reinventing herself as an apocalyptic Martha Stewart. Door prizes will be awarded.

Thursday

Friday,
November 5, 1999

7:00 a.m.

| 2028 | 7:00-7:50 a.m. | PDR 3 | Third Floor | Chicago Hilton |

COMMUNITY COLLEGE SECTION BUSINESS MEETING

Sponsor: Community College Section

| 2046 | 7:00-7:50 a.m. | McCormick Board Rm | Fourth Floor | Chicago Hilton |

EXPERIENTIAL LEARNING IN COMMUNICATION COMMISSION BUSINESS MEETING

Sponsor: Experiential Learning in Communication Commission

| 2047 | 7:00-9:15 a.m. | Pullman Board Rm | Fourth Floor | Chicago Hilton |

PI KAPPA DELTA NATIONAL COUNCIL BUSINESS MEETING

Sponsor: Pi Kappa Delta

8:00 a.m.

| 2107 | 8:00-9:15 a.m. | Continental BR B | Lobby Level | Chicago Hilton |

CRAYONS IN COMPUTER-MEDIATED COMMUNICATION PEDAGOGY: CONCEPTS FOR COLORING OUTSIDE THE LINES

Sponsor: Human Communication and Technology Commission
Chair: Ken Williams, Marshall University
"Click Here and You're There: Exploring and Teaching Metaphors On-Line." Andrew F. Wood, San Jose State University
"Coming to a Web Page Near You - Communication Theory: The Role of Computers as a Pedagogy Strategy in Today's Communication Classroom." Nina C. Persi, Ohio University
"Evaluating Resources on the WWW: Moving the Lessons from Distributing Prescriptive Handouts to Teaching Critical Inquiry." Matthew J. Smith, Miami University, Hamilton
"Organizing Relational Expectations Through Computer-Mediated Communication: Theory and Pedagogy." Krishna P. Kandath, Ohio University
"Understanding Communication: Technologies in an Educational Environment." Patrick B. O'Sullivan, Illinois State University

Respondent: Stephanie Coopman, San Jose State University

| 2108 | 8:00-9:15 a.m. | Continental BR C | Lobby Level | Chicago Hilton |

MAPPING INTERNAL THIRD WORLDS

Sponsor: Critical and Cultural Studies Division

Chair: Bernardo Attias, California State University, Northridge
  "For Entertainment's Sake: Orientalism and Erasure in the Embodied Narrative of
    Mountaineering." Derek T. Buescher, University of Utah
  "Internal Colonies Thirty Years Later: Continuing *Racial Oppression in America.*" Kent A.
    Ono, University of California, Davis, Bob Blauner, University of California, Berkeley
  "Border Patrols: Investigating Third Worlds in Los Angeles." Bernardo Attias, California
    State University, Northridge, Karyl K. Kicenski, George Mason University, Deepak
    Narang Sawhney, The Union Institute

2111   8:00-9:15 a.m.   Int'l Ballroom North   Second Floor   Chicago Hilton

PERFORMING ILLNESS

Sponsor: Performance Studies Division
Chair: Beverly W. Long, University of North Carolina, Chapel Hill

Panelists: Gretchen A. Case, University of California, Berkeley
            Paul H. Gray, University of Texas, Austin
            Timothy Gura, Brooklyn College
            Jodi Kanter, Northwestern University
            Killian E. Manning, University of Utah
            Mark J.V. Olson, University of North Carolina, Chapel Hill
            Joanne R. Gilbert, Alma College

Understanding illness in and as performance, this panel addresses tensions between being the
body-object of others' performances and being an embodied subject who performs.

2112   8:00-9:15 a.m.   Int'l Ballroom South   Second Floor   Chicago Hilton

INNOVATIVE TECHNIQUES FOR TRAINING PROFESSIONALS

Sponsor: Training and Development Division
Chair: Mittie J. A. Nimocks, University of Wisconsin, Platteville
  "Boundary-Breaking." Maurine C. Eckloff, University of Nebraska, Kearney
  "From Controversy to Common Ground: Forging Team Agreements." Peter A. Glaser,
    Glaser & Associates, Inc.
  "Constructive Candor: Giving Interpersonal Feedback." Susan R. Glaser, University of
    Oregon
  "The Multicultural Meanings of Hand Gestures." Akbar Javidi, University of Nebraska,
    Kearney
  "Participative Decision-Making." Carol Koehler, University of Missouri, Kansas City
  "Visualization and Relaxation Exercise." Linda S. Kurz, University of Missouri, Kansas City
  "Managing Organizational Culture Change from the Inside: The Use of Peer Consulting
    Pairs." Gregory H. Patton, University of Southern California
  "Creativity-Building." Jan Skourup, University of Nebraska, Kearney
  "Behavior Modification Through Impromptu Incorporation of Communication Skills."
    Denise Spemizza, Southern Illinois University, Edwardsville
  "Introductions with a Purpose: Are You Deceiving Me?" Don R. Swanson, Monmouth
    University
  "Improving Relationships with Diverse Others: Increasing Cultural Sensitivity." Sonia
    Zamanou-Erickson, Southern Illinois University, Edwardsville

This program includes eleven innovative training techniques that will be presented in a
ten-minute time period format by experienced professionals in the field of Training and
Development. This program provides a unique opportunity for Training and Development
professionals to be acquainted with many innovative training techniques.

2114   8:00-9:15 a.m.   Boulevard A   Second Floor   Chicago Hilton

THE K-12 SPEAKING, LISTENING, AND MEDIA LITERACY STANDARDS: CLASSROOM ACTIVITIES THAT COLOR OUTSIDE THE LINES

Sponsor: Elementary & Secondary Education Section
Chair: Jean A. Streiff, Oakland Catholic High School, Pennsylvania

"Standards 1 - 8: Implementing 'Field Experience' and 'Observation' in the Study of Communication Fundamentals." David A. Yastremski, Ridge High School, New Jersey
"Standard 2: Using Rhetorical Analysis to Study Crisis Communication." Jill K. Gerken, Seton Hall Preparatory, New Jersey
"Standards 6 and 17: Grouping Standards to Analyze the Role of Conflict in Oral Communication. Standard 11: The Importance of Clarity and Shared Meaning During Oral Communication." Valerie A. Whitecap, Ft. Couch Middle School, Pennsylvania
"Standard 12: Overcoming Communication Anxiety Through Strategies That Work." Fran P. Bogos, North Allegheny High School, Pennsylvania
"Standard 13: Improving Listening Competency by Focusing on Speaking." Jean A. Streiff, Oakland Catholic High School, Pennsylvania

---

2115   8:00-9:15 a.m.   Boulevard B   Second Floor   Chicago Hilton

COLORING OUTSIDE THE LINES OF SOCIAL MOVEMENT STUDIES: A PANEL IN HONOR OF LELAND GRIFFIN

Sponsor: NCA First Vice President
Chair: Valeria Fabj, Emerson College

Panelists: Valeria Fabj, Emerson College
          E. Anne Laffoon, University of Colorado, Boulder
          Margaret R. LaWare, Iowa State University
          Kathryn M. Olson, University of Wisconsin, Milwaukee
          Catherine H. Palczewski, University of Northern Iowa
          Matthew J. Sobnosky, College of William and Mary

Griffin's teachings and writings encourage scholars to keep challenging the existing theories of social movements. This panel colors outside the lines of social movement theory.

2116   8:00-9:15 a.m.   Boulevard C   Second Floor   Chicago Hilton

PLACES FOR RACE, GENDER, AND POSTCOLONIAL THEORY IN INTERCULTURAL COMMUNICATION

Sponsor: International & Intercultural Communication Division
Chair: Anupama Mandavilli, University of Southern California
    "Racial Discourse in Japan's Internationalization: Yearning for Westernization (Whitenization)." Etsuko Fujimoto, Arizona State University
    "The Place of Postcolonial Theory in the Intercultural Communication Field." William Kelly, University of New Mexico
    "The Impact of Race and Gender on the Expression of Anger." Susan Steen, University of Southern Mississippi, Sheri Crowley Rooks, University of Maryland, European Division, Charles H. Tardy, University of Southern Mississippi
    "Gender and Relational Distance Influences on Japanese Use of Interpersonal Conflict Styles." Mark Cole, Phoenix Community College, Lisa Bradford, University of Wisconsin, Milwaukee

Respondent: Lisa A. Flores, University of Utah

2118   8:00-9:15 a.m.   Waldorf   Third Floor   Chicago Hilton

STUDENT PAPERS IN FAMILY COMMUNICATION

Sponsor: Family Communication Division
Chair: Kandi L. Walker, University of Denver
    "Maternal Reading Strategies, Child Vocabulary Scores and Socio-Economic Indicators." Laura L. Winn, University of Georgia
    "Growing Up in Dexterville: Communication, Quest and the Search for a Masculine Identity." William Jay Baglia, University of South Florida

Friday

"Effects of Parental Monitoring and Involvement on Adolescent Problem Behavior."
Stephen Yungbluth, University of Kentucky, Nancy G. Harrington, University of
Kentucky, Steven M. Giles, Tanglewood Research, Gregory J. Feeney, University of
Kentucky/Lexington Community College
"Coloring Outside the Methodological Lines: An Argument for the Use of Triangulation in
Family Communication Research." Kandi L. Walker, University of Denver, Tamara S.
Bollis-Pecci, University of Denver

Respondent: Michelle A. Miller, Penn State University

2119   8:00-9:15 a.m.   Astoria   Third Floor   Chicago Hilton

RHETORIC AND COLLECTIVE MEMORY

Sponsor: Public Address Division
Chair: Lynne Derbyshire, University of Rhode Island
"Dorothy Day's Contested Legacy: 'Humble Irony' as a Constraint on Memory." Carol J.
Jablonski, University of South Florida
"Metaphors of Memory: Characterizations of the Titanic Recovery Site." Cheryl R.
Jorgensen-Earp, Lynchburg College
"Collective Memory, Political Nostalgia, and the Rhetorical Presidency: Bill Clinton's
Commemoration of the March on Washington, August 28, 1998." Shawn J. Parry-Giles,
University of Maryland, Trevor Parry-Giles, Campaign Performance Group

Respondent: Stephen H. Browne, Penn State University

2121   8:00-9:15 a.m.   Williford A   Third Floor   Chicago Hilton

AFRICAN AMERICAN AUDIENCES, MEDIA AND IDENTITY

Sponsor: African American Communication & Culture Commission
Chair: Robin R. Means Coleman, New York University
"I Sing, Therefore I Am: The (De)construction of Identity Through the Jazz Lyrics of African
American Women." Kim L. Verdell, University of Georgia
"Up in Smoke: Black Women and Cigarette Advertising in *Essence* Magazine." Dwight E.
Brooks, University of Georgia, Hanna Norton, University of Georgia
"Reader Response: African American Movie Audiences and *Menace II Society, Juice,* and
Boyz 'N the Hood." Celeste A. Fisher, Marymount Manhattan College
"Black Talk Radio Listeners: Common-Sense Media Critics." Catherine R. Squires,
University of California, Santa Barbara
"Solidifying the Emergent Field of African American Audience Study: A Call for Papers."
Robin R. Means Coleman, New York University

Respondent: Trevy A. McDonald, North Carolina Central University

---

2122   8:00-9:15 a.m.   Williford B   Third Floor   Chicago Hilton

CYBER-POLITICS: THE EMERGENCE OF DIGITAL POLITICS IN AMERICAN
POLITICAL COMMUNICATION

Sponsor: Political Communication Division
Chair: Timothy B. Rumbough, Bloomsburg University
"A Tangled Web: The Internet's Influence on Political Attitudes." Barbara K. Kaye, Valdosta
State University, Thomas J. Johnson, Southern Illinois University
"Techno-Targeting: Analyzing Traffic Data for Campaign Web Sites." James E. Tomlinson,
Bloomsburg University
"Political Attack Web Sites: Mudslinging in Cyberspace." Timothy B. Rumbough,
Bloomsburg University
"The Political Valence of the World Wide Web: In Search of the 'Real' of a New
Technology." James B. McOmber, Valdosta State University
"The World According to Me: A Visual Analysis of the Web Sites of the Clinton/Gore and
Dole/Kemp 1996 Presidential Campaigns." Kristin K. Froemling, University of Oklahoma
"Patterns of 1998 Congressional Cyber-Campaigning." Ammar A. Bakkar, University of
Oklahoma

| 2123 | 8:00-9:15 a.m. | Williford C | Third Floor | Chicago Hilton |

POWER/GENDER/RACE: THE REPRODUCTION OF PRIVILEGE

Sponsor: Feminist and Women Studies Division
Chair: Lynda D. Dixon, Bowling Green State University
   "The Aliens in the *Alien* Quatrology: Representations of Women and Race." Lisa M.
      Schreiber, University of Nebraska, Lincoln
   "Positioning Non-Unitary Subjectivities: Adolescent Love Poetry and Girls' Discursive
      Power." Emily J. Plec, University of Utah
   "Propertied Investments: De-Constructions of White Femininity Under a Victimized
      Regime*." Aimee M. Carrillo Rowe, University of Washington, Samm Lindsay, University
      of Washington
   "Interlocking Oppressions and Marginalization: Rethinking the Application of Feminist
      Standpoint Theory." Matthew H. Barton, University of Nebraska, Lincoln

Respondent: K. E. Supriya, University of Wisconsin, Milwaukee

*Top Student Paper

| 2124 | 8:00-9:15 a.m. | Marquette | Third Floor | Chicago Hilton |

TOP THREE COMPETITIVE PAPERS IN ORGANIZATIONAL COMMUNICATION

Sponsor: Organizational Communication Division
Chair: Theodore E. Zorn, University of Waikato, New Zealand
   "It's Not a Matter of *If* but *When*: Exploring the Model of Situated Identifications Among
      Members of a Dispersed Organization." Craig R. Scott, University of Texas, Austin, Craig
      E. Carroll, University of Texas, Austin
   "Bending (But Not Breaking) the Rules of 'Professional' Display: Emotion Negotiation in
      Caregiver Performances." Jayne M. Morgan, University of Northern Iowa, Kathleen J.
      Krone, University of Nebraska, Lincoln
   "Are Organizations Rational?" James R. Taylor, University of Montreal

Respondent: Noshir S. Contractor, University of Illinois, Urbana-Champaign

| 2125 | 8:00-10:45 a.m. | Joliet | Third Floor | Chicago Hilton |

COMMUNICATION DEPARTMENT CHAIRS BREAKFAST

Sponsors: NCA First Vice President
              Association for Communication Administration
Chairs: Orlando L. Taylor, Howard University
         Alison Alexander, University of Georgia
   "The Role of Service-Learning in the Engaged Campus." Edward Zlotkowski, American
      Association for Higher Education

Respondent: James L. Applegate, University of Kentucky

TICKET REQUIRED

This program will feature a presentation by Zlotkowski, followed by a response from NCA
Second Vice President Applegate. Attendees will then be given time to discuss service-learning
within small groups of similar institutions.

| 2126 | 8:00-9:15 a.m. | PDR 1 | Third Floor | Chicago Hilton |

COMMUNICATION APPREHENSION AND AVOIDANCE COMMISSION BUSINESS MEETING

Sponsor: Communication Apprehension & Avoidance Commission

Friday

| 2127 | 8:00-9:15 a.m. | PDR 2 | Third Floor | Chicago Hilton |

TOP PAPERS IN ENVIRONMENTAL COMMUNICATION

Sponsor: Environmental Communication Commission
Chair: Bryan C. Taylor, University of Colorado
   "Rethinking the Irreparable." Terence P. Check, St. John's University
   "Genesis of an Environmental Controversy: The Rhetorical Negotiation of the National
      Park Concept During the Formative Years, 1872-1916." Daniel O. Buehler, University of
      Maryland, College Park
   "Source Credibility in Environmental Health-Risk Controversies: Application of Meyer's
      Credibility Index." Katherine A. McComas, Cornell University, Craig W. Trumbo,
      University of Wisconsin, Madison
   "Strategic and Tactical Dimensions of Green Communication: A Critical Analysis." Dirk C.
      Gibson, University of New Mexico

Respondent: James G. Cantrill, Northern Michigan University

| 2128 | 8:00-9:15 a.m. | PDR 3 | Third Floor | Chicago Hilton |

LANGUAGE AND SOCIAL INTERACTION DIVISION BUSINESS MEETING

Sponsor: Language and Social Interaction Division

| 2129 | 8:00-9:15 a.m. | PDR 4 | Third Floor | Chicago Hilton |

CROSS EXAMINATION DEBATE ASSOCIATION BUSINESS MEETING

Sponsor: Cross Examination Debate Association

| 2130 | 8:00-9:15 a.m. | PDR 5 | Third Floor | Chicago Hilton |

AFRICAN AMERICAN COMMUNICATION AND CULTURE DIVISION
BUSINESS MEETING

Sponsor: African American Communication & Culture Commission

| 2131 | 8:00-9:15 a.m. | PDR 6 | Third Floor | Chicago Hilton |

COMMUNICATION ASSESSMENT COMMISSION BUSINESS MEETING

Sponsor: Commission on Communication Assessment

| 2132 | 8:00-9:15 a.m. | PDR 7 | Third Floor | Chicago Hilton |

COMMUNICATION ETHICS COMMISSION BUSINESS MEETING

Sponsor: Communication Ethics Commission

| 2133 | 8:00-9:15 a.m. | Conf 4A | Fourth Floor | Chicago Hilton |

ASIAN/AMERICAN TRANSNATIONAL CONSTRUCTIONS OF IDEOLOGY,
COMMUNITIES AND IDENTITIES

Sponsor: Asian Pacific American Communication Studies Division
Chair: Kathleen Wong (Lau), Arizona State University
   "Wedding Celebrations: Examining Asian-Indian Culture and Identity." Anu S. Chitgopekar,
      Arizona State University
   "Nani Lal Chuni and the Big Bad Wolf: Transnationalism, Identity and Values in an Indian
      American Folk Performance." Christine L. Garlough, University of Minnesota
   "Dialectic Nature of Japanese American Buddhist Ceremony: Rhetorical Analysis of
      Buddhist Communication." Takashi Kosaka, Monterey Institute of International Studies

"Economic Mismanagement: Ideological Control of Thailand." David Airne, University of Missouri, Columbia

---

2134   8:00-9:15 a.m.   Conf 4B   Fourth Floor   Chicago Hilton

MOBILE IDENTITIES, MOBILIZED KNOWLEDGES: CULTURAL AND LEGAL MANAGEMENT OF SUBJECT POPULATIONS

Sponsor: Critical and Cultural Studies Division
Chair: Shawn Miklaucic, University of Illinois, Urbana-Champaign
    "'League-al' Identity: Mobility, the Passport and the League of Nations." Craig Robertson, University of Illinois, Urbana-Champaign
    "Modes of Identification/Processes of Subjectification: Truth, Epiphanies, and Governing Through Mobility." Jeremy Packer, University of Illinois, Urbana-Champaign
    "The Knowledge Gangsters: African American Conspiracy Theories, Political Rationality, and the Governance of Dissent." Jack Bratich, University of Illinois, Urbana-Champaign
    "Mobilizing Identity in the Transnational Art Community: Mona Hatoum and the Politics of Representation." Natasha Ritsma, University of Illinois, Urbana-Champaign

Respondent: Cameron R. McCarthy, University of Illinois, Urbana-Champaign

---

2135   8:00-9:15 a.m.   Conf 4C   Fourth Floor   Chicago Hilton

MYTH, FANTASY AND THE CONSTRUCTION OF IDENTITY

Sponsor: Student Section
    "Villainous Metaphor in Rhetoric: A Critical Examination of the Metaphoric Creation of Enemy in the Case of Saddam Hussein." Terry A. Robertson, University of Oklahoma
    "Powerlessness, Physical Inadequacy, and Sexual Doubt: The Construction of Masculinity in Upscale Men's Magazines." Robyn C. Walker, University of Utah
    "PeTA(people Equal to animals?): A Fantasy Theme and Rhetorical Vision Analysis*." Dawn Madura, Purdue University, Calumet
    "A Critique: From the 'Cosmic Zora'." Joni M. Johnson-Jones, University of Akron

Respondent: Ernest G. Bormann, University of Minnesota

*Debut Paper

2136   8:00-9:15 a.m.   Conf 4D   Fourth Floor   Chicago Hilton

COMMUNICATION EDUCATION IN THE PHARMACY COLLEGE

Sponsor: Health Communication Division
Chair: Mary Fong, California State University, San Bernardino

Panelists: Kenneth Leibowitz, University of the Sciences, Pennsylvania
           Helen M. Meldrum, Massachusetts College of Pharmacy and Allied Health
           Bruce L. Lambert, University of Illinois, Chicago
           Mei-ling Wang, University of the Sciences, Pennsylvania

Leaders in the development of communication education in pharmacy schools will discuss curriculum design, teaching methods, assessment methods and issues, research agendas, and collaboration with professional organizations and the pharmaceutical industry.

2137   8:00-9:15 a.m.   Conf 4E   Fourth Floor   Chicago Hilton

EFFECTIVELY COMMUNICATING WITH STREET GANGS

Sponsor: Community College Section
Chair: Edward A. Schwarz, Prairie State College
    "Teaching Tolerance: Directing/Molding Classroom Response When the Student Speaker Is a Gang Member." Marla Chisolm, University of Texas, Permian Basin
    "Recruitment, Retention, and Retrospective Empowerment of Gang Members." Raymond C. Puchot, El Paso Community College

Friday

"A Gangster's Perspective." Linda C. Brown, El Paso Community College, Transmountain Campus

This panel will provide examples of successful retention efforts with culturally diverse populations. Panelists will discuss methods of encouraging student disclosure to enlighten and educate others.

2138   8:00-9:15 a.m.   Conf 4F   Fourth Floor   Chicago Hilton

COMPETITIVE PAPERS IN MEDIA STEREOTYPING OF GENDER AND RACE STUDIES OF CONTENT AND EFFECTS

Sponsor: Mass Communication Division
Chair: Charles F. Aust, Kennesaw State University
   "'Drip, Drip' or 'Drench': Effects of Gender Stereotyping in the Media." Patrice A.
      Oppliger, Northeastern University
   "Race and the Misrepresentation of Victimization on Local Television News*." Travis L.
      Dixon, University of Michigan, Daniel G. Linz, University of California, Santa Barbara
   "Media Exposure and Stereotypes of Race and the Justice System." Ren-He Huang,
      Michigan State University, Ron C. Tamborini, Michigan State University

Respondent: Mary Beth Oliver, Penn State University

*Top 3 Competitive Paper

2139   8:00-9:15 a.m.   Conf 4G   Fourth Floor   Chicago Hilton

ORIENTING THE EMPLOYEE, ORIENTING THE CORPORATION: TRAINING ISSUES IN NEW EMPLOYEE ORIENTATION PROGRAMS

Sponsor: Training and Development Division

Panelists: Robert R. Boren, Boise State University
           Laurel T. Hetherington, Boise State University
           Ed Phillips, Southern Illinois University
           Lori A. Sefton, Southern Illinois University
           Michelle Wilkes-Carilli, University of Tennessee, Knoxville

This panel will address the theoretical and practical utility of the 'transactional orientation' model. The current paradigm in corporations and small companies alike is the one-way model: Orienting the employee to the workplace. Yet, the two-way or transactional model is theoretically and practically sound. Selected case studies will be presented to provide evidence of the workability of two-way or transactional orientation models. Audience members are invited to join in our activities and discussion.

2140   8:00-9:15 a.m.   Conf 4H   Fourth Floor   Chicago Hilton

MYTHS OF TECHNOLOGY AND ROMANTIC LOVE IN JAMES CAMERON'S TITANIC

Sponsor: Media Forum Series
Chair: Thomas S. Frentz, University of Arkansas, Fayetteville
   "Myths of Technology and Romantic Love: James Cameron's Titanic." Janice H. Rushing,
      University of Arkansas, Fayetteville, Thomas S. Frentz, University of Arkansas, Fayetteville

Respondent: Sharon D. Downey, California State University, Long Beach

Taking issue with accounts of Titanic that localize its impact in either the love story or the technological effects, this program historicizes the film within three classic myths—"Pygmalion and Galatea," "Tristan and Iseult," and "Eros and Psyche" — recovering the gendered tensions between romantic love and technological progress. Film clips are used to show how Cameron, by allowing the action to flow from the memory of old Rose, casts his film as a feminine descent that constrains the masculine excesses of technology.

2141   8:00-9:15 a.m.   Conf 4I   Fourth Floor   Chicago Hilton

EXAMINING APPLIED COMMUNICATION ON THE FRONT LINES: WHAT CAN COMPUTER-MEDIATED SYSTEMS, CONSUMER WARM LINES, AND ALCHOLICS ANONYMOUS TELL US?

Sponsor: Applied Communication Division
Chair: Michelle T. Violanti, University of Tennessee
  "Unusual Routines and Computer-Mediated Communication Systems*." Stephen D.
    Cooper, Rutgers University
  "Ideological Dilemmas on Consumer-Run Warm Lines: Making a Case for Applied
    Ethnographic Research." Christopher J. Pudlinski, Central Connecticut State University
  "Do You Have a Better Idea?: The Sponsor Relationship in Alcoholics Anonymous." David
    B. Jackson, University of Nebraska, Lincoln

Respondent: Kelby K. Halone, Clemson University

*Top Student Paper

2142   8:00-9:15 a.m.   Conf 4J   Fourth Floor   Chicago Hilton

SPEAKING-INTENSIVE COURSES: CURRICULAR AND ADMINISTRATIVE PROBLEMS

Sponsor: Senior College & University Section
Chair: Theodore F. Sheckels, Randolph-Macon College
  "Mary Washington College's Speaking Across the Curriculum Goals and Objectives: The
    Gap Between Theory and Practice." Robin A. Gurien, Mary Washington College
  "A Speaking-Intensive Course: Points of Commonality; Points of Variety." Pamela C. Miller,
    DePauw University
  "Inventing the Wheel: Implementing Speaking-Intensive Programs Across the Curriculum."
    Maria M. Scott, Randolph-Macon College
  "Defining and Developing Speaking-Intensive Courses: A Programmatic Model." Tamara L.
    Burk, College of William and Mary

2143   8:00-9:15 a.m.   Conf 4K   Fourth Floor   Chicago Hilton

INFLUENCE PROCESSES I: THEORY AND RESEARCH ON THE DOOR-IN-THE-FACE INFLUENCE STRATEGY

Sponsor: Interpersonal Communication Division
Chair: Kyle J. Tusing, University of Wisconsin, Madison
  "Explaining the Door-in-the-Face: Is It Really Time to Abandon Reciprocal Concessions?"
    Jerold L. Hale, University of Georgia, Melanie K. Laliker, University of Georgia
  "Two-and-a-Half Arguments Against the Reciprocal-Concessions Explanation of
    Door-in-the-Face Effects." Daniel J. O'Keefe, University of Illinois, Urbana-Champaign
  "A Meta-Analysis of the Ceiling Effect in the Door-in-the-Face Influence Strategy." Thomas
    H. Feeley, SUNY, Geneseo
  "A Study of Door-in-the-Face: A Guilt-Based Interpretation." Mark A. deTurck, SUNY,
    Buffalo, Christine Derme, SUNY, Buffalo

2144   8:00-9:15 a.m.   Conf 4L   Fourth Floor   Chicago Hilton

ASSESSMENT IN PUBLIC RELATIONS EDUCATION

Sponsor: Public Relations Division
Chair: Jeffrey L. Courtright, University of North Dakota
  "What Defines an Excellent Student Campaign: Issues of Assessment." Diane A. Gorcyca,
    Missouri Western State College, Charles A. Lubbers, Kansas State University
  "Show Me! Portfolios as Instruments of Student Evaluation." Dan P. Millar, Indiana State
    University

Friday

"Applying the Assessment Process to a Public Relations Degree Program: A
    Curriculum-Based Assessment Approach to Program Outcomes." Thomas R. Flynn,
    Slippery Rock University
"New Assessment Strategies and Tools." Dean A. Kruckeberg, University of Northern Iowa

---

2146   8:00-9:15 a.m.   McCormick Board Rm   Fourth Floor   Chicago Hilton

DELTA SIGMA RHO - TAU KAPPA ALPHA BUSINESS MEETING

Sponsor: Delta Sigma Rho-Tau Kappa Alpha

2149   8:00-9:15 a.m.   Conf 5B   Fifth Floor   Chicago Hilton

PEDAGOGICAL CONCERNS IN THE BASIC COURSE

Sponsor: Basic Course Division
Chair: Karla J. Huffman, Illinois State University
    "Organizing the Basic Communication Course—Critical Dialogue, Performance and
        Identity: A Review of Literature." Cathy Glenn, San Francisco State University
    "Count Time: Teaching the Basic Course in a Correctional Environment." Clark W. Friesen,
        Lee College
    "New Approaches: The Basic Course as Part of an Integrated First Year Program." Cary W.
        Horvath, Westminster College
    "Analyzing C-Span in the Basic Communication Course." James A. Schnell, Ohio
        Dominican College

Respondent: Jacquelyn J. Buckrop, Ball State University

2151   8:00-9:15 a.m.   Conf 5D   Fifth Floor   Chicago Hilton

CASTING A WIDE TEACHING NET: SPANNING THE DISCIPLINE WITH JUDY
C. PEARSON

Sponsor: Teachers on Teaching
Chair: Richard L. West, University of Southern Maine

Panelists: Richard L. West, University of Southern Maine
            Judy C. Pearson, Virginia Tech University

As a teacher who has dedicated her career to teaching in such diverse areas of the discipline
as gender communication, communication theory, family communication, and
communication education, Professor Pearson's commitment to excellence in teaching
resonates throughout the country. She has touched literally thousands of students by engaging
them with her broad-based knowledge of the field, her humor, and her commitment to
underprivileged populations.

2152   8:00-9:15 a.m.   Conf 5E   Fifth Floor   Chicago Hilton

COLORING OUTSIDE THE LINES: INTERDISCIPLINARY PERSPECTIVES ON
NARRATIVE AS RHETORIC

Sponsor: Rhetorical and Communication Theory Division
Chair: Edward Schiappa, University of Minnesota, Twin Cities
    "The Teller and the Tale: Ethos and the Implied Author in the Economic Narratives of
        Adam Smith." Paul Turpin, University of Southern California
    "A Narrative Criticism of The Apostle." David A. Thomas, University of Richmond, James
        W. Fuller, Jr., University of Richmond
    "Neurocognitive Studies, Narratives, and Reflections of Action." Charles Bazerman,
        University of California, Santa Barbara
    "As It Really Was: Memoir and Science." Deirdre N. McCloskey, University of Iowa

---

2153   8:00-9:15 a.m.   Conf 5F   Fifth Floor   Chicago Hilton

THE IMPEACHMENT CONTROVERSY: ARGUING OUTSIDE THE LINES

Sponsor: American Forensic Association
Chair: Margaret D. Zulick, Wake Forest University
   "Political Communication Outside the Lines: Arguing the Impeachment Controversy."
   Allan Louden, Wake Forest University
   "Folklore Outside the Lines: Arguing the Impeachment Controversy." Andrew W. Leslie,
   Wake Forest University
   "Rhetoric Outside the Lines: Arguing the Impeachment Controversy." Margaret D. Zulick,
   Wake Forest University
   "Ethics Outside the Lines: Arguing the Impeachment Controversy." Michael J. Hyde, Wake
   Forest University
   "History Outside the Lines: Arguing the Impeachment Controversy." Thomas Kane,
   University of Pittsburgh

2154   8:00-9:15 a.m.   Conf 5G   Fifth Floor   Chicago Hilton

LOOKING AT IMMEDIACY FROM A DIFFERENT PERSPECTIVE

Sponsor: Instructional Development Division
Chair: Danette E. Ifert, West Virginia Wesleyan College
   "Variations in Learning, Motivation, and Perceived Immediacy Between Live and Distance
   Education Classrooms." Lori J. Carrell, University of Wisconsin, Oshkosh, Kent E.
   Menzel, DePauw University
   "Training Teachers to Use Verbal Immediacy." Karla K. Jensen, Texas Tech University
   "Immediacy in the Classroom: Effects of Student Behaviors." Doreen K. Baringer,
   University of Oklahoma, James C. McCroskey, West Virginia University

Respondent: Danette E. Ifert, West Virginia Wesleyan College

2155   8:00-9:15 a.m.   Conf 5H   Fifth Floor   Chicago Hilton

TOP FOUR PAPERS IN LESBIAN/GAY COMMUNICATION STUDIES

Sponsor: Gay/Lesbian Transgender Communication Studies Division
Chair: Ralph R. Smith, Southwest Missouri State University
   "The Rhetoric of Identity: A Queer Aesthetic." Davin A. Grindstaff, Penn State University
   "Coming out of the Closets: *Ellen* and the Emergence of Gay Characters on Network TV."
   Michael S. Warren, Northeastern Illinois University
   "Between Law and Love: Politics, Christianity, and Sexual Citizenship." William J. Earnest,
   University of Texas, Austin
   "Gay Men and Lesbian Readings of Popular Culture: Searching [to] Out the Subtext." Mark
   Lipton, New York University

Respondent: Edward M. Alwood, University of North Carolina, Chapel Hill

---

2156   8:00-9:15 a.m.   Conf 5I   Fifth Floor   Chicago Hilton

THE 'HEART' OF INTRAPERSONAL COMMUNICATION RESEARCH: THE PROCESSING AND EXPRESSING OF EMOTION

Sponsor: Intrapersonal Communication/Social Cognition Commission
Chair: Gina C. Wesley, University of Wisconsin, Oshkosh
   "The Effect of Emotion on Persuasive Message Processing: The Contingent Tendency
   Model." Kristen B. Leslie, University of Illinois, Urbana-Champaign
   "The Heart of the Matter: Introducing Emotion into Action Assembly Theory." Matthew B.
   Sprinkle, Texas A&M University
   "Support Provider Mood and Familiar versus Unfamiliar Events: An Investigation of Social
   Support Quality." Nichole L. Egbert, University of Georgia
   "The Role of Nonconscious Affect in Perception." Claude H. Miller, University of Arizona

Friday

"The Relationship Between Attachment Style and Efficacy: The Use of Fear and Danger Control in the Threat of Relationship Dissolution." Jenny Moon Sung, University of Hawaii, Manoa, Krystyna S. Aune, University of Hawaii, Manoa

Respondent: Susanne Jones, Arizona State University

2157	8:00-9:15 a.m.	Conf 5J	Fifth Floor	Chicago Hilton

CONTEMPORARY RHETORICAL ANALYSIS: ARE CONSERVATIVE THEORISTS BEING MARGINALIZED?

Sponsors: Emeritus/Retired Members Section
          Rhetorical and Communication Theory Division
Chair: Gerald H. Sanders, Miami University, Ohio
"Killing the Public: Contradictions in the Rhetorical Scholarship of the Abortion Controversy." James A. Aune, Texas A&M University
"The Death of Argument from Principle: A Neo-Weaverian History." Ronald F. Reid, University of Massachusetts
"The Rhetorical Paradigm in Psychiatric History: Thomas Szasz and the Myth of Mental Illness." Richard E. Vatz, Towson University, Lee S. Weinberg, University of Pittsburgh

Respondent: Robert D. Kully, California State University, Los Angeles

2158	8:00-10:45 a.m.	Lake Ontario	Eighth Floor	Chicago Hilton

SHORT COURSE #9. ORAL COMMUNICATION ACROSS THE CURRICULUM: DESIGNING, IMPLEMENTING, AND ASSESSING A UNIVERSITY-WIDE PROGRAM

Sponsor: Short Courses

Instructors: Michael W. Cronin, Radford University
             George L. Grice, Radford University

Fee required. See complete Short Course descriptions elsewhere in the program.

2159	8:00-10:45 a.m.	Lake Michigan	Eighth Floor	Chicago Hilton

SHORT COURSE #10. ACTIVITY-BASED LEARNING IN THE SMALL GROUP COMMUNICATION CLASSROOM

Sponsor: Short Courses

Instructors: David R. Neumann, Rochester Institute of Technology
             Keith B. Jenkins, Rochester Institute of Technology

Fee required. See complete Short Course descriptions elsewhere in the program.

2160	8:00-10:45 a.m.	Lake Huron	Eighth Floor	Chicago Hilton

SHORT COURSE #11. DIRECTING THE COMMUNICATION INTERNSHIP PROGRAM

Sponsor: Short Courses

Instructors: Karen M. Roloff, DePaul University
             Eldra Rodriguez-Gilman, CBS News

Fee required. See complete Short Course descriptions elsewhere in the program.

2161	8:00-10:45 a.m.	Lake Erie	Eighth Floor	Chicago Hilton

SHORT COURSE #12. RESEARCH PROTOCOLS FOR USENET APPLICATIONS

Sponsor: Short Courses

Instructors: G. Jon Hall, University of Northern Iowa

Shing-Ling S. Chen, University of Northern Iowa

Fee required. See complete Short Course descriptions elsewhere in the program.

2162   8:00-9:15 a.m.   Essex Court   Second Floor   Essex Inn

NURTURING SPIRITUAL GROWTH THROUGH COMMUNICATION COURSEWORK

Sponsor: Religious Communication Association
Chair: Debra-Lynn Sequeira, Seattle Pacific University

Panelists: Deborah S. Dunn, Westmont College
Diane F. Witmer, California State University, Fullerton
Kevin Kersten, Boston College
Ann Marie Barry, Boston College
Lyall Crawford, Weber State University
John A. Campbell, University of Memphis

This panel will discuss ways we promote spiritual growth in our students through our communication coursework. The panelists, from both public and private universities, from Eastern and Western religious traditions, will examine issues of spiritual and personal growth raised by the content and context of interpersonal, organizational, rhetoric, and communication theory courses.

2163   8:00-9:15 a.m.   Windsor Court   Second Floor   Essex Inn

BODY, MIND, AND THEORY: AUTOETHNOGRAPHIC ACCOUNTS OF STIGMA

Sponsor: Ethnography Division
Chair: Patricia Geist, San Diego State University
"Looking Different: Negotiating the Minor Bodily Stigma of Crossed Eyes." Joan A. George, University of South Florida
"One Hundred Pounds in a Size Four Dress: An Autoethnographic Account of Stigma and Weight Consciousness." Elena C. Strauman, University of South Florida
"What's Wrong With Her?: The Stigmatizing Effects of an Invisible Stigma." Melissa J. Frame, University of South Florida
"Mirroring Identities: Facing and Reflecting the Duplicity of Abuse." Maggie Z. Miller, San Diego State University
"Voices in My Head: Living With the Stigmas of Impairment and Disfigurement." Laura L. Ellingson, University of South Florida

Respondent: Patricia Geist, San Diego State University

2164   8:00-9:15 a.m.   Buckingham Court   Second Floor   Essex Inn

MEMORIALIZING THE PAST—GUIDANCE FOR THE FUTURE

Sponsor: American Studies Commission
Chair: David Descutner, Ohio University
"The Cross By the Side of the Road: The Rhetoric of Place, Warning, and Mourning in Roadside Memorials." Celeste C. Lacroix, Ohio University
"The Full Circle of Time: A University and Community's Struggle with Tragedy and Commemoration." Becky A. McDonald, Ball State University
"Bearing Witness to the Holocaust: Remembering the Unbelievable, Articulating the Incomprehensible." Beth A. Messner, Ball State University
"Remember Jimmy: A Small Town Memorializes James Dean." Laura L. Shue, Ball State University

Respondent: David Descutner, Ohio University

Friday

2165   8:00-9:15 a.m.   Park East Walk   Second Floor   Essex Inn

COLORING OUTSIDE THE LINES OF CRITICISM: BURKE AND POPULAR CULTURE

Sponsor: Kenneth Burke Society, NCA Branch
Chair: Phyllis M. Japp, University of Nebraska, Lincoln
   "Identifying Cashiers and Customers: Comic Framing and the FDA ID Campaign." Thomas
      A. Workman, University of Nebraska, Lincoln
   "Professional Basketball and Mediated Discourse: A Burkean Analysis of the WNBA." Jean
      M. Dufresne, University of Nebraska, Lincoln
   "Political Cartoons and Impeachment: A Comic Transformation of the Clinton
      Impeachment." Timothy A. Borchers, Moorhead State University
   "Visual Art and Coping with Breast Cancer: A Burkean Analysis." Susanne L. Williams,
      Moorhead State University

2166   8:00-9:15 a.m.   Cohn Rm   Second Floor   Spertus Institute

THE INTERPLAY OF AUTHORIZATION AND LEGITIMACY IN THE RHETORIC OF SCIENCE

Sponsor: American Association for Rhetoric of Science & Technology
Chair: Dale L. Sullivan, Michigan Technological University
   "Taking Advantage of Authorized Speech to Build Legitimacy: An Analysis of David M.
      Raup's Presidential Address to the Paleontological Society, 1977." Harrison Carpenter,
      Michigan Technological University
   "The Prospects and Problems of Authorized Discourse: The Case of Gifford Pinchot and
      The Foresters." Margaret L. FalerSweany, Michigan Technological University
   "Constraints and Authority in Public Policy Hearings." Dale L. Sullivan, Michigan
      Technological University

2167   8:00-9:15 a.m.   Krensky Rm   Second Floor   Spertus Institute

BRIDGING BOTH WORLDS: ETHICAL, METHODOLOGICAL, AND PRACTICAL CONSIDERATIONS FOR ACADEMICS AND PROFESSIONAL LEGAL CONSULTANTS

Sponsor: Communication and Law Commission
Chair: David G. Levasseur, West Chester University

Panelists: Teresa M. Rosado, Zagnoli McEvoy Foley Ltd.
            Debra L. Worthington, University of Central Arkansas
            Samuel R. Tepper, Northwestern University
            David G. Levasseur, West Chester University
            Merrie Jo Stallard, Center for Trial Insights
            Shelley C. Spiecker, Tsongas & Associates

This panel explores issues that affect academics and professional consultants engaging in
individual or joint research projects in courtroom communication. Panelists will present "case
studies" of their experiences on recent research projects.

2168   8:00-9:15 a.m.   Rm 902   Ninth Floor   Spertus Institute

WESTERN AND CHINESE WAY OF COMMUNICATION: DIFFERENCES AND SIMILARITIES

Sponsor: Chinese Communication Association
Chair: D. Ray Heisey, Kent State University
   "An Analysis of Differences and Similarities Between Western and Chinese Theoretical
      Principles in Organizational Communication." Qingwen Dong, University of the Pacific,
      Stockton, Kenneth D. Day, University of the Pacific, Stockton

"Chinese Dialogue and Western Complexity: The Intersection of Ancient and Modern Paradigms in Educational Reform." Scott C. Hammond, Brigham Young University, Gao Hongmei, Brigham Young University
"Explore the Interaction Zone: The Reading of Advertising by the Chinese Audience." Zhihong Gao, University of Illinois, Urbana-Champaign

Respondents: Jensen Chung, San Francisco State University
          Wenjie Yan, East Stroudsburg University

2169   8:00-9:15 a.m.   Rm 903   Ninth Floor   Spertus Institute

AN EXPLORATION OF THE INSTRUCTOR'S ROLE IN DEVELOPING STUDENTS' MULTICULTURALISM THROUGH EXPERIENTIAL ACTIVITIES

Sponsor: Experiential Learning in Communication Commission
Chair: Michael E. Balmert, Carlow College
    "'When the Diversity Is You': An Indian Instructor's Approach to Teaching Diversity in the Introductory Communication Course." Devika Chawla, Central Michigan University
    "Sexual Orientation as a Resource for Teaching Diversity." Andy Bonin, Michigan University
    "Race as a Resource for Increasing Multicultural Understanding." Derrick Rosenoir, Central Michigan University
    "'White Females Can Teach Diversity, Too!': A Perspective from a Caucasian Female Instructor." Cindy Moore, Central Michigan University

Respondent: Shelly Hinck, Central Michigan University

2170   8:00-9:15 a.m.   Rm 904   Ninth Floor   Spertus Institute

RE-SEARCHING THE INTERNET: A MULTI-PERSPECTIVE REVIEW OF INTERNET COMMUNICATION IN CHINA

Sponsor: Association for Chinese Communication Studies
Chair: Ringo Ma, SUNY, Fredonia
    "Internet Communication and Interconnectivity: A Comparative Study of Cyberpractice in China and USA." Jinguo Shen, Richard Stockton College of New Jersey
    "Visions of Internet in Education: A Comparative Study of Educational Function of Internet in Canada and China." Dejun Liu, University College of Cape Breton, Canada
    "An Exploration of Internet Use in a Provincial Government Department: A Case Study on the Development of China's Internet Infrastructure." Jin Jianbin, Hong Kong Baptist University
    "Scapegoating Pornography: Issues of Regulation in Chinese Internet Communication." Changfu Chang, Purdue University

Respondent: Yanmin Yu, University of Bridgeport

2171   8:00-9:15 a.m.   Rm 906   Ninth Floor   Spertus Institute

CONTEMPORARY PEDAGOGY FOR CLASSICAL RHETORIC

Sponsor: American Society for the History of Rhetoric
Chair: Jane Sutton, Penn State University, York
    "Averting the Reductionism of Classical Oppositions." David M. Timmerman, Wabash College
    "What's in a Curriculum?: Exploring the Logon Techne and the 'Problem' of Pre-Disciplinarity." Davis W. Houck, Florida Atlantic University
    "Transgressing Teleologies in Teaching Classical Rhetoric." Mari Lee Mifsud, University of Richmond

Respondents: John Poulakos, University of Pittsburgh
          Takis Poulakos, University of Iowa

Friday

2172   8:00-9:15 a.m.   Rm 907   Ninth Floor   Spertus Institute

FOOLISH CONSISTENCIES: THE ROLE AND FUNCTION OF
CONTRADICTION IN ARGUMENT

Sponsor: Cross Examination Debate Association
Chair: David L. Steinberg, University of Miami
   "Muting the Subaltern Voice: Polarity, Performative Contradiction and the Postmodern
      Critic." Kristina L. Schriver, California State University, Chico
   "A Brechtian Affirmation: A Case for a Self-Critical Approach to Advocacy." Kenneth T.
      Broda-Bahm, Towson University
   "Framing Consistency: Building Argumentative Rationales for Departures from
      Conventional Entailments." Stephen C. Koch, Capital University
   "Consideration or Contradiction? The Role of Argument Salience in Opinion Formation."
      Todd C. Trautman, University of Illinois, Urbana-Champaign

---

2173   8:00-9:15 a.m.   Rm 908   Ninth Floor   Spertus Institute

IS OUR VISION CLEAR?: PERCEPTIONS OF THE LINES BETWEEN TWO-YEAR
AND FOUR-YEAR COLLEGE FORENSICS PROGRAMS

Sponsor: Phi Rho Pi
Chair: Cynthia E. Dewar, City College of San Francisco
   "Where They See the Lines: Perceptions of Two-Year Programs Held by Two- and Four-Year
      Forensics Students." Lori A. Polacheck, Itawamba Community College
   "The Event Lines in Two-Year and Four-Year Forensics Circuits: Student Perceptions." Jody
      Rice, Southeastern Illinois College, Gary Allen, Southeastern Illinois College, Mark Lucus,
      Southeastern Illinois College, Jack Mummert, Southeastern Illinois College
   "Where We See the Lines: Perceptions of Two-Year Programs Held by Two- and Four-Year
      Forensics Coaches." Christina L. Moss, Young Harris College
   "Both Sides Now: Perceptions From a Coach to Two- and Four-Year Programs." Gary C.
      Dreibelbis, Solano College
   "Distinction? What Distinction: How One Region Erased the Lines Between Two- and
      Four-Year Programs." M'Liss Hindman, Tyler Junior College

Respondent: Randolph Richardson, Berry College

2174   8:00-9:15 a.m.   Auditorium   Second Floor   Spertus Institute

WHERE DO WE GO FROM HERE?: A CRITICAL LOOK AT MENTORING,
MEMBERSHIP AND MISSION OF THE NCA THEATRE DIVISION

Sponsor: Theatre Division
Chair: Julie R. Patterson-Pratt, University of Minnesota, Morris

Panelists: Deryl B. Johnson, Kutztown University
           Sharon Ammen, St. Mary of the Woods College
           Michele A. Pagen, California University of Pennsylvania
           James M. Brandon, Hillsdale College
           Barbara Parisi, Long Island University, Brooklyn
           Gail S. Medford, Bowie State University
           Douglas L. Caskey, Goshen College
           Patti P. Gillespie, University of Maryland
           Ronald E. Shields, Bowling Green State University
           Gerald Lee Ratliff, SUNY, Potsdam
           Marilyn A. Hetzel, Metropolitan State College of Denver
           Renee Vincent, University of North Carolina, Wilmington
           John C. Countryman, Berry College
           Thomas E. Ruddick, Edison Community College
           Laura Facciponti, University of North Carolina, Asheville
           Monica F. Anderson, Franciscan University

This open forum discussion will continue to address the concerns, the needs and the diversification of the Theatre Division. We will share our successes and move forward with sound ideas on how we can best serve our membership and the discipline of theatre in general. Audience participation is greatly encouraged.

2178   8:00-9:15 a.m.   **Conrad Suite   Chicago Hilton**

NCA COUNCIL ON PH.D. PROGRAMS BUSINESS MEETING

Sponsor: Council on Ph.D. Programs

9:30 a.m.

2206   9:30-10:45 a.m.   **Continental BR A   Lobby Level   Chicago Hilton**

COMPETITIVE PAPERS IN EXPLORATIONS OF USES AND EFFECTS OF THE INTERNET

Sponsor: Mass Communication Division
Chair: Rebecca A. Carrier, California State Polytechnic University, Pomona
   "How Others Are Affected by the Internet: The Role of Reference Group Size in the
      Third-Person Effect*." David Tewksbury, University of Illinois, Urbana-Champaign
   "To Do Is to Empower: Relationships Between Experience with Networked Computing,
      Efficacy, and Attitudes Toward Life On-Line." Thomas A. McCain, Ohio State University,
      Scott B. Morris, Ohio State University, Cable T. Green, Ohio State University, Talal
      Al-Najran, Kuwait University
   "Gratifications Sought and Obtained by Male College Students' Use of Internet
      Pornography." Rick A. Buerkel, Central Michigan University, Nancy Buerkel-Rothfuss,
      Central Michigan University
   "Internet Pornography: Cultivation Analysis and the New Technologies." Nancy
      Buerkel-Rothfuss, Central Michigan University, Rick A. Buerkel, Central Michigan
      University

Respondent: James R. Walker, Saint Xavier University

*Top 3 Competitive Paper

2207   9:30-10:45 a.m.   **Continental BR B   Lobby Level   Chicago Hilton**

RETHINKING VIRTUAL COMMUNICATION

Sponsor: Human Communication and Technology Commission
Chair: Clark Germann, Metropolitan State College of Denver
   "New Aspects in Channel Choice: The Influence of Communication Avoidance and
      Avoidance Intentions." Volker Frank, University of Texas, Austin
   "Virtual Reality as a New Communication Medium: Moving to Meet Unfulfilled
      Expectations." Clark Germann, Metropolitan State College of Denver
   "The Technical Code of the Internet/WWW." Andrew J. Flanagin, University of California,
      Santa Barbara, Wendy Jo Maynard Farinola, University of California, Santa Barbara
   "You Know the Virtual Honeymoon is Over When. . .." Craig R. Scott, University of Texas,
      Austin, C. Erik Timmerman, University of Texas, Austin, Diana M. Sage, University of
      Texas, Austin, Laura Quinn, University of Texas, Austin
   "Rethinking Virtual Reality: Simulation and the Deconstruction of the Image." David J.
      Gunkel, Northern Illinois University

Respondent: Karen L. Lollar, University of Denver

2208   9:30-10:45 a.m.   **Continental BR C   Lobby Level   Chicago Hilton**

CAPITAL FLOWS AND CULTURAL ANTAGONISMS: GLOBALIZATION AND ITS DISCONTENTS

Sponsor: Critical and Cultural Studies Division

Friday

Chair: Dilip P. Gaonkar, Northwestern University
  "The Planner's Dream Undone: Think Tanks and Neoliberal Economic Orthodoxy." Amos
    A. Tevelow, University of Pittsburgh
  "You Say Global, I Say Cabal: Conspiracy Theories and Articulation of Contexts." Jack
    Bratich, University of Illinois, Urbana-Champaign
  "It Will Not Soil Your Breakfast Cloth: *The New York Times* and NAFTA." Brian Gross,
    University of Illinois
  "Globalony and Labor: Labor's Corporate Campaign Strategy During the Staley Lockout."
    Deepa Kumar, University of Pittsburgh

Respondent: Dilip P. Gaonkar, Northwestern University

2201	9:30-4:45 p.m.	Northwest Exhibit Hall	Lower Level	Chicago Hilton

NCA POSTER SESSION

Sponsor: Poster Session
  1. "Service Learning Projects Imbedded in a Public Relations Curriculum." Noreen M.
     Schaefer-Faix, Defiance College
  2. "Teaching Issues Management in the Introductory Public Relations Course." Debra A.
     Kernisky, Northern Michigan University
  3. "Teaching Research Methods: Strategic Public Communication Campaign Design."
     Cornelius B. Tyson, Central Connecticut State University
  4. "The First Day of Public Relations Writing Lab: How NOT to Write a News Release."
     Jeffrey L. Courtright, University of North Dakota
  5. "Incorporating Global/Multicultural Perspectives in PR Education: Exploring Pedagogical
     Strategies." Nilanjana Bardhan, Southern Illinois University, Carbondale
  6. "Using Cases and Case Analysis in Public Relations Education." Dan P. Millar, Indiana
     State University
  7. "Internet Explorations: Online Assignments for the Introductory Public Relations
     Course." Michael F. Smith, La Salle University
  8. "Getting the Message Out." Diane M. Harney, Pacific Lutheran University
  9. "Understanding College Students' Sex Risk Perception: A Health Communication
     Perspective." John R. Chapin, Penn State University, Beaver
  10. "Sexual Harassment: Case Law and its Influence on Sexual Harassment Policies." M.
      Carla Schenone-Stevens, St. Ambrose University
  11. "Perceived Instructor Affinity-Seeking and Student Learning in the Chinese College
      Classroom." Scott A. Myers, Creighton University, Mei Zhong, San Diego State
      University
  12. "'Body Slamming' the Two Party System: An Analysis of Jesse Ventura and the 1998
      Minnesota Gubernatorial Debates." Ann Marie Mongeau, Minnesota State University
  13. "Assessing the Strategies and Effectiveness of Guerrilla Media Campaigns: An Applied
      Speech and Effectiveness Analysis." Frederick W. Isaacson, San Francisco State
      University
  14. "Computer-Mediated Communication and Communication-Related Anxieties:
      Predictors of Computer Use." Tania K. Gojdycz, West Virginia University, Brian R.
      Patterson, West Virginia University
  15. "Navajo Communication: Changing Patterns and Contemporary Realities." Robert A.
      Barraclough, West Virginia University
  16. "Adolescent Perceptions of Sexual Abstinence Compliance-Gaining Strategies Used by
      Parents and Teachers." Michael C. Germano, West Virginia University, Theodore A.
      Avtgis, St. John's University, Christine Adamko, West Virginia University
  17. "Arousal Styles During Public Speaking." Maili Porhola, University of Jyvaskyla, Finland
  18. "Interethnic Communication Apprehension and Relational Maintenance Strategy
      Usage." Mary C. Toale, West Virginia University
  19. "Crossing the Color Lines: Regional Approaches and Activities in the Communication
      Classroom." Nanette Potee, Northeastern Illinois University, Patricia J. English,
      Southern Illinois University, Janet M. Hoffmann, Mercer University, David W. Worley,
      Indiana State University
  20. "How Individuals Strategize to Dissolve Romantic Relationships: An Analysis Using
      McCraken's Long Interview." James C. Roux, Horry-Georgetown Technical College

21. "Connecting the Dots: Linking Research and Community Needs." Barbara J. Kappler, University of Minnesota
22. "The Future of CMC Pedagogy: Courses, Concepts, and Texts." Norman E. Clark, Appalachian State University
23. "Sound Arguments: Rock Music and the Construction of Authenticity, Taste, and Value." Theodore Matula, California State University, Monterey Bay
24. "Transformational Leadership, Follower Self-Esteem, Communication Satisfaction and Circles of Influence." Christine E. Trinastich, University of Texas, Austin
25. "Confessions and Consumer Desires: Visualizing Women's Place in Modernity." Roseann M. Mandziuk, Southwest Texas State University
26. "Pedagogies of 'Empowerment': Critical Alternatives for Teaching Public Speaking." Wade S. Davis, University of Iowa, Thomas Burkhart, University of Iowa, Kathryn A. Cady, University of Iowa, Julie E. Ferris, University of Iowa, Kyra L. Pearson, University of Iowa, Christopher J. Skiles, University of Iowa
27. "The Violence Cycle of Victimage and Shame: A Rhetorical Criticism of *Cops*." Tracy L. Murphy, Minnesota State University, Mankato
28. "Downward Communication: Its Affect on Subordinate Perceptions and Organizational Climate." Tony Boehler, Minnesota State University, Mankato
29. "Vernacular Discourse: A Localized Community in Dialogue with Mainstream Culture." Jolane Flanigan, University of Montana, Missoula
30. "Work/Text: A New Approach to Mass Communication." Cynthia W. Walker, Rutgers University

---

2211   9:30-10:45 a.m.   Int'l Ballroom North   Second Floor   Chicago Hilton

OPEN WORKSHOP WITH HOLLY HUGHES

Sponsor: Performance Studies Division
Chair: Jules A. Odendahl, University of North Carolina, Chapel Hill

Panelist: Holly Hughes, Performance Artist, New York City

Holly Hughes, premiere performance artist, political activist (infamous member of the "NEA 4"), and Obie award-winning writer, will lead improvisational, movement and writing exercises.

2214   9:30-10:45 a.m.   Boulevard A   Second Floor   Chicago Hilton

RICHARD E. VATZ ON RHETORIC AND PSYCHIATRY

Sponsor: Challenging Boundaries Series
Chair: Mark H. Wright, Embry-Riddle University
  "Rhetoric and Psychiatry." Richard E. Vatz, Towson University

---

2215   9:30-10:45 a.m.   Boulevard B   Second Floor   Chicago Hilton

ALTERNATIVE PRACTICES IN GROUP COMMUNICATION PEDAGOGY

Sponsor: Group Communication Division
Chair: Carole A. Barbato, Kent State University, East Liverpool
  "Contextualizing the Teaching Moment in Group Communication." Joann Keyton, University of Memphis
  "Small Group Pedagogy and Community Organizational Needs: A Marriage That Works." Carolyn M. Anderson, University of Akron
  "Apprehending the Proverbial Elephant: A Dialectical, Developmental Perspective for Understanding Group Communication." Lawrence R. Frey, University of Memphis
  "Meeting Group Communication Students' Needs for Learning and Application: Challenges Presented by Students with Busy Agendas." Bruce L. Riddle, Kent State University

| 2216 | 9:30-10:45 a.m. | Boulevard C | Second Floor | Chicago Hilton |

INTERCULTURAL COMMUNICATION IN THREE ORGANIZATIONAL CONTEXTS

Sponsor: International & Intercultural Communication Division
Chair: Timothy A. Simpson, Ohio University
  "Place, Non-Place, and Communication in Thailand." Timothy A. Simpson, Ohio
    University
  "What Causes Conflict in Multinational Organizations? Do Cultural Differences Matter?"
    Kumiko Tsutsui, University of Texas, Austin
  "Communication in Thai Employment Interview: Process, Structure, and Foci of
    Talk/Discussion." Nongluck Sriussadaporn-Charoenngam, Chulalongkorn University,
    Thailand

Respondent: Samuel M. Edelman, California State University, Chico

| 2218 | 9:30-10:45 a.m. | Waldorf | Third Floor | Chicago Hilton |

MULTIPLE PERSPECTIVES ON PARENTAL INFLUENCES IN THE FAMILY

Sponsor: Family Communication Division
Chair: Rebecca L. Mikesell, University of Scranton
  "The Communication of Parental Favoritism." Anne E. Lucchetti, North Carolina State
    University
  "Individual and Relationship-Specific Tension and Young Adult Decisions to Seek Advice
    from Parents." Rhonda J. Sprague, University of Wisconsin, Stevens Point
  "Gender and Sports: Parents' Influence on Their Children's Perceptions of Sports." Karla K.
    Jensen, Texas Tech University, Mary Kate Leonard, Texas Tech University
  "Presence, Absence, or Something In-Between: An Explication of the Construct Father
    Involvement." Jennifer M. Heisler, Michigan State University

Respondent: Thomas J. Socha, Old Dominion University

| 2219 | 9:30-10:45 a.m. | Astoria | Third Floor | Chicago Hilton |

TOP DEBUT PAPERS IN PUBLIC ADDRESS

Sponsor: Public Address Division
Chair: Anne T. Demo, Vanderbilt University
  "Gender Myths and Media Coverage of Hillary Rodham Clinton's Involvement with Health
    Care: What *Is* Woman's Proper Place?" Christina R. Foust, University of Nebraska,
    Lincoln
  "The Taft-Hartley Act in a Global Rhetorical Conjecture." Jayson Harsin, Northwestern
    University
  "The Rhetoric of Contrition and Bill Clinton: Denial and Responsibility in Presidential
    Discourse." Matthew H. Barton, University of Nebraska, Lincoln
  "Whitefield as Rhetorician: A Textual Analysis of Whitefield's 'Marriage of Cana'." Jerome
    D. Mahaffey, University of Memphis

Respondent: Robert E. Terrill, Indiana University

| 2221 | 9:30-10:45 a.m. | Williford A | Third Floor | Chicago Hilton |

AFRICAN AMERICAN RHETORIC COLORING OUTSIDE NATIONAL LINES

Sponsor: African American Communication & Culture Commission
Chair: Andrew Ann Lee, Albany State University
  "Early Roots of Black Nationalism: The Rhetorical Transformation of the Black Subject."
    Dexter B. Gordon, University of Alabama
  "Edward Wilmot Blyden: Black Nationalism and the Rhetoric of Contradiction." Stephen
    A. King, Delta State University

"Minister Louis Farrakhan and Spike Lee as Contemporary Prophets: An Analysis of Their Rhetoric in Consideration of Prophetic Strategies." Charmetra Chatmon, Biola University
"'Sick and Tired of Being Sick and Tired': The Rhetoric of Civil Rights Leader Fannie Lou Hamer." Shauntae R. Brown-White, University of Kansas

Respondent: Thurmon Garner, University of Georgia

2222	**9:30-10:45 a.m.**	**Williford B**	**Third Floor**	**Chicago Hilton**

COOPERATIVE RESEARCH ON THE 2000 ELECTIONS: FORMING TEAMS TO MAXIMIZE POLITICAL COMMUNICATION INQUIRY

Sponsor: Political Communication Division

Panelists: Lynda Lee Kaid, University of Oklahoma
Dianne G. Bystrom, Iowa State University
John C. Tedesco, Virginia Tech University

With the 2000 elections approaching, researchers in political communication have expressed a desire to work together in research teams as a way of maximizing the financial resources they have, as well as to find ways to enhance generalization of results and coordinate similar studies in different locations. Interested political communication researchers are invited to attend this session to discuss the possibilities of working with other colleagues on 2000 election projects. Researchers working with any theoretical or methodological approach are welcome.

2223	**9:30-10:45 a.m.**	**Williford C**	**Third Floor**	**Chicago Hilton**

RE-TURNING THE GAZE: FEMINIST READINGS OF CINEMA

Sponsor: Feminist and Women Studies Division
Chair: Dreama G. Moon, California State University, San Marcos
"Framing the Feminine: Diasporic Readings of Gender in Indian Cinema*." Anjali Ram, Clark University
"Women as Touchtone: Relationships Built Around Women." Amy E. Capwell-Burns, Bowling Green State University
"The Other Mother: Revenge of the Female Fetish in Indian Cinema." Ishita Sinha Roy, University of Southern California
"Bucking Authority: The Dynamics of Sexual Relations in Films." Danette M. Watt, Southern Illinois University, Edwardsville

Respondent: Linda C. Steiner, Rutgers University

*Top Paper

2224	**9:30-10:45 a.m.**	**Marquette**	**Third Floor**	**Chicago Hilton**

ORGANIZATIONAL COMMUNICATION DIVISION BUSINESS MEETING

Sponsor: Organizational Communication Division

2226	**9:30-10:45 a.m.**	**PDR 1**	**Third Floor**	**Chicago Hilton**

INSTRUCTIONAL DEVELOPMENT DIVISION EXECUTIVE BOARD MEETING

Sponsor: Instructional Development Division

2227	**9:30-10:45 a.m.**	**PDR 2**	**Third Floor**	**Chicago Hilton**

LA RAZA CAUCUS AND LATINA/LATINO COMMUNICATION STUDIES DIVISION EXECUTIVE OFFICERS MEETING

Sponsors: La Raza Caucus
Latina/Latino Communication Studies Division

Friday

| 2228 | 9:30-10:45 a.m. | PDR 3 | Third Floor | Chicago Hilton |

APPLIED COMMUNICATION MOVES TO THE WEB: REPORTS FROM REGIONAL COMMUNICATION ASSOCIATION WEBMASTERS

Sponsor: Applied Communication Division
Chair: Kevin T. Wright, University of Oklahoma
  "The Evolution of a Web Site: Issues Involved in Changing a Web Site and Web Site Manager." Lawrence A. Hosman, University of Southern Mississippi
  "Options for Housing a Web Site: Domain Names Versus Directories." Lyle J. Flint, Ball State University
  "My Web Site and Billions & Billions of Dollars." John A. Cagle, California State University, Fresno
  "A Regional Web Site in Search of an Identity." Paul E. Scovell, Salisbury State University

| 2229 | 9:30-10:45 a.m. | PDR 4 | Third Floor | Chicago Hilton |

PHI RHO PI BUSINESS MEETING

Sponsor: Phi Rho Pi

| 2230 | 9:30-10:45 a.m. | PDR 5 | Third Floor | Chicago Hilton |

EASTERN COMMUNICATION ASSOCIATION EXECUTIVE COUNCIL MEETING

Sponsor: Eastern Communication Association

| 2231 | 9:30-10:45 a.m. | PDR 6 | Third Floor | Chicago Hilton |

ARGUMENTATION AND FORENSICS DIVISION BUSINESS MEETING

Sponsor: Argumentation and Forensics Division

| 2232 | 9:30-10:45 a.m. | PDR 7 | Third Floor | Chicago Hilton |

NATIONAL EDUCATION DEBATE ASSOCIATION BUSINESS MEETING

Sponsor: National Educational Debate Association

| 2233 | 9:30-10:45 a.m. | Conf 4A | Fourth Floor | Chicago Hilton |

TOP FOUR PAPERS IN COMMUNICATION APPREHENSION AND AVOIDANCE

Sponsor: Communication Apprehension & Avoidance Commission
Chair: Brian L. Heuett, Southern Utah University
  "An Examination of the Impact of Performance Visualization." Joe Ayres, Washington State University, Brian L. Heuett, Southern Utah University
  "Effects of the Penn State Reticence Program on Beliefs About Communication and Fear of Negative Evaluation." James A. Keaten, University of Northern Colorado, Lynne Kelly, University of Hartford, Cynthia Finch, Penn State University
  "The Multidimensional Model: Teaching Students to Self-Manage Communication Apprehension by Self-Selecting Treatments." Karen K. Dwyer, University of Nebraska, Omaha
  "Vividness and Control: Factors in the Effectiveness of Performance Visualization." Joe Ayres, Washington State University, Tim S. Hopf, Washington State University, Patricia A. Edwards, Washington State University

| 2234 | 9:30-10:45 a.m. | Conf 4B | Fourth Floor | Chicago Hilton |

AFRICAN AMERICAN COMMUNICATION AND CONFLICT: FOCUSING ON INTERSECTIONS OF RACE AND GENDER

Sponsor: Black Caucus
Chair: Mark P. Orbe, Western Michigan University
 "Coloring, Conflict, and Collaboration Within the Cuticle: A Critical Examination of Communication and Perception Between African American Women and Vietnamese Nail Technicians." Nikita Y. Harris, Howard University, Andrew Critchfield, Howard University
 "The Semiotics of 'Good Hair' and 'Bad Hair' in George C. Wolfe's 'The Colored Museum'." Teri L. Varner, University of Texas, Austin
 "Conflict Among Sister-Friends: Conceptualizations of Facework Within African American Female Friendships." Trina J. Wright, Howard University
 "'Real World' Interracial Conflict: Thematizing Perceptions Based on Race and Gender." Kiesha T. Warren, Western Michigan University, Mark P. Orbe, Western Michigan University

Respondent: Karen L. Dace, University of Utah

| 2235 | 9:30-10:45 a.m. | Conf 4C | Fourth Floor | Chicago Hilton |

COMMUNICATION THEORY AND INTERNET USE: IMPLICATIONS FOR POLICY, PRACTICE, AND RESEARCH ON THE INTERNET

Sponsor: Commission on Communication in the Future
Chair: Ron C. Tamborini, Michigan State University
 "Internet Search Behavior and Mood Alteration: A Selective Exposure Approach." Dana E. Mastro, Michigan State University, Matthew Eastin, Michigan State University
 "Anxiety and Cognitive Processing in Mediated Doctor-Patient Interactions: A Telemedicine Application." Rebecca M. Chory, Michigan State University
 "The Digital Millennium Copyright Act: A First Analysis of Copyright Law in the Electronic Age." Jay Newell, Michigan State University
 "Exploring the Impact of Message and Involvement on Banner Ad Likability Ratings." Terry Daugherty, Michigan State University

Respondent: Dean H. Krikorian, Cornell University

| 2236 | 9:30-10:45 a.m. | Conf 4D | Fourth Floor | Chicago Hilton |

TOP THREE PAPERS IN LANGUAGE AND SOCIAL INTERACTION

Sponsor: Language and Social Interaction Division
Chair: Christina S. Beck, Ohio University
 "Inviting Interplay in Panel Format News Interviews." David Olsher, University of California, Los Angeles
 "Speaking Your Piece and the *Dugri* Talk: A Cross-Cultural Comparison of Two Direct Speech Events." Sara J. Parker, SUNY, Albany
 "Negotiating Who Presents the Problem: Consequences of Selection in Pediatric Consultations." Tanya Stivers, University of California, Los Angeles

Respondent: Phillip J. Glenn, Southern Illinois University, Carbondale

| 2237 | 9:30-10:45 a.m. | Conf 4E | Fourth Floor | Chicago Hilton |

INTEGRATING COMMUNIBIOLOGICAL PERSPECTIVES INTO GRADUATE AND UNDERGRADUATE CURRICULA

Sponsor: Table Talk Series
Chair: James C. McCroskey, West Virginia University

Panelists: Michael J. Beatty, University of Missouri, St. Louis
          Patricia Kearney, California State University, Long Beach

Friday

Sherwyn P. Morreale, NCA National Office
John L. Sherry, Purdue University

Within the research community, increasing attention is being addressed to the genetic bases of human communication. Most current curricula reflect the assumptions and instructional strategies appropriate to the social learning model of communication development. This panel will encourage discussion exploring whether, and if so how, the communibiological perspective should be integrated into contemporary curricula in communication studies.

2238   9:30-10:45 a.m.   **Conf 4F   Fourth Floor   Chicago Hilton**

LEARNING OUTSIDE THE CLASSROOM LINES: EXPERIENTIAL DESIGNS FOR THE ORGANIZATIONAL COMMUNICATION CURRICULUM

Sponsor: Experiential Learning in Communication Commission
Chair: Melissa K. Gibson, Western Michigan University
    "Watch, Listen, and Learn: Organizational Analysis in the Introductory Organizational Communication Course." Matthew J. Smith, Miami University
    "If Not You, Then Who?: Lessons Learned About Service Learning in the Training and Development Course." Melissa K. Gibson, Western Michigan University, Eleanor M. Kostecki, Western Michigan University
    "Organizational Communication Assessments: Merging Teaching and Research Interests with Grant Support." Wendy Z. Ford, Western Michigan University
    "Experiential Learning in the Graduate Consulting Course: Serving the Community and Recognizing the Talent of Graduate Students." Sue DeWine, Ohio University

---

2239   9:30-10:45 a.m.   **Conf 4G   Fourth Floor   Chicago Hilton**

THE TRAINING PROCESS: COMMUNICATION ISSUES, SKILLS, AND STRATEGIES

Sponsor: Training and Development Division
    "Training Accelerators: Increasing the Trainer's and Trainee's ROI." Michael L. Fahs, California Polytechnic State University
    "Translucent Colors? Learning May be More Important Than Training." Jeffrey F. Anderson, Kennesaw State University
    "Connecting Outside the Lines: Strategies for Trainers Using Communication Styles Theory." Basma Ibrahim DeVries, Concordia University
    "Evaluate Before It Is Too Late!" Richard Linder, Berry College, William J. Wardrope, Stephen F. Austin State University

---

2240   9:30-10:45 a.m.   **Conf 4H   Fourth Floor   Chicago Hilton**

COLORING OUTSIDE THE LINES OF MEDIA RESEARCH AND PEDAGOGY: RACE, GENDER AND MEDIA IMAGES AND AUDIENCES

Sponsor: Media Forum Series
Chair: Veronica Davison, University of Pennsylvania
    "Lil' Kim and Foxy Brown: Images of Strength or Weakness?" Karen M. Bowdre, University of Southern California
    "What's Love Got to Do with the Projects?: An Analysis of The PJs." Dwight E. Brooks, University of Georgia
    "Reactions to Visual Texts in the Interracial Classroom." Tina M. Harris, University of Georgia

Respondent: Navita C. James, University of South Florida

2241   9:30-10:45 a.m.   **Conf 4I   Fourth Floor   Chicago Hilton**

TOP THREE PANEL IN PUBLIC RELATIONS

Sponsor: Public Relations Division
Chair: Rachel L. Holloway, Virginia Tech University

"Community Relations and Risk Communication: A Longitudinal Study of the Impact of Emergency Response Messages." Robert L. Heath, University of Houston, Michael J. Palenchar, University of Houston

"An Empirical Analysis of Image Restoration: Texaco's Racism Crisis." W. Timothy Coombs, Illinois State University, Jennifer Frank, Illinois State University, Geisun Kim, Illinois State University, Chante Lacour, Illinois State University, Kristy Schickel, Illinois State University, Lainen Schmidt, Illinois State University

"Public Relations Practice in Japan: Testing the Relevance of Japanese Management 'Stream' to Grunig's Excellence Theory." David R. Watson, Ketchum Public Relations, Georgia, Lynne M. Sallot, University of Georgia

Respondent: Becky A. McDonald, Ball State University

2242   9:30-10:45 a.m.   Conf 4J   Fourth Floor   Chicago Hilton

FINDING A JOB IS THE EASY PART!: YOUNG TEACHERS REFLECT ON THEIR TRANSITIONS INTO A FULL-TIME TEACHING POSITION

Sponsor: Senior College & University Section
Chair: Jessica M. Henry, St. Cloud State University
"The Perks and Perils of Being a Young Female Faculty Member in a New Job: An Analysis of Interviews with Women Faculty Members." Jessica M. Henry, St. Cloud State University

"The Transition: Moving from a Four-Year Institution to a Community College." Jeff F. Przybylo, William Rainey Harper College

"Redefining Community: From a University-Based Community to a Metropolitan University." Audra L. Colvert, Towson University

"'Toto, We're Not at the University Anymore. . .': The Phenomenological Experience of Teaching the Small, Private, Liberal Arts Student." John R. Perlich, North Central College

Respondent: Ray A. Slagle, St. Cloud State University

2243   9:30-10:45 a.m.   Conf 4K   Fourth Floor   Chicago Hilton

RELATING AT A DISTANCE: RECENT STUDIES ON LONG-DISTANCE COMMUNICATION

Sponsors: Interpersonal Communication Division
              Human Communication and Technology Commission
Chair: Emily J. Langan, Arizona State University
"Presences, Quasi-Presences, and Absences: An Investigation of Long-Distance Relational Types." Erin M. Sahlstein, University of Iowa

"Using Routine and Strategic Communication and Activities to Maintain Friendships: Examining Geographically Close and Long-Distance Friendships." Amy J. Johnson, Michigan State University

"Suspicion in Cyberspace: Deception and Detection in the Context of Internet Relay Chat Rooms." Karen M. Wolff, University of Texas, Austin

"IRC: A New Frontier For Relationships." Kevin S. Trowbridge, Union University, Valerie Howell, University of Memphis

"Distance Makes the Heart Work Harder: Relationship Maintenance in Long-Distance and Proximal Relationships." Kathryn C. Maguire, University of Texas, Austin

Respondent: John P. Caughlin, University of Nebraska, Lincoln

---

2244   9:30-10:45 a.m.   Conf 4L   Fourth Floor   Chicago Hilton

UNDERSTANDING SPIRITUAL PERSPECTIVES THROUGH METAPHOR

Sponsor: Spiritual Communication Commission
Chair: Linda M. Pledger, University of Arkansas, Little Rock
"Unifying Souls: A Metaphorical Analysis of Spirituality in the Unitarian Church." Allan L. Ward, University of Arkansas, Little Rock

Friday

"Spiritual Poems: A Metaphorical Analysis of Spirituality Among Yoga Practitioners in America as Compared to Mainstream Christianity." Carol L. Thompson, University of Arkansas, Little Rock, Michael Kleine, University of Arkansas, Little Rock
"The Uneasy Relationship Between Buddhism and New Age Spirituality: Ancient Metaphors/New Interpretations." Christy C. Standerfer, University of Colorado, Boulder
"Metaphorical Investigations into Magical Traditions." Marceline E. Thompson, University of Memphis

Respondent: Michael Kleine, University of Arkansas, Little Rock

---

2245   9:30-10:45 a.m.   Conf 4M   Fourth Floor   Chicago Hilton

DOING SPONSORED RESEARCH IN ORGANIZATIONS: THE ETHICAL AND PRACTICAL IMPLICATIONS OF COLORING OUTSIDE THE LINES

Sponsor: Organizational Communication Division
Chair: Noshir S. Contractor, University of Illinois, Urbana-Champaign
    "The Balancing Act of Funded Research." Gail T. Fairhurst, University of Cincinnati
    "Out of the Tower and into the Fire: Negotiating and Securing Private Funding for Organizational Research." James D. Patterson, University of Kansas
    "Inside the Frame/Outside of the Lines: Implications for Critical Researchers 'Doing' Sponsored Organizational Research." Kasey L. Walker, Purdue University
    "The Stories We Tell: Reflexivity and Identity in Sponsored, Critical-Interpretive Research." Heather M. Hank, Purdue University

Respondent: Dennis K. Mumby, Purdue University

2246   9:30-10:45 a.m.   McCormick Board Rm   Fourth Floor   Chicago Hilton

RACIAL AND ETHNIC DIVERSITY ADVISORY COUNCIL MEETING

Sponsor: Ethnic and Racial Diversity Committee

2247   9:30-10:45 a.m.   Pullman Board Rm   Fourth Floor   Chicago Hilton

COMMUNICATION NEEDS OF STUDENTS AT-RISK COMMISSION BUSINESS MEETING

Sponsor: Communication Needs of Students at Risk Commission

2249   9:30-10:45 a.m.   Conf 5B   Fifth Floor   Chicago Hilton

ETHICS AND STUDENT INVOLVEMENT IN THE BASIC COURSE

Sponsor: Basic Course Division
Chair: Cathy A. Fleuriet, Southwest Texas State University
    "Teaching Ethics as a Process Application of the Isocratean Method of Teaching Ethics to the Basic Course." LeAnn M. Brazeal, University of Missouri, Columbia, Andrew A. Klyukovski, University of Missouri, Columbia
    "Ethical Issues in the Basic Course: Training Graduate Teaching Assistants in Decision-Making." Janice R. Stuckey, Jefferson State Community College, Mark D. Nelson, University of Alabama, Tuscaloosa
    "ESL Students and the Basic Speech Course: A Scaffolding Approach to Confidence and Skills Development." Eric Kendrick, Georgia State University
    "Public Speaking is Rafting the Rapids: Student-Generated Metaphors." Lisa Daigle, Georgia State University, Kristi A. Schaller, Georgia State University

Respondent: Roger C. Pace, University of San Diego

2252   9:30-10:45 a.m.   Conf 5E   Fifth Floor   Chicago Hilton

THE ACHIEVEMENT OF RICHARD HARVEY BROWN: THE CONVERGENCE OF SOCIAL AND RHETORICAL THEORY

Sponsor: Rhetorical and Communication Theory Division

Chair: Alan G. Gross, University of Minnesota, Twin Cities
   "Civic Artistry, Social Theory, and Democratic Knowledge." Robert Hariman, Drake
      University
   "At Last, A Social Theory Grounded in Rhetoric." Alan G. Gross, University of Minnesota,
      Twin Cities
   "'Welcome Home': Richard Harvey Brown and the Rhetorical Tradition." Allen M. Scult,
      Drake University

Respondent: Richard Harvey Brown, University of Maryland

2253   9:30-10:45 a.m.   Conf 5F   Fifth Floor   Chicago Hilton

CONSTRUCTIONS OF ENVIRONMENTAL PLACE AND IDENTITY: CONTESTED SPACE, CONTESTED ROLES, AND CONTESTED DOCTRINES

Sponsor: Environmental Communication Commission
Chair: Patricia Paystrup, Southern Utah University
   "Environmental Communication and Action Research: Researching and Creating a
      Sustainable Food System." Hollis F. Glaser, University of Nebraska, Omaha
   "Creating a Christian Environmentalist Identity: The EEN and the Declaration of the Care
      for Creation." Caitlin M. Wills, University of Georgia
   "Contested Environmental Space: Incinerators, Mothers, and Social Justice." Jennifer A.
      Peeples, University of Washington

Respondent: Judith E. Hendry, University of New Mexico

2254   9:30-10:45 a.m.   Conf 5G   Fifth Floor   Chicago Hilton

TEACHER AND STUDENT CHARACTERISTICS IN THE LEARNING PROCESS

Sponsor: Instructional Development Division
Chair: Marjorie Keeshan Nadler, Miami University
   "The Relationship Among Teacher Characteristics, Student Learning, and Teacher
      Evaluation." Jason J. Teven, Northwest Missouri State University
   "In Search of a Gender Connection: An Investigation of Gender Roles and Learning Style."
      Kay E. Payne, Western Kentucky University, Holly J. Payne, University of Kentucky, Larry
      M. Caillouet, Western Kentucky University
   "Teacher Clarity: A Definition, Review, and a Profile of the Clear Teacher." Joseph L.
      Chesebro, West Virginia University

Respondent: Marjorie Keeshan Nadler, Miami University

2255   9:30-10:45 a.m.   Conf 5H   Fifth Floor   Chicago Hilton

NARRATIVES OF HUMAN DISABILITY AS COMMUNICATIVE EXPERIENCES

Sponsor: Caucus on Disability Issues
Chair: James Ferris, University of Wisconsin, Madison
   "The Language of a Sort of Disability or How I Explain that My Son Can't See Across a
      Room." Elaine B. Jenks, West Chester University
   "The Social Practice of Disciplining Pain in and by Polio Survivors*." S. Renee Gillespie,
      University of Colorado, Boulder
   "Hide and Seek in the Discourse of Disability: Peter's Story." James G. Crawford, Ohio
      University

*Top Paper

2256   9:30-10:45 a.m.   Conf 5I   Fifth Floor   Chicago Hilton

FROM CRAYOLAS TO POWER POINT: HOW FAR HAVE WE REALLY COME IN ORAL COMMUNICATION INSTRUCTION?

Sponsor: Elementary & Secondary Education Section
Chair: Norman S. Greer, Illinois University

Friday

"The Status of Oral Communication in K-12 Districts in the State of Illinois." Mary C. Hogg, Eastern Illinois University, David W. Worley, Indiana State University

"Speaking Up and Speaking Out: The State of the State of K-8 Oral Communication Instruction." Tamara L. Burk, College of William and Mary

"Coming In the Back Door: A Speech Teacher's Journey on the Way to Teaching Speech." Erik Hammerstrom, Wheeling High School

"What Is Our Discipline Doing?: Help for the K-12 Teacher." Morris E. Snively, Belleville East High School, Illinois

Respondent: Mary E. Bozik, University of Northern Iowa

2257   9:30-10:45 a.m.   Conf 5J   Fifth Floor   Chicago Hilton

COMMUNICATION ETHICS THROUGH THE EYES OF LEVINAS AND BAKHTIN

Sponsor: Communication Ethics Commission
Chair: Jeffrey W. Murray, University of Pittsburgh

"Ethics as Response and Responsibility: Perspectives by Emmanual Levinas, Mikhail Bakhtin and Zygmunt Bauman*." Spoma Jovanovic-Mattson, University of Denver

"Teaching as an Inherently Ethical Endeavor: Utilizing Levinas as a Foundation." Alison P. Peticolas, University of Denver

"In Word and Deed: Ethics and Bakhtinian Dialogism*." Alexandre Lopez de Miranda, Purdue University

*Top Three Paper

2262   9:30-10:45 a.m.   Essex Court   Second Floor   Essex Inn

STUDIES IN RHETORIC AND THE CHALLENGES OF/TO EVANGELICAL CHRISTIAN COMMUNITY

Sponsor: Religious Communication Association
Chair: Michael E. Eidenmuller, Northwestern State University

"Doxa, Decorum, and Orders of Desire: The Functions of Rhetoric in the ECT Controversy." Nathan A. Baxter, Indiana University

"Caught in the Crossfire: Max Lucado Addressing the National Prayer Breakfast." Carl M. Cates, Valdosta State University

"The Rhetoric of Meaning, Truth, and Authority in Contemporary Evangelicals' Use of Biblical Scripture: 'Proof-Texting' vs. the 'Scriptual Implant'." Michael E. Eidenmuller, Northwestern State University

"Methods of Conversion: Charles G. Finney and Alternatives to Revivalism." Gary C. Hiebsch, College of the Ozarks

"Conceptualizing a Corrective to the Rhetorical Deficiencies of the Evangelical Christian Tradition: 'Humility' as Representative Anecdote." Mark Allan Steiner, Loyola University, Chicago

"Evangelical Public Prayer as Sermon." Robert A. Stewart, Texas Tech University

Respondent: John L. Pauley, Saint Mary's College

2263   9:30-10:45 a.m.   Windsor Court   Second Floor   Essex Inn

GERRY PHILIPSEN'S SIGNIFICANCE TO ETHNOGRAPHIC STUDIES IN COMMUNICATION

Sponsor: Ethnography Division
Chair: Nick L. Trujillo, California State University, Sacramento

Panelists: Charles A. Braithwaite, University of Montana
          Donal A. Carbaugh, University of Massachusetts, Amherst
          Kristine L. Fitch, University of Iowa

Respondent: Gerry F. Philipsen, University of Washington

2264	9:30-10:45 a.m.	Buckingham Court	Second Floor	Essex Inn

SIGNS, CODES AND CULTURE: STRETCHING THE LIMITS OF SEMIOTICS

Sponsor: Semiotics and Communication Commission
Chair: Stanley A. Deetz, University of Colorado, Boulder
"Culture, Codes and the Network Society: 'Real Virtuality'." Joseph Pilotta, Ohio State University
"Significant Practices: A Structurationist Approach to the Study of Codes and Culture." Christopher J. Richter, Hollins University
"Vocalization as Culture Milieu: A Semiotics of Sound." Jane Tumas-Serna, Hollins University
"Other Levels of Speaking: Continuity, Transformation and Invention." Algis Mickunas, Ohio University

Respondent: Stanley A. Deetz, University of Colorado, Boulder

2265	9:30-10:45 a.m.	Park East Walk	Second Floor	Essex Inn

KENNETH BURKE AND KARL MARX: HISTORICAL AND THEORETICAL PERSPECTIVES

Sponsor: Kenneth Burke Society, NCA Branch
"Something Wicked This Way Comes." Wade R. Kenny, University of Dayton
"The Effect of Marxoid Rays on Man-in-the-Moon Marxism." Michael C. McGee, University of Iowa
"Kenneth Burke, Karl Marx, and the Problem of Warrantable Outrage." Herbert W. Simons, Temple University
"KB Saves Karl from the Embarrassment of History." Richard H. Thames, Duquesne University

2266	9:30-10:45 a.m.	Cohn Rm	Second Floor	Spertus Institute

VOICES OF DISSENT ALONG THE FRONTIER

Sponsor: American Association for Rhetoric of Science & Technology
Chair: Henry P. Krips, University of Pittsburgh
"Peter Duesberg and the AIDS Dissent Movement: Is Science Driving AIDS Policy?" Anand Rao, Clarion University
"Suicide Machines: Medicine Responds to Kevorkian's Critique." Deborah J. Voss, University of Pittsburgh
"An Incongruous Perspective: Robert Sinsheimer's Evolutionary Critique of Recombinant DNA Research." James R. Pickett, Marian College
"Waldemar Kaempffert: Critic of the Endless Frontier." Timothy M. O'Donnell, University of Pittsburgh

Respondent: Michael D. Hazen, Wake Forest University

2267	9:30-10:45 a.m.	Krensky Rm	Second Floor	Spertus Institute

CURRENT EMPIRICAL STUDIES IN JURY DECISION-MAKING

Sponsor: Communication and Law Commission
Chair: Shelley C. Spiecker, Tsongas & Associates
"Unlocking the Jury Box: Structuring the Leadership in Real-Life Jury Deliberations*." Sunwolf, Santa Clara University
"Judge Nonverbal Communication on Trial: Do Jurors Notice?" Ann K. Burnett, North Dakota State University
"Reducing the Hindsight Bias: Can the Expert Witness Help?" Debra L. Worthington, University of Central Arkansas, Merrie Jo Stallard, Center for Trial Insights

Respondent: Shelley C. Spiecker, Tsongas & Associates

*Top Paper—Quantitative Method

Friday

2268   9:30-10:45 a.m.   Rm 902   Ninth Floor   Spertus Institute

THE ILLUSION OF OBJECTIVE REALITY

Sponsor: Visual Communication Commission
Chair: Charles R. Metts, Berry College
  "William Eggleston: Photographic Communication and the Burden of Representation."
    Joseph John Kotlowski, Regent University
  "On the Politics of 'Having Been There': Understanding Journalism Through 'The
    Eyewitness' Frame." Barbie Zelizer, University of Pennsylvania
  "Poetic Expression in Time-Based Media." Charles R. Metts, Berry College

Respondent: Ken Burke, Mills College

2269   9:30-10:45 a.m.   Rm 903   Ninth Floor   Spertus Institute

COLORING OUTSIDE THE LINES: HONORING THE STUDENT AS CONTRIBUTOR

Sponsor: Experiential Learning in Communication Commission
Chair: Charlotte M. Jones, Carroll College
  "Honoring the Student as Contributor: Constructing a Gender Museum." Leslie H. Jarmon,
    University of Texas, Austin
  "Walking the Narrow Edge: Encouraging Personal Growth and Service in Communication
    Courses." Brent Northup, Carroll College
  "Honoring the Student as Contributor: Undergraduate Conference Presentations."
    Charlotte M. Jones, Carroll College
  "Speaking Outside the Lines: The Case of VICA." Lawrence M. Modaff, Waubonsee
    Community College
  "Broadcasting Experience: The Speech Student as Contributor." Daniel P. Modaff, Ohio
    University

2270   9:30-10:45 a.m.   Rm 904   Ninth Floor   Spertus Institute

PRACTICAL APPROACHES FOR RESOLVING CONFLICTS IN DIVERSE, REAL-LIFE CONTEXTS

Sponsor: Peace and Conflict Communication Commission
Chair: D. Ray Heisey, Kent State University
  "Chinese Approaches to Resolving Conflicts in Joint Business Ventures." Tai Ping Chen,
    Beijing Industrial Development Company, China
  "Community Mediation Practices in a Metropolitan Development Corporation." Ian S.
    Heisey, Bellaire-Puritas Development Corporation, Ohio
  "Volunteer Peacemakers in World Trouble Spots." Joshua Yoder, Christian Peacemaker
    Teams, Illinois
  "Resolving Inner as Well as Outer Conflicts for Eastern European Refugees." Christine Lee,
    Migration Refugee Service, Ohio

2271   9:30-10:45 a.m.   Rm 906   Ninth Floor   Spertus Institute

MYTHOPOESIS, NOMOS AND PHYSIS: A VOLATILE MIXTURE

Sponsor: American Society for the History of Rhetoric
Chair: Dale L. Sullivan, Michigan Technological University
  "Singing the Muses' Song: Myth, Wisdom, and Speech in Ancient Greece." Christopher
    Johnstone, Penn State University
  "Rhetoric Between Orality and Literacy: Oral Memory, Writing and Performance in
    Isocrates and Aristotle*." Ekaterina V. Haskins, University of Iowa
  "The *Khora* of *Khoras*: Aitionic Argument in Isocrates' *Panegyricus*." Jon Leon Torn,
    Northwestern University

Respondent: Robert G. Sullivan, Ithaca College

*Outstanding Student Paper

2272   9:30-10:45 a.m.   Rm 907   Ninth Floor   Spertus Institute

MASCULINE AND FEMININE SPEAKING STYLES: NEW PERSPECTIVES ON COMPETITIVE SPEECH AND DEBATE

Sponsor: Cross Examination Debate Association
Chair: Valerie R. Renegar, University of Kansas
    "Feminist Ethics in Competition: Fostering Healthy Interpersonal Relationships in Debate."
      Sue E. Lowrie, Pepperdine University
    "Evaluator/Audience Feedback Toward Male/Female Competitive Speakers." John Nash,
      Hastings College
    "American Me? Questioning Male Minority Identity in College Debates over Civil Rights."
      Richard D. Pineda, Wayne State University
    "Relational Language and Post Round Disclosure: Pathways to Change?" Valerie R.
      Renegar, University of Kansas
    "E-Debate and Community Organization: The Affirmative Action Issue." Christina M.
      Sabee, Northwestern University, Shannon S. Dyer, Northwestern University

Respondent: Stacey K. Sowards, University of Kansas

2273   9:30-10:45 a.m.   Rm 908   Ninth Floor   Spertus Institute

COMPETITIVE PAPERS IN FORENSICS

Sponsor: National Forensic Association
Chair: Barbara S. Baron, Brookdale Community College
    "Competitive and Cooperative Dimensions in Intercollegiate Forensics: A
      Phenomenological Investigation of Motivation." Jeff S. Cook, University of Nebraska,
      Lincoln
    "Competitive Forensics Persuasion: Re-Examining the Model." Steven N. Blivess, Penn
      State University
    "Extemporaneous Speaking and Gender: Leveling the Playing Field." Clark D. Olson,
      Arizona State University

2274   9:30-10:45 a.m.   Auditorium   Second Floor   Spertus Institute

IDENTITY, ROLES, AND RECEPTION: WOMEN IN NON-TRADITIONAL 'ROLES'

Sponsor: Theatre Division
Chair: M. Susan Anthony, University of Maryland, College Park
    "Broken Boundaries: Maude Gonne's Nationalism and the Abbey Theatre." Robin
      Boisseau, University of Maryland, College Park
    "Transculturating Gender, Carnivalizing National Identity: Mafifa and the Performative
      Transgressions of the Last(?) Conga Queen." Denise Corte, University of Maryland,
      College Park
    "'Presumptuous Incompetence': The Hamlet of Anna Elizabeth Dickinson." Stacey
      Stewart, University of Maryland, College Park

Respondent: Anne Fliotsos, University of Missouri, Columbia

This panel investigates the performativity of woman, specifically the performativity of self (or character with its symbiotic carryover), its reception by society, and the often painful results of stepping outside social boundaries. These analyses reveal the structures of society which define 'woman' as well as the challenges these women struck upon the theatre and its surrounding world.

Friday

11:00 a.m.

Raymie E. McKerrow, NCA First Vice President and Primary Convention Planner has selected the following programs as exemplary. These programs are "highlighted" on Friday and Saturday during the 11:00 a.m.– 12:15 p.m. time period.

2306   11:00-12:15 p.m.   Continental BR A   Lobby Level   Chicago Hilton

ADULT LEARNERS: PEDAGOGICAL CONCERNS AND STRATEGIES FOR THE NEW FACES IN THE OLD CLASSROOMS

Sponsor: Senior College & University Section
Chair: Chrys Gabrich, Carlow College

Panelists: Martha Ezzell, Carlow College
         Janie M. Harden Fritz, Duquesne University
         Ann D. Jabro, Robert Morris College
         Jennifer K. Wood, University of Pittsburgh
         Chrys Gabrich, Carlow College

2307   11:00-12:15 p.m.   Continental BR B   Lobby Level   Chicago Hilton

RE-VISIONING FEMINISM: GENERATIONS AND THE INTERROGATION OF HISTORY

Sponsor: Feminist and Women Studies Division

Panelists: Karlyn K. Campbell, University of Minnesota
         Carolyn Calloway-Thomas, Indiana University, Bloomington
         Celeste M. Condit, University of Georgia
         Melissa D. Deem, University of Iowa

2308   11:00-12:15 p.m.   Continental BR C   Lobby Level   Chicago Hilton

POSITIONING LSI IN THE DISCIPLINE: VISIONS FOR THE NEW MILLENNIUM

Sponsor: Language and Social Interaction Division

Panelists: Donald G. Ellis, University of Hartford
         Sandra L. Ragan, University of Oklahoma
         Karen Tracy, University of Colorado
         Robert E. Sanders, SUNY, Albany

Featuring four prominent scholars in the area of language and social interaction, this panel will focus on how LSI can celebrate interdisciplinary links while continuing to highlight its importance and centrality as a specialization within the discipline of communication.

2311   11:00-12:15 p.m.   Int'l Ballroom North   Second Floor   Chicago Hilton

QUEERING PERFORMANCE: POSITIONS AND PROBLEMATICS

Sponsor: Performance Studies Division
Chair: Jill Dolan, CUNY

Panelists: Randall T. Hill, St. Lawrence University
         Holly Hughes, Performance Artist, New York City
         E. Patrick Johnson, University of North Carolina, Chapel Hill
         Donna M. Nudd, Florida State University
         Eric Rosen, Northwestern University/About Face Theatre Company
         Lisa Wolford, Bowling Green State University

| 2314 | 11:00-12:15 p.m. | Boulevard A | Second Floor | Chicago Hilton |

ROUNDTABLE DISCUSSION OF INTERDISCIPLINARY APPROACHES TO TEACHING AND CONDUCTING RESEARCH IN FAMILY COMMUNICATION

Sponsor: Family Communication Division
Chair: Michelle A. Miller, Penn State University

Panelists: Tiffany Townsend, Penn State University
Tanya Afifi, Penn State University
Michelle A. Miller, Penn State University
Steve Duck, University of Iowa
Anita L. Vangelisti, University of Texas, Austin
Eva L. Lefkowitz, Penn State University

Respondent: Marceline E. Thompson, University of Memphis

| 2315 | 11:00-12:15 p.m. | Boulevard B | Second Floor | Chicago Hilton |

VISIONS OF COMMUNITY: ETHICAL ISSUES IN PUBLIC RELATIONS AND COMMUNITY BUILDING

Sponsors: Public Relations Division
Communication Ethics Commission
Chair: Sharon L. Bracci, University of North Carolina, Greensboro

Panelists: James F. Klumpp, University of Maryland
Kevin M. Deluca, Penn State University
Virginia T. Rodino, University of Maryland
Dean A. Kruckeberg, University of Northern Iowa
Sharon L. Bracci, University of North Carolina, Greensboro
Richard M. Dubiel, University of Wisconsin, Stevens Point

The audience will join the panelists for an open discussion following the panel presentations.

| 2316 | 11:00-12:15 p.m. | Boulevard C | Second Floor | Chicago Hilton |

ROUNDTABLE: IDEOLOGY AND THE STUDY OF CULTURAL IDENTITY IN INTERCULTURAL COMMUNICATION

Sponsor: International & Intercultural Communication Division
Chair: Young Yun Kim, University of Oklahoma

Panelists: Donal A. Carbaugh, University of Massachusetts, Amherst
Kristine L. Fitch, University of Iowa
Young Yun Kim, University of Oklahoma
Judith N. Martin, Arizona State University
Jolene Koester, California State University, Sacramento
Dreama G. Moon, California State University, San Marcos

Participants reflect on and discuss how their personal political ideology may influence their academic investigations into the phenomenon of cultural identity in intercultural communication.

| 2319 | 11:00-12:15 p.m. | Astoria | Third Floor | Chicago Hilton |

PUTTING THE NCA COMMUNICATION ETHICS CREDO TO WORK

Sponsor: Communication Ethics Commission
Chair: Kenneth E. Andersen, University of Illinois, Urbana-Champaign
"In the Association." Sherwyn P. Morreale, NCA National Office
"In the Classroom." Paula S. Tompkins, St. Cloud State University
"In the Workplace." Matthew W. Seeger, Wayne State University
"In the Public Sphere." Kenneth E. Andersen, University of Illinois, Urbana-Champaign

Friday

2321   11:00-12:15 p.m.   **Williford A**   **Third Floor**   **Chicago Hilton**

EXPLORING RESEARCH BOUNDARIES: SUCCESSES AND CHALLENGES IN SOCIAL CONSTRUCTIONIST, EMPIRICAL RESEARCH

Sponsor: Challenging Boundaries Series
Chair: John R. Stewart, University of Washington

Panelists: Theresa R. Castor, College of William and Mary
          Lawrence R. Frey, University of Memphis
          Roberta L. Gray, University of Washington
          Wendy Leeds-Hurwitz, University of Wisconsin, Parkside
          John Shotter, University of New Hampshire, Durham
          Tasha J. Souza, University of Wisconsin, Parkside
          Shawn Spano, San Jose State University

Until recently, most social constructionist writing has been theoretical rather than empirical. Now there are a few researchers who are broadening the scope of social constructionism to include empirical research. This panel brings these researchers together in a timely, boundary-expanding conversation. Panelists will share highlights from brief essays describing the most important successes and challenges they experienced in the course of specific social constructionist, empirical research projects. The chair will pose questions designed to encourage dialogue between and among the panelists and the audience based on the common themes and differences in the essays and presentations.

2322   11:00-12:15 p.m.   **Williford B**   **Third Floor**   **Chicago Hilton**

THE EXPERIENCE OF LEARNING: EXPLORING THE "STUDENT AS CONSUMER" METAPHOR

Sponsor: Experiential Learning in Communication Commission
Chair: Pat Arneson, Duquesne University

Panelists: John A. Campbell, University of Memphis
          George E. Cheney, University of Montana
          Thom Gillespie, Indiana University
          Michael Leff, Northwestern University
          Jill J. McMillan, Wake Forest University
          Michael M. Osborn, University of Memphis
          Roy J. Schwartzman, University of South Carolina
          Anastacia D. Serro-Boim, St. John's University
          Ronald F. Wendt, University of South Dakota
          Ted A. Wendt, Murray State University
          Julia T. Wood, University of North Carolina, Chapel Hill

This roundtable discussion will explore the "student as consumer" metaphor by addressing questions central to this topic, including: Why are the metaphors of the market and the consumer so popular for reconfiguring higher education? How are metaphors applied in higher education? How can symbols be appropriated, transformed, or undermined to the advantage of the academy? How is academe more and less than a market? How are students more and less than consumers?

2323   11:00-12:15 p.m.   **Williford C**   **Third Floor**   **Chicago Hilton**

WHAT COUNTS AS SCHOLARSHIP

Sponsor: Research Board
Chair: Roderick P. Hart, University of Texas, Austin

Panelists: Thomas W. Benson, Penn State University
          Carole Blair, University of California, Davis
          Judee K. Burgoon, University of Arizona
          Mark Hickson, University of Alabama, Birmingham

Our discipline has become the site of controversy about how to define scholarship and how to assess levels of scholarly achievement. Can we count scholarship in any direct, quantitative fashion? What biases enter into our conventional standards of recognizing and assessing scholarship? Should we change these standards? If so, how? The participants in this panel will make a short statement about what they think counts as scholarship, and a general discussion will follow.

2324	11:00-12:15 p.m.	Marquette	Third Floor	Chicago Hilton

TEACHING OUTSIDE THE LINES: ROUNDTABLE ON POLITICS AND PEDAGOGY OF AFRICAN AMERICAN WOMEN'S STUDIES IN COMMUNICATION

Sponsors: Black Caucus
          Women's Caucus
Chair: Katherine G. Hendrix, University of Memphis

Panelists: Olga I. Davis, Arizona State University
           Janice D. Hamlet, Shippensburg University
           Marsha Houston, Tulane University
           Venita A. Kelley, University of Nebraska, Lincoln
           Charles I. Nero, Bates College
           Karla D. Scott, Saint Louis University
           Sherri Smith, University of Alabama, Huntsville

The participants in this roundtable will discuss the politics of proposing and teaching courses about African American women and communication at predominantly white institutions, and the strategies that enabled them successfully to offer such courses. They will share sample syllabi and recommend print and visual resources for courses about African American women and communication in a variety of areas within the discipline.

2326	11:00-12:15 p.m.	PDR 1	Third Floor	Chicago Hilton

A PANEL DISCUSSION: WHAT SHOULD BE THE RELATIONSHIP BETWEEN COMPETITIVE SPEECH/DEBATE TEAMS AND THE UNIVERSITY/DEPARTMENT OF COMMUNICATION

Sponsor: Argumentation and Forensics Division
Chair: Jean L. DeHart, Appalachian State University

Panelists: Robert E. Frank, Morehead State University
           Thomas J. Hynes, State University of West Georgia
           Michael J. Janas, Samford University
           Allan Louden, Wake Forest University
           Michael R. Moore, Morehead State University
           Edward M. Panetta, University of Georgia
           Kimberly A. Powell, Luther College
           Randolph Richardson, Berry College
           Kellie W. Roberts, University of Florida
           Glenda J. Treadaway, Appalachian State University
           Carol K. Winkler, Georgia State University
           David Zarefsky, Northwestern University

This panel of coaches and administrators will examine questions such as: Do competitive programs serve the missions of the departments of communication and the universities overall? Should competitive teams be a part of the communication department? Should there be a move toward a professional coaching staff? What should be the role of graduate coaching assistants? How can/should programs be adequately financed? How should universities determine the results of competitive teams? At the end, audience members will be encouraged to respond.

Friday

2327   11:00-12:15 p.m.   PDR 2   Third Floor   Chicago Hilton

POSTCOLONIAL SCHOLARSHIP IN COMMUNICATION: DIVERSE APPROACHES

Sponsor: Spotlight on Scholarship
Chair: Thomas K. Nakayama, Arizona State University

Participants: Raka Shome, University of California, Davis
        Radha S. Hegde, Rutgers University
        K. E. Supriya, University of Wisconsin, Milwaukee

This panel examines how postcolonial theory has shaped the protocols and practices in the discipline of communication, including postcolonial critiques in relation to communication inquiry and method.

2328   11:00-12:15 p.m.   PDR 3   Third Floor   Chicago Hilton

WHAT IS THE SHAPE OF THE RIVER?: AFFIRMATIVE ACTION IN THE TWENTY-FIRST CENTURY

Sponsor: Table Talk Series
Chair: Ronald L. Applbaum, Kean University

Panelists: Judy C. Pearson, Virginia Tech University
        Paul E. Nelson, Ohio University
        Sidney A. Ribeau, Bowling Green State University
        Orlando L. Taylor, Howard University

The program examines the role of Affirmative Action in the twenty-first century. It explores whether Affirmative Action is an outdated policy or the best way to promote equal opportunity for all members of society. The central focus will be on strategies for reviving the progressive challenge of equitable participation and affirming the removal of inequity in admissions and hiring in higher education.

12:30 p.m.

2406   12:30-1:45 p.m.   Continental BR A   Lobby Level   Chicago Hilton

NUTS AND BOLTS OF MANAGING A STATE ASSOCIATION I: INTERNAL ISSUES

Sponsor: States Advisory Council
Chair: Tamara L. Burk, College of William and Mary

Panelists: Tamara L. Burk, College of William and Mary
        Jonathan H. Millen, Rider University
        Barbara I. Hall, University of Illinois, Urbana-Champaign
        Jerry L. Buley, Arizona State University
        Robert M. Smith, University of Tennessee, Martin
        Carl M. Cates, Valdosta State University
        Patricia S. Nelson, Georgia Perimeter College

Group leaders discuss convention planning, communicating with state association members, rebuilding a state association, and issues for new presidents.

2407   12:30-1:45 p.m.   Continental BR B   Lobby Level   Chicago Hilton

TECHNOLOGY ISSUES IN THE UNIVERSITY SETTING: OUT WITH THE OLD AND ON WITH THE NEW

Sponsor: Human Communication and Technology Commission
Chair: James D. Wallace, Cameron University

Panelists: Karen R. Krupar, Metropolitan State College of Denver
            Maurine C. Eckloff, University of Nebraska, Kearney
            Clark Germann, Metropolitan State College of Denver
            Ronna M. Thornock, University of Denver
            Mary Y. Mandeville, Oklahoma State University

Respondents: Andrew Glickman, University of Texas
            Heather M. McKissick, Lower Colorado River Authority

Technology has emerged as an important issue in institutions of higher education. What are important factors in defining this technology for our campuses? What are the problems and the strategies in creating successful programs? What role do departments of speech communication play in the context of their institutions' technology mission? This discussion will be for audience members who have existing programs using technology, who are in the process of planning programs, or who believe that such programs benefit their institutions. Active audience interaction and participation will be encouraged.

2408   12:30-1:45 p.m.   Continental BR C   Lobby Level   Chicago Hilton

NATION, NEO/COLONIALISM, AND CULTURE: POSTCOLONIAL CRITICAL APPROACHES

Sponsor: Critical and Cultural Studies Division
Chair: Raka Shome, University of California, Davis
   "Breathing Life into the Victim: Recuperating White Masculinity Through the Trope of the Primitive." Aimee M. Carrillo Rowe, University of Washington
   "Postcolonial Performance and Cultural Identity." Jennifer M. Huss, Claremont Graduate School
   "Media Assemblages and Policy Logics: Rethinking the Nation in the Context of Globalization." Stephen B. Wiley, North Carolina State University
   "Leopold II, King of the Belgians, the Rhetoric of 'Belgian Congo' and 'Recolonization'." Marouf Hasian, University of Utah
   "The Problem of Representing the Other: Re-Evaluation of Cultural Studies Concept for Journalistic Practice." Elfriede Fursich, Boston College

---

2411   12:30-1:45 p.m.   Int'l Ballroom North   Second Floor   Chicago Hilton

HERE AND GONE: MEMORY, ARCHIVES AND PLAY

Sponsor: Performance Studies Division
Chair: Della Pollock, University of North Carolina, Chapel Hill
   "Peoples of Memory: James Luna Performs for Dino." Jane M. Blocker, University of Minnesota
   "Pulling Ribbons from Mouths: Umbilical Ties to the Referent." Carol Mavor, University of North Carolina, Chapel Hill
   "On Archives, Clones, and Clowns." Rebecca Schneider, Cornell University

Respondent: Jose Munoz, New York University

2412   12:30-1:45 p.m.   Int'l Ballroom South   Second Floor   Chicago Hilton

GIFTS—GREAT IDEAS FOR TEACHING SPEECH

Sponsor: GIFTS Series
Chair: Lori E. Zakel, Sinclair Community College
   1. "'But I Hate This Text': The Reflective Thinking Process and the Selection of a Text in a Small Group Class." M. Carla Schenone-Stevens, St. Ambrose University
   2. "Interpersonal Communication Icebreaker." Timothy B. Rumbough, Bloomsburg University
   3. "Hollywood! A Simulation for Mass Communication." Carol Pauli, Marist College
   4. "Name That Interview." Nancy J. Eckstein, University of Nebraska, Lincoln
   5. "Attribution Theory in Practice: Introducing a Classmate." Thomas R. Wagner, University of Central Florida

Friday

6. "The Brown Paper Bag Exercise." Jayne L. Violette, Georgetown College
7. "Discussion: Intercultural Communication Activity." Lisa Daigle, Georgia State University
8. "Have You Heard the One About the Three Theorists Who Walked into a Bar?: Humanizing Theory." Brooks Aylor, La Salle University
9. "The Gift Of G.A.B.." Abigail Gray Briggs, Air University
10. "Crisis Management: Setting the Stage for Speaking in Groups." Wade S. Davis, University of Iowa
11. "Coloring Outside the Lines: The First Public Speech." Roxane Lulofs, Azusa Pacific University
12. "Facts vs. Opinion: The Pundits Speak." W. Bradford Mello, Trinity College, Washington, D.C.
13. "Groupteach: A Communication Workshop Assignment." Barbara A. Penington, University of Wisconsin, Whitewater
14. "My Values: My Culture." R. Rennae Elliott, Oakwood College
15. "Encouraging Cooperative Argumentation in the Basic Course." Theodore Matula, California State University, Monterey Bay
16. "Babe: A Lesson in Self-Concept." Julie Weeks Simanski, Des Moines Area Community College
17. "Roll Call Questions in the Public Speaking Course." Carolyn M. Wiethoff, Ohio State University
18. "Color Me Outside the Lines: Coloring My Fantasy Adventure." Priscilla A. Schneider, California University of Pennsylvania

The above GIFTS will be presented by their creators in small, roundtable format. The number to the left of the GIFT indicates the table number where the creator/presenter will be located.

2414	12:30-1:45 p.m.	Boulevard A	Second Floor	Chicago Hilton

BLURRING GLOBAL BOUNDARIES: INDIGENOUS NEGOTIATIONS WITH IMPORTED MEDIA TEXTS

Sponsor: Challenging Boundaries Series
Chair: Scott R. Olson, Ball State University
"How the Teenage Pakistani Diaspora in London Watch Imported Soap Operas such as the Australian Television Program *Neighbours*." Marie Gillespie, University of Wales
"The Hybrid Cultural Environment of Israeli Teenagers: Where Elements of Local Culture and of Globalized (Mostly American) Culture Mix and Negotiate." Tamar Liebes, Hebrew University of Jerusalem
"Reception of Western Media in Nigeria: *Communalism* as an Option to Individualism or Collectivism in the Reading of Media Texts." Andrew A. Moemeka, Central Connecticut State University
"The Narratology of Hollywood Media and Its Global Reception: Native American Reception of Media Texts." Scott R. Olson, Ball State University
"Reception of Global Media by Teenagers in Poland: Traditional Communication Patterns and the Western Media Influence." John Parrish-Sprowl, Indiana University-Purdue University, Fort Wayne
"The Reception of Global Media in Zambia: The Juxtaposition of the Imported South African Soap Opera *Egoli: Place of Gold* with Indigenous Programming Like *Sakala Brothers Folk Music* and the News." Cornelius B. Pratt, Michigan State University
"Theorizing Resistance to Global Television, the Debate About Global Television Audiences, and Possible Future Research Questions: Audience Negotiation with Imported Media in Latin America." Silvio Waisbord, Rutgers University

2415	12:30-1:45 p.m.	Boulevard B	Second Floor	Chicago Hilton

THIRTY YEARS OF IRVING J. REIN AT NORTHWESTERN UNIVERSITY: RIDING RUDY'S RED WAGON TO A LIFETIME OF ACHIEVEMENT

Sponsor: NCA First Vice President

Chair: Donald Fishman, Boston College
"Irving J. Rein as a Researcher." Richard A. Kallan, California State Polytechnic University
"Irving J. Rein: Changing the Contours of the Discipline." Robert Shuter, Marquette University
"A View of Rein from the Chair's Perspective." Michael Leff, Northwestern University
"A View of Rein from the Dean's Office." Roy V. Wood, University of Denver
"Culture Shock: Irving J. Rein as a Mentor." Stephen A. Smith, University of Arkansas
"Closing Remarks on Coloring Outside the Lines for Thirty Years." Joyce Lindmark, Boston College, Donald Fishman, Boston College

This program is designed to honor the contributions of Irving J. Rein to the Department of Communication Studies at Northwestern University during the past thirty years. In Reinian style, the program will be both a tribute and a roast. Colleagues, former students and friends will speak about various aspects of Rein's career at Northwestern University. In addition, current students will be asked in an open mike session to offer their comments as the Reinian tradition continues.

2416	12:30-1:45 p.m.	Boulevard C	Second Floor	Chicago Hilton

TOP STUDENT PAPERS IN INTERCULTURAL, INTERNATIONAL, AND CULTURAL COMMUNICATION

Sponsor: International & Intercultural Communication Division
Chair: Todd Imahori, Seinan Gakuin University, Japan
"Life or Death for Public Service Broadcasting? Pascal's Wager for a Twenty-First Century Europe*." Christian Christensen, University of Texas, Austin
"Perceptions of Performance Feedback Messages** ***." Yuko Morimoto Yoshida, San Francisco State University
"Apology on the Occasion of the Fiftieth Anniversary of the End of the Pacific War: Murayama Tomiichi, Prime Minister of Japan, August 15, 1995, Tokyo Japan***." Jane W. Yamazaki, Wayne State University

Respondent: Todd Imahori, Seinan Gakuin University, Japan

*Top One Student Paper   **Top Two Student Paper   ***Debut

2418	12:30-1:45 p.m.	Waldorf	Third Floor	Chicago Hilton

CHILDREN IN THE FAMILY: AN EXAMINATION OF SIBLING RELATIONSHIPS

Sponsor: Family Communication Division
Chair: Amy M. Bippus, University of Texas, Austin
"Maintaining Long-Distance Sibling Relationships." Lindsay M. Timmerman, University of Texas, Austin
"The Everyday Interaction Rules of Young Adult Siblingship: Focus on Conflict and Dealing with Parents." Lisa A. Roghaar, University of Georgia
"Sibling Alliance Rules." John H. Nicholson, Angelo State University
"The Experience, Expression and Perceived Appropriateness of Jealousy in the Family." Krystyna S. Aune, University of Hawaii, Manoa, Jamie Comstock, University of West Florida

Respondent: Glen H. Stamp, Ball State University

2419	12:30-1:45 p.m.	Astoria	Third Floor	Chicago Hilton

CONTEMPORARY AFRICAN AMERICAN LEADERS REDRAWING THE LINES: RHETORICS OF SOCIAL CHANGE, ALLIANCE, AND RESPONSIBILITY

Sponsor: Public Address Division
Chair: Kathryn M. Olson, University of Wisconsin, Milwaukee
"Second Persona and Moral Rhetoric in Fannie Lou Hamer's 1971 Address to the NAACP Legal Defense Fund." Ljiljana Komnenic, University of Wisconsin, Milwaukee

Friday

"Politics, Ethical Judgment, and Social Action: Transcending Normative Criteria and Revisioning the Rules." Steven R. Goldzwig, Marquette University, Patricia A. Sullivan, SUNY, New Paltz

"The Rhetorical Potentials and Problems of Imagery: Issues of Association and Jesse Jackson's Million Man March Speech." Kathryn M. Olson, University of Wisconsin, Milwaukee

Respondent: Detine Bowers, University of Wisconsin, Milwaukee

---

2421   12:30-1:45 p.m.   Williford A   Third Floor   Chicago Hilton

TOP FOUR PAPERS IN AFRICAN AMERICAN COMMUNICATION AND CULTURE

Sponsor: African American Communication & Culture Commission
Chair: Peter Nwoso, California State University, Sacramento

"W.E.B. Dubois on Woman Suffrage: A Rhetorical Analysis of His Crisis Writings*." Garth E. Pauley, Calvin College

"Confronting the Politics of Race: Rhetorical Paradoxes in Clarence Thomas' Address to the National Bar Association." Timothy J. Brown, Buffalo State College

"Inter-Racioethnic Communication and Organizational Assimilation: An African American Perspective** ***." Patricia C. Phillips-Gott, Southwest Texas State University

"A Critique of Fictional Self-Help: Oprah Winfrey's Book Club Looks at Domestic Violence***." Rita L. Van Zant, University of Georgia

Respondent: Veronica J. Duncan, University of Georgia

*Top Paper **Top Student Paper ***Student Debut

2422   12:30-1:45 p.m.   Williford B   Third Floor   Chicago Hilton

THINKING ABOUT PRESIDENTIAL DEBATE FORMATS FOR 2000: ARE PAST APPROACHES TO DEBATES AS GOOD AS IT GETS?

Sponsor: Political Communication Division
Chair: Janet S. Horne, Salisbury State University

"Let's Put 'Debate' into Presidential Debates." William L. Benoit, University of Missouri, Columbia

"An Examination of Selected Experiments with Different Debate Formats: Have We Learned Anything Since 1960?" John T. Morello, Mary Washington College

"Negotiating Presidential Debate Formats in 2000: Can Sponsors Have More Influence over the Process?" Diana B. Carlin, University of Kansas

"The Meta-Format for Presidential Campaign Debates." David S. Birdsell, Baruch College

Respondent: Michael Pfau, University of Wisconsin, Madison

2423   12:30-1:45 p.m.   Williford C   Third Floor   Chicago Hilton

FEMINIST AND WOMEN'S STUDIES SPOTLIGHT ON SCHOLARSHIP: PAULA A. TREICHLER

Sponsor: Feminist and Women Studies Division
Chair: Radha S. Hegde, Rutgers University

Respondents: Ellen A. Wartella, University of Texas, Austin
                Anne Balsamo, Xerox Palo Alto Research Center
                Lawrence Grossberg, University of North Carolina

The Feminist and Women's Studies Division presents this panel to honor the contribution of "Spotlight Scholar" Paula A. Treichler, University of Illinois, Urbana-Champaign, to feminist scholarship and pedagogy.

2424	12:30-1:45 p.m.	Marquette	Third Floor	Chicago Hilton

ACTIVE AND COLLABORATIVE LEARNING STRATEGIES FOR COMMUNICATION COURSES

Sponsor: Table Talk Series
Chair: Bruce C. McKinney, James Madison University

Panelists: Anita K. Foeman, West Chester University
Deborah Borisoff, New York University
Lynne Kelly, University of Hartford
Ann B. Frymier, Miami University
James A. Keaten, University of Northern Colorado

Panelists discuss how they have incorporated active learning and/or collaborative learning strategies in their own courses and the outcomes of this process. Courses in interviewing, research methods, intercultural communication and persuasion are examined.

2426	12:30-1:45 p.m.	PDR 1	Third Floor	Chicago Hilton

PUBLIC RELATIONS DIVISION BUSINESS MEETING

Sponsor: Public Relations Division

2427	12:30-1:45 p.m.	PDR 2	Third Floor	Chicago Hilton

ENVIRONMENTAL COMMUNICATION COMMISSION BUSINESS MEETING

Sponsor: Environmental Communication Commission

2428	12:30-1:45 p.m.	PDR 3	Third Floor	Chicago Hilton

COMMISSION ON COMMUNICATION AND LAW BUSINESS MEETING

Sponsor: Communication and Law Commission

2429	12:30-1:45 p.m.	PDR 4	Third Floor	Chicago Hilton

PUBLIC ADDRESS DIVISION BUSINESS MEETING

Sponsor: Public Address Division

2430	12:30-1:45 p.m.	PDR 5	Third Floor	Chicago Hilton

BASIC COURSE DIVISION EXECUTIVE BOARD MEETING

Sponsor: Basic Course Division

2431	12:30-1:45 p.m.	PDR 6	Third Floor	Chicago Hilton

DEPARTMENT ENTREPRENEURSHIP

Sponsor: Association for Communication Administration
Chair: John A. Courtright, University of Delaware

Panelists: Robert K. Avery, University of Utah
Bill Balthrop, University of North Carolina
Gary L. Kreps, Hofstra University
J. Gregory Payne, Emerson College
Patricia Witherspoon, University of Texas, Austin

Respondent: John A. Courtright, University of Delaware

Friday

Departments are increasingly being asked to raise money to buy equipment, endow scholarships and chairs, and support activities which were previously underwritten by their institutions. Some departments have been successful in such endeavors. How did they do it?

2432   12:30-1:45 p.m.   PDR 7   Third Floor   Chicago Hilton

NCA AND AFFILIATE ORGANIZATIONS BUSINESS MEETING

Sponsor: National Communication Association

2433   12:30-1:45 p.m.   Conf 4A   Fourth Floor   Chicago Hilton

MEDIA MESSAGES, PUBLIC POLICY, AND HEALTH CARE DECISIONS

Sponsor: Health Communication Division
Chair: Charlotte M. Jones, Carroll College
  "Explaining Illness Through the Mass Media: The Problem-Solving Perspective." Katherine E. Rowan, Purdue University
  "Rhetorical Dimensions of Decriminalization." Richard E. Vatz, Towson University, Lee S. Weinberg, University of Pittsburgh
  "The Health Knowledge Gap and its Differential Health Outcomes: Questions, Causes, and Considerations." Rebecca M. Chory, Michigan State University, Charles T. Salmon, Michigan State University
  "Competing Voices in the World of Health Care." Michael L. Spangle, University of Denver

Respondent: Charlotte M. Jones, Carroll College

2434   12:30-1:45 p.m.   Conf 4B   Fourth Floor   Chicago Hilton

THE AFA AT FIFTY: A LEADERSHIP RETROSPECTIVE

Sponsor: American Forensic Association
Chairs: Patricia M. Ganer, Cypress College
        Gerald H. Sanders, Miami University

A video presentation from interviews with many past AFA presidents.

2435   12:30-1:45 p.m.   Conf 4C   Fourth Floor   Chicago Hilton

INFLUENCES ON THE EFFICACY OF HEALTH PROMOTION MESSAGES

Sponsor: Health Communication Division
Chair: Vincent R. Waldron, Arizona State University West
  "Empathy, Intimacy and the Motivation to Perform Cancer Self-Examinations." Mark T. Morman, Baylor University
  "Hearing Loss and Hearing Protection Messages Using the Extended Parallel Process Model to Prevent Noise-Induced Hearing Loss Among Coal Miners in Appalachia." Lisa M. Murray-Johnson, Michigan State University, Kim Witte, Michigan State University, Dhaval S. Patel, Michigan State University, Cynthia E. Zuckerman, Michigan State University, Victoria Orrego, Michigan State University
  "The Barriers to Action Model (BAM): Understanding Barriers to Preventative Health Actions for Occupational Noise-Induced Hearing Loss." Dhaval S. Patel, Michigan State University, Kim Witte, Michigan State University, Cynthia E. Zuckerman, Michigan State University, Lisa M. Murray-Johnson, Michigan State University, Victoria Orrego, Michigan State University, Andrew M. Maxfield, CDC-NIOSH, Washington DC, Julie Tisdale, Office of Communication NIOSH, Washington, DC, Suzanne Meadows-Hogan, Office of Communication NIOSH, District of Columbia, Edward D. Thimons, Pittsburgh Research Lab NIOSH
  "Understanding the Role of Empathy Arousal in Responses to Persuasive Health Communication: Developing a Theory and Empirical Method." Rose G. Campbell, Butler University, Austin S. Babrow, Purdue University

Respondent: Vincent R. Waldron, Arizona State University West

---

2436   12:30-1:45 p.m.   Conf 4D   Fourth Floor   Chicago Hilton

COLORING OUTSIDE THE LINES? ARE YOU IN YOUR RIGHT MIND?

Sponsor: Community College Section
Chair: Donald M. Ehret, Columbus State Community College

Panelists: Libby A. McGlone, Columbus State Community College
             Christiana M. Hopkins, Columbus State Community College
             Donald M. Ehret, Columbus State Community College

Respondent: Christiana M. Hopkins, Columbus State Community College

This panel will discuss the rationale for and use of right-brain activities in communication arts at a community college.

2437   12:30-1:45 p.m.   Conf 4E   Fourth Floor   Chicago Hilton

ACCOMPLISHING CULTURAL COMPETENCY: LANGUAGE AND SOCIAL INTERACTION CONCERNS ACROSS CULTURES

Sponsor: Language and Social Interaction Division
Chair: Charles A. Braithwaite, University of Montana
   "Japanese Acknowledgement Tokens and Speakership Incipiency: The Nasal Token and the So-Token." Juanita E. Handy Bosma, University of Texas, Austin, Izumi Funayama, University of Texas, Austin
   "Authentic Conversation as a Model for Textbook Dialogue." Jean Wong, College of New Jersey
   "'Sometimes I Don't Know When to Give a Tip or Just Say Thank You': 'Cultural Learning' in Intercultural Contact." Alan D. Hansen, SUNY, Albany
   "Pragmatics of the Evil Eye in Egyptian Arabic." Mustafa Mughazy, Georgia State University

Respondent: Michaela R. Winchatz, Southern Illinois University

---

2438   12:30-1:45 p.m.   Conf 4F   Fourth Floor   Chicago Hilton

COMPETITIVE PAPERS IN GENDER AND THE MEDIA: FINDINGS FROM CONTENT ANALYSES

Sponsor: Mass Communication Division
Chair: Elizabeth M. Perse, University of Delaware
   "Gender, Intelligence, and the Media: The Presentation and Treatment of Female Television Talk-Show Experts." Lisa B. Holderman, Beaver College
   "Sportscasting and Sports Reporting: The Power of Gender Bias." Susan T. Eastman, Indiana University, Andrew C. Billings, Indiana University, Bloomington
   "Television's World of Work in the Nineties*." Nancy Signorielli, University of Delaware, Susan Kahlenberg, Muhlenberg College
   "The Framing of Feminists and Feminism in U.S. Electronic Media." Rebecca A. Lind, University of Illinois, Chicago, Colleen Salo, University of Illinois, Chicago

Respondent: Margaret J. Haefner, Illinois State University

*Top 3 Competitive Paper

2439   12:30-1:45 p.m.   Conf 4G   Fourth Floor   Chicago Hilton

TRAINING OUR FUTURE TRAINERS: ESTABLISHING A STUDENT CHAPTER OF THE AMERICAN SOCIETY FOR TRAINING AND DEVELOPMENT

Sponsor: Training and Development Division

Panelists: Melissa K. Gibson, Western Michigan University
             Dave Jennings, ASTD Area Manager
             James A. Gilchrist, Western Michigan University
             Eleanor M. Kostecki, Western Michigan University

Mary Lucas, Western Michigan University

This panel discusses the advantages and challenges of establishing a student chapter of ASTD at institutions of higher learning. The program can give advice and instruction to speech communication educators and students on establishing their own chapter of ASTD. Because colleges and universities are the foundation for future trainers, this professional organization can give students a "head start" in learning about the profession and focusing their curriculum choices.

2440   12:30-1:45 p.m.   Conf 4H   Fourth Floor   Chicago Hilton

TELEVISION, FEMINISMS, AND CULTURAL MEMORY: SCHOLARLY AND PEDAGOGICAL INQUIRY

Sponsor: Media Forum Series
Chair: A. Susan Owen, University of Puget Sound
  "Technological Forms and Visual Tropes: Gertrude Berg and the Early Years of Television."
    Caren J. Deming, University of Arizona
  "'Burning Questions': Mediated Feminism, Cultural Memory, and the 1968 Miss America
    Pageant Protest." Bonnie J. Dow, University of Georgia
  "Sabrina, the Teenage. . .?: Girls, Witches, Mortals and Other Gendered Fantasy
    Concepts." Sarah Projansky, University of California, Davis, Leah R. Vande Berg,
    California State University, Sacramento
  "Re-Producing U.S. Feminist Histories: Television and Paramnesia in the National
    Imaginary." Melissa D. Deem, University of Iowa
  "Old Predators and New Hero(ine)s in 'Buffy': Growing Up Postmodern in a Post-Feminist
    World." A. Susan Owen, University of Puget Sound

2441   12:30-1:45 p.m.   Conf 4I   Fourth Floor   Chicago Hilton

EXPLORATIONS OF ORGANIZATIONAL APOLOGETICS

Sponsor: Public Relations Division
Chair: Michael L. Kent, SUNY, Fredonia
  "Organizations and Apologia: The State of the Art." Keith M. Hearit, Western Michigan
    University
  "The Rhetoric of Arrogance: The Public Relations Response of the Standard Oil Trust."
    Joshua Boyd, Purdue University
  "Failed Legitimacy: The Case of the National College Registration Board*." Rebecca J.
    Meisenbach, Wake Forest University
  "Dysfunctional Patterns Leading to an Adrenaline-Rush." Curt Bechler, Aquinas College

Respondent: Jeffrey L. Courtright, University of North Dakota

*Student Paper

2442   12:30-1:45 p.m.   Conf 4J   Fourth Floor   Chicago Hilton

REX MIX'S PROGRAMS OF EXCELLENCE: PAST, PRESENT, FUTURE

Sponsor: Senior College & University Section
Chair: Cindy Buell, Wesleyan College
  "History and Goals of the 'Programs of Excellence' Competition." Joseph W. MacDoniels,
    Hope College
  "Characteristics of the Award-Winning Schools." Jacqueline Schmidt, John Carroll
    University
  "Judges' Perspectives on Winning Programs of Excellence." George C. Wharton, Curry
    College, Mary E. Beadle, John Carroll University
  "Applying for the 'Programs of Excellence' Awards." Stephen L. Coffman, Montana State
    University, Billings
  "The 1999 'Programs of Excellence' Competition." Theodore F. Sheckels,
    Randolph-Macon College

2443   12:30-1:45 p.m.   Conf 4K   Fourth Floor   Chicago Hilton

TOP FOUR PAPERS: STUDENT SECTION

Sponsor: Student Section
"Just Give It to Me Straight: Deception Between Patients and Providers*." Juliann C.
   Scholl, University of Oklahoma, Kevin T. Wright, University of Oklahoma
"Where Politicians Fear to Tread: Advertising for Internet Security**." John W. Jordan,
   University of Georgia
"Doing Right: Towards a Bakhtinian Communicative Ethics." Alexandre Lopez de Miranda,
   Purdue University
"Neonatal Intensive Care Unit: Care Givers Taking Care of Themselves." Derek C. Clapp,
   Texas Tech University

Respondents: Kathleen Farrell, University of Iowa
              David R. Roskos-Ewoldsen, University of Alabama

*Top Paper in Interpersonal Communication for the Student Section **Top Paper in Rhetorical
Studies for the Student Section, Debut Paper

2444   12:30-1:45 p.m.   Conf 4L   Fourth Floor   Chicago Hilton

EXAMINING THE LINES: FEMALE ACADEMICIANS ADDRESS POWER, MEANING, ISOLATION AND ESTRANGEMENT

Sponsor: Women's Caucus
Chair: Shawn Townes, Ohio University

Panelists: Marilyn D. Hunt, Missouri Western State College
           Carolyn Calloway-Thomas, Indiana University, Bloomington
           Enid S. Waldhart, University of Kentucky
           Lou D. Tillson, Murray State University
           Tracy C. Russo, University of Kansas
           Jenny Nelson, Ohio University
           Virginia P. Richmond, West Virginia University

Respondent: Pamela A. Dawes-Kaylor, Ohio University

This roundtable brings together a wide range of female administrators and academicians to
share their experiences, trials, treasures, and paradigms about women and the academy.

2445   12:30-1:45 p.m.   Conf 4M   Fourth Floor   Chicago Hilton

SUPPORTIVE COMMUNICATION II: EXPLAINING COMPETENCE AND INCOMPETENCE THROUGH COGNITIVE, CULTURAL, SITUATIONAL, AND DISCURSIVE FACTORS

Sponsors: Group Communication Division
          Interpersonal Communication Division
Chair: Wendy Samter, University of Delaware
   "Supportive Communication as a Strategic Enterprise: The Effects of Support Providers'
      Attributions on Their Interaction Goals." Erina L. MacGeorge, University of Illinois,
      Urbana-Champaign
   "Verbal and Nonverbal Elements of Comforting Behavior in Interactive Contexts: Some
      Effects of Target Blame and Behavioral Reciprocity." Wendy Samter, University of
      Delaware, Walid A. Afifi, Penn State University
   "The Dark Side of Cognitive Complexity: The Production of Hurtful Messages." Aaron E.
      Bacue, University of Arizona
   "The Effects of Indirectness in Support Elicitation on Support Evaluation." Wendy L. Falato,
      Penn State University, Susan J. Messman, Penn State University
   "Cultural Differences in Rules for Communicating Emotional Support: Effects of
      Individualism-Collectivism on Expressing and Managing Emotion." Steven T. Mortenson,
      Purdue University, Brant R. Burleson, Purdue University

---

2446   12:30-1:45 p.m.   McCormick Board Rm   Fourth Floor   Chicago Hilton

SOUTHERN STATES COMMUNICATION ASSOCIATION NOMINATING COMMITTEE MEETING

Sponsor: Southern States Communication Association

2447   12:30-1:45 p.m.   Pullman Board Rm   Fourth Floor   Chicago Hilton

WORLD COMMUNICATION ASSOCIATION BUSINESS MEETING

Sponsor: World Communication Association

2449   12:30-1:45 p.m.   Conf 5B   Fifth Floor   Chicago Hilton

NOW THAT WE HAVE TECHNOLOGY IN THE CLASSROOM, WHAT DO WE DO WITH IT?

Sponsor: Basic Course Division
Chair: Marilyn M. Shaw, University of Northern Iowa

Panelists: Laura L. Sohl, University of Northern Iowa
       Susan Cusmano, University of Northern Iowa
       Marilyn M. Shaw, University of Northern Iowa

Panelists will discuss the options and activities available with the use of technology in multiple classroom settings. Audience participation is encouraged.

2451   12:30-1:45 p.m.   Conf 5D   Fifth Floor   Chicago Hilton

THE COMMUNICATION PREDICAMENTS OF AGING AS CONSTRUED ACROSS CULTURES

Sponsor: Communication and Aging Commission
Chair: Mary Lee Hummert, University of Kansas
   "Talking Age and Aging Talk: Communication and Aging Around the Pacific-Rim." Howard Giles, University of California, Santa Barbara

---

2452   12:30-1:45 p.m.   Conf 5E   Fifth Floor   Chicago Hilton

DISTINGUISHED SCHOLAR IN RHETORIC AND COMMUNICATION THEORY

Sponsor: Rhetorical and Communication Theory Division
Chair: Gerard A. Hauser, University of Colorado, Boulder

This panel will feature a lecture by the 1999 recipient of the award for the Distinguished Scholar in Rhetoric and Communication Theory.

2453   12:30-1:45 p.m.   Conf 5F   Fifth Floor   Chicago Hilton

TOP THREE PAPERS: COMMISSION ON COMMUNICATION IN THE FUTURE

Sponsor: Commission on Communication in the Future
Chair: Nancy J. Hoar, Western New England College
   "Love on the Line: A Study of Romantic Relationships in an On-Line Context." Sue M. Wildermuth, University of Minnesota, Minneapolis
   "Hope for a New Century: Transporting Environmental Communication Across International Boundaries." Lea J. Parker, Northern Arizona University
   "Why Chat? Motives for Communicating via the Internet." Michelle E. Fournier, Ohio University

Respondent: Sue Barnes, Fordham University

2454   12:30-1:45 p.m.   Conf 5G   Fifth Floor   Chicago Hilton

THE NATURE OF COMMUNICATION IN THE CLASSROOM

Sponsor: Instructional Development Division
Chair: Ann L. Darling, University of Utah
   "An Exploratory Study of Teacher Communication Knowledge in the College Classroom."
      Carol S. Cawyer, University of North Texas, Gustav W. Friedrich, Rutgers University
   "A Communication-Based Model of College Student Persistence." Rachel E.
      Karpanty-Yantis, Illinois Institute of Art
   "The Social Construction of Communication Climate: An Analysis of At-Risk Students in an
      Alternative High School." Tasha J. Souza, University of Wisconsin, Parkside

Respondent: Ann L. Darling, University of Utah

2455   12:30-1:45 p.m.   Conf 5H   Fifth Floor   Chicago Hilton

BACKLASH AND TALKING TRASH: RHETORICAL RESISTANCE TO THE DISABILITY RIGHTS MOVEMENT

Sponsor: Caucus on Disability Issues
Chair: Spoma Jovanovic-Mattson, University of Denver
   "Seeking Common Ground via Appeals to Common Sense: Counter Persuasion and the
      Disability Rights Movement." Bruce R. Dorries, Radford University
   "Disability and Dependence: A Case Study of Groupthink and the Million Dollar
      Exploitation of a Closed-Head-Injured Family Member." Kelly P. Herold, Winona State
      University, Karen Johnson, Winona State University
   "Against the ADA: News Narratives and Backlash." Beth A. Haller, Towson University

---

2456   12:30-1:45 p.m.   Conf 5I   Fifth Floor   Chicago Hilton

REMEMBERING THE COLONY IN A POSTCOLONIAL AND GLOBAL WORLD

Sponsor: Latina/Latino Communication Studies Division
Chair: Nathaniel I. Cordova, University of Maryland
   "Romanticizing Remembrance: Castro Cuba and the Colony." Myra Mendible, Florida Gulf
      Coast University
   "Preface to a Postcolonial Mythology: Puerto Rico, Memories of Citizenship, and the
      Rhetoric of Decolonization in 1998." Nathaniel I. Cordova, University of Maryland
   "Discursive Amnesia/Amnesty and San Jose Chinatown." Wenshu Lee, San Jose State
      University
   "(Re)Building a Nation: South Africa's Heritage Day as a Site of Renaming, Reimaging, and
      Remembering." Scott M. Schonfeldt-Aultman, San Francisco State University, Gust A.
      Yep, San Francisco State University

Respondent: Kent A. Ono, University of California, Davis

2457   12:30-1:45 p.m.   Conf 5J   Fifth Floor   Chicago Hilton

COLORING OUTSIDE THE LINES

Sponsor: Lambda Pi Eta
Chair: Frances M. Broderick, College of Mount Saint Vincent
   "The Use of Female Sexuality Within Alcohol Advertising*." Christi Stern, College of
      Wooster
   "The Importance of Understanding Culture When Dealing with Public Relations."
      Margaret Paynor, College of Mount Saint Vincent
   "Exploring the Reality: The Effects of Prime-Time Television on College-Age Women."
      Bridget M. Beherns, Marist College, Jessica Holden, Marist College, Meghan
      O'Shaughnessy, Marist College
   "Rhetorical Fiction: An Examination of the Rhetorical Value of the Fictional Novel
      Blackwater." Ryan Elizabeth Clark, College of Wooster

*This paper was selected as the top paper presented by a Lambda Pi Eta Communication Honor Society member and will be awarded the 1999 Stephen A. Smith Award for Outstanding Undergraduate Scholarship in Communication.

| 2458 | 12:30-3:15 p.m. | Lake Ontario | Eighth Floor | Chicago Hilton |

SHORT COURSE #13. TEACHING THE COLLEGE COURSE IN LEADERSHIP COMMUNICATION

Sponsor: Short Courses

Instructors: Michael Z. Hackman, University of Colorado, Colorado Springs
Craig E. Johnson, George Fox University

Fee required. See complete Short Course descriptions elsewhere in the program.

| 2459 | 12:30-3:15 p.m. | Lake Michigan | Eighth Floor | Chicago Hilton |

SHORT COURSE #14. CONQUER YOUR SPEECHFRIGHT: TEACHING A WORKSHOP OR A MODULE IN A BASIC SPEECH COURSE FOR HIGH APPREHENSIVES

Sponsor: Short Courses

Instructor: Karen K. Dwyer, University of Nebraska, Omaha

Fee required. See complete Short Course descriptions elsewhere in the program.

| 2460 | 12:30-3:15 p.m. | Lake Huron | Eighth Floor | Chicago Hilton |

SHORT COURSE #15. BEYOND THE UNIVERSITY, INTO THE COMMUNITY: SERVICE-LEARNING IN THE COMMUNICATION COURSE

Sponsor: Short Courses

Instructors: Carolyn L. Karmon, Washburn University
Russell D. Lowery-Hart, West Texas A&M University
Carol J. Bruess, University of St. Thomas
Lori A. Byers, Spalding University
Laura L. Shue, Ball State University

Fee required. See complete Short Course descriptions elsewhere in the program.

| 2461 | 12:30-3:15 p.m. | Lake Erie | Eighth Floor | Chicago Hilton |

SHORT COURSE #16. TEACHING THE COLLEGE COURSE IN GROUP COMMUNICATION

Sponsor: Short Courses

Instructor: Joann Keyton, University of Memphis

Fee required. See complete Short Course descriptions elsewhere in the program.

| 2462 | 12:30-1:45 p.m. | Essex Court | Second Floor | Essex Inn |

FROM CREATION TO APOCALYPSE: EXISTENTIAL READINGS OF TIME

Sponsor: Religious Communication Association
Chair: Michael J. Hyde, Wake Forest University
"History, Memory, and Motive: An Inquiry into the Lived Past." Bryan Crable, Villanova University
"The Compulsion of the Present." Wade R. Kenny, University of Dayton
"Futuralness as Freedom: Moving Toward the Past That Will Have Been." Corey Anton, Grand Valley State University

Respondent: Calvin L. Schrag, Purdue University

2463   12:30-1:45 p.m.   **Windsor Court**   **Second Floor**   **Essex Inn**

EVOCATIVE WRITING IN ETHNOGRAPHY

Sponsor: Ethnography Division
Chair: Diane F. Witmer, California State University, Fullerton
    "Almost Them, Almost Me: Doing Fieldwork at Beth Israel Messianic Congregation." Leigh
      Berger, University of South Florida
    "Hunting for the Militia: An Ethnographic Account of Seeking Organizational Access."
      Janel A. Crider, Purdue University
    "Citywest Emergency: (A Fiction Depicting) A Day in the Life of a 911 Call-Taker." Sarah J.
      Tracy, University of Colorado, Boulder
    "Woman's Body Found in River: An Autobiography of Murder, Fear, and Survival."
      Stephanie Poole Martinez, Southern Illinois University

Respondent: Arthur P. Bochner, University of South Florida

2464   12:30-1:45 p.m.   **Buckingham Court**   **Second Floor**   **Essex Inn**

"THE EYE IS THE FIRST CIRCLE; THE HORIZON IT FORMS, THE SECOND": SPECTATORSHIP, IDENTITY, AND PLACE IN AMERICA

Sponsor: American Studies Commission
Chair: Diane Gruber, Arizona State University West
    "The Emergence of a Spectator Culture: Place and Placelessness at the Picture Palace*."
      Janna Jones, University of South Florida
    "'The World Is Not Like Celebration': Rhetorical Displacement and Replacement in
      Disney's Celebration." Andrew F. Wood, San Jose State University
    "From Discourse to Golf Course: The Serious Play of Imagining Community Space." D.
      Robert DeChaine, Claremont Graduate University
    "The Mass Consumption of Merchandized Identities." Joseph V. Gemin, University of
      Wisconsin, Oshkosh

*Top Three Paper

2466   12:30-1:45 p.m.   **Cohn Rm**   **Second Floor**   **Spertus Institute**

SCIENCE AND ITS RHETORICS AT THE INTERSECTION: CASE STUDIES IN ENVIRONMENTAL SCIENCE AND POLICY

Sponsor: American Association for Rhetoric of Science & Technology
Chair: Steve Fuller, University of Durham
    "Business and the Environment: Selling Development to an Environmentally-Conscious
      Public." Anand Rao, Clarion University
    "Where There's Smoke, There's . . . PM-10, SOX, NOX, VOC, Petroleum Hydrocarbons
      and Lead." Kirk W. Junker, Queen's University/Dublin City University
    "Intellectual Property Rights: New Strategies for Stealing Global/Local Resources." Peter K.
      Bsumek, James Madison University

Respondent: Steve Fuller, University of Durham

2468   12:30-1:45 p.m.   **Rm 902**   **Ninth Floor**   **Spertus Institute**

THE MANY COLORS OF COMMUNICATION: TEACHING COMMUNICATION IN THE CHINESE CLASSROOM

Sponsor: Chinese Communication Association
Chair: Laura K. Hahn, Humboldt State University

Panelists: Lyall Crawford, Weber State University
        Victoria L. DeFrancisco, University of Northern Iowa
        Melissa McCalla, University of Colorado, Denver

Friday

Sharon M. Varallo, Augustana College
Laura K. Hahn, Humboldt State University

2469   12:30-1:45 p.m.   Rm 903   Ninth Floor   Spertus Institute

FROM PEDOGOGY TO ASSESSMENT IN EXPERIENTIAL LEARNING WITH AN INTERNSHIP TWIST

Sponsor: Experiential Learning in Communication Commission
Chair: Eileen M. Perrigo, University of West Florida
  "Bloome's Taxonomy as a Formative Assessment Technique: It's Not New, but It's Still Innovative." Denise Ann Vrchota, Iowa State University
  "The Role of Computerized Adaptive Testing in Experiential Learning." Susan Brown Zahn, Indiana State University
  "Assessing Job Skills of Interns and Graduates in Speech Communication." Frederick W. Isaacson, San Francisco State University
  "Communication Faculty Internships: Adding Practice to Theory." Dirk C. Gibson, University of New Mexico
  "Public Relations Internship System Evaluation: Evaluation Criteria and a Preliminary Instrument." Dirk C. Gibson, University of New Mexico

Respondent: Donald R. Martin, DePaul University

2470   12:30-1:45 p.m.   Rm 904   Ninth Floor   Spertus Institute

COMPETITIVE PAPERS IN CHINESE COMMUNICATION STUDIES: STYLES OF COMMUNICATION

Sponsor: Association for Chinese Communication Studies
Chair: Becky Yeh, University of Oklahoma
  "Self-Disclosure and the Chinese-Canadians: A Case Study." Jianglong Wang, Western Washington University
  "Masculinity Index and Communication Style: An Asian View*." John C. Hwang, California State University, Sacramento

Respondent: Rueyling Chuang, St. John's University/College of St. Benedict

*Top Paper

2471   12:30-1:45 p.m.   Rm 906   Ninth Floor   Spertus Institute

READINGS OF JAMES DARSEY'S *THE PROPHETIC TRADITION AND RADICAL RHETORIC IN AMERICA*

Sponsor: American Society for the History of Rhetoric
Chair: James M. Tallmon, South Dakota State University
  "The Toad in the Garden: Women As Prophets." Karlyn K. Campbell, University of Minnesota
  "Prophetic Ethos and Political Theories in Conflict with the American Tradition." Mari Boor Tonn, University of New Hampshire
  "The Radical, the Prophet and the Critic: Ethical Considerations." John A. Campbell, University of Memphis

Respondent: James Darsey, Georgia State University

Darsey's book won the 1998 Diamond Book Award, the 1998 Winans-Wichelns Award for Distinguished Scholarship in Rhetoric and the 1998 Marie Hochmuth Nichols Award.

2472   12:30-1:45 p.m.   Rm 907   Ninth Floor   Spertus Institute

INTERCOLLEGIATE DEBATE AS INVITATIONAL RHETORIC: AN OFFERING AND ILLUSTRATION

Sponsor: Cross Examination Debate Association
Chair: Jodee Hobbs, Northeast Louisiana University

"Intercollegiate Debate as Invitational Rhetoric: An Offering." Jeffrey D. Hobbs, Abilene Christian University, Jeffrey T. Bile, University of Utah, Kristina Campos, Abilene Christian University, Jodee Hobbs, Northeast Louisiana University, Sue E. Lowrie, Pepperdine University, Amanda M. Wilkins, Emerson College

Respondents: Sonja K. Foss, University of Colorado, Denver
Cindy L. Griffin, Colorado State University
Josina M. Makau, California State University, Monterey Bay

"Intercollegiate Debate as Invitational Rhetoric: An Illustration", Four of the panelists will debate the 1999-2000 intercollegiate debate topic demonstrating debate as invitational rhetoric.

2473   12:30-1:45 p.m.   Rm 908   Ninth Floor   Spertus Institute

A SELECTION OF AWARD-WINNING ORAL INTERPRETATIONS FROM THE 1999 PHI RHO PI NATIONAL FORENSICS TOURNAMENT

Sponsor: Phi Rho Pi
Chair: Cynthia E. Dewar, City College of San Francisco

Respondent: Gretchen E. Wheeler, Casper College

In addition to award-winning prose, poetry, drama, dramatic duo, and programmed oral interpretations from the 1999 Phi Rho Pi National Forensics Tournament, this program also provides information on literature selection, thematic appeals, and performance techniques. Audience members will have an opportunity to interact with the student performers.

2474   12:30-1:45 p.m.   Auditorium   Second Floor   Spertus Institute

A CARL SANDBURG READING HOUR: CELEBRATION AND CELEBRITY

Sponsor: Theatre Division
Chair: Gerald Lee Ratliff, SUNY, Potsdam

Panelists: Susan Kay Tomasovic, George Mason University
Deryl B. Johnson, Kutztown University
Gail S. Medford, Bowie State University
Roberta L. Crisson, Kutztown University
Julie R. Patterson-Pratt, University of Minnesota, Morris

Carl Sandburg, the celebrity, celebrates his 90th anniversary in his favorite city, Chicago. Join the celebration of Sandburg the poet and his place in American literature.

2478   12:30-3:15 p.m.   Conrad Suite   Chicago Hilton

NCA PAST PRESIDENTS BUSINESS MEETING AND LUNCHEON

Sponsor: National Communication Association

2:00 p.m.

2506   2:00-3:15 p.m.   Continental BR A   Lobby Level   Chicago Hilton

NEW RESEARCH IN TELEVISION PROGRAM PROMOTION

Sponsor: Mass Communication Division
Chair: Susan T. Eastman, Indiana University
"Applying Audience Activity Theory to the Practice of Promotion." Elizabeth M. Perse, University of Delaware
"Structural and Content Factors Affecting the Effectiveness of Promotion." Susan T. Eastman, Indiana University, Paul D. Bolls, Indiana University
"Television Branding as Promotion: Rationale, Practice, and Effects." Robert V. Bellamy, Duquesne University, Paul J. Traudt, University of Nevada, Las Vegas

Friday

"Using Sex and Violence in Network Program Promotion." James R. Walker, Saint Xavier University

Respondent: Jennings Bryant, University of Alabama

2507   2:00-3:15 p.m.   Continental BR B   Lobby Level   Chicago Hilton

SELF-PRESENTATION IN ON-LINE TEACHING/LEARNING ENVIRONMENTS

Sponsor: Human Communication and Technology Commission
Chair: Dianne L. Blomberg, Metropolitan State College of Denver
 "Creating Interpersonalness in the On-Line Teaching/Learning Relationship." Dianne L. Blomberg, Metropolitan State College of Denver
 "The Personal Narrative On-Line: A Re-examination of Fisher's Paradigm." Beth A. Weigel, University of Denver
 "The Constitution of Self In and Through Technology." Roger W. Smith, J.D. Edwards & Company
 "The Teaching and Assessment of Interpersonal Skills On-Line." Shawn Worthy, Metropolitan State College of Denver
 "Technology and the Self." Jennifer L. Coburn-Engquist, University of Denver

Respondents: C. Erik Timmerman, University of Texas, Austin
     Jennifer M. MacLennan, University of Saskatchewan

We are called upon to communicate in the on-line forum in educational settings and an "interpersonal" relationship will likely emerge. Creating interpersonalness, performance of self, uncovering the personal narrative, assessing interpersonal skill, and creating "self" on-line are all variables of this act. Reaching an understanding of these technologies is required of those who perform here. Most of us have little or no formal training in these areas. This interactive panel discussion will present suggestions for a greater understanding of the phenomenon.

2508   2:00-3:15 p.m.   Continental BR C   Lobby Level   Chicago Hilton

SPOTLIGHT FORUM: SPEAKING THE UNSPEAKABLE—WHITENESS AND THE POLITICS OF OUR DISCIPLINE

Sponsor: Critical and Cultural Studies Division
Chair: Raka Shome, University of California, Davis

Panelists: Marsha Houston, Tulane University
    Thomas K. Nakayama, Arizona State University
    Philip C. Wander, San Jose State University

Respondent: Raymie E. McKerrow, Ohio University

This forum will interrogate the problem of whiteness in our discipline. The focus is on examining whiteness not just as an epistemological problem, but as an epistmological problem that has "real life" material effects on the lives and careers of people of color in our field (and sometimes on whites who challenge the whitness of our field). This forum is centrally focused on the ways in which marginalized racial groups "pay a price" for the continuing problem of whiteness in our discipline. Audience participation and views will be heavily encouraged.

2511   2:00-3:15 p.m.   Int'l Ballroom North   Second Floor   Chicago Hilton

PERFORMING ETHNOGRAPHY

Sponsor: Ethnography Division
Chair: Christina W. Stage, Arizona State University
 "Cultural Performance Analysis Shells (CPAS): An Integrated Ethnographic Methodology." Kristin B. Valentine, Arizona State University, Gordon T. Matsumoto, Arizona State University
 "Performing Research: Mediated Possibilities for Scholarly Discourse." Michelle A. Miller, Penn State University

Respondent: Stacy L. Holman Jones, University of Texas, Austin

---

2514   2:00-3:15 p.m.   Boulevard A   Second Floor   Chicago Hilton

SHAPING UP TECHNOLOGY AND SHIPPING OUT COMMUNICATION EXPERTISE

Sponsor: Challenging Boundaries Series
Chair: Mark A. Aakhus, Rutgers University
  "Technology Design and Communication." Sally A. Jackson, University of Arizona
  "Technology Design Communities." Michele H. Jackson, University of Colorado
  "Technology Design and Communication Professionals." Mark A. Aakhus, Rutgers University
  "Technology Design and Research Partnerships with Organizations." Marshall S. Poole, Texas A&M University

---

2515   2:00-3:15 p.m.   Boulevard B   Second Floor   Chicago Hilton

PERSPECTIVES ON RATIONAL AND NON-RATIONAL ARGUMENT IN GROUPS

Sponsor: Group Communication Division
Chair: Sandra M. Ketrow, University of Rhode Island

Panelists: Dale E. Brashers, University of Illinois, Urbana-Champaign
        Dennis S. Gouran, Penn State University
        Michael Mendelson, Iowa State University
        Renee A. Meyers, University of Wisconsin, Milwaukee

This interactive panel engages perspectives on argument (formal vs. informal, rational vs. non-rational) in groups, including intergroup and mixed-motive orientations (such as labor vs. management-type bargaining), and examines the growing criticism of the rational perspective and its perceived deficiencies, as well as the need to understand better the ways in which decision makers actually make choices.

2516   2:00-3:15 p.m.   Boulevard C   Second Floor   Chicago Hilton

JUSTIFICATION, PERSUASION, AND REFUTATION: RHETORICAL EXPLORATION IN INTERCULTURAL COMMUNICATION

Sponsor: International & Intercultural Communication Division
Chair: Paul N. Lakey, Abilene Christian University
  "The Organization of Justificatory Discourse in Interaction: A Comparison Within and Across Cultures." Barbara Warnick, University of Washington, Valerie L. Manusov, University of Washington
  "'Feminine Style' Intersecting High-Context Communication: A Rhetorical Case Study of a Japanese Feminist Discourse." Shinobu Suzuki, Hokkaido University
  "Testing the Moderating Effect of Message Sidedness on Explicit Conclusion and Implicit Conclusion: A Cross-Cultural Study." Rie Ohashi, Michigan State University, Mary Jiang I. Bresnahan, Michigan State University, Reiko Nebashi, Rikkyo University, Japan

Respondent: William J. Starosta, Howard University

2518   2:00-3:15 p.m.   Waldorf   Third Floor   Chicago Hilton

MARRIAGE: ISSUES THAT RELATE TO RELATIONAL MAINTENANCE

Sponsor: Family Communication Division
Chair: Rick A. Buerkel, Central Michigan University
  "Predicting Maintenance Enactment from Couple Type, Partner Behavior, and Relational Characteristics." Marianne Dainton, La Salle University, Laura L. Stafford, Ohio State University
  "Affect and Behavioral Involvement in Spousal Complaints and Compliments." Jeanne K. Flora, California State University, Fullerton, Chris Segrin, University of Arizona

Friday

"Don't Sweat the Small Stuff: The Role of Conflict in Later-Life Marriages." Fran Dickson, University of Denver, Tamara S. Bollis-Pecci, University of Denver, Patrick C. Hughes, University of Denver, Linda D. Manning, University of Denver, Kandi L. Walker, University of Denver, Scott D. Gratson, University of Denver

"Maintaining Marriages in the United States and Russia: Comparing the Influence of Maintenance Behaviors on Indicators of Marital Quality." Deborah S. Ballard-Reisch, University of Nevada, Reno, Daniel J. Weigel, University of Nevada, Reno, Marat Zaguidoulline, University of Bergen, Norway

Respondent: Anita L. Vangelisti, University of Texas, Austin

2521   2:00-3:15 p.m.   Williford A   Third Floor   Chicago Hilton

FINDING MEANING IN AFRICAN AMERICAN DISCOURSE

Sponsor: African American Communication & Culture Commission
Chair: Anntarie L. Sims, College of New Jersey
    "Negotiating Societal Stereotypes: Analyzing 'Real World' Discourse By and About African American Men." Mark P. Orbe, Western Michigan University, Kiesha T. Warren, Western Michigan University
    "Perceptual and Behavioral Profiles of Race and Dialect." Andrew C. Billings, Indiana University, Bloomington
    "Out of the Frying Pan and into the Fire: A Look at Who Really Put the 'Anglo' and 'African' in the Anglo and African American Word." Juandalynn L. Taylor, University of Texas, Austin
    "Deconstructing Bell Hooks: Messages and Meaning." Lisa M. Schreiber, University of Nebraska, Lincoln

Respondent: Jeffrey L. Woodyard, Stetson University

2522   2:00-3:15 p.m.   Williford B   Third Floor   Chicago Hilton

PERSUASION AND SOCIAL MOVEMENTS: RHETORICAL ALTERNATIVES TO THE RESOURCE MOBILIZATION MODEL

Sponsor: Political Communication Division
Chair: Patricia A. Sullivan, SUNY, New Paltz
    "Reconfiguring the Rhetoric of Social Movements: Concepts and Approaches in Transition." Steven R. Goldzwig, Marquette University, Patricia A. Sullivan, SUNY, New Paltz
    "Argument from Conspiracy." Charles J. Stewart, Purdue University
    "The Pro-Choice and Pro-Life Autobiographies of 'Jane Roe': Counter-Narratives by the Same Person." Sharon L. Maney, University of North Carolina, Greensboro
    "Patriot Movement or Domestic Terrorism?: Violence as a Source of Rhetorical Invention." Craig A. Smith, University of North Carolina, Greensboro

---

2523   2:00-3:15 p.m.   Williford C   Third Floor   Chicago Hilton

AFFECT IN THE ETHNOGRAPHIC INTERVIEW: A ROUNDTABLE DISCUSSION OF METHODOLOGICAL CONCERNS FACING RESEARCHERS

Sponsor: Feminist and Women Studies Division
Chair: Nina J. Truch, University of Arizona

Panelists: Julia T. Wood, University of North Carolina, Chapel Hill
        Eileen B. Ray, Cleveland State University
        Beth H. Ellis, Ball State University
        George B. Ray, Cleveland State University
        Lora Lempert, University of Michigan, Dearborn

The discussion will address the emotional impact that ethnographic interviews have on researcher and participant when investigating topics of abuse and violence against women, and coping mechanisms available for each.

| 2524 | 2:00-3:15 p.m. | Marquette | Third Floor | Chicago Hilton |

LEARNING COMMUNITIES AS A CURRICULUM REFORM TECHNIQUE IN THE DISCIPLINE OF COMMUNICATION

Sponsor: Table Talk Series
Chair: Dale A. Bertelsen, Bloomsburg University
  "Defining the Role of Learning Communities: An Overview." Mary Mino, Penn State University, DuBois
  "Teaching in a Communication-Linked Learning Community: An Experiential Report." Joseph Mitchell, Indiana State University
  "Measuring Learning Community Effectiveness." James W. Chesebro, Indiana State University, Kevin J. G. Snider, Indiana State University, Ruth L. Green, North Carolina State University

Designed to encourage experimentation, these papers examine how the discipline of communication might incorporate learning communities as a new curriculum design.

| 2525 | 2:00-3:15 p.m. | Joliet | Third Floor | Chicago Hilton |

LAMBDA PI ETA: HOW AND WHY TO START A CHAPTER

Sponsor: Lambda Pi Eta

Panelists: James L. Gaudino, NCA National Office
  Sherwyn P. Morreale, NCA National Office
  Omari Sanders, NCA National Office
  Orlando L. Taylor, Howard University
  Spiro G. Yulis, College of New Jersey

Lambda Pi Eta, the National Communication Honor Society, currently has over 200 chapters across the country. LPH encourages excellence among undergraduate communication students, fosters cooperation among students and faculty, and encourages responsibility and leadership. If your institution does not have a chapter, this is an opportunity to meet with NCA and LPH leaders and find out how (and why) to begin one.

| 2526 | 2:00-3:15 p.m. | PDR 1 | Third Floor | Chicago Hilton |

SPIRITUAL COMMUNICATION COMMISSION BUSINESS MEETING

Sponsor: Spiritual Communication Commission

| 2527 | 2:00-3:15 p.m. | PDR 2 | Third Floor | Chicago Hilton |

PERFORMANCE STUDIES DIVISION BUSINESS MEETING

Sponsor: Performance Studies Division

| 2528 | 2:00-3:15 p.m. | PDR 3 | Third Floor | Chicago Hilton |

STUDENT SECTION BUSINESS MEETING

Sponsor: Student Section

| 2529 | 2:00-3:15 p.m. | PDR 4 | Third Floor | Chicago Hilton |

ASIAN PACIFIC AMERICAN COMMUNICATION STUDIES DIVISION BUSINESS MEETING

Sponsor: Asian Pacific American Communication Studies Division

Friday

| 2530 | 2:00-3:15 p.m. | PDR 5 | Third Floor | Chicago Hilton |

BASIC COURSE DIVISION BUSINESS MEETING

Sponsor: Basic Course Division

| 2531 | 2:00-3:15 p.m. | PDR 6 | Third Floor | Chicago Hilton |

TOP COMPETITIVE PAPERS IN FREEDOM OF EXPRESSION

Sponsor: Freedom of Expression Commission
Chair: Paul Siegel, Gallaudet University
   "The Centerwall Study: The Rhetorical Use of Evidence in the Violence Debate*." Craig R.
   Smith, California State University, Long Beach
   "Virility? Hostility? Incompatibility?: Sexual Harassment, Free Speech and Public
   Spheres**." Marilyn E. Bordwell, Allegheny College
   "Support for Censorship of Television Violence: The Third-Person Effect, News Exposure,
   and Other Predictors." Cynthia A. Hoffner, Illinois State University, Martha Buchanan,
   Illinois State University, Joel David Anderson, Illinois State University, Laura Kowalczyk,
   Illinois State University, Angela Pastorek, Illinois State University, Richard S. Plotkin,
   Illinois State University, Lisa A. Ricciotti, Illinois State University, Stacy Schneider, Illinois
   State University, Kelsey Silberg, Illinois State University

Respondent: Paul Siegel, Gallaudet University

*Top Paper   **Top Student Paper

| 2532 | 2:00-3:15 p.m. | PDR 7 | Third Floor | Chicago Hilton |

NCA AND STATE COMMUNICATION ASSOCIATION PRESIDENTS BUSINESS MEETING

Sponsors: National Communication Association
        States Advisory Council

| 2533 | 2:00-3:15 p.m. | Conf 4A | Fourth Floor | Chicago Hilton |

FEMINIST AND WOMEN'S STUDIES DIVISION GENERAL BUSINESS MEETING

Sponsor: Feminist and Women Studies Division

| 2534 | 2:00-4:45 p.m. | Conf 4B | Fourth Floor | Chicago Hilton |

LICENSED TO KILL: COMMUNICATION AND THE CONSTRUCTION OF A CLIMATE OF HATE

Sponsor: Gay/Lesbian Transgender Communication Studies Division
Chair: Ray A. Slagle, St. Cloud State University

Panelists: Walter L. Atkinson, Northern Illinois University
          Paula S. Tompkins, St. Cloud State University
          Russel R. Windes, CUNY

The number of violent attacks on gay men, lesbians, bisexuals, and transgendered people rises every year. What is surprising is the increase of anti-gay crimes, despite an overall decrease in the general crime rate. This panel will discuss how communication has created a climate that spurs such violence. Participants will watch and discuss the award winning documentary Licensed to Kill which examines the lives of seven men whose contempt for homosexuals lead them to murder.

| 2535 | 2:00-3:15 p.m. | Conf 4C | Fourth Floor | Chicago Hilton |

RESULTS OF A LONGITUDINAL STUDY OF GRADUATE STUDENTS: IMPLICATIONS FOR GRADUATE EDUCATION IN COMMUNICATION

Sponsor: Educational Policies Board
Chair: Richard L. West, University of Southern Maine
  "Overview of the Multi-Campus, Multi-Year Research Program." Jo Sprague, San Jose State University
  "Voices of the Future Professoriate: What Do Graduate Students Learn About Teaching?" Claire S. Calcagno, San Jose State University
  "Voices of the Future Professoriate: What Do Graduate Students Learn About Research?" Laura M. Manning, University of Washington
  "Implications for TA Trainers and Course Supervisors." Donald H. Wulff, University of Washington
  "Reconceptualizing Graduate Education: Implications for Higher Education's Leaders." Jody D. Nyquist, University of Washington

| 2536 | 2:00-3:15 p.m. | Conf 4D | Fourth Floor | Chicago Hilton |

REDRAWING THE LINES: WOMEN'S RHETORICAL CONSTRUCTION OF SELF IN POP CULTURE

Sponsor: Public Address Division
Chair: Carol J. Jablonski, University of South Florida
  "Women of Mystery: The Female Detective in Fiction." Suzanne M. Daughton, Southern Illinois University
  "The Swimsuit Issue: *Cathy* vs. *Sports Illustrated*." Kathleen J. Turner, Tulane University
  "Modeling Generation X: Kate Moss' Construction of a Twenty-Something Femininity." D. Lynn O'Brien Hallstein, Babson College
  "Sexuality and Selfhood: *Ellen* and Media Constructions of Lesbian Identity." Bonnie J. Dow, University of Georgia

Respondent: Carol J. Jablonski, University of South Florida

| 2537 | 2:00-3:15 p.m. | Conf 4E | Fourth Floor | Chicago Hilton |

ISSUES IN MEDIA ETHICS

Sponsor: Communication Ethics Commission
Chair: Matthew W. Seeger, Wayne State University
  "Beyond Heroics: Praiseworthy Compromises and Other Strategies for Resisting Business Demands in the Professions*." Sandra L. Borden, Western Michigan University
  "Communication Ethics and the Use of Technological Distortion Within Televised Political Advertising: A Case Study." Gary A. Noggle, Bethel College
  "Branded with the Mark of Cain: Issues Surrounding New York State's Offender Registration Act." Pamela D. Schultz, Alfred University

Respondent: Pat Arneson, Duquesne University

*Top Three Paper

| 2538 | 2:00-3:15 p.m. | Conf 4F | Fourth Floor | Chicago Hilton |

THE CHALLENGING TERRAIN OF APPLIED COMMUNICATION RESEARCH: NEGOTIATING TRADITIONAL AND NOVEL CONTEXTS

Sponsor: Applied Communication Division
Chair: Lyle J. Flint, Ball State University
  "An Exploratory Study of Department Heads/Chairs and Senior Administrators' Perceptions of the Performance Appraisal Interview." Earl E. McDowell, University of Minnesota

Friday

"Effects of Interviewer Race on Response Extremity of African Americans." Robin L. Nabi, University of Arizona, Paula Lazili, University of Pennsylvania, Robert Hornik, University of Pennsylvania

"Compliance Gaining and Communication in Coach-Athlete Dyads." Jeffrey W. Kassing, Arizona State University West, Dominic A. Infante, Kent State University

"Trait Verbal Aggression, Sport Fan Identification, and Perceptions of Appropriate Sports Fan Communication." Kelly A. Rocca, West Virginia University, Sally M. Vogl-Bauer, University of Wisconsin, Whitewater

Respondent: Kenneth J. Levine, Illinois State University

2539   2:00-3:15 p.m.   Conf 4G   Fourth Floor   Chicago Hilton

GENDER AND POLITICAL COMMUNICATION

Sponsor: Political Communication Division
Chair: Jerry L. Miller, Ohio University

"An Analysis of Media Coverage Toward Female Candidates in Senatorial Campaign Debates." Terry A. Robertson, University of Oklahoma

"'The Buck Stops with Me': Attorney General Janet Reno's Defensive Discourse in Response to the Branch Davidian Crisis." Shannon R. Davis, University of Colorado, Boulder

"The Effects of Counter-Stereotypical Messages for Female Candidates." Arla G. Bernstein, Penn State University

"It Was All About Images: Glendening vs. Sauerbrey for Governor of Maryland in 1996." Theodore F. Sheckels, Randolph-Macon College

"Gender Differences in Candidate Evaluation, Issue Preference, and Vote Choice in the 1996 U.S. Presidential Election: A Test of Competing Theoretical Explanations." Henry C. Kenski, University of Arizona, Brooks Aylor, La Salle University, Kate M. Kenski, University of Pennsylvania

"Why Not a Woman? Reactions to the Presidential Candidacy of Elizabeth Dole." Dianne G. Bystrom, Iowa State University

---

2540   2:00-3:15 p.m.   Conf 4H   Fourth Floor   Chicago Hilton

COMMEMORATING AN UNCERTAIN FUTURE: THE RHETORIC OF THE CIVIL RIGHTS MEMORIAL

Sponsor: Media Forum Series
Chairs: Carole Blair, University of California, Davis
          Neil Michel, Axiom Photo & Design

This presentation tours the Civil Rights Memorial and its setting in Montgomery, Alabama, and seeks to stimulate critical readings of the Memorial, using the conceptual resources available in theories of symbolicity, visuality, materiality, and race.

2541   2:00-3:15 p.m.   Conf 4I   Fourth Floor   Chicago Hilton

ASSOCIATION FOR COMMUNICATION ADMINISTRATION EXECUTIVE COMMITTEE MEETING

Sponsor: Association for Communication Administration

2542   2:00-3:15 p.m.   Conf 4J   Fourth Floor   Chicago Hilton

MENTOR AS TEACHER, ADVISOR AND FRIEND: FACULTY COLORING OUTSIDE THE LINES OF TRADITIONAL ACADEME

Sponsor: Senior College & University Section
Chair: Alan C. Lerstrom, Luther College

"A Student Mentoring Program: Alumni as Model and Mentor." Chrys Gabrich, Carlow College

"Faculty Mentoring Faculty: Learning the Rules of Academe." Vickie L. Harvey, St. John's University

"Mentors: The Wind Beneath Our Wings." Penny L. Krampien, Adrian College
"To What Extent Does a Peer Mentoring Program Aid in Student Retention?" Mary P. Lahman, Manchester College
"A University Wide Program for Faculty Mentoring New Faculty." Kristin L. Marshall, Clarion University

---

2543   2:00-3:15 p.m.   Conf 4K   Fourth Floor   Chicago Hilton

FRIENDSHIP DILEMMAS

Sponsor: Interpersonal Communication Division
Chair: Paul A. Mongeau, Miami University, Ohio
"What If Harry Met Sally in 1999? Sex as Management Strategy in Cross-Sex Friendships." Walid A. Afifi, Penn State University, Sandra L. Faulkner, Penn State University
"To Confront or Not to Confront: The Masquerade Paradox." Nathan Miczo, University of Arizona
"Men's Expectations of Tactics Utilized by Women to Initiate a Sexual Encounter." M. Sean Limon, Michigan State University, Betty H. LaFrance, Wake Forest University
"Between Gay and Straight: Dilemmas and Possibilities of Friendship." Lisa M. Tillmann-Healy, University of South Florida

Respondent: Paul A. Mongeau, Miami University, Ohio

2544   2:00-3:15 p.m.   Conf 4L   Fourth Floor   Chicago Hilton

SHADES OF GRAY: ETHICAL DILEMMAS AND ON-LINE RESEARCH

Sponsor: Society for the Study of Symbolic Interaction
Chair: G. Jon Hall, University of Northern Iowa
"From Cornerville to Cyberville: The Ethics of Studying Real People in Virtual Places." Steve Jones, University of Illinois, Chicago
"The Ethics of Doing Naturalistic Discourse Research on the Internet." Barbara F. Sharf, Texas A&M University
"The Ethical Antinomies of Internet Research: Is there a Balance?" Jim Thomas, Northern Illinois University
"Research Papparazzi in Cyberspace: Ethical Guidelines and Protocols for On-Line Research." G. Jon Hall, University of Northern Iowa, Shing-Ling S. Chen, University of Northern Iowa

Respondent: Steve Jones, University of Illinois, Chicago

2545   2:00-3:15 p.m.   Conf 4M   Fourth Floor   Chicago Hilton

ADVANCED COLLABORATION TOOLS TO SUPPORT MULTI-UNIVERSITY DISTRIBUTED LEARNING IN ORGANIZATIONAL COMMUNICATION

Sponsor: Organizational Communication Division

Panelists: Peter R. Monge, University of Southern California
Barbara J. O'Keefe, University of Michigan
Cynthia Stohl, Purdue University
Pascal R. Yammine, University of Illinois, Urbana-Champaign
Noshir S. Contractor, University of Illinois, Urbana-Champaign

The purpose of this panel is to describe and demonstrate the convergence of communication, computer, and collaborative technologies to create a distributed learning environment for teaching courses in organizational communication across time, space, and institutional boundaries

---

2546   2:00-3:15 p.m.   McCormick Board Rm   Fourth Floor   Chicago Hilton

AMERICAN STUDIES COMMISSION BUSINESS MEETING

Sponsor: American Studies Commission

Friday

2547   2:00-3:15 p.m.   **Pullman Board Rm**   **Fourth Floor**   **Chicago Hilton**

INTERNATIONAL FORENSICS ASSOCIATION BUSINESS MEETING

Sponsor: International Forensic Association

2549   2:00-3:15 p.m.   **Conf 5B**   **Fifth Floor**   **Chicago Hilton**

THE BASIC COMMUNICATION COURSE: CONCERNS AND SOLUTIONS FROM THE DIRECTORS, THE TEACHING ASSISTANTS, AND THE STUDENTS

Sponsor: Basic Course Division
Chair: Craig R. Hullett, Michigan State University
   "Leading the Troops: The Trials and Tribulations of the Basic Course Director." Jennifer M. Heisler, Michigan State University
   "The Neutral Zone: Surviving the GTA Experience." Stacie A. Beery, Michigan State University
   "In the Trenches: Students Speak Out About the Basic Course." Dhaval S. Patel, Michigan State University
   "Plan of Attack: Common Themes Among Basic Course Personnel." Shanna R. Speakman, Michigan State University

2551   2:00-3:15 p.m.   **Conf 5D**   **Fifth Floor**   **Chicago Hilton**

GIRL CULTURES: THE GLOBALIZATION OF POPULAR CULTURE

Sponsor: Women's Caucus
Chair: Anne Cooper Chen, Ohio University
   "Popular Culture for Girls: From Japan to the World." Anne Cooper Chen, Ohio University
   "Popular Culture for Girls: From the U.S. to the World." Norma Pecora, Ohio University
   "The Sudan." Saadia Ali Malik, Ohio University
   "Japan." Kimkio Akita, Ohio University
   "India." Gayathri Chandran, Ohio University
   "Taiwan." Yu-Li Chang, Ohio University

Respondent: Sharon R. Mazzarella, Ithaca College

2552   2:00-3:15 p.m.   **Conf 5E**   **Fifth Floor**   **Chicago Hilton**

VISUAL RHETORICS AND THE PICTORIAL TURN: THREE STUDIES IN CRITICAL VIEWING

Sponsor: Rhetorical and Communication Theory Division
Chair: John L. Lucaites, Indiana University
   "Picturing Yellowstone: Art, Tourism, and America's Wonderland." Kevin M. Deluca, Penn State University
   "Entering America: The Changing Visual Rhetoric of U.S. Immigrants." Anne T. Demo, Vanderbilt University
   "Visual Rhetorics and the Myth of the Migrant: The FSA Visualizes 'The Real Joads'." Cara A. Finnegan, University of Illinois, Urbana-Champaign

Respondents: W. J. T. Mitchell, University of Chicago
                John L. Lucaites, Indiana University

2553   2:00-3:15 p.m.   **Conf 5F**   **Fifth Floor**   **Chicago Hilton**

CIVIC DISCOURSE FOR THE THIRD MILLENNIUM: FUTURE TRAJECTORIES FOR INTERNATIONAL COMMUNICATION SCHOLARSHIP

Sponsors: Commission on Communication in the Future
            International & Intercultural Communication Division
Chair: K. S. Sitaram, Southern Illinois University, Carbondale

"Civic Discourse, Civil Society and Chinese Communities: Social Conversation in the Third Millennium." Randy Kluver, Oklahoma City University, John H. Powers, Hong Kong Baptist University

"Culture and Technology in the New Europe: Civic Discourse in Transformation in Post-Socialist Nations." Laura B. Lengel, American International University, London

"Working at the Bar: Thailand, Civic Discourse, and Commercial Sex." Thomas M. Steinfatt, University of Miami

"Chinese 'Face' Now and in the Future: Evolving Chinese Communication Patterns." Wenshan Jia, Truman State University

"Images of Human Rights in the Caribbean and Latin America: Recent Films and Still Photography." William Over, St. John's University

Respondent: Michael H. Prosser, Rochester Institute of Technology

---

2554   2:00-3:15 p.m.   Conf 5G   Fifth Floor   Chicago Hilton

TOP PAPERS IN INSTRUCTIONAL DEVELOPMENT

Sponsor: Instructional Development Division
Chair: Ann B. Frymier, Miami University
   "Perceived Teacher Confirmation: The Development and Validation of an Instrument and Two Studies of the Relationship to Cognitive and Affective Learning." Kathleen S. Ellis, University of Colorado, Colorado Springs
   "Mutual Influence in Teacher-Student Relationships: Applying IAT to Assess Teacher Adaptation to Student Classroom Involvement." Jamie Comstock, University of West Florida
   "Interactive Television Instructor's Perceptions of Students' Nonverbal Responsiveness and Their Influence on Distance Teaching." Timothy P. Mottet, Southwest Texas State University

Respondent: Ann B. Frymier, Miami University

2555   2:00-3:15 p.m.   Conf 5H   Fifth Floor   Chicago Hilton

A CROSS-CULTURAL LOOK AT COMMUNICATION APPREHENSION: FINDING THE BARRIERS

Sponsor: Communication Apprehension & Avoidance Commission
Chair: Tanichya K. Wongprasert, Washington State University
   "Communication Apprehension, Bullying, and Relational Stress: A Comparison of Japanese and American Students." John O'Mara, University of Connecticut, Joan O'Mara, University of Hartford, Jerry L. Allen, University of New Haven, Ben Judd, University of New Haven
   "Japanese Fear of Communication Focus Groups." Masahiro Sakamoto, Hokuriku University, Charles B. Pribyl, Hokuriku University, James A. Keaten, University of Northern Colorado, Fusako Koshikawa, Waseda University
   "A Cross-Cultural Investigation of Communication Apprehension Between Koreans and Americans: Re-Examining the Issue." Eunkyong L. Yook, James Madison University

---

2556   2:00-3:15 p.m.   Conf 5I   Fifth Floor   Chicago Hilton

CONSULTING THAT WORKS: MAKING A REAL WORLD IMPACT

Sponsor: Roundtable Series
Chair: Susan R. Glaser, University of Oregon
   "Show Me the Money: Winning Your First Contract and Getting Invited Back." Carl Campton, Kelly Services
   "Transforming Organizational Cultures: Changing How People Resolve Conflict and Solve Problems." Peter A. Glaser, Glaser & Associates, Inc.
   "Bridging Theory and Practice in Communication Consulting." David R. Seibold, University of California, Santa Barbara
   "Using Communication Templates to Coach Organizational Leaders." Randall K. Stutman, Temple University

Friday

2557   2:00-3:15 p.m.   Conf 5J   Fifth Floor   Chicago Hilton

COLORING OUTSIDE THE LINES: THE ROLE OF RESEARCH AND APPLICATION IN THE COMMUNITY COLLEGE

Sponsor: Community College Section
Chair: Lynn M. Disbrow, Sinclair Community College
  "Research as Curriculum Enhancement." Teri J. Avis, Normandale Community College
  "Research as Promotion and Tenure Tool." John D. Reffue, Hillsborough Community
    College
  "Research as Pedagogical Revitalization." Reeze L. Hanson, Haskell Indian Nations
    University, Kansas

2562   2:00-3:15 p.m.   Essex Court   Second Floor   Essex Inn

DAUGHTERS OF THE CLOTH: CONSTRUCTION OF CHRISTIAN IDENTITY IN THE 1990s

Sponsor: Religious Communication Association
Chair: Helen M. Sterk, Calvin College

Panelists: Tina M. Harris, University of Georgia
          Patricia S. Hill, Cleveland State University
          Davina A. Jones, Bowling Green State University
          Nneka I. Ofulue, University of Georgia
          Jennifer F. Wood, Bowling Green State University

This panel will discuss theories and concepts that contribute to an understanding of identity. Specifically, panelists will address how their gendered, racial, and Christian standpoints have been directly influenced, and possibly shaped, through experiences within the context of family, and the degree to which these experiences have effected the type of research methodology each panel member employs.

2563   2:00-3:15 p.m.   Windsor Court   Second Floor   Essex Inn

THE NOVEL AS CULTURAL ANALYSIS

Sponsor: Ethnography Division
Chair: Carolyn S. Ellis, University of South Florida
  "From Fact to Fiction: Gayness Writes On." Frederick C. Corey, Arizona State University
  "Echoes of Silence." Robin P. Clair, Purdue University
  "Moving Between the Lines: A Search for Other, a Search for Self, a Search for Meaning."
    Catherine B. Becker, University of Hawaii, Hilo

Respondent: Carolyn S. Ellis, University of South Florida

2564   2:00-3:15 p.m.   Buckingham Court   Second Floor   Essex Inn

SPOTLIGHT ON THE SCHOLARSHIP OF WENDY LEEDS-HURWITZ

Sponsor: Semiotics and Communication Commission
Chair: Deborah L. Eicher-Catt, Penn State University, Wilkes-Barre
  "The Theoretical and Pedagogical Implications of *Semiotics and Communication* by
    Leeds-Hurwitz." Nicole A. Wendel, University of Oklahoma
  "Looking at Transformative Rituals Across Cultures: An Application of Leeds-Hurwitz'
    Approach to Semiotics." Jonathan G. Shailor, University of Wisconsin, Parkside
  "Playing with Symbols: Studying Semiotics and Communication." Victoria Chen, San
    Francisco State University

Respondent: Wendy Leeds-Hurwitz, University of Wisconsin, Parkside

This panel honors the scholarship of Wendy Leeds-Hurwitz, author of the groundbreaking text, *Semiotics and Communication: Signs, Codes, Culture.* All the panelists will speak to the value of applying Leeds-Hurwitz' approach to their on-going research and teaching. Dr.

Leeds-Hurwitz will respond by contextualizing this discussion in light of her on-going research and writing in the area of semiotics.

2565   2:00-3:15 p.m.   Park East Walk   Second Floor   Essex Inn

KENNETH BURKE SOCIETY TOP THREE COMPETITIVE PAPERS

Sponsor: Kenneth Burke Society, NCA Branch
Chair: Bryan Crable, Villanova University
  "Looking Under the Hood and Tinkering with Voter Cynicism: Ross Perot and Perspective by Incongruity*". Mari Boor Tonn, University of New Hampshire, Valerie A. Endress, University of Hartford
  "Attitudes Toward Freud: Burke and Freudianism in Context 1930-1950**". Steven Bailey, University of Illinois, Urbana-Champaign
  "Man-Hands, Close Talkers, and Scapegoats: A Burkean Criticism of Seinfeld***". Melissa Cotter, Villanova University

Respondent: Ekaterina V. Haskins, University of Iowa

*Top Paper   **Top Graduate Student Paper   ***Top Undergraduate Paper

---

2566   2:00-3:15 p.m.   Cohn Rm   Second Floor   Spertus Institute

RHETORIC OF SCIENCE AND TECHNOLOGY IN THE CLASSROOM

Sponsor: American Association for Rhetoric of Science & Technology
Chair: John Lyne, University of Pittsburgh
  "Between Handbook and Theory: Teaching Rhetoric of Science to Journalists." Joan Leach, Imperial College of London
  "Teaching the Undergraduate Course in Rhetoric of Technology." David J. Depew, University of Iowa, Joanna S. Ploeger-Tsoulos, University of Iowa
  "Science Literacy, Science Education, and Teaching Rhetoric of Science." Karen M. Taylor, University of Pittsburgh
  "Productivist Performance in the Rhetoric of Science Classroom." Gordon R. Mitchell, University of Pittsburgh

---

2567   2:00-3:15 p.m.   Krensky Rm   Second Floor   Spertus Institute

THE CHANGING FACE OF JURIES: UNDERSTANDING GENERATION-X

Sponsor: Communication and Law Commission
Chair: Ann E. Burnette, Southwest Texas State University

Panelists: Teresa M. Rosado, Zagnoli McEvoy Foley Ltd.
        Andrienne LeFevre, Zagnoli McEvoy Foley Ltd.
        Patricia J. McEvoy, Zagnoli McEvoy Foley Ltd.
        William T. Grimes, Zagnoli McEvoy Foley Ltd.

This panel explores the political, economic and social events that have shaped the feelings and attitudes of this generational group through qualitative and quantitative analyses. The participants will focus specifically on communication content and styles that may be relevant for case themes and visual courtroom presentations.

2569   2:00-3:15 p.m.   Rm 903   Ninth Floor   Spertus Institute

MAINTAINING THE COMPREHENSIVE FORENSICS PROGRAM IN THE NEW MILLENNIUM

Sponsor: Pi Kappa Delta
Chair: Edward S. Inch, Pacific Lutheran University
  "Defining a Comprehensive Program." Joel L. Hefling, South Dakota State University
  "A Comprehensive Forensics Program in a Liberal Arts College." John E. McCabe-Juhnke, Bethel College

Friday

"Directing Tournaments to Encourage Comprehensive Programs." Scott L. Jensen, Webster University
"Special Challenges to Comprehensive Programs in the New Millennium." Bob R. Derryberry, Southwest Baptist University

Respondent: Susan P. Millsap, Otterbein College

2570   2:00-3:15 p.m.   Rm 904   Ninth Floor   Spertus Institute

AFTER THE BATTLES ARE OVER: TRUTH, RECONCILIATION, AND RE-BUILDING COMMUNITIES AND COUNTRIES

Sponsor: Peace and Conflict Communication Commission
Chair: Rod L. Troester, Penn State University, Erie
  "Bonhoeffer's Warning: Community as Building, Renovation, Patience, and Endurance." Ronald C. Arnett, Duquesne University
  "Healing History's Wounds: Reconciliation Communication Efforts to Build Community Between Native American and Non-Indian Peoples." Sheryl L. Dowlin, Mankato State University
  "South Africa's Truth and Reconciliation Commission's Final Report: Building Peace by Committee?" Paul E. Scovell, Salisbury State University
  "The Commission for the Historical Clarification of Human Rights Violation and Acts of Violence: Working for Peace in Guatemala After 35 Years of Violence." Rod L. Troester, Penn State University, Erie, Cathy S. Mester, Penn State University, Erie
  "Justice and Healing Through Peace-Talk: The Truth and Reconciliation Commission in Bosnia and Herzegovina." Colleen E. Kelley, Penn State University, Erie

---

2572   2:00-3:15 p.m.   Rm 907   Ninth Floor   Spertus Institute

A ROUNDTABLE DISCUSSION AMONG YOUNG FEMALE DEBATE COACHES

Sponsor: Cross Examination Debate Association
Chair: Valerie R. Renegar, University of Kansas

Panelists: Lisa K. Heller, University of Richmond
          Sue E. Lowrie, Pepperdine University
          Sarah T. Partlow, University of Kansas
          Valerie R. Renegar, University of Kansas
          Tara Tate, University of North Texas

Discussion will focus on a number of issues in debate that are of concern to women, or where the panelists feel their perspective can be valuable. Issues include, but are not limited to, affirmative action, the retention of women, becoming role models, humanizing debate, community building, and creating ties between women in this activity.

2573   2:00-3:15 p.m.   Rm 908   Ninth Floor   Spertus Institute

HELPING AND/OR HINDERING OUR OCCUPATIONAL, RELATIONAL, SOCIAL AND PHYSICAL LIVES: A PANEL ON WELLNESS ISSUES THAT AFFECT THE FORENSICS COMMUNITY

Sponsor: National Forensic Association
Chair: Ann K. Burnett, North Dakota State University
  "Tournament Structure and Wellness: The Explosion of and 'Evils' Resulting from the Swing Tournament Format." Scott G. Dickmeyer, Concordia College, Minnesota, Larry Schnoor, Communication Links
  "Forensics and Career: Wellness from the Perspective of Balancing Teaching, Scholarship, Service and Forensics." Cynthia R. Carver, Concordia College
  "Wandering by the Oasis of Wellness: Implications of Mentoring and Modeling Behaviors in Forensics." Daniel D. Cronn-Mills, Minnesota State University, Mankato
  "Wellness and Family: The Impact of Forensics on Family Life." Linda B. Dickmeyer, Concordia College, Minnesota

Respondent: Ann K. Burnett, North Dakota State University

| 2574 | 2:00-3:15 p.m. | Auditorium | Second Floor | Spertus Institute |

TRASHING THE CANON

Sponsor: Theatre Division
Chair: Barbara Parisi, Long Island University, Brooklyn
    "Trailers, Gun-racks and Spam: The Visual Rhetoric of White Trash in Theatre." Jim B. Williams, Bowling Green State University
    "Iconoclastic or Innocuous: Images of Whiteness in Contemporary Theatre." Becky K. Becker, Truman State University, Heath A. Diehl, Bowling Green State University

Respondent: Gerald Lee Ratliff, SUNY, Potsdam

This panel explores and examines the issues and ramifications of whiteness in the theater within a presentation and discussion format.

| 2578 | 2:00-4:45 p.m. | | | Off Site |

CHALLENGING BOUNDARIES: FRANCES WILLARD AND THE WCTU

Sponsor: Challenging Boundaries Series
Chair: Jean Goodwin, Northwestern University
    "Our 'House Beautiful': The Woman's Temple and the WCTU's Domesticity on Display, 1887-1917." Rachel Bohlmann, University of Iowa
    "Translating Women from the Passive to the Active Voice." Carolyn DeSwarte Gifford, Editor, *Writing out My Heart: Selections from the Journals of Frances E. Willard, 1855-1896*
    "Feminizing the Public Platform: Willard's Campaign to Loosen Women's Tongues." Amy R. Slagell, Iowa State University

Respondent: Richard W. Leeman, University of North Carolina, Charlotte

This program will be held at the Frances Willard Home and WCTU headquarters in Evanston, IL. It will include a special tour of the Willard museum by the Frances Willard Historical Association. Information concerning making the trip from the conference hotel to the program is available by contacting Amy Slagell at aslagell@iastate.edu prior to the convention.

3:30 p.m.

| 2606 | 3:30-4:45 p.m. | Continental BR A | Lobby Level | Chicago Hilton |

ROUNDTABLE: LIFE HISTORY, IDENTITY, AND THE MEDIA—TOWARD A THEORY OF SUBJECTIVE RESPONSE

Sponsor: Mass Communication Division
Chair: Ellen A. Wartella, University of Texas, Austin

Panelists: Victor Federico Sampedro Blanco, University of Salamanca, Spain
          Tania Cordeiro, State University of Bahia, Brazil
          Kevin G. Barnhurst, University of Illinois, Chicago
          Navita C. James, University of South Florida

Respondents: Ellen A. Wartella, University of Texas, Austin
            Joli K. Jensen, University of Tulsa

| 2607 | 3:30-4:45 p.m. | Continental BR B | Lobby Level | Chicago Hilton |

SETTING THE TONE FOR COMPUTER-MEDIATED COMMUNICATION

Sponsor: Human Communication and Technology Commission
Chair: Lance A. Strate, Fordham University
    "Tuning Up." Frank E. X. Dance, University of Denver
    "Oral Echoes in E-mail." Dennis L. Wignall, Saginaw Valley State University
    "The Ghosts of Literacy in the House of Digitality." David E. Weber, University of Denver

Friday

"'E-pals' as an Exercise in the Seduction of Student Technophobes." Susan L. Cook, Gonzaga University

"Building the Global Village in the Big City." Dennis Gallagher, Regis University

Respondents: Patrick B. O'Sullivan, Illinois State University
             Alice L. Crume, SUNY, Brockport

2608   **3:30-4:45 p.m.**   **Continental BR C**   **Lobby Level**   **Chicago Hilton**

KNOWLEDGE, AESTHETICS, AND SCHOLARSHIP

Sponsor: Critical and Cultural Studies Division
Chair: Nathan E. Stormer, University of Maine, Orono
   "Scholarship in the Ruins." Robert Hariman, Drake University
   "The Aesthetic Imperative and Critical Discourse." Carole Blair, University of California, Davis
   "An Appropriating Aesthetic: An Examination of Politics and Power in the Discourse of Critical Scholarship." Helene A. Shugart, Augusta State University
   "Gearheads and Werkelhufers: Theory as Performative Aesthetic." Nathan E. Stormer, University of Maine, Orono

---

2611   **3:30-4:45 p.m.**   **Int'l Ballroom North**   **Second Floor**   **Chicago Hilton**

REHEARSING HISTORY: ROUNDTABLE ON PERFORMANCE HISTORIOGRAPHY

Sponsor: Performance Studies Division
Chair: Tracy Davis, Northwestern University

Panelists: Ruth L. Bowman, Louisiana State University
          Kirk W. Fuoss, St. Lawrence University
          Shannon P. Jackson, University of California, Berkeley
          Lisa Merrill, Hofstra University

Panelists will identify key issues (ethical, political, representational) in the process of having written performance histories, focusing on how performance shapes broader debates in historiography.

2612   **3:30-4:45 p.m.**   **Int'l Ballroom South**   **Second Floor**   **Chicago Hilton**

THE ANNUAL GRADUATE STUDENT OPEN HOUSE: A STUDENT NETWORK TO GRADUATE SCHOOL

Sponsor: Student Section
Chair: Colleen M. Carey, Northwestern University

Panelists: Danna E. Prather, University of Iowa
          Diana L. Tucker, Southern Illinois University, Carbondale

This program provides students with an opportunity to meet informally with representatives from various graduate programs across the country. Faculty members and graduate students have been invited to share materials describing their various programs. In lieu of formal presentations, students who would like information are invited to meet with school representatives to discuss education and career opportunities.

2614   **3:30-4:45 p.m.**   **Boulevard A**   **Second Floor**   **Chicago Hilton**

WIDENING THE BOUNDARIES: IDEOLOGY, WHITENESS, AND CHAOS

Sponsor: Challenging Boundaries Series
Chair: David Descutner, Ohio University
   "Rethinking False Consciousness Ideology Through the Collapse of Subject/Object." Nessim J. Watson, Westfield State College
   "Critiquing Whiteness: Vice President Gore's Speech on M. L. K. Day 1998." Kevin D. Kuswa, University of Texas, Austin

"Chaos and Complexity: Expanding the Boundaries." James G. Crawford, Ohio University

| 2615 | 3:30-4:45 p.m. | Boulevard B | Second Floor | Chicago Hilton |

(FE)MENTORING NCA: REDISCOVERING FIVE EXTRAORDINARY VOICES

Sponsor: NCA First Vice President
Chair: Patti P. Gillespie, University of Maryland
  "Henrietta Prentiss, President of NCA, 1932." Judith S. Trent, University of Cincinnati
  "Maud May Babcock, President of NCA, 1936." Sharon A. Ratliffe, Golden West College
  "Magdalene Kramer, President of NCA, 1947." Beverly W. Long, University of North
    Carolina, Chapel Hill
  "Elise Hahn, President of NCA, 1958." Anita Taylor, George Mason University
  "Marie Hochmuth Nichols, President of NCA, 1969." Jane Blankenship, University of
    Massachusetts

In the 85 years of the National Communication Association, eleven women have served as president. This program brings together six of them to discuss the professional lives and contributions made by the earlier five. The program is the first in a series of collaborative projects on female leadership in NCA.

| 2616 | 3:30-4:45 p.m. | Boulevard C | Second Floor | Chicago Hilton |

DEVELOPMENT, TECHNOLOGY, AND INFORMATION CONTROL: GLOBAL IMPLICATIONS OF INTERCULTURAL COMMUNICATION

Sponsor: International & Intercultural Communication Division
Chair: Hui-Ching Chang, University of Illinois, Chicago
  "Who Speaks for Asia: Media and Information Control in the Global Economy." Gerald
    Sussman, Portland State University, John A. Lent, Third World Media Associates
  "As Nigeria Opens Its Market: Where Does Rural Development Communication Stand?"
    Chukwuka A. Onwumechili, Bowie State University, Joy Arungwa, Bowie State
    University
  "Kultura/Technologie Mladych: Youth Culture and Technology in the Czech Republic."
    Zdenka Telnarova, University of Ostrava, Czech Republic, Laura B. Lengel, American
    International University, London, Eva Burianova, University of Ostrava, Czech Republic

Respondent: Paul N. Lakey, Abilene Christian University

| 2618 | 3:30-4:45 p.m. | Waldorf | Third Floor | Chicago Hilton |

FAMILY SYSTEMS: AN EXPLORATION OF AFFECT AND MAINTENANCE IN THE FAMILY

Sponsor: Family Communication Division
Chair: Jane E. Jorgenson, University of South Florida
  "Exploring the Affective Dimension of Relational Commitment." Daniel J. Weigel,
    University of Nevada, Reno, Deborah S. Ballard-Reisch, University of Nevada, Reno
  "Cooking is Like Food for the Soul: The Cultural Maintenance of Family Identity in the
    Films *Soul Food* and *Eat, Drink, Man, Woman*." Tina M. Harris, University of Georgia,
    Rosalinda Cantu, Bowling Green State University
  "Applying Family System Theory to the Genesis of Codependence." Katherine L. Nelson,
    Barry University
  "The Inevitable Postponed: Factors that Affect the Family Disclosure of a Subsequent
    Pregnancy Following a Pregnancy Loss." Francine R. MacBride, Eastern Michigan
    University, Dennis P. Grady, Eastern Michigan University

Respondent: Paul L. Yelsma, Western Michigan University

Friday

2619   3:30-4:45 p.m.   Astoria   Third Floor   Chicago Hilton

COMPETITIVE PAPERS IN GROUP COMMUNICATION: ETHNIC, MINORITY, AND GENDER GROUP COMMUNICATION

Sponsor: Group Communication Division
Chair: Jane Macoubrie, North Carolina State University
   "Double Minority Influence in Work Teams." Celeste M. Walls, Arizona State University
   "Members' Perceptions of Ethnic and Opinion Minorities' Participation in Group
     Decision-Making." William J. Farrar, University of California, Santa Barbara, David R.
     Seibold, University of California, Santa Barbara
   "An Analysis of the Rhetorical Devices and Group Movement Patterns in a Black
     Self-Analytic Study Group." Rufus L. Barfield, II, University of Central Florida
   "Leadership, Dominance, and Deception in Mixed-Gender, Long-Term Groups." Scott D.
     Johnson, University of Richmond, Benjamin Muldrew, Arnold Communications

Respondent: Carolyn M. Anderson, University of Akron

2621   3:30-4:45 p.m.   Williford A   Third Floor   Chicago Hilton

EXPERIENCES AND TOOLS TO FACILITATE COLORING OUTSIDE THE LINES IN AFRICAN AMERICAN EDUCATION

Sponsor: African American Communication & Culture Commission
Chair: Teresa A. Nance, Villanova University
   "Joel Chandler Harris' Uncle Remus: An Example of Teaching Using Dialect and Moral
     Lessons in Folklore*." Melanie J. Selfridge, Penn State University
   "The Effects of Integration on Black Students in Predominantly White Schools." Holly
     Jones, Howard University
   "How Can We Enhance Self-Confidence in the Classroom?" Adeline L. Evans, Florida
     A&M University, O. Sylvia Lamar, Florida A&M University, Anna M. Evans, SUNY,
     Oswego

Respondent: Rhunette C. Diggs, University of Louisville

*Student Debut Paper

2622   3:30-4:45 p.m.   Williford B   Third Floor   Chicago Hilton

CENTRAL STATES COMMUNICATION ASSOCIATION BUSINESS MEETING

Sponsor: Central States Communication Association

2623   3:30-4:45 p.m.   Williford C   Third Floor   Chicago Hilton

COLORING OUTSIDE THE LINES: CURRICULAR DECISIONS IN GENDER AND FEMINIST STUDIES

Sponsor: Feminist and Women Studies Division
Chair: Trudy L. Hanson, West Texas A&M University

Panelists: Suzanne McCorkle, Boise State University
           Cory L. Young, Bowling Green University
           Michelle T. Violanti, University of Tennessee
           Susan M. Ross, Hamilton College
           Michelle A. Holling, California State University, Monterey Bay
           Diana K. Ivy, Texas A&M University
           B. Christine Shea, California Polytechnic State University, San Luis Obispo

Scholars from a variety of philosophical and academic perspectives will discuss the direction
that gender/feminist studies curriculum has taken and prospects for the future.

2626	3:30-4:45 p.m.	PDR 1	Third Floor	Chicago Hilton

INSTRUCTIONAL DEVELOPMENT DIVISION BUSINESS MEETING

Sponsor: Instructional Development Division

2627	3:30-4:45 p.m.	PDR 2	Third Floor	Chicago Hilton

OUTSTANDING HEALTH COMMUNICATION SCHOLAR

Sponsor: Health Communication Division
Chair: Roxanne Parrott, University of Georgia

Panelists: James W. Dearing, Michigan State University
Arvind Singhal, Ohio University
Tom Valente, Johns Hopkins University

This program features the scholarship of the 1999 Winner of the Outstanding Health Communication Scholar Award, Everett M. Rogers, University of New Mexico. This award is given jointly by the ICA/NCA Divisions of Health Communication to a senior scholar who has significantly influenced the field. A panel of respondents will discuss Rogers's work.

2628	3:30-4:45 p.m.	PDR 3	Third Floor	Chicago Hilton

REMEMBERING LYNDREY NILES: CELEBRATING THE LIFE OF A TRUE SCHOLAR AND GENTLEMAN

Sponsors: Black Caucus
African American Communication & Culture Commission

Chair: Melbourne S. Cummings, Howard University
"Remembering Niles: More Than a Professor." Michon Hicks, Howard University
"Knowing Niles: Lives Being Revolutionized." Carlos D. Morrison, Clark Atlanta University
"Remembering Niles: A Mentor, Scholar, and Friend." Brenda J. Allen, University of Colorado, Boulder
"No One Like Niles: Truly a Remarkable Scholar and Friend." Orlando L. Taylor, Howard University
"Remembering Niles: A Legacy Unforgotten." Melbourne S. Cummings, Howard University

Respondent: Ronald L. Jackson, Penn State University

2629	3:30-4:45 p.m.	PDR 4	Third Floor	Chicago Hilton

RELIGIOUS COMMUNICATION ASSOCIATION BUSINESS MEETING

Sponsor: Religious Communication Association

2630	3:30-4:45 p.m.	PDR 5	Third Floor	Chicago Hilton

COMMUNICATION AND RISK: PEDAGOGICAL IMPLICATIONS FOR COMMUNICATION EDUCATORS

Sponsor: Communication Needs of Students at Risk Commission
Chair: David W. Worley, Indiana State University
"Defining and Refining At-Riskness in Higher Education." Mary Hinchcliff-Pelias, Southern Illinois University, Carbondale
"Virtue Ethics and the Teaching of Language Arts." Virginia Kohl, University of South Florida
"The Technological Have-Nots: Defining a New Category of At-Risk Students." Paul J. Siddens, University of Northern Iowa
"Communication and Risk: Examining the Communication Needs of Students At-Risk." Stephen K. Hunt, Illinois State University, Lance R. Lippert, Southern Illinois University

Friday

Respondent: Brian S. Titsworth, Moorhead State University

| 2631 | 3:30-4:45 p.m. | PDR 6 | Third Floor | Chicago Hilton |

FREEDOM OF EXPRESSION COMMISSION BUSINESS MEETING

Sponsor: Freedom of Expression Commission

| 2632 | 3:30-4:45 p.m. | PDR 7 | Third Floor | Chicago Hilton |

ELEMENTARY AND SECONDARY EDUCATION SECTION BUSINESS MEETING

Sponsor: Elementary & Secondary Education Section

| 2633 | 3:30-4:45 p.m. | Conf 4A | Fourth Floor | Chicago Hilton |

ASIAN/PACIFIC AMERICAN CAUCUS BUSINESS MEETING

Sponsor: Asian/Pacific American Caucus

| 2635 | 3:30-4:45 p.m. | Conf 4C | Fourth Floor | Chicago Hilton |

TOP THREE PAPERS IN PUBLIC ADDRESS

Sponsor: Public Address Division
Chair: Mary L. Kahl, SUNY, New Paltz
    "A Gentleman's History of Geology: The Fall and Rise of Rhetoric in Charles Lyell's
    Principles of Geology." Andrew C. Hansen, Penn State University
    "Irony, Decorum, and the Space-Time Continuum in Frederick Douglass' 'What to the
    Slave Is the Fourth of July'?" Robert E. Terrill, Indiana University
    "Rhetorical Invention During World War I: Suffrage Cartoons in *The Woman Citizen.*"
    Michele E. Ramsey, University of Georgia

Respondent: Stephen E. Lucas, University of Wisconsin, Madison

| 2636 | 3:30-4:45 p.m. | Conf 4D | Fourth Floor | Chicago Hilton |

REPORT FROM THE UNIVERSITY OF TEXAS CONFLICT RESOLUTION CENTER PROJECT: RESEARCH, CURRICULUM, AND ADMINISTRATION

Sponsor: Peace and Conflict Communication Commission
Chair: Madeline M. Maxwell, University of Texas, Austin

Panelists: Katerine A. Zilkha, University of Texas, Austin
    Amanda Babcock, University of Texas, Austin
    Briana Chua, University of Texas, Austin
    Cory A. Schneider, University of Texas, Austin

The panelists will present preliminary research findings from the first year of operation of the
Conflict Resolution Center at the University of Texas, Austin.

| 2637 | 3:30-4:45 p.m. | Conf 4E | Fourth Floor | Chicago Hilton |

LINGUISTIC LINES: THE SOCIAL CONSTRUCTION OF SEPARATENESS

Sponsor: Language and Social Interaction Division
Chair: Susan L. Kline, Ohio State University
    "Discursive Constructions of Racial Boundaries and Self-Segregation on Campus." Richard
    Buttny, Syracuse University
    "Women's Narratives of Life in a Thin-Is-In U.S. Culture: Weight Issues and Metaphors."
    Renee Maday, Arizona State University
    "Nude Dancers, Beavers and Homeless People in My Backyard: A Study of Resident
    Identity Invoked in the Public Hearing." Cynthia A. Suopis, University of Massachusetts,
    Amherst

"Gender as a Discursive Practice in Talk About Rape." Lee West, University of Iowa

Respondent: Eric M. Kramer, University of Oklahoma

2638	3:30-4:45 p.m.	Conf 4F	Fourth Floor	Chicago Hilton

NEW RESEARCH ON INFORMATIONAL RECEPTIVITY: ASSOCIATIONS AND CONSEQUENCES

Sponsor: Intrapersonal Communication/Social Cognition Commission
Chair: Lawrence R. Wheeless, University of North Texas
   "The Relations of Informational Receptivity to State-Receiver Apprehension and
      State-Interaction Involvement." Chance Spiker, The Saber Group, Lawrence R.
      Wheeless, University of North Texas
   "The Associations of Informational Receptivity, State Communication Anxiety, and Selected
      Demographic Factors." Brenda K. Ritz, Academy for Research and Professional
      Development, Suzanne Terry, University of North Texas
   "Information Reception Apprehension, Educational Motivation, and Achievement." Tisha
      L. Lackey, University of North Texas, Karen M. Ptacek, University of North Texas, Paul
      Schrodt, University of North Texas
   "The Relationship of Informational Receptivity to Trait Interaction Involvement and Other
      Factors." Janet S. McEwen, American College of Emergency Physicians, William R. Reed,
      Abbott Labs

Respondent: Ray W. Preiss, University of Puget Sound

2639	3:30-4:45 p.m.	Conf 4G	Fourth Floor	Chicago Hilton

ANALYZING POLITICAL MESSAGES

Sponsor: Political Communication Division
Chair: Julia A. Spiker, University of Akron
   "Testing the Use of Technological Distortion of Mass Media Channels Within Televised
      Political Advertising: A Case Study." Gary A. Noggle, Bethel College
   "Effects of Distorted Political Ads: Manipulating Voter Responses." Lynda Lee Kaid,
      University of Oklahoma
   "The Lexicon of Mistrust: The Historical Use of Veracity in Political Language." William P.
      Jennings, University of Texas, Austin
   "Voter Perceptions of Modalities for Political Advertising: Television, Newspaper, Radio,
      and Door-to-Door Canvassing." Scott D. Wells, University of Oklahoma, L. Clark
      Callahan, University of Oklahoma
   "The Brain and The Body Politic: What Human Cognition Means for Nonviolent Politics."
      Ellen W. Gorsevski, Washington State University

2640	3:30-4:45 p.m.	Conf 4H	Fourth Floor	Chicago Hilton

THE NEW FACE OF TELEVISION NEWS PLUGOLA

Sponsor: Media Forum Series
Chair: Matthew P. McAllister, Virginia Tech University

This presentation will take a critical look at the concept of "plugola," described as television
news stories about other television programming. Showing various examples, including news
stories about the last episode of Seinfeld, the causes, forms and implications of plugola will be
examined.

2641	3:30-4:45 p.m.	Conf 4I	Fourth Floor	Chicago Hilton

ASSOCIATION FOR COMMUNICATION ADMINISTRATION GENERAL BUSINESS MEETING

Sponsor: Association for Communication Administration

Friday

2642	3:30-4:45 p.m.	Conf 4J	Fourth Floor	Chicago Hilton

BEYOND THE BORDERS: ADJUNCT FACULTY RECONSIDERED

Sponsor: Senior College & University Section
Chair: George C. Wharton, Curry College
   "Expanding the Canvas: Portraits of Adjuncts for the Millennium." Joel P. Litvin,
      Bridgewater State College
   "Changing the Object of Judgment: The Adjunct as Administrator/Teacher." Jacqueline
      Schmidt, John Carroll University
   "The Positive Consequences of the Use of Adjuncts: An Administrator's Perspective."
      Ralph R. Donald, Southern Illinois University, Edwardsville
   "Adjuncts on the Loose: What Happens When Adjunct Faculty Take Over the Basic
      Course?" Cynthia M. Gottshall, Mercer University
   "Insuring Quality and Consistency: A Creative Approach to Managing Adjuncts." Thomas
      Spann, University of Nebraska, Lincoln

Respondent: Ina R. Ames, Curry College

2643	3:30-4:45 p.m.	Conf 4K	Fourth Floor	Chicago Hilton

THE ROLE OF ARGUMENTATION IN SOCIETY: THE CASUAL ANTECEDENTS AND CONSEQUENCES OF ARGUMENTATIVENESS AND VERBAL AGGRESSIVENESS

Sponsor: Argumentation and Forensics Division
Chair: James C. McCroskey, West Virginia University
   "Does Argumentation Training Inhibit Verbal Aggressiveness?" Paul J. Mineo, University of
      Connecticut, Mark A. Hamilton, University of Connecticut
   "The Role of Nonverbal Behavior on Perceptions of Aggressive Communication." Andrew
      S. Rancer, University of Akron
   "Verbal Aggression in Decision-Making." Matthew M. Martin, West Virginia University,
      Alan D. Heisel, West Virginia University, Kristin M. Valencic, West Virginia University
   "Personality Antecedents of Verbal Aggression, Passive Aggression, Relational Negativism,
      and Assault." Mark A. Hamilton, University of Connecticut, Paul J. Mineo, University of
      Connecticut
   "The Effects of Personality on Argumentative Style." Gerhald Blicke, University of Landau

2644	3:30-4:45 p.m.	Conf 4L	Fourth Floor	Chicago Hilton

MOVING FOLLOWERSHIP OUT OF THE SHADOW OF LEADERSHIP: NEW METAPHORS AND INTERDISCIPLINARY PERSPECTIVES

Sponsor: Organizational Communication Division
Chairs: Vincent R. Waldron, Arizona State University West
        Billy W. Catchings, University of Indianapolis
   "Removing Followership from the Shadow of Leadership: A Brief Introduction." Vincent R.
      Waldron, Arizona State University West
   "Followers as Mystics and Prophets." Kathleen J. Krone, University of Nebraska, Lincoln
   "Developing Situated Responsiveness: Followership, Consent and the Dialectic of
      Control." Stanley A. Deetz, University of Colorado, Boulder
   "Can One Follow Freely?" Ramsey Eric Ramsey, Arizona State University West
   "Performance, Apprenticeship, and Audience: Following from an Artistic Perspective." Billy
      W. Catchings, University of Indianapolis
   "Framing and Reframing Followership: Questions for Discussion." Gail T. Fairhurst,
      University of Cincinnati

Respondents: Jeffrey W. Kassing, Arizona State University West
             Marilyn D. Hunt, Missouri Western State College
             Douglas Kelly, Arizona State University West
             Lynn Cherry, College of Charleston
             Gail T. Fairhurst, University of Cincinnati

2645   3:30-4:45 p.m.   Conf 4M   Fourth Floor   Chicago Hilton

APPROACHES AND FRONTIERS IN ORGANIZATION SOCIALIZATION RESEARCH: EXAMINING THE INDIVIDUAL/ORGANIZATION RELATIONSHIP

Sponsor: Organizational Communication Division
Chair: Paaige K. Turner, Saint Louis University
  "Learning Theory and Organizational Socialization: Toward a Synthesis." Karen R. Stout,
    University of Utah, Connie A. Bullis, University of Utah
  "Socialization in New Organizational Forms: The Case of the Virtual Organization." Janel
    A. Crider, Purdue University
  "Introducing Communication Assessments into Organizational Socialization Survey
    Instruments." Vernon D. Miller, Michigan State University, Janie M. Harden Fritz,
    Duquesne University, Zachary P. Hart, University of Missouri, Columbia
  "Socializing Contingent Labor: The Process of Gendering Vocation and Organizations."
    Nikki C. Townsley, Purdue University
  "Expanding the Research Agenda in Assimilation Research." Michael W. Kramer, University
    of Missouri, Columbia
  "Narrativizing the Individual/Organization Relationship: An Alternative Organizational
    Socialization Perspective." Paaige K. Turner, Saint Louis University, Robert L. Krizek,
    Saint Louis University

2646   3:30-4:45 p.m.   McCormick Board Rm   Fourth Floor   Chicago Hilton

SOUTHERN STATES COMMUNICATION ASSOCIATION EXECUTIVE COUNCIL MEETING

Sponsor: Southern States Communication Association

2647   3:30-4:45 p.m.   Pullman Board Rm   Fourth Floor   Chicago Hilton

INTERNATIONAL FORENSICS ASSOCIATION BUSINESS MEETING

Sponsor: International Forensic Association

2649   3:30-4:45 p.m.   Conf 5B   Fifth Floor   Chicago Hilton

ADMINISTERING THE BASIC COURSE: MEETING THE NEEDS OF DIVERSE INSTRUCTORS

Sponsor: Basic Course Division
Chair: Roberta A. Davilla, University of Northern Iowa

Panelists: Melissa L. Beall, University of Northern Iowa
         April Chatham-Carpenter, University of Northern Iowa
         Roberta A. Davilla, University of Northern Iowa
         Leah E. White, University of Northern Iowa
         Penny O'Connor, University of Northern Iowa
         Bruce F. Wickelgren, University of Northern Iowa
         Sondra Webb Craft, University of Northern Iowa
         Laura L. Sohl, University of Northern Iowa

Respondent: Paul E. Nelson, Ohio University

2651   3:30-4:45 p.m.   Conf 5D   Fifth Floor   Chicago Hilton

TOP PAPERS IN COMMUNICATION AND AGING

Sponsor: Communication and Aging Commission
Chair: Susan A. Fox, Western Michigan University
  "Computer-Mediated Social Support, Older Adults and Coping." Kevin T. Wright,
    University of Oklahoma

"Communication Across and Within Generations: Taiwanese, Chinese-American and Euro-Americans Perceptions of Communication." Howard Giles, University of California, Santa Barbara, Beatrice Liang, University of California, Santa Barbara, Kimberly A. Noels, University of Saskatchewan
"The Issue is Frailty or Is Frailty the Issue?" Roberta L. Gray, University of Washington

Respondent: Sherry J. Holladay, Illinois State University

2652   3:30-4:45 p.m.   Conf 5E   Fifth Floor   Chicago Hilton

COLORING OUTSIDE THE LINES: VERBAL, VISUAL, AND HYPERTEXTUAL COMPOSITION

Sponsor: Rhetorical and Communication Theory Division
Chair: David M. Cheshier, Georgia State University
   "The Role of the Speechwriting Process in Rhetorical Theory." Peter J. Bicak, Rockhurst College
   "The Next Step: Homelessness as Meme." Kathleen M. Torrens, California State University, Fresno
   "Patriotic Paranoia and the Fantasmic Body: 'Unpacking the Tacit Dimension' of 1940s Visual Culture." James P. McDaniel, Indiana University
   "The Reader as Author/The Consumer as Producer: Towards a Rhetoric of Hypertextuality." Roy Joseph, Texas A&M University

---

2653   3:30-4:45 p.m.   Conf 5F   Fifth Floor   Chicago Hilton

ROUNDTABLE DISCUSSION: COMMUNICATION AND NUCLEAR WEAPONS—TOWARD THE DEVELOPMENT OF A NATIONAL CONSORTIUM OF COLLABORATIVE RESEARCH AND SUPPORT

Sponsor: Environmental Communication Commission

Panelists: Stephen P. Depoe, University of Cincinnati
           Bryan C. Taylor, University of Colorado
           Judith E. Hendry, University of New Mexico

Interested participants are invited to share their ideas in this discussion.

2654   3:30-4:45 p.m.   Conf 5G   Fifth Floor   Chicago Hilton

ACADEMIC FORENSICS AS A PEDAGOGY OF INCLUSION

Sponsor: National Federation Interscholastic Speech & Debate Association
Chair: Stefan A. Bauschard, Cathedral Preparatory School
   "From City to Suburb: Supporting Inner City Students Through Forensics." Barbara Stone, Imagination Group
   "Can Debate Be a Pedagogy for the Oppressed? Reflecting on the Writings of Paolo Friere." Joel D. Rollins, University of Texas
   "Mirror, Mirror on the Wall, Who Is the Most Intelligent of Them All? Exploring the Potential for Policy Debate to Provide Opportunities for Students with Non-Traditional Intelligences." Stefan A. Bauschard, Cathedral Preparatory School

Respondents: David M. Berube, University of South Carolina
             Roy J. Schwartzman, University of South Carolina

---

2655   3:30-4:45 p.m.   Conf 5H   Fifth Floor   Chicago Hilton

DISABILITY, RESEARCH, AND INVOLVEMENT: A ROUNDTABLE DISCUSSION OF RESEARCH BY AND WITH PERSONS WITH DISABILITIES

Sponsor: Caucus on Disability Issues
Chair: Joy M. Cypher, West Chester State University

Panelists: Paula Michal-Johnson, Villanova University
           Mary F. Keehner, Purdue University

Julie D. Phillips, Purdue University
Joy M. Cypher, West Chester State University

2656   3:30-4:45 p.m.   Conf 5I   Fifth Floor   Chicago Hilton

FACILITATING PROGRAM ASSESSMENT: DEMYSTIFYING THE PROCESS

Sponsor: Commission on Communication Assessment
Chair: Richard L. Quianthy, Broward Community College
   "Assuring and Assessing Skill Development." Lori E. Zakel, Sinclair Community College
   "Assessment in Action: Faculty and Program Development." Tamara L. Burk, College of
      William and Mary
   "Assessment: Linking Programs, Accountability, and Strategic Planning." Nancy R. Dunbar,
      Brown University
   "Organizational Development: Educational Assessment and Program Marketing." Pat
      Arneson, Duquesne University

2657   3:30-4:45 p.m.   Conf 5J   Fifth Floor   Chicago Hilton

COLORING OUTSIDE THE LINES: INNOVATIONS IN STATE ASSOCIATIONS

Sponsor: States Advisory Council
Chair: Thomas G. Endres, University of St. Thomas
   "Faculty Scholarships, Training, and Development in North Dakota." Jeffrey D. Brand,
      North Dakota State University, Timothy L. Sellnow, North Dakota State University
   "Curriculum Development and Teacher Preparation in California." Judith A. Barnes, San
      Jose State University, Edwina L. Stoll, De Anza College
   "Hosting High School State Forensics Championships in Florida." Bonnie L. Clark, St.
      Petersburg Junior College
   "Foundation-Funded Traveling Workshops in Minnesota." Thomas G. Endres, University of
      St. Thomas, Larry Schnoor, Communication Links
   "Performing Arts Auditions and All-State Recognitions in Oklahoma." Robert Greenstreet,
      East Central University
   "Joint Meeting with Eastern Communication Association RPA Division in Pennsylvania."
      Chrys Gabrich, Carlow College

2658   3:30-4:45 p.m.   Lake Ontario   Eighth Floor   Chicago Hilton

TOP PAPERS IN VISUAL COMMUNICATION

Sponsor: Visual Communication Commission
Chair: Janis L. Edwards, Western Illinois University
   "Clinton's Visual Image Defense in the Lewinsky Debacle: Toward a New Taxonomy of
      Visual Apologia." Lini Allen, University of Northern Colorado, David L. Palmer,
      University of Northern Colorado
   "The Educated Eye." Shannon Skarphol Kaml, University of Minnesota
   "Toon In, Turn On, Drop Out: Animation, *The Simpsons*, and Postmodern Mediated
      Form." Jonathan H. Bruning, University of Kansas
   "Outside the Boundaries: Visual Evaluation for the World Wide Web." Sue Barnes,
      Fordham University

Respondent: Janis L. Edwards, Western Illinois University

2661   3:30-4:45 p.m.   Lake Erie   Eighth Floor   Chicago Hilton

DUELING EAGLES: IMMIGRATION ISSUES REVISITED

Sponsor: Latina/Latino Communication Studies Division
Chair: Myrna Pietri, California State University, Los Angeles
   "Re-Defining the Role of Undocumented Women in the Immigrant Rights Movement: The
      Case of Mujeres Unidas y Activas*." Maria Rogers-Pascual, San Francisco State
      University

Friday

"Fortifying Borders: Materializing Whiteness." Aimee M. Carrillo Rowe, University of Washington

Respondent: Leda M. Cooks, University of Massachusetts, Amherst

*Top Paper

| 2662 | 3:30-4:45 p.m. | Essex Court | Second Floor | Essex Inn |

C. S. LEWIS IN THE NEXT MILLENNIUM

Sponsor: Religious Communication Association
Chair: Russell K. Hirst, University of Tennessee
   "C. S. Lewis and the New Science: The Abolition of Man as Prophetic Argument." James A. Herrick, Hope College
   "From A Grief Observed to Shadowlands—and Beyond: To Whom Will Lewis Speak?" Elvera B. Berry, Roberts Wesleyan College
   "Embalming Images: Lewis and the Inkling of Film." Terrence R. Lindvall, Regent University

Respondent: Dale L. Sullivan, Michigan Technological University

---

| 2663 | 3:30-4:45 p.m. | Windsor Court | Second Floor | Essex Inn |

COLORING AGAINST THE LINES: NATIVE ETHNOGRAPHY AS INTERCULTURAL PRAXIS

Sponsor: Ethnography Division
Chair: Marwan M. Kraidy, University of North Dakota
   "The Native and the 'Other': Negotiating Identity in Hawaii." Fay Y. Akindes, University of Wisconsin, Parkside
   "Power, Positionality, and Ethnographic Knowledge: Can There Be a Feminist 'Native' Ethnography?" Anjali Ram, Clark University
   "Doing Indigenous Ethnography in Mexico as a Cultural Outsider: Lessons from the 'Four Seasons'." S. Lily Mendoza, Arizona State University
   "Native Ethnography, Thick and Thin." Marwan M. Kraidy, University of North Dakota

Respondent: Raul E. Gonzalez-Pinto, ITESM Campus Queretaro, Mexico

---

| 2664 | 3:30-4:45 p.m. | Buckingham Court | Second Floor | Essex Inn |

"A COUNTER FRICTION TO STOP THE MACHINE": STUDIES IN AMERICAN RHETORICAL RESISTANCE

Sponsor: American Studies Commission
Chair: Shawny Anderson, Saint Mary's College of California
   "Domestications of the Hearth: Containing the Reform Potential of Public Broadcasting*." Glenda R. Balas, DePauw University
   "Social Engineering and Photographic Representation: Resistance of the Icon to the Logos in Survey Graphic*." Cara A. Finnegan, University of Illinois, Urbana-Champaign
   "Battle for the Real America: A Dramatistic Analysis of the Rhetoric of the Militia of Montana." Sarah E. Mahan-Hays, Ohio University Eastern

*Top Three Paper

| 2665 | 3:30-4:45 p.m. | Park East Walk | Second Floor | Essex Inn |

THE KENNETH BURKE COLORING BOOK: INSTRUCTIONS AND CRIB SHEETS

Sponsor: Kenneth Burke Society, NCA Branch
Chair: Ray R. Benkendorf, Southwestern College
   "Heroes, Villains, Clowns, and Fools: The Pathology of B(urkean) O(ccupational) P(sychosis)." W. Lance Haynes, University of Missouri, Rolla
   "The Importance of Being Earnest, and the Dangers." James F. Klumpp, University of Maryland

"Kenneth Burke and Criticism as Activism." Tony J. Palmeri, University of Wisconsin, Oshkosh

Respondent: Barry Brummett, University of Wisconsin, Milwaukee

---

2666   3:30-4:45 p.m.   Cohn Rm   Second Floor   Spertus Institute

RHETORIC OF SCIENCE AS A 'STALLED PROJECT': TOWARD A METHODOLOGICAL SELF CRITIQUE

Sponsor: American Association for Rhetoric of Science & Technology
Chair: John A. Campbell, University of Memphis
   "Rhetoriography: An Essay in Method." John A. Campbell, University of Memphis
   "Working in the Academy and Working in the Polis: Can We Make Everybody Happy?" Steven A. Claas, University of Minnesota
   "The Hermeneutic Role of the Habermasian Participant in the Rhetoric of Science." Ruth J. Cronje, University of Minnesota
   "The Fusion of Horizons: Historical and Rational Reconstruction in the Rhetoric of Science." Andreea Decui, University of Bucharest

---

2667   3:30-4:45 p.m.   Krensky Rm   Second Floor   Spertus Institute

WHEN CULTURE AND LAW COLLIDE: PAST AND PRESENT LEGAL CASES

Sponsor: Communication and Law Commission
Chair: Ronald J. Matlon, Towson University
   "Moral Argument and the George Reynolds Case." Janice E. Schuetz, University of New Mexico
   "Typhoid Mary, Bacteriology, and Progressive Law Courts." Marouf Hasian, University of Utah
   "A Foreigner in American Courts." Jane W. Yamazaki, Wayne State University

Respondent: Ronald J. Matlon, Towson University

2668   3:30-4:45 p.m.   Rm 902   Ninth Floor   Spertus Institute

STUDIES OF NEWS COVERAGE, CAMPAIGN RHETORIC AND INTERNET DISCOURSE ABOUT CHINESE AROUND THE WORLD

Sponsor: Chinese Communication Association
Chair: Peter A. DeCaro, Buena Vista University
   "One Country, Two Pictures: President Clinton's 1998 China Visit as Portrayed in Two Chinese and Two American Elite Newspapers." Shupeng Li, Southern Illinois University, Dennis T. Lowry, Southern Illinois University
   "The First Taiwanese Presidential Election of 1996: An Analysis of the Campaign Rhetoric." Lin-Lee Lee, University of Minnesota
   "Civic Discourse on Internet in the Chinese Virtual Community in North America." Dejun Liu, University College of Cape Breton, Canada

Respondent: Gary B. Wilson, Hong Kong Baptist University

2669   3:30-4:45 p.m.   Rm 903   Ninth Floor   Spertus Institute

FIRST WE GET THE CRAYONS . . . ORGANIZING THE NUTS AND BOLTS OF SERVICE-LEARNING EXPERIENCES IN COMMUNICATION

Sponsor: Experiential Learning in Communication Commission
Chair: Eileen M. Perrigo, University of West Florida
   "Creating Projects and Connecting with the Community." Jeffrey L. Woodyard, Stetson University
   "Crystalizing the Service-Learning Experience: Using Reflection Techniques to Maximize Student Learning." Charles A. Lubbers, Kansas State University
   "Assessing the Service-Learning Component in the Communication Curriculum: Areas and Strategies for Measurement." Paul A. Soukup, Santa Clara University

Friday

"Creating a Bond: Gaining Administrative Support for Service-Learning." Toni S. Whitfield, University of West Florida

"The Art of Publishing Your Service-Learning Experiences: Scholarship at Work." Edward Zlotkowski, American Association for Higher Education

---

2670   3:30-4:45 p.m.   Rm 904   Ninth Floor   Spertus Institute

INDIGENOUS TERMS, CULTURAL CONCEPTS, AND COMMUNICATIVE FUNCTIONS

Sponsor: Association for Chinese Communication Studies
Chair: Alberto Gonzalez, Bowling Green State University
"The Cultural Connotation and Communicative Function of China's Kinship Terms." Shaorong Huang, University of Cincinnati
"The Chinese Concept of Face and a Family of its Related Terms." Wenshan Jia, Truman State University
"Native Terms for Chinese Small Talk and Implications for Communication Theory." Shuming Lu, Brooklyn College, CUNY
"Old Words and New Meanings in Post-Mao China." Mei Zhang, University of Pittsburgh

Respondent: D. Ray Heisey, Kent State University

2671   3:30-4:45 p.m.   Rm 906   Ninth Floor   Spertus Institute

MINING THE RHETORICAL VEIN

Sponsor: American Society for the History of Rhetoric
Chair: Hanns J. Hohmann, San Jose State University
"Style and Persuasion Through Character in Aristotle's *Rhetoric*." Richard J. Graff, Northwestern University
"Walter Pater and the Rhetorical Tradition: Finding Common Sense in the Particular." Lois P. Agnew, Texas Christian University
"George Mackenzie on Judicial Eloquence in Post-Restoration Scotland." Beth I. Manolescu, University of Illinois

Respondent: Barbara Warnick, University of Washington

2672   3:30-4:45 p.m.   Rm 907   Ninth Floor   Spertus Institute

ALTERNATIVE WAYS OF TEACHING, VIEWING AND EVALUATING DEBATE

Sponsor: Cross Examination Debate Association
Chair: Roxann L. Knutson, Appalachian State University
"Negotiating a Change in the Argumentation Course: Teaching Cooperative Argument." David E. Williams, Texas Tech University, Brian R. McGee, Texas Tech University
"A Call for the Novelization of Debate: Bakhtin and the Question of Authoritative Evidence." Benjamin R. Bates, University of Georgia
"Seeing the 'Big Picture': A Prescription to the Activity to Hit the Boards Running." Jason Stone, Middle Tennessee State University
"Disclosure as the Discovery Phase: Applying Legal System Procedures to Academic Debate." Bob E. Alexander, Northeast Louisiana State University

Respondent: Roxann L. Knutson, Appalachian State University

2673   3:30-4:45 p.m.   Rm 908   Ninth Floor   Spertus Institute

A ROUNDTABLE DISCUSSION: COMMUNITY COLLEGE COACHING IN THE UNIVERSITY-DRIVEN WORLD OF POLICY DEBATE

Sponsor: Phi Rho Pi
Chair: Cynthia E. Dewar, City College of San Francisco

Panelists: K. C. Boylan, Sacramento City Community College
          Joe Corcoran, Santa Rosa Junior College
          Dean P. Gundlach, College of Eastern Utah

Bob Lechtreck, Bakersfield College
Mark Nelson, Santa Rosa Junior College
Mark J. Woolsey, Fresno City College

Respondent: Terrence C. Winebrenner, California Polytechnic State University, San Luis Obispo

Focus will be placed on the challenges community college coaches face in preparing their students to be competitive with university policy debate programs.

2674	3:30-4:45 p.m.	Auditorium	Second Floor	Spertus Institute

REACHING ACROSS BORDERS: ACTING EXERCISES FROM UNUSUAL SOURCES

Sponsor: Theatre Division
Chair: Katherine Sullivan, Saint Mary's College

This is a practical workshop which demonstrates and teaches acting exercises drawn from "outside the lines" of theatre, having their origins instead in Fritz Perls-based encounter groups, martial arts, dance, poetry, and art therapy. These can help actors to develop vulnerability and create a better ensemble. Gentle and positive, these activities can prove to be exhilarating on a personal level as well.

5:00 p.m.

2706	5:00-6:15 p.m.	Continental BR A	Lobby Level	Chicago Hilton

NUTS AND BOLTS OF MANAGING A STATE ASSOCIATION II: OUTREACH

Sponsor: States Advisory Council
Chair: Tamara L. Burk, College of William and Mary

Panelists: Barbara I. Hall, University of Illinois, Urbana-Champaign
Jerry L. Buley, Arizona State University
Raymie E. McKerrow, Ohio University
Tamara L. Burk, College of William and Mary

Panel leaders discuss state association/NCA partnerships, involving non-academic communication professionals in a state association, K-12 Education Standards across the states and regional networking.

2707	5:00-6:15 p.m.	Continental BR B	Lobby Level	Chicago Hilton

PUBLISHING ON-LINE

Sponsor: Human Communication and Technology Commission
Chair: John C. Sherblom, University of Maine, Orono
  "The Evolution of an On-Line Publication: Com Resources On-Line." Joan E. Aitken, University of Missouri, Kansas City
  "Editing a Special Issue of EJC/REC On-Line." Dudley D. Cahn, SUNY, New Paltz
  "Co-editing a New On-Line Publication: Communication Teacher Resources On-Line." Leonard J. Shedletsky, University of Southern Maine
  "EJC/REC on the Eve of Its Second Decade." Teresa M. Harrison, Rensselaer Polytechnic Institute, Timothy D. Stephen, Rensselaer Polytechnic Institute

Respondent: William F. Eadie, NCA National Office

2708	5:00-6:15 p.m.	Continental BR C	Lobby Level	Chicago Hilton

ETHNOGRAPHIES IN THE HOMEPLACE: VOICE, SPACE, AND CRITICAL REFLEXIVITY

Sponsor: Critical and Cultural Studies Division
Chair: Philip C. Wander, San Jose State University

Friday

"An Ethnographic Study of Comfort Women." Jong-Hwa Lee, Ohio University
"Li'l Africa: An Ethnography of the Black Diaspora at Ohio University." Shawn A. Torres, Ohio University
"Doing Field Research in South India as an Indian Feminist Ethnographer: Rethinking Reflexivity." Ruma J. Sen, Ohio University

Respondent: Wenshu Lee, San Jose State University

2711   5:00-6:15 p.m.   Int'l Ballroom North   Second Floor   Chicago Hilton

ETHNOGRAPHIC VENTRILOQUISM AND THE NEW ETHNOGRAPHY

Sponsor: Performance Studies Division
Chair: Elizabeth C. Fine, Virginia Tech University
    "The Ethnographer as Ventriloquist in the New Ethnography." Elizabeth C. Fine, Virginia Tech University
    "Discursive Re-contextualizations in Ethnographies of Discourse: An Argument for an Empirical Postmodernism." Anita Puckett, Virginia Tech University
    "Ethnographic Resistance: Searching for Identity in the Postmodern Community." Nathan P. Stucky, Southern Illinois University, Carbondale

Respondent: Richard Bauman, Indiana University

2714   5:00-6:15 p.m.   Boulevard A   Second Floor   Chicago Hilton

CHALLENGING BOUNDARIES: DEAF CULTURE AND COMMUNICATION

Sponsor: Challenging Boundaries Series
Chair: Shelley D. Lane, Collin County Community College
    "'Handicapped We're Not': The Deaf Culture Perspective." Marianne Sasseen, Texas Education Service Center, Region 10
    "Meaning and Method: How Deaf Culture Influences the Interpreting Process." Helene Gilbert, Collin County Community College
    "Testing and Topics: How Deaf Culture Influences the Teaching of Communication." Shelley D. Lane, Collin County Community College
    "Survival Signs: An Audience Participation ASL Lesson." Henry Whalen, Collin County Community College

---

2715   5:00-6:15 p.m.   Boulevard B   Second Floor   Chicago Hilton

COLORING OUTSIDE THE LINES: HAMMERBACK AND JENSEN'S *THE RHETORICAL CAREER OF CESAR CHAVEZ*

Sponsor: NCA First Vice President
Chair: Alberto Gonzalez, Bowling Green State University

Panelists: Alberto Gonzalez, Bowling Green State University
          Rosalinda Cantu, Bowling Green State University
          Fernando P. Delgado, Arizona State University West
          Dolores V. Tanno, California State University, San Bernardino

Respondents: John C. Hammerback, North Carolina State University
            Richard J. Jensen, University of Nevada, Las Vegas

---

2716   5:00-6:15 p.m.   Boulevard C   Second Floor   Chicago Hilton

INDIVIDUALISM, COLLECTIVISM, HARMONY, AND DESIRE: VALUE ORIENTATIONS ACROSS CULTURES

Sponsor: International & Intercultural Communication Division
Chair: Ling Chen, Hong Kong Baptist University

"Harmony as Performance: The Turbulence Under Chinese Interpersonal Communication." Hui-Ching Chang, University of Illinois, Chicago
"Desire and Power: A Cultural Reading of Individuality and Social Collectivity in Tian Zhuangzhuang's *The Blue Kite*." Hong Wang, Southern Illinois University
"Individualist Collectivist Values: American, Indian and Japanese Cross-Cultural Study." Catherine W. Konsky, Illinois State University, Mariko Eguchi, Illinois State University, Janet Blue, Illinois State University, Suraj P. Kapoor, Illinois State University

Respondent: John H. Powers, Hong Kong Baptist University

| 2718 | 5:00-6:15 p.m. | Waldorf | Third Floor | Chicago Hilton |

DECISION-MAKING AND THE MANAGEMENT OF UNCERTAINTY

Sponsor: Health Communication Division
Chair: Melanie Booth-Butterfield, West Virginia University
"Decision-Making, Competency, and Medical Ethics: Measurement of Communication Differences Amongst Professional Groups." Susan Zickmund, University of Iowa
"Communication in the Management of Uncertainty." Dale E. Brashers, University of Illinois, Urbana-Champaign, Judith L. Neidig, Ohio State University, Stephen M. Haas, Rutgers University, Linda K. Dobbs, Ohio State University, Linda W. Cardillo, Ohio State University, Jane A. Russell, Ohio State University
"The Impact of the Endorsing Channel upon Physicians' Decisions to Adopt Clustered and Unclustered Drug Treatment Innovations." Toby J. Arquette, Northwestern University
"Life in an Evolving Hospital: Nurses' Reactions to Changes in Communication and Communication About Change." Julie A. Apker, Wayne State University, Katherine I. Miller, Texas A&M University, Lori J. Joseph, University of Kansas
"Communication in Advance Care Planning: Preferences for Surrogate Involvement." Stephen C. Hines, West Virginia University, Alan D. Heisel, West Virginia University, Mary C. Toale, West Virginia University, Rikki D. Amos, West Virginia University, Doreen K. Baringer, University of Oklahoma, Jennifer S. Burkett, West Virginia University, Jeffrey D. Cline, West Virginia University, John V. Dalesio, West Virginia University, Christopher E. Davis, West Virginia University, Kimberly J. Franey, West Virginia University, Lisa N. George, West Virginia University, Tania K. Gojdycz, West Virginia University, Christian A. Hall, West Virginia University, Meg S. Lyons, West Virginia University, Jill N. Mattiello, West Virginia University

| 2719 | 5:00-6:15 p.m. | Astoria | Third Floor | Chicago Hilton |

CONSPIRACY RHETORIC: GAINING PERSPECTIVE BY INCONGRUITY

Sponsor: Public Address Division
Chair: Carol K. Winkler, Georgia State University
"The Anatomy of a Conspiracy: Salmon P. Chase's 'Appeal of the Independent Democrats'." Robert A. Kraig, University of Wisconsin, Madison
"Social Movements and Constitutive Rhetoric: Which Public Does the Militia Address?" Joseph G. Bellon, University of Georgia
"Sumner, Garrison and the Slave-Power Conspiracy: Between Two Traditions." Michael W. Pfau, Northwestern University
"Just Because I'm Paranoid Doesn't Mean They're Not After Me: A Comparative Analysis of the Use of Conspiracy in Public Address." Robert J. McKown, Northwestern University

Respondent: David Zarefsky, Northwestern University

| 2721 | 5:00-6:15 p.m. | Williford A | Third Floor | Chicago Hilton |

DIVERSE IDENTITIES AS ESTABLISHED THROUGH MUSIC AND TELEVISION

Sponsor: African American Communication & Culture Commission
Chair: Dwight E. Brooks, University of Georgia
"An Expanded View of Understanding Black Women n' Jazz: An Unintentionally Introspective Endeaver." Kim L. Verdell, University of Georgia

Friday

"Yours, Mine and Ours: A Look at Rhythm and Blues as a Cultural Archetype." Sharnine S. Herbert, Howard University

"Gangsta Rap Trailblazers: Expressions of Womanism." Shannon B. Campbell, University of Florida

"Rap: Asserting Poetics Against the Popular." Gregory J. Dimitriadis, University of Illinois, Urbana-Champaign

"Reclaiming Aesthetic Diversity: A Genre of African American Situation Comedy." Timothy Havens, Indiana University, Bloomington

Respondent: Eric K. Watts, Wake Forest University

2722   5:00-6:15 p.m.   Williford B   Third Floor   Chicago Hilton

THE 1998 DISTINGUISHED APPLIED COMMUNICATION SCHOLARSHIP WINNERS AND RUNNERS-UP: WHAT LESSONS AND ADVICE CAN THEY SHARE?

Sponsor: Applied Communication Division
Chair: Jim L. Query, Loyola University, Chicago
　　"The Fragile Community: Living Together with AIDS." Mara B. Adelman, Seattle University, Lawrence R. Frey, University of Memphis
　　"The Silicone Breast Implant Story: Communication and Uncertainty." Marsha L. Vanderford, University of South Florida, David H. Smith, University of South Florida
　　"Looking For Justice in All the Wrong Places: On a Communication Approach to Social Justice." Lawrence R. Frey, University of Memphis, W. Barnett Pearce, Pearce Walters Associates, Mark A. Pollock, Loyola University, Chicago, B. Lee Artz, Loyola University, Chicago, Bren O. Murphy, Loyola University, Chicago
　　"Hooked on Expectations: An Analysis of Influence and Relationships in the Tailhook Reports." Michelle T. Violanti, University of Tennessee

---

2723   5:00-6:15 p.m.   Williford C   Third Floor   Chicago Hilton

PERFORMING GENDER, GENDERING PERFORMANCE

Sponsor: Feminist and Women Studies Division
Chair: Anne F. Mattina, Stonehill College
　　"'We Ought to Know Better': Meta-Shame and the Performance of Weight Consciousness in Women's Friendships." Elena C. Strauman, University of South Florida, Laura L. Ellingson, University of South Florida
　　"Ani Difranco's Palimpsest of Public Performance: 'Taken Out of Context I Must Seem So Strange'." Kelly C. McLaughlin, University of Iowa
　　"'The Story of Her Life': The Filmic Construction of the Woman Artist in *Carrington*." Jennifer L. Borda, Penn State University
　　"Harnessing Dildos and Desire: An Ethnography of a Feminist Sex Toy Store." Lynn Comella, University of Massachusetts

Respondent: Sujata Moorti, Old Dominion University

2724   5:00-7:45 p.m.   Marquette   Third Floor   Chicago Hilton

CAUCUS ON GAY AND LESBIAN CONCERNS BUSINESS MEETING AND RECEPTION

Sponsor: Gay & Lesbian Concerns Caucus

2725   5:00-7:45 p.m.   Joliet   Third Floor   Chicago Hilton

WOMEN'S CAUCUS BUSINESS MEETING AND FRANCINE MERRITT AWARD RECEPTION

Sponsor: Women's Caucus

| 2726 | 5:00-6:15 p.m. | PDR 1 | Third Floor | Chicago Hilton |

SENIOR COLLEGE AND UNIVERSITY SECTION GENERAL BUSINESS MEETING

Sponsor: Senior College & University Section

| 2727 | 5:00-7:45 p.m. | PDR 2 | Third Floor | Chicago Hilton |

MASS COMMUNICATION DIVISION BUSINESS MEETING AND RECEPTION

Sponsor: Mass Communication Division

| 2728 | 5:00-6:15 p.m. | PDR 3 | Third Floor | Chicago Hilton |

COMMUNICATION SCHOLARS: POWER, POLICY, AND (IM)POTENCY?

Sponsor: Table Talk Series
Chair: Gary Gumpert, Communication Landscapers

Panelists: Robert K. Avery, University of Utah
Deborah Borisoff, New York University
Susan J. Drucker, Hofstra University
Gary Gumpert, Communication Landscapers
Gary L. Kreps, Hofstra University
Thomas A. McCain, Ohio State University

How close are communication scholars to those who have a voice in determining policy and how close should we be? Do we have access to granting sources and funds; to governmental agencies? What is the hierarchical position of departments/schools of communication within the university setting? How are they regarded by administrators? University politics can alter the impact of communication scholars upon the community. This panel will explore these issues from diverse perspectives including the view from administrators, consultants, and researchers.

| 2729 | 5:00-6:15 p.m. | PDR 4 | Third Floor | Chicago Hilton |

RHETORICAL AND COMMUNICATION THEORY DIVISION BUSINESS MEETING

Sponsor: Rhetorical and Communication Theory Division

| 2730 | 5:00-6:15 p.m. | PDR 5 | Third Floor | Chicago Hilton |

COMMUNICATION ETHICS COMMISSION BUSINESS MEETING

Sponsor: Communication Ethics Commission

| 2731 | 5:00-6:15 p.m. | PDR 6 | Third Floor | Chicago Hilton |

THEATRE DIVISION BUSINESS MEETING

Sponsor: Theatre Division

| 2732 | 5:00-6:15 p.m. | PDR 7 | Third Floor | Chicago Hilton |

ETHNOGRAPHY DIVISION BUSINESS MEETING

Sponsor: Ethnography Division

Friday

2733   5:00-6:15 p.m.   Conf 4A   Fourth Floor   Chicago Hilton

COLORING OUTSIDE THE LINES: A NEW LIFE FOR THE NCA SECTION NEWSLETTER?

Sponsor: Community College Section
Chair: Thomas J. Sabetta, Jefferson Community College
   "The Newsletter as a Revenue Enhancer." Thomas E. Ruddick, Edison Community College
   "The Newsletter as a Recruiting Tool." Robert C. Bohan, St. Petersburg Junior College
   "The Newsletter as a Link to the Section Community." David L. Bodary, Sinclair
      Community College

This panel discussion is designed to allow brainstorming and creative problem-solving surrounding the changing role of the NCA Section Newsletter. While the newsletter serves as a vital information source, is it possible to use it for other equally important purposes without violating the section mission? All NCA section newsletter editors or interested parties are encouraged to attend.

2734   5:00-6:15 p.m.   Conf 4B   Fourth Floor   Chicago Hilton

THE 'PLACE' OF ORATORY IN GREEK POLITICAL LIFE: PHYSICAL SETTING AND RHETORICAL PRACTICE IN CLASSICAL GREECE

Sponsor: American Society for the History of Rhetoric
Chair: Audrey M. Van Mersbergen, University of Minnesota, Duluth
   "The Secret Composition Practices of the Ancient Spartans: A Reconstruction of Material
      Evidence." Richard Enos, Texas Christian University
   "Communicating in Classical Contexts: The Centrality of Delivery." Christopher Johnstone,
      Penn State University
   "Discontent with Discourse: The Influence of Physical Context on Political Deliberation in
      Athens." David M. Timmerman, Wabash College

Respondent: Edward Schiappa, University of Minnesota, Twin Cities

---

2735   5:00-6:15 p.m.   Conf 4C   Fourth Floor   Chicago Hilton

ROLE OF SILENCE IN PEACE AND CONFLICT COMMUNICATION: IMPLICATIONS FOR RESEARCH AND EDUCATION

Sponsor: Peace and Conflict Communication Commission
Chair: Benjamin J. Broome, George Mason University
   "Functions of Silence in Intrapersonal Conflict: Some Ghandian Concepts." Nemi C. Jain,
      Arizona State University, Puvana Ganesan, Arizona State University
   "Role of Silence and Avoidance in Interpersonal Conflict." Alexia S. Jazayeri, Arizona State
      University
   "Silent Strategies in Managing Intergroup and Organizational Conflicts." Pamela J. Zaug,
      Arizona State University
   "Silence and International Conflict: Some Cross-Cultural and Global Perspectives." Tamie
      Kanata, Arizona State University, Nemi C. Jain, Arizona State University

---

2736   5:00-6:15 p.m.   Conf 4D   Fourth Floor   Chicago Hilton

OUTCOME BASED ASSESSMENT IN CROSS-CURRICULAR ENDEAVORS

Sponsor: Commission on Communication Assessment
Chair: Lisa M. Skow, University of North Carolina
   "National Conversations Regarding Assessment in Higher Education." John A. Daly,
      University of Texas, Austin
   "Telling Our Story and Telling It Well: Programmatic Assessment of Communication Across
      the Curriculum." Ann L. Darling, University of Utah
   "Assessment as Pedagogy: Training TA's to Evaluate Undergraduate Communication Across
      the Curriculum." Maureen A. Mathison, University of Utah

"Disciplinary Assessment of Oral Presentations: Initial Steps and Strategies." Deanna P. Dannels, University of Utah

| 2737 | 5:00-6:15 p.m. | Conf 4E | Fourth Floor | Chicago Hilton |

TALK ON TELEVISION: EXPLORATIONS OF MEDIATED DISCOURSE

Sponsor: Language and Social Interaction Division
Chair: Kathleen C. Haspel, University of Denver
   "Rhetorical Discourse in Interactive Commerce Systems: Strategies in Television Home Shopping." Susan L. Kline, Ohio State University
   "The Institution of Active Listening: An Analysis of a Public Demonstration of Active Listening Techniques." Samuel G. Lawrence, SUNY, Albany
   "Teasing in the Late Night Television Interview: Two Major Discursive Strategies." Leah Wingard, University of California, Los Angeles

Respondent: Stuart J. Sigman, Emerson College

| 2738 | 5:00-6:15 p.m. | Conf 4F | Fourth Floor | Chicago Hilton |

PERSUASION AND PERCEPTION

Sponsor: Intrapersonal Communication/Social Cognition Commission
Chair: Janet R. Meyer, Kent State University
   "Cognitive Dissonance Theory and Compliance-Gaining Strategies: Applications and Limitations." Carma L. Bylund, Northwestern University
   "Metaphor and Persuasion: Role of Structural Coherence, Attitude Accessibility and Prior Knowledge." Pradeep Sopory, University of Memphis
   "Perceptions of Romantic Partners' Nonverbal and Verbal Social Skills: Associations with Attachment Style and Relational Satisfaction." Laura K. Guerrero, Arizona State University, Susanne Jones, Arizona State University
   "A Meta-Analysis of the Relative Influence and Influencability of Men and Women." Mark A. Hamilton, University of Connecticut, Paul J. Mineo, University of Connecticut

Respondent: Robert N. Bostrom, University of Kentucky

| 2739 | 5:00-6:15 p.m. | Conf 4G | Fourth Floor | Chicago Hilton |

POLITICS 'OUTSIDE THE LINES': MINNESOTA GOVERNOR JESSE 'THE BODY' VENTURA

Sponsor: Political Communication Division
Chair: Debra L. Petersen, University of St. Thomas
   "'Political Harmonic Convergence': The Unthinkable Election of Jesse Ventura." Kevin O. Sauter, University of St. Thomas
   "'A Pipe Straight into Our Hands': Governor Jesse Ventura's Internet Rhetoric." Adrienne E. Christiansen, Macalester College, Sally A. Caudill, Macalester College
   "'Our Governor Can Beat Up Your Governor': A Feminist Cluster-Analysis of Jesse Ventura's Macho-Political Style." Debra K. Japp, St. Cloud State University, Phyllis M. Japp, University of Nebraska, Lincoln
   "The Role of First Lady in a Masculinized Governorship: First Lady Terry Ventura." Debra L. Petersen, University of St. Thomas
   "Re-Contextualization of the Public's Agenda: A Study of Public Opinion, Internet Discussion, and Newspapers in the 1998 Minnesota Gubernatorial Election." Jong-Gil Song, University of Oklahoma, Scott D. Wells, University of Oklahoma, Justin D. Walton, University of Oklahoma

| 2740 | 5:00-6:15 p.m. | Conf 4H | Fourth Floor | Chicago Hilton |

POLITICAL CARTOONS: CONTINUING COMMUNICATION WITH A BITE

Sponsor: Media Forum Series
Chair: Bonnie L. Clark, St. Petersburg Junior College

Friday

"Exploding the Pop Culture Paradigm in Political Cartoon Research." Janis L. Edwards, Western Illinois University

"Iconicity, Indexicality, and Propositional Syntax: The Making of a Painful Political Cartoon." Suzanne W. Chapman, University of Iowa

"No Laughing Matter: Cartoonist Depictions of Sexual Harassment." Janette K. Muir, George Mason University

"Editorial Cartooning in the Gay Press." Edward Sewell, Virginia Tech University

"Presidential Humor: The Framing of William Jefferson Clinton as Everyman." Jan Joseph Younger, Heidelberg College

---

2741   5:00-6:15 p.m.   Conf 4I   Fourth Floor   Chicago Hilton

CRITERIA FOR SELECTING COMMUNICATION CONSULTANTS: CORPORATIONS SPEAK OUT

Sponsor: Roundtable Series
Chair: Sue DeWine, Ohio University

This panel discussion will feature corporate executives from McDonald's Corporation, Anderson Consulting, and Ameritech discussing what criteria they use when hiring outside consultants. Discussion will focus on what communication consultants can offer the corporate world and how communication consultants can market themselves to corporations so that corporate executives realize the value of a consulting intervention based on communication practices.

2742   5:00-6:15 p.m.   Conf 4J   Fourth Floor   Chicago Hilton

EDUCATIONAL POLICIES BOARD BUSINESS MEETING

Sponsor: Educational Policies Board

2743   5:00-6:15 p.m.   Conf 4K   Fourth Floor   Chicago Hilton

NONVERBAL AND RELATIONAL MESSAGES: FUNCTIONS AND INTERPRETATIONS

Sponsor: Interpersonal Communication Division
Chair: Beth A. Le Poire, University of California, Santa Barbara

"Attributions for Nonverbal Expressions of Liking and Disliking: An Extension of the Self-Serving Bias." Kory Floyd, Cleveland State University

"Marital Couples' Perceptions of Touch Behavior and Marital Satisfaction." Jenny A. Taylor, California State University, Fullerton

"Re-conceptualizing Relational Transgressions as Relational Messages: Predicting Responses from Changes in Relational Definitions." Artemio Ramirez, University of Arizona, Laura R. Roberts, University of Arizona

"Emotional Support: Targeting Attributions to Change Emotions." Craig R. Hullett, Michigan State University

Respondent: Beth A. Le Poire, University of California, Santa Barbara

---

2744   5:00-6:15 p.m.   Conf 4L   Fourth Floor   Chicago Hilton

TEACHING PUBLIC RELATIONS ON-LINE

Sponsor: Public Relations Division
Chair: Jeff K. Springston, University of Georgia

"Teaching Public Relations On-Line: The Myths and Opportunities." Bonita Dostal Neff, Valparaiso University

"Teaching Totally via the Internet." Becky A. McDonald, Ball State University

"Course Web Sites: A View from Both Sides." W. Timothy Coombs, Illinois State University

"New Communication Media, New Public Relations Practices, New Teaching Ways." Daradirek Ekachai, Southern Illinois University

| 2745 | 5:00-6:15 p.m. | | Conf 4M | Fourth Floor | Chicago Hilton |

BALANCING FRIENDSHIPS, FAMILY, AND WORK: DEVELOPMENTAL INFLUENCES, SOCIALIZATION AND COMMUNICATION

Sponsor: Organizational Communication Division
Chair: Caryn E. Medved, Michigan State University
    "Understudied Communication: Balancing Work and Family in Organizations*." Erika L. Kirby, Creighton University
    "Toward a New Construct Influencing Communication at Work: Work Friendship Orientation within the Narrative Organization." Janie M. Harden Fritz, Duquesne University, Ronald C. Arnett, Duquesne University
    "Developmental Influences and Communication in Peer Workplace Friendships." Patricia M. Sias, Washington State University, Guy Smith, Washington State University, Tatyana Avdeyeva, Washington State University
    "Three Competing Models of Communication During Organizational Socialization." Zachary P. Hart, University of Missouri, Columbia, Vernon D. Miller, Michigan State University

Respondent: Cynthia Stohl, Purdue University

*Top Student Paper

| 2746 | 5:00-6:15 p.m. | McCormick Board Rm | Fourth Floor | Chicago Hilton |

COMMISSION ON COMMUNICATION AND AGING BUSINESS MEETING

Sponsor: Communication and Aging Commission

| 2747 | 5:00-6:15 p.m. | Pullman Board Rm | Fourth Floor | Chicago Hilton |

SEMIOTICS AND COMMUNICATION COMMISSION BUSINESS MEETING

Sponsor: Semiotics and Communication Commission

| 2749 | 5:00-6:15 p.m. | | Conf 5B | Fifth Floor | Chicago Hilton |

ASSESSMENT ISSUES IN THE BASIC COURSE

Sponsor: Basic Course Division
Chair: William J. Seiler, University of Nebraska, Lincoln
    "Instructor Degree Status, Gender, and Grades in Basic Speech." Christopher Power, Wichita State University, L. Keith Williamson, Wichita State University
    "Defining the Rules and Roles of the Basic Course: A Preliminary Assessment of Student Perceptions." Michael W. Shelton, University of Kentucky, Derek R. Lane, University of Kentucky, Enid S. Waldhart, University of Kentucky
    "A Review of Assessment of the Basic Communication Course and the Influence of the Course and Its Instructors on Learning." Jennifer Jones-Corley, Penn State University

Respondent: Amy R. Slagell, Iowa State University

| 2751 | 5:00-6:15 p.m. | | Conf 5D | Fifth Floor | Chicago Hilton |

COLORING iNSIDE/OUTSIDE THE LINES: WOMEN NEGOTIATE SPIRITUAL PRACTICES OF RESISTANCE

Sponsor: Spiritual Communication Commission
Chair: S. Renee Gillespie, University of Colorado, Boulder
    "Women's Cosmetics Rituals as Negotiated Resistance to Gender Norms." S. Renee Gillespie, University of Colorado, Boulder
    "Reclaiming the Power of the Great Mother Archetype: Responses to Representations of the Virgin Mary in Mexico." M. Cristina Gonzalez, Arizona State University

Friday

"Feminism in the Catholic Church: An Analysis of the Recitation of the Rosary and Marian Devotion." Marceline E. Thompson, University of Memphis

"Traditional Views of Femininity in New Age Spirituality: Tensions, Paradoxes, and Questions." Christy C. Standerfer, University of Colorado, Boulder

"Subtle Paths of Resistance: Spiritual Manifestations of Soul." Carol L. Thompson, University of Arkansas, Little Rock

Respondent: Tarla R. Peterson, Texas A&M University

2752   5:00-6:15 p.m.   Conf 5E   Fifth Floor   Chicago Hilton

WALT WHITMAN AND DEMOCRATIC COMMUNICATION

Sponsor: Rhetorical and Communication Theory Division
Chair: Robert L. Ivie, Indiana University

"Walt Whitman and Democratic Testimony." Kenneth Cmiel, University of Iowa

"Whitman, Tocqueville, and the Possibilities of Democratic Art." Joli K. Jensen, University of Tulsa

"Walt Whitman and Democratic Mass Mediation." Peter D. Simonson, Allegheny College

Respondent: Ed Folsom, University of Iowa

2753   5:00-6:15 p.m.   Conf 5F   Fifth Floor   Chicago Hilton

THE AFA CODE OF ETHICS AT 50: A PANEL DISCUSSION

Sponsor: American Forensic Association
Chair: James F. Klumpp, University of Maryland

Panelists: John E. Fritch, Southwest Missouri State University
            Gina E. Lane, William Jewell College
            Gretchen E. Wheeler, Casper College
            Guy P. Yates, West Texas A&M University
            George W. Ziegelmueller, Wayne State University

2754   5:00-6:15 p.m.   Conf 5G   Fifth Floor   Chicago Hilton

CULTIVATING HUMANITY IN A NEGOTIATED AGE: COMMUNICATION CLASSROOMS IN ACTION

Sponsor: Instructional Development Division
Chair: Scott D. Johnson, University of Richmond

"Cultivating Humanity in the Interpersonal Communication Course: Negotiating Perceptions of Self and Other." David E. Engen, Millikin University, Scott D. Johnson, University of Richmond

"Hearing Other Voices: Listening in the Age of Negotiation." Curt Bechler, Aquinas College

"On the Idea of Audience: Cultivating Humanity in Rhetorical Design Processes." Mari Lee Mifsud, University of Richmond

"Cultivating Imagination Through the Use of Feature Films in the Communication Classroom." Russell F. Proctor, Northern Kentucky University

---

2755   5:00-6:15 p.m.   Conf 5H   Fifth Floor   Chicago Hilton

THE POLITICS OF QUEER IDENTITY AND VISIBILITY

Sponsor: Gay/Lesbian Transgender Communication Studies Division
Chair: John R. Butler, Northern Illinois University

"Speaking and Spoken-For: Coming Out Stories and Political Strategy." John Lynch, University of Pittsburgh

"Sexual Behavior As 'Immaterial': The Compromise of Identity in the Struggle For Equal Protection." Anthony Marsowicz, Northern Illinois University

"The Illusionary Prize of Visibility and Its Cultural Implications For a Queer Community." Guillermo G. Caliendo, University of Pittsburgh

Respondent: James Darsey, Georgia State University

This panel examines the politics of queer identity by surveying three cultural spaces where the queer community is negotiating its identity. The panel intends to raise serious questions about the way in which a queer community is being represented—through narratives, legal rhetoric, and media—during a time of political gains and strategic negotiations.

2756	5:00-6:15 p.m.	Conf 5I	Fifth Floor	Chicago Hilton

CRITICAL THINKING, LITERATURE AND THE COMMUNICATION CLASSROOM

Sponsor: Elementary & Secondary Education Section

Panelists: Adrian W. Frana, Rich East High School, Illinois
Jan Heiteen, Downers Grove South High School, Illinois
Robert D. Neuleib, University High School/Illinois State University

The panel members will discuss approaches, concepts and materials that demonstrate the links between critical thinking, literature and the communication classroom.

2757	5:00-6:15 p.m.	Conf 5J	Fifth Floor	Chicago Hilton

WRITING ETHNOGRAPHIC ALTERNATIVES

Sponsor: Society for the Study of Symbolic Interaction
Chair: Arthur P. Bochner, University of South Florida

Panelists: Stacy H. Jones, University of Texas, Austin
Anna Banks, University of Idaho
Stephen P. Banks, University of Idaho
Annette N. Markham, Virginia Tech University
Robert S. Drew, Saginaw Valley State University

Respondent: Laurel Richardson, Ohio State University

2758	5:00-6:15 p.m.	Lake Ontario	Eighth Floor	Chicago Hilton

POWERFUL STYLE: WOMEN IN POLITICS NEGOTIATING A SUITABLE LOOK

Sponsor: Visual Communication Commission
Chair: Ann J. Atkinson, Penn State University, Altoona
"Looking the Part: Playing with Style." Ann J. Atkinson, Penn State University, Altoona
"Choosing the Right Uniform: Margaret Chase Smith's Fashion Sense." Sandra J. Sarkela, SUNY, Potsdam
"Like Night and Day: Eleanor Roosevelt's Conflicting Looks." Rita M. Miller, Keene State College
"An Extraordinary Turn: Hillary Rodham Clinton on the Pages of Vogue." Kathryn A. Wiss, Western Connecticut State University
"Fashion States: Madeleine Albright's Use of Pins." Kathryn M. Gunderson, National University

2759	5:00-6:15 p.m.	Lake Michigan	Eighth Floor	Chicago Hilton

FORMATIONS OF TRANSNATIONAL ASIAN PACIFIC AMERICAN IDENTITIES THROUGH SPECIFIC INSTANCES AND TRANSCENDENCES OF NATION(S)/STATE(S)

Sponsors: Asian/Pacific American Caucus
Asian Pacific American Communication Studies Division
Chair: Shujen Wang, Emerson College
"The Multiplicity of Pan-Asian Pacific American Identities in the Transnational Diaspora: Examinations of Relationships to the Nation/State." Kathleen Wong (Lau), Arizona State University
"Crafting a New Indian Identity: Dissolving Borders in Cyberspace." Ananda Mitra, Wake Forest University

Friday

"Let the Chinese Wetback Do It!: Official and Vernacular Representations of Asian American Diasporic Communities and Transnational Identities." Gordon W. Nakagawa, California State University, Northridge

---

2761   5:00-6:15 p.m.   Lake Erie   Eighth Floor   Chicago Hilton

CROSSING GEOGRAPHIC, SPATIAL, AND POPULAR LINES: CONTEXTUALIZING LATINA/OS IN VARIOUS MEDIA COMMUNITIES

Sponsors: La Raza Caucus
              Latina/Latino Communication Studies Division
Chair: Myrna Pietri, California State University, Los Angeles
    "Internationalizing Ricardo Flores-Magon and Regeneracion*." Raul Tovares, University of North Dakota
    "Zonians in Cyberspace: The Imagining of Individual, Community and Nation on the Panama-L Listserve.." Leda M. Cooks, University of Massachusetts, Amherst
    "Corridos, Rock n' Roll, and Chicano Rap: Popular Musical Articulations as Ideology Critique." Christopher J. Skiles, University of Iowa

Respondent: Carlos G. Aleman, James Madison University

*Top Paper

2762   5:00-6:15 p.m.   Essex Court   Second Floor   Essex Inn

COMPETITIVE PAPERS FROM THE RELIGIOUS COMMUNICATION PUBLIC ADDRESS DIVISION

Sponsor: Religious Communication Association
Chair: Bohn D. Lattin, University of Portland
    "St. Paul, Ethos and the Charisma of Grace." Craig R. Smith, California State University, Long Beach
    "Keeping the Faith: Apocalyptic and Jeremiadic Discourse at the End of the Millennium." Jennifer R. Mercieca, University of Illinois, Urbana-Champaign
    "Exoneration and Emergence in Mary Baker Eddy's *Christian Science in Tremont Temple* Address." Kimber C. Pearce, St. Anselm College
    "The *Clean Up TV* Campaign 1977-1981." Robert C. Chandler, Pepperdine University

Respondent: Bohn D. Lattin, University of Portland

2763   5:00-6:15 p.m.   Windsor Court   Second Floor   Essex Inn

ETHNOGRAPHIES OF PUBLIC AND PRIVATE SPACES

Sponsor: Ethnography Division
Chair: Theodore E. Zorn, University of Waikato, New Zealand
    "Supple/mental: Gaming and Rhizomatic Spatial Negotiation." Steven S. Vrooman, Arizona State University
    "Runaway Trains in a Land of Opportunity: Understanding 'At-Risk'." Deanna L. Fassett, Southern Illinois University
    "Listening with the Third Eye: An Ethnography of Animal-Human Communicators." Susan Hafen, University of Wisconsin, Eau Claire
    "'Chop Talk': Stylists' Ways of Speaking in the Salon." Merry C. Buchanan, University of Oklahoma, Steven B. Pratt, University of Central Oklahoma

Respondent: Alice L. Crume, SUNY, Brockport

6:30 p.m.

2815   6:30-7:45 p.m.   Boulevard B   Second Floor   Chicago Hilton

NCA 1999 NOMINATING COMMITTEE BUSINESS MEETING

Sponsor: 1999 NCA Nominating Committee

8:00 p.m.

2911   8:00-9:15 p.m.   Int'l Ballroom North   Second Floor   Chicago Hilton

A SWANK EVENING PERFORMANCE SALON

Sponsor: Performance Studies Division
Chair: Derek Goldman, University of North Carolina, Chapel Hill
    "Whitman." Eric Rosen, Northwestern University/About Face Theatre Company
    "Strange Case: Jekyll and Hyde." Steve Totland, Lifeline Theatre
    "Chicago Ghost Stories." Jessica Thebus, Steppenwolf Theatre
    "Kaddish for Allen Ginsburg." Peter Carpenter, StreetSigns, Derek Goldman, University of
        North Carolina, Chapel Hill
    "I Am Not a Cartoonist." Natsu Onoda, Northwestern University

Respondents: Peter Amster, Roosevelt University
                Paul C. Edwards, Northwestern University
                Frank Galati, Northwestern University/Goodman Theatre
                Martha Lavey, Steppenwolf Theatre
                Mary Zimmerman, Northwestern University

An evening of performances of literature by Chicago-based companies, featuring discussion of
performance studies on the professional stage. Dedicated to the memory of Dr. Leslie Irene
Coger.

2978   9:00-11:00 p.m.   Lakeside Green   Chicago Hilton

SPECIAL MUSICAL PERFORMANCE BY "GOOD ENOUGH"

Sponsor: National Communication Association

As the only all brother musical group with two NCA members, "Good Enough" will give a
special performance in the Lakeside Green Lounge. John, Larry and Dan Modaff are an
acoustic trio who play a brand of music that incorporates a little folk, a little rock n' roll, a little
soul and a whole lot of rhythm.

Friday

Saturday,
November 6, 1999

7:00 a.m.

3028   7:00-7:50 a.m.   **PDR 3**   **Third Floor**   **Chicago Hilton**

COMMUNITY COLLEGE SECTION BUSINESS MEETING

Sponsor: Community College Section

3032   7:00-7:50 a.m.   **PDR 7**   **Third Floor**   **Chicago Hilton**

ENVIRONMENTAL COMMUNICATION COMMISSION BUSINESS MEETING

Sponsor: Environmental Communication Commission

8:00 a.m.

3106   8:00-9:15 a.m.   **Continental BR A**   **Lobby Level**   **Chicago Hilton**

PLURAL WORLDS OF RITUAL COMMUNICATION

Sponsor: Mass Communication Division
Chair: Peter D. Simonson, Allegheny College
   "The Persuasive Powers of Ritual." Eric W. Rothenbuhler, University of Iowa, Gregory J.
      Shepherd, University of Kansas
   "Journalism as Ritual of Moral Engagement." James S. Ettema, Northwestern University
   "Spectacular Association: Local Ritual and Mass-Mediated Civic Life." Peter D. Simonson,
      Allegheny College
   "How Texts Endanger the Body Politic." Carolyn A. Marvin, University of Pennsylvania

Respondent: Elihu Katz, University of Pennsylvania

3107   8:00-9:15 a.m.   **Continental BR B**   **Lobby Level**   **Chicago Hilton**

GEORGE BUSH AND THE RHETORIC OF PRUDENCE

Sponsor: Public Address Division
Chair: Martin J. Medhurst, Texas A&M University
   "Bush and the Religious Right: Family Values and the 1992 Campaign." Amy M. Tilton,
      Texas A&M University
   "In Search of a Vision: Bush's Rhetoric of a Renewed America." Catherine L. Langford,
      Texas A&M University
   "Political Truancy: George Bush's Claim to the Mantle of 'Education President'." Holly G.
      McIntush, Texas A&M University
   "Economically Speaking: George Bush and the Price of Perception." Wynton C. Hall, Texas
      A&M University

Respondent: Craig R. Smith, California State University, Long Beach

3108   8:00-9:15 a.m.   Continental BR C   Lobby Level   Chicago Hilton

CRITICAL RACE STUDIES

Sponsor: Critical and Cultural Studies Division
Chair: Kent A. Ono, University of California, Davis
   "Civil Unrest in Los Angeles 1992: A Marxist Drama." Sherry R. Shepler, Wayne State
      University
   "The Failure of the Afro-Centric Project." Charlton McIlwain, University of Oklahoma
   "Opposition and Undecidability in Spike Lee's *Do the Right Thing.*" Bill Yousman,
      University of Massachusetts
   "The Rhetoric of Difference and Resistance: The Effects of Discrimination Against African
      Americans and the Burakumin of Japan." Sherick A. Hughes, Wake Forest University,
      Michael D. Hazen, Wake Forest University
   "Defacing Blackness: Pro-Slavery's Narrative of Oppression." Dexter B. Gordon, University
      of Alabama

3110   8:00-9:15 a.m.   Grand Ballroom   Second Floor   Chicago Hilton

WRITING UP, WRITING DOWN: PRESENTING PERFORMANCE WORK ON THE PAGE

Sponsor: Performance Studies Division
Chair: Ronald J. Pelias, Southern Illinois University, Carbondale

Panelists: Gayle M. Austin, Georgia State University
           Daun G. Kendig, St. Cloud State University
           Lesa Lockford, Centenary College
           Linda M. Park-Fuller, Southwest Missouri State University
           Ronald J. Pelias, Southern Illinois University, Carbondale
           Tami L. Spry, St. Cloud State University
           Jill Taft-Kaufman, Central Michigan University
           Linda S. Welker, Northern Kentucky University

3114   8:00-9:15 a.m.   Boulevard A   Second Floor   Chicago Hilton

KALEIDOSCOPIC CHAOS: THE RHETORIC Y2K, MILLENNIAL, APOCALYPTIC, AND END TIME DISCOURSE

Sponsor: Challenging Boundaries Series
   "Millennial Politics: Apocalyptic Power in the Liminal Kingdom." Ted Daniels, Millennial
      Watch Institute
   "Refracting Wisdom: Thoughts on Mining the Apocalyptic Interface." Charles Cameron,
      Arlington Institute
   "Charting the End of Civilization as We Know It: The Abyssal Rhetoric of Gary North's Y2K
      Secular Eschatology." Ned Vankevich, Eastern Nazarene College

3116   8:00-9:15 a.m.   Boulevard C   Second Floor   Chicago Hilton

'COLORING OUTSIDE' INTERCULTURAL TRUISMS

Sponsor: International & Intercultural Communication Division
Chair: Anjali Ram, Clark University
   "Beyond the Rhetoric of Binarism: Postcolonial Alternatives to Teaching Intercultural
      Communication." Anjali Ram, Clark University
   "Center/Peripheral and Dominant/Marginal: A Critical Examination of Intercultural
      Communication." Rueyling Chuang, St. John's University/College of St. Benedict
   "Coloring Outside the Book: Implications for the Future of Intercultural Communication."
      Leda M. Cooks, University of Massachusetts, Amherst
   "Cultural Diversity Training: Its Cartographies of Silence." Susan Hafen, University of
      Wisconsin, Eau Claire

"Framing Differences: Employing Burke's Frames to 'Accept' Barriers to Diversity." Thomas A. Workman, University of Nebraska, Lincoln

Respondent: Wenshu Lee, San Jose State University

| 3119 | 8:00-9:15 a.m. | Astoria | Third Floor | Chicago Hilton |

TOP FOUR PAPERS IN INTERPERSONAL COMMUNICATION

Sponsor: Interpersonal Communication Division
Chair: Judee K. Burgoon, University of Arizona
"An Individual Difference Explanation of Why Married Couples Engage in the Demand/Withdraw Pattern of Communication." John P. Caughlin, University of Nebraska, Lincoln, Anita L. Vangelisti, University of Texas, Austin
"Relationship Maintenance in Gay Couples Coping with HIV/AIDS." Stephen M. Haas, Rutgers University
"First Date Expectations: The Impact of Sex of Initiator, Alcohol Consumption, and Partner Knowledge." Mary Clair Morr, Arizona State University, Paul A. Mongeau, Miami University, Ohio
"Relationship Development Trajectories and Relational Well-Being." Jeanne K. Flora, California State University, Fullerton, Chris Segrin, University of Arizona

Respondent: Sally Planalp, University of Montana

| 3121 | 8:00-9:15 a.m. | Williford A | Third Floor | Chicago Hilton |

COLORING OUTSIDE THE LINES: INTERROGATING AFRICAN AMERICAN IDENTITY IN MASS MEDIA

Sponsor: African American Communication & Culture Commission
Chair: Robin R. Means Coleman, New York University
"Alternative Explanation: A Textual Analysis of Rap Music Lyrics." Sonja M. Brown, University of Georgia
"Lost in Space: A Textual Analysis of African American in Science Fiction*." Keith E. McHenry, New York University
"A Textual Analysis of *Windows* in *Essence* Magazine." Tina M. Harris, University of Georgia
"Portrayals of Black Families on Television." Jannette L. Dates, Howard University, Carolyn A. Stroman, Howard University
"Coloring the Literature: A Call for Continued Research." Robin R. Means Coleman, New York University

Respondent: Ronald B. Scott, Miami University

*Student Debut Paper

| 3122 | 8:00-9:15 a.m. | Williford B | Third Floor | Chicago Hilton |

DECEMBER 19, 1998: THE SCANDAL, THE SPEAKER, SADDAM . . . AND THE FALLOUT

Sponsor: Political Communication Division
Chair: Suzanne McCorkle, Boise State University
"I'll Take the High Road and You Take the Low Road: British Newspaper Responses to the Clinton Affair and its Aftermath." Marilyn J. Matelski, Boston College
"Chinese 'Checkmate': Understanding the Chinese Media Response." Nancy L. Street, Bridgewater State College
"Solo of a Superpower: U.S. Politics as Seen by German Media." Elfriede Fursich, Boston College
"Arab Press Reactions to the Clinton Scandal: Political Suicide, Fireworks, and Real Death." Jabbar A. Al-Obaidi, Bridgewater State College
"Sex, Lies, Videotapes, and Missiles: A Computer-Assisted Text Analysis on Korean Newspapers' Coverage of President Clinton's Scandal and the Iraqi War." Joohoan Kim, Boston College

---

3123   8:00-9:15 a.m.   Williford C   Third Floor   Chicago Hilton

SITUATING WOMEN IN DISCURSIVE STRUCTURES

Sponsor: Feminist and Women Studies Division
Chair: Anita Taylor, George Mason University
   "Women and Medical Discourse: A Necessary Unification of Speech Codes Theory and
      Muted Group Theory." Kerrie M. Smyres, Arizona State University
   "Written Out of Her Own Story: The Silencing of the Expatriate Spouse." Stephanie M.
      Reding, Purdue University
   "Creating a Female Language in China's Hunan Province: The Rhetorical Study of *Nushu.*"
      Lin-Lee Lee, University of Minnesota
   "Gender Equity as Sexual Disguise in Education Discourse." Kimberly D. Golombisky,
      University of South Florida

Respondent: Roseann M. Mandziuk, Southwest Texas State University

---

3125   8:00-10:45 a.m.   Joliet   Third Floor   Chicago Hilton

COMMUNICATION DOCTORAL PROGRAM CHAIRS BREAKFAST

Sponsors: NCA First Vice President
             Association for Communication Administration
Chairs: Orlando L. Taylor, Howard University
          Alison Alexander, University of Georgia

Panelists: Jules LaPidus, Council of Graduate Schools
             Jim Voytuk, National Research Council

Respondent: Michael Leff, Northwestern University

TICKET REQUIRED

Discussion Topics: "The Methodology for the Upcoming NRC Ranking Report"
                      "The Importance of Category Systems in National Databases
                      for Higher Education".

3126   8:00-9:15 a.m.   PDR 1   Third Floor   Chicago Hilton

FUTURE DIRECTIONS IN GAY/LESBIAN SCHOLARSHIP

Sponsor: Spotlight on Scholarship

Introduction: Ralph R. Smith, Southwest Missouri State University

   "The Young Conservatives: Queer Theory and the Future of Gay/Lesbian Studies in the
      Academy." Dana L. Cloud, University of Texas, Austin
   "Queer Studies and the Discovery of the Future Subjunctive." James Darsey, Georgia State
      University
   "Research and Theory in Gay and Straight Interpersonal Relationships." Joseph DeVito,
      Hunter College, CUNY
   "OK, We're Visible. Now What?" Larry Gross, University of Pennsylvania
   "Challenging Assumptions in Lesbian/Gay Research." Fred E. Jandt, California State
      University, San Bernardino
   "Precious Enclaves and Academic Tricks: The Prospects of Queer Studies in
      Communication." Charles E. Morris, Denison University
   "The Emergence of Queer Theory in Communication Studies." Ray A. Slagle, St. Cloud
      State University

3127   8:00-9:15 a.m.   **PDR 2**   **Third Floor**   **Chicago Hilton**

INTERNATIONAL AND INTERCULTURAL COMMUNICATION DIVISION BUSINESS MEETING

Sponsor: International & Intercultural Communication Division

---

3128   8:00-9:15 a.m.   **PDR 3**   **Third Floor**   **Chicago Hilton**

DOES THIS SHOE FIT?: ASSESSING THE IMPACT OF PRESENTATIONAL TECHNOLOGIES IN THE CLASSROOM

Sponsor: Commission on Communication Assessment
Chair: Susan A. Jasko, California University of Pennsylvania

Panelists: Susan A. Jasko, California University of Pennsylvania
Wayne S. Bond, Montclair State University
Sue Barnes, Fordham University
Patrick Miller, California University of Pennyslvania
Roy J. Schwartzman, University of South Carolina

This roundtable discussion will address the following questions: How does the introduction of this technology affect student interaction? Does it affect the student-teacher relationship? Is learning enhanced?

3129   8:00-9:15 a.m.   **PDR 4**   **Third Floor**   **Chicago Hilton**

TOP THREE PAPERS IN APPLIED COMMUNICATION

Sponsor: Applied Communication Division
Chair: Jim L. Query, Loyola University, Chicago
"Media Selection During the Implementation of Planned Organizational Change." C. Erik Timmerman, University of Texas, Austin
"Intercultural Communication Between Patients and Health Care Providers: An Exploration of Intercultural Communication Effectiveness, Cultural Sensitivity, Stress and Anxiety." Patricia Amason, University of Arkansas, Fayetteville
"Employee Turnover and Network Centrality: Testing Feeley and Barnett's (1997) Erosion Model." Thomas H. Feeley, SUNY, Geneseo

Respondent: Joann Keyton, University of Memphis

3130   8:00-9:15 a.m.   **PDR 5**   **Third Floor**   **Chicago Hilton**

THEATRE DIVISION BUSINESS MEETING

Sponsor: Theatre Division

3131   8:00-9:15 a.m.   **PDR 6**   **Third Floor**   **Chicago Hilton**

HUMAN COMMUNICATION AND TECHNOLOGY COMMISSION BUSINESS MEETING

Sponsor: Human Communication and Technology Commission

3132   8:00-9:15 a.m.   **PDR 7**   **Third Floor**   **Chicago Hilton**

TOP PAPERS IN ARGUMENTATION AND FORENSICS

Sponsor: Argumentation and Forensics Division
Chair: Kirstin J. Cronn-Mills, Minnesota State University, Mankato
"The Death of Public Evaluation: An Examination of the Public Arguments Surrounding the TWA Flight 800 Crash." Shane A. Miller, Eastern Illinois University
"Uncontestable Topic Choice, Persuasive Speaking, and the Education of Citizens." Christina R. Foust, University of Nebraska, Lincoln

Saturday

"Argumentative Style as a Predictor of Critical Thinking Competence and Social Tolerance."
   Carol Koehler, University of Missouri, Kansas City, Michael R. Neer, University of
   Missouri, Kansas City
"Cognition and Communication: Students' Cognitive Styles and the Argumentation and
   Debate Course." Stephen K. Hunt, Illinois State University

Respondent: Daniel D. Cronn-Mills, Minnesota State University, Mankato

---

3133   8:00-9:15 a.m.   Conf 4A   Fourth Floor   Chicago Hilton

IDEOLOGY, RESISTANCE, AND THE GAZE

Sponsor: Critical and Cultural Studies Division
Chair: Henry P. Krips, University of Pittsburgh
   "The Value of Misreading Lacan: Screen Theory, Structuralism, and the Gaze." Jennifer
      Friedlander, University of Pittsburgh
   "Resistance and the Gaze." Henry P. Krips, University of Pittsburgh
   "Close Encounters of the Visual Kind: The Picture and the Gaze." Vanda Rakova,
      University of Pittsburgh

Respondent: Lawrence Grossberg, University of North Carolina, Chapel Hill

---

3134   8:00-9:15 a.m.   Conf 4B   Fourth Floor   Chicago Hilton

DRAWING THE LINES AT A DIFFERENT PLACE: VISUALIZING POPULAR CULTURE WITH KENNETH BURKE

Sponsor: Visual Communication Commission
Chair: Jeff L. Bineham, St. Cloud State University
   "'EnviroPop': Nature as Visual 'Psychosis' in Popular Culture." Mark Meister, North Dakota
      State University
   "Visualizing the 'Good Life': 'Back to Nature' with 'Style'." Phyllis M. Japp, University of
      Nebraska, Lincoln, Debra K. Japp, St. Cloud State University
   "'When You Care Enough': A Burkean Analysis of the Visual Aspects of Greeting Cards."
      Diana L. Rehling, St. John's University
   "Visual Taste, Space, and Saving Face: Guilt and Redemption in Martha Stewart's 'Living'."
      Marla R. Kanengieter, St. Cloud State University
   "Visualizing the Technological Imperative in Medical Dramas: The Melding of Science,
      Technology, and Healing in Popular Discourses of Health." Lynn M. Harter, Moorhead
      State University, Phyllis M. Japp, University of Nebraska, Lincoln

---

3135   8:00-9:15 a.m.   Conf 4C   Fourth Floor   Chicago Hilton

TEACHING COMMUNICATION EXPERIENTIALLY ACROSS THE CURRICULUM: THEORY, APPLICATIONS AND PROCESS

Sponsor: Experiential Learning in Communication Commission
Chair: Donald R. Martin, DePaul University
   "When Experience is Not Enough: Finding Leverage for Interpersonal Change." David A.
      Brenders, DePaul University
   "Systems Thinking: Bridging the Gap Between Theory and Practice in the Organizational
      Communication Classroom." Alexandra G. Murphy, DePaul University
   "Using Data to Make the Point in Teaching Communication Research Methods." Tim D.
      Cole, DePaul University
   "Teaching Interviewing Experientially: Content, Context and Skills." Jill L. O'Brien, DePaul
      University
   "On-Line Experiential Learning Tools for 'Small Group Communication'." J. C. Bruno
      Teboul, DePaul University

Respondent: Gregory H. Patton, University of Southern California

| 3136 | 8:00-9:15 a.m. | Conf 4D | Fourth Floor | Chicago Hilton |

BLACK CAUCUS BUSINESS MEETING

Sponsor: Black Caucus

| 3137 | 8:00-9:15 a.m. | Conf 4E | Fourth Floor | Chicago Hilton |

NEGOTIATION, CONFLICT, AND RELATIONAL COMMUNICATION IN
STUDENT-INSTRUCTOR INTERACTION

Sponsor: Instructional Development Division
Chair: Matthew J. Smith, Miami University, Hamilton
   "'Um. . . About This Grade on My. . .Uh. . .Paper': Student-Instructor Informal
   Negotiations." Elizabeth R. Bernat, Ohio University
   "Role Transitions in Student-Teacher Relationships: Friendship Rules Between Teachers and
   Students." Chris L. Nix, University of Louisville
   "On the Flip Side: Student Immediacy Behaviors in the Classroom." Brian S. Titsworth,
   Moorhead State University
   "'Let's Talk After Class': Instructor Accounts of Grade Disputes." Charles A. Braithwaite,
   University of Montana

Respondent: William J. Seiler, University of Nebraska, Lincoln

| 3138 | 8:00-9:15 a.m. | Conf 4F | Fourth Floor | Chicago Hilton |

ACROSS THE GREAT DIVIDE: CONVERGENCES OF RHETORICAL/CRITICAL
AND MASS COMMUNICATION APPROACHES TO MEDIA ARTIFACTS

Sponsor: Rhetorical and Communication Theory Division
Chair: Bruce E. Gronbeck, University of Iowa
   "The Semiotics of Digital Storytelling." Marisa S. Olson, University of California, Berkeley
   "Medium and The Motive: Toward a Rhetorical Critical Approach to Medium Theory and
   Orality/Literacy Studies." Ralph J. Beliveau, University of Iowa
   "Redrawing the (Chalk) Lines: Cultivation, Identification, and Hyper-Realistic Police
   Dramas." Seth Kahn Egan, Syracuse University, Chrys Kahn-Egan, Longwood College
   "Re-Focusing the Critical Lens: Feminist Coding in the Cinematic Depiction of Single
   Motherhood." Lisa R. Barry, Albion College

| 3139 | 8:00-9:15 a.m. | Conf 4G | Fourth Floor | Chicago Hilton |

METAPHORS, HEGEMONY, AND IDEOLOGY: THE CHALLENGES OF SEXUAL
HARASSMENT, HIDDEN POWER, ACTIVISM, AND CONSUMERISM

Sponsor: Organizational Communication Division
Chair: Adelina M. Gomez, University of Colorado, Colorado Springs
   "Hidden Power in Organizations: False Reality and Metaphors in W.L. Gore and
   Associates." Christopher D. Salinas, Wayne State University
   "Observing Power and Ideology in a Corporate Language Class." Myria W. Allen,
   University of Arkansas
   "(Inter)acting Hegemony: Discursive Positioning and Sexual Harassment." Nikki C.
   Townsley, Purdue University, Patricia Geist, San Diego State University
   "Commodifying Activism/Challenging Consumerism: Discursive Practices of Hegemony in
   a Non-Profit Organization." Kathleen S. Valde, University of Iowa

Respondent: Donald D. Morley, University of Colorado, Colorado Springs

| 3140 | 8:00-9:15 a.m. | Conf 4H | Fourth Floor | Chicago Hilton |

CO-CONSTRUCTING CO-ORIENTATIONS: THE ART OF CONVERSATIONAL
MANAGEMENT

Sponsor: Language and Social Interaction Division

Saturday

Chair: Tanya Stivers, University of California, Los Angeles
   "Participation Structure in Collaborative Writing Episodes: The Use of Footing in the
      Management of Conflict and Disagreement." Joseph A. Bonito, University of Arizona,
      Robert E. Sanders, SUNY, Albany
   "Creating Expectations of Appreciation by Animating Mock Figures." Heidi L. Muller,
      University of Colorado, Boulder
   "That's the Ticket: The Pragmatic Functions of Prosody in Communication." Leah E. Polcar,
      University of Arizona

Respondent: Kent G. Drummond, University of Wyoming

3141   8:00-9:15 a.m.   Conf 4I   Fourth Floor   Chicago Hilton

THE INCREDIBLE SHRINKING MAN, XENA (WARRIOR PRINCESS), THE ATTACK OF THE 50-FOOT WOMAN, MR. MOM—AND OTHER REVERSALS OF ROMANTIC RELATIONSHIP STEREOTYPES IN THE MASS MEDIA

Sponsor: Media Forum Series

Panelists: Mary-Lou Galician, Arizona State University
            David Natharius, California State University, Fresno

---

3142   8:00-9:15 a.m.   Conf 4J   Fourth Floor   Chicago Hilton

COLORING OUTSIDE THE LINES: IDEOLOGY, SYMBOLS, AND PURIFICATION IN POPULAR MEDIA

Sponsor: Religious Communication Association
Chair: Loren O. Murfield, Eastern College
   "Coloring the World Wide Web: Culture Types and Ideology in Religious Organizations'
      Websites." Jeffrey L. Courtright, University of North Dakota
   "A Question of Color: Religious Symbols in The Negro Soldier." Kathleen M. German,
      Miami University, Ohio
   "Color My World: The Color of Sin, Guilt, and Purification in Pleasantville." Alan D.
      Winegarden, Concordia University, Michael J. Charron, Concordia University, Minnesota

---

3143   8:00-9:15 a.m.   Conf 4K   Fourth Floor   Chicago Hilton

A REPORT ON THE STANDARD BEARERS PROJECT

Sponsor: Elementary & Secondary Education Section
Chair: Kimberly A. Klorer, El Paso Community College
   "An Overview of the Standard Bearers Project." Sherwyn P. Morreale, NCA National Office
   "A Survey of the NCA Standard Bearers." Cecelia M. Blotkamp, Robert E. Lee High School,
      Virginia, Virginia P. O'Keefe, Tidewater Community College
   "The State of Standards in Nebraska." John R. Heineman, Lincoln High School, Nebraska
   "New Jersey Standards in Speaking, Listening, and Media Literacy." David A. Yastremski,
      Ridge High School, New Jersey
   "A View of Standards from Texas." Gwen Miraglia Lindsay, Milby Senior High School, Texas
   "The Implementation of Standards." Morris E. Snively, Belleville East High School, Illinois

Respondent: Deborah Hefferin, Broward Community College

3144   8:00-9:15 a.m.   Conf 4L   Fourth Floor   Chicago Hilton

TRAINING AND DEVELOPMENT: ACADEMICS AND PRACTITIONERS AT THE CROSSROADS

Sponsor: Training and Development Division
Chair: Carley H. Dodd, Abilene Christian University
   "The Corporate University: New Ground, or Filling in the Educational Gap." Alicia Woods,
      Safeguard Business Systems
   "Applications of Communication Style Profiles to the Classroom and Training." Paul N.
      Lakey, Abilene Christian University

"Advances in T&D Delivery via a Corporate Intranet." Diane St. Clair, Arthur Andersen
  Consulting
"University Administrative Use and Abuse of T&D." Joseph J. Cardot, Abilene Christian
  University
"I Sent You An E-Mail." David Partain, Nike Securities L.P.

Respondent: Carley H. Dodd, Abilene Christian University

The purpose of this panel is to present trends in T&D in both the academic and corporate
contexts. The panelists will each take a specific area and present the current state-of-the
industry. The program will provide an interpretation of the issues, challenges, frustrations, and
successes faced and experienced by those in this explosive growth industry.

| 3145 | 8:00-9:15 a.m. | Conf 4M | Fourth Floor | Chicago Hilton |

COMMUNICATING WITH LEADERS: CULTURE, CHANGE, AND COMPETENCE

Sponsor: Organizational Communication Division
Chair: Jane E. Jorgenson, University of South Florida
  "Finding a Leader: Culture and Change at a Suzuki Music School." Terri Toles-Patkin,
    Eastern Connecticut State University
  "Leader-Member Exchange, Gender, and Subordinates' Communication Expectations with
    Supervisors." Jaesub Lee, University of Houston
  "Communicating with Management: Relating Trust to Job Satisfaction and Organizational
    Effectiveness." Kathleen S. Ellis, University of Colorado, Colorado Springs, Pamela S.
    Shockley-Zalabak, University of Colorado, Colorado Springs
  "Leadership and Communication Competence: A Forward-Looking Review." Jordana M.
    K. Signer, University of Southern California
  "Superior-Subordinate Relationship Quality as a Determinant of Employee Dissent." Jeffrey
    W. Kassing, Arizona State University West

Respondent: Tracy C. Russo, University of Kansas

| 3146 | 8:00-9:15 a.m. | McCormick Board Rm | Fourth Floor | Chicago Hilton |

INTRAPERSONAL COMMUNICATION/SOCIAL COGNITION COMMISSION BUSINESS MEETING

Sponsor: Intrapersonal Communication/Social Cognition Commission

| 3147 | 8:00-9:15 a.m. | Pullman Board Rm | Fourth Floor | Chicago Hilton |

NATIONAL FEDERATION INTERSCHOLASTIC SPEECH AND DEBATE ASSOCIATION BUSINESS MEETING

Sponsor: National Federation Interscholastic Speech & Debate Association

| 3149 | 8:00-9:15 a.m. | Conf 5B | Fifth Floor | Chicago Hilton |

BASIC COURSE ASSESSMENT: THE POST-TEST

Sponsor: Basic Course Division
Chair: Beth M. Waggenspack, Virginia Tech University

Panelists: Donald D. Yoder, University of Dayton
          Jacquelyn J. Buckrop, Ball State University
          William L. Robinson, Purdue University, Calumet
          Samuel P. Wallace, University of Dayton
          Lawrence W. Hugenberg, Youngstown State University

Faculty who have "been there" discuss assessment information-gathering instruments and
methods, the scores/outcomes and their meanings, and the administrative response to the
assessment process and outcomes.

Saturday

3151   8:00-9:15 a.m.   Conf 5D   Fifth Floor   Chicago Hilton

STUDENTS, TEACHER, SUBJECT, SPACE: HONORING THE CLASSROOM ARCHITECTURE OF LYNN TURNER

Sponsor: Teachers on Teaching
Chair: Richard L. West, University of Southern Maine

Panelists: Richard L. West, University of Southern Maine
          Lynn H. Turner, Marquette University

Dedicated to the belief that classrooms should be safe spaces for students to speak, Professor Turner is remembered as an inclusive and supportive teacher for marginalized populations. This panel will center on the types of teaching strategies that she uses in classrooms with students from diverse backgrounds.

3152   8:00-9:15 a.m.   Conf 5E   Fifth Floor   Chicago Hilton

RETHINKING SUBJECTIVITY IN RHETORIC AND COMMUNICATION THEORY

Sponsor: Rhetorical and Communication Theory Division
Chair: Maurice Charland, Concordia University, Montreal
   "Philosophy of Communication as Constitutive Intersubjectivity: Furthering a Definition."
     Robert A. Cole, SUNY, Oswego
   "Explanatory Theories and Praxial Theories: Debatable Ideas on Selfhood." Corey Anton,
     Grand Valley State University
   "The Rhetorical Function of the Abject Body: Transgressive Corporeality in *Trainspotting*."
     Christine L. Harold, Penn State University
   "Ontology and Cyberspace: Contemplating the Virtual Self." Kenneth A. Rufo, University
     of Georgia

3154   8:00-9:15 a.m.   Conf 5G   Fifth Floor   Chicago Hilton

THE INFLUENCE PERSONALITY PREDISPOSITIONS IN THE TEACHING-LEARNING RELATIONSHIP

Sponsor: Instructional Development Division
Chair: K. David Roach, Texas Tech University
   "Students' Motives for Communicating with Their Instructors III: Considering
     Socio-Communicative Style and Sex Differences." Matthew M. Martin, West Virginia
     University, Timothy P. Mottet, Southwest Texas State University, Scott A. Myers,
     Creighton University
   "Perceived Instructor Argumentativeness, Verbal Aggressiveness, and Student Participation
     in the College Classroom." Kelly A. Rocca, West Virginia University, Scott A. Myers,
     Creighton University
   "Instructional Strategies Mediating Compulsive Communicators' Impact on Classroom
     Communication: Color Me Competent." Danette E. Ifert, West Virginia Wesleyan
     College, Kathleen M. Long, West Virginia Wesleyan College, Shirley D. Fortney, West
     Virginia Wesleyan College

Respondent: K. David Roach, Texas Tech University

3155   8:00-9:15 a.m.   Conf 5H   Fifth Floor   Chicago Hilton

UNDERSTANDING SHADES OF INTERPERSONAL COMMUNICATION AND COMMUNICATION APPREHENSION

Sponsor: Communication Apprehension & Avoidance Commission
Chair: Debbie M. Ayres-Sonandre, Tacoma Community College
   "Partner Communication Apprehension: Measurement Confirmation and Extension."
     William G. Powers, Texas Christian University, Don E. Love, Eastern New Mexico
     University

"An Examination of the Effect of 'Initiating' on Communication Apprehension and Other Variables in Initial Interactions Between Able-and Disable-Bodied Individuals." Joe Ayres, Washington State University, Debbie M. Ayres-Sonandre, Tacoma Community College
"Pain as a Factor in Willingness to Communicate." Deborah B. Shelley, University of Houston, Downtown

| 3156 | 8:00-9:15 a.m. | Conf 5I | Fifth Floor | Chicago Hilton |

EMERITUS/RETIRED MEMBERS SECTION BUSINESS MEETING

Sponsor: Emeritus/Retired Members Section

| 3157 | 8:00-9:15 a.m. | Conf 5J | Fifth Floor | Chicago Hilton |

PEDAGOGICAL STRATEGIES FOR INFUSING CULTURAL PERSPECTIVES INTO THE CLASSROOM

Sponsor: Senior College & University Section
Chair: Dacia Charlesworth, Southeast Missouri State University
   "Cultural Activities for the Interpersonal Communication Classroom." Nancy J. Curtin-Alwardt, Southern Illinois University
   "Cultural Activities for the Business and Professional Communication Classroom." Elizabeth Gullickson-Tolman, Southern Illinois University, Carbondale
   "Cultural Activities for the Public Speaking Classroom." Maggie M. Sullivan, Loras College
   "Cultural Activities for the Creative and Critical Thinking Classroom." Dacia Charlesworth, Southeast Missouri State University

| 3158 | 8:00-10:45 a.m. | Lake Ontario | Eighth Floor | Chicago Hilton |

SHORT COURSE #17. TEACHING COMMUNICATION COURSES WITH THE WORLD WIDE WEB: COGNITIVE TECHNOLOGY

Sponsor: Short Courses

Instructors: Leonard J. Shedletsky, University of Southern Maine
             Howard E. Sypher, University of Kansas
             Melissa L. Beall, University of Northern Iowa
             Joan E. Aitken, University of Missouri, Kansas City

Fee required. See complete Short Course descriptions elsewhere in the program.

| 3159 | 8:00-10:45 a.m. | Lake Michigan | Eighth Floor | Chicago Hilton |

SHORT COURSE #18. TEACHING MEDIA LITERACY IN THE CLASSROOM

Sponsor: Short Courses

Instructor: Gary A. Noggle, Bethel College

Fee required. See complete Short Course descriptions elsewhere in the program.

| 3160 | 8:00-10:45 a.m. | Lake Huron | Eighth Floor | Chicago Hilton |

SHORT COURSE #19. HOW TO DESIGN A COURSE IN MISCOMMUNICATION

Sponsor: Short Courses

Instructor: C. David Mortensen, University of Wisconsin, Madison

Fee required. See complete Short Course descriptions elsewhere in the program.

Saturday

3161   8:00-10:45 a.m.   Lake Erie   Eighth Floor   Chicago Hilton

SHORT COURSE #20. INNOVATIVE APPROACHES TO ADR COURSES

Sponsor: Short Courses

Instructors: Michael L. Spangle, University of Denver
                 Myra Warren Isenhart, Denver University

Fee required. See complete Short Course descriptions elsewhere in the program.

3162   8:00-9:15 a.m.   Essex Court   Second Floor   Essex Inn

COLORING OUTSIDE THE LINES: INNOVATIVE ROLE PERFORMANCE IN AN EVANGELICAL UNIVERSITY

Sponsor: Religious Communication Association
Chair: Roxane Lulofs, Azusa Pacific University
   "Performing an Oxymoron: Proclaiming and Practicing Christian Feminism in an
      Evangelical University." Roxane Lulofs, Azusa Pacific University
   "Performing Media Connections: Living in Hollywood and the Evangelical University."
      Monica C. Ganas, Azusa Pacific University
   "Performing Forensics: Competition in the Evangelical Environment." Kevin T. Jones, Azusa
      Pacific University
   "Performing as a Veteran/Academic: Living a Life of Peace After a Time of War." Ray
      McCormick, Azusa Pacific University

3163   8:00-9:15 a.m.   Windsor Court   Second Floor   Essex Inn

BLACK ON BLACK ETHNOGRAPHY: AFRICAN AMERICAN ETHNOGRAPHERS DISCUSS ETHICAL AND PROBLEMATIC ISSUES SURROUNDING 'DOING' ETHNOGRAPHIC RESEARCH ON/IN OUR OWN

Sponsor: Ethnography Division
Chair: Myron M. Beasley, Ohio University
   "Liminality Betwixted and Between: The Interview Process and the African American Male
      Administrators on Predominately White Campuses." Rex L. Crawley, Ohio University
   "Promoting a Critical Consciousness: The African American Community in Danger Due to
      a Blind Eye '—What is the Native Researcher to Do'?" Shawn Townes, Ohio University
   "Imagined and Interpretive African American Communities: But What Happens When
      They Say What They Are not Supposed to Say?" Jeffrey L. Tyus, Ohio University

Respondent: Katrina E. Bell, Northeastern Illinois University

---

3164   8:00-9:15 a.m.   Buckingham Court   Second Floor   Essex Inn

AMERICAN FOREIGN POLICY AND THE LEGACY OF THE COLD WAR

Sponsor: American Studies Commission
Chair: Thomas Kane, University of Pittsburgh
   "America's 'War on Terrorism': The Rhetorical Construction of the Next Cold War." Kevin J.
      Ayotte, University of Pittsburgh
   "The U.S. as Paper Tiger?: The Rhetoric of Deterrence in the Post-Cold-War World." Heidi
      E. Hamilton, Augustana College
   "Rogues and Superpowers: New Threats and Nostalgia for Cold War Moral Order." Daniel
      McGee, University of Illinois, Urbana-Champaign
   "At What Price Security?: Institutional Argument and the Possibility of Public Deliberation
      in the Defense Counterproliferation Initiative." Jon Wiebel, University of Iowa

Respondent: G. Thomas Goodnight, Northwestern University

3165   8:00-9:15 a.m.   **Park East Walk**   **Second Floor**   **Essex Inn**

KENNETH BURKE AND SOCIAL MOVEMENTS

Sponsor: Kenneth Burke Society, NCA Branch
Chair: Valeria Fabj, Emerson College
   "The Contrary Method: Revisiting Kenneth Burke, Leland Griffin and William Blake." Eric
      Franklin Healy, Emerson College
   "The Gay Community Faces the Religious Right's 'Ex-Gay Campaign': A Rhetorical Analysis
      of the Universal Fellowship of Metropolitan Community Churches' Response."
      Mao-Chen Chang, Emerson College
   "AGAPE: A Rhetorical Analysis." Sharon A. Hoey, Emerson College
   "The ERA Movement and the Illinois Campaign: A Dramatistic Perspective." Malia Lazu,
      Emerson College

Respondent: Kathleen A. DeHaan, College of Charleston

3166   8:00-9:15 a.m.   **Cohn Rm**   **Second Floor**   **Spertus Institute**

IS THERE A RHETORIC OF ENGINEERING?

Sponsor: American Association for Rhetoric of Science & Technology
Chair: Helen Constantinides, University of Minnesota
   "The Limits of Rhetorical Theory: Redefining 'Audience' and 'Persuasion' Within the
      Context of Engineering." David Coogan, Illinois Institute of Technology
   "Technical Rhetoric and Professional Practice." Michael Davis, Illinois Institute of
      Technology
   "Writing and Thinking Like an Engineer." John Way, Illinois Institute of Technology

---

3169   8:00-9:15 a.m.   **Rm 903**   **Ninth Floor**   **Spertus Institute**

COLORING OUTSIDE THE LINES: DEBATING IN FRONT OF DIVERSE AUDIENCES

Sponsor: Pi Kappa Delta
Chair: Greggory D. Simerly, Idaho State University
   "Public Debate: A Public Service or a Public Nuisance?" Robert O. Weiss, DePauw
      University
   "Public Palatable Propositions." Heather Norton, Penn State University
   "Learning to Accommodate Public Judgement." Larry R. Underberg, Southeast Missouri
      State University
   "Style versus Substance in Public Debate: Smoke and Mirrors?" Virginia L. Chapman,
      Anderson University

Respondent: Michael H. Bauer, Ball State University

3170   8:00-9:15 a.m.   **Rm 904**   **Ninth Floor**   **Spertus Institute**

POLITICAL DISCOURSE, POWER DYNAMICS, AND PERSONAL MEMOIRS OF CHINA'S CULTURAL REVOLUTION

Sponsor: Association for Chinese Communication Studies
Chair: Shuming Lu, Brooklyn College, CUNY
   "Leninism in Chinese Political Discourse: Ideology and Power in the Cultural Revolution."
      Randy Kluver, Oklahoma City University
   "Rhetorical Themes and Styles of Big-Character Posters During the Cultural Revolution."
      Xing (Lucy) Lu, DePaul University
   "Power Struggle, Power Negotiation, and Power Sharing During China's Cultural
      Revolution Movement from 1966-1969." Shaorong Huang, University of Cincinnati
   "Cultural Revolution and Chinese Consciousness: An Interpretive Cultural Study of
      Memoirs of Lived Experiences." Minmin Wang, Rider University

Respondent: David A. Frank, University of Oregon

Saturday

3171   8:00-9:15 a.m.   Rm 906   Ninth Floor   Spertus Institute

TOP TWO PAPERS IN PEACE AND CONFLICT COMMUNICATION

Sponsor: Peace and Conflict Communication Commission
Chair: Anna L. Eblen, Western Washington University
  "'Good Behavior' as an Interpretive Frame in Latino Conflict Negotiation Processes: A
  Focus Group Analysis." Mitchell R. Hammer, American University, Randall Rogan, Wake
  Forest University
  "Oppositional Argument, Civil Disobedience, and the Norms of Appearance: The Body in
  Protest." Courtney L. Dillard, University of Texas, Austin

3172   8:00-9:15 a.m.   Rm 907   Ninth Floor   Spertus Institute

A LOOK AT JUDGE EFFECTIVENESS: DO WE REALLY HAVE A CLEAR PICTURE OF WHAT WE DO?

Sponsor: Cross Examination Debate Association
Chair: Michael A. Fisher, Arkansas State University
  "Viewing the Debate Round as an Interpersonal Transaction." Jack E. Rogers, University of
  Texas, Tyler
  "A Classification of Humor in Debate Rounds: Does it Impact the Judge?" Don C. Govang,
  Lincoln University
  "Is There a Link Between Judge Personality Type and Decisions in Competitive Debate
  Rounds? So What!" Dennis White, Arkansas State University
  "Do Variables of Initial Attraction Impact the Judges' Decision in College Debate Rounds?"
  Michael A. Fisher, Arkansas State University

Respondent: Scott L. Jensen, Webster University

3173   8:00-9:15 a.m.   Rm 908   Ninth Floor   Spertus Institute

FORENSICS AT THE MILLENNIUM: REVIEWING THE TWENTIETH CENTURY AND PLANNING FOR THE TWENTY-FIRST

Sponsors: National Forensic Association
          Pi Kappa Delta
Chair: Phil A. Martin, North Central Technical College
  "From Elocution and Declamation to Rhetorical Criticism and Poetry: Individual Events on
  the College Level." Lisa D. Shemwell, Morehead State University, Noel Earl, Morehead
  State University
  "From Literary Societies to CEDA and Lincoln Douglas: Debate on the College Level."
  Mark S. Hickman, West Chester University, Eddie Myers, Louisiana State University
  "From an English Class to a Speech Discipline: Forensics on the High School Level."
  Virginia B. Landreth-Etherton, Rowan County Senior High School, Mark Etherton,
  Murray High School

Respondent: Cathy L. Thomas, Morehead State University

3174   8:00-9:15 a.m.   Auditorium   Second Floor   Spertus Institute

DEVISED THEATRE: THEORY AND PRACTICE

Sponsor: Theatre Division
Chair: Mark W. Burnette, Bowling Green State University

Panelists: Sunwill Swaroop, Bowling Green State University
           Melissa Friesen, Bowling Green State University
           Christine Williams, Bowling Green State University
           Mary Jo Lodge, Bowling Green State University
           James Williams, Bowling Green State University
           Julie Schmitt, Bowling Green State University
           Bethanie Monroe, Bowling Green State University

Taylore Doherty, Bowling Green State University

This panel addresses the devised theatre methodology of major contemporary theatre practitioners. Excerpts from performance pieces, utilizing these techniques, will be performed.

9:30 a.m.

3206   9:30-10:45 a.m.   Continental BR A   Lobby Level   Chicago Hilton

COMPETITIVE PAPERS IN RESEARCH ON VIEWERS' RESPONSES TO NEWS STORIES

Sponsor: Mass Communication Division
Chair: Robert V. Bellamy, Duquesne University
  "More Bad News: Disaster Proximity and Severity as Determinants of Apprehension, Victimization Risk and Risk Locus of Control." Charles R. Berger, University of California, Davis, C. Mo Bahk, University of Cincinnati
  "At the Scene of the Crime: Grief in the Media." Michelle M. Pulaski, University of Connecticut, Megan A. Sheehan, University of Connecticut, Lesley A. Withers, University of Connecticut, Cynthia D. Mohr, University of Connecticut
  "The Influence of Relationship and Gender on Television Viewers' Responses to Rape Stories." Bradley S. Greenberg, Michigan State University, Lynn A. Rampoldi-Hnilo, Michigan State University, Rick Busselle, Washington State University

Respondent: Lawrence J. Mullen, University of Nevada, Las Vegas

---

3207   9:30-10:45 a.m.   Continental BR B   Lobby Level   Chicago Hilton

POSITION PAPERS ON COMPUTER-MEDIATED COMMUNICATION AND ITS RHETORICAL AND SOCIAL IMPLICATIONS

Sponsor: Human Communication and Technology Commission
Chair: Todd S. Frobish, Penn State University
  "Social Interaction and the Chat Room: The New Way to Reach Out and Touch Someone." Steven N. Blivess, Penn State University
  "Utopia or Dystopia? An Exploration of the Computer-Mediated Public Sphere." David P. Schultz, Penn State University
  "Mpegs, Gifs, and Emoticons: Pedagogical and Rhetorical Implications of On-Line Iconography." Anthony J. Wainwright, Penn State University
  "Inquiries into the Religious Employment of Computer-Mediated Strategies." Todd S. Frobish, Penn State University

---

3208   9:30-10:45 a.m.   Continental BR C   Lobby Level   Chicago Hilton

SIGHTING/SITING GLOBALIZATION: CULTURE-ECONOMY IN CHINA, TAIWAN AND U.S. FEMINISM

Sponsor: Critical and Cultural Studies Division
Chair: Daniel Vukovich, University of Illinois, Urbana-Champaign
  "Most Favored Nation: Sinological-Orientalism, or, the West's 'Post-Mao' China." Daniel Vukovich, University of Illinois, Urbana-Champaign
  "Global Identities? Gender, Consumption, and Reconfigurations of the Domestic." Fang-Chih Yang, University of Illinois, Urbana-Champaign
  "Feminism and Globalization: Provincializing U.S. Feminism." Radhika Mongia, University of Illinois, Urbana-Champaign

Respondent: Lawrence Grossberg, University of North Carolina, Chapel Hill

Saturday

| 3201 | 9:30-3:45 p.m. | Northwest Exhibit Hall | Lower Level | Chicago Hilton |

NCA POSTER SESSION

Sponsor: Poster Session

1. "Listening Behavior in the Instructional Context." Joseph L. Chesebro, West Virginia University
2. "Value Perception in the Soap Opera, 'Another Life'." J. Lynn Reynolds, Pepperdine University
3. "The Paradox of Structure: How Using a Structural Template to Analyze the Organizational Communication Case Study Can Facilitate 'Thinking Outside of the Lines'." Sheryl L. Williams, University of Wisconsin, Whitewater
4. "'Take the Lead': A Fantasy-Theme Analysis of MADD's Initiative to Stop Underage Drinking." Melissa Groot, Trinity Christian College
5. "Ethnocentrism: Measurement, Origins, and Impact." Alan D. Heisel, West Virginia University
6. "Giving Voice to the Voiceless: Homelessness, Counter-Memory, and Rhetorical Resistance on the Streets of Memphis." Bernard J. Armada, University of St. Thomas
7. "In the Spirit of Healing: An Analysis of Spirituality Courses in Medical School Curriculum." Darci L. Graves, Southwest Missouri State University
8. "Oxherding to Enlightenment: Teaching Awareness as a Communication Competency." Gray Matthews, University of Memphis
9. "Service Learning and Public Speaking: A Winning Combination." Mikiko L. Crawford, Ohio University, Southern Campus
10. "Sacred Ground: An Analysis of Public Grief, Vengeance, Irony, and Catharsis at the Oklahoma Bombing Site." Kristin K. Froemling, University of Oklahoma, Terry A. Robertson, University of Oklahoma
11. "Understanding the Player - Coach Relationship: An Analysis of Leadership Behaviors in *Hoosiers*." Paul D. Turman, University of Nebraska, Lincoln
12. "The Effect of the Mass Media on Occupational and Organizational Beliefs." Rebecca M. Chory, Michigan State University
13. "Structuration in Diffusion of Interactive Innovation: Alternative Perspectives to Critical Mass in Japanese Mobile-Phone Systems." Toru Kiyomiya, Michigan State University
14. "R U Sure?: Changing the Culture of College Drinking Through Mediated and Interpersonal Interventions." Linda C. Lederman, Rutgers University, Lea P. Stewart, Rutgers University, Sherrey L. Barr, Rutgers University
15. "Academic Tenure: The Judicial System and Dismissal for Cause." Joseph J. Hemmer, Jr., Carroll College
16. "We Don't Talk Anymore: Or at Least the Way We Use To." John Chetro-Szivos, University of Massachusetts, Amherst
17. "Attachment Style and Responses to Distressed Relationships Using the Rusbult Exit, Voice, Loyalty, and Neglect Typology." William A. Maze, Minnesota State University, Mankato
18. "Political Candidates and Mass Media: Techniques Employed for Achieving Free Media Publicity in Statewide and Local Elections." Scott D. Wells, University of Oklahoma
19. "Split-Personalities: Examining Organizational Identification Among Temporary Workers." Loril M. Gossett, University of Colorado, Boulder
20. "Cartoons as Communication: Stereotypes of the Aged." Gene Burd, University of Texas, Austin
21. "Orientations Toward the Online Romantic Involvements: The Implications for Social Support of Computer-Mediated Relationships." Traci L. Anderson, University of Oklahoma
22. "The Relationship Among Teacher Immediacy, Student Motivation and Learning: A Comparative Analysis of Russian Perspectives." Diane M. Millette, University of Miami, Ludmilla Gricenko Wells, Florida Gulf Coast University
23. "Secondary Circuits in Globalization of Television Programming Interactive World Wide Web Presentation." Sorin Matei, University of Southern California, Kathryn Sasina, University of Southern California, Tamar Ginosar, University of Illinois, Urbana-Champaign, Nikki C. Townsley, Purdue University

---

3210   9:30-10:45 a.m.   Grand Ballroom   Second Floor   Chicago Hilton

PERFORMING LOVE IN HISTORY: A DEBATE/DISCUSSION

Sponsor: Performance Studies Division
Chair: Erik Doxtader, University of North Carolina, Chapel Hill

Panelists: Judith A. Hamera, California State University, Los Angeles
          Craig S. Gingrich-Philbrook, Southern Illinois University, Carbondale

Inspired by Luce Irigaray's controversial *Love Between Us: A Sketch of the Possibility of Felicity in History*, the discussants will ask: How does or doesn't performance as romance in motion, as embodied desire, as a politics of love and longing make "felicity" possible?

3212   9:30-10:45 a.m.   Int'l Ballroom South   Second Floor   Chicago Hilton

EXTENDING OUR CREATIVE BOUNDARIES: INTEGRATING SERVICE-LEARNING IN COMMUNICATION COURSES—A DISCUSSION CIRCLES APPROACH

Sponsor: Instructional Development Division
Chair: Toni S. Whitfield, University of West Florida

Panelists: Roberta A. Davilla, University of Northern Iowa
          Carol J. Bruess, University of St. Thomas
          Deborah R. Gaut, University of West Florida
          Barbara A. Danuser, Johnson County Community College
          Sara C. Weintraub, Bentley College
          Joseph M. Ganakos, University of West Florida

This interactive program will consist of course-specific discussion circles where experienced communication educators will provide creative examples of integrating service-learning into all communication courses. A brief introduction of the pedagogy will be given and each presenter will describe his or her topic; then attendees can visit in any of the discussion circles. Bring questions, an inquiring mind, and examples or syllabi.

3214   9:30-10:45 a.m.   Boulevard A   Second Floor   Chicago Hilton

CHALLENGING THE BORDERS WITHOUT AND WITHIN: RACIAL/ETHNIC IDENTITY DEVELOPMENT IN OUR STUDENTS

Sponsor: Challenging Boundaries Series
Chairs: Deborah A. Brunson, University of North Carolina, Wilmington
        Evelyn J. Plummer, Seton Hall University

Panelists: Catherine M. Blackburn, Brookdale Community College
          Deborah A. Brunson, University of North Carolina, Wilmington
          Sandra W. Holt, Tennessee State University
          Keith B. Jenkins, Rochester Institute of Technology
          Evelyn J. Plummer, Seton Hall University

Ethnicity, race, and culture constrain our behavior from both inside and outside of the lines. The effective contemporary communicator should work to move beyond imposed boundaries in order to create an operational paradigm which honors cultural traditions yet is situationally and personally relevant. Panelists will explore the implications of such externally and internally imposed borders as whiteness, racial norms, gender roles, and cultural expectations and will engage attendees in exercises designed to foster a more flexibly tolerant mode of cultural self-definition.

Saturday

3215   9:30-10:45 a.m.   Boulevard B   Second Floor   Chicago Hilton

DANGEROUS NOTIONS: ISSUES IN CENSORSHIP AND INTELLECTUAL FREEDOM

Sponsor: Theatre Division
Chair: Michele A. Pagen, California University of Pennsylvania

Panelists: Mary Cutler, University of North Dakota, Grand Forks
Teresa E. Durbin, Bowling Green State University
Michael M. O'Hara, Ball State University
Elizabeth Burow Flak, Valparaiso University
Carol Burbank, University of Maryland, College Park
C. David Frankel, University of South Florida
Annie McGregor, Penn State University

3216   9:30-10:45 a.m.   Boulevard C   Second Floor   Chicago Hilton

NATION BUILDING, VISUAL REPRESENTATION, AND THE WAR-MACHINE

Sponsor: Critical and Cultural Studies Division
Chair: Mary S. Strine, University of Utah
"The Subject of National Strategy and the Strategy of National Subjects." Bernardo Attias, California State University, Northridge
"Nationalism, Women, and the War-Machine: Revisiting the *Women in Military Service of America Memorial*." Barbara A. Biesecker, University of Iowa
"Nuclear Iconography in Post-Cold War Culture." Bryan C. Taylor, University of Colorado

---

3219   9:30-10:45 a.m.   Astoria   Third Floor   Chicago Hilton

INTERPERSONAL COMMUNICATION DIVISION BUSINESS MEETING

Sponsor: Interpersonal Communication Division

3221   9:30-10:45 a.m.   Williford A   Third Floor   Chicago Hilton

INTERRACIAL COMMUNICATION: THEORETICAL PERSPECTIVES, RELATIONSHIP-BUILDING, AND ACTION PLANS

Sponsor: African American Communication & Culture Commission

Panelists: Carolyn Calloway-Thomas, Indiana University, Bloomington
Rhunette C. Diggs, University of Louisville
Tina M. Harris, University of Georgia
Patricia S. Hill, Cleveland State University
Ronald L. Jackson, Penn State University
Davina A. Jones, Bowling Green State University
Teresa A. Nance, Villanova University
Dorthy Pennington, University of Kansas
Ronald B. Scott, Miami University
Lee West, University of Iowa

This panel brings together scholars and graduate students to present perspectives and action plans, including issues of pedagogy, identity, self-esteem, mass media research, spirituality, friendships, and a model for the implementation of interracial communication and diversity at the systems level.

3222   9:30-10:45 a.m.   Williford B   Third Floor   Chicago Hilton

RHETORIC AND POLITICS IN THE IMPEACHMENT AND AFTERMATH OF PRESIDENT WILLIAM JEFFERSON CLINTON

Sponsor: Political Communication Division

Chair: Richard E. Vatz, Towson University
   "Political Party Images in the Clinton Impeachment Case." Kathleen E. Kendall, SUNY,
      Albany
   "Doing the 'People's Business' in the Midst of Impeachment: The Rhetorical and Political
      Impact of President Clinton's 1999 State of the Union Address." Mary L. Kahl, SUNY,
      New Paltz
   "Classical Forms of Argument: The Legal Defense Rhetoric of President Clinton on
      Impeachment." Paula J. Wilson, Lynchburg College
   "Finessing the Divide in the Aftermath of Impeachment: An Analysis of Presidential and
      Congressional Strategies for Image Restoration and Reconciliation." Valerie A. Endress,
      University of Hartford
   "Sax, Lies and Videotapes." James Benjamin, University of Toledo
   "'Spinning' Out of Control: How the House Got 'Disconnected' from the Public on the
      Clinton-Lewinsky Matter." Dan F. Hahn, New York University

---

3223   9:30-10:45 a.m.   Williford C   Third Floor   Chicago Hilton

PUTTIN' IT ON: UNDERSTANDING THE PERFORMATIVITY OF GENDER

Sponsor: Feminist and Women Studies Division
Chair: Catherine E. Waggoner, Wittenberg University
   "Performance as Subversive Strategy: Deflecting the Male Gaze in *ELLEN*." Helene A.
      Shugart, Augusta State University
   "Nigerian Women and Cultural Politics." Joni L. Jones, University of Texas, Austin
   "Performing Femininity: From the Page to the Screen." M. Heather Carver, University of
      Texas, Austin
   "Preserving the Pedestal: Paradoxical Performances of Femininity in the South." Catherine
      E. Waggoner, Wittenberg University

Respondent: Elizabeth E. Bell, University of South Florida

3224   9:30-10:45 a.m.   Marquette   Third Floor   Chicago Hilton

THREE FACETS OF DIVERSITY IN ORGANIZATIONS

Sponsor: Black Caucus
Chair: Lyndrey A. Niles, Howard University
   "The Need for 'Deep' Diversity in the Communication of Corporate America." Heather E.
      Harris, Howard University
   "Predicting Communicative Resistance to Diversity Initiatives in Organizations: A Viable
      Option for Success." Mary E. Kinnard, Howard University
   "Diversity in the Church: An Analysis Based on Gender, Age, and Race." Debyii S.
      Thomas, Howard University

3226   9:30-10:45 a.m.   PDR 1   Third Floor   Chicago Hilton

CAUCUS ON GAY AND LESBIAN CONCERNS BUSINESS MEETING

Sponsor: Gay & Lesbian Concerns Caucus

3227   9:30-10:45 a.m.   PDR 2   Third Floor   Chicago Hilton

TOP THREE PAPERS IN INTERCULTURAL, INTERNATIONAL, AND CULTURAL COMMUNICATION

Sponsor: International & Intercultural Communication Division
Chair: Mark L. McPhail, University of Utah
   "Reinvention and Performativity of Cultural Identity*." Jolanta A. Drzewiecka, Washington
      State University
   "Blooding a Race: Cultural Identity and the Legal (Mis)Recognition of Hawaiians**." Rona
      T. Halualani, San Jose State University
   "Is the Chinese Self-Construal in Transition?***." Nagesh Rao, Ohio University, Arvind
      Singhal, Ohio University, Li Ren, Ohio University, Jianying Zhang, Ohio University

Respondent: Casey M. K. Lum, William Paterson University

*Top One Paper   **Top Two Paper   ***Top Three Paper

3228   9:30-10:45 a.m.   PDR 3   Third Floor   Chicago Hilton

INTERSECTIONS BETWEEN RHETORIC AND POSTSTRUCTURALISM

Sponsor: Student Section
Chair: Danna E. Prather, University of Iowa
  "Perception and Phenomena: Derrida and Visual Rhetoric." Daniel L. Emery, University of
    Iowa
  "Rhetoric as a Link Between Marxissant Ideologiekritik and Foucauldian Power." Brian
    Lain, University of Iowa
  "Sovereignty/Discipline/Government: National Identities and Foucault's Triangle of
    Governmentality." Wade S. Davis, University of Iowa
  "Never the Same by Any Other Name." William C. Trapani, University of Iowa

---

3229   9:30-10:45 a.m.   PDR 4   Third Floor   Chicago Hilton

APPLIED COMMUNICATION DIVISION BUSINESS MEETING

Sponsor: Applied Communication Division

3230   9:30-10:45 a.m.   PDR 5   Third Floor   Chicago Hilton

LA RAZA CAUCUS AND LATINA/LATINO COMMUNICATION STUDIES DIVISION BUSINESS MEETING

Sponsors: La Raza Caucus
          Latina/Latino Communication Studies Division

3231   9:30-10:45 a.m.   PDR 6   Third Floor   Chicago Hilton

VISUAL COMMUNICATION COMMISSION BUSINESS MEETING

Sponsor: Visual Communication Commission

3232   9:30-10:45 a.m.   PDR 7   Third Floor   Chicago Hilton

STATES ADVISORY COUNCIL BUSINESS MEETING

Sponsor: States Advisory Council

3233   9:30-10:45 a.m.   Conf 4A   Fourth Floor   Chicago Hilton

FINDING THE LINES: PREDICTORS AND COMMUNICATION ANXIETY

Sponsor: Communication Apprehension & Avoidance Commission
Chair: Jerry L. Allen, University of New Haven
  "Task Sensitization and Exposure to Speaker as Predictors of Audience Detection of Public
    Speaking State Anxiety." Tina K. Hearne, Texas Christian University, Chris R. Sawyer,
    Tarrant County Junior College, Ralph R. Behnke, Texas Christian University
  "Self-Perceived Speaker Competence and Anxiety Sensitivity as Predictors of Anxiety
    During Public Speaking." Lega K. Strain, Texas Christian University, Chris R. Sawyer,
    Tarrant County Junior College, Ralph R. Behnke, Texas Christian University
  "Anxiety Sensitivity, Adolescent Speech Trait Anxiety, and Communication Satisfaction as
    Predictors of Speech Trait Anxiety in College." Sara E. Strader, Texas Christian University,
    Chris R. Sawyer, Tarrant County Junior College, Ralph R. Behnke, Texas Christian
    University
  "Anxiety Sensitivity and Speech Trait Anxiety as Predictors of State Anxiety During Public
    Speaking." Jennifer D. Mladenka, Texas Christian University, Chris R. Sawyer, Tarrant
    County Junior College, Ralph R. Behnke, Texas Christian University

"Competence or Confidence?: Public Speaking Apprehension, Demand for Speech Planning Skills, and Anticipatory State Anxiety." Michael J. Beatty, University of Missouri, St. Louis, Kristin M. Valencic, West Virginia University

---

3234   9:30-10:45 a.m.   Conf 4B   Fourth Floor   Chicago Hilton

FILM, RHETORIC, AND MEMORY: CRITICAL INTERSECTIONS

Sponsor: American Studies Commission

Panelists: Peter C. Ehrenhaus, Pacific Lutheran University
Marouf Hasian, University of Utah
James Jasinski, University of Puget Sound
John L. Lucaites, Indiana University
A. Susan Owen, University of Puget Sound

Because film is both popular medium and rhetorical discourse, it is situated at critical intersections among film studies, rhetoric and public address, continental theory, and cultural memory. Readings of *Saving Private Ryan* will explore: A) how film as rhetoric shapes remembrance of critical moments in American history, and B) potential points of theoretical intersection among these literatures.

3235   9:30-10:45 a.m.   Conf 4C   Fourth Floor   Chicago Hilton

SUCCULENT WOMEN: AN AUTOETHNOGRAPHIC EXPLORATION OF GRADUATE ASSISTANT EXPERIENCES

Sponsor: Feminist and Women Studies Division

Presentation: Bernadette M. Calafell, Arizona State University
Felicia B. Van Deman, Arizona State University

Discussion: Bernadette M. Calafell, Arizona State University
Felicia B. Van Deman, Arizona State University
Kristin B. Valentine, Arizona State University

This is a two part presentation which will involve a performance of autoethnographic narratives of women graduate students followed by a discussion of the issues raised.

3236   9:30-10:45 a.m.   Conf 4D   Fourth Floor   Chicago Hilton

POLITICS AND PEDAGOGY FOR TEACHING GENDER AND VIOLENCE: EXPANDING THE CONFINES OF TRADITIONAL ACADEMIC PRACTICE

Sponsor: Women's Caucus
Chair: Jamey A. Piland, Trinity College

Panelists: Katherine L. Adams, California State University, Fresno
Diana K. Ivy, Texas A&M University
David Natharius, California State University, Fresno
Rose Pascarell, George Mason University
Jamey A. Piland, Trinity College
Anita Taylor, George Mason University

Calling on tenets of feminist pedagogy, this program will address issues involved in teaching gender and violence, including specific pedagogical practices critical to the creation of "safe space."

3237   9:30-10:45 a.m.   Conf 4E   Fourth Floor   Chicago Hilton

LEARNING OUR BOUNDARIES AND LEARNING HOW TO CROSS THEM: A PRESENTATION OF LESSONS LEARNED AT THE NCA-NORTHWESTERN DOCTORAL HONORS' CONFERENCE

Sponsor: Organizational Communication Division
Chair: Brant R. Burleson, Purdue University

"Leading Young Scholars into the New Millennium of Organizational Communication Studies: A Seminar Faculty Perspective." Randy Y. Hirokawa, University of Iowa

"Scrutinizing and Extending the Research on Organizational Socialization." Jennifer H. Waldeck, University of California, Santa Barbara

"Coloring Outside the Lines in Organizational Emotion Research." Sarah J. Tracy, University of Colorado, Boulder

"Workplace Aggression as an Organizational Phenomenon: It's More Than Just Interpersonal." Diane M. Monahan, Temple University

Respondent: David R. Seibold, University of California, Santa Barbara

---

3238   9:30-10:45 a.m.   Conf 4F   Fourth Floor   Chicago Hilton

EXOTIC VISUALIZING THE OTHER: THE HERMENEUTICS OF AN AMERICAN IN INDIA

Sponsor: Semiotics and Communication Commission
Chair: Elliot I. Gaines, Ashland University

Panelists: Marwan M. Kraidy, University of North Dakota
Nilanjana Bardhan, Southern Illinois University, Carbondale
Trevellya Ford-Ahmed, West Virginia State College
Mukhbir Singh, Ohio University

This panel will discuss mediated representations of cultural identity based upon a video produced as a scholarly interpretation of sound and images acquired in India. The video is intended to represent the lived-experience of an American visiting India. The organization of signs is structured to suggest the embodied perception of the viewer.

3239   9:30-10:45 a.m.   Conf 4G   Fourth Floor   Chicago Hilton

LOOKING BACK ONTO THE SOUTH AFRICAN EXPERIENCE

Sponsor: Association for Rhetoric & Communication in Southern Africa]
Chair: Philippe J. Salazar, University of Cape Town/International College of Philosophy, Paris
"Intercultural Perceptions: White/Black." Melissa E. Steyn, University of Cape Town
"The Serious Consequences of Comedy: Negotiating Cultural Change and Difference Through Humour." Dorothy M. Roome, Towson University
"Vigil (aunties) and Ministers: A Feminist Rhetorical Analysis of Black Sash Hauntings of Government Officials." Scott M. Schonfeldt-Aultman, San Francisco State University
"A Zambian Example: Oratorical Style in the Speeches of President FTJ Chiluba." Charles Calder, University of Zambia

---

3240   9:30-10:45 a.m.   Conf 4H   Fourth Floor   Chicago Hilton

CO-CONSTRUCTING IDENTITY: THE IMPLICATIVENESS OF INTERACTIONAL CHOICES FOR SOCIAL SELVES

Sponsor: Language and Social Interaction Division
Chair: Robert G. Westerfelhaus, University of Houston, Downtown
"Commonalities in Shared Meaning Among Organizational Members." Mary M. Eicholtz, Ohio University
"Surname Decisions at Marriage: Women's Descriptions of Choice, Deterministic Act, and Dynamic Process." Evelyn Y. Ho, University of Iowa
"Inferring Selves from Stories: Speakers' and Listeners' Reactions to Narrative Enactments of Self in Two Languages." Michele E. J. Koven, University of Illinois
"Narrating American Transgressions: The Meanings and Discourses of One Version of Socializing Practice." Peggy J. Miller, University of Illinois, Urbana-Champaign, Todd L. Sandel, University of Illinois, Urbana-Champaign, Chung-hui Liang, University of Illinois, Urbana-Champaign, Heidi Fung, Academia Sinica

Respondent: Gerry F. Philipsen, University of Washington

| 3241 | 9:30-10:45 a.m. | Conf 4I | Fourth Floor | Chicago Hilton |

USING C-SPAN TO STUDY ROSS PEROT'S EXPRESSION OF SENSITIVITY AND INSENSITIVITY WITH DIVERSITY ISSUES DURING THE 1992 PRESIDENTIAL CAMPAIGN

Sponsor: Media Forum Series

Panelist: James A. Schnell, Ohio Dominican College

| 3242 | 9:30-10:45 a.m. | Conf 4J | Fourth Floor | Chicago Hilton |

RESEARCH METHODOLOGY AND ORGANIZATIONAL DEVELOPMENT

Sponsor: Training and Development Division
  "Facilitation Protocol for Researching Organizational Objectives." Anthony B. Schroeder, Eastern New Mexico University
  "Focus Group Protocol and the Assessment of a Diversity Initiative." Don R. Swanson, Monmouth University
  "Building Interview Agendae for Prospective Trainees." Michael L. Fahs, California Polytechnic State University
  "Conducting An On-Line Research Study with Human Relations Professionals." Joseph Basso, Monmouth University

| 3244 | 9:30-10:45 a.m. | Conf 4L | Fourth Floor | Chicago Hilton |

FROM VISION TO BEHAVIOR TO CONTENTION IN A PUBLIC RELATIONS PARADIGM SHIFT: COLORING OUTSIDE THE LINES AS THE MILLENNIUM TURNS

Sponsor: Public Relations Division
Chair: Charles A. Lubbers, Kansas State University
  "Rhetorical Enactment: Building a Wholistic Sense of the Organization as Enactor of Relationships." Robert L. Heath, University of Houston
  "Positioning not Framing; Orienting not Informing: A Paradigm Shift Becomes a Dance." Bonita Dostal Neff, Valparaiso University
  "Frontstage: Shifting from Communication Roles in the Past to Enacting Interpersonal Relationships in the Future." G. Vonne Meussling, Indiana State University
  "Community-Building: From Public Opinion to Relationship-Building to Community-Building in Public Relations." Dean A. Kruckeberg, University of Northern Iowa

Respondent: Jeff K. Springston, University of Georgia

| 3245 | 9:30-10:45 a.m. | Conf 4M | Fourth Floor | Chicago Hilton |

CONSULTANTS, THERAPISTS AND CHANGE AGENTS: IDENTITY AND CONTROL IN CONTEMPORARY ORGANIZATIONS

Sponsor: Organizational Communication Division
Chair: George E. Cheney, University of Montana
  "In Search of Heroes, Followers, and Villains: Identity and Control in the Discourse of Popular Management Books." Theodore E. Zorn, University of Waikato, New Zealand, Deborah Page, University of Waikato, New Zealand
  "The Possibilities and Limits of Workplace Identity: Constituting Subjects Through Self-Help/Business Discourse." David A. Carlone, University of Colorado, Boulder
  "Workers' Identity and Control During Downsizing: The Therapeutic Management of Emotion." Steven K. May, University of North Carolina, Chapel Hill
  "'Just Who Are We Y'all?' Identity Formation in the Academic Organization: Looking at a Very Old, Southern Liberal Arts College in the Process of Contemporary Redefinition." Kathleen A. DeHaan, College of Charleston, Lynn Cherry, College of Charleston

---

3246   9:30-10:45 a.m.   McCormick Board Rm   Fourth Floor   Chicago Hilton

SOCIETY FOR THE STUDY OF SYMBOLIC INTERACTION BUSINESS MEETING

Sponsor: Society for the Study of Symbolic Interaction

3247   9:30-10:45 a.m.   Pullman Board Rm   Fourth Floor   Chicago Hilton

DELTA SIGMA RHO - TAU KAPPA ALPHA BUSINESS MEETING

Sponsor: Delta Sigma Rho-Tau Kappa Alpha

3249   9:30-10:45 a.m.   Conf 5B   Fifth Floor   Chicago Hilton

WHERE WE LIVE AND WORK: THE MANY FACES IN AND OF THE BASIC COURSE

Sponsor: Basic Course Division
Chair: Karen A. Smith, The College of Saint Rose

Panelists: Nanci M. Burk, Phoenix College
Maggie M. Sullivan, Loras College
Diana L. Tucker, Southern Illinois University, Carbondale
Rebecca A. Wolniewicz, Southwestern College

This panel encourages an interactive exchange of ideas designed to help teachers of the basic course adapt their course to the region and school in which they live and work.

3251   9:30-10:45 a.m.   Conf 5D   Fifth Floor   Chicago Hilton

NATIVE AMERICAN SPIRITUALITY AND ITS REPRESENTATIONS: EXAMINING AMERICAN INDIAN ARTIFACTS, STORYTELLING, PRAYER AND RITUAL AS RHETORICAL FORM

Sponsor: Spiritual Communication Commission
Chair: Anne Marie Czerwinski, University of Missouri, Columbia
"The Sacred Inipi Ceremony: Understanding the Rite of Purification Through Dramatic Form." Anne Marie Czerwinski, University of Missouri, Columbia
"Eloquence as Refusal: Mystification and Materialism in the Rhetoric of *Indian Art*." Lini Allen, University of Northern Colorado, Angela Koponen, University of Northern Colorado
"Native American Rhetoric: Exploring the Rhetorical Use of Narrative in Native American Story and Drama." Daniel D. Gross, Montana State University
"Life Among the Spirits: Native American Interspiritual Communication." Joseph C. Chilberg, SUNY, Fredonia

---

3252   9:30-10:45 a.m.   Conf 5E   Fifth Floor   Chicago Hilton

COUNTERPUBLICS AND THE STATE: A ROUNDTABLE DISCUSSION

Sponsor: Rhetorical and Communication Theory Division
Chairs: Robert B. Asen, University of Wisconsin, Madison
Daniel C. Brouwer, Loyola University, Chicago

This roundtable will focus on the interactions between counterpublics and states. The panelists, all of whom are contributors to a new volume titled *Counterpublics and the State*, wish to open up a guided discussion to address the various consequences of state-counterpublic tensions. The book contributors invite those interested in public sphere theory, social movements, and political communication to add their voices to this discussion.

3253	9:30-10:45 a.m.	Conf 5F	Fifth Floor	Chicago Hilton

CMC: SOCIAL AND PEDAGOGICAL IMPLICATIONS FOR THE FUTURE

Sponsor: Commission on Communication in the Future
Chair: Wilfred Tremblay, University of Wisconsin, Whitewater
"A Futuristic Vision of Communication Pedagogy: Toward a Computational Theory and Praxis." Dacia Charlesworth, Southeast Missouri State University, William J. McKinney, Southeast Missouri State University
"Facilitating or Impeding Mechanism for Electronic Commerce?: The Case of the Proposed National IC Card System in Taiwan." Huichuan Liu, Tamkang University
"Silencing the Internet: Technological Measures and Proposed Counter Measures." Brian C. Snow, Northern Arizona University, Richard A. Parker, Northern Arizona University
"Teleconferencing as a Means to Increase Access to Cancer Information and Support: The Case of Cancer Care Inc.." Roxanne Parrott, University of Georgia, Kelly A. Dorgan, University of Georgia
"Growing Pains: Effective Integrating of New Technologies in the Communication Classroom of the Future." Jacqueline M. Layng, University of Toledo

Respondent: Edwin J. Abar, Westfield State College

3254	9:30-10:45 a.m.	Conf 5G	Fifth Floor	Chicago Hilton

ENHANCING STUDENT LEARNING AND MOTIVATION

Sponsor: Instructional Development Division
Chair: Kent E. Menzel, DePauw University
"Organizational Lecture Cues and Notetaking Facilitate Student Information Processing." Brian S. Titsworth, Moorhead State University, Kenneth A. Kiewra, University of Nebraska, Lincoln
"College Teachers' Use of Self-Disclosive Messages and Students' Affective Learning." Susan R. Walker, California State University, Long Beach, Terre H. Allen, California State University, Long Beach
"Student Interest, Empowerment, and Motivation." Keith Weber, Marist College

Respondent: Kent E. Menzel, DePauw University

3255	9:30-10:45 a.m.	Conf 5H	Fifth Floor	Chicago Hilton

ART, ACTIVISM, AND ADVOCACY: GAY AND LESBIAN DISCOURSE

Sponsor: Gay/Lesbian Transgender Communication Studies Division
Chair: Billy W. Catchings, University of Indianapolis

Panelists: John D. Anderson, Emerson College
Billy W. Catchings, University of Indianapolis
John R. Butler, Northern Illinois University
Cindy J. Kistenberg, University of Houston, Downtown

Panelists will share brief position statements reviewing scholarship and reflecting on current thinking, research, and art regarding sexuality and language. Perspectives will cover a broad range of discourses inluding literary subtexts of and essays on Henry James, rhetoric of AIDS activism, advocacy and opposition regarding same-sex marriage and adoption, and queer theory. Audience members are invited to participate in this discussion and to share their own research interests.

3256	9:30-10:45 a.m.	Conf 5I	Fifth Floor	Chicago Hilton

METHODS AND INSTRUMENTS USED IN THE STUDY OF INTRAPERSONAL COMMUNICATION AND SOCIAL COGNITION

Sponsor: Intrapersonal Communication/Social Cognition Commission
Chair: Ron C. Tamborini, Michigan State University

Saturday

"Message Processing Quality: Initial Development of a Close-Ended Measure of Elaboration Depth." Stacy L. Wolski, University of Arizona, Robin L. Nabi, University of Arizona

"Development and Validation of a New Method for Measuring Equivocation." Richard S. Bello, Nicholls State University, Renee Edwards, Louisiana State University

"When I'm Within My Rights: An Expectancy-Based Model of Actor Evaluative and Behavioral Responses to Compliance-Resistance Strategies." Craig R. Hullett, Michigan State University, Ron C. Tamborini, Michigan State University

"The Latent Bias of Acquiescence Contained in the Need for Cognition Scale (NCS)." R. Lance Holbert, University of Wisconsin, Madison, Stephen J. Zubric, University of Wisconsin, Madison, Michael Pfau, University of Wisconsin, Madison

"The Message Is in the Metaphor: Assessing the Comprehension of Metaphors and Analogies in Advertisements." Susan E. Morgan, University of Kentucky, Tom Reichert, University of North Texas

Respondent: Mark A. Hamilton, University of Connecticut

3257   9:30-10:45 a.m.   Conf 5J   Fifth Floor   Chicago Hilton

MORE COLORING OUTSIDE THE LINES

Sponsor: Lambda Pi Eta
Chair: Susan Kay Tomasovic, George Mason University
   "One Voice, Many Responses: A Rhetorical Analysis of 'On the White Man's and Red Man's Religion'." Jill Nicole Tappa, Abilene Christian University
   "An Analysis of Nurse Training on Infant Touch." Lee Orthmann, Marist College, Cynthia Scott, Marist College
   "A Paper Examining Newspaper Coverage of Affirmative Action Using the Community Structure Approach." Michael Shomesh, College of New Jersey, Anthony Shissias, College of New Jersey
   "Verbal Diversion Theory." Erika Rae Scott, Ohio University
   "Changing Forms of Self-Presentations: Analysis of E-mail Messages Based on Current Literature." Kristan Falkowski, Penn State University

---

3262   9:30-10:45 a.m.   Essex Court   Second Floor   Essex Inn

COLORING OUTSIDE THE LINES: CURRICULUM AND INSTRUCTIONAL IMPLICATIONS OF LEADERSHIP EDUCATION IN THE VIRTUAL CLASSROOM

Sponsor: Religious Communication Association
Chair: Matthew Melton, Lee University
   "Coloring Outside the Lines of Traditional Adult Education: The Interactive Issues of Computer-Mediated Communication in a Leadership Program." Linda D. Grooms, Virginia Beach City Public Schools/Regent University
   "Coloring Outside the Lines: Mentoring and Spirituality in the Virtual Classroom of a Leadership Program." Kathaleen Reid-Martinez, Regent University
   "Coloring Outside the Lines: Assessing Psychological Types and Critical Thinking Skills to Enhance Leadership Education for the Twenty-First Century." Patricia J. Stewart, Chesapeake Public Schools

Respondent: Emeka J. Okoli, Norfolk State University

3263   9:30-10:45 a.m.   Windsor Court   Second Floor   Essex Inn

TEACHING ETHNOGRAPHY AT THE GRADUATE LEVEL

Sponsor: Ethnography Division
Chair: H.L. (Bud) Goodall, University of North Carolina, Greensboro

Panelists: Carolyn S. Ellis, University of South Florida
            Patricia Geist, San Diego State University
            M. Cristina Gonzalez, Arizona State University
            Nick L. Trujillo, California State University, Sacramento

3264   9:30-10:45 a.m.   **Buckingham Court   Second Floor   Essex Inn**

SEMIOTICS AND THE FINE ARTS

Sponsor: Semiotics and Communication Commission
Chair: Jane Tumas-Serna, Hollins University
    "Museum Design as Text: A Semiotic Tapestry." Billie J. Jones, Pennsylvania College of
      Technology
    "Talking-Stories of 'Ghosts': Lexical Foregrounding in *The Woman Warrior.*" Huihui Li,
      Texas A&M University
    "A Frame for Semiotic Analysis of Painting." Kyong L. Kim, Mount Vernon Nazarene
      College
    "Perspectives on Silence: From Binarism to Semiosis*." Angeli R. Diaz, Purdue University

Respondent: Heidi M. Rose, Villanova University

*Top Student Paper

3265   9:30-10:45 a.m.   **Park East Walk   Second Floor   Essex Inn**

SHADES OF FREEDOM, SHADES OF RESPONSIBILITY: HOW ACTORS IN SOCIAL CONTROVERSIES EXPLOIT AMBIGUITY TO REDEFINE SITUATIONS

Sponsor: Kenneth Burke Society, NCA Branch
    "Economic Freedom and Social Responsibility: A Pentadic Analysis of Two Episodes in the
      Nike Controversy." Daniel Foster, University of Wisconsin, Milwaukee
    "The 'Dark Underside' of Freedom: Governmental Responsibility and Postmodern
      Democracy." Michael R. Kramer, University of Wisconsin, Milwaukee
    "Sharing the Responsibility of AIDS: Mary Fisher's Address to the 1992 Republican
      National Convention." Daniel J. Ryan, University of Wisconsin, Milwaukee
    "Framing the Watergate Debate: Legal Responsibility in Barbara Jordan's 'Statement of the
      Articles of Impeachment' and Richard Nixon's 'The Watergate Investigation'." Ralph W.
      Siddall, University of Wisconsin, Milwaukee

3266   9:30-10:45 a.m.   **Cohn Rm   Second Floor   Spertus Institute**

FROM CYBERDIVAS TO CYBERDOGMAS: CONTEXTUALIZING THE RHETORIC OF VIRTUAL COMMUNITY

Sponsor: American Association for Rhetoric of Science & Technology
Chair: Carol Stabile, University of Pittsburgh
    "Commerce and On-Line Community: Going to the 'WELL' One Time Too Many." Steve
      Jones, University of Illinois, Chicago
    "The Rhetoric of Global Cybercommunity and the Capitalist Imaginary." Michelle L.
      Rodino, University of Pittsburgh
    "Virtual Community Networks: Geographically Centered, Culturally Conditioned, and
      Rhetorically Constructed." Joseph Schmitz, University of Tulsa
    "Third-World Cyberdivas and the Rhetoric of the Global Village: Dangerous Meetings in
      (In)visible Contexts." Radhika Gajjala, Bowling Green State University

Respondent: Alberto Gonzalez, Bowling Green State University

3267   9:30-10:45 a.m.   **Krensky Rm   Second Floor   Spertus Institute**

EXPLORATORY STUDIES IN COMMUNICATION AND LAW

Sponsor: Communication and Law Commission
Chair: Ann K. Burnett, North Dakota State University
    "Uncivil Communication in Law: Examining the Problem, Evaluating the Solutions, and
      Exploring Diverse New Directions Using Communication Research and Theory."
      Shannon S. Dyer, Northwestern University
    "Integrative Complexity and the Rhetoric of Court Budgeting." Kari C. Kelso, University of
      Texas, Austin

Saturday

"A Study of How Trial Consultants Plan, Conduct, and Analyze Focus Groups." Peggy Y. Byers, Ball State University

Respondent: Ann K. Burnett, North Dakota State University

| 3269 | 9:30-10:45 a.m. | Rm 903 | Ninth Floor | Spertus Institute |

MANAGING PARADOX IN FORENSICS

Sponsor: Pi Kappa Delta
Chair: Edward A. Hinck, Central Michigan University
   "Understanding Directors of Forensics as Organizational Leaders: The Role of Paradox in Changing Team Culture." Edward A. Hinck, Central Michigan University
   "Managing the Paradox of Boundaries: Negotiating the Tension Between One's Identity as a Student and a Team Member." Katherine L. Hatfield, Central Michigan University
   "Examining the Paradox of Risk-Taking in Intercollegiate Forensics." Kristi Gerding, Central Michigan University
   "Confronting the Paradox of Creativity and Formula in Impromptu Speaking." Jeff Taylor, Central Michigan University

| 3270 | 9:30-10:45 a.m. | Rm 904 | Ninth Floor | Spertus Institute |

COMPETITIVELY REVIEWED PAPERS IN PEACE AND CONFLICT COMMUNICATION

Sponsor: Peace and Conflict Communication Commission
Chair: Randall Rogan, Wake Forest University
   "Toward a Comprehensive Model for the Assessment and Management of Intraorganizational Conflict." Jessica K. Jameson, Temple University
   "The Causal Relationship Between Gender, Anger, Hostility, and Verbal and Physical Aggressiveness." Terry A. Kinney, University of Minnesota, Sue M. Wildermuth, University of Minnesota
   "Abraham's 'Dysfunctional Family' in the Middle East: A Rhetorical Analysis of Sis Levin's Peace Rhetoric." Margaret Cavin, Biola University

Respondent: Michael F. Smith, La Salle University

| 3271 | 9:30-10:45 a.m. | Rm 906 | Ninth Floor | Spertus Institute |

COMPETITIVE PAPERS IN ANCIENT RHETORIC

Sponsor: American Society for the History of Rhetoric
Chair: Mari Lee Mifsud, University of Richmond
   "De Oratore Book I: Rewoven Strands of the Classical Tradition." William R. Harris, University of Memphis
   "Plato's Rhetorical Theory: Subjectivity and Agency in Ancient Greek Conceptions of Orality." Christopher J. Skiles, University of Iowa
   "Ciceronian Rhetorical Guidelines for History: A Dialogue and A Letter." Ilon M. Lauer, University of Georgia

| 3272 | 9:30-10:45 a.m. | Rm 907 | Ninth Floor | Spertus Institute |

SYNERGIES AND VISIONS: AN EXAMINATION OF THE FUTURE ROLE OF DEBATE IN BOTH PUBLIC AND TOURNAMENT SETTINGS

Sponsor: Cross Examination Debate Association
Chair: Nina-Jo Moore, Appalachian State University
   "Serving our Students: Expectations for the Total Skills Package of the Debate-Trained Advocate in the Twenty-First Century." Stephen C. Koch, Capital University
   "Reinventing the Public Sphere: Public Debate as a Force of Social Change." Kerith Woodyard, Northern Illinois University
   "Local Politics and Foreign Policy: A Cross-Cultural Study of Argument in the Public Sphere." David L. Steinberg, University of Miami

Respondent: Nina-Jo Moore, Appalachian State University

3273   9:30-10:45 a.m.   Rm 908   Ninth Floor   Spertus Institute

EDUCATION AND/OR COMPETITION: ESTABLISHING GOALS FOR CONTEMPORARY FORENSICS PROGRAMS

Sponsor: National Forensic Association
Chair: Guy P. Yates, West Texas A&M University
  "The More Things Change the More They Stay the Same: The Historical Evolution of
    Program Goals in Forensics." Larry Schnoor, Communication Links
  "Forensics As Co-Curricular Activity: Suggestions for Developing an Educational Philosophy
    for the Intercollegiate Individual Events Program." John R. Perlich, North Central College
  "So What's So Wrong with a Little Competition? A Defense of Competitive Goals."
    Michael W. Kirch, Purdue University, Tom Zeidler, Illinois State University
  "Goals and the Challenge of Rapid Change: Challenges Faced by Forensics Programs
    Experiencing Rapid Growth." Daniel L. Smith, Bradley University
  "Balancing Educational and Competitive Goals in Forensics: The Quest for the Golden
    Mean." Richard E. Paine, North Central College

Respondent: Vicki L. Karns, Suffolk University

3274   9:30-10:45 a.m.   Auditorium   Second Floor   Spertus Institute

ADVICE FROM THE TRENCHES: CHICAGO ARTISTS SPEAK

Sponsor: Theatre Division
Chair: Julie R. Patterson-Pratt, University of Minnesota, Morris

Panelists: Brian McCartney, Stone Circle Theatre Ensemble
            Jessica McCartney, Stone Circle Theatre Ensemble
            Arlene Hill, Freelance Actor
            Chris McCaleb, Stone Circle Theatre Ensemble
            Charissa Armon, Stone Circle Theatre Ensemble

11:00 a.m.

Raymie E. McKerrow, NCA First Vice President and Primary Convention Planner has
selected the following programs as exemplary. These programs are "highlighted" on
Friday and Saturday during the 11:00 a.m. – 12:15 p.m. time period.

3306   11:00-12:15 p.m.   Continental BR A   Lobby Level   Chicago Hilton

AFRICANA/AFRICAN AMERICAN/BLACK STUDIES, WOMEN'S STUDIES: CONTRIBUTIONS TO AFRICAN AMERICAN COMMUNICATION RESEARCH

Sponsor: Spotlight on Scholarship
Presiding Officer: Ronald L. Jackson, Penn State University

Participants: Molefi K. Asante, Temple University
                Brenda J. Allen, University of Colorado, Boulder
                Cecil A. Blake, University of Nebraska, Lincoln
                Olga I. Davis, Arizona State University
                Veronica J. Duncan, University of Georgia
                Ronald J. Stephens, University of Nebraska, Lincoln

This panel examines the role of particular theoretical approaches (e.g., Afrocentricity, feminist
theories) in the development of African American communication theory and methods.

Saturday

3307   11:00-12:15 p.m.   Continental BR B   Lobby Level   Chicago Hilton

THE FUTURE OF ASSESSMENT PUBLICATIONS BY NCA: A ROUNDTABLE DISCUSSION

Sponsor: Commission on Communication Assessment
Chair: Richard L. Quianthy, Broward Community College

Panelists: Philip M. Backlund, Central Washington University
William G. Christ, Trinity University
Ruth A. Hulbert-Johnson, University of Colorado, Colorado Springs
Donna Surges Tatum, University of Chicago

The discussion will explore the future of publication of assessment projects, the role of CAC in NCA assessment, and related issues. Audience participation is encouraged.

3308   11:00-12:15 p.m.   Continental BR C   Lobby Level   Chicago Hilton

SPEAKING ACROSS THE CURRICULUM: FOE OR FRIEND

Sponsor: Senior College & University Section
Chair: Robert O. Weiss, DePauw University

Panelists: John A. Daly, University of Texas, Austin
Roy J. Schwartzman, University of South Carolina
John T. Morello, Mary Washington College
A. A. Bowers, Jr, University of Phoenix

This session will be conducted as a public debate with opportunity for audience participation.

3310   11:00-12:15 p.m.   Grand Ballroom   Second Floor   Chicago Hilton

MESSAGE PRODUCTION: A COLLOQUIUM

Sponsors: Interpersonal Communication Division
Group Communication Division
Chair: Charles R. Berger, University of California, Davis

Panelists: Judee K. Burgoon, University of Arizona
Brant R. Burleson, Purdue University
James P. Dillard, University of Wisconsin, Madison
John O. Greene, Purdue University
Dale Hample, Western Illinois University
Janet R. Meyer, Kent State University
Vincent R. Waldron, Arizona State University West
Steven R. Wilson, Northwestern University

Knowing when or when not to speak during a conversation and knowing what to say and how to say it when one does speak are vitally dependent on message production skills. Message production skills are also critical to communicative success in unmediated public communication contexts as well as mediated communication situations. The purpose of this colloquium is to explore the nature of these message production skills. Audience questions will be invited.

3314   11:00-12:15 p.m.   Boulevard A   Second Floor   Chicago Hilton

SERVICE-LEARNING AND COMMUNICATION EDUCATION

Sponsor: Educational Policies Board
Chair: Carolyn Calloway-Thomas, Indiana University, Bloomington

Panelists: James L. Applegate, University of Kentucky
David Droge, University of Puget Sound
Sherwyn P. Morreale, NCA National Office
John Saltmarsh, Campus Compact

Edward Zlotkowski, American Association for Higher Education

The panelists bring their expertise and experience to bear on a discussion about the implications of service-learning for communication educators.

| 3315 | 11:00-12:15 p.m. | Boulevard B | Second Floor | Chicago Hilton |

POST COLD WAR DISCOURSE IN THE ABSENCE OF AN ENEMY

Sponsor: NCA First Vice President
Chair: Robert P. Newman, University of Iowa

Panelists: Marilyn J. Young, Florida State University
David C. Williams, University of Puerto Rico
Robert L. Ivie, Indiana University
Carol K. Winkler, Georgia State University
Richard B. Gregg, Penn State University
Theodore O. Windt, University of Pittsburgh

Ten years have passed since the Berlin Wall came down, effectively ending the Cold War. Scholars who have studied the Cold War period will discuss the ways in which the United States is responding to a world where the centering focus of the dominant enemy—the Soviet Union— has been lost. Among the themes to be discussed: the changes in metaphors and other descriptors now that "the Evil Empire" no longer fits; the recurrent need for "an enemy"—in particular the construction of terrorists states as the new enemy; and the ways in which we are resurrecting Russia as a force of evil to be feared.

| 3316 | 11:00-12:15 p.m. | Boulevard C | Second Floor | Chicago Hilton |

HOMOPHOBIA IN OUR COURSES: RESOURCES AND STRATEGIES WHEN DEALING WITH GAY, LESBIAN, BISEXUAL, TRANSGENDERED ISSUES IN CLASSROOM TEACHING

Sponsor: Gay/Lesbian Transgender Communication Studies Division
Chair: Carol L. Benton, Central Missouri State University

Panelists: Carol A. Atkinson, Central Missouri State University
Carol L. Benton, Central Missouri State University
Frederick C. Corey, Arizona State University
Dennis P. Grady, Eastern Michigan University
Timothy Gura, Brooklyn College
John R. Heineman, Lincoln High School, Nebraska
Peter M. Pober, University of Texas
Jeanne S. Posner, Western Connecticut State University
Cory L. Young, Bowling Green University

Discussion issues may include: coming out, texts with strong gay-related themes, texts that ignore or marginalize homosexuality, homophobic comments and behavior. The panelists will present a brief overview of the types of problems encountered when teaching particular communication courses, summary of example cases, and strategy for intervention. Audience participation is encouraged.

| 3319 | 11:00-12:15 p.m. | Astoria | Third Floor | Chicago Hilton |

IRONING OUT THE WRINKLES: ISSUES IN INCORPORATING DISTANCE EDUCATION IN THE COMMUNICATION CLASSROOM

Sponsor: Instructional Development Division
Chair: Carole A. Barbato, Kent State University, East Liverpool

Panelists: Mary E. Bozik, University of Northern Iowa
John A. Courtright, University of Delaware
Mikiko L. Crawford, Ohio University, Southern Campus

Saturday

Elizabeth E. Graham, Ohio University
Elizabeth M. Perse, University of Delaware
Jessica Street, Ohio University
Candice E. Thomas-Maddox, Ohio University
Rodney A. Reynolds, Regent University

This panel will explore—in an interactive format—issues and challenges associated with implementing distance education in the communication classroom. Topics include: interaction and classroom relationships, faculty compensation, technological support, promotion and tenure, copyright and issues of ownership of intellectual property, evaluation and applied research, faculty development, credibility of on-line sources, and creating effective learning environments.

3321	11:00-12:15 p.m.	Williford A	Third Floor	Chicago Hilton

FEMINISM, GENDER, AND DIVERSITY ISSUES: THE CHILLY CLIMATE IN HIGHER EDUCATION

Sponsor: Table Talk Series
Chair: Trudy L. Hanson, West Texas A&M University

Panelists: Katherine Hawkins, Wichita State University
Teri S. Gamble, College of New Rochelle
Michael W. Gamble, New York Institute of Technology
Dreama G. Moon, California State University, San Marcos
Fern L. Johnson, Clark University

The climate in higher education institutions in the United States has become increasingly colder regarding issues of diversity and multiculturalism. This discussion focuses specifically on what directions feminist and women's studies programs are taking, and addressing concerns about philosophical, as well as curricular issues.

3323	11:00-12:15 p.m.	Williford C	Third Floor	Chicago Hilton

FROM TEACHER TO KEEPER: THE TRANSITION FROM FACULTY TO ADMINISTRATION

Sponsor: Table Talk Series
Chair: Susan A. Jasko, California University of Pennsylvania

Panelists: Gary L. Kreps, Hofstra University
Lance A. Strate, Fordham University
Dencil K. Backus, California University of Pennsylvania
John Parrish-Sprowl, Indiana University-Purdue University, Fort Wayne
Susan J. Drucker, Hofstra University

This panel will address the following questions: How does one re-negotiate role expectations? Can you name three guidelines for discerning administrative priorities? What advice do you have for someone contemplating this move? *Why* administer?

3324	11:00-12:15 p.m.	Marquette	Third Floor	Chicago Hilton

ASSESSING OUTCOMES OF TECHNOLOGICALLY-DELIVERED EDUCATION

Sponsors: Training and Development Division
Human Communication and Technology Commission

Panelists: Clark Germann, Metropolitan State College of Denver
Karen R. Krupar, Metropolitan State College of Denver
Dennis L. Wignall, Saginaw Valley State University
Terre H. Allen, California State University, Long Beach
Patricia Kearney, California State University, Long Beach
Timothy G. Plax, California State University, Long Beach
Jennifer H. Waldeck, University of California, Santa Barbara

Technology is being used more and more in the teaching and delivery of communication education. Yet, very little attention has been paid to the assessment of the quality. These panelists will discuss current trends in the assessment of technology and instruction.

3326	11:00-12:15 p.m.	PDR 1	Third Floor	Chicago Hilton

DISTANCE EDUCATION: CHALLENGES AND SUCCESSES IN DEVELOPMENT AND DELIVERY

Sponsor: Community College Section
Chair: Linda C. Brown, El Paso Community College

Panelists: Cindy Carley, Amarillo College
         Janna L. Holt-Day, South Plains College
         Lynn M. Disbrow, Sinclair Community College

Panel members will provide an overview of the distance learning program at their institutions. This seminar will include a discussion of the challenges and successes in the development and delivery of classes, compensation issues, faculty training, and administrative policies and procedures.

12:30 p.m.

3406	12:30-1:45 p.m.	Continental BR A	Lobby Level	Chicago Hilton

COMPETITIVE PAPERS IN CULTURAL AND RHETORICAL EXPLORATIONS OF POPULAR COMMUNICATION AND ADVERTISING

Sponsor: Mass Communication Division
Chair: J. Emmett Winn, Auburn University
   "Faithful or Foolish: The Emergence of the 'Ironic Cover Album' and Rock Culture*."
      Steven Bailey, University of Illinois, Urbana-Champaign
   "Punk Rock and the Myth of Nihilism." Peter G. Ross, Central Michigan University
   "'Defeat Talk': Expressing Partisanship in a Sports Broadcast When the Favored Team is
      Losing. Alan D. Hansen, SUNY, Albany
   "Understanding Images in Advertising: A Neo-Sophistic Approach." Jerome D. Mahaffey,
      University of Memphis

Respondent: Matthew P. McAllister, Virginia Tech University

*Top Student Paper

3407	12:30-1:45 p.m.	Continental BR B	Lobby Level	Chicago Hilton

COMPUTER-MEDIATED EDUCATION: THE HUMAN ELEMENT

Sponsor: Human Communication and Technology Commission
Chair: Diane F. Witmer, California State University, Fullerton
   "A Computer-Mediated Communication Retrospective: Has it Really Been Twenty Years?"
      James D. Wallace, Cameron University
   "The E-Rate: Bridging the Information Access Gap Created by the Digital Divide."
      Omerosa Manigault, Howard University
   "Cyberspace as Frontier." Kenzie A. Cameron, University of Georgia, Franklin J. Boster,
      Michigan State University
   "A Perspective and Research Agenda for Computer-Mediated Communication: CMC as a
      Hypercontextual, Hyperconscious, and Co-Constructed Drama." Charles E. Soukup,
      University of Nebraska, Lincoln
   "Uses of Technology for Teaching in International Internships: The Farthest Reaches of
      Distance Education." John C. Sherblom, University of Maine
   "Thinking in Virtuality: The Computer-Human Interface in Human Communication
      Courses." Dennis L. Wignall, Saginaw Valley State University

Respondents: Lori J. Charron, Concordia University, Minnesota
         Dianna R. Wynn, Midland College

Saturday

3408   12:30-1:45 p.m.   Continental BR C   Lobby Level   Chicago Hilton

TECHNOLOGIES OF CITIZENSHIP

Sponsor: Critical and Cultural Studies Division
Chair: Toby Miller, New York University
   "Governing Speech: Speech Education as a Technology of Citizenship." Darrin K. Hicks,
      University of Denver, Ronald Greene, University of Texas, Austin
   "Putting the 'P' in PBS: Citizenship, the State, and the New Right." Theodore G. Striphas,
      University of North Carolina, Chapel Hill
   "Spaces of Surveillance: Cybercitizenship in Postcolonial Britain." Ashley Dawson,
      University of Iowa
   "Citizenship Lessons: National Anxiety and the New Woman." Melissa D. Deem,
      University of Iowa, Christopher Kamrath, Northwestern University

Respondent: Toby Miller, New York University

3410   12:30-1:45 p.m.   Grand Ballroom   Second Floor   Chicago Hilton

VIOLENCE PERFORMED

Sponsor: Performance Studies Division
Chair: Lawrence Grossberg, University of North Carolina, Chapel Hill
   "Border Racism: Performance, Performativity and the U.S./Mexico Border." Anthony T.
      Perucci, New York University
   "Public Violence/Private Neglect: Performances of Trauma and Risk in a Post-Queer, Deep
      South." Patrick W. Anderson, University of California, Berkeley
   "The Evolution of Rage." Kathy Randels, Artspot Productions

Respondent: Dwight Conquergood, Northwestern University

3412   12:30-1:45 p.m.   Int'l Ballroom South   Second Floor   Chicago Hilton

CIRCUS OF CONSULTING PRACTICES

Sponsor: Roundtable Series
Chair: Sue DeWine, Ohio University
   "The Lion Tamer: Working with Unruly Participants." Mary M. Eicholtz, Ohio University
   "The Snake Charmer: Engaging Participants." Melissa K. Gibson, Western Michigan
      University
   "The Clown: Using Humor in Training and Consulting." Todd T. Holm, Ohio University
   "The Magician: Using Magic Tricks in Training." Rex L. Crawley, Ohio University
   "The Juggler: Balancing Organizational Priorities." Elizabeth R. Bernat, Ohio University
   "The Fortune Teller: Working with Perceptions." Susan R. Glaser, University of Oregon
   "The Hypnotist: Working for Consensus with Clients." Peter A. Glaser, Glaser & Associates,
      Inc.
   "The Choreographer: Putting It All Together." Anita C. James, Ohio University
   "The Tight-Wire Walker: Working Without a Net in Strategic Planning." Sue DeWine,
      Ohio University

This program will provide participants with an opportunity to talk with practicing consultants
on a variety of topics. Every 15 minutes participants will be asked to move to another station.

3414   12:30-1:45 p.m.   Boulevard A   Second Floor   Chicago Hilton

COMMUNICATION AND THE CONFIGURATION OF SPACE

Sponsor: Challenging Boundaries Series
Chair: Roger C. Aden, Ohio University
   "Urban Congregations of Capital and Communications: Redesigning Social and Spatial
      Boundaries." Gerald Sussman, Portland State University
   "Trespassing City Borders and Boundaries: Graffiti as Urban Communication." Gene Burd,
      University of Texas, Austin

"La Gente de la Frontera: A Cross-Cultural Perspective on Border Identity." Melissa Martinez, New Mexico State University

---

3416   12:30-1:45 p.m.   Boulevard C   Second Floor   Chicago Hilton

CODING, COMPETENCE AND COLLABORATION ACROSS CULTURALLY DIVERSE STUDENT POPULATIONS

Sponsor: International & Intercultural Communication Division
Chair: Chukwuka A. Onwumechili, Bowie State University
  "Socializing Experience of Japanese Student Sojourners in the USA: Cultural Coding of 'Japanese-ness'." Izumi Funayama, University of Texas, Austin
  "Host Communication Competence, Host Interpersonal Communication, and Cross-Cultural Adaptation: A Study of International Students in Japan." Masazumi Maruyama, Nagasaki University
  "On-Line Collaboration Among Culturally Diverse Students: An Analysis of an International and Multicultural CMC Project in London." Laura B. Lengel, American International University, London, Catherine Scott, University of North London, Susi Peacock, American International University, London

Respondent: Gary B. Wilson, Hong Kong Baptist University

3418   12:30-3:15 p.m.   Waldorf   Third Floor   Chicago Hilton

NCA LEGISLATIVE COUNCIL BUSINESS MEETING

Sponsor: NCA Legislative Council

3419   12:30-1:45 p.m.   Astoria   Third Floor   Chicago Hilton

THE RHETORIC OF GEORGE WASHINGTON: ESSAYS COMMEMORATING THE WASHINGTON BICENTENNIAL

Sponsor: Public Address Division
Chair: Stephen E. Lucas, University of Wisconsin, Madison
  "A Wise, a Good, and a Great Man: Washington's Use of Credibility as a Rhetorical Strategy." Robert V. Friedenberg, Miami University, Ohio
  "Washington's First Inaugural Address: A Study of Presidential Ethos." Linda D. Horwitz, Hamilton College
  "Washington's Farewell: Geographical Distance as Bane and Blessing." Michael J. Hostetler, St. John's University
  "A Test of the Rhetorical Prerogatives of the Presidency: Washington's Proclamation of Impartiality of 1793." Jon W. Paulson, Bethany College

Respondent: Stephen E. Lucas, University of Wisconsin, Madison

---

3421   12:30-1:45 p.m.   Williford A   Third Floor   Chicago Hilton

AFRICAN AMERICAN RHETORIC WITHIN THE GOVERNMENT SECTOR

Sponsor: African American Communication & Culture Commission
Chair: Myron M. Beasley, Ohio University
  "Wishbones, Earmuffs and Splattered Bugs: Re-Examining the 90s Controversy over Application of the Voting Rights Act to Congressional Reappointment*." Jon Leon Torn, Northwestern University
  "Clarence Thomas: Intellectual Slave or Sagacious Commentator of the Struggle for Justice?*." Sabrina Bradley, Morgan State University
  "Classical Elements in Selected Addresses by Barbara Charline Jordan*." Adrienne Jene Mayo, Morgan State University

Respondent: Solomon W. Obotetukudo, Clarion University

*Student Debut Paper

Saturday

3422   12:30-1:45 p.m.   Williford B   Third Floor   Chicago Hilton

CONSTRUCTING EVENTS THROUGH POLITICAL NARRATIVE AND DISCOURSE

Sponsor: Political Communication Division
Chair: Robert E. Denton, Virginia Tech University
  "Sports Metaphors and Gunslinger Narratives: Campaigns on Thin Ice." Janis L. Edwards,
    Western Illinois University
  "Crafting the Negative Narrative of Controversy: The News Media and Framing." Courtney
    L. Dillard, University of Texas, Austin
  "The New Soviets: The Rhetorical Uses of Terrorism in the Clinton White House." Gary C.
    Woodward, College of New Jersey
  "Privacy, Publicity, and Propriety in Congressional Eulogies for Representative Stewart
    McKinney (R-CT)." Daniel C. Brouwer, Loyola University, Chicago

Respondent: Bruce E. Gronbeck, University of Iowa

3423   12:30-1:45 p.m.   Williford C   Third Floor   Chicago Hilton

FEMINIST PERSPECTIVES ON SOCIAL CHANGE: A CONTINUUM OF TRANSFORMATION

Sponsor: Feminist and Women Studies Division
Chair: Cindy L. Griffin, Colorado State University
  "A Rhetoric of Reorientation: Activating Change Through Women's Spirituality Rituals."
    Kimberly D. Barnett Gibson, Saint Mary's University, Cindy L. Griffin, Colorado State
    University
  "Materiality and Discourse in Social Change." Dana L. Cloud, University of Texas, Austin
  "Metaphorical Hauntings in the Rhetoric of the Mothers of the Plaza de Mayo: A Theory of
    Personal and Social Transformation." Karen A. Foss, University of New Mexico, Kathy L.
    Domenici, Domenici Littlejohn, New Mexico

Respondent: Sonja K. Foss, University of Colorado, Denver

3424   12:30-1:45 p.m.   Marquette   Third Floor   Chicago Hilton

MASS COMMUNICATION AND AFRICAN AMERICANS

Sponsors: Black Caucus
          African American Communication & Culture Commission
Chair: Bishetta D. Merritt, Howard University
  "The Portrayal of African Americans in Television Advertising." B. Jordan Brookins, Howard
    University
  "Between the Color Lines of Prime-Time: White Viewers Perceptions of African American
    Television Images." Chontrese Doswell, University of Maryland
  "Who's Laughing at Who?: The Use of Parody in Black Film." Kimberly R. Moffitt, Howard
    University
  "Mass Media Perceptions and the Labeling of African American Athletes: Social Deviants
    or News Media Scapegoats?" Tamara Scott, Howard University
  "Black Aesthetics: Rhythm and Blues in Advertising, Television, and Film." Sharnine S.
    Herbert, Howard University

3427   12:30-3:15 p.m.   PDR 2   Third Floor   Chicago Hilton

ACADEMIC PROGRAMS THAT PROMOTE EMPOWERMENT FOR PEOPLE WITH DISABILITIES: COMMUNICATION PERSPECTIVES

Sponsor: Caucus on Disability Issues
Chair: Gary L. Kreps, Hofstra University
  "Disability Issues: Communication Strategies on Campus to Confront the Challenges."
    Susan A. Fox, Western Michigan University

"Dusting the Floors of Academia and Polishing the Community Using the Disability Rag."
Kelly P. Herold, Winona State University
"Addressing the Pedagogical Challenges of the Visually Impaired." S. Diane McFarland,
D'Youville College
"Helping Educators Facilitate the Journey of Learning Disabled Students: Implications for
Organizational Development and Communication Instruction." Ellen W. Bonaguro,
Ithaca College, Jim L. Query, Loyola University
"The Bridge to Employment Program: An Innovative Partnership to Promote
Empowerment and Self-Sufficiency for People with Physical Disabilities." Gary L. Kreps,
Hofstra University

3428   12:30-1:45 p.m.   PDR 3   Third Floor   Chicago Hilton

CHANGING NOTIONS OF GENDER AND THE DREAM GIRL: RECONSIDERING "BARBIE-NESS"

Sponsor: Women's Caucus
Chair: Elizabeth J. Whitney, University of Utah
"Let's Play Barbie: Adolescent Memoirs of Life in the Dream House." Elizabeth J. Whitney,
University of Utah
"I Enjoy Being a Girl." Theresa M. Carilli, Purdue University, Calumet
"The Barbie Zone: To Mattel and Back." Amy S. Burt, Georgia College and State University
"Pearls and Pastels or the Making of a Lady From the Mess of a Daughter." Laila A. Farah,
Southern Illinois University

3429   12:30-1:45 p.m.   PDR 4   Third Floor   Chicago Hilton

COMPETITIVE PAPERS: RHETORICAL AND MEDIA STUDIES IN ASIAN PACIFIC AMERICAN COMMUNICATION

Sponsors: Asian/Pacific American Caucus
Asian Pacific American Communication Studies Division
Chair: Todd Imahori, Seinan Gakuin University, Japan
"Power and the Rhetoric of Rearticulation: Asian Indians at a Hindu Temple*." Pravin A.
Rodriquez, Carroll College
"Three Themes of Japanese American Stories: Story Analysis of Japanese American History
and Experience." Takashi Kosaka, Monterey Institute of International Studies
"Images of Asians/Pacific Islanders in Star Trek." Marquita L. Byrd, San Jose State University
"Asian Filmmakers Moving Into Hollywood—Genre Regulation and Auteur Aesthetics."
Pei-Chi Cheng, Indiana University

Respondent: Rueyling Chuang, St. John's University/College of St. Benedict

---

3430   12:30-1:45 p.m.   PDR 5   Third Floor   Chicago Hilton

COLORING OUTSIDE THE LINES: EXAMINING THE MULTIPLE CONTEXTS OF AT-RISKNESS

Sponsor: Communication Needs of Students at Risk Commission
Chair: Susanne L. Williams, Moorhead State University
"Perceived Messages from Schools Regarding Adolescent Tobacco Use." Melanie
Booth-Butterfield, West Virginia University, Robert Anderson, West Virginia University,
Kimberly Williams, West Virginia University
"Young Men in Residential Treatment: The Nature of Their Communication in the
Therapeutic Milieu and Elsewhere*." Erica Michaels Hollander, University of Denver
"Don't Drop Out!: A University's Use and Evaluation of Residential Colleges and Their
Impact on Student Satisfaction, Communication Implications, and Enhanced Retention."
Camisha Pierce, Murray State University, Timothy S. Todd, Murray State University
"A Taste of the Real Thing: Public Speaking Activities for Deaf Students." Raed A. Mohsen,
Lebanese American University
"A Short Course for the Instruction of Public Speaking Skills." James A. Schnell, Ohio
Dominican College

Saturday

*Debut Paper

3431   12:30-1:45 p.m.   PDR 6   Third Floor   Chicago Hilton

ADMINISTRATIVE ISSUES IN COMMUNICATION DISTANCE LEARNING INITIATIVES

Sponsor: Association for Communication Administration
Chair: Robert K. Avery, University of Utah

Panelists: Cassandra L. Book, Michigan State University
          Kathy A. Krendl, Ohio University
          Thomas A. McCain, Ohio State University
          Alan Stavitsky, University of Oregon

Respondent: Robert K. Avery, University of Utah

As the face of higher education is being remolded to incorporate funding shortfalls, increased accountability, and competency-based directives, various forms of mediated instruction are being explored as solutions to meeting these and other challenges. This panel will share the experiences of communication colleagues who have had direct experiences with managing distance learning initiatives.

3432   12:30-3:15 p.m.   PDR 7   Third Floor   Chicago Hilton

'THE NUREMBURG FILES' V. PLANNED PARENTHOOD COALITION

Sponsor: Freedom of Expression Commission
     Advocates for the Plaintiffs: Brian M. O'Connell, Central Connecticut State University,
     Juliet L. Dee, University of Delaware, Thomas R. Flynn, Slippery Rock University
     Advocates for the Respondents: Dale A. Herbeck, Boston College, Christopher D. Hunter,
     University of Pennsylvania, Frank Harrison, Trinity University
     Presiding Judges: Joseph S. Tuman, San Francisco State University, Stanley Morris,
     Attorney-at-Law, Donald Fishman, Boston College

3433   12:30-1:45 p.m.   Conf 4A   Fourth Floor   Chicago Hilton

A DIAGNOSTIC LOOK FROM THE 'OUTSIDE IN AND THE INSIDE OUT': AN EMPIRICAL STUDY OF AN AFROCENTRIC ORGANIZATIONAL MODEL

Sponsor: African American Communication & Culture Commission
Chair: Marcia J. Clinkscales, Howard University

Panelists: Laura K. Dorsey, Howard University
          Nikita Y. Harris, Howard University
          Heather E. Harris, Howard University
          Sherry B. Scott, Howard University
          Cherylann Charles-Williamson, Howard University

The members of this panel will provide a discussion on their organizational diagnostic findings of a Washington, DC organization grounded in an Afrocentric model of organizing. Discussion will include the assessment analysis of communication processes as it relates to leadership and management functions in an organization.

3434   12:30-1:45 p.m.   Conf 4B   Fourth Floor   Chicago Hilton

MADE IN HIS/HER IMAGE: RELIGIOUS CONTROVERSY AND QUEER USURPARE IN MCNALLY'S CORPUS CHRISTI

Sponsor: Gay/Lesbian Transgender Communication Studies Division
Chair: Landon Coleman, Georgia Perimeter College
     "To Hold as 'Twere the Mirror up to Hate': Religio-Conservative Rhetoric in the Reportage
     of the Corpus Christi Controversy." Richard K. Sisson, Georgia Perimeter College

"What a Friend We Have in Jesus!: McNally's Gay Messiah and His Dramatic Context."
   Landon Coleman, Georgia Perimeter College
"Theatrical Bombs vs Molotov Cocktails: Some Thoughts on Staging Controversial
   Dramas." David Zak, Bailiwick Repertory Theatre, Chicago

Respondent: Joel Fink, Roosevelt University

From the beginning of the modern lesbian and gay movement, dramatic discourse has proven
a potent rhetorical force in social change. In 1998, the Manhattan Theatre Club's staging of
Terence McNally's controversial play *Corpus Christi* ignited protest and condemnation. The
playwright "colored outside the lines" by depicting a gay messiah and his apostles; the public's
response was heavily chronicled by the press. From a rhetorical, dramaturgical, and directorial
perspective, panel members will discuss the drama's role in a social context. Video clips of
salient sections of *Corpus Christi* will be shown; a question and answer session will follow.

3435   12:30-1:45 p.m.   Conf 4C   Fourth Floor   Chicago Hilton

STEPPING OVER NEW LINES: ISSUES FACING CONTEMPORARY FAMILY LIFE

Sponsor: Family Communication Division
Chair: Lindsay M. Timmerman, University of Texas, Austin
   "Values Talk at Family Dinner: Variety in Content and Practice." Deborah J. Wooldridge,
      Coe College
   "How Do Adolescents Resist Drug Offers from Family and What Family Factors Affect the
      Resistance Strategy?" Yvonne B. Kellar-Guenther, Western Illinois University
   "Points of Convergence: The Study of Family and Television." David T. McMahan,
      University of Iowa
   "Long-Distance Kin-Keeping." Erin M. Sahlstein, University of Iowa

Respondent: Carol J. Bruess, University of St. Thomas

3436   12:30-1:45 p.m.   Conf 4D   Fourth Floor   Chicago Hilton

THE EFFECTIVENESS OF PUBLIC HEALTH CAMPAIGNS

Sponsor: Health Communication Division
Chair: Sandra L. Ragan, University of Oklahoma
   "A Meta-Analysis of U.S. Health Campaign Effects on Behavior: The Impact of Message
      Factors, Exposure, Control Group Trends, and Campaign Length." Leslie B. Snyder,
      University of Connecticut, Mark A. Hamilton, University of Connecticut
   "The Effects of Anti-Tobacco Advertisements Based on Risk-Taking Tendencies: Realistic
      Fear Ads versus Gross Humor Ads." Moon Jeong Lee, University of Florida, Mary Ann
      Ferguson, University of Florida, Fred Sowder, University of Florida
   "The Recall of a Health Campaign Message: Is There a Relationship Among Gender, Sex,
      and Ego-Involvement?" Kenneth J. Levine, Illinois State University, Judith M. Berkowitz,
      Emerson College
   "An Organizational Theory of Health Communication Campaigns: Evidence from the
      Uganda AIDS Campaign." James Kiwanuka-Tondo, University of Connecticut, Leslie B.
      Snyder, University of Connecticut

Respondent: Sandra L. Ragan, University of Oklahoma

3437   12:30-1:45 p.m.   Conf 4E   Fourth Floor   Chicago Hilton

ISSUES IN COMMUNICATION BETWEEN PATIENTS AND HEALTH CARE
PROVIDERS

Sponsor: Health Communication Division
Chair: Charles H. Grant, University of Tennessee
   "On-Line Commentary in Acute Medical Visits: A Method of Shaping Patient
      Expectations." John C. Heritage, University of California, Los Angeles, Tanya Stivers,
      University of California, Los Angeles
   "Applying Politeness Theory to Compliance-Gaining in Health Care Environments." Carma
      L. Bylund, Northwestern University

"A Case Study of an Intercultural Health Care Visit: An African American Woman and Her White Male Physician." Lynda D. Dixon, Bowling Green State University

"Satisfaction with the Medical Interview Team: An Analysis of Patients' Stories." Carolyn M. Anderson, University of Akron

Respondent: Charles H. Grant, University of Tennessee

3438   12:30-1:45 p.m.   Conf 4F   Fourth Floor   Chicago Hilton

BALANCING THE 'SEE SAW': SUCCESSFULLY IMPLEMENTING GENDER EQUITY STRATEGIES IN THE COMMUNICATION CLASSROOM

Sponsor: Community College Section
Chair: Audrey J. Cunningham, University of Indianapolis

Panelists: Jay G. Bourne, Asbury College
Gary D. Deaton, Transylvania University
Robert J. Glenn, Owensboro Community College
Eileen M. Lewandowski, Prestonsburg Community College
James E. Reppert, Southern Arkansas University

3439   12:30-1:45 p.m.   Conf 4G   Fourth Floor   Chicago Hilton

THE TIMES THEY ARE A-CHANGING: MANAGING AND MEASURING ORGANIZATIONS IN FLUX

Sponsor: Applied Communication Division
Chair: Scott C. Ratzan, Academy for Educational Development

"Deconstructing and Reconstructing the Organization: A Technology Shift into the Twenty-First Century." Robert C. Rock, American Society of Clinical Pathologists

"What Happens When Everybody Is Trained in Teamwork? A Case Study." Theresa M. Somrak, American Society of Clinical Pathologists

"Culture Shift: Managing Change in the Hospital Setting." Judy Schueler, University of Chicago Hospitals

"Meaningful Measurement: Tools for Action Plans and Follow-Up." Donna Surges Tatum, University of Chicago

Respondent: William P. Fisher, Jr., Louisiana State University Medical Center

---

3440   12:30-1:45 p.m.   Conf 4H   Fourth Floor   Chicago Hilton

CONVERSATION ANALYSIS DATA SESSION

Sponsor: Language and Social Interaction Division

Panelists: Phillip J. Glenn, Southern Illinois University, Carbondale
Charlotte M. Jones, Carroll College
Daniel P. Modaff, Ohio University
Jeffrey D. Robinson, University of California, Los Angeles

Facilitated by the panel, attendees will discuss possible claims that can be advanced about a segment of videotaped data by employing conversation analytic methods.

3441   12:30-1:45 p.m.   Conf 4I   Fourth Floor   Chicago Hilton

TELEVISION AESTHETICS AND IDEOLOGY: MODELS FOR CRITICISM AND THE CLASSROOM

Sponsor: Media Forum Series

Panelists: Brenton J. Malin, University of Iowa
Chul Heo, University of Iowa

3442   12:30-1:45 p.m.   Conf 4J   Fourth Floor   Chicago Hilton

VISUALIZING *LOLITA*: EXPLORATIONS OF INTERTEXTUALITY

Sponsor: Visual Communication Commission
Chair: Richard L. Ward, University of South Alabama
   "Novel to Film, Frame to Window: *Lolita* Manifested in Text and Image." Ken Burke, Mills
      College
   "*Lolita*: Visual Representation of Seduction." Gail J. Chryslee, University of South Alabama,
      Michelle Moreau, University of South Alabama
   "Two Visions of *Lolita*: The Visual Styles of Kubrick and Lyne." Richard L. Ward, University
      of South Alabama

Respondent: Sharon L. Bracci, University of North Carolina, Greensboro

3443   12:30-1:45 p.m.   Conf 4K   Fourth Floor   Chicago Hilton

WHEN THE FABRIC TEARS I: THE EXPERIENCE AND MANAGEMENT OF JEALOUSY, UNCERTAINTY, AND EXPECTANCY VIOLATIONS IN CLOSE RELATIONSHIPS

Sponsor: Interpersonal Communication Division
Chair: Denise H. Solomon, University of Wisconsin
   "Understanding the Role of Intrapersonal Uncertainty in the Experience and Expression of
      Jealousy in Cross-Sex Friendships." Jennifer Bevan, University of Delaware
   "The Role of Intimacy and Relational Uncertainty in the Experience of Romantic Jealousy."
      Leanne K. Knobloch, University of Wisconsin, Madison, Denise H. Solomon, University
      of Wisconsin
   "Toward a Model of Jealousy Experience and Expression: Associations Between Threat,
      Emotion, Cognition, Goals, Communication, and Relational Consequences." Laura K.
      Guerrero, Arizona State University, Melanie R. Trost, Arizona State University, Stephen
      M. Yoshimura, Arizona State University
   "A Preliminary Test of a Model of Information-Seeking Following Violations in Close
      Relationships." Walid A. Afifi, Penn State University, Judith L. Weiner, Penn State
      University, Josephine W. Lee, Penn State University

3444   12:30-1:45 p.m.   Conf 4L   Fourth Floor   Chicago Hilton

ALTERNATIVE STRATEGIES AND APPROACHES FOR TEACHING PUBLIC RELATIONS

Sponsor: Public Relations Division
Chair: Charles A. Lubbers, Kansas State University
   "Teaching 'Themeing' in Public Relations Message Design and Campaigns." Donald J.
      Rybacki, Northern Michigan University, Karyn C. Rybacki, Northern Michigan University
   "Stimulating Active Learning and Creative Problem Solving in Public Relations Courses."
      Cynthia E. King, California State University, Fullerton
   "Linking Rhetoric, Ideology and Public Relations: Teaching Public Relations Campaigns
      from a Rhetorical Perspective." Michele A. Najor, Wayne State University
   "Developing Integrated Communications Courses and Programs: Definitely Coloring
      Outside the Lines." Mark P. McElreath, Towson State University

3445   12:30-1:45 p.m.   Conf 4M   Fourth Floor   Chicago Hilton

THE DIVERSE FACES OF THEORY DEVELOPMENT

Sponsor: Organizational Communication Division
Chair: Cynthia A. Irizarry, Hofstra University
   "Facultative Identity: An Integrative Solution to the Tension Between the Socially
      Constructed and Essential Conceptions of Identity for Individuals and Organizations."
      Brian Sandine, University of Colorado, Boulder

"Organizational Identification, Image, and Change: A Reconceptualization of Dutton, Dukerich, and Harquail's (1994) Model." Jolie C. Fontenot, University of Texas, Austin
"Stumbling Toward Ontology in Organizational Communication Theorizing." Kelby K. Halone, Clemson University
"Surmounting Obstacles to Theory Development: The Need for Critical Realism in Organizational Communication." Timothy R. Kuhn, Arizona State University

Respondent: Steven R. Corman, Arizona State University

3447   12:30-1:45 p.m.   Pullman Board Rm   Fourth Floor   Chicago Hilton

PEACE AND CONFLICT COMMUNICATION COMMISSION BUSINESS MEETING

Sponsor: Peace and Conflict Communication Commission

3449   12:30-1:45 p.m.   Conf 5B   Fifth Floor   Chicago Hilton

CRITICAL ISSUES FOR SOCIALIZATION AND TRAINING MASTER'S LEVEL COMMUNICATION GTAs

Sponsor: Basic Course Division
Chair: Cheri J. Simonds, Illinois State University

Panelists: Carol S. Cawyer, University of North Texas
          Scott A. Myers, Creighton University
          K. David Roach, Texas Tech University

Panelists will share results of a nation-wide survey of basic course directors as well as share effective components of their own programs. Audience discussion will follow.

3451   12:30-1:45 p.m.   Conf 5D   Fifth Floor   Chicago Hilton

TEACHER AS COACH AND MENTOR: A DISCUSSION OF EFFECTIVE TEACHING TECHNIQUES WITH ROBERT C. ROWLAND

Sponsor: Teachers on Teaching
Chair: Kelly M. McDonald, Western Washington University

Panelists: Jeffrey W. Jarman, Wichita State University
          Kelly M. McDonald, Western Washington University
          Robert C. Rowland, University of Kansas

This discussion will center on effective teaching techniques of Professor Rowland. In exploring the teacher as "coach," panelists will investigate traditional expectations for teaching.

3452   12:30-1:45 p.m.   Conf 5E   Fifth Floor   Chicago Hilton

CHALLENGING BOUNDARIES IN RHETORICAL AND COMMUNICATION THEORY

Sponsor: Rhetorical and Communication Theory Division
Chair: Gerard A. Hauser, University of Colorado, Boulder
    "Communication in the Conversation of Disciplines*." Robert T. Craig, University of Colorado, Boulder
    "Misrepresenting Aristotle's Heirs: Rhetorical Scholarship on Gadamer's *Phronesis**." John Arthos, SUNY, Fredonia
    "Critical Rhetoric: Modernist Assumption, Postmodern Quagmire: A Tentative Beginning." Sherry R. Shepler, Wayne State University
    "Foundations Like Flowing Water: The Influence of Ancient Rhetoric on Nieztsche's Perspectival and Anti-Metaphysical Turn." Ned Vankevich, Eastern Nazarene College

*Top Three Paper in Rhetoric and Communication Theory

3453   12:30-1:45 p.m.   Conf 5F   Fifth Floor   Chicago Hilton

KEY COMMUNICATION CONCEPTS FOR THE TWENTY-FIRST CENTURY: A ROUNDTABLE DISCUSSION

Sponsor: Commission on Communication in the Future
Chair: Lance A. Strate, Fordham University
   "'The Medium is the Message' and 'Oscillation'." Edward Lee Lamoureux, Bradley University
   "Organizational Communication, Learning, and Design: A Model for Integration." Sandra L. Herndon, Ithaca College
   "Media Literacy." Nancy J. Hoar, Western New England College
   "Spirit." Raymond Gozzi, Ithaca College

3454   12:30-1:45 p.m.   Conf 5G   Fifth Floor   Chicago Hilton

THE AGE OF ELECTRONIC INFORMATION AND ITS IMPACT ON HIGH SCHOOL FORENSIC COMPETITION: WHERE ARE THE LINES BEING DRAWN?

Sponsor: National Federation Interscholastic Speech & Debate Association
Chairs: Ruth E. Kay, Detroit Country Day School
         Treva Dayton, National Federation Interscholastic Speech and Debate Association

Panelists: Jana M. Riggins, University of Texas
           Richard E. Edwards, Baylor University
           Timothy A. Borchers, Moorhead State University

The panel will address the impact electronic media is having on high school forensic competition in interpretation events, policy debate and public speaking, including the issues of ethics and the evolving rules governing speech and debate contests.

3455   12:30-1:45 p.m.   Conf 5H   Fifth Floor   Chicago Hilton

EXPLANATORY FACTORS IN COMMUNICATION APPREHENSION AND SHYNESS

Sponsor: Communication Apprehension & Avoidance Commission
Chair: Chia-Fang Hsu, Washington State University
   "Actual and Preferred Casual Attributions of Shyness." Brent K. Pollitt, California State University, Fresno, Vincent L. Bloom, California State University, Fresno
   "Pavlovian Temperament and Reinforcement History as Predictors of Communication Apprehension: An Empirical Test of the Communibiological Paradigm." Chris R. Sawyer, Tarrant County Junior College, Ralph R. Behnke, Texas Christian University
   "Actual and Preferred Causal Attributions of Communication Apprehension." Brent K. Pollitt, California State University, Fresno, Vincent L. Bloom, California State University, Fresno
   "The Effect of Self-Construals on Communication Apprehension Towards Informative and Persuasive Public Speaking." Allison D. Hu, University of Hawaii, Manoa, Norman C. H. Wong, University of Hawaii, Manoa

---

3456   12:30-1:45 p.m.   Conf 5I   Fifth Floor   Chicago Hilton

COGNITION UBER ALLES?

Sponsor: Intrapersonal Communication/Social Cognition Commission
Chair: Susanne Jones, Arizona State University
   "Looking Below the Surface of Attitude Expression: Integrating Accessibility Measures and Political Communication." R. Kirkland Ahern, University of Pennsylvania, David J. Dutwin, University of Pennsylvania
   "The Role of Vision in Visual Communication." Shannon Skarphol Kaml, University of Minnesota

Saturday

"Socializing the Theory of Reasoned Action." Eric B. Meiners, Michigan State University, William D. Crano, Michigan State University

"The Importance of Cognition and Emotion in the Comforting Process." Susanne Jones, Arizona State University

"Imagined Interactions (II): More Than a Decade of Research and Current Developments." James M. Honeycutt, Louisiana State University, Sherry G. Ford, Louisiana State University

Respondent: Janet R. Meyer, Kent State University

3458   12:30-3:15 p.m.   Lake Ontario   Eighth Floor   Chicago Hilton

SHORT COURSE #21. INCORPORATING TECHNOLOGY INTO THE INTERCULTURAL COMMUNICATION COURSE

Sponsor: Short Courses

Instructors: Lisa A. Stefani, Grossmont College
Itsuo Shirono, Meikai University

Fee required. See complete Short Course descriptions elsewhere in the program.

3459   12:30-3:15 p.m.   Lake Michigan   Eighth Floor   Chicago Hilton

SHORT COURSE #22. RACIALIZING COMMUNICATION: TEACHING INTERRACIAL COMMUNICATION ON THE UNDERGRADUATE AND GRADUATE LEVELS

Sponsor: Short Courses

Instructors: Tina M. Harris, University of Georgia
Colleen A. Coleman, Bowling Green State University
Jennifer F. Wood, Bowling Green State University

Fee required. See complete Short Course descriptions elsewhere in the program.

3461   12:30-1:45 p.m.   Lake Erie   Eighth Floor   Chicago Hilton

REACHING ACROSS THE LINES FOR HELP: THE COLONIZED ASPECTS OF A DOCTORAL EDUCATION IN MEXICO AND THE NEED FOR HELP FROM U.S. LATINA/O SCHOLARS

Sponsor: La Raza Caucus
Chair: M. Cristina Gonzalez, Arizona State University

"Morosidad in Mexico: Cultural Reasons Why Mexicans Can't Say No." Luz Elvia Rascon, Escuela Libre de Psicologia, A.C.

"Forcing the Raramuri into the Lines of the Urban Mexico: Aspects of Forced Cultural and Linguistic Accommodation and Assimilation." Jesus Vaca Cortes, Escuela Libre de Psicologia, A.C.

"Mexican Women's Attitudes Toward Their Bodies: When Worrying About Your Own Health Is a Bad Thing." Rosario Valdes Caraveo, Escuela Libre de Psicologia, A.C.

"Borderland Viewpoints: How Exposure to U.S. Scholars in the Classroom Colors the Experience with Mexican Higher Education." Pedro Barrera Valdivia, Escuela Libre de Psicologia, A.C.

Respondents: Francisco Cabrer, Universidad Nacional Autonoma de Mexico
M. Cristina Gonzalez, Arizona State University

3462   12:30-1:45 p.m.   Essex Court   Second Floor   Essex Inn

COLORING OUTSIDE THE LINES OF TRADITIONAL APOLOGIA

Sponsor: Religious Communication Association
Chair: David C. Klope, Trinity Christian College

"Extending the Second Order Ideograph: Monica Lewinsky as the 'Family Values' Bookend of Clinton's Presidency." Loren O. Murfield, Eastern College

"Political Confession as a Perlocutionary Act: An Interpretation of the Public Response to Clinton's August 17th Address." Ronald E. Lee, University of Nebraska, Karen King Lee, University of Nebraska

"President Clinton's Apologia at the White House Prayer Breakfast." Joseph R. Blaney, Northwest Missouri State University

"William Jefferson Clinton's Rhetoric of Self-Defense in the Monica Lewinsky Scandal: 'Coloring Outside the Lines' of Traditional Apologia." Mary A. Brockett, Hiram College, Nancy E. Mitchell, Kent State University, Kim S. Phipps, Messiah College

"Unanswered Prayers: A Study of Apologia of God in the Matter of Prayer." Dann L. Pierce, University of Portland, Bohn D. Lattin, University of Portland

Respondent: David C. Klope, Trinity Christian College

3463	12:30-1:45 p.m.	**Windsor Court**	**Second Floor**	**Essex Inn**

SHIFTS AND SHADES BETWEEN THE LINES: FEMINISM AND VIGILANCE

Sponsor: Ethnography Division
Chair: Eric E. Peterson, University of Maine, Orono

"My Life as a Lacuna." Nathan E. Stormer, University of Maine, Orono

"Sleeping On/With It: Narrative Reflections on Feminism (Hetero) Sexuality, and Self-Surveillance." Mary F. Keehner, Purdue University

"Raising Eyebrows and Raising Children Raising Questions: Inspection and Introspection in Feminist Parenting." Amber E. Kinser, East Tennessee State University

"Imagining an Impossibility of How to Force an Identity into Existence." Shiv Ganesh, Purdue University

Respondent: Eric E. Peterson, University of Maine, Orono

3464	12:30-1:45 p.m.	**Buckingham Court**	**Second Floor**	**Essex Inn**

TOP STUDENT PAPERS IN AMERICAN STUDIES

Sponsor: American Studies Commission
Chair: Michael W. Barberich, University of Pittsburgh

"Cultural Breakdown on the Plains: Subverting Crow Dog's Tribe by Controlling Its Politics and Economy." Deborah J. Clark, Howard University

"Memory's Rise and Fall: Armistice Day in America." Andrew J. Gooding, University of Illinois, Urbana-Champaign

"The Magic of Whoopi: Politics and Difference within Mainstream American Cinema*." Colette S. Jung, Purdue University

"Speech, Silence, and *Young Mr. Lincoln*." Brian J. Snee, Rochester Institute of Technology

Respondent: Janna Jones, University of South Florida

*Debut Paper

3465	12:30-1:45 p.m.	**Park East Walk**	**Second Floor**	**Essex Inn**

RHETORICAL THEORY AND BEYOND: TEACHING KENNETH BURKE IN . . .

Sponsor: Kenneth Burke Society, NCA Branch
Chair: Julie D. Phillips, Purdue University

"Complete and Total Identification: Teaching Kenneth Burke in the Rhetorical Theory Course." Bryan Crable, Villanova University

"Language and World: Teaching Kenneth Burke in the Introductory Honors Course." Joy M. Cypher, West Chester State University

"Is that Kenneth Burke Rolling Over in His Grave? . . : Teaching Kenneth Burke in Public Relations." Michael L. Kent, SUNY, Fredonia

"Learning Burke Through Burke's Letters: Teaching Kenneth Burke in the Communication Theory Course." David G. Levasseur, West Chester University

Saturday

"The Body and Universal Experience: Teaching Burke in Women's Studies." Julie D. Phillips, Purdue University

---

3466   12:30-1:45 p.m.   Cohn Rm   Second Floor   Spertus Institute

RHETORIC, SCIENCE, AND HISTORY IN THE MODERN WORLD

Sponsor: American Association for Rhetoric of Science & Technology
Chair: Charles E. Morris, Denison University
"The Art of Forgetting: John W. Draper and the Rhetorical Invention of History." Bradford J. Vivian, Penn State University
"The Rhetoric of E.O. Wilson's *Consilience*: Modeling the Future on the Dreams of a Scientific Past." Leah M. Ceccarelli, University of Washington
"'No Neutral Ground': Frederick Douglass and the Politics of Science." Stephen H. Browne, Penn State University

Respondent: John A. Campbell, University of Memphis

3467   12:30-1:45 p.m.   Krensky Rm   Second Floor   Spertus Institute

AMERICAN LEGAL EDUCATION'S IMPACT UPON LEGAL ARGUMENTATION

Sponsor: Communication and Law Commission
Chair: Teresa M. Rosado, Zagnoli McEvoy Foley Ltd.
"Rhetorical Legal Education in American Law Schools." Lisa A. Perry, Minnesota State University, Mankato
"Langdellian Legal Oratory: The Consequences of the Case Law Method For Courtroom Argumentation." Terence S. Morrow, Gustavus Adolphus College
"Framing the Law: The Press, the FBI and Minority Portrayals of the Incident at Waco." Phillip A. Voight, Gustavus Adolphus College

Respondent: Teresa M. Rosado, Zagnoli McEvoy Foley Ltd.

3471   12:30-1:45 p.m.   Rm 906   Ninth Floor   Spertus Institute

INEBRIATION, POLARIZATION AND INAUGURATION

Sponsor: American Society for the History of Rhetoric
Chair: Robert W. Cape Jr., Austin College
"Political Spectacle and Presidential Vulgarity: Andrew Johnson's 1866 Swing Around the Circle." Angela G. Ray, University of Minnesota
"Bryan's Cross of Gold Speech: The Rhetoric of Division." William D. Harpine, University of Akron
"Justifying Divorce: Jefferson Davis' Confederate Inaugural Address as an Occasional Rhetorical Hybrid." Kevin M. Minch, University of Kansas

Respondent: Michael R. Schliessmann, South Dakota State University

---

3472   12:30-1:45 p.m.   Rm 907   Ninth Floor   Spertus Institute

CEDA/NDT POLICY DEBATE TOPIC PAPERS: 2000-2001

Sponsor: Cross Examination Debate Association
Chair: Greg Achten, Pepperdine University

Each contributor will present the topic area by discussing the following issues: rationale for topic area, possible affirmative positions, possible negative positions, possible wordings of resolutions and a bibliography. These Topic Area Papers will be on topic areas suggested for inclusion on the Topic Ballot for 2000-2001. All members of the debate community are encouraged to contribute to this discussion.

| 3473 | 12:30-1:45 p.m. | Rm 908 | Ninth Floor | Spertus Institute |

UNDERSTANDING THE INVISIBLE BARRIERS TO DIVERSITY IN THE FORENSICS COMMUNITY

Sponsor: Phi Rho Pi
Chair: Cynthia E. Dewar, City College of San Francisco
   "Judicial Activism in Policy Debate: The Ethics of Intervention." K. C. Boylan, Sacramento City Community College
   "Interpreters' Theatre: A Forum for Marginalized Voices." Joe Corcoran, Santa Rosa Junior College
   "From the Back of the Room: An Examination of Sensitivity in Forensics." Lisa M. Kawamura, California Polytechnic State University, San Luis Obispo
   "Oral Interpretation: Listening for and Hearing the Voice of the 'Other'." Cynthia Valdivia-Sutherland, Butte Community College
   "The Margins are Not a Desert: Voices, Voicing, and the Forensics Environment." Kristina L. Schriver, California State University, Chico

Respondent: Kimo Ah Yun, California State University, Sacramento

| 3474 | 12:30-1:45 p.m. | Auditorium | Second Floor | Spertus Institute |

CREATING PERFORMANCE SYNERGY

Sponsor: Theatre Division
Chair: Christie A. Logan, California State University, Northridge
   "Connecting with the Audience: Augusto Boal's Techniques." David T. Kottenstette, Metropolitan State College of Denver
   "Connecting with the Ensemble: Building an Effective Social System." Marilyn A. Hetzel, Metropolitan State College of Denver
   "Connecting with the Interior Self: Psychological Techniques." M. Lee Potts, University of Colorado, Boulder

2:00 p.m.

| 3506 | 2:00-3:15 p.m. | Continental BR A | Lobby Level | Chicago Hilton |

COMPETITIVE PAPERS IN CRITICAL EXPLORATIONS OF POLITICAL AND ECONOMIC MEDIA ISSUES

Sponsor: Mass Communication Division
Chair: Chris Schroll, Wayne State University
   "Deciphering Pocahontas: Unpackaging the Commodified Native American Woman." Kent A. Ono, University of California, Davis, Derek T. Buescher, University of Utah
   "The Strategic Marketing Value of the Internet for Mass Media." Sylvia Chan-Olmsted, University of Florida
   "Talking in Golden Tongues: An Economic Analysis of The Rush Limbaugh Show and The Howard Stern Show." Marjorie Lynne Yambor, Michigan State University
   "Global AIDS/HIV News Narratives: Eliciting a Response from Reporters and Stakeholders." Nilanjana Bardhan, Southern Illinois University, Carbondale

Respondent: Leonard Shyles, Villanova University

| 3507 | 2:00-3:15 p.m. | Continental BR B | Lobby Level | Chicago Hilton |

SERVICE-LEARNING AND TECHNOLOGY: ENCOURAGING COMMUNICATION STUDENTS AND FACULTY TO "COLOR OUTSIDE THE LECTURE LINES"

Sponsor: Human Communication and Technology Commission
Chair: Sue M. Wildermuth, University of Minnesota, Minneapolis

Saturday

"Cyber Buddies: A Creative and Colorful Way to Integrate Interpersonal Communication, Service-Learning, and Computer-Mediated Interaction into the Classroom." Sue M. Wildermuth, University of Minnesota, Minneapolis

"Artificial Intelligence and Service-Learning in the Communication Classroom: Encouraging Students to 'Put Their Heads Together' to Help Those Less Fortunate." Ryan D. Mills, Miami University

"Using Technology to Facilitate Service-Learning: A Case Study from an Environmental Communication Classroom." Micheal R. Vickery, Alma College

"Communication Technology in a Service-Learning Journalism Course: A 'Do It Yourself' Guide." Eleanor M. Novek, Monmouth University

---

3508   2:00-3:15 p.m.   Continental BR C   Lobby Level   Chicago Hilton

HEGEMONY, IDEOLOGY, AND THE DISCURSIVE MANAGEMENT OF CRISIS

Sponsor: Critical and Cultural Studies Division
Chair: Lawrence Grossberg, University of North Carolina, Chapel Hill
    "The Rhetoric of Capital in Crisis: Managing the Asian Economic Collapse." Kevin J. Ayotte, University of Pittsburgh
    "Stabilizing Cold War Fear: The Rosenbergs and the Maintenance of Crisis." Gretchen Soderlund, University of Illinois, Urbana-Champaign
    "Producing Panics: Television, Cultural Studies, and the Mass Audience." Carol Stabile, University of Pittsburgh

Respondent: Jonathan E. Sterne, University of Illinois, Urbana-Champaign

---

3510   2:00-3:15 p.m.   Grand Ballroom   Second Floor   Chicago Hilton

EXCESSIVE PERFORMANCES

Sponsor: Performance Studies Division
Chair: Stacy E. Wolf, George Washington University
    "Over the Top and Everything Wrong." Terry Galloway, Independent Artist
    "Losing My Dirty Mind: Epilepsy, Autobiography, and Excess." Andrea T. Wagner, University of Pennsylvania
    "Performative Transvestism: An Ex-Drag-Vaganza Celebrating Largess, or Enlarge! Enliven! Enlighten! An Info-Training in Drag." Bud Coleman, University of Colorado, Boulder
    "Excessively Jewish, Excessively Queer: Thoughts on Women and Musicals." Stacy E. Wolf, George Washington University

---

3514   2:00-3:15 p.m.   Boulevard A   Second Floor   Chicago Hilton

COLORING OUTSIDE THE LINES: TEXTBOOK DEVELOPMENT—TRADITION VERSUS INNOVATION

Sponsor: Challenging Boundaries Series
Chair: Mark V. Redmond, Iowa State University

Panelists: Philip M. Backlund, Central Washington University
          Steven A. Beebe, Southwest Texas State University
          Cynthia Berryman-Fink, University of Cincinnati
          Mark V. Redmond, Iowa State University
          Denise Ann Vrchota, Iowa State University

A panel and audience discussion on the impact of textbooks in interpersonal, small group, and organizational communication, public speaking and special topics coloring outside the lines.

3515   2:00-3:15 p.m.   Boulevard B   Second Floor   Chicago Hilton

OUT OF BOUNDS: AN INTERACTIVE DIALOGUE ABOUT THE ROLE OF CULTURE IN DOCTOR-PATIENT INTERACTIONS

Sponsor: NCA First Vice President
Chair: Nagesh Rao, Ohio University
 "Doctor-Patient Interaction in the Context of Culture: An Empathic Response." Kenneth Tuefel, M.D., Texas
 "Culturally Sensitive Care by Medical Providers: Case Studies from Minnesota and New Mexico." Everett M. Rogers, University of New Mexico, Corinne Shefner-Rogers, Private Consultant, New Mexico
 "Using Personal Video Cameras to Develop New Frames of Reference About Doctor-Patient Interactions." Gregory Makoul, Northwestern University
 "How Do We Deal with Culturally Diverse Patients?: Exploratory Data from Medical Students and Doctors in the United States, Brazil, and India." Nagesh Rao, Ohio University

3516   2:00-3:15 p.m.   Boulevard C   Second Floor   Chicago Hilton

TRADITION, MODERNITY, AND BEYOND: MEDIA CONSTRUCTIONS OF THE NATION

Sponsor: International & Intercultural Communication Division
Chair: Marwan M. Kraidy, University of North Dakota
 "Of Tacos, Amigos and Fiesta: Mexican Cultural Identity Constructed as the Other." Ute Sartorius Kraidy, University of North Dakota
 "Redefining Turkish National Identity Through Radio and Music." Ece Algan, Ohio University
 "Virtually Contested Constructions: The Nation in Burma Webspace." Lisa B. Brooten, Ohio University
 "Markets, Morals, and Mediations: Television and Cultural Identity in Lebanon." Marwan M. Kraidy, University of North Dakota

Respondent: Marwan M. Kraidy, University of North Dakota

3519   2:00-3:15 p.m.   Astoria   Third Floor   Chicago Hilton

SHIFTING FORMATIONS, PUBLIC CULTURE, AND RHETORICAL STRATEGIES OF NATION

Sponsor: Public Address Division
Chair: Dilip P. Gaonkar, Northwestern University
 "Rhetorical (Dis)Embodiments of the Nation: Counter-Memory and Strategies of Reversal in John Dos Passos' 1919." Christopher Kamrath, Northwestern University
 "Detecting Knowledges: Rhetorical Strategy and the Politics of Film Genre." Shawn Shimpach, New York University
 "Dying to Get In: Tonic Rhetoric in the New York Times Obituaries." Robert McCarthy, University of Chicago
 "Aestheticizing the Body Marked by Muscles and Maternity: Public Pregnancies, Black Female Sexuality, and Citizenship." Kyra L. Pearson, University of Iowa

Respondent: Dilip P. Gaonkar, Northwestern University

3521   2:00-3:15 p.m.   Williford A   Third Floor   Chicago Hilton

BLACK WOMAN AS COMMUNICATIVE MOSAIC: SPEAKING IN TON(GU)ES OF LIBERATION?

Sponsors: African American Communication & Culture Commission

Saturday

Feminist and Women Studies Division
Chair: Melbourne S. Cummings, Howard University
  "Her Story: Race(ing) the Myths and Metaphors of the African-Descended Woman." Diane
    A. Forbes, Howard University
  "Grandmother as Ancestral Memory: Expressions of Structural Agency Within Oppressive
    and Hegemonic Social Structures." Omowale T. Elson, Howard University
  "African American Female Small Group Communication: An Exploratory Analysis." Laura
    K. Dorsey, Howard University

Respondent: William J. Starosta, Howard University

3522   2:00-3:15 p.m.   Williford B   Third Floor   Chicago Hilton

LANGUAGE, RHETORIC, AND POLITICAL IDENTITY

Sponsor: Political Communication Division
Chair: Maureen C. Minielli, Saint Joseph's College
  "Reconstructions of Race, Religion, and National Identity in the Discourse of
    Contemporary White Supremicists." Jody M. Roy, Ripon College, Matthew W. Belling,
    Ripon College
  "Political Discourses on Identity: Opposition and Alternatives in Lesbian/Gay Legislative
    Advocacy." Ralph R. Smith, Southwest Missouri State University
  "Identification for Purpose: The Founding of the Students for a Democratic Society." David
    C. Deifell, University of Iowa
  "Back to the Wall: Bill Clinton and the Rhetoric of Investiture." Brian J. Snee, Rochester
    Institute of Technology
  "Populism, Political Legitimacy and Civic Community: The 'Outsider' Public Character of
    Lamar Alexander." Stephen A. Klien, Boston University

3523   2:00-3:15 p.m.   Williford C   Third Floor   Chicago Hilton

MEET BLONDE VENUS, G.I. JANE, FEMALE SLEUTHS AND, OF COURSE, MS. McBEAL

Sponsor: Feminist and Women Studies Division
Chair: Lynn Cockett, Rutgers University
  "Blonde Venus: Feminist Coding in the Cinematic Depiction of Single Motherhood*." Lisa
    R. Barry, Albion College
  "A Female Hero in an Action Film: Transformation Through G.I. Jane?" Deidra D.
    Donmoyer, Bowling Green State University
  "Differential Detecting: Female Sleuths Disrupting a Masculine Tradition." Grace A.
    Giorgio, University of Illinois, Urbana-Champaign
  "The Good, the Bad and the Ally: A Look at Subjectivity, Sexuality and Masculine Power in
    Prime Time's *Ally McBeal*." Danna E. Prather, University of Iowa, Brian Lain, University
    of Iowa

Respondent: Kathleen C. Haspel, University of Denver

*Top Student Paper

3524   2:00-3:15 p.m.   Marquette   Third Floor   Chicago Hilton

"OH, TO SEE WHAT THE FUTURE HOLDS!": SHOWCASING AFRICAN AMERICAN GRADUATE STUDENT RESEARCH

Sponsor: Black Caucus
Chair: Mark P. Orbe, Western Michigan University
  "Cultural Diversity in the Workplace: How Do African Americans Define Success." Denise
    Gates, Western Michigan University
  "The Superficiality of Inter-Ethnic Communication: A Socio-Historical Approach*."
    Jacqueline James-Hughes, Howard University
  "The Image of Africa in the U.S. American Press: A Critical Analysis of *The New York Times*
    and *The Washington Post*, 1996-1999*." M. H. Sani, Western Michigan University

"Intercultural Features in *The New York Times*: A Corpus Linguistics Probe." Ruth A. Seymour, Wayne State University

Respondent: Jeffrey L. Woodyard, Stetson University

*Student Debut Paper

3526   2:00-3:15 p.m.   PDR 1   Third Floor   Chicago Hilton

TOP FOUR PAPERS IN SPIRITUAL COMMUNICATION: THEORY, CRITICISM AND PEDAGOGY

Sponsor: Spiritual Communication Commission
Chair: Warren G. Koch, George Fox University
    "Karl Jaspers: On Cipher, Myth, and Existenz." Ronald D. Gordon, University of Hawaii, Hilo
    "Spirituality in *Daughters in the Dust*: Assessing the Potentials of an Oral Cinematic Form." Warren G. Koch, George Fox University
    "A Jungian Analysis of Spirituality in Twelve-Step Conference Narratives." Maggie A. Wills, Fairfield University
    "Taoism and Pedagogy: An Application of Taoism to Contemporary Communication Pedagogy." Sydne E. Kasle, Syracuse University

---

3529   2:00-3:15 p.m.   PDR 4   Third Floor   Chicago Hilton

LOOKING BEYOND CONVENTIONAL WISDOM OF COMMUNICATION AND EMPLOYMENT INTERVIEWS

Sponsor: Applied Communication Division
Chair: William G. Kirkwood, East Tennessee State University
    "'Tell Me, Can You be Vicious'?: Implications of 'Real World' Interviews on Interpersonal Communication and Interviewing Training." Deborah Borisoff, New York University
    "Cognitive Strategies and the Prediction of Theft in Pre-Employment Integrity Measures: A Comparison of Structured Interviews versus Paper-and-Pencil Formats." John C. Hollwitz, Loyola College, Baltimore, Donna R. Pawlowski, Creighton University
    "Do I 'Fit' Here? Exploring Importance of Candidate-Recruiter Perceptions of Shared Values Communicated During the Screening Interview." Janet R. Bodenman, Bloomsburg University

Respondent: Steven M. Ralston, East Tennessee State University

---

3530   2:00-3:15 p.m.   PDR 5   Third Floor   Chicago Hilton

NATIONAL FORENSIC ASSOCIATION BUSINESS MEETING

Sponsor: National Forensic Association

3531   2:00-3:15 p.m.   PDR 6   Third Floor   Chicago Hilton

PHILOSOPHICAL APPROACHES TO INDIVIDUAL EVENTS INSTRUCTION: BEYOND PAINT-BY-NUMBER PERFORMANCE

Sponsor: Argumentation and Forensics Division
Chair: Andrew F. Wood, San Jose State University
    "Playing to Win: Pragmatic Coaching and the Development of Competitive Skills for Real Life." Bonnie L. Clark, St. Petersburg Junior College
    "Directing Individual Events: A Classical Perspective." Robert L. Frank, Berry College
    "All the Forensic World's a Stage: A Dramatistic Approach to Forensic Instruction." Randolph Richardson, Berry College
    "Individual Events Instruction: Lessons from Feminist Scholarship." Christina L. Moss, Young Harris College, Karen L. Holmes, Berry College
    "Fear and Loathing in Forensics: The View from Postmodern Suburbia." B. Keith Murphy, Fort Valley State University

Respondent: Thomas A. Workman, University of Nebraska, Lincoln

---

3533   2:00-3:15 p.m.   Conf 4A   Fourth Floor   Chicago Hilton

USING CRISIS TO IMPROVE PUBLIC RELATIONSHIPS

Sponsor: Public Relations Division
Chair: Maureen Taylor, Rutgers University
  "The Internet as a Crisis Communication Tool." Danielle Perry, Rutgers University
  "Crisis and the Internet: An Opportunity to Build Dialogic Relationships." Michael L. Kent,
    SUNY, Fredonia
  "Crisis Communication: Conflict Resolution and Media Relations." Jessica Barnes, Rutgers
    University

Respondent: Maureen Taylor, Rutgers University

3534   2:00-3:15 p.m.   Conf 4B   Fourth Floor   Chicago Hilton

THE RHETORIC OF GOD'S VOICE: FROM LITTLE BOYS AND BURNING BUSHES IN POPULAR AMERICAN CINEMA/A MEDIA FORUM

Sponsor: Religious Communication Association
Chair: Marc T. Newman, Palomar College
  "'...And a Little Child Shall Lead Them': Burkean Rhetoric in the Film, *Simon Birch*." Erick
    J. Roebuck, Biola University
  "God's Voice in the Burning Bush: Archetypal Metaphors in the Rhetoric of the Film, *The
    Prince of Egypt*." Todd V. Lewis, Biola University

Respondent: Marc T. Newman, Palomar College

3535   2:00-3:15 p.m.   Conf 4C   Fourth Floor   Chicago Hilton

FEMINISTS AND TECHNOLOGY: VOICES AND REPRESENTATION

Sponsor: Feminist and Women Studies Division
  "Feminists and Technology: Critiques of Technological Imaginary in Relation to 'Other'
    Cyberfeminisms." Radhika Gajjala, Bowling Green State University
  "Women, Technology, and the United Nations: An Analysis of the Recommendations of
    the 1995 Platform for Action." Barbara S. Monfils, University of Wisconsin, Whitewater
  "Feminists and Technology: The Electronic Panopticon and Around-the-Clock
    Accountability." Paige P. Edley, Bowling Green State University
  "Feminists and Technology: Cultural Identity." Lynda D. Dixon, Bowling Green State
    University
  "Technologies of the 'Nation': Media Spectacle, Transnationalism, and Princess Diana."
    Raka Shome, University of California, Davis

3537   2:00-3:15 p.m.   Conf 4E   Fourth Floor   Chicago Hilton

MEDIA AND POLITICS

Sponsor: Political Communication Division
Chair: Robert H. Gobetz, University of Indianapolis
  "How Television News Framed the First Presidential Debate of 1996." April I. Franklin,
    University of Oklahoma, James S. O'Geary, University of Oklahoma
  "A Content Analysis of 1996 Primary and General Election Ad Watches." John C. Tedesco,
    Virginia Tech University, Lori M. McKinnon, University of Alabama
  "Effects of Media Exposure on Political Processing." Todd C. Trautman, University of
    Illinois, Urbana-Champaign
  "A Collision on the Dance Floor: The Political Communication of George Bush." William T.
    Horner, University of Texas, Austin, M. Heather Carver, University of Texas, Austin
  "My Boss, Me and Them: Unraveling the Congressional Press Secretary's Relationships
    with the Member of Congress and the Media." Edward J. Downes, Boston University

| 3538 | 2:00-3:15 p.m. | Conf 4F | Fourth Floor | Chicago Hilton |

COLORING OUTSIDE THE LINES: THE ROLE OF THE COMMUNICATION DEPARTMENT IN THE COMMUNITY

Sponsor: Community College Section
Chair: John W. Griggs, Glendale Community College
  "Foundations for the College in the Community." Tessa Martinez Pollack, Glendale Community College
  "Service-Learning: Bringing the Classroom to the Community." Helena R. Mays, Glendale Community College
  "Teaching Public Speaking in the Elementary School." Pamela J. Joraanstad, Glendale Community College
  "Coloring Outside the Lines: The Communication Department and Its Broader Community." James W. Reed, Glendale Community College

Respondent: Mark Joraanstad, Horizon Elementary School, Arizona

| 3539 | 2:00-3:15 p.m. | Conf 4G | Fourth Floor | Chicago Hilton |

CROSS-CULTURAL ANALYSIS OF LANGUAGE, COMMUNICATION ADAPTATION, AND IDENTITY IN KOREAN-AMERICAN CONTEXT

Sponsor: Korean American Communication Association
Chair: Kyong L. Kim, Mount Vernon Nazarene College
  "A Connotative Semiological Analysis: An Analysis of Koreans' of the Acronym 'IMF' as Myth." Eunkyong L. Yook, James Madison University
  "Korean Students' Self-Perception and Cultural Adaptation in American University." Yang-Soo Kim, University of Oklahoma
  "Loneliness, Relational Satisfaction, and Self/Partner Relationship Behavior: A Cross-Cultural Comparison Between the U.S. and Korea." Young-Ok Yum, University of Hawaii, Manoa
  "Group Conversation of Korean Couples in America: Gender, Power, and Social Structures." Oh-Hyeon Lee, University of Massachusetts, Amherst
  "Korean Americans' Relational Ethnic Identity and Mental Health." Eura Jung, Penn State University
  "Sex and Violence: A Textual Analysis of Korean Primetime Television." Jong G. Kang, Illinois State University

Respondent: Jaihyun Lee, Western Illinois University

| 3540 | 2:00-3:15 p.m. | Conf 4H | Fourth Floor | Chicago Hilton |

CHARTING AN INTERACTIONAL PATH: RESOURCES FOR INTERPERSONAL ALIGNMENT AND PERSUASION

Sponsor: Language and Social Interaction Division
Chair: Samuel G. Lawrence, SUNY, Albany
  "Preventatives and Dispreferreds Between Stylist and Client: A Conversation Analytic Study in the Salon." Merry C. Buchanan, University of Oklahoma
  "Talks of Trouble and Closings: A Conversation Analytic Perspective of Getting from Here to There." Margaret M. Sargent, North Central College
  "Metaphorical Language and Intra-Attitudinal Structural Consistency." Pradeep Sopory, University of Memphis
  "Gender and Simultaneous Speech: A Meta-Analytic Review." Stewart C. Alexander, University of Illinois, Lance Rintamaki, University of Illinois, Urbana-Champaign, Markus Pomper, University of Illinois

Respondent: Glen H. Stamp, Ball State University

Saturday

3541   2:00-3:15 p.m.   Conf 4I   Fourth Floor   Chicago Hilton

PRODUCING THE DEPARTMENT OF COMMUNICATION VIDEO

Sponsor: Media Forum Series

Panelist: Sarah R. Stein, North Carolina State University

3542   2:00-3:15 p.m.   Conf 4J   Fourth Floor   Chicago Hilton

ADVERTISING ISSUES: IMAGES FOR CONSUMPTION

Sponsor: Visual Communication Commission
Chair: Eric A. Zimmer, University of Pennsylvania
   "Reading Sports Advertisements: An Investigation of Youth Interpretations." Allison T.
      Butler, New York University
   "Sit-Up Straight and Smile: Construction of the Postmenopausal Woman in Pharmaceutical
      Advertising." Angela Z. Djurovic, DePaul University
   "The Ideological Function of Automobile Design: The 1955 Chevrolet Bel Air as Rhetorical
      Artifact." Christopher J. Skiles, University of Iowa
   "Comparing the Effectiveness of PSAs in Black and White versus Color." Eric A. Zimmer,
      University of Pennsylvania, Robin L. Nabi, University of Arizona, Martin Fishbein,
      University of Pennsylvania, Kathleen Jamieson, University of Pennsylvania

Respondent: Robin Andersen, Fordham University

3543   2:00-3:15 p.m.   Conf 4K   Fourth Floor   Chicago Hilton

WHEN THE FABRIC TEARS II: JEALOUSY, CONFLICT AND FACE THREATS

Sponsor: Interpersonal Communication Division
Chair: Laura K. Guerrero, Arizona State University
   "Why Do We React the Way We Do? The Effect of Lovestyles, Satisfaction, Trust, and
      Experience of Jealousy on Communicative Responses to Jealousy." Lindsay M.
      Timmerman, University of Texas, Austin
   "Fueling the Flames of the Green-Eyed Monster: The Role of Ruminative Thought in
      Reaction to Perceived Relationship Threat." Christy L. Carson, Illinois State University,
      William R. Cupach, Illinois State University
   "The Dialectics of Marital Satisfaction: Assesing the Aftermath of Marital Conflict
      Interaction." Larry A. Erbert, Cleveland State University
   "Request Refusals as Face-Threatening Acts: A Preliminary Investigation from the
      Coordinated Management of Meaning." Masayuki Nakanishi, Tsuda College, Tokyo

Respondent: Laura K. Guerrero, Arizona State University

3544   2:00-3:15 p.m.   Conf 4L   Fourth Floor   Chicago Hilton

REFRAMING THE MENTORING RELATIONSHIP TO PROMOTE WOMEN'S
ADVANCEMENT IN THE DISCIPLINE

Sponsor: Women's Caucus
Chair: Diana L. Tucker, Southern Illinois University, Carbondale

Panelists: Laurel T. Hetherington, Boise State University
           Elizabeth Gullickson-Tolman, Southern Illinois University, Carbondale
           Teddi Joyce, Southern Illinois University
           Mary E. Rohlfing, Boise State University
           Diana L. Tucker, Southern Illinois University, Carbondale

This panel asks audience members to help devise a program on implementing mentoring skills
in the classroom.

| 3545 | 2:00-3:15 p.m. | Conf 4M | Fourth Floor | Chicago Hilton |

INTEGRATING ORGANIZATIONAL COMMUNICATION AND HUMAN RESOURCES: CROSSING BETWEEN THE ORGANIZATIONAL LINES

Sponsor: Organizational Communication Division
Chair: Anne P. Hubbell, Michigan State University
  "The Integration of Communication Theory and Human Resource Functions in
  Organizations." Caryn E. Medved, Michigan State University
  "The Many Voices and Faces of Human Resource Professionals in the Role of Change
  Agent." Laurie K. Lewis, University of Texas, Austin
  "Strategizing Human Resource Issues: The Use of Message Strategies During Union
  Organization." Janet M. Lillie, Michigan State University
  "Communication Complexities in Multinational Human Resources." Nancy Burgas,
  Phronesis, Patrice M. Buzzanell, Northern Illinois University

Respondent: Sue DeWine, Ohio University

| 3546 | 2:00-3:15 p.m. | McCormick Board Rm | Fourth Floor | Chicago Hilton |

COMMISSION ON COMMUNICATION IN THE FUTURE BUSINESS MEETING

Sponsor: Commission on Communication in the Future

| 3547 | 2:00-3:15 p.m. | Pullman Board Rm | Fourth Floor | Chicago Hilton |

PEACE AND CONFLICT COMMUNICATION COMMISSION BUSINESS MEETING

Sponsor: Peace and Conflict Communication Commission

| 3549 | 2:00-3:15 p.m. | Conf 5B | Fifth Floor | Chicago Hilton |

WHAT SHOULD WE TEACH IN THE BASIC COURSE?

Sponsor: Basic Course Division
Chair: Kristi A. Schaller, Georgia State University

Panelists: Jacquelyn J. Buckrop, Ball State University
           Lawrence W. Hugenberg, Youngstown State University
           Cheri J. Simonds, Illinois State University
           Mark D. Nelson, University of Alabama, Tuscaloosa
           Donald D. Yoder, University of Dayton

Panelists and audience members will debate the content of the basic course.

| 3552 | 2:00-3:15 p.m. | Conf 5E | Fifth Floor | Chicago Hilton |

CONTEXT AND CRITICISM IN RHETORICAL STUDIES

Sponsor: Rhetorical and Communication Theory Division
Chair: Mark A. Pollock, Loyola University, Chicago
  "Orchestrating Idioms and Voices: Performative Traditions in King's A Time to Break
  Silence." James Jasinski, University of Puget Sound
  "Robert Kennedy and Lyndon Johnson on Vietnam: Text and Context in the Shadow of
  JFK." John M. Murphy, University of Georgia
  "The 'Contexts' of Rhetorical Analysis." Thomas Rosteck, University of Arkansas,
  Fayetteville

Respondent: Carole Blair, University of California, Davis

Saturday

3553   2:00-3:15 p.m.   Conf 5F   Fifth Floor   Chicago Hilton

FRAMING THE EARTH: GLOBAL WARMING, GLOBAL RESPONSIBILITY, AND GLOBAL DIRECT SALES MARKETING???

Sponsor: Environmental Communication Commission
Chair: Anand Rao, Clarion University
    "Equinox International: Utilizing the Comic Frame in Direct Sales Marketing." Irene Grau,
    California State University, Los Angeles
    "Everything You Need to Know or Just Hot Air?" Michael E. Nitz, University of Idaho,
    Volker Janssen, University of Hamburg, Marc Hermann, University of Hamburg, Stefanie
    Huber, University of Hamburg
    "Bridging the North-South Divide: The Global Responsibility Frame at Earth Summit +5."
    Marie A. Mater, Nanyang Technological University

Respondent: Jonathan I. Lange, Southern Oregon State College

3554   2:00-3:15 p.m.   Conf 5G   Fifth Floor   Chicago Hilton

AFFINITY-SEEKING AND COMPLIANCE-GAINING: EXTENDING RESEARCH

Sponsor: Instructional Development Division
Chair: Timothy P. Mottet, Southwest Texas State University
    "Behavioral Alteration Techniques and Behavioral Alteration Messages as Compliance
    Gaining Behaviors: A Review of Literature from a Message Production Perspective."
    Christina M. Sabee, Northwestern University
    "Is Affinity-Seeking Truly Strategic? A Study Examining the Role of Strategy in Instructional
    Communication Research." Linda B. Dickmeyer, Concordia College, Minnesota
    "The Impact of Teacher Immediacy, Teacher Affinity-Seeking, and Teacher Misbehaviors
    on Student-Perceived Teacher Credibility*." Katherine S. Thweatt, West Virginia
    University

Respondent: Timothy P. Mottet, Southwest Texas State University

*Top Student Paper

3555   2:00-3:15 p.m.   Conf 5H   Fifth Floor   Chicago Hilton

ANXIETY PATTERNS AND TECHNOLOGY REGARDING COMMUNICATION APPREHENSION

Sponsor: Communication Apprehension & Avoidance Commission
Chair: Terence S. Schliesman, Western State College of Colorado
    "Anticipatory Anxiety Patterns of Male and Female Public Speakers." Ralph R. Behnke,
    Texas Christian University, Chris R. Sawyer, Tarrant County Junior College
    "The Effect of Computer Anxiety, Communication Apprehension, and Writing
    Apprehension on Computer-Mediated Communication Technology Use." Michael D.
    Rapp, University of Houston, Craig R. Scott, University of Texas, Austin
    "The Relationship Between Computing Time and Communication
    Apprehension/Communication Competence Among Adolescents." Terence S.
    Schliesman, Western State College of Colorado, Joe Ayres, Washington State University

---

3556   2:00-3:15 p.m.   Conf 5I   Fifth Floor   Chicago Hilton

GLOBAL CONSULTING: INTERACTION BETWEEN FUNCTIONALITY AND NATIONALITY

Sponsor: Roundtable Series
Chair: Michael J. Vivion, F. Hoffmann-La Roche Ltd., Basel Switzerland
    "Clinic Speak." Bradley Hayden, F. Hoffmann-LaRoche Ltd., California
    "The Language of the Laboratory." Sarah Duncan, F. Hoffmann-LaRoche Ltd., New Jersey
    "Interaction Between Functions and Nations." Michael J. Vivion, F. Hoffmann-La Roche
    Ltd., Basel Switzerland

3557   2:00-3:15 p.m.   Conf 5J   Fifth Floor   Chicago Hilton

SCHOLARSHIP AFTER RETIREMENT: THE DEMAND AND THE POSSIBILITIES

Sponsor: Emeritus/Retired Members Section
Chair: Gerald H. Sanders, Miami University, Ohio

Panelists: Bernard L. Brock, Wayne State University
         Gary Gumpert, Communication Landscapers
         Austin J. Freeley, John Carroll University
         Ernest G. Bormann, University of Minnesota

This panel will discuss their own research and publishing after retirement as well as their perception of possibilities for others.

3561   2:00-3:15 p.m.   Lake Erie   Eighth Floor   Chicago Hilton

WHAT ARE WE WATCHING?: AN EXAMINATION OF SPANISH LANGUAGE MEDIA

Sponsor: Latina/Latino Communication Studies Division
Chair: Leda M. Cooks, University of Massachusetts, Amherst
    "*Dame Un Beso:* A Content Analysis of Sexual Activity on Telenovelas." Kristin C. Engstrand, University of Washington
    "Differences in the Uses and Gratifications Among Spanish-Speaking Viewers of the Television Program *Sabado Gigante*." Martha I. Chew, University of New Mexico

Respondent: Aimee M. Carrillo Rowe, University of Washington

3563   2:00-3:15 p.m.   Windsor Court   Second Floor   Essex Inn

THE PRACTICE OF DOING ETHNOGRAPHIC RESEARCH

Sponsor: Ethnography Division
Chair: Shirley K. Drew, Pittsburg State University
    "Ethnography as Spiritual Practice: A Change in the Taken for Granted." M. Cristina Gonzalez, Arizona State University
    "Ruth's Paper." Diane S. Grimes, Syracuse University
    "Reflecting on the Gifts and the Graciousness of the Seasons: Ethnography as an Exercise in Trust and Receptiveness." S. Lily Mendoza, Arizona State University
    "The Socialization of an Ethnographer: Coloring Outside the Lines in the Dissertation Process." Charlotte G. Burke, Bob Jones University

Respondent: Steven K. May, University of North Carolina, Chapel Hill

---

3564   2:00-3:15 p.m.   Buckingham Court   Second Floor   Essex Inn

DECODING SIGNS ACROSS ORGANIZATIONAL AND CULTURAL BOUNDARIES

Sponsor: Semiotics and Communication Commission
Chair: James C. Lundy, Doane College
    "Interaction as a Text: A Semiotic Analysis of an Organizing Process*." Daniel Robichaud, University of Colorado, Boulder
    "Life in Semiotic Square, or New Signs on the Block." Igor E. Klyukanov, Penn State University, Berks
    "Semiotic Theory in Icon Design for International Audiences." Michelle Keyser, North Carolina State University, Steven B. Katz, North Carolina State University
    "Reading Across Codes: Managerial Preferences in Consuming Popular Management Theories." Sonya K. Pagel, Seattle Pacific University

Respondent: Jacqueline M. Martinez, Purdue University

*Top Paper

| 3565 | 2:00-3:15 p.m. | Park East Walk | Second Floor | Essex Inn |

KENNETH BURKE'S MASTER TROPES REVISITED

Sponsor: Kenneth Burke Society, NCA Branch
Chair: Ekaterina V. Haskins, University of Iowa
  "Kenneth Burke's Constitutive Metaphor." Ekaterina V. Haskins, University of Iowa
  "Metonymy: The Reduction of Sex to Parts in David Reuben's *Everything You Always Wanted to Know About Sex. . . but Were Afraid to Ask.*" Valerie V. Peterson, University of Iowa
  "Synechdoche: The Violent Trope." David C. Hoffman, Temple University
  "Kenneth Burke's Dialogical Trope: The Ethical Ground of Irony." Jeffrey W. Murray, University of Pittsburgh

| 3566 | 2:00-3:15 p.m. | Cohn Rm | Second Floor | Spertus Institute |

THE RHETORIC OF THE RHETORIC OF SCIENCE

Sponsor: American Association for Rhetoric of Science & Technology
Chair: Alan G. Gross, University of Minnesota, Twin Cities
  "Rhetorical Situation, Context, and Performative Tradition: Engaging in the 'Hermeneutic' Project of 'Thickening' Rhetorical Criticism." Doreen Starke-Meyerring, University of Minnesota
  "Unrealistic, Unjustified, Retrograde—or Right?" Margaret Hamilton, University of Minnesota
  "Transgressing Gaonkar: Thickening *Ethos.*" Helen Constantinides, University of Minnesota

| 3567 | 2:00-3:15 p.m. | Krensky Rm | Second Floor | Spertus Institute |

EXAMINING THE BRAVE NEW WORLD: THE MEDIA, THE COURTS AND THE LAW

Sponsor: Communication and Law Commission
Chair: Todd F. McDorman, Wabash College
  "Communication Variables of Litigation Public Relations." Dirk C. Gibson, University of New Mexico
  "The Impact of Media Coverage of the Courts: Televised Trials." Paul Haridakis, Kent State University

Respondent: Todd F. McDorman, Wabash College

| 3569 | 2:00-3:15 p.m. | Rm 903 | Ninth Floor | Spertus Institute |

L-D AND PARLIAMENTARY DEBATE IN THE NEW MILLENNIUM

Sponsor: Pi Kappa Delta
Chair: Joel L. Hefling, South Dakota State University
  "The State-of-the-Art of Case Construction in Parliamentary Debate." Susan E. Hellbusch, Creighton University
  "The Influence of Critic Experience in the Evaluation of Lincoln-Douglas Debate: Individual Events Backgound vs Debate Background." Audra Diers, University of Wyoming
  "The Nature of Critic Decisions in Parliamentary Debate: Toward a Discovery." Daniel A. West, Rice University
  "The Influence of Judging Paradigm on Critic Decision-Making in Lincoln-Douglas Debate." Marty J. Birkholt, Creighton University
  "The Influence the Nature of the Resolution May Have on Win/Loss Ratios in Parliamentary Debate." Renea B. Gernant, Concordia University, Seward

Respondent: Harold Lawson, Central Missouri State University

3570   2:00-3:15 p.m.   Rm 904   Ninth Floor   Spertus Institute

THE IMAGE AND PERCEPTION OF CHINESE IN AMERICAN MEDIA

Sponsor: Association for Chinese Communication Studies
Chair: Ling Chen, Hong Kong Baptist University
    "Media Coverage and Cultural Misperceptions: Chinese and Americans at the Centennial
        Olympic Games." Shuming Lu, Brooklyn College, CUNY
    "China's Image Seen from the U.S. Media: Why is It Largely Negative." Yanmin Yu,
        University of Bridgeport
    "From Ideographic Gestalt to Holistic Ontology: The American Image of Chinese Language
        and Culture." Zhenbin Sun, Harvard University
    "Model or Peril? A Content Analysis of Asian American Coverage in the Mainstream
        Newspapers: 1990-1997." Jung-kuang Sun, SUNY, Buffalo
    "From the Virtuous Hua Mu Lan to the Bad Boy Jiang Ze-min: The Politics and Political
        Economy of U.S. Coverage of the Chinese Cultural Group." Mei-ling Wang, University of
        the Sciences, Pennsylvania

3571   2:00-3:15 p.m.   Rm 906   Ninth Floor   Spertus Institute

RHETORIC AND THE SOCIAL BOND

Sponsor: American Society for the History of Rhetoric
Chair: Beth S. Bennett, University of Alabama
    "Platonic Dialectic as Torture: On-Line Rhetoric, the Public, and the Good." Todd S.
        Frobish, Penn State University
    "Infinite Substance and Limited Perception: Imagination and Desire in Spinoza's *Ethics* and
        Lacan's *Four Fundamental Concepts of Psycho-Analysis*." Daniel L. Emery, University of
        Iowa
    "Vico, Heidegger, Grassi: Rhetoric of Science as 'Postmodern Humanism'." Amos A.
        Tevelow, University of Pittsburgh

3572   2:00-3:15 p.m.   Rm 907   Ninth Floor   Spertus Institute

THE IMPACT OF INTERCOLLEGIATE DEBATE ON PARTICIPANTS' QUALITY
OF LIFE

Sponsor: Cross Examination Debate Association
Chair: Warren D. Decker, George Mason University

Panelists: David L. Steinberg, University of Miami
        David M. Romanelli, Loyola University, Chicago
        William T. Sheffield, California State University, Northridge
        Glen Frappier, Gonzaga University
        Monte Stevens, Kansas State University

The panelists will present data gathered from the ongoing efforts of the CEDA's Quality of Life
Project Team and lead a structured discussion on issues related to the impact of intercollegiate
debate on participants' quality of life.

3574   2:00-3:15 p.m.   Auditorium   Second Floor   Spertus Institute

LABON MOVEMENT FOR ACTORS

Sponsor: Theatre Division
Chair: Renee Vincent, University of North Carolina, Wilmington

Workshop for actors, directors, teachers to introduce the fundamentals of Labon Technique.
Comfortable clothes and shoes are recommended and a learned monologue is helpful but not
required. No prior movement experience is required.

Saturday

3:30 p.m.

3606   3:30-4:45 p.m.   Continental BR A   Lobby Level   Chicago Hilton

COMPETITIVE PAPERS IN EMOTIONAL RESPONSES TO MEDIA CONTENT

Sponsor: Mass Communication Division
Chair: Stephanie L. Sargent, Virginia Tech University
   "Commercial Humor Enhancement of Program Enjoyment: Gender and Program Appeal as Mitigating Factors." Stephen D. Perry, Illinois State University
   "Preference for Frightening Films: The Role of Empathy, Sensation-Seeking, and Content Features." Cynthia A. Hoffner, Illinois State University, Rissa Robertson, Illinois State University, Seok Kang, Illinois State University, Carlene Malley, Illinois State University, Edwin A. Reed, Illinois State University, Andrew Sievert, Illinois State University
   "The Death of a Princess: Media-Related Factors Affecting Emotional Response and Intensity." Melissa J. Frame, University of South Florida
   "Integrating Emotion and Cognition: An Exploration of Appraisal Theory and Motivated Television Viewing." Mary M. Step, Case Western Reserve University

Respondent: James B. Weaver, Virginia Tech University

3607   3:30-4:45 p.m.   Continental BR B   Lobby Level   Chicago Hilton

EMBRACING DIFFERENCES IN LIFE AND LEARNING THROUGH COMPUTER-MEDIATED COMMUNICATION

Sponsor: Human Communication and Technology Commission
Chair: Diane F. Witmer, California State University, Fullerton
   "Faculty Development at SUNY: Shifting from Teaching to Learning." Dudley D. Cahn, SUNY, New Paltz
   "Commonality and Community: Developing Friendships Through Discourse." Michael J. Cody, University of Southern California, Deborah S. Dunn, Westmont College, Diane F. Witmer, California State University, Fullerton
   "Evaluation of Cognitive, Affective, and Skill-Based Outcomes Associated with On-Line Courses." Tracy C. Russo, University of Kansas

Respondents: Howard E. Sypher, University of Kansas
             Matt Stoner, University of Arizona

As the use of computer technology continues to expand, it is important to recognize that for increasing numbers of people, life experiences also include "cyber experiences," both relational and pedagogical. This panel addresses such experiences by exploring differences, contradictions, and similarities in the ways in which computer technology may catalyze relationships and learning.

3608   3:30-4:45 p.m.   Continental BR C   Lobby Level   Chicago Hilton

REFLECTING ON ERNEST BOYER: SCHOLARSHIP AND THE LIBERAL ARTS COLLEGE

Sponsor: Senior College & University Section
Chair: Alan C. Lerstrom, Luther College
   "'We Are Who We Are': Repositioning Boyer's Dimensions of Scholarship." Robert L. Heinemann, Messiah College
   "Implementing New Models of Scholarship: Strategies for Faculty at Undergraduate Institutions." Roger Smitter, North Central College
   "Definition and Direction: A Reexamination of 'Creative Scholarship' in a Liberal Arts Context." Gerald Lee Ratliff, SUNY, Potsdam
   "The Scholarship of Application: Using Theory in Practice." Alan C. Lerstrom, Luther College

| 3610 | 3:30-4:45 p.m. | Grand Ballroom | Second Floor | Chicago Hilton |

KILLING DILLINGER: A 'MYSTORY'

Sponsor: Performance Studies Division
Chair: Ruth L. Bowman, Louisiana State University
  "'Mystory' Pedagogy and Practice." Ruth L. Bowman, Louisiana State University
  "Killing Dillinger: A Mystory." Michael S. Bowman, Louisiana State University
  "Guns and Mothers." Alan J. Shapiro, University of North Carolina, Chapel Hill

Respondent: Alan J. Shapiro, University of North Carolina, Chapel Hill

| 3612 | 3:30-4:45 p.m. | Int'l Ballroom South | Second Floor | Chicago Hilton |

'CRAFT': COACHING, RUNNING, ADMINISTERING FORENSICS TIPS

Sponsor: Phi Rho Pi
Chair: Cynthia E. Dewar, City College of San Francisco
  "Boldly Going Where Nobody Has Gone Before: Creating a Competitive Forensics
    Program." Lisa Bennedetti, Ohlone College
  "What Do You Mean Our Budget is Cut?: Innovative and Proven Strategies for
    Fundraising." K. C. Boylan, Sacramento City Community College
  "Tag Team Impromptu: Teaching Students How to Build a Mental Database." Kelly M.
    Hughes, Pasadena City College
  "Roses are Red. Violets are Blue. Classical Poetry is Valuable Too!" Jennifer L. Jones,
    University of Illinois, Urbana-Champaign
  "Lights, Camera, Action! Using Videotape as a Coaching Tool." Jennifer L. Peterson,
    University of Illinois, Urbana-Champaign
  "CD-ROM-Based Coaching Techniques: The Wave of the Future." Rolland C. Petrello,
    Moorpark College
  "The 'Team' Meeting: Strategies for Making the Most of Meeting as a Team." Jeff F.
    Przybylo, William Rainey Harper College
  "Transforming Mr. or Ms. Hyde into Dr. Jekyll: Nurturing Your Forensics Students Egos."
    Raymond C. Puchot, El Paso Community College
  "Interpreters Theatre: Integrating Students into the Development Process." Stephen P.
    Schroeder, College of DuPage
  "Informative Speaking: Back to the Basics." Stacy Seibert, Purdue University

| 3614 | 3:30-4:45 p.m. | Boulevard A | Second Floor | Chicago Hilton |

USING METADISCOURSE TO RESPOND TO CRAIG'S METAMODEL OF COMMUNICATION: A COLORFUL AND DIALECTICAL APPROACH TO CROSSING THE BOUNDARIES OF OUR DISCIPLINARITY LINES

Sponsor: Challenging Boundaries Series
Chair: Thomas B. Farrell, Northwestern University
  "Theories of Verbal Aggression, Argumentation (Ad Hominem), and Agenda Setting: An
    Unlikely Team to Uncover Negative Communicative Strategies." Shannon S. Dyer,
    Northwestern University, Josh Compton, Southwest Missouri State University
  "Attribution, Negotiation and Narrative: Revisiting the Ethnographic/Scientific Balance."
    Elizabeth R. Bernat, Ohio University, Hilary R. Altman, Northwestern University
  "Image Restoration in the Interpersonal Arena: Politeness Theory with a 'Benoit' Twist."
    Carma L. Bylund, Northwestern University, Brett A. Miller, Southwest Baptist University
  "Dramatistic Conversation: An Application of Burkean Rhetorical Theory to Conversation
    Analysis in Interpersonal Interactions." Christina M. Sabee, Northwestern University,
    Michael Geiser, Northwestern University

Respondent: Robert T. Craig, University of Colorado, Boulder

Saturday

3615   3:30-4:45 p.m.   **Boulevard B**   **Second Floor**   **Chicago Hilton**

COLORING OUTSIDE THE LINES: COMMUNICATIVE BEHAVIOR AS THE NEXUS OF SEXUALITY, IDENTITY, AND POLITICS

Sponsor: NCA First Vice President
Chair: John M. Sloop, Vanderbilt University
   "On-Line Sexuality: Performing and Resisting Identity in Second-Order Space." Gary W.
      Larson, Wichita State University
   "Blurring the Lines: News Reporting of On-Line Pornography and Issues of Harm, Effects,
      Identity, Legality and Reality." J. M. Metz, University of Central Florida
   "The 'Pornographic' Voice in the Clinton Impeachment: Intersections of Identity and
      Space." A. Susan Owen, University of Puget Sound

Respondent: John M. Sloop, Vanderbilt University

3616   3:30-4:45 p.m.   **Boulevard C**   **Second Floor**   **Chicago Hilton**

GROUP COMMUNICATION IN CONTEXT: STUDIES OF BONA FIDE GROUPS

Sponsor: Group Communication Division
Chair: Lawrence R. Frey, University of Memphis
   "Multiple Identities in Teams in a Cooperative Supermarket: A Bona Fide Group
      Perspective." John G. Oetzel, University of New Mexico, Jean Robbins, University of
      New Mexico
   "On the Verge of Collaboration: Identifying Group Structure and Process." Joann Keyton,
      University of Memphis, Virginia Stallworth, Child Advocacy Center
   "Influences on the Communication and Recommendations of International Business
      Consulting Teams." John C. Sherblom, University of Maine, Orono

Respondent: Lawrence R. Frey, University of Memphis

3619   3:30-4:45 p.m.   **Astoria**   **Third Floor**   **Chicago Hilton**

RADICAL RHETORICS: ANTEBELLUM REFORM AND CONSPIRACY

Sponsor: Public Address Division
Chair: Leroy G. Dorsey, Texas A&M University
   "Black Bogey as Radical Prototype: David Walker's *Appeal*." Charles E. Morris, Denison
      University
   "Exposing the Papal Plot: The Rhetorical Development of a Conspiracy Theory." Jody M.
      Roy, Ripon College
   "'Rough Instruments are Used for Rough Work': Wendell Phillips Attacks Daniel Webster
      in the 'Surrender of Sims'." Julie Tryboski, Penn State University

Respondent: Michael Leff, Northwestern University

3621   3:30-4:45 p.m.   **Williford A**   **Third Floor**   **Chicago Hilton**

COLORING OUTSIDE TRADITIONAL ORGANIZATIONAL LINES BY INCLUDING AFRICAN AMERICANS

Sponsor: African American Communication & Culture Commission
Chair: Dawna I. Ballard, University of California, Santa Barbara
   "African American Communication, Organizations, and Assimilation: A Co-Cultural
      Perspective*." Patricia C. Phillips-Gott, Southwest Texas State University
   "Rethinking Diversity Training: A Postmodern Analysis of Organizational Diversity
      Education*." Shawn D. Long, University of Kentucky

"Racial Group Orientation and Social Outcomes: Summarizing Relationships Using Meta-Analysis." Mike Allen, University of Wisconsin, Milwaukee, Lisa Bradford, University of Wisconsin, Milwaukee, Erica F. Cooper, Indiana University, Bloomington, Loretta Howard, University of Wisconsin, Milwaukee, Undraye Howard, University of Wisconsin, Milwaukee

Respondent: Anne M. Nicotera, Howard University

*Student Debut Paper

3622   3:30-4:45 p.m.   Williford B   Third Floor   Chicago Hilton

POLITICAL COMMUNICATION IN THE CLINTON SCANDALS

Sponsor: Political Communication Division
Chair: Mary Alice Baker, Lamar University
   "The Rhetorical Construction of Role in the Impeachment of William Jefferson Clinton." David J. Dutwin, University of Pennsylvania
   "Answering the Clinton Character Question: Source Evaluation in the 1996 U.S. Presidential Election." Brooks Aylor, La Salle University
   "Surprise, You're on National Television: An Analysis of Clinton's Grand Jury Testimony." Andrew A. Klyukovski, University of Missouri, Columbia, William L. Benoit, University of Missouri, Columbia
   "Pizza, Cigars, and Sex: The Comeback Kid Rides Again." Bernadette Mink, University of Arkansas
   "I'm Sorry, Now Let's Move On: Bill Clinton's Rhetorical Strategy in 'Monica-Gate'." Larry J. King, Lamar University, R. Scott Britten, Bowling Green State University, Jim Towns, Stephen F. Austin State University

---

3623   3:30-4:45 p.m.   Williford C   Third Floor   Chicago Hilton

RHETORICAL CONSTRUCTIONS OF FEMINISM

Sponsor: Feminist and Women Studies Division
Chair: Mary E. Triece, University of Akron
   "Popular Culture and the Rhetorical Definition of 'Woman': Implications for Feminism." Tressa M. Kelly, Wayne State University
   "Rhetorics of Consciousness-Raising: Multiple 'Stylistic-Features' in U.S. Second-Wave Feminism." David C. Deifell, University of Iowa
   "Mapping Rhetorical Interventions in Localized and National Feminist Histories: 'Second Wave Feminism' and 'Ain't I a woman'." Kyra L. Pearson, University of Iowa
   "The Personal, the Political, and Others: Audre Lorde Denouncing 'The Second Sex Conference'." Lester C. Olson, University of Pittsburgh

Respondent: Lisa A. Flores, University of Utah

3624   3:30-4:45 p.m.   Marquette   Third Floor   Chicago Hilton

SQUARING THE CIRCLE IN THE INTRODUCTION TO THEATRE COURSE: SHARING INNOVATIVE IDEAS IN TEACHING

Sponsor: Theatre Division
Chair: Gail S. Medford, Bowie State University
   "Dramaturgy as Pedagogy in the Introductory Theatre Course." Angela J. Latham, Triton College
   "Technology Enters Introduction to Theatre." Michael M. O'Hara, Ball State University
   "Performance in Teaching and Learning in Introduction to Theatre." Lynne Greeley, University of Vermont
   "Service-Learning in Theatre Arts." Gail S. Medford, Bowie State University

Saturday

3625   3:30-4:45 p.m.   **Joliet   Third Floor   Chicago Hilton**

COMPETITIVE PAPERS IN INTERPERSONAL COMMUNICATION

Sponsor: Student Section
  "Beyond the Marriage Partners: The Impact of Divorce on Children's Communication."
    Tawnya Taddiken, Washburn University
  "Total Eclipse: The Bright and Dark Side of Reciprocal Self-Disclosure." Emily J. Langan,
    Arizona State University
  "Coloring Outside the Lines: The Weinlick Way*." Angie Seifert, Concordia University, St.
    Paul, Christopher J. Ohland, Concordia University, St. Paul, Nasha Toland, Concordia
    University, St. Paul, Joanne Chudzik, Concordia University, St. Paul
  "Communication Apprehension in Cases of an Attractive Other." Benjamin J. Rabe,
    Augustana College

Respondent: Kristine L. Fitch, University of Iowa

*Deput Paper

3626   3:30-4:45 p.m.   **PDR 1   Third Floor   Chicago Hilton**

MEET THE NCA EDITORS

Sponsor: Publications Board
Chair: Judee K. Burgoon, University of Arizona
  Communication Education. Joe Ayres, Washington State University
  Communication Monographs. Michael J. Beatty, University of Missouri, St. Louis
  Communication Teacher. Lawrence W. Hugenberg, Youngstown State University
  Critical Studies in Mass Communication. James W. Chesebro, Indiana State University
  Free Speech Yearbook. Matthew W. Seeger, Wayne State University
  International and Intercultural Annual. Mary Jane Collier, University of Denver
  Journal of Applied Communication Research. H. Dan O'Hair, University of Oklahoma
  Quarterly Journal of Speech. Andrew A. King, Louisiana State University
  Text and Performance Quarterly. Judith A. Hamera, California State University, Los Angeles

This informal session provides members an opportunity to learn about the editorial policies of
the association. Editors will be available for questions from the audience.

3627   3:30-4:45 p.m.   **PDR 2   Third Floor   Chicago Hilton**

HEALTH COMMUNICATION DIVISION BUSINESS MEETING

Sponsor: Health Communication Division

3628   3:30-4:45 p.m.   **PDR 3   Third Floor   Chicago Hilton**

FAMILY COMMUNICATION DIVISION GENERAL BUSINESS MEETING

Sponsor: Family Communication Division

3629   3:30-4:45 p.m.   **PDR 4   Third Floor   Chicago Hilton**

CONTRIBUTED PAPERS

Sponsor: Association for Communication Administration
Chair: Don M. Boileau, George Mason University
  "Publication Patterns of Male and Female Faculty Members in the Communication
    Discipline." Lawrence Nadler, Miami University, Marjorie Keeshan Nadler, Miami
    University
  "Peer Recognition of Scholarly Productivity: A Descriptive Study of National
    Communication Association Research Award Winners, 1961-1998." George W.
    Musambira, Western Kentucky University

"From Elimination to Enhancement: Building Stronger Departments of Communication."
   Mary J. Smythe, University of Missouri

| 3630 | 3:30-4:45 p.m. | PDR 5 | Third Floor | Chicago Hilton |

KENNETH BURKE SOCIETY BUSINESS MEETING

Sponsor: Kenneth Burke Society, NCA Branch

| 3631 | 3:30-4:45 p.m. | PDR 6 | Third Floor | Chicago Hilton |

CRITICAL AND CULTURAL STUDIES DIVISION BUSINESS MEETING

Sponsor: Critical and Cultural Studies Division

| 3632 | 3:30-4:45 p.m. | PDR 7 | Third Floor | Chicago Hilton |

WEAPONS OF MASS DESTRUCTION: UNITED STATES FOREIGN POLICY DISCOURSE AND THE RHETORICAL CONSTRUCTION OF THREAT

Sponsor: Argumentation and Forensics Division
Chair: Gordon R. Mitchell, University of Pittsburgh
   "News Media and the Rhetorical Uses of Terror: Constructing the Threat of Weapons of
   Mass Destruction." Kevin J. Ayotte, University of Pittsburgh
   "Simulations of Terror: U.S. Foreign Policy Discourse and the Case of Sudan." Marcy L.
   Halpin, University of Pittsburgh
   "From Ebola to Anthrax: The Priming of the Biological Warfare Threat." Daniel McGee,
   University of Illinois, Urbana-Champaign

Respondent: Cori E. Dauber, University of North Carolina, Chapel Hill

---

| 3633 | 3:30-4:45 p.m. | Conf 4A | Fourth Floor | Chicago Hilton |

AFRICAN AMERICAN COMMUNICATION AND CULTURE DIVISION/BLACK CAUCUS BUSINESS MEETING

Sponsors: African American Communication & Culture Commission
          Black Caucus

| 3634 | 3:30-4:45 p.m. | Conf 4B | Fourth Floor | Chicago Hilton |

PI KAPPA DELTA BUSINESS MEETING

Sponsor: Pi Kappa Delta

| 3635 | 3:30-4:45 p.m. | Conf 4C | Fourth Floor | Chicago Hilton |

CROSS EXAMINATION DEBATE ASSOCIATION BUSINESS MEETING

Sponsor: Cross Examination Debate Association

| 3636 | 3:30-4:45 p.m. | Conf 4D | Fourth Floor | Chicago Hilton |

RELIGIOUS COMMUNICATION ASSOCIATION BUSINESS MEETING

Sponsor: Religious Communication Association

| 3637 | 3:30-4:45 p.m. | Conf 4E | Fourth Floor | Chicago Hilton |

PUBLIC RELATIONS DIVISION BUSINESS MEETING

Sponsor: Public Relations Division

Saturday

3638   3:30-4:45 p.m.   Conf 4F   Fourth Floor   Chicago Hilton

MEDIATING FOR UPSTREAM EFFECTS: TRANSFORMATIVE MEDIATION PROGRAMS

Sponsor: Peace and Conflict Communication Commission
Chair: Gilda C. Parrella, Loyola University, Chicago

Panelists: Joseph Folger, Temple University
Terese Lynch, U.S. Postal Service REDRESS Program
Dorothy J. DellaNoce, Temple University

Panelists will discuss the transformative mediation model and its uses in effecting large scale cultural change in organizations. The program will feature video excerpts of mediation training and interactive panel and audience participation.

3639   3:30-4:45 p.m.   Conf 4G   Fourth Floor   Chicago Hilton

THEORIZING DIGITAL MEDIA THROUGH KOREAN EXPERIENCES

Sponsor: Korean American Communication Association
Chair: Jong G. Kang, Illinois State University
   "Belief in Modernization and Hope in Information Society: South Korean Media Industry."
   Doobo Shim, University of Wisconsin, Madison
   "Impact of New Media Technology on South Korean Labor Movements' Resource
   Management Strategies." Taehyun Kim, Ohio State University
   "The New Media in the Old Media: Reporting Communication Technologies in the Mass
   Media." Mee-Eun Kang, Cleveland State University
   "Homo Telephonicus: The Emergence of New Communication Pattern in Korea."
   Shin-Dong Kim, Hallym University, South Korea
   "Taking Privacy Seriously in the Age of Homo Digitals: Dataveillance and the Korean
   National Identification Card System." Joohoan Kim, Boston College

Respondent: Eunkyong L. Yook, James Madison University

3640   3:30-4:45 p.m.   Conf 4H   Fourth Floor   Chicago Hilton

CONVERSATION ANALYSIS AND ETHNOMETHODOLOGY: REFLECTIONS ON ACCOMPLISHMENTS AND GOALS

Sponsor: Language and Social Interaction Division

Panelists: Wayne A. Beach, San Diego State University
John C. Heritage, University of California, Los Angeles
D. Lawrence Wieder, University of Oklahoma

Three leading scholars will share perspectives on the impacts that conversation analysis and ethnomethodology have had on the field of communication, and reflections on directions for future research.

3641   3:30-4:45 p.m.   Conf 4I   Fourth Floor   Chicago Hilton

FEMINIST NARRATIVE EXPRESSION: WOMEN'S VOICES ABOUT WISDOM

Sponsor: Media Forum Series

Panelist: Jennifer A. Machiorlatti, University of Windsor, Ontario

Respondent: Esther A. Kramer, Milwaukee, Wisconsin

Screening of "Wise Woman Wisdom: Holding the Blood" with discussion and response.

| 3642 | 3:30-4:45 p.m. | Conf 4J | Fourth Floor | Chicago Hilton |

THE DYNAMICS OF CRITICAL THINKING

Sponsor: Elementary & Secondary Education Section
Chair: Cecelia M. Blotkamp, Robert E. Lee High School, Virginia
"Developing Thinking Skills Through Poetry: A Project with Third Graders." Virginia P. O'Keefe, Tidewater Community College
"Computer-Based Problem-Solving in the Middle School." Kathryn Schweers, Corporate Landing Middle School, Virginia
"Teaching Students to Critically Analyze Their Assumptions: The Critical Thinking Project in El Paso Secondary Schools." Linda C. Brown, El Paso Community College, Kimberly A. Klorer, El Paso Community College

| 3643 | 3:30-4:45 p.m. | Conf 4K | Fourth Floor | Chicago Hilton |

DIALECTICS, DISCLOSURE AND RELATIONSHIP TALK

Sponsors: Interpersonal Communication Division
                  Language and Social Interaction Division
Chair: Joseph A. Bonito, University of Arizona
"Dream-Recollection and Dialectical-Disclosure Within Established Relationships: An Exploratory Study." Karen A. Ijams, Northeastern Illinois University
"The Dialectical Connection Between Persona-Adoption, Affinity-Seeking, and Self-Disclosure." Norman C. H. Wong, University of Hawaii, Manoa, Karie Leigh Baum, University of Hawaii, Manoa, Krystyna S. Aune, University of Hawaii, Manoa
"Car Talk: Connecting Setting, Communication, and Relationship in a Unique Environment." Christine E. Trinastich, University of Texas, Austin, Brian K. Richardson, University of Texas, Austin, Larry D. Browning, University of Texas, Austin, Mark L. Knapp, University of Texas, Austin
"What Did You Say? Explorations of Couple Type and Message Interpretation." Andrea T. Scott, Louisiana State University
"A Qualitatively Constructed Interpersonal Communication Model: A Grounded Theory Analysis." Glen H. Stamp, Ball State University

| 3644 | 3:30-4:45 p.m. | Conf 4L | Fourth Floor | Chicago Hilton |

COMICS AND VISUAL CULTURE

Sponsor: Visual Communication Commission
Chair: Lisa M. Cuklanz, Boston College
"Critical Analysis of Comic Strips." Jeffrey A. Miller, Utica College of Syracuse University
"The Visual Agenda of Women Comic Artists in Hong Kong." Wendy Siuyi Wong, Hong Kong Baptist University
"Toward a Theory of Comic Book Communication." Randy Duncan, Henderson State University

| 3645 | 3:30-4:45 p.m. | Conf 4M | Fourth Floor | Chicago Hilton |

DIVERSE WAYS OF KNOWING: APPROACHES TO CONFLICT, SOCIALITY, CUSTOMS, TECHNOLOGY, AND CLIMATE DATA

Sponsor: Organizational Communication Division
Chair: Timothy R. Kuhn, Arizona State University
"Appropriateness and Effectiveness of Conflict Styles: An Application of the Competence Model to Rahim's Organizational Conflict Inventory." Michael A. Gross, Arizona State University, Laura K. Guerrero, Arizona State University
"Toward the Development of a Sociality Scale and its Relationship to Customer Satisfaction." Chas D. Koermer, Baldwin-Wallace College, Curtis Brant, Baldwin-Wallace College

Saturday

"A Communication Climate Approach to Collecting Sensitive Date About Intergroup Relations in Organizations." Cathy Boggs, University of California, Santa Barbara
"Technology Use and Organizational Socialization." Jennifer H. Waldeck, University of California, Santa Barbara, Andrew J. Flanagin, University of California, Santa Barbara

Respondent: Katherine I. Miller, Texas A&M University

3646	3:30-4:45 p.m.	McCormick Board Rm	Fourth Floor	Chicago Hilton

EDUCATIONAL POLICIES BOARD BUSINESS MEETING

Sponsor: Educational Policies Board

3647	3:30-4:45 p.m.	Pullman Board Rm	Fourth Floor	Chicago Hilton

COMMISSION ON AMERICAN PARLIAMENTARY PRACTICE BUSINESS MEETING

Sponsor: Commission on American Parlimentary Practice

3649	3:30-4:45 p.m.	Conf 5B	Fifth Floor	Chicago Hilton

TEACHING ACTIVITIES IN AND FOR THE BASIC COURSE

Sponsor: Basic Course Division
Chair: William J. Seiler, University of Nebraska, Lincoln
"Holistic Listening: The Key to Effective Communication." Lisa J. Goodnight, Purdue University, Calumet, Lee M. Rademacher, Purdue University, Calumet
"One Cannot Not Communicate: An Exercise in Impression Formation." Sue M. Wildermuth, University of Minnesota, Minneapolis
"The Best Bank in Town: A Small Group Problem-Solving Assignment." Belinda A. Bernum, University of Central Arkansas
"Gorgias and the Ethical Ideal: Bridging the Past to the Present and Beyond For Students in the Basic Course." Orin G. Johnson, University of Memphis

3651	3:30-4:45 p.m.	Conf 5D	Fifth Floor	Chicago Hilton

COMMUNICATING FAMILY RELATIONSHIPS IN LATER LIFE

Sponsor: Communication and Aging Commission
Chair: Lisa Sparks Bethea, University of Texas, San Antonio
"Differential Accounts of Closeness in Adult Grandchild-Grandparent Relationships." Annette L. Folwell, Western Oregon University, Jo Anna Grant, Arkansas State University
"A Comparison of Relational Qualities in Grandchildren's Relationships with Grandparents and Step-Grandparents." Sherry J. Holladay, Illinois State University
"Looking for Mother in Conversations of Mother-Care." Margaret Z. Ostrenko, University of South Florida

Respondent: Loretta L. Pecchioni, Louisiana State University

3652	3:30-4:45 p.m.	Conf 5E	Fifth Floor	Chicago Hilton

DIALOGICAL IMAGININGS IN RHETORIC AND COMMUNICATION THEORY

Sponsor: Rhetorical and Communication Theory Division
Chair: Dilip P. Gaonkar, Northwestern University
"The Voice of Expert: A Bakhtinian Speech Genre." Karen L. Lollar, University of Denver
"Coloring Outside the Lines, But Inside the Discipline: Associative Rhetoric and Interpersonal Communication*." Lynette M. Long, James Madison University
"Dialogical Rhetoric: An Application of Martin Buber's Philosophy of Dialogue." Jeanine L. Czubaroff, Ursinus College

Respondent: Richard Bauman, Indiana University

*Top Three Paper in Rhetoric and Communication Theory

3653   3:30-4:45 p.m.   Conf 5F   Fifth Floor   Chicago Hilton

SETTING THE AGENDA: EXECUTIVE LEADERSHIP AND THREE TOUGH ISSUES

Sponsor: American Forensic Association
Chair: Barbara A. Pickering, James Madison University
"Clinton's Race Initiative Address: Agency, Performative Contradiction, and Human Rights in Civil Rights Discourse." Bridget Godes, University of Northern Iowa, Catherine H. Palczewski, University of Northern Iowa, Jennifer Rawe, University of Northern Iowa
"Post Cold War Rhetoric Toward China: A Reappraisal of Realism." Matthew G. Gerber, University of Kansas
"The Global Warming Controversy: The Intersection of Science and Politics." Kelly P. Dunbar, Baylor University

---

3654   3:30-4:45 p.m.   Conf 5G   Fifth Floor   Chicago Hilton

TECHNOLOGY AND THE CLASSROOM

Sponsor: Instructional Development Division
Chair: Candice E. Thomas-Maddox, Ohio University
"Video Interactive Distance Learning: A Test of Student Motivation, Satisfaction with Interaction and Mode of Delivery, and Perceived Effectiveness." Ruth M. Guzley, California State University, Chico, Susan Avanzino, California State University, Chico, Aaron Bor, California State University, Chico
"Students' Uses of New Media to Shrink the Lecture Hall." John R. Chapin, Penn State University, Beaver, Barna Donovan, Rutgers University
"Learning as Coloring Outside the Lines in the Age of Expansion: Information Interaction Styles." Robert F. Brooks, Florida State University, Kathleen M. Burnett, Florida State University, C. Edward Wotring, Florida State University

Respondent: Mary E. Bozik, University of Northern Iowa

3655   3:30-4:45 p.m.   Conf 5H   Fifth Floor   Chicago Hilton

DISABILITY, PEDAGOGY, AND CONCERNS

Sponsor: Caucus on Disability Issues
Chair: Krishna P. Kandath, Ohio University
"Dyslexia as Pathological/A Dyslexic Paradigm: Critiquing and Continuing Our Understanding of Dyslexia." Keith C. Pounds, Southern Illinois University
"Alternative Approaches to Teaching Communication Between Disabled and Ablebodied Persons." Kari P. Soule, Northwestern University, Joy Christina Shih, Northwestern University
"Distance Education and Teacher Student Interactions: The Impact of Students with Disabilities." Kim M. Kozicki, University of Idaho

---

3656   3:30-4:45 p.m.   Conf 5I   Fifth Floor   Chicago Hilton

BREAKING THE MOLD AND THINKING OUTSIDE THE BOX: UNIQUE ASSESSMENT PROGRAMS, PROJECTS, AND LESSONS LEARNED

Sponsor: Commission on Communication Assessment
Chair: William G. Christ, Trinity University
"Assessment as a Driver for Planning: The Role of Outcomes and Program Assessment in a University Planning Process." Philip M. Backlund, Central Washington University
"Performance-Based Funding of Department Programs Using Multiple Assessments." Robert M. Smith, University of Tennessee, Martin
"Lessons Learned from Implementing Departmental Assessment Plans." Susan R. Hatfield, Winona State University
"Assessment: Demonstrating Outcomes in a Culture of Potential." Christine R. Helsel, Eastern Illinois University

"Are We Meeting the Needs of K-12 School Systems?: Assessment Report on the Status of Teacher Education Programs in Speech Communication." Mary C. Hogg, Eastern Illinois University

---

3657   3:30-4:45 p.m.   Conf 5J   Fifth Floor   Chicago Hilton

A DIALOGUE ON VOICES OF CARE AND JUSTICE

Sponsor: Communication Ethics Commission
Chair: Brent Northup, Carroll College
   "Applications of a Feminist Ethic of Care in the Public Sphere." Richard L. Johannesen, Northern Illinois University
   "Beyond the Heinz Dilemma: Argument, Ethics and Professional Epistemology in the Voices of Care and Justice." Susan Zickmund, University of Iowa

Respondent: Jon A. Hess, University of Missouri, Columbia

3658   3:30-4:45 p.m.   Lake Ontario   Eighth Floor   Chicago Hilton

NEW TECHNOLOGIES FOR TEACHING FREEDOM OF SPEECH

Sponsor: Freedom of Expression Commission
Chair: Jean Goodwin, Northwestern University
   "Take a Stand: An Interactive CD on the Hit Man/Murder Manual Case." Jean Goodwin, Northwestern University
   "Using the World Wide Web in Teaching Free Expression." Stephen A. Smith, University of Arkansas
   "Web Site Development and Use." Dale A. Herbeck, Boston College
   "A is for Access: Rural Undergraduates and Virtual Law Libraries." Susan Mallon Ross, SUNY, Potsdam

The presenters will demonstrate (and, if possible, give away) some new technologies, and discuss how they can be used in teaching the undergradute free speech course.

3659   3:30-4:45 p.m.   Lake Michigan   Eighth Floor   Chicago Hilton

"STRANGERS" FROM DIFFERENT SHORES: A TRANSNATIONAL COMPARISON OF ASIANS AND ASIAN PACIFIC AMERICANS

Sponsors: Asian/Pacific American Caucus
              Asian Pacific American Communication Studies Division
Chair: Roichi Okabe, Nanzan University
   "The Comparison of Cultural Value Judgments Between Chinese-American Children and Chinese Children." Joyce Cheng, University of Northern Iowa
   "Japanese and Japanese Americans in the Continental U.S.: Interethnic Communication Competence." Todd Imahori, Seinan Gakuin University, Japan
   "How Different Are They Really? Asians and Asian Americans in Hawaii: The Case of Japanese and Koreans." Akira Miyahara, Seinan Gakuin University, Japan, Min-Sun Kim, University of Hawaii, Manoa

Respondent: Kathleen Wong (Lau), Arizona State University

3661   3:30-4:45 p.m.   Lake Erie   Eighth Floor   Chicago Hilton

IN OUR IMAGE?: AN EXPLORATION OF LATINA/O CULTURE

Sponsor: Latina/Latino Communication Studies Division
Chair: Fernando P. Delgado, Arizona State University West
   "Transforming Religious Experience: The Cult of Our Lady of Guadalupe As an Art of the Contact Zone." Robert G. Westerfelhaus, University of Houston, Downtown, Rafael Obregon, Penn State University, Arvind Singhal, Ohio University
   "In Our Own Image?!: A Rhetorical Criticism of Latina Magazine." Bernadette M. Calafell, Arizona State University

Respondent: Leda M. Cooks, University of Massachusetts, Amherst

3662	3:30-4:45 p.m.	Essex Court	Second Floor	Essex Inn

PERFORMANCE HOUR: BEE BEE GUNS AND COMBAT BOOTS

Sponsor: Religious Communication Association
Chair: Edwin A. Hollatz, Wheaton College

Panelist: Renton Rathbun, Bob Jones University

This original, one-person show dramatizes two levels of memory: a child making sense of his grandmother's Alzheimer's disease and a soldier's first encounter with a brutal military culture. Issues of cruelty and hatred on both levels are finally resolved by forgiveness.

3663	3:30-4:45 p.m.	Windsor Court	Second Floor	Essex Inn

ETHNOGRAPHIES OF RACE, GENDER, AND CULTURE

Sponsor: Ethnography Division
Chair: Kara KW Chan, Hong Kong Baptist University
   "Observer, Participant, Native, Ethnographer: Reflections on Shifting Identities." Esther
      Schely Newman, Hebrew University of Jerusalem
   "Constructing Gender: The Roles of 'Feminine' and 'Masculine' as Done by a Female
      Pediatric Nursing Team." Daniel Stuart Wilber, Purdue University
   "From Queens to Calabashes: Touring the Native." Rona T. Halualani, San Jose State
      University
   "African American Me: An Ethnography of Identity Construction in Miami, Florida."
      Juandalynn L. Taylor, University of Texas, Austin

Respondent: Patricia J. Sotirin, Michigan Technological University

3664	3:30-4:45 p.m.	Buckingham Court	Second Floor	Essex Inn

COLORING OUTSIDE THE LINES IN MEDIA CRITICISM: POWER, RESISTANCE, AND CONNECTION IN RADIO, FILM, AND THE INTERNET*

Sponsor: American Studies Commission
Chair: Barbara L. Baker, Central Missouri State University
   "Acts of Power/Acts of Resistance: NPR Teenage Diaries." Kristin A. Brown-Owens, Central
      Missouri State University
   "'The Resistance Manifesto': The Rhetorical Vision of Neo-Nazi Propaganda." Jose E.
      Cabrera, Central Missouri State University
   "A Feminist Critique of The Wedding: Remembering Zucca's Daughters." Mary A. Costley,
      Central Missouri State University
   "Being and Seeming: How the Beanie Baby Craze Affects Internet Relationships." Rebecca
      M. Held, Central Missouri State University
   "Postmodernity and the Reaffirmation of Dominance in Waiting for Guffman." Kristie
      Pennock-Delgado, Central Missouri State University

*Student Debut Panel

3665	3:30-4:45 p.m.	Park East Walk	Second Floor	Essex Inn

EXTENDING SEMIOTIC THEORY

Sponsor: Semiotics and Communication Commission
Chair: Frank J. Macke, Mercer University
   "Toward a Theory of Imbrication." James R. Taylor, University of Montreal
   "Alfred Schutz and the Meaning of Reflection: Inadequacies, Correctives, and Examplars."
      Corey Anton, Grand Valley State University
   "Ecosemiotics." James C. Lundy, Doane College

Respondent: Algis Mickunas, Ohio University

Saturday

3666   3:30-4:45 p.m.   **Cohn Rm**   **Second Floor**   **Spertus Institute**

FAILURES OF DISCOURSE

Sponsor: American Association for Rhetoric of Science & Technology
Chair: Joan Leach, Imperial College of London
   "What Do You Get When You Fall in Love? The Rhetoric of Medical Authority and the
      Immunology of Love." Greg Spicer, California University of Pennsylvania
   "Without a Voice: Determining End-of-Life Treatment Choice in the Communicatively
      Impaired." Deborah J. Voss, University of Pittsburgh
   "Breast Cancer Controversy: A Case Study in the Rhetoric of Clinical Experiments and
      Public Information." Lisa A. Belicka, University of Pittsburgh

Respondent: Joan Leach, Imperial College of London

3667   3:30-4:45 p.m.   **Krensky Rm**   **Second Floor**   **Spertus Institute**

TELEVISION PROGRAMS AS LEGAL TEXTS: WHAT DO THEY TELL US ABOUT THE AMERICAN CRIMINAL JUSTICE SYSTEM?

Sponsor: Communication and Law Commission
Chair: Jeffrey D. Brand, North Dakota State University
   "ALLY McBEAL: Law as Sexual Persona." Susan E. Fillippeli, Auburn University
   "Law and Order: The White Guys Are Still Running the Show." David L. Sutton, Auburn
      University, Melissa Britts, Auburn University, Margaret Landman, Auburn University
   "The Practice: An Ethnographic Analysis." Britton McMullian, Auburn University, Dusty
      Shaffer, Auburn University, John Spitler, Auburn University, Georgia Wilson, Auburn
      University

Respondent: Jeffrey D. Brand, North Dakota State University

3670   3:30-4:45 p.m.   **Rm 904**   **Ninth Floor**   **Spertus Institute**

COMPETITIVE PAPERS IN CHINESE COMMUNICATION STUDIES: MEDIA AND CULTURE IN CHINA

Sponsor: Association for Chinese Communication Studies
Chair: Michael D. Hazen, Wake Forest University
   "Technical Hegemony vs. Cultural Hegemony: Impact of Television on the Sociocentric
      Chinese Society*." Hong Wang, Southern Illinois University
   "An Analysis of the One-Child-Per-Family Policy in the People's Republic of China." Pei
      Wang, University of Cincinnati, James A. Schnell, Ohio Dominican College
   "The Political Nature of the Modern Chinese Press: 1815-1949." Dejun Liu, University
      College of Cape Breton, Canada

Respondent: Mei Zhong, San Diego State University

*Student Paper

3671   3:30-4:45 p.m.   **Rm 906**   **Ninth Floor**   **Spertus Institute**

RHETORIC, IDENTITY AND VIRTUE: ISOCRATEAN APPROACHES TOWARD POLITICAL ACTION

Sponsor: American Society for the History of Rhetoric
Chair: Ron Vonburg, University of Pittsburgh
   "Who the Hellas are We? Identity and Identification in Isocratean Rhetoric." John Weibel,
      University of Iowa
   "Isocrates Gets the Vote: How the Isocratean Encomium Finds Its Way to the Campaign
      Podium." Julie E. Ferris, University of Iowa
   "Politics as Virtue and Collective Memory: Lessons Learned from Isocrates' On the Peace."
      Wade S. Davis, University of Iowa
   "The Post-Isocratean Condition: Calling Virtuous Subjects into Being Through Rhetorical
      Praxis." Kathryn A. Cady, University of Iowa

Respondent: John Poulakos, University of Pittsburgh

3672   3:30-4:45 p.m.   Rm 907   Ninth Floor   Spertus Institute

WHAT ROLE OUGHT FORENSICS PLAY IN THE TWENTY-FIRST CENTURY COMMUNICATION STUDIES DEPARTMENT

Sponsor: Cross Examination Debate Association
Chair: Bruce F. Wickelgren, University of Northern Iowa

Panelists: G. Jon Hall, University of Northern Iowa
Melissa L. Beall, University of Northern Iowa
Larry G. Ehrlich, University of Missouri, Kansas City
Leah E. White, University of Northern Iowa
Tara Tate, University of North Texas

Respondent: Bill Henderson, University of Northern Iowa

Decisions relating to the nature and goals of forensics are an ongoing topic of concern. Choices to hire or retain, funding, release time, as well as support services are made by non-forensic members of the academic community. This panel will probe these issues from a variety of perspectives.

3673   3:30-4:45 p.m.   Rm 908   Ninth Floor   Spertus Institute

TRANSFORMING STUDENTS, FACULTY, COMMUNITIES, AND FORENSICS PROGRAMS THROUGH SERVICE-LEARNING

Sponsor: National Forensic Association
Chair: Edward A. Hinck, Central Michigan University
"Walking the Forensic Tightrope: Using Service-Learning to Improve Team Academic and Competitive Performance." Russell D. Lowery-Hart, West Texas A&M University
"Transforming Self-Concept and Community Through Persuasive Speaking Activities in a Correctional Facility." James Zeigler, Ionia Temporary Correctional Facility, Edward A. Hinck, Central Michigan University
"Integrating Service-Learning in Faculty Tenure and Promotion Guidelines for Directors of Forensics." Shelly Hinck, Central Michigan University
"Aligning University and Community Resources in Service-Learning Projects Involving Speech Programs." Pam Fitzgerald, Isabella County United Way, Shawna Ross, Central Michigan University Volunteer Office

---

3674   3:30-4:45 p.m.   Auditorium   Second Floor   Spertus Institute

PERFORMANCE: A WAY TO COMMUNICATE CULTURE

Sponsor: Theatre Division
Chair: Gary L. Balfantz, Sauk Valley Community College
"Positive Experiences: Voices of HIV/AIDS." Scott E. Dillard, Fort Valley State University, Amy S. Burt, Georgia College and State University
"Using the Performing Arts to Interpret Heritage." Daniel Dahlquist, University of Wisconsin, Platteville, Tim Merriman, National Association for Interpretation

Saturday

5:00 p.m.

3711   5:00-6:15 p.m.   Int'l Ballroom North   Second Floor   Chicago Hilton

NCA PRESIDENTIAL ADDRESS

Sponsor: National Communication Association
Chair: Raymie E. McKerrow, Ohio University

Presidential Address. Orlando L. Taylor, Howard University

6:30 p.m.

3811   6:30-7:45 p.m.   Int'l Ballroom North   Second Floor   Chicago Hilton

NCA AWARDS PRESENTATION

Sponsor: National Communication Association
Chair: Raymie E. McKerrow, Ohio University

Presentation of awards by Sharon Ratliffe, Golden West College and Lloyd Bitzer, Northwestern University. Please join together to honor the recipients of the NCA Awards.

8:00 p.m.

3912   8:00-9:15 p.m.   Int'l Ballroom South   Second Floor   Chicago Hilton

SCRAP METTLE SOUL: COMMUNITY-BASED PERFORMANCE

Sponsor: Theatre Division

Performers: Beatrice Bosco, Chicago Arts Program
             Allison Trimarco, Chicago Arts Program

Scrap Mettle SOUL is Chicago's only community performance ensemble and uses the performance process to strengthen community both on stage and behind the scenes. True stories are gathered from the community and, with the help of writers, directors, composers, designers and others from the Chicago arts community, original scripts and songs are created and performed by community members. This performance is a sampling of their work.

Sunday,
November 7, 1999

8:00 a.m.

4108   **8:00-9:15 a.m.**   **Continental BR C**   **Lobby Level**   **Chicago Hilton**

CULTURAL STUDIES POTPOURRI

Sponsor: Critical and Cultural Studies Division
Chair: Lisa A. Flores, University of Utah
   "Free Spree: Toward an 'Overreading' of Professional Basketball." Anthony T. Perucci, New
      York University
   "The Interplay of Familial and National Morality: The Politics of Forrest Gump's Postwar
      Family Values." J. Christian Spielvogel, James Madison University
   "Representations of Modern Living: A Study of Household Products and Appliance
      Advertisements in Hong Kong." Wendy Wong, Hong Kong Baptist University
   "Creating 'New Generation': An Althusserian Analysis of New Generation Discourse of
      Mass Media in Korea, 1993-1997." Oh-Hyeon Lee, University of Massachusetts,
      Amherst
   "Serial Killers are Invariably Unfunny: Critical Sarcasm's Antimanifesto." Eric Shouse,
      University of South Florida

4110   **8:00-9:15 a.m.**   **Grand Ballroom**   **Second Floor**   **Chicago Hilton**

PERFORMING ETHNOGRAPHIC THEORY AND RESEARCH

Sponsor: Performance Studies Division
Chair: Mindy E. Fenske, Louisiana State University
   "X-Rays and Catholic Schoolgirls: Performing Medical and Personal History." Gretchen A.
      Case, University of California, Berkeley
   "The Limits of Liminality: History, Ritual and Culture in the Context of Greek Theatrical
      Experience." Gregory L. Cavenaugh, Louisiana State University
   "Seeing Red." Jill Hildebrant, Southern Illinois University, Carbondale
   "Vision Quest and Liminal Experience: Beyond Catharsis." Rebecca M. Kennerly, Louisiana
      State University
   "Ethnography in the Ether." Kelly Rowett, University of North Carolina, Chapel Hill
   "Auto-Critique of the Performative Ethnographer." Ross Louis, Louisiana State University

Respondent: Joni L. Jones, University of Texas, Austin

4115   **8:00-9:15 a.m.**   **Boulevard B**   **Second Floor**   **Chicago Hilton**

WHAT IS IN MY FILE?: PREPARING FOR TENURE AND POST-TENURE REVIEW

Sponsor: Theatre Division
Chair: Anne R. Berkeley, Montgomery College
   "Teaching Portfolios." John C. Countryman, Berry College, Sara L. Nalley, Columbia
      College, Ronald E. Shields, Bowling Green State University

"The Post-Tenure Review." Roberta L. Crisson, Kutztown University, Barbara Parisi, Long Island University, Brooklyn, Dorothy Webb, Indiana University-Purdue University, Indianapolis

---

4116   8:00-9:15 a.m.   Boulevard C   Second Floor   Chicago Hilton

SELF-OTHER: SPECIFYING HISTORICAL, POLITICAL, CULTURAL AND RACIAL CONDITIONS

Sponsor: Critical and Cultural Studies Division
Chair: Thomas K. Nakayama, Arizona State University
   "Shifting Sands of Whiteness: The Return of the Repressed in White South African Identity." Melissa E. Steyn, University of Cape Town
   "Asian American Identities: The Insufficiency of the 'Other' Framework." Kathleen Wong (Lau), Arizona State University
   "Polish Americans and Jewish Americans: Self-Other Relations Through Historical and Transnational Struggles." Jolanta A. Drzewiecka, Washington State University
   "Over-Determined Limits and Possibilities for 'Native Identity': Cultural Studies and Re-Theorizing Identity." Rona T. Halualani, San Jose State University
   "Subject Positioning as Translation: Reframing the Postmodern Debates on Identities." S. Lily Mendoza, Arizona State University

Respondent: Wenshu Lee, San Jose State University

4118   8:00-9:15 a.m.   Waldorf   Third Floor   Chicago Hilton

NCA LEGISLATIVE COUNCIL BUSINESS MEETING

Sponsor: NCA Legislative Council

4119   8:00-9:15 a.m.   Astoria   Third Floor   Chicago Hilton

RACE, SCIENCE, AND MEMORY IN SEGREGATIONIST RHETORIC

Sponsor: Public Address Division
Chair: Robert B. Asen, University of Wisconsin, Madison
   "Boundary Work in the Public Rhetoric of Intellectuals: Franz Boas' Atlanta University Commencement Address as a Refutation of White Supremacist Science." David Droge, University of Puget Sound
   "Social Darwinism and Post-Reconstruction African American Rhetoric." Richard W. Leeman, University of North Carolina, Charlotte
   "Alabama's Collective Memory and the Segregationist Structure of Governor Fob James' Religious Crusade." Michael J. Janas, Samford University

Respondent: John A. Campbell, University of Memphis

4121   8:00-9:15 a.m.   Williford A   Third Floor   Chicago Hilton

STUDENT PAPERS IN VISUAL COMMUNICATION

Sponsor: Visual Communication Commission
Chair: April Dupree, University of South Alabama
   "Swastika as Icon: Visual Rhetoric Using Burke's 'Ultimate Term'." Danna E. Prather, University of Iowa
   "The Visual Image and Aristotelian Rhetoric." Diana L. Tucker, Southern Illinois University, Carbondale
   "Autobiography, Dialogic Engagement and Madness in *Complaints of a Dutiful Daughter*." Teresa G. Bergman, University of California, Davis
   "An Historical Look at the Photographic Image." Michelle I. Seelig, Florida State University

Respondent: Marla R. Kanengieter, St. Cloud State University

4122   8:00-9:15 a.m.   Williford B   Third Floor   Chicago Hilton

THE RHETORIC OF POPULAR ECONOMICS

Sponsor: Political Communication Division
Chair: Michael Weiler, Emerson College
    "Huey Long and the Populist Economics of Despair and Hope." Bernard K. Duffy,
      California Polytechnic State University, San Luis Obispo
    "The Agrarian Movement vs. Impulses Toward Economic Success: When Two Historical
      Ideologies Clashed in Print, and Orality Tipped the Scales in Favor of One." Ronald H.
      Carpenter, University of Florida, Gainesville
    "Building the Post-War Economic Consensus: The Seeds of Conservative Triumph."
      Michael Weiler, Emerson College

Respondent: Edward M. Panetta, University of Georgia

4123   8:00-9:15 a.m.   Williford C   Third Floor   Chicago Hilton

WRITING WOMEN INTO POLITICAL AND SOCIAL SPACES

Sponsor: Feminist and Women Studies Division
Chair: Nikki C. Townsley, Purdue University
    "Women's Participation in Computer-Mediated Communication: A Discovery Process."
      Melissa Camacho, Michigan State University
    "Hakoiri Musume (Daughter[s] in a Box): The 1883 Speech of Kishida Toshiko." Jane W.
      Yamazaki, Wayne State University
    "Rewriting Women into Rhetorical History: Adding Intersections to the Corporeal Body via
      New Alliances." Mark J. Jones, Ohio University
    "Privileged and Marginalized: A Politically Conservative Discourse on Family." Janice
      Haynes, University of Massachusetts, Amherst

Respondent: Catherine H. Palczewski, University of Northern Iowa

---

4124   8:00-9:15 a.m.   Marquette   Third Floor   Chicago Hilton

DEVELOPMENT COMMUNICATION IN AFRICA: NEW MILLENNIUM CHALLENGES

Sponsors: Black Caucus
    African American Communication & Culture Commission
Chair: Cecil A. Blake, University of Nebraska, Lincoln
    "The New Information and Communication Technologies and Their Application in
      Development Communications for Africa." Cecil A. Blake, University of Nebraska,
      Lincoln
    "Integrating Uses and Dependency into Communication and National Development in
      Africa." Donald S. Taylor, California State University, Sacramento, Peter Nwoso,
      California State University, Sacramento
    "Development Communication and the New Millennium: Which Way for Africa." Andrew
      A. Moemeka, Central Connecticut State University

Respondent: Charles C. Okigbo, North Dakota State University

4125   8:00-9:15 a.m.   Joliet   Third Floor   Chicago Hilton

NCA 2000 CONVENTION PLANNERS SECOND MEETING

Sponsor: 2000 NCA Convention Planners Committee

4127   8:00-9:15 a.m.   PDR 2   Third Floor   Chicago Hilton

EXPLAINING ILLNESS: ISSUES OF THEORY, STRATEGIES, AND POPULATIONS

Sponsor: Health Communication Division
Chair: Bryan B. Whaley, University of San Francisco

Sunday

"The Nature and Language of Illness Explanations." Teresa L. Thompson, University of Dayton

"Managing Uncertainty in Illness Explanation: An Application of Problematic Integration Theory." Austin S. Babrow, Purdue University, Stephen C. Hines, West Virginia University, Chris R. Kasch, Bradley University

"Explaining Illness as Bad News: Individual Differences in Sharing Illness-Related Information." Cathy M. Gillotti, Purdue University, Calumet, James L. Applegate, University of Kentucky

"Explaining Illness to Older Adults: The Complexities of the Provider-Patient Interaction as We Age." Jon F. Nussbaum, Penn State University, Loretta L. Pecchioni, Louisiana State University, Jo Anna Grant, Arkansas State University, Annette L. Folwell, Western Oregon University

"Explaining Illness to Asian Americans: Culture, Communication and Boundary Regulation." Gust A. Yep, San Francisco State University

Respondent: H. Dan O'Hair, University of Oklahoma

4128　　8:00-9:15 a.m.　　　　　　PDR 3　　　Third Floor　　Chicago Hilton

THE EMERGENCE OF SELF THROUGH FAMILY INTERACTION: PERSONAL NARRATIVES OF FAMILY COMMUNICATION

Sponsor: Family Communication Division
Chair: Glen H. Stamp, Ball State University
　"My Walk with the Venerable One." Tai Du, Ball State University
　"An Unlikely Pair." Andrea M. McClanahan, Ball State University
　"The Fictitious Child." Amanda M. Wilson, Ball State University
　"My Own Words Through Different Ears." Jill McCall, Ball State University
　"Love and Tragedy: A Narrative Analysis." Natasha Tiff, Ball State University
　"The Kaleidoscope of Life: A Narrative Analysis." Jennifer A. Becker, Ball State University

Respondent: Glen H. Stamp, Ball State University

4129　　8:00-10:45 a.m.　　　　　　PDR 4　　　Third Floor　　Chicago Hilton

CREATIVE LINKS BETWEEN MASTER'S PROGRAMS AND CONTEMPORARY CAREER PATHWAYS

Sponsor: Table Talk Series
Chair: Janice M. Barrett, Boston University

Panelists: Don M. Boileau, George Mason University
　　　　　Martha D. Cooper, Northern Illinois University
　　　　　Kenneth D. Day, University of the Pacific
　　　　　Edward J. Downes, Boston University
　　　　　Craig A. Dudczak, Syracuse University
　　　　　Marlene G. Fine, Simmons College
　　　　　Katherine Hawkins, Wichita State University
　　　　　Susan A. Jasko, California University of Pennsylvania
　　　　　Stephen A. Klien, Boston University
　　　　　Robert L. Krizek, Saint Louis University
　　　　　Roseann M. Mandziuk, Southwest Texas State University
　　　　　Sue Parenio, Boston University
　　　　　Warren G. Sandmann, Minnesota State University, Mankato
　　　　　Roy J. Schwartzman, University of South Carolina
　　　　　Anastacia D. Serro-Boim, St. John's University
　　　　　Xing (Lucy) Lu, DePaul University

Careers for students entering our field are changing so rapidly that we need to explore how our MA programs can best meet the needs of current and prospective students in the workplace. This panel highlights how different higher education institutions are providing appropriate training and professional connections and focuses on seventeen distinct career options for M.A./M.S. graduates in communication. Audience participation.

4130   8:00-9:15 a.m.   PDR 5   Third Floor   Chicago Hilton

LOVE, COMMITMENT AND RELATIONSHIP MAINTENANCE

Sponsors: Interpersonal Communication Division
          Family Communication Division
Chair: Anita L. Vangelisti, University of Texas, Austin
   "Making Sense of Humor in Young Romantic Relationships: Understanding Partners'
      Perceptions." Amy M. Bippus, University of Texas, Austin
   "Communicating Commitment in Premarital Relationships." Cailin Kulp, University of
      Texas, Austin
   "Perceptions of Commitment in Marriage: Assessing the Influence of Relational
      Preferences." Daniel J. Weigel, University of Nevada, Reno, Deborah S. Ballard-Reisch,
      University of Nevada, Reno
   "Applying a 'New' Model to the Communicative Phenomenon of Codependents'
      Relational Maintenance." Katherine L. Nelson, Barry University

Respondent: Anita L. Vangelisti, University of Texas, Austin

4132   8:00-9:15 a.m.   PDR 7   Third Floor   Chicago Hilton

COLORING OUTSIDE THE LINES OF DRAMATIC INTERPRETATION: YOU BE THE JUDGE

Sponsor: Argumentation and Forensics Division
Chair: Thomas A. Workman, University of Nebraska, Lincoln

Panelists: Karen R. Piercy, University of Wisconsin, Eau Clair
            Thomas A. Workman, University of Nebraska, Lincoln
            Tom Zeidler, Illinois State University

In April of 1999, The National Forensic Association offered the experimental event "Dramatic
Dialogue Interpretation" or DDI. The objective of the event was to explore the somewhat lost
art of performing multiple characters in dialogue, an aspect often missing in many
performances of Dramatic Interpretation. This panel seeks to extend the learning from that
event by "coloring outside the lines" in two directions. First, students will perform different
styles of Dramatic Interpretation—monologue, dialogue, and mixed. Then panel and
audience will discuss the different styles, looking at judging criteria and competitive issues in
Dramatic Interpretation, and will define and evaluate the lines drawn in judging the event.
The goal is to create a discussion among forensics professionals about standardization in
judging Dramatic Interpretation, and about ways we can allow students to extend boundaries
for educational purposes.

4134   8:00-9:15 a.m.   Conf 4B   Fourth Floor   Chicago Hilton

ENACTING 'BELONGING': DISPLAYING LEGITIMATE MEMBERSHIP IN RELATIONSHIPS

Sponsor: Language and Social Interaction Division
Chair: Chris L. Nix, University of Louisville
   "Serial Interactions in the Dense Layering of Social Support." Mary Jiang I. Bresnahan,
      Michigan State University, Lisa M. Murray-Johnson, Michigan State University
   "Relationship Maintenance in Action: Talking About Future Activities at Dinner." Susan D.
      Corbin, University of Texas, Austin
   "The Relationship in Talk: Explicit and Implicit Influences on Persuasion." Erin M.
      Sahlstein, University of Iowa
   "Claiming Partner Knowledge I: On the Exigencies and Utility of a Profoundly Intimate
      Conversational Claim." Shirley A. Staske, Eastern Illinois University

Respondent: Sandra L. Ragan, University of Oklahoma

Sunday

4135   8:00-9:15 a.m.   Conf 4C   Fourth Floor   Chicago Hilton

THE INTIMATE ART OF THE PREGNANT BELLYMASK: PERFORMING GENDER THROUGH AN INTERPERSONAL ARTIFACT

Sponsor: Feminist and Women Studies Division

Performers: Julie E. Ferris, University of Iowa
                  Amie D. Kincaid, Eastern Illinois University

Respondent: Karen A. Foss, University of New Mexico

This is a performance and critical analysis of the artwork of women who created masks of their pregnant form including the mask, interviews and videos.

4136   8:00-9:15 a.m.   Conf 4D   Fourth Floor   Chicago Hilton

ORGANIZATIONAL COMMUNICATION IN INTERNATIONAL CONTEXTS: CULTURES, CHANGE, TECHNOLOGY, AND SATISFACTIONS

Sponsor: Organizational Communication Division
Chair: Timothy R. Kuhn, Arizona State University
   "Building the Relational Theory of Motivational Communication and Calling for Testing the Theory and Its Cultural Variability in the Organizational Context." Xuejian Yu, Stonehill College
   "Sustainable Development, New Information Technology and NGOs in India: A Critical Approach Toward Development and Technology." Shiv Ganesh, Purdue University
   "American Expatriates in Russia: Cultural Expectations and Job Satisfaction of Russian Subordinates." Tatyana Avdeyeva, Washington State University
   "Interpreting Organizational Culture of State-Owned Enterprises in China." Shuang Liu, Hong Kong Baptist University

Respondent: B. Christine Shea, California Polytechnic State University, San Luis Obispo

---

4138   8:00-9:15 a.m.   Conf 4F   Fourth Floor   Chicago Hilton

MEDIA EFFECTS OR MEDIA SCAPEGOATING?: A ROUNDTABLE DISCUSSION

Sponsor: Mass Communication Division
Chair: Gwenyth L. Jackaway, Fordham University

Panelists: Joanne R. Cantor, University of Wisconsin, Madison
                Ed Donnerstein, University of California, Santa Barbara
                Jeb Fowles, University of Houston, Clear Lake
                Gwenyth L. Jackaway, Fordham University

Respondent: Ellen A. Wartella, University of Texas, Austin

4139   8:00-9:15 a.m.   Conf 4G   Fourth Floor   Chicago Hilton

A DISCUSSION OF TEACHING TECHNOLOGY IN MIDDLETOWN, USA

Sponsor: Human Communication and Technology Commission
Chair: Glynis C. Hiebner, Central Connecticut State University
   "Matching Student Learning Styles to Internet Technology Strategies." Scott R. Olson, Ball State University
   "Incorporating Technology into the Classroom: BSU Students' Perceptions." Beth A. Messner, Ball State University
   "But Communication Is a Process: Why Do We Make the Web so Static?" Lyle J. Flint, Ball State University
   "Contrasting Methods of Internet Use." Richard G. Nitcavic, Ball State University
   "The Good, the Bad, and the Ugly: Using Technology in the Required University Course." Jacquelyn J. Buckrop, Ball State University

Respondents: Peggy Y. Byers, Ball State University
             Scott A. Chadwick, Iowa State University

4140   8:00-9:15 a.m.   Conf 4H   Fourth Floor   Chicago Hilton

ARE MY VALUES THEIR VALUES? OR DO THEIR VALUES HAVE TO BECOME MY VALUES? THE TRAINER'S ROLE IN COMMUNICATING VALUES WITHIN THE ORGANIZATION

Sponsor: Training and Development Division
Chairs: Nanci M. Burk, Phoenix College
        Robert R. Boren, Boise State University
        Laurel T. Hetherington, Boise State University
        Ed Phillips, Southern Illinois University
        Lori A. Sefton, Southern Illinois University
        Michelle Wilkes-Carilli, University of Tennessee, Knoxville

Trainers in the twenty-first century will continue to witness companies intent on clarifying and communicating their values to internal and external audiences. Whether the trainer is involved directly in the articulation of values or simply has a tacit understanding of the organization's values statement, it is clear that trainers are often expected to conduct educational sessions within the context of the company's values system. This panel will tackle issues of communicating values from a trainer's perspective.

4142   8:00-9:15 a.m.   Conf 4J   Fourth Floor   Chicago Hilton

COMMUNICATION LABORATORIES AND PEDAGOGY: FACULTY/STAFF DEVELOPMENT IMPLICATIONS AND THE POTENTIAL AND CHALLENGES OF SELECTED APPROACHES

Sponsor: Senior College & University Section
Chair: Linda B. Hobgood, University of Richmond
    "Faculty Development and Staff Training: Providing Incentives Which Promote Use." Linda B. Hobgood, University of Richmond
    "Dialectical Tensions of Running a Speaking Center at a College Without a Required Communication Course." Robin A. Gurien, Mary Washington College
    "Faculty Development and Oral Communication Labs: A Model Partnership." Tamara L. Burk, College of William and Mary

---

4143   8:00-9:15 a.m.   Conf 4K   Fourth Floor   Chicago Hilton

BOUNDARY WORK

Sponsor: American Association for Rhetoric of Science & Technology
Chair: Margaret Hamilton, University of Minnesota
    "Falsifiability Revisited: Friend or Foe of Rhetoric." James B. McOmber, Valdosta State University
    "William Jennings Bryan: Science as Learning, or as Guesswork?" Matthew W. Segaard, University of Minnesota
    "Demarcation, Translation, and Boundary Work in the Rhetorical Reconstruction of Nuclear Fusion." William J. Kinsella, Lewis & Clark College

---

4144   8:00-9:15 a.m.   Conf 4L   Fourth Floor   Chicago Hilton

CULTURAL ARTIFACTS OF POST-FEMINISM

Sponsor: American Studies Commission
Chair: Margaret K. Dick, St. Mary's College, California
    "Putting Ally on Trial: Contesting Post-Feminism in Popular Culture." Mary D. Vavrus, University of Minnesota
    "A Sign of the Times: The Cultural Politics of Ophelia-as-Discourse." Maria Mastronardi, University of Illinois, Chicago

Sunday

"'She Thinks Just Like I Do': College Women's Identification with Ally McBeal." Shawny Anderson, Saint Mary's College of California

Respondent: Bonnie J. Dow, University of Georgia

| 4149 | 8:00-9:15 a.m. | Conf 5B | Fifth Floor | Chicago Hilton |

CONSIDERING THE COLORS AND LINES IN BASIC COURSE TEXTBOOKS

Sponsor: Basic Course Division
Chair: David W. Worley, Indiana State University
   "A Descriptive Analysis of Best-Selling Basic Course Texts." David W. Worley, Indiana State University, David T. McMahan, University of Iowa, Mary C. Hogg, Eastern Illinois University
   "An Author's View of Textbooks in the Basic Communication Course." Lawrence W. Hugenberg, Youngstown State University
   "Basic Course Textbooks: A Pedagogical Tool for Teaching Assistants." Elyse L. Pineau, Southern Illinois University, Carbondale
   "The Role of the Text in Basic Communication Course Classrooms." Barbara S. Hugenberg, Bowling Green State University
   "Using Technology to Enhance Teaching and Textbooks." Melissa L. Beall, University of Northern Iowa

| 4151 | 8:00-9:15 a.m. | Conf 5D | Fifth Floor | Chicago Hilton |

HOW DO WE LISTEN TO OTHER CULTURES? ECOLOGICAL HEALING AND SPIRITUALITY

Sponsor: Spiritual Communication Commission
Chair: Lois J. Einhorn, SUNY, Binghamton
   "Following the Circle: Understanding Four Sacred Herbs of Native American Spirituality." Cindi Elliott, Columbia College
   "Crying for a Vision: Narrative Accounts of the Sacred Rite of Hanblecheyapi." Anne Marie Czerwinski, University of Missouri, Columbia
   "Why Do Women Live Longer? Holistic Communication: Integration of the Social Spiritual and Physical." Robert I. Thompson, University of Kentucky

| 4152 | 8:00-9:15 a.m. | Conf 5E | Fifth Floor | Chicago Hilton |

THEORIZING PRACTICE, PRACTICING THEORY: RHETORIC AND PEDAGOGY

Sponsor: Rhetorical and Communication Theory Division
   "Deliberating Bodies: Classroom as Proto-Public Spaces." Rosa A. Eberly, University of Texas, Austin
   "A Return to Rhetoric's Origins? Using the Phaedrus as a Basic Course Text." Susan M. Ross, Hamilton College
   "The Will to Believe . . . in Rhetoric." Glen A. McClish, Southwestern University

| 4153 | 8:00-9:15 a.m. | Conf 5F | Fifth Floor | Chicago Hilton |

PERFORMING JUDGMENT AND JUDGING PERFORMANCE: THE FUTURE OF FORENSICS

Sponsor: American Forensic Association
Chair: William E. Shanahan, Fort Hays State University

Panelists: Brian Lain, University of Iowa
       William C. Trapani, University of Iowa
       Joseph P. Zompetti, Mercer University
       Maxwell Schnurer, University of Pittsburgh

Respondent: William E. Shanahan, Fort Hays State University

4154	8:00-9:15 a.m.	Conf 5G	Fifth Floor	Chicago Hilton

BRINGING THEORIES AND CONCEPTS TO LIFE: EXPERIENTIAL LEARNING ACTIVITIES FOR THE COMMUNICATION CLASSROOM

Sponsor: Instructional Development Division
"Experiential Learning Activities for Classes in Organizational Communication." Shawn Beckett, Ohio University
"Experiential Learning Activities for Classes in Gender Communication." Carol J. Bruess, University of St. Thomas
"Experiential Learning Activities for Classes in Small Group Communication." Lori A. Byers, Spalding University
"Experiential Learning Activities for Classes in Intercultural Communication." Russell D. Lowery-Hart, West Texas A&M University
"Experiential Learning Activities for Classes in Public Relations." Marjorie Keeshan Nadler, Miami University
"Experiential Learning Activities for Classes in Interpersonal Communication." Nina C. Persi, Ohio University
"Experiential Learning Activities for Classes in Family Communication." Candice E. Thomas-Maddox, Ohio University
"Experiential Learning Activities for Classes in Persuasion." Melissa B. Wanzer, Canisius College

4157	8:00-9:15 a.m.	Conf 5J	Fifth Floor	Chicago Hilton

PARADIGMS LOST: A PERFORMANCE ETHNOGRAPHY

Sponsor: Society for the Study of Symbolic Interaction
Chair: Carolyn S. Ellis, University of South Florida
"Paradigms Lost." Laurel Richardson, Ohio State University

Respondent: Lynn C. Miller, University of Texas, Austin

4160	8:00-9:15 a.m.	Lake Huron	Eighth Floor	Chicago Hilton

CABLE TELEVISION 1949-1999: FIFTY YEARS OF WIRED EXPRESSION

Sponsor: Freedom of Expression Commission
Chair: Bruce E. Drushel, Miami University
"Threatening Invader or Favored Child: First Amendment Implications of Regulators' Perspectives on Cable Television." Bruce E. Drushel, Miami University
"'I Know It When I See It': And I See It on Cable." Kenneth J. Levine, Illinois State University
"Scrambled Legs and Glam: An Examination of the Indecency Provisions of the Telecommunications Act of 1996." Howard M. Kleiman, Miami University
"Has Cable TV Really Changed the Substance of News Reporting?: Scandal Broadcast News from Winchell to Drudge." Kevin M. Minch, University of Kansas

4162	8:00-9:15 a.m.	Essex Court	Second Floor	Essex Inn

CONFLICT MANAGEMENT IN RELIGIOUS ORGANIZATIONS

Sponsor: Religious Communication Association
Chair: Joseph J. Cardot, Abilene Christian University
"Conflict Management Among Baptists." Mary E. Collins, Sam Houston State University
"Religious Conflict Among Latter Day Saints." Becky L. Johns, Weber State University
"Church Conciliation Services." Paul N. Lakey, Abilene Christian University
"Conflict Management Among Roman Catholics." Lynda D. Dixon, Bowling Green State University
"Conflict Culture in Private, Church-Related Universities." Christy L. King, University of Oklahoma

Respondent: Barry C. Poyner, Truman State University

Sunday

4163   8:00-9:15 a.m.   Windsor Court   Second Floor   Essex Inn

AUTOETHNOGRAPHY AND PERSONAL INVOLVEMENT IN ETHNOGRAPHIC RESEARCH

Sponsor: Ethnography Division
Chair: Paaige K. Turner, Saint Louis University
   "Autoethnography: Narrating Experiences of Other(ed) Selves." Nicole A. Wendel,
      University of Oklahoma, Krishna P. Kandath, Ohio University
   "Just Who Is Telling the Story? The Implied Author in Autoethnography." Elaine B. Jenks,
      West Chester University
   "Furry Hugs and Sloppy Kisses: An Ethnographic Investigation into the Role of
      Animal-Assisted Therapy." Angela F. Brumley-Shelton, University of Kentucky
   "Losing Sammy: A Catalyst for Exiting an Abusive Relationship." Pam L. Secklin, St. Cloud
      State University

Respondent: Melanie B. Mills, Eastern Illinois University

4164   8:00-9:15 a.m.   Buckingham Court   Second Floor   Essex Inn

DE-FAMILIARIZING STRANGERS IN THE POSTMODERN WORLD: PART II

Sponsor: Semiotics and Communication Commission
Chair: Tom Craig, Brock University, Canada
   "Familiarizing the Chicana and De-Familiarizing the Feminist: Methodology for Liberation
      Theory and Praxis." Jacqueline M. Martinez, Purdue University
   "Reading the Familiar Through the Stranger: Suzan-Lori Parks' *Venus and the Black Female
      Body*." Lisa Anderson, Purdue University
   "Cultural Semiosis of the 'Familiar' and the 'Strange': Reciprocities of Consciousness in
      Communicology." Isaac E. Catt, Millersville University

9:30 a.m.

4208   9:30-10:45 a.m.   Continental BR C   Lobby Level   Chicago Hilton

COLORING OUTSIDE THE PEDAGOGICAL LINES: CRITICAL INTERVENTIONS, RESISTANCES, AND RHETORICS

Sponsor: Critical and Cultural Studies Division
Chair: Gerard A. Hauser, University of Colorado
   "Dissent, Controversy, and the Basic Course: The Question of Cathexis." Kendall R.
      Phillips, Central Missouri State University
   "Critical Rhetoric and Resistance: Performance, Power and Pedagogy." Cathy Glenn, San
      Francisco State University
   "Is the Classroom a Public Sphere?" Susan Wells, Temple University
   "The Paradox of Empowerment: Critical Response to 'Efficient' Education." Ronald F.
      Wendt, University of South Dakota

4210   9:30-10:45 a.m.   Grand Ballroom   Second Floor   Chicago Hilton

OUTSIDE THE LINES AND BETWEEN THE NOTES: ADAPTING AND STAGING RALPH ELLISON'S *INVISIBLE MAN*

Sponsor: Performance Studies Division
Chair: Patricia H. Suchy, Louisiana State University

Panelists: Ross Louis, Louisiana State University
            Terrance Tucker, Louisiana State University

Respondent: Derek Goldman, University of North Carolina, Chapel Hill

This panel will describe and demonstrate polyphony, collage, blues' "stop time", and
synaesthesia in the adaptation and staging of Ralph Ellison's *Invisible Man*.

| 4215 | 9:30-10:45 a.m. | Boulevard B | Second Floor | Chicago Hilton |

MENTORING ISSUES IN THEATRE PROGRAMS

Sponsor: Theatre Division
Chair: Ken W. McCoy, Stetson University

Panelists: Patrick Faherty, Texas A&M University, Kingsville
Gerald Lee Ratliff, SUNY, Potsdam
Jerry Eisenhour, Eastern Illinois University
Nina M. LeNoir, Bradley University
Gerry Large, University of Wisconsin, Madison
Tim Good, Elmhurst College

A panel discussion of mentoring issues unique to college and university theatre programs. Content includes the relationship between student, mentoring and funding at small institutions, faculty mentoring plans and procedures, and student mentoring for special projects and theatre productions.

| 4216 | 9:30-10:45 a.m. | Boulevard C | Second Floor | Chicago Hilton |

CROSSING THE LINE: ACADEMICS AS ACTIVISTS

Sponsor: Challenging Boundaries Series
Chair: J. Robert Cox, University of North Carolina
"Academic Scholarship and Activism: An Overview." J. Robert Cox, University of North Carolina
"Raising a Voice for the Voiceless: Shared Perspectives on Current Issues Within the Animal Rights Movement." Courtney L. Dillard, University of Texas, Austin
"Cultural Studies at the Crossroads: Revisiting the Theory-Practice Discussion." Deepa Kumar, University of Pittsburgh
"Opportunities and Risks of Using Communication Theory for Praxis: Studying and Struggling for Environmental Justice." Phaedra C. Pezzullo, University of North Carolina

Respondent: Dana L. Cloud, University of Texas, Austin

| 4219 | 9:30-10:45 a.m. | Astoria | Third Floor | Chicago Hilton |

SPEAKING OUTSIDE SYMPATHETIC LINES: PRESIDENTIAL RESPONSES TO HOSTILE AUDIENCES

Sponsor: Public Address Division
Chair: Wilmer A. Linkugel, University of Kansas
"Adapting to the Audience Without Pulling any Punches: FDR at Commonwealth Club." Tammy R. Vigil, University of Kansas
"Truman's Farewell Address: A Forthright Style and a Forthright President." Keri A. Bodensteiner, University of Kansas, Mary M. Carver, Northern Illinois University
"The Guardian Genius of Democracy: Lyndon Johnson and the Elementary and Secondary Education Act of 1965." Julie Davis, University of Kansas
"A Rhetorical Analysis of Ronald Reagan's 1976 Presidential Campaign." John M. Jones, University of Kansas

Respondent: Judith Hoover, Western Kentucky University

| 4222 | 9:30-10:45 a.m. | Williford B | Third Floor | Chicago Hilton |

GEORGE BUSH AND THE RHETORIC OF FOREIGN POLICY

Sponsor: Political Communication Division
Chair: Kurt Ritter, Texas A&M University
"George Bush's Rhetoric in Response to the Tiananmen Square Massacre." Nicolas Rangel, Texas A&M University
"Bush's War on Drugs: A Rhetorical Analysis." Joel T. Whittemore, Texas A&M University

"The Failure at Rio: Diplomacy, Ecology, and Election Politics." Martin Carcasson, Texas A&M University

"In Search of a New World Order: George Bush and the Post-Cold-War Era." Roy Joseph, Texas A&M University

Respondent: Mary E. Stuckey, University of Mississippi

4223	9:30-10:45 a.m.	Williford C	Third Floor	Chicago Hilton

WOMAN AS EVIL: HER ROOTS AND HER RECLAMATION

Sponsor: Feminist and Women Studies Division
Chair: Karen Rasmussen, California State University, Long Beach
   "Not Just Virgen Pura: Chicana Writers Reclaim Herstory." Lisa A. Flores, University of Utah
   "I Am a Woman: The Lilith Myth in Works by Alice Walker and Toni Morrison." Karen Rasmussen, California State University, Long Beach, Angela J. Aguayo, California State University, Long Beach
   "So Is it Her War? The Fate of the Feminine in Films Featuring Women in the Military." Sharon D. Downey, California State University, Long Beach
   "The Witch as Archetypal Metaphor: Feminist Folklorists Counter Her Demonization." Nina M. Reich, California State University, Long Beach

Respondent: A. Cheree Carlson, Arizona State University

4224	9:30-10:45 a.m.	Marquette	Third Floor	Chicago Hilton

MASS COMMUNICATION AND AFRICAN AMERICAN COLLEGE STUDENTS

Sponsor: Black Caucus
Chair: Andrea H. Jackson, Howard University
   "Assessing Perceptions of Computer-Mediated (CMC) Competence in African American College Students." Vernon Harper, Howard University
   "Television Exposure and Ideal Body Image: Racial Identity and Self-Esteem Among African American College Women—A Critical Analysis." Rockell A. Brown, Howard University
   "Information Processing of HIV/AIDS Prevention Messages Among African American College Students." Carolyn A. Stroman, Howard University

4225	9:30-10:45 a.m.	Joliet	Third Floor	Chicago Hilton

NCA 2000 NOMINATING COMMITTEE BUSINESS MEETING

Sponsor: 2000 NCA Nominating Committee

4226	9:30-10:45 a.m.	PDR 1	Third Floor	Chicago Hilton

RUSSIA IN TRANSITION: STUDIES IN THE DEVELOPMENT OF BUSINESS DISCOURSE IN ORGANIZATIONAL COMMUNICATION

Sponsor: Applied Communication Division
Chair: Mark G. Borzi, Eastern Illinois University
   "An Analysis of Communication Competence of Russian Professionals in Their Organizational Interactions: Three Case Studies." Olga Matyash, Syracuse University
   "The Development of Market-Based Communication Skills in Russian Women's Organizations: An Ethnographic Investigation." Deborah S. Ballard-Reisch, University of Nevada, Reno
   "An Analysis of American-Russian Business Interactions: Developing Market Competence Across the Cultural Divide." Yulia Gordeyeva, Indiana University-Purdue University, Fort Wayne
   "From Communism to Capitalism: A Transformative Grammar of Organizational Discourse in Russia and Eastern Europe." John Parrish-Sprowl, Indiana University-Purdue University, Fort Wayne

4227	9:30-10:45 a.m.	PDR 2	Third Floor	Chicago Hilton

THE INFLUENCE OF TECHNOLOGY ON HEALTH COMMUNICATION

Sponsor: Health Communication Division
Chair: Jeff K. Springston, University of Georgia
  "Developing Hyperpersonal: In the Media or in the Relationship? An Exploration of CMC Support Communities and Traditional Support." Jeanine W. Turner, Georgetown University, Jean Grube, Georgetown University, Jennifer McCann, Association for Professionals in Infection Control
  "Predicting Communication Networks of Health Educators." Gary S. Meyer, Marquette University
  "Technology and Health Promotion: Using the THUS Framework as an Organizing Principle." Bradford M. Millay,
  "The Social Construction of Social Support: An Analysis of the alt.support.eating-disord News Group." Christine L. North, Jamestown College, Sandra L. Ragan, University of Oklahoma
  "The Unknown Victims: A Thematic Analysis of an On-Line Male Breast Cancer Support Group." Jennifer L. Peterson, University of Illinois, Urbana-Champaign

4228	9:30-10:45 a.m.	PDR 3	Third Floor	Chicago Hilton

FAMILY SYSTEMS: PUBLIC AND PRIVATE NOTIONS OF FAMILY

Sponsor: Family Communication Division
Chair: Linda D. Manning, University of Denver
  "Commodified Families." Diana L. Rehling, St. John's University
  "The Public and Private Dialogue About the American Family on Television." Kelly J. Fudge, East Carolina University
  "Constructing Family Identity: An Analysis of American Holiday Letters." George B. Ray, Cleveland State University, Susan B. Poulsen, Portland State University
  "It Takes a Cyber-Village: Pregnancy Bulletin Boards as Support Communities." Lorin B. Arnold, Rowan University

Respondent: Donna R. Pawlowski, Creighton University

4230	9:30-10:45 a.m.	PDR 5	Third Floor	Chicago Hilton

INFLUENCE PROCESSES II: PERSUADING, RESISTING, CREATING AND REPAIRING CREDIBILITY

Sponsor: Interpersonal Communication Division
Chair: Thomas H. Feeley, SUNY, Geneseo
  "The Persuasive Effect of Affective and Cognitive Messages: A Test of Conflicting Hypotheses." Kenzie A. Cameron, University of Georgia, Franklin J. Boster, Michigan State University
  "The Social Processes of Drug Resistance in a Relational Context." Michelle A. Miller, Penn State University
  "Um, Can Credibility Be Repaired?" Heather Freeman, Illinois State University, Renee Tessmann, Illinois State University
  "The Interpersonal Functions of Tattoos." Lisa M. Schreiber, University of Nebraska, Lincoln

Respondent: Thomas H. Feeley, SUNY, Geneseo

4231	9:30-10:45 a.m.	PDR 6	Third Floor	Chicago Hilton

AMERICAN INFLUENCES ON COMMUNICATION EDUCATION AND PEDAGOGY IN JAPANESE SCHOLARSHIP

Sponsor: International & Intercultural Communication Division
Chair: Shigeru Matsumoto, Tokai University

Sunday

"A Critical Analysis of the Rhetoric of Anti-English 'Linguistic Imperialism' Movement."
   Naoto Usui, Aikoku Gakuen University
"Occidentalism: Japanese Uniqueness of Communication?" Hideki Kakita, Aoyama Gakuin
   University
"American Model of Eloquence and Message Production as Ideal Japanese
   Communication: A Critical Examination of Communication Education in Japan."
   Yoshihisa Itaba, Dokkyo University

Respondent: Shigeru Matsumoto, Tokai University

4232   9:30-10:45 a.m.   PDR 7   Third Floor   Chicago Hilton

ARGUING ACROSS THE LINES: DEBATE, DISSENT AND ARGUMENTATIVE CONSTRUCTS

Sponsor: Argumentation and Forensics Division
Chair: Bonnie L. Clark, St. Petersburg Junior College
   "The Use of Oppositional Arguments Within the Context of a People's Claim to
   Uniqueness." Chantal Benoit-Barne, University of Colorado, Boulder
   "A Functional Analysis of the 1988 Bush-Dukakis Presidential Debates." William L. Benoit,
   University of Missouri, Columbia, LeAnn M. Brazeal, University of Missouri, Columbia
   "Modernism is Nothing New: Uncovering the Hidden Fallacy of Postmodernism." William
   D. Harpine, University of Akron
   "Militias and the Regulation of Dissent: The Collapse of Public Reason." Kevin J.
   Cummings, Denver University

Respondent: Robert E. Frank, Morehead State University

4233   9:30-10:45 a.m.   Conf 4A   Fourth Floor   Chicago Hilton

THE FORM AND THE POWER: IMAGES OF RELIGION IN POPULAR AMERICAN FILM

Sponsor: Religious Communication Association
Chair: Annalee R. Ward, Trinity Christian College
   "The Land of Faery as Cheat: A Lewisian Analysis of Robert Zemeckis' Film *Contact*." Marc
   T. Newman, Palomar College
   "Provocation in Scorsese's Film, *The Last Temptation of Christ*." Robin Riley, Kansas
   Wesleyan University
   "The Marginalization of Traditional Southern Religion in the Film *The Grass Harp*." Michael
   P. Graves, Regent University

Respondent: Annalee R. Ward, Trinity Christian College

4234   9:30-10:45 a.m.   Conf 4B   Fourth Floor   Chicago Hilton

BUILDING BRIDGES: LINKING CONVERSATION ANALYSTS AND MEDICAL PRACTITIONERS

Sponsor: Language and Social Interaction Division

Panelists: Wayne A. Beach, San Diego State University
            John C. Heritage, University of California, Los Angeles
            Anita M. Pomerantz, Temple University

Panelists will discuss ways to establish mutually beneficial relationships with healthcare
practitioners, especially in terms of positioning CA-related concerns as valuable to healthcare
practitioners and educators.

4235   9:30-10:45 a.m.   Conf 4C   Fourth Floor   Chicago Hilton

REDRAWING BOUNDARIES: DISCURSIVE MEDIATIONS OF WAR, LAW, AND THE CITY

Sponsor: Commission on Communication in the Future
Chair: Mary Rose Williams, Lane Community College
  "Mediating the Sounds and Sights of War." Laurette Alkidas, Wayne State University
  "Censorship in Cyberspace: Incipient Cyberlaw and the Mediation of Future On-Line Communication." Robert Carr, Wayne State University
  "Communicating the Common Image: Hard Work, Mutual Forbearance, and Consumerism in the Inner-City." Valerie Kinloch, Wayne State University

Respondent: Frances J. Ranney, Wayne State University

4236   9:30-10:45 a.m.   Conf 4D   Fourth Floor   Chicago Hilton

NAVIGATING FROM THE MARGINS: ORGANIZATIONAL STRUCTURES AND STRICTURES

Sponsor: Organizational Communication Division
Chair: Anne M. Nicotera, Howard University
  "A Structurational Analysis of Communication Patterns in a Predominantly African American Organization." Anne M. Nicotera, Howard University, Marcia J. Clinkscales, Howard University
  "Negotiating Multiple Identities In and Around Organizational Margins: A Case Study in Co-Cultural Theory." Mark P. Orbe, Western Michigan University
  "The Institutional Marginalization of Black Male Identity." Ronald L. Jackson, Penn State University
  "Gender as Psychic Prisons: Opening the Organizational Doors to a New Vision." Diane A. Forbes, Howard University

Audience response encouraged.

4238   9:30-10:45 a.m.   Conf 4F   Fourth Floor   Chicago Hilton

FAMILY SYSTEMS: STRAINS IN FAMILY BONDS

Sponsor: Family Communication Division
Chair: Rhonda J. Sprague, University of Wisconsin, Stevens Point
  "Keeping the Relationship Alive: An Analysis of Relational Maintenance Strategies Employed by Non-Custodial Parents and Their Children Following Divorce." Candice E. Thomas-Maddox, Ohio University
  "Describing Work and Family Conflict Situations: Sources and Strategies." Caryn E. Medved, Michigan State University, Kelly Morrison, Michigan State University, Jennifer Butler-Ellis, Michigan State University, Deidre L. Popovich, Michigan State University, Jennifer M. Heisler, Michigan State University, Amy J. Johnson, Michigan State University
  "Take My Mother-in-Law (But Bring Her Back!): Ambivalence in In-Law Relationships." Mittie J. A. Nimocks, University of Wisconsin, Platteville, Patricia Bromley, University of Wisconsin, Platteville
  "Codependency Scale Development." Beth A. Le Poire, University of California, Santa Barbara, Margaret E. Prescott, University of California, Santa Barbara

Respondent: Sherilyn R. Marrow-Ferguson, University of Northern Colorado

---

4240   9:30-10:45 a.m.   Conf 4H   Fourth Floor   Chicago Hilton

BEYOND ROLE PLAYING: INTERACTIVE PERFORMANCE AS A CORPORATE TRAINING TOOL

Sponsor: Training and Development Division

Panelists: Laura A. Terlip, University of Northern Iowa
    Karen S. Mitchell, University of Northern Iowa

Sunday

Interactive performance techniques are based on the work of Augusto Boal's Forum Theatre and Jonathan Fox's Playback Theatre. This panel will focus on the use of interactive performance in training and development, especially for those interested in its application to conflict management, diversity issues, and management development. The interactive session will consist of a description of the techniques, a short demonstration, and a follow-up discussion with the audience.

4241   9:30-10:45 a.m.   Conf 4I   Fourth Floor   Chicago Hilton

CONNECTING THE DOTS: UNITING THEORY, INSTRUCTION AND PRACTICE

Sponsor: Public Relations Division
Chair: Barbara A. Mastrolia, Indiana University Northwest
   "Communication Theory and Public Relations: Facing the Interface." James H. Tolhuizen, Indiana University Northwest
   "Implementing with Integrity: Balancing Campaign Effectiveness Strategies and Ethical Accountability to the Target Audience." Lori Montalbano-Phelps, Indiana University Northwest
   "Increasing Public Relations Through Campus Television and Service-Learning." Dorothy W. Inge, Indiana University Northwest

Respondent: Philip M. Backlund, Central Washington University

---

4242   9:30-10:45 a.m.   Conf 4J   Fourth Floor   Chicago Hilton

OF THEE I SING: IN HONOR OF UNSUNG MENTORS

Sponsor: Senior College & University Section
Chair: Kenneth E. Andersen, University of Illinois, Urbana-Champaign
   "Deldee Herman, Western Michigan University." Sharon A. Ratliffe, Golden West College
   "Wendell Crow, California State University, Fullerton." Tasha L. Van Horn, Citrus College
   "Lillian R. Wagner, Northern Iowa University." Kenneth E. Andersen, University of Illinois, Urbana-Champaign

---

4243   9:30-10:45 a.m.   Conf 4K   Fourth Floor   Chicago Hilton

RHETORICAL TENSIONS IN MEDICAL DISCOURSE

Sponsor: American Association for Rhetoric of Science & Technology
Chair: Thomas J. Darwin, University of Memphis
   "Figures of Speech: The Rhetorical Construction of Autism." Katherine J. DeMaria, University of Pittsburgh
   "Rhetoric, Science, and the *Kairos* of Medicine." Thomas J. Darwin, University of Memphis
   "The Reconciliation of Hygeia and Asklepios: Managing the Tension Between Conventional and Alternative Medicine." Cyd C. Ropp, University of Memphis

---

4244   9:30-10:45 a.m.   Conf 4L   Fourth Floor   Chicago Hilton

IS A RHETORICAL THEORY OF FIGURES POSSIBLE?

Sponsor: American Society for the History of Rhetoric
Chair: Arthur E. Walzer, University of Minnesota
   "Recognizing a Rhetorical Theory of Figures: What Aristotle Tells Us About the Relationship Between the Figures of Speech." Sara J. Newman, Kent State University
   "How a Rhetorical Theory of Figures Works: Is 'is' a Metaphor? Reexamining Bio-Rhetoric." Robert A. Brookey, Stonehill College
   "How a Rhetorical Theory of Figures Serves a Persuasive Function: Perelman's Views." Alan G. Gross, University of Minnesota, Twin Cities

Respondent: Arthur E. Walzer, University of Minnesota

4249   9:30-10:45 a.m.   Conf 5B   Fifth Floor   Chicago Hilton

TEACHING AND ASSESSING VALUES AND ETHICS IN THE BASIC COURSE

Sponsor: Basic Course Division
Chair: Robert N. Jackson, Nebraska Wesleyan University

Panelists: Beth M. Waggenspack, Virginia Tech University
           Donald D. Yoder, University of Dayton
           Cheri J. Simonds, Illinois State University
           Robert N. Jackson, Nebraska Wesleyan University

All teachers deal with issues of plagiarism, cheating, and respect in their classrooms. Panelists will present position papers on how, why and whether we should assess our students' growth and progress in these areas.

4252   9:30-10:45 a.m.   Conf 5E   Fifth Floor   Chicago Hilton

COLORING OUTSIDE THE LINES: GENRE, CONTEXT, VALIDITY, AND IMPLICIT COGNITIVE PROCESSES IN COMMUNICATION

Sponsor: Rhetorical and Communication Theory Division
Chair: Dale E. Brashers, University of Illinois, Urbana-Champaign
   "Genre and the Micro-Macro Problem in Communication Theory." Donald G. Ellis, University of Hartford
   "Communication as Configurations of Context, Environment, Framing, Rules and Power." Tricia L. Hansen-Horn, University of Northern Iowa
   "Another Look at the Validity of the Role Category Questionnaire." Harry W. Weger, Indiana University, Southeast, Leah E. Polcar, University of Arizona
   "Locating Implicit Cognitive Processes in the Realm of Public Discourse." Dale Cyphert, University of Northern Iowa

---

4254   9:30-10:45 a.m.   Conf 5G   Fifth Floor   Chicago Hilton

USING A CASE STUDY INSTRUCTIONAL METHOD: APPLYING SCHOLARSHIP IN THE CLASSROOM SETTING

Sponsor: Instructional Development Division
Chairs: Dawn O. Braithwaite, University of Nebraska, Lincoln
        Julia T. Wood, University of North Carolina, Chapel Hill

Panelists: Melissa L. Beall, University of Northern Iowa
           Dawn O. Braithwaite, University of Nebraska, Lincoln
           Betsy W. Bach, University of Montana
           Sandra Metts, Illinois State University
           Sandra Petronio, Arizona State University
           Brian H. Spitzberg, San Diego State University
           Brian S. Titsworth, Moorhead State University
           Julia T. Wood, University of North Carolina, Chapel Hill

Panelists will discuss the use of a case study teaching method, web applications and research opportunities from this teaching approach.

4255   9:30-10:45 a.m.   Conf 5H   Fifth Floor   Chicago Hilton

INTERROGATING IDENTITY ON THE STREETS OF GAY CHICAGO

Sponsor: Gay/Lesbian Transgender Communication Studies Division
Chair: Trung T. Tieu, University of Wisconsin, Milwaukee
   "Is It Really a SPACE OF OUR OWN?: Identity, Space, and African American 'same gender loving men' of Chicago." Myron M. Beasley, Ohio University
   "Memory, Identity, and Orgasmic Misery." Frederick C. Corey, Arizona State University

"Rhetorical Investigations into Identity in Gay Chicago." Trung T. Tieu, University of Wisconsin, Milwaukee

Respondent: Scott E. Dillard, Fort Valley State University

4257   9:30-10:45 a.m.   Conf 5J   Fifth Floor   Chicago Hilton

TAKING INVENTORY AND TAKING ACTION: A DEPARTMENT MODEL FOR SUCCESS

Sponsor: Community College Section
Chair: Patti A. Redmond, Sacramento City College

Panelists: Patti A. Redmond, Sacramento City College
     K. C. Boylan, Sacramento City Community College
     Chris Iwata, Sacramento City College
     Patty Harris-Jenkinson, Sacramento City College

Sacramento City College has examined and implemented methods that are helping to provide a competitive academic program while maintaining an amiable working environment.

4260   9:30-10:45 a.m.   Lake Huron   Eighth Floor   Chicago Hilton

COLORING BEYOND THE LINES OF REASON: THE RHETORIC OF HATE CRIMES

Sponsor: Freedom of Expression Commission
Chair: Ben D. Voth, Miami University
     "'Reflection on Matthew Shepard': The Strategic Use of Metaphor in Solving Dialectical Tensions Between Free Speech and Tolerance." Gillian Teubner, Miami University
     "Is Scapegoating Really Necessary?: Victimage, Frames of Rejection, and Matthew Shepard, A.B.P (ad bellum purificandum)." Jeffrey L. Courtright, University of North Dakota
     "Hate Crimes as Symbolic Constructions: Understanding the Rhetorical Exigencies of Fabricated Hate Crimes." Ben D. Voth, Miami University

Respondent: Kathleen M. German, Miami University, Ohio

4261   9:30-10:45 a.m.   Lake Erie   Eighth Floor   Chicago Hilton

CONSUMERS AND THE MEDIA: RAMIFICATIONS OF IDENTIFYING AND ACCESSING THE HISPANIC MARKET

Sponsors: La Raza Caucus
          Latina/Latino Communication Studies Division
Chair: Nathaniel I. Cordova, University of Maryland
     "Hispanics, Advertising, and Alcohol: A Cultivation Analysis of Beer Commercials on the Univision Television Network." Frank G. Perez, University of New Mexico
     "Advertising to American Hispanic Audiences: Barriers and Problems." Dirk C. Gibson, University of New Mexico
     "Sabado Gigante as an Element of Homogenization Among Spanish-Speaking Viewers*." Martha I. Chew, University of New Mexico

Respondent: Michelle A. Holling, California State University, Monterey Bay

*Student Debut Paper

4262   9:30-10:45 a.m.   Essex Court   Second Floor   Essex Inn

GETTING TO KNOW YOU: INTERPERSONAL COMMUNICATION IN RELIGIOUS CONTEXTS

Sponsor: Religious Communication Association
Chair: Gordon L. Forward, Point Loma Nazarene University

"Promise Keepers and Women: Depiction of Relationships in Personal Narratives." Mary E. Collins, Sam Houston State University, Chad Bird, Sam Houston State University

"Creating a Typology of Persuasive Messages in Church: An Exploration of Upward Influence Tactics Used by Parishioners in Interpersonal Interactions with Clergy." Isolde G. Anderson, Northwestern University, Shannon S. Dyer, Northwestern University, Mary Trujillo, Northwestern University, Hiromi Endo, Northwestern University

"Personal Prayer and Relationships with God." E. James Baesler, Old Dominion University, Mark Hillis, Old Dominion University, Mandi Greene, Old Dominion University, Mary Anderson, Old Dominion University, Jessica Bradshaw, Old Dominion University

"Individualism and Collectivism as Predictions of Functional Roles and Communicator Style of Individual Members of Multicultural Teams." Glen Martin, Regent University, Rodney A. Reynolds, Regent University, William J. Brown, Regent University

---

4263   9:30-10:45 a.m.   Windsor Court   Second Floor   Essex Inn

VOICES FROM THE HEARTLAND: POVERTY, PROPHETS, AND PRIVATE EYES

Sponsor: Ethnography Division
Chair: Kathleen M. Golden, Edinboro University of Pennsylvania
   "Tales of the Strong Poet: *The Day Jesus Came to My Town**." Joseph A. Kloss, Edinboro University of Pennsylvania
   "Giving Refuge: A Homeless Diary." Sarah J. Glover, Edinboro University of Pennsylvania
   "The Men That Make the Majority: An Ethnography of the County Detectives of Lake City*." Danette R. Parrett, Edinboro University of Pennsylvania
   "Beating the Blues: A Brief Single-Source Ethnographic Study of a Non-Profit Health Maintenance Organization*." David A. Waples, Edinboro University of Pennsylvania
   "The Meter Reader: An Ethnography of a Woman in a Non-Traditional Trade." Alice Dalmaso, State Correctional Institution, Pennsylvania

Respondent: Lawrence R. Frey, University of Memphis

*Debut Paper

4264   9:30-10:45 a.m.   Buckingham Court   Second Floor   Essex Inn

OBSTACLES TO MEDIA LITERACY IN THE UNITED STATES

Sponsor: American Studies Commission
Chair: Mary D. Vavrus, University of Minnesota
   "The (Popular) Cultural is Not Political: Public Resistance to Popular Culture Controversies in the United States." Naomi R. Rockler, University of Minnesota
   "Structural Obstacles to the Development of Media Education in the United States." Robert W. Kubey, Rutgers University
   "Locating the Viewer: Exploring Barriers to Media Literacy Through Audience Analysis." Patricia A. Ryden, Purdue University
   "Culture Wars: Audiences Negotiate Meaning in the Xenaverse." Erika Caswell, University of Minnesota

Respondent: Rebecca A. Lind, University of Illinois, Chicago

11:00 a.m.

4308   11:00-12:15 p.m.   Continental BR C   Lobby Level   Chicago Hilton

USES AND ABUSES OF CULTURE: DISPLAYS OF POWER

Sponsor: Critical and Cultural Studies Division
Chair: Tony L. Kirschner, Western Maryland College
   "X-Rated Culture: Extreme Sports, Youth Culture, and Media Conglomeration." Craig Robertson, University of Illinois, Urbana-Champaign
   "David Hammons's White Space(ing)s." Catherine Michele Adams, University of Iowa

"Museums and Motorcycle Mayhem: Racing Toward New Museum Practices." Mary Coffey, University of Illinois, Urbana-Champaign, Jeremy Packer, University of Illinois, Urbana-Champaign

Respondent: Tony L. Kirschner, Western Maryland College

4310   11:00-12:15 p.m.   Grand Ballroom   Second Floor   Chicago Hilton

TORCH SONG POSSIBILITY: VISIONS AND VOICES OF THE TORCH SINGER

Sponsor: Performance Studies Division
Chair: Stacy L. Holman Jones, University of Texas, Austin
    "Passing the Torch: Torch Stylings from the 1920s to the Present." Catherine Berry, Singer-Songwriter
    "Breath, Body, Torch." Teri L. Varner, University of Texas, Austin
    "Motion, Text, Voice." Deanna B. Shoemaker, University of Texas, Austin
    "My Torch Story." Stacy L. Holman Jones, University of Texas, Austin

Respondents: Carolyn S. Ellis, University of South Florida
             Laurel Richardson, Ohio State University

4315   11:00-12:15 p.m.   Boulevard B   Second Floor   Chicago Hilton

CONTRIBUTED PAPERS

Sponsor: Theatre Division
Chair: Deryl B. Johnson, Kutztown University
    "*The Wild Duck*: A Play of Play." Matthew Smith, Columbia University
    "Running Head: PERFORMING SELF AND OTHERS." Michael W. Kirch, Purdue University
    "Old Coat, New Hat: An After-Modernist Look at the Modern Mime Theatre of Angna Enters." frances anne Pici, Georgia State University
    "The World According to Paula Vogel." Robert M. Post, University of Washington

Respondents: Monica F. Anderson, Franciscan University
             Patti P. Gillespie, University of Maryland

4316   11:00-12:15 p.m.   Boulevard C   Second Floor   Chicago Hilton

COLORING OUTSIDE THE LINES IN THE COMMUNICATION CLASSROOM: EXPERIENTIAL CONSIDERATIONS AND CONSTERNATIONS

Sponsor: Experiential Learning in Communication Commission
    "Coloring Outside Aristotle's Lines: Evolving Premises for the Basic Public Speaking Course." Nancy Rost Goulen, Kansas State University
    "Bringing Performance Together Across the Miles: Teaching Performance Studies via the Iowa Communication Network." Leah E. White, University of Northern Iowa
    "'Communicative Chaos' or 'Common Sense?': The Role of Group and Dyadic Testing in the Communication Classroom." Kelby K. Halone, Clemson University
    "Coloring Outside the Lines? Diversity as Normality in the Inter/Multicultural Classroom." Trudy E. Burtis, University of New Mexico
    "Coloring Outside the Lines: Themes and Trends in Experiential Learning in Communication-Commission-Sponsored Programs at the (S)NCA 1993-1998." Diane S. Krider, Central Michigan University, Peter G. Ross, Central Michigan University

---

4319   11:00-12:15 p.m.   Astoria   Third Floor   Chicago Hilton

CONSTITUTIVE RHETORICS OF LABOR, COMMUNISM, AND AMERICAN CITIZENSHIP

Sponsor: Public Address Division
Chair: Susan Zickmund, University of Iowa
    "Domestic Architecture and Industrial Utopia: The Rhetoric of Pullman, Illinois." Cynthia Duquette Smith, University of Texas, Austin

"When Revolution Meets Reform: The American Young Communist League's Use of
   Contradictory Appeals in the *Young Worker*." Jennifer L. Young, Penn State University
"The American Legion, Public Speaking, and Education for Citizenship in the Cold War."
   Elizabeth W. Mechling, Core Communication, Jay Mechling, University of California,
   Davis

Respondent: Mark Meister, North Dakota State University

4321   11:00-12:15 p.m.   Williford A   Third Floor   Chicago Hilton

DEBATE AND FORENSICS PROGRAM MANAGEMENT ROUNDTABLE

Sponsor: Cross Examination Debate Association
Chair: Roy J. Schwartzman, University of South Carolina
   "Creating Programs in Settings Without Any Prior Forensic/Debating Histories." Sam
      Nelson, University of Rochester
   "Converting National Programs from Regional Programs." David M. Berube, University of
      South Carolina
   "Creating a National Program: A Case Study at the University of Missouri at Kansas City."
      Linda M. Collier, University of Missouri, Kansas City
   "The Relationship of Debate Team Funding and Competitive Success Among South Florida
      Debate Programs." Ernesto Querido, University of Miami

Respondent: A. C. Snider, University of Vermont

4322   11:00-12:15 p.m.   Williford B   Third Floor   Chicago Hilton

CAMPAIGN STYLES, MESSAGES, AND AUDIENCES

Sponsor: Political Communication Division
Chair: Janet L. Murphy, Oklahoma Christian University of Science and Arts
   "Interpersonal Communication Styles of Political Candidates: Predicting Winning and
      Losing Candidates in Three U.S. Presidential Elections." Timothy D. Stephen, Rensselaer
      Polytechnic Institute, Teresa M. Harrison, Rensselaer Polytechnic Institute, William
      Husson, Emerson College, David Albert, Albany City School District, New York
   "News Narrative and Presidential Campaigns: Telling the Story Through Presidential
      Debates." Mitchell S. McKinney, University of Oklahoma
   "The Iowa Caucus Attender: Sources of Information in the Decision-Making Process—Past
      and Future." G. Jon Hall, University of Northern Iowa, Allen Bronson Brierly, University
      of Northern Iowa
   "Presidential Campaign Promises, 1948-1996." Felicity McKevitt, University of Texas,
      Austin, Sharon E. Jarvis, University of Texas, Austin
   "Rhetorical Analysis of Osage Campaign Literature." Karola M. Schwartz, University of
      Oklahoma

Respondent: Theodore F. Sheckels, Randolph-Macon College

4323   11:00-12:15 p.m.   Williford C   Third Floor   Chicago Hilton

FRAMING WOMEN, WORK AND THE WORKPLACE

Sponsor: Feminist and Women Studies Division
Chair: Marlene G. Fine, Simmons College
   "Taking Our Ambivalences Seriously: Mothering Practices in the Corporate Context."
      Patricia J. Sotirin, Michigan Technological University
   "En-Visioning Change: Narratives of Struggle and the Rhetoric of Possibility in *Life and
      Labor* Magazine, 1911-1917." Mary E. Triece, University of Akron
   "Diversity as Organizational Etiquette: A Critique of Organizational Treatment of
      Difference and Communicative Democracy." Colette S. Jung, Purdue University
   "Revisioning Theory About Women and Leadership." Marcy E. Meyer, Ball State University,
      Beth H. Ellis, Ball State University

Respondent: Deborah Borisoff, New York University

4325   11:00-12:15 p.m.   Joliet   **Third Floor   Chicago Hilton**

DISSERTATION DEFENSE: BERNARD BROCK

Sponsor: Kenneth Burke Society, NCA Branch
Chair: Wade R. Kenny, University of Dayton
   "The Doctoral Dissertation of Bernard Brock: Precis and Assessment." James F. Klumpp,
      University of Maryland
   "Defense Committee Member One: Critique." John J. Miller, Wayne State University
   "Defense Committee Member Two: Critique." Sherry R. Shepler, Wayne State University
   "Defense Committee Member Three: Critique." Nathaniel I. Cordova, University of
      Maryland

Respondent: Bernard L. Brock, Wayne State University

4326   11:00-12:15 p.m.   PDR 1   **Third Floor   Chicago Hilton**

OUTSIDE THE LINES: COMMUNICATION EDUCATION IN THE
TWENTY-FIRST CENTURY

Sponsor: Educational Policies Board
Chair: Andrew D. Wolvin, University of Maryland

Panelists: James W. Chesebro, Indiana State University
         Gustav W. Friedrich, Rutgers University
         James C. McCroskey, West Virginia University
         Jo Sprague, San Jose State University

The panelists will bring their extensive theoretical and research perspectives to bear on issues
about and projections for the state of communication education 2000.

4327   11:00-12:15 p.m.   PDR 2   **Third Floor   Chicago Hilton**

LIVING AT THE MARGINS OF HEALTH CARE: ISSUES AND IMPLICATIONS
FOR HEALTH COMMUNICATION SCHOLARS

Sponsor: Health Communication Division
Chair: Patrice M. Buzzanell, Northern Illinois University
   "Coming Out: The Patient with Chronic Pain." Kenzie A. Cameron, University of Georgia
   "Speaking Out Loud: Female Cancer Survivors, Impairment, and Alternative Medicine."
      Laura L. Ellingson, University of South Florida
   "At Least We Know What It Is: Examining the Experience of Illness, Uncertainty and Social
      Support in the Stories of People with Chronic Fatigue Syndrome." Pamela J. Lannutti,
      University of Georgia
   "Uncertainty in Brain Injury: A Survivor's Perspective." Kami J. Silk, University of Georgia
   "Living with Invisible Disability: Media Representations of Chronic Fatigue Syndrome."
      Elena C. Strauman, University of South Florida

Respondent: Elaine B. Jenks, West Chester University

4328   11:00-12:15 p.m.   PDR 3   **Third Floor   Chicago Hilton**

FRONT PORCH STORIES: FAMILY NARRATIVES THAT INSTRUCT OUR
YOUTH

Sponsor: African American Communication & Culture Commission
Chair: Veronica J. Duncan, University of Georgia
   "The Role of Narrative: My Family's Stories." Jack L. Daniel, University of Pittsburgh
   "Ralph Ellison and Me: An Adventure with the *Invisible Man*." Molefi K. Asante, Temple
      University
   "You Have Eyes! I Know that You Hear Me." Thurmon Garner, University of Georgia
   "The Gospel According to Big Daddy: Can't Died a Long Time Ago." Virgie N. Harris, Fort
      Valley State University
   "The Only Dog I Ever Loved Had Mange." Scott E. Dillard, Fort Valley State University

"Me Mere Stories: Our Grandmother's Stories." Kristin M. Langellier, University of Maine, Orono

Using narrative as the rhetorical paradigm, the panel will tell stories that were and are used to instruct Afro-American, Euro-American, and Franco-American youth about their cultural, political, and socio-psychological experiences in the United States.

4329	11:00-12:15 p.m.	PDR 4	Third Floor	Chicago Hilton

MYTH AS REALITY: THE INTERPLAY OF MASS MEDIA OFFERING AND PUBLIC REACTIONS IN MAINLAND CHINA, TAIWAN AND HONG KONG

Sponsor: Table Talk Series
Chair: Minmin Wang, Rider University

Panelists: Bei Cai, Bowling Green State University
Hui-Ching Chang, University of Illinois, Chicago
Ling Chen, Hong Kong Baptist University
Xing (Lucy) Lu, DePaul University
Ringo Ma, SUNY, Fredonia

The relationship among Mainland China, Taiwan, Hong Kong, and the United States is a complex one and has attracted the attention of many scholars. The mass media in each of these four regions has played a major role in shaping the public's perceptions of this dynamic situation. This panel invites scholars from Mainland China, Taiwan, and Hong Kong to engage in a lively dialogue about their own region's perceptions and opinions of the other two Chinese regions and the United States. This panel strives to present what the American media often misses: a current "true" picture of Chinese people—what they think, what they talk about, what they care about, and what they believe.

4330	11:00-12:15 p.m.	PDR 5	Third Floor	Chicago Hilton

COLORING OUTSIDE THE LINES: TEACHERS NEGOTIATING SELF AND OTHERNESS

Sponsor: Communication Needs of Students at Risk Commission
Chair: Bryant K. Alexander, California State University, Los Angeles

Respondent: Nanci M. Burk, Phoenix College

The panel discussion seeks to re-vision the notion of at-risk, not as a specified and exclusive feature of students, but as a transactional disposition created between students and teachers. Through the use of instructional narratives, the panelists seek to open up discussion related to the following questions: Who can talk for what, and when, and why? What happens when interactive education leads to burnout? How can we use theories of active/passive resistance to talk about at-risk? What happens when teachers are the ones "at-risk" in the classroom?

4331	11:00-12:15 p.m.	PDR 6	Third Floor	Chicago Hilton

'SELF' AND 'OTHER' IN INTERCULTURAL COMMUNICATION

Sponsor: International & Intercultural Communication Division
Chair: Yahya R. Kamalipour, Purdue University, Calumet
    "The Semiotics of the Other and Physical Beauty." Masako Isa, University of Okinawa
    "Presenting Oneself as an 'Ingratiator' or 'Intimidator': An Experimental Analysis of Nonverbal Self-Presentation Behaviors in Japan-U.S. Conflict Interactions." Tamie Kanata, Arizona State University
    "Assessing the Validity of Cross-Cultural Self-Construal Measurement: The Relative Impact of Self-Construal Type, Culture, and Biological Sex on Leadership Style." Michael Z. Hackman, University of Colorado, Colorado Springs, Kathleen S. Ellis, University of Colorado, Colorado Springs, Craig E. Johnson, George Fox University, Constance Staley, University of Colorado, Colorado Springs

Respondent: Naomi Sugimoto, Ferris State University

Sunday

4332   11:00-12:15 p.m.   **PDR 7**   **Third Floor**   **Chicago Hilton**

SHADES OF GRAY: DE-MYSTIFYING THE RATING SCALE IN FORENSICS

Sponsor: Argumentation and Forensics Division
  "Reading Between the Lines: Students' Perspectives on the Rating Scale." Susan J. Collie,
    Winona State University
  "Mixed Messages: Comparing and Contrasting the Rating Scales of the AFA and NFA."
    Doug Binsfield, University of Wisconsin, Stout
  "What Are We Teaching? The Rating Scale in an Educational Context." Joel L. Hefling,
    South Dakota State University
  "As Clear as Black and White: Prescribing a Superior Rating Scale." Bruce F. Wickelgren,
    University of Northern Iowa, Tracy Routsong, University of Northern Iowa
  "A Judge's Frame of Reference: Unwritten Rules of the Rating Scale." Kelly J. Peters,
    University of Wisconsin, Eau Claire

4333   11:00-12:15 p.m.   **Conf 4A**   **Fourth Floor**   **Chicago Hilton**

ENTERTAINMENT VIOLENCE AND CULTURAL STABILITY: THREE STUDIES OF THE PROACTIVE INFLUENCES OF VIOLENCE IN POPULAR FILM

Sponsor: Religious Communication Association
Chair: William D. Romanowski, Calvin College
  "Good Violence: The Redemption Theme in *Saving Private Ryan*." David A. Thomas,
    University of Richmond
  "Piety and Penance: Media Violence as Mortification of Cultural Sins." Matthew Melton,
    Lee University
  "Violent Rituals and the Maintenance of Society in the Film *Lethal Weapon 4*." Doris Riley,
    Kansas Wesleyan University

Respondent: William D. Romanowski, Calvin College

4334   11:00-12:15 p.m.   **Conf 4B**   **Fourth Floor**   **Chicago Hilton**

ALTERNATIVE PATHS TO AN ETHNOGRAPHY OF COMMUNICATION

Sponsor: Language and Social Interaction Division
Chair: D. Lawrence Wieder, University of Oklahoma
  "When is an Ethnography of Communication?" Wendy Leeds-Hurwitz, University of
    Wisconsin, Parkside
  "The Conceptual Structure of Hymes' Ethnography of Speaking and Its Alternatives." D.
    Lawrence Wieder, University of Oklahoma
  "Toward a Sociologically Oriented Ethnography of Communication." Stuart J. Sigman,
    Emerson College
  "An Ethnography of Communication That Foregrounds the Immediate Encounter." Michael
    Fairly, Southeast Oklahoma State University, Faye G. Mangrum, Southeast Oklahoma
    State University

4335   11:00-12:15 p.m.   **Conf 4C**   **Fourth Floor**   **Chicago Hilton**

THINKING OUTSIDE THE BOUNDARIES: FUTURE VISIONS OF EDUCATION AND TECHNOLOGY

Sponsor: Commission on Communication in the Future
Chair: Lance A. Strate, Fordham University

Panelists: Sue Barnes, Fordham University
         J. M. Metz, University of Central Florida
         Maureen C. Minielli, Saint Joseph's College
         Raymond Gozzi, Ithaca College

Intelligent agents, Web-based learning, and CD-ROMs are new technological approaches to
education. This panel will discuss new technology and the future of education.

| 4336 | 11:00-12:15 p.m. | Conf 4D | Fourth Floor | Chicago Hilton |

ORGANIZING WORKERS AND COMMUNITIES FOR THE NEW MILLENNIUM: NEW STRATEGIES, NO BOUNDARIES

Sponsor: Organizational Communication Division
Chair: James A. Aune, Texas A&M University
  "Caring for the Community's People: University of Iowa Hospitals and Clinics Get a Union." Kathleen Farrell, University of Iowa
  "(High-Tech) Workers of the World, Unite!" Michelle L. Rodino, University of Pittsburgh
  "A New Organizational Paradigm: Organizing Community Through Collaboration, Commitment and Caring." Bethany C. Goodier, University of South Florida
  "From the Ethics of Ambiguity to Building a Collaborative Action Agenda: The Non-Christian Left in Florida Devises a Counter-Statement to the Christian Coalition." Virginia Kohl, University of South Florida, Jerome Lieberman, University of South Florida

Respondent: Ekaterina V. Haskins, University of Iowa

| 4338 | 11:00-12:15 p.m. | Conf 4F | Fourth Floor | Chicago Hilton |

ADVANCING THE DISCIPLINE: FINDINGS, DIRECTIONS, AND IMPLICATIONS FOR THE USE OF META-ANALYSIS IN INTERPERSONAL COMMUNICATION

Sponsor: Interpersonal Communication Division
Chair: Daniel J. Canary, Penn State University
  "A Meta-Analysis of Sex Differences in Self-Esteem: Directions for Communication Research and Theory." Erin M. Sahlstein, University of Iowa, Mike Allen, University of Wisconsin, Milwaukee
  "Comparing the Production of Power in Language on the Basis of Sex." Lindsay M. Timmerman, University of Texas, Austin
  "Behavior After Learning Positive HIV Results: A Meta-Analysis." Mike Allen, University of Wisconsin, Milwaukee, Mary K. Casey, University of Wisconsin, Milwaukee, Tara M. Emmers-Sommer, University of Oklahoma, Lisa Bradford, University of Wisconsin, Milwaukee
  "Understanding Interpersonal Communication Through Meta-Analysis." Daniel J. Canary, Penn State University, Michelle J. Mattrey, Penn State University

| 4341 | 11:00-12:15 p.m. | Conf 4I | Fourth Floor | Chicago Hilton |

MARKING THE 40TH ANNIVERSARY OF THE CASTRO REVOLUTION: A PUBLIC RELATIONS PERSPECTIVE

Sponsor: Public Relations Division
Chair: Pamela G. Bourland-Davis, Georgia Southern University
  "Castro's First Media Tour of the United States in the Spring of 1960: A Media Relations Analysis." Jason Berger, University of Missouri, Kansas City
  "Castro's Convertibles: The Cuban Revolution and the New York Jewish Intellectuals." Robert E. Brown, Salem State College
  "The Godfather, His Family and His Entourage Fleeing Cuba: The Image of Castro in the Godfather Trilogy." Donald Fishman, Boston College
  "Guns, Advisors & Publicity: Castro's Influence in Sub-Sahara Africa." Cornelius B. Pratt, Michigan State University
  "Beauty and the Beast: Fidel Castro." Rise J. Samra, Barry University

| 4342 | 11:00-12:15 p.m. | Conf 4J | Fourth Floor | Chicago Hilton |

THE NEW CONSUMER PARADIGM: I'VE PAID MY TUITION, NOW GIVE ME MY DEGREE

Sponsor: Senior College & University Section

Sunday

Chair: Ina R. Ames, Curry College
"The New Consumer Paradigm: An Administrative Perspective." Thomas Spann, University of Nebraska, Lincoln
"The New Consumer Paradigm: A Faculty Perspective." George C. Wharton, Curry College
"The New Consumer Paradigm: A Student Perspective." Ina R. Ames, Curry College
"The New Consumer Paradigm: A Liberal Arts Perspective." Ralph R. Donald, Southern Illinois University, Edwardsville

---

4344   11:00-12:15 p.m.   Conf 4L   Fourth Floor   Chicago Hilton

ON THE INTERACTIONAL ACHIEVEMENT OF "FAMILY": CONSTRUCTING FAMILY TIES AND FAMILY UNDERSTANDINGS IN TALK

Sponsor: Family Communication Division
Chair: Phillip J. Glenn, Southern Illinois University, Carbondale
"The Malignancy Calls: Understanding How Families Talk Through Cancer." Wayne A. Beach, San Diego State University
"The Ownership of Grandchildren as an Interactional Achievement." John C. Heritage, University of California, Los Angeles
"Changing the Rules: College-Age Children and Their Parents Negotiating New Relational Boundaries." Shirley A. Staske, Eastern Illinois University

Respondent: Anita M. Pomerantz, Temple University

4351   11:00-12:15 p.m.   Conf 5D   Fifth Floor   Chicago Hilton

NATURE OF A SISTUH: RESEARCH IN PERFORMANCE

Sponsor: Women's Caucus
Chair: Joyce Ellis, North Carolina Central University
"Sistuhs in the Ivory Tower: Experiences in the Academy." Trevellya Ford-Ahmed, West Virginia State College, Janice D. Hamlet, Shippensburg University, Karen E. Strother-Jordan, Oakland University
"Sistuhs Breaking Down Barriers: Black Women Experience Corporate America." Jeanne L. Porter, North Park University
"Sistuhs at the Well: Quenching Our Spiritual Thirsts." Deborah A. Austin, University of South Florida, Vanessa W. Quainoo, University of Rhode Island
"Sistuhs Watching and Reading: Representations in Mass Media." Katrina E. Bell, Northeastern Illinois University, Trevy A. McDonald, North Carolina Central University, Doris Y. Dartey, Mount Mercy College

---

4352   11:00-12:15 p.m.   Conf 5E   Fifth Floor   Chicago Hilton

CASE STUDIES IN RHETORICAL PERSONAE

Sponsor: Rhetorical and Communication Theory Division
Chair: Robert B. Asen, University of Wisconsin, Madison
"Death Goes Public: Jack Kevorkian as Critical Rhetorician and Representational Ideograph." Todd F. McDorman, Wabash College
"'Well, That Depends on What the Meaning of 'Is' Is, Doesn't It': The Clinton Scandal and the Death of Meaning." Jennifer R. Mercieca, University of Illinois, T. G. Potts, University of Illinois
"Boris Yeltsin's Ascent to Power: *Personae* and the Rhetoric of Revolution." Matthew T. Althouse, Louisiana College
"'Just the Facts, Ma'am': Starr's Image Repair Discourse Viewed in *20/20*." William L. Benoit, University of Missouri, Columbia, John P. McHale, University of Missouri, Columbia

---

4353   11:00-12:15 p.m.   Conf 5F   Fifth Floor   Chicago Hilton

ENVIRONMENTAL JUSTICE, ACTIVISM, AND ETHNOGRAPHY: REPORTS FROM THE FIELD

Sponsor: Environmental Communication Commission
Chair: Stephen P. Depoe, University of Cincinnati
    "Doing and Writing Ethnography: Corporeal and Spatial Implications of Environmental
      Communication." Phaedra C. Pezzullo, University of North Carolina, Chapel Hill
    "History in the Making: Inside the Fernald Living History Project." Rhonda Barnes-Kloth,
      University of Cincinnati, Stephen P. Depoe, University of Cincinnati, Jennifer J.
      Hamilton, University of Cincinnati, Amy J. Lombardo, University of Cincinnati
    "Environmental Conflict Methodologies and Standpoints in Struggle: The Activist Potential
      of the Intensive Interview." Frederick K. Goshorn, University of Pennsylvania
    "Power, Language, and Perspective: The Lived Experiences in the Siting of a Low-Level
      Radioactive Waste Facility." John P. Linney, University of Texas, El Paso

Respondents: John W. Delicath, Allegheny College
             Susan L. Senecah, SUNY, Syracuse

4354   11:00-12:15 p.m.   Conf 5G   Fifth Floor   Chicago Hilton

USING NEW CRAYONS TO COLOR THE INSTRUCTIONAL DEVELOPMENT DISCIPLINE

Sponsor: Instructional Development Division
Chair: Richard L. West, University of Southern Maine
    "Paint by Numbers, Connect the Dots, Paint by Numbers, Connect the Dots: Challenging
      Instructional Communication Scholars to Color Outside of the Lines." Nelle Bedner,
      Ohio University
    "Jamieson Meets Lucas: Eloquence and Pedagogical Model(s) in *The Art of Public
      Speaking.*" Todd S. Frobish, Penn State University
    "Reconceptualizing the Instructional Process Through an Ethic of Care." Lynn M. Harter,
      Moorhead State University, Brian S. Titsworth, Moorhead State University, Patricia R. W.
      Clasen, Buena Vista University
    "Can't You See Me?: Reflections of an Invisible Black Professor." Katherine G. Hendrix,
      University of Memphis

Respondent: Richard L. West, University of Southern Maine

4355   11:00-12:15 p.m.   Conf 5H   Fifth Floor   Chicago Hilton

COMPETITIVE PAPERS ON ISSUES OF SEXUALITY

Sponsor: Gay/Lesbian Transgender Communication Studies Division
Chair: Carol L. Benton, Central Missouri State University
    "Communication in Asian American Families with Queer Members: A Relational Dialectics
      Perspective." Gust A. Yep, San Francisco State University, Karen E. Lovaas, San Francisco
      State University, Philip C. Ho, San Francisco State University
    "Examination of HIV Prevention Campaigns That Target African American Men Who Have
      Sex with Men Living in the Southeast." Roger K. Myrick, Auburn University
    "Measuring Sexual Harassment: Perceptions of Same-Sex Harassment at the Workplace."
      Andrew C. Billings, Indiana University, Bloomington
    "Perceptions of Sexual Harassment in Interaction and Relational Scenarios." Ronald A.
      Perger, Cleveland State University, Kory Floyd, Cleveland State University
    "Femme to Femme." Elizabeth J. Whitney, University of Utah

---

4357   11:00-12:15 p.m.   Conf 5J   Fifth Floor   Chicago Hilton

EXPLORING ETHICAL FOUNDATIONS FOR COMMUNICATION

Sponsor: Communication Ethics Commission
Chair: Richard M. Dubiel, University of Wisconsin, Stevens Point

Sunday

"The Ethics of Chaos: An Analogical Argument for Narrative as Ground for Communication Ethics." Timothy J. Ellis, Canyon City, Oregon

"A Meaning-Centered Ethic." Brian R. Betz, SUNY, Oswego

"Stephen Covey's *The Seven Habits of Highly Effective People* as Boundary-less Ethics: Organizational Control Through Values Training." Gregory Larson, University of Colorado, Boulder, David A. Carlone, University of Colorado, Boulder

Respondent: Alexandre Lopez de Miranda, Purdue University

4360   11:00-12:15 p.m.   Lake Huron   Eighth Floor   Chicago Hilton

WHERE DO YOU DRAW THE LINE? REGULATING SPEECH IN CYBERSPACE

Sponsor: Freedom of Expression Commission
Chair: Marilyn J. Matelski, Boston College

"Regulating Speech in Cyberspace: Justice O'Connor's Enigmatic Opinion in *Reno v. ACLU*." Dale A. Herbeck, Boston College

"CDA Version 2.0: COPA and the Legislative Road to Internet Content Regulation." Christopher D. Hunter, University of Pennsylvania

"Converging Technologies, Converging Nations, Converging Regulations." Susan J. Drucker, Hofstra University, Gary Gumpert, Communication Landscapers

---

4361   11:00-12:15 p.m.   Lake Erie   Eighth Floor   Chicago Hilton

OPEN WIDE AND SAY 'AHH': AN EXPLORATION OF CULTURALLY APPROPRIATE DELIVERY OF HEALTH SERVICES

Sponsor: Latina/Latino Communication Studies Division
Chair: Leda M. Cooks, University of Massachusetts, Amherst

"Diagnosing and Treating Depression in Mexican Immigrants." Deborah J. Clark, Howard University

"Multicultural Persuasion: Analyzing the Effect of Message Designs to Change Individual Attitude and Health Promotion Behavior in Multicultural Populations Through Growth Curve Analysis." Rachel Smith, University of Arizona

Respondent: Aimee M. Carrillo Rowe, University of Washington

4363   11:00-12:15 p.m.   Windsor Court   Second Floor   Essex Inn

RECOVERING FROM THE EIGHTIES: CULTURAL STUDIES OF URBANA-CHAMPAIGN, ILLINOIS

Sponsor: Ethnography Division
Chair: Elizabeth Perea, University of Illinois, Urbana-Champaign

"Rebirthing the Freak: Film Culture, the Local Community, and the Avant-Garde." Steven Bailey, University of Illinois, Urbana-Champaign

"Relationships of Power and Gender: An Ethnographic Cultural Study of Women in Popular Music in Champaign-Urbana, Illinois." Elizabeth Perea, University of Illinois, Urbana-Champaign

"Tuning-In: The Use of Music as Survival Strategy Among Gay, Lesbian, Bisexual, and Transgendered College Students in Urbana-Champaign." Lance Rintamaki, University of Illinois, Urbana-Champaign

"Articulations of Denial: A Lesbian Community's Non-Response to Woman-to-Woman Abuse." Grace A. Giorgio, University of Illinois, Urbana-Champaign

Respondent: Andrea Press, University of Illinois, Urbana-Champaign

Call for Papers for the 2000 Convention of the National Communication Association

Seattle
November 8 - 12, 2000

This call for papers will be continuously updated on the NCA home page at
http://www.natcom.org/convention/2000/call2000.htm

Please check the latest version before submitting papers and panels.

The 86th Annual Meeting of the National Communication Association will be held in Seattle at the Seattle Convention and Trade Center from November 8 - 12. The primary convention planner is James L. Applegate, NCA First Vice President.

CONVENTION THEME: The theme for the 2000 convention is **Communication: The Engaged Discipline**. With the end of the Cold War and the reconfiguration of society's demographic, economic, and social character at the dawn of a new Millennium, has come the demand that higher education and the disciplines within it reconsider our role. We are traditionally the institution primarily charged with the generation and dissemination of knowledge that challenges and enriches the human condition. Society is demanding we justify the huge investment being made in our research and teaching institutions. **Engagement** is a theme that has captured the spirit of much of this effort over the last decade. Societal leaders call for "engaged campuses" that create partnerships with local, state, national, and international communities improving our intellectual, spiritual, and material lives. Disciplines within higher education are being asked to look outward for opportunities for similar partnerships.

Communication is uniquely positioned to become a disciplinary leader in this 21st Century movement. Our intellectual focus is increasingly the concern of many areas of society: communication and the maintenance of diverse communities; communication as the goal of information technology; communication as the key to improved public health; communication as the cornerstone of productive work; communication as the heart of education through traditional and new forms of pedagogy; communication criticism as core to improved social ethics and justice; and so on. In addition, as a discipline, historically we, more than most, have maintained a central commitment to engaging our basic research and teaching in ways that improve social and communication practices at individual and societal levels. We have a great opportunity in the year 2000 in Seattle to propel our discipline into the center of the important conversations of our time and provide leadership in defining our future. The theme is a challenge to each individual member and subgroup of NCA to think carefully about who our important constituencies are, how we can engage them in productive partnerships, and what we can contribute to the improvement of 21st Century society. The various series described below elaborate the ways the convention is designed to support efforts to focus the intellectual power of the convention outward even as we solidify our internal connections through the normal and important rituals of the national meeting.

SPECIAL NOTE: All members and planners are strongly encouraged to submit programs using innovative formats that involve more people on fewer panels in more interactive formats. *Our goal is to maintain the level of member participation while reducing the NUMBER of programs by at least 10%.* Such formats should include but not be limited to:

Poster sessions: See the call for poster sessions below. These may be submitted to program planners or directly to Vince Waldron who is planning a special emphasis on these sessions.

High density programs: Eight or more presenters in a program present brief summaries. Each then is available for program attendees who wish to engage them in individual or small group dialogues.

Roundtables: Six or more participants discuss issues arising from mutual review of papers/themes prior to the session with audience participation.

CONVENTION THEME SUBMISSIONS: Papers, panels, programs, forums, workshops, courses and other creative programs that emphasize the convention theme are welcome. In particular, unit planners are urged to encourage programs which engage NCA scholars with important external constituencies (academic and those outside academe). More generally, programs are encouraged that explore areas of communication scholarship that are, or should be, engaged with important issues on the agenda of the human community.

HOW TO SUBMIT PAPERS AND PANEL/PROGRAM PROPOSALS: See the individual calls for the unit planner's name, contact information, number of copies to submit, deadline, whether to indicate "student" or "debut" paper and maximum length. In addition to traditional program formats, planners encourage high density programming formats that involve as many or more participants in fewer programs. **Participants should submit only one paper per unit.** Consistent with the goal of maximizing participation by as many people as possible who wish to present papers or participate on panels, the convention planners for each unit listed below have been asked to accept only one paper from any person submitting as first author. Although chairing or responding for a program does not count as such participation, members are asked to limit their acceptance of such invitations to spread participation as widely as possible. Convention presentations also should be made within the spirit of NCA's Affirmative Action Statement.

Proposals for panels/programs: A detachable cover page should include the panel/program title, complete identification of all participants (name, affiliation, address, phone/fax number and e-mail address of each participant). The remainder of the proposal should include a rationale for the panel/program, a 50-75 word abstract of each paper or presenter's topic, and all audio-visual requests. Submissions need to be accompanied by a completed NCA program proposal form found in the December issue of *Spectra* and include convention program copy if needed. Send the requested number of copies by the deadline listed. All submissions should be typed, using a 12 pt. font. See unit's individual call for any additional requirements.

Papers: Include a detachable cover page with the title, author's name, affiliation, address, phone/fax number, e-mail address and a 50-75 word abstract. Papers authored solely by students or persons who have never presented at a national convention should be marked "student" or "debut" on the upper right hand corner of the removable title page if applicable. Papers must be typed, double-spaced, use 12 pt. font and be limited to the length specified by each unit. Send the requested number of copies by the deadline listed. See unit's individual call for any additional requirements.

BUSINESS MEETINGS: Requests for business meetings should be completed on a Business Meeting Request Form and submitted and prioritized along with your unit's programs. Units will be limited to one business meeting. Additional meetings will be scheduled on a space available basis.

AUDIO-VISUAL EQUIPMENT NEEDS: Audio-visual equipment is expensive, and participants are encouraged to keep needs to a minimum. Requests for specific equipment must accompany proposals and must meet the same submission deadlines as for paper and program proposals. NCA policy statements on AV equipment can be secured from the NCA National Office 703-750-0533 or from the NCA web site: http://www.natcom.org. The policy also appears at the end of this call for papers.

CONVENTION PAPER DISTRIBUTION CENTER: The Paper Distribution Center is a centralized location for convention papers presented at the 2000 NCA Convention. In the event that convention participants are unable to attend a program or secure a copy of papers at a specific program, papers (by the last name of the first author) will be available for a nominal charge at the Paper Distribution Center. Details regarding the center will be published in *Spectra*.

AUTHORSHIP ETHICS: Whenever an item is submitted for a convention panel or program, the author(s) must give credit to those who were involved in the creation of the product in a direct or substantive way. Acknowledgment of assistance, student or otherwise, should be given. If materials have been presented at a previous convention or in some other public setting, the presentation history of the submission should be made clear on the cover page when the paper or abstract is submitted.

NEW SERIES

The Engaged Discipline

James L. Applegate, Dept of Communication, 230 Grehan Bldg, Univ of Kentucky, Lexington, KY 40506-0042; office 606-257-3622; fax 606-257-4103; japple@pop.uky.edu
Copies: 4
Deadline: February 15, 2000

This series includes programs directly speaking to the convention theme—**Communication: The Engaged Discipline.** The format is open: a program with 3-4 papers with or without a respondent; a program featuring an engaged scholar or program of scholarship with or without respondents; a program engaging important external constituencies with our own scholars (e.g., funding agency representatives, higher education or government leaders, scholars from other disciplines, artists, or corporate leaders); programs exploring opportunities, strategies/models for, and barriers to engagement of communication research and teaching; highly interactive programs using face-to-face or mediated formats with remote sites. Especially of interest are programs engaging communication teaching and research with those concerns most pressing for society as we move into a new millennium (e.g., sustaining community in a diverse, international society; creating inclusive, effective information technologies; fostering free and responsible speech that enhances public discourse; ensuring communication literacy—oral, written, and electronic; improving public health; promoting a human shape for work; contributing to life-long learning through developing more effective pedagogy K-16 and beyond; and enhancing the quality of personal relationships in impersonal times). Programs should engage our scholarship and teaching with people and issues outside the comfortable boundaries that normally contain our work. The primary convention planner is responsible for this series. Think creatively. Programs that best embrace the theme are eligible for limited financial support from the primary planner.

The Scholarship of Teaching

Jo Sprague, Office of Faculty Affairs, One Washington Square, San Jose State Univ, San Jose, California 95192-0012; office 408-924-2450; fax 408-924-2425; josprague@aol.com
Copies: 4
Deadline: February 15, 2000

This series integrates the GIFTS series and the TEACHERS ON TEACHING series into one series, more broadly focused on the scholarship of teaching as that concept has developed since the writing of Ernest Boyer's *Scholarship Reconsidered.* Proposals demonstrating good teaching practice and honoring great teaching are still welcome; however, this new series primarily encourages programs that explore the ways we can best enrich our campuses' educational mission. Programs may focus on best practices for communication pedagogy both with communication students and in general education efforts; use of new instructional technologies; assessment research on both learning outcomes and teaching itself accommodating to diversity both inside and outside the classroom; policy issues that effect the valuing of teaching at department, university, and international levels; the role of research in fostering good teaching; the relation of teaching scholarship to other forms of scholarship: application, integration, and discovery; models for communication departments taking leadership roles on their campuses in fostering teaching and learning; and so on. NCA is currently partnering with the Carnegie Foundation and the PEW Charitable Trusts in funded efforts to enhance the scholarship of teaching across higher education. Those involved in this new series may have the opportunity to be a part of this engagement effort. This new series, a variety of preconferences, and other activities are designed to display and enhance our leadership role in the creation of not only improved communication education, but of student learning across the academy. You are encouraged to be creative in developing program formats that engage scholars from within and outside the discipline (e.g., PEW Scholars) in exploring, teaching, and assessing dimensions of the scholarship of teaching and the communication discipline's role in fostering that scholarship. Poster sessions, preconferences, seminars, high density program formats are encouraged.

CONTINUING SERIES

Communication Consulting Series

Susan and Paul Glaser, Glaser & Associates, Inc, Executive Offices, 1740 Craigmont, Eugene, OR 97405; office 541-343-7575; fax 541-3343-1706; glaser@continet.com
Copies: 4
Deadline: February 15, 2000

This series will bring together individuals interested in exploring the practical, academic, and ethical issues of consulting. Consulting activity is one clear way our discipline is **engaged** in meeting needs of external constituencies. Issues to be considered include but are not limited to (1) consulting as an enterprise, (2) consulting as an academic endeavor, (3) consulting and tenure consideration, (4) consulting as research, (5) ethical issues, (6) NCA's role in enhancing our placement of graduates in non-academic enterprises, (7) gaining and keeping clients, and (8) gender issues in consulting. Refer to "HOW TO SUBMIT PAPERS AND PANEL/PROGRAM PROPOSALS" at the beginning of the call. *Also see "Convention Paper Distribution Center" and "Special Note" at the beginning of the call.*

Media Forum Series

Gail Chryslee, Dept of Communication, Univ of South Alabama, 1000 UCOM, Mobile, AL 36688-0001; office 334-380-2800; fax 334-380-2850; gchrysle@jaguar1.usouthal.edu
Copies: 4
Deadline: February 15, 2000

This series solicits proposals for programs in which media presentations play an essential role. Programs that include critical analysis of significant media texts and **engage** scholars with external constituencies (e.g., industry, government regulatory agencies) are especially encouraged. Active audience participation is expected. Submissions involving the creative process, pedagogy, demonstrations of new technologies, or screenings of significant works would be appropriate as long as their successful presentation requires media viewing and/or listening as a central element. Specific equipment requirements MUST be detailed in the proposal. Send four copies of a clearly articulated proposal following the format in the December 2000 *Spectra*, 1) detailing the media texts to be used, as well as 2) the reasons for and manner of their use, and 3) identifying participants, their affiliations, and their roles. Again, programs that engage participants across disciplines, industry, government that generate dialogue on ethical, technical, policy, and theoretical issues confronting mediated forms of communication are especially encouraged. *Also see "Convention Paper Distribution Center" and "Special Note" at the beginning of the call.*

Poster Sessions

Vincent R. Waldron, Dept of Communication Studies, Arizona State Univ West, 4701 W Thunderbird Road, Phoenix, AZ 85069-7100; office 602-543-6634; fax 602-543-6612; vincew@asu.edu
Copies: 4
Deadline: February 15, 2000

The Poster Sessions continue as a special series for the 2000 convention. Our location at a beautiful convention center in Seattle allows us to further enhance poster sessions in several new ways. First, the sessions will be located in a central area of the convention center near other popular displays and booths. Second, the sessions will feature food and beverage service. Engaged discussions of research can occur over good food and drink. This new Series will allow any current NCA member to submit a single or co-authored project ("project" is a generic term covering a variety of possible submissions—posters based on completed papers, a compilation of prior work, current work, and proposed work, etc. This series is not limited to traditional "completed research" or papers based on completed research. Those unit planners who have included acceptance of poster submissions in their call will be invited to forward those submitted to the Poster Session planner by the specified deadline. If in doubt about where to submit, send your poster proposal to the Poster Session planner, especially if the session conforms to the convention theme. For those considering submission, the following may be helpful. Depending on the subject and method, the poster's content may vary widely. Generally, such posters will contain the primary argument or rationale being portrayed, the primary results or conclusions drawn. At the poster session, the presenter may elect to provide a brief oral summary; however, the majority of time should be allocated for interaction with those attending the session. If the paper is based on a completed paper, a copy of that paper should be submitted to the Convention Paper Distribution Center, so that those interested in attending and discussing the paper may be able to secure a copy and read it in advance or, at least, secure a copy for further perusal after the session. Submission restrictions: Consistent with the "one paper per unit" goal noted earlier, you may submit only one project as first author (this does permit a second project submission as second or third author). In addition, the expectation is that the first author will be present for the poster session interaction with interested attendees. Submission protocol: Submit four copies of a 500 word abstract along with a concise but clear description of what is envisioned as the presentation poster and a list of key terms (as this will allow for easier subject matter classification). Where possible, notification will be made either by e-mail or fax.

Seminar Series

Roxanne Parrott, Dept of Speech Communication, 127 Terrell Hall, Univ of Georgia, Athens, GA 30602; office 706-542-3269; fax 706-542-3245; rparrott@arches.uga.edu
Copies: 4
Deadline: February 15, 2000

This series seeks proposals for seminars that focus on issues or lines of inquiry that are significant to the theory, criticism and practice of communication. Seminars should in some way display, advance, or enrich the discipline's areas of **engagement** with important constituencies in other disciplines or outside the academy. Seminars might (1) rethink traditional theories, approaches, or methods of research in light of contemporary social needs and challenges with the goal of enriching communication's contributions; (2) identify boundaries within and between disciplinary approaches that could be blurred or broached by communication researchers in ways that better enable us to contribute to the common good; or perhaps most importantly, (3) bring colleagues from business, government, and non-profits together with communication scholars to explore areas of **engagement** that improve the public health, preserve the environment, enhance inclusiveness, bridge international boundaries, increase learning, pursue social justice, make clear communication's valuable position in a higher education community itself focused on **engagement**, and so on. Proposals should include a title, name and address of a seminar leader who has agreed to serve, an outline of the issues to be addressed, and audio-visual equipment needed. All submissions must be accompanied by a brief description of the seminar and should include detailed instructions for participants. In some cases, commitments for participation or plans to include persons outside the discipline could be included as well. Seminars will be scheduled on the pre-convention day.

Short Courses

Kathleen M. Kougl, Dept of Communication and Theater, Youngstown State Univ, Youngstown, OH 44555; office 216-742-3631; kmkougl@cc.ysu.edu
Copies: 10
Deadline: February 1, 2000

Short courses encourage intense focus on a selected topic in a concentrated three-hour instructional format. In addition to the selected topics that reflect specific areas relevant to the courses, scholarship, or project activities of communication specialists, the following short courses are being solicited: (1) courses in new research methods or pedagogy; (2) courses in "Teaching the College Course in . . ."; (3) courses addressing the convention theme of **engagement**; (4) courses in curriculum development or applied instructional strategies; and (5) courses that advance new communication technologies and methodologies. All short course submissions must follow the format outlined in the December issue of *Spectra*. The review committee recommends proposals in terms of (1) value of the short course content for NCA members; (2) qualifications of the suggested instructor/staff to teach the content; (3) continuing education demand of the field, and (4) potential effectiveness of the instructional procedures.

Spotlight on Scholarship

Sandra Metts, Dept of Communication, Fell Hall, Illinois State Univ, Normal, IL 61790-4480; office 309-438-7883; fax 309-438-3048; smmetts@mvs.cmp.ilstu.edu

Copies: 4
Deadline: February 15, 2000

Three types of proposals are solicited: (1) proposals summarizing and analyzing the work of a distinguished senior researcher-scholar; (2) proposals enabling a distinguished senior researcher-scholar to make an extended presentation from a major scholarly work in progress and to obtain responses of distinguished critics; and (3) proposals summarizing and offering exemplars of major research programs. Programs that celebrate scholarship that exemplifies the convention theme of **engagement** are especially encouraged. Letters of nomination for programs based on individual scholarship or programs of research should be accompanied by current vita of an individual scholar if that is the focus, current vitae of all panel participants, and a statement describing the dominant themes and impact of the research being analyzed. A program organized around a research program also should include in two pages or less, the name of participants, and a brief description of each participant's role.

Table Talk Series

Alison Alexander, Grady College of Journalism and Mass Communication, Univ of Georgia, Athens, GA 30606; office 706-542-3785; fax 706-542-4785; alison@arches.uga.edu
Copies: 4
Deadline: February 15, 2000

This series will bring together individuals interested in addressing diverse issues: (1) professional issues (e.g., ways to encourage engagement within universities; creating curricula that meet the needs of increasingly diverse populations of students; tension between professional and liberal arts education; the need for a united focus and mission for the speech communication discipline in threatening times; alternative organizational models for departments and colleges; the conflict between politically correct language sensitivity and first amendment rights; finding common ground between teaching and scholarship for K-12 and higher education; public concerns about the primacy of research in the retention, tenure, and promotion process; higher education in a period of declining public support for affirmative action, diversity, and multiculturalism; re-discovering the utilitarian and applied purpose of communication studies; improving K-12's preparation of students for higher education); (2) NCA-centered issues (e.g., NCA taking political positions on issues not directly related to the professional purpose of the association; NCA's role in accrediting programs; NCA's role in developing instruments to evaluate and certify the oral competency of K-12 and higher education faculty; NCA's responsibilities in providing consulting opportunities for its members; NCA requiring diversity of nominees for its elections); and (3) action issues (e.g., preparing agenda items for the Policy Platform Committee, Administrative Committee, Resolution Committee, or Legislative Council including preparation of background material and motions which could be based on deliberations in #1 and #2 above). Proposals for Table Talk sessions should identify the discussion topic, explain the significance to others, identify a discussion leader, indicate participants, if available, and audience likely to join Table Talk.

"Town Hall" Meetings

James L. Applegate, Dept of Communication, 230 Grehan Bldg, Univ of Kentucky, Lexington, KY 40506-0042; office 606-257-3622; fax 606-257-4103; japple@pop.uky.edu
Copies: 4
Deadline: February 15, 2000

One of the oldest forms of self governance in this country is the "Town Hall" Meeting. The history of this governance form shows that the rhetoric flowed freely as public issues were debated. We are looking for innovative proposals and suggestions as to panelists and issues for debate. They may be of a serious or humorous nature. Of course, audience participation is central to any "Town Hall" Meeting. Topics that embrace or challenge the convention theme calling for an **engaged discipline** are especially encouraged.

Preconferences

James L. Applegate, Dept of Communication, 230 Grehan Bldg, Univ of Kentucky, Lexington, KY 40506-0042; office 606-257-3622; fax 606-257-4103; japple@pop.uky.edu
Copies: 4
Deadline: February 15, 2000

Members interested in conducting a Preconference should submit the following information, *through an NCA unit or affiliate,* to the primary convention planner. Submissions must include (1) title of the pre-convention conference and name of sponsoring unit(s); (2) brief statement of purpose and objectives of the conference; (3) a draft of the conference agenda—including beginning and ending times; (4) an estimate of the attendance; (5) a detailed budget, expected expenses for audio-visual equipment, food, speaker fees, transportation costs, handouts, and other relevant items associated with running the conference (conference fees will be set by the NCA National Office based on this information); and (6) name, address, phone and fax numbers, and e-mail address of the Pre-conference Coordinator. Pre-conferences that realize the convention **engagement** theme either through topic or participants are especially encouraged.

UNITS & AFFILIATES

African American Communication and Culture Division

Virgie N. Harris, Fine Arts Dept, Fort Valley State Univ, 110 Founders Hall, Fort Valley, GA 31030; office 912-825-6387; fax 912-825-6132; harrisv@mail.fvsu.edu
Copies: 4
Deadline: February 1, 2000
Specify student papers: yes
Specify debut papers: yes
Maximum length: 25 pages, excluding references

The Division invites submissions of competitive papers that advance understanding of communication involving and/or affecting individuals of African descent throughout the Diaspora. Examinations of African-African American culture are also welcome. Papers may be theoretical, methodological, rhetorical, qualitative, ethnographic, or empirical in nature. New and different perspectives are welcome. Only completed papers will be considered. Refer to "HOW TO SUBMIT PAPERS AND PANEL/PROGRAM PROPOSALS" at the beginning of the call. *Also see "Convention Paper Distribution Center," "Poster Sessions," and "Special Note" at the beginning of the call.*

American Association for the Rhetoric of Science and Technology

Joan Leach, Humanities Program, 313C Mechanical Engineering Bldg, Imperial College of Science, Technology, and Medicine, London, SW7 2AX United Kingdom; office 0171-594-8753; j.leach@ic.ac.uk
Copies: 3
Deadline: February 15, 2000
Specify student papers: no
Specify debut papers: no

The American Association for the Rhetoric of Science and Technology invites submission of program proposals and papers. Submissions may cover any area of rhetoric of science, including the rhetorical analysis of science policy debates, the analysis of scientific texts, the transfer of scientific rhetoric into literary or other contexts, and the rhetorical impact of popular representations of science. Refer to "HOW TO SUBMIT PAPERS AND PANEL/PROGRAM PROPOSALS" at the beginning of the call. *Also see "Convention Paper Distribution Center," "Poster Sessions," and "Special Note" at the beginning of the call.*

American Forensics Association

Karla Leeper, P.O. Box 97368, Baylor Univ, Waco, TX 76798, office 254-710-6919; fax 254-710-1563; karla_leeper@baylor.edu
Copies: 4
Deadline: February 1, 2000
Specify student papers: no
Specify debut papers: no
Maximum length: article length

The Association invites individual papers and program proposals relating to any aspect of forensic activity or argumentation. Papers and programs addressing the broad interests of the forensic community are encouraged, although quality programs and papers relevant to a particular subset of the community will also be considered. All submissions will be blind reviewed, and there will be one or more panels composed of competitively selected papers if submissions indicate. Refer to "HOW TO SUBMIT PAPERS AND PANEL/PROGRAM PROPOSALS" at the beginning of the call. *Also see "Convention Paper Distribution Center," "Poster Sessions," and "Special Note" at the beginning of the call.*

American Society for the History of Rhetoric

Mari Lee Mifsud, Dept of Speech Communication, Univ of Richmond, Richmond, VA 23228; office 804-261-5594; mmifsud@richmond.edu
Copies: 4
Deadline: February 15, 2000
Specify student papers: yes
Specify debut papers: no

The American Society for the History of Rhetoric invites submission of program proposals and competitive papers. ASHR welcomes work that examines both the theory and practice of rhetoric in all periods and languages and its relationship with poetics, politics, religion, law, and other cultural influences. To be considered for the Society's Student Paper Award, all student-authored papers should be marked "student paper." All papers accepted for presentation during each calendar at ASHR scholarly meetings are eligible for consideration in the Society's annual *Advances in the History of Rhetoric.* Refer to "HOW TO SUBMIT PAPERS AND PANEL/PROGRAM PROPOSALS" at the beginning of the call. *Also see "Convention Paper Distribution Center," "Poster Sessions," and "Special Note" at the beginning of the call.*

American Studies Commission

Barbara R. Burke, Dept of Speech Communication, Univ of Minnesota, Morris, 600 E 4th Street, Morris, MN 56267-2132; office 320-589-6243; burkebr@mrs.umn.edu
Copies: 4
Deadline: February 15, 2000
Specify student papers: yes
Specify debut papers: yes

The American Studies Commission invites paper and thematic panel submissions that address communication and the diverse texts, artifacts, practices, and traditions of American culture(s) from an interdisciplinary perspective. The commission invites papers and thematic panels. Submissions related to the convention theme are especially encouraged. Refer to "HOW TO SUBMIT PAPERS AND PANEL/PROGRAM PROPOSALS" at the beginning of the call. *Also see "Convention Paper Distribution Center," "Poster Sessions," and "Special Note" at the beginning of the call.*

Applied Communication Division

Sunwolf, Dept of Communication, Santa Clara Univ, 500 El Camino Real, Santa Clara, CA 95053-0277; office 408-554-4911; fax 408-554-4913; sunwolf@acu.edu
Copies: 5
Deadline: February 15, 2000
Specify student papers: yes
Specify debut papers: yes
Maximum length: 25 pages excluding references

The Applied Communication Division invites submission of papers, thematic panels, and proposals for other types of programs (e.g., poster sessions) that focus on how communication theory, research, and/or practice contribute to addressing real, pragmatic, social problems. Papers, panels, and programs may be theoretical, methodological, or empirical in nature. We also encourage programs which are interactive (e.g., dialogues, debates, round table discussions, etc.). If papers have multiple authors, the name of the most likely presenter of the paper should be circled. Top papers are formally recognized. No fax or e-mail submissions accepted. Refer to "HOW TO SUBMIT PAPERS AND PANEL/PROGRAM PROPOSALS" at the beginning of the call. *Also see "Convention Paper Distribution Center," "Poster Sessions," and "Special Note" at the beginning of the call.*

Argumentation and Forensics Division

Tom Workman, Dept of Communication Studies, Univ of Nebraska, 430 Oldfather Hall, Lincoln, NE 68588; office 715-836-3305; fax 715-836-3820; workman@unlinfo.edu
Copies: 4
Deadline: February 15, 2000
Specify student papers: yes
Specify debut papers: yes
Maximum length: article length

The Division invites submissions of both thematic panels and individual papers for competitive review. The Division accepts programs and papers on argumentation theory and/or criticism, and on the theory and practice of any aspect of forensic activity. Refer to "HOW TO SUBMIT PAPERS AND PANEL/PROGRAM PROPOSALS" at the beginning of the call. *Also see "Convention Paper Distribution Center," "Poster Sessions," and "Special Note" at the beginning of the call.*

Asian/Pacific American Caucus

Mary Fong, Dept of Communication Studies, California State Univ, San Bernardino, 5500 University Parkway, San Bernardino, CA 92407; office 909-880-5891; fax 909-880-7009; mfong@csusb.edu
Copies: 4
Deadline: February 15, 2000
Specify student papers: yes
Specify debut papers: yes

The Caucus invites program proposals and papers that fulfill its mission to promote and advocate for the improved status, representation, understanding and opportunities for Asian Pacific Americans. Of special interest is scholarship that address these issues for Asian Pacific Americans within the discipline of Communication as well as society at large. Refer to "HOW TO SUBMIT PAPERS AND PANEL/PROGRAM PROPOSALS" at the beginning of the call. *Also see "Convention Paper Distribution Center," "Poster Sessions," and "Special Note" at the beginning of the call.*

Asian/Pacific American Communication Studies Division

Mary Fong, Dept of Communication Studies, California State Univ, San Bernardino, 5500 University Parkway, San Bernardino, CA 92407; office 909-880-5891; fax 909-880-7009; mfong@csusb.edu
Copies: 4
Deadline: February 15, 2000
Specify student papers: yes
Specify debut papers: yes

The Division invites thematic program proposals and papers that promote communication research advancing understanding about heterogeneous identities and cultures of Asian Pacific Americans, and Asians and Pacific Islanders in the Diaspora. Of special interest is scholarship exploring interconnectedness among identity, culture, race, ethnicity, gender, sexuality, community and communication. The Division encourages submission of co-sponsored programs and program proposals with alternative or innovative formats (round table discussions, debates, etc.). A top-ranked paper will be recognized at the APAC business meeting. Refer to "HOW TO SUBMIT PAPERS AND PANEL/PROGRAM PROPOSALS" at the beginning of the call. *Also see "Convention Paper Distribution Center," "Poster Sessions," and "Special Note" at the beginning of the call.*

Association for Chinese Communication Studies

Mary Fong, Dept of Communication Studies, California State Univ, San Bernardino, 5500 University Parkway, San Bernardino, CA 92407; office 909-880-5891; fax 909-880-7009; mfong@csusb.edu
Copies: 5
Deadline: February 1, 2000
Specify student papers: no
Specify debut papers: no

Maximum length: 25 pages

The Association for Chinese Communication Studies (ACCS) invites submissions of competitive papers, panel programs and other programs addressing theoretical, research, and/or methodological issues in Chinese culture and communication studies. Refer to "HOW TO SUBMIT PAPERS AND PANEL/PROGRAM PROPOSALS" at the beginning of the call. *Also see "Convention Paper Distribution Center," "Poster Sessions," and "Special Note" at the beginning of the call.*

Association for Communication Administration

Don Boileau, Communication Dept, George Mason Univ, Fairfax, VA 22030; office 703-993-1105; dboileau@gmu.edu
Copies: 3
Deadline: February 1, 2000
Specify student papers: no
Specify debut papers: no

The ACA invites submissions for contributed papers in communication and thematic panels. Essays should be capable of presentation in 15 minutes. Refer to "HOW TO SUBMIT PAPERS AND PANEL/PROGRAM PROPOSALS" at the beginning of the call. *Also see "Convention Paper Distribution Center," "Poster Sessions," and "Special Note" at the beginning of the call.*

Association for Rhetoric and Communication in Southern Africa

Philippe-Joseph Salazar, Centre for Rhetoric Studies, Univ of Cape Town, Private Bag 7001, Rondebosch South Africa; office +27216502895; fax +27216505530; salazar@beattie.uct.ac.za
Copies: 1
Deadline: February 15, 2000
Specify student papers: no
Specify debut papers: no

The Association invites the submission of competitive proposals for a thematic session comprised of four selected papers on intercultural rhetoric in emerging democracies. Full papers need not be submitted. E-mail submissions are encouraged. Refer to "HOW TO SUBMIT PAPERS AND PANEL/PROGRAM PROPOSALS" at the beginning of the call. *Also see "Convention Paper Distribution Center," "Poster Sessions," and "Special Note" at the beginning of the call.*

Basic Course Division

Jacquelyn Buckrop, Dept of Communication Studies, Ball State Univ, Muncie, IN 47306; office 765-285-1882; fax 765-285-2736; jbuckrop@gw.bsu.edu
Copies: 5
Deadline: February 1, 2000
Specify student papers: yes
Specify debut papers: yes
Maximum length: 25 pages

The Division invites submissions of papers, and program proposals that focus on research, instruction, or administration in the basic course. Completed papers are encouraged, but comprehensive abstracts (3-5 pages) will be accepted and judged competitively. Refer to "HOW TO SUBMIT PAPERS AND PANEL/PROGRAM PROPOSALS" at the beginning of the call. *Also see "Convention Paper Distribution Center," "Poster Sessions," and "Special Note" at the beginning of the call.*

Black Caucus

Eric Watts, Dept of Speech Communication, Wake Forest Univ, Winston-Salem, NC 27109; office 910-759-4691; watts@wfu.edu
Copies: 4
Deadline: February 1, 2000
Specify student papers: yes
Specify debut papers: yes

The Black Caucus invites program proposals (no papers, please) that address its mission, which is to advocate for the improved status, representation, and opportunities for African Americans in the discipline. In keeping with the spirit of its mission, the Caucus invites innovative formats (in addition to standard paper and panel presentations) that encourage wide participation and involvement. We especially welcome the participation of students and newer scholars. Program proposals should include a statement committing all proposed participants to attend if the proposal is accepted. Refer to "HOW TO SUBMIT PAPERS AND PANEL/PROGRAM PROPOSALS" at the beginning of the call. *Also see "Convention Paper Distribution Center," "Poster Sessions," and "Special Note" at the beginning of the call.*

Chinese Communication Association

Junhao Hong, Dept of Communication, SUNY Buffalo, Buffalo, NY 14261; office 716-645-2141 x112; fax 716-645-2086; jhong@acsu.buffalo.edu
Copies: 4
Deadline: February 1, 2000
Specify student papers: no
Specify debut papers: no

CCA invites papers and panel proposals addressing the broad interests of the CCA community. Papers and panel proposals may include, but are not limited to, critical assessment of the state of art in Chinese communication research, the inter-cultural and/or cross-cultural dynamics of the Chinese-speaking community, the changing relationship among China, Taiwan, and Hong Kong, and the role of communication in this process. Topics related to intercultural communication, cross-cultural comparison on group identity, negotiation, cultural change and the media are particularly welcome. All submissions will be judged in a blind-review process. Preference will be given to programs featuring participation from different institutions. No e-mail submissions will be accepted. Refer to "HOW TO SUBMIT PAPERS AND PANEL/PROGRAM PROPOSALS" at the beginning of the call. *Also see "Convention Paper Distribution Center," "Poster Sessions," and "Special Note" at the beginning of the call.*

Commission on American Parliamentary Practice

Martha Haun, School of Journalism, Univ of Houston, Houston, TX 77204-3768; office 713-747-5305; mhaun@uh.edu
Copies: 4
Deadline: February 15, 2000
Specify student papers: no
Specify debut papers: no
Maximum length: article length

The Commission invites competitive papers and panel proposals on the history, theory, practice or teaching of parliamentary law or procedures. Refer to "HOW TO SUBMIT PAPERS AND PANEL/PROGRAM PROPOSALS" at the beginning of the call. *Also see "Convention Paper Distribution Center," "Poster Sessions," and "Special Note" at the beginning of the call.*

Communication and Aging Commission

Sherry Holladay, Dept of Communication 4480, Illinois State Univ, Normal, IL 61790-4480; office 309-438-7630; sjholla@rs6000.cmp.ilstu.edu
Copies: 5
Deadline: February 15, 2000
Specify student papers: yes
Specify debut papers: no
Maximum length: 25 pages excluding references and tables

The Commission invites full papers, interactive (poster) proposals and thematic panel proposals concerning basic and applied research on communication and aging. Submissions may focus on the relationship of various communication contexts to communication and aging (e.g., intergenerational relationships, physician-elderly patient communication, communication within organizations such as nursing homes, representation of older persons in the media), impression formation processes (e.g., age stereotypes and communication), sociolinguistic studies of discourse and aging (e.g., patronizing talk, identity across the lifespan), communication and public policy on aging, pedagogy on communication and aging, etc .

Student papers should be marked "Student" on the title page *and* the first page of the text. Interactive (poster) proposals may be submitted in either full paper format or as extended abstracts of 2-3 pages (preference will be given to full papers). Refer to "HOW TO SUBMIT PAPERS AND PANEL/PROGRAM PROPOSALS" at the beginning of the call. *Also see "Convention Paper Distribution Center," "Poster Sessions," and "Special Note" at the beginning of the call.*

Communication Apprehension and Avoidance Commission

Chris Sawyer, Tarrant County Junior College NW, 4801 Marine Creek Parkway, Fort Worth, TX 76179; office 817-515-7228; fax 817-515-7007; csawyer@tcjc.cc.tx.us
Copies: 4
Deadline: February 15, 2000
Specify student papers: no
Specify debut papers: no

The Commission invites papers, extended abstracts, and program proposals related to basic research, educational programs, and treatment programs in the area of communication apprehension, communication avoidance, reticence, and shyness. Submission of research papers and instructional papers will be evaluated separately. Refer to "HOW TO SUBMIT PAPERS AND PANEL/PROGRAM PROPOSALS" at the beginning of the call. *Also see "Convention Paper Distribution Center," "Poster Sessions," and "Special Note" at the beginning of the call.*

Communication Ethics Commission

Sharon Bracci, 102 Ferguson Bldg, Univ of North Carolina, Greensboro, Greensboro, NC 27402-6170; office 336-334-3836; fax 336-334-3618; slbracci@uncg.edu
Copies: 5
Deadline: February 1, 2000
Specify student papers: yes
Specify debut papers: no

The Commission invites papers, extended abstracts and program proposals on any aspect of communication ethics, including theory, practice, history or pedagogy. Traditional or alternative perspectives are welcome. Graduate students are especially encouraged to contribute. Preference will be given to completed manuscripts. If a paper is accepted, the first author agrees to send the respondent a copy one month prior to the NCA panel date. Refer to "HOW TO SUBMIT PAPERS AND PANEL/PROGRAM PROPOSALS" at the beginning of the call. *Also see "Convention Paper Distribution Center," "Poster Sessions," and "Special Note" at the beginning of the call.*

Communication in the Future Commission

Susan B. Barnes, Dept of Communication and Media Studies, Fordham Univ, 441 E Fordham Road, Bronx, NY 10458; office 718-817-4855; fax 718-817-4868; barnes@murray.fordham.edu
Copies: 4
Deadline: February 15, 2000
Specify student papers: yes
Specify debut papers: yes

The Commission invites completed papers, extended abstracts (2-4 pages) and panel submissions. Topic categories include (1) legal/ethical; (2) social/technological; and (3) pedagogical/ teaching about the future of communication. Graduate student submissions are encouraged. Refer to "HOW TO SUBMIT PAPERS AND PANEL/PROGRAM PROPOSALS" at the beginning of the call. *Also see "Convention Paper Distribution Center," "Poster Sessions," and "Special Note" at the beginning of the call.*

Communication and Law Commission

Todd F. McDorman, Wabash College, P.O. Box 352, Crawfordsville, IN 47933; office 765-361-6183; fax 765 361-6341; mcdormat@wabash.edu
Copies: 4
Deadline: February 15, 2000

Specify student papers: yes
Specify debut papers: yes

The Commission invites the submission of competitive papers and proposals for program panels that advance the understanding of communication within the legal arena. Studies of jury decision-making, pre-trial processes, interaction within the courtroom, mass communication, interviewing, alternative dispute resolution, negotiation, and legal rhetoric are welcome. The Commission welcomes both quantitative and qualitative methods. Please indicate if you wish your submissions to be considered for poster sessions. Refer to "HOW TO SUBMIT PAPERS AND PANEL/PROGRAM PROPOSALS" at the beginning of the call. *Also see "Convention Paper Distribution Center," "Poster Sessions," and "Special Note" at the beginning of the call.*

Communication Assessment Commission

Ellen Hay, Augustana College, Office of the Dean of the College, Rock Island, IL 61201; office 309-794-7312; fax 309-794-7422; adceh@augustana.edu
Copies: 4
Deadline: February 15, 2000
Specify student papers: no
Specify debut papers: no

The Communication Assessment Commission invites submissions of papers or panels dealing with any aspect of the assessment or measurement of communication programs, knowledge bases, or skills. The Commission encourages papers or programs that focus on assessment instrument research and development, the role of assessment in program and student development, and the role of culture in assessment. Proposals for thematic panels should also include a statement of intention to attend for all participants. Refer to "HOW TO SUBMIT PAPERS AND PANEL/PROGRAM PROPOSALS" at the beginning of the call. *Also see "Convention Paper Distribution Center," "Poster Sessions," and "Special Note" at the beginning of the call.*

Communication Needs of Students at Risk Commission

John R. Heineman, 1116 S 17th Street, Lincoln High School, Lincoln, NE 68508; office 402-436-1301; fax 402-436-1540; jheineman@aol.com
Copies: 4
Deadline: February 15, 2000
Specify student papers: yes
Specify debut papers: yes

The Commission invites the submission of completed papers and proposals for program panels that advance the understanding of communication needs of students at risk. We are particularly interested in papers and panels which connect the NCA convention theme to the examination of theory, pedagogy, and practices dealing with the challenges, roles of communication professionals, solutions, models of instruction, and assessment processes. Please indicate if you wish your submission to be considered for poster sessions. Refer to "HOW TO SUBMIT PAPERS AND PANEL/PROGRAM PROPOSALS" at the beginning of the call. *Also see "Convention Paper Distribution Center," "Poster Sessions," and "Special Note" at the beginning of the call.*

Community College Section

Robert C. Bohan, Humanities/Fine Arts Div (SP/G), St. Petersburg Junior College, P.O. Box 13489, St. Petersburg, FL 33733-3489; office 727-341-4784; fax 727-341-4744; bohanr@email.spjc.cc.fl.us
Copies: 5
Deadline: February 1, 2000
Specify student papers: yes
Specify debut papers: yes

The Community College Section invites submissions of program proposals, thematic panels, and/or papers pertaining to all community college concerns in communication. Completed papers will be reviewed through a blind review process. Ideas for short courses and seminars are also invited. Refer to "HOW TO SUBMIT PAPERS AND PANEL/PROGRAM PROPOSALS" at the beginning of the call. *Also see "Convention Paper Distribution Center," "Poster Sessions," and "Special Note" at the beginning of the call.*

Critical and Cultural Studies Division

Kent Ono, American Studies, Hart Hall, Univ of California, Davis, Davis, CA 95616; office 530-752-4901; fax 530-752-9260; kaono@ucdavis.edu
Copies: 4
Deadline: February 15, 2000
Specify student papers: no
Specify debut papers: no
Maximum length: 25 pages

In the effort to promote the teaching and scholarly inquiry of the languages of knowledge, power, and disciplinarity as they affect cultural and social practices in both historical and contemporary contexts, the division invites submissions of program proposals and papers that emphasize the careful and creative theorization, interpretation, and evaluation—from multiple perspectives—of discourses and practices that empower and/or hinder groups, subcultures, or inflect on the practice of "everyday life." The division also encourages submissions which encourage teaching and scholarship that goes beyond the boundaries of the academy in fostering social action and promoting social change. Alternative panel formats and panels on the conference theme are especially encouraged. Only completed papers will be considered and a 50-word abstract should accompany each paper. For panels, include a statement committing all proposed participants to attend should the program be accepted. No e-mail submissions will be accepted. Refer to "HOW TO SUBMIT PAPERS AND PANEL/PROGRAM PROPOSALS" at the beginning of the call. *Also see "Convention Paper Distribution Center," "Poster Sessions," and "Special Note" at the beginning of the call.*

Cross Examination Debate Association

Greg Achten, Communication Division, 24255 PCH, Pepperdine Univ, Malibu, CA, 90263; office 310-456-4524; fax 310-456-3083; gachten@pepperdine.edu
Copies: 5
Deadline: February 1, 2000
Specify student papers: no
Specify debut papers: no

The Cross Examination Debate Association invites submissions for "Contributed Papers in Argumentation and Debate" relevant to policy debate and thematic panels. Essays should be capable of presentation in 15 minutes. Refer to "HOW TO SUBMIT PAPERS AND PANEL/PROGRAM PROPOSALS" at the beginning of the call. *Also see "Convention Paper Distribution Center," "Poster Sessions," and "Special Note" at the beginning of the call.*

Disability Issues Caucus

Beth Haller, 8000 York Rd, Dept of Mass Communication/Communication Studies, Towson State Univ, Towson, MD 21252-0001; office 410-830-2442; fax 410-830-3656; bhalle@towson.edu
Copies: 5
Deadline: February 15, 2000
Specify student papers: yes
Specify debut papers: yes
Maximum length: 30 pages

The two goals behind the Disability Issues Caucus are to promote greater participation by people with disabilities in NCA and the discipline at large, and to encourage quality scholarship on issues concerning disability and communication. The Caucus invites program proposals and papers exploring any aspect of issues related to disability and communication, and it especially encourages programs that will promote participation by people with disabilities. The caucus invites innovative or alternative program formats as well as more traditional paper and panel presentations. Program proposals should include a statement committing all proposed participants to attend should the program be accepted. Refer to "HOW TO SUBMIT PAPERS AND PANEL/PROGRAM PROPOSALS" at the beginning of the call. *Also see "Convention Paper Distribution Center," "Poster Sessions," and "Special Note" at the beginning of the call.*

Elementary and Secondary Section

Robert Stockton, Western High School, 501 S Western Ave, Anaheim, CA 92804-1615; office 714-871-9274; fax 714-220-4027
Copies: 4
Deadline: February 15, 2000
Specify student papers: no
Specify debut papers: no

The Section invites the submission of papers and program panels that enhance the teaching of communication in the elementary and secondary classroom. Research in any discipline field which ties directly to K-12 is encouraged. Additionally, programs on the practice of teaching communication are needed. Refer to "HOW TO SUBMIT PAPERS AND PANEL/PROGRAM PROPOSALS" at the beginning of the call. *Also see "Convention Paper Distribution Center," "Poster Sessions," and "Special Note" at the beginning of the call.*

Environmental Communication Commission

Jean Retzinger, 301 Campbell Hall, Univ of California, Berkeley, Berkeley, CA 94720-2992; office 510-643-1960; fax 510-642-4607; jpretz@uclink4.berkeley.edu
Copies: 5
Deadline: February 1, 2000
Specify student papers: yes
Specify debut papers: yes

The commission invites submissions for both competitively selected papers and thematic panels reflecting the link between communication practices and environmental affairs. Papers will be juried. Refer to "HOW TO SUBMIT PAPERS AND PANEL/PROGRAM PROPOSALS" at the beginning of the call. *Also see "Convention Paper Distribution Center," "Poster Sessions," and "Special Note" at the beginning of the call.*

Ethnography Division

Ron Wendt, Dept of Speech Communication, Univ of South Dakota, Vermillion, SD 57069; office 319-524-2542; rwendt@sunbird.usd.edu
Copies: 5
Deadline: February 15, 2000
Specify student papers: yes
Specify debut papers: yes
Maximum length: 30 pages

The Division invites papers and panels that (1) discuss ethnography as a communicative stance and way of knowing/living in the world; (2) critically examine ethnographic practices and theoretical understandings; (3) use ethnographic approaches such as participant observation, in-depth interviewing, grounded theory, ethnography of speaking, critical theory, feminism, postmodernism, or auto-ethnography; and (4) experiment with ethnographic forms such as literary, poetic, multi-voiced, conversational, visual, and performative. No e-mail submissions accepted. Refer to "HOW TO SUBMIT PAPERS AND PANEL/PROGRAM PROPOSALS" at the beginning of the call. *Also see "Convention Paper Distribution Center," "Poster Sessions," and "Special Note" at the beginning of the call.*

Experiential Learning in Communication Commission

Karen M. Roloff, DePaul Univ, 2320 N Kenmore Ave, Chicago, IL 60614; office 773-325-7586; fax 773-325-7584; kroloff@wppost.depaul.edu
Copies: 4
Deadline: February 15, 2000
Specify student papers: yes
Specify debut papers: no

The Commission invites submissions of program ideas, panels and papers on any area of experiential learning in communication. The Commission is especially interested in assessment, evaluation and measurement of experiential learning and facilitation, as well as other applied aspects of learning situations, internships, qualitative and quantitative research and curriculum designs. Programs may be invited or competitive in nature and submitted papers may be reports of research, theoretical considerations, or practical applications of experiential learning in and out of the classroom. Refer to "HOW TO SUBMIT PAPERS AND PANEL/PROGRAM PROPOSALS" at the beginning of the call. *Also see "Convention Paper Distribution Center," "Poster Sessions," and "Special Note" at the beginning of the call.*

Family Communication Division

Lynn H. Turner, Dept of Communication Studies, Johnston Hall, Room 118, P.O. Box 1881, Marquette Univ, Milwaukee, WI 53201-1881; office 414-288-6351; fax 414-288-3923; 6046turnerl@vms.csd.mv.edu
Copies: 5
Deadline: February 15, 2000
Specify student papers: yes
Specify debut papers: yes
Maximum length: 25 pages

The Family Communication Division encourages innovative approaches to the study of communication in families and family relationships (e.g., marriage, post-divorce, parent-child, siblings, extended families, and family relationships with professionals and the community), and solicits papers and panel proposals from members of all NCA sections and divisions. The Division values diversity in approaches to theory, method, and pedagogy as well as culture, and encourages submissions of work about a broad array of families. Papers and proposals are submitted to blind review. Refer to "HOW TO SUBMIT PAPERS AND PANEL/PROGRAM PROPOSALS" at the beginning of the call. *Also see "Convention Paper Distribution Center," "Poster Sessions," and "Special Note" at the beginning of the call.*

Feminist and Women's Studies Division

Michelle Violanti, Dept of Speech Communication, Univ of Tennessee, 105 McClung Tower, Knoxville, TN 37996-0405; office 432-974-7072; fax 423-974-4879; violanti@utkvx.utcc.utk.edu
Copies: 4
Deadline: February 1, 2000
Specify student papers: yes
Specify debut papers: no
Maximum length: 25 pages

The Division invites papers on any aspect of women's studies in communication and particularly papers that (1) honor women's diversity in race, class, sexual orientation and nationality and (2) challenge existing theoretical paradigms that have excluded diverse women's voices. Papers will be selected competitively and, when possible, grouped into appropriate themes. Only completed papers that follow the submission guidelines will be considered. The Division provides a $50 award to the top student-authored paper. In addition to individual papers, panel proposals may also be submitted in competition for sponsorship by the Division or co-sponsorship with other divisions. Alternative panel formats are encouraged. Program proposals should include a statement committing all proposed participants to attend should panel be accepted. Please be certain no members of the panels have agreed to serve on more than one non-competitive program. Refer to "HOW TO SUBMIT PAPERS AND PANEL/PROGRAM PROPOSALS" at the beginning of the call. *Also see "Convention Paper Distribution Center," "Poster Sessions," and "Special Note" at the beginning of the call.*

Freedom of Expression Commission

Warren Sandmann, Speech Communication Dept #89, Minnesota State Univ, Mankato, Mankato MN 56002-8400; office 507-389-2213; fax 507-389-5887; warren.sandmann@mankato.msus.edu
Copies: 4
Deadline: February 15, 2000
Specify student papers: yes
Specify debut papers: yes

The Commission invites papers and program proposals concerning all aspects of freedom of expression. Submissions may deal with any issue pertinent to free speech including the justification for protecting expression, historical cases or episodes in suppression, the state of current or pending legal tests or standards, the tension between speech and privacy, issues pertaining to media law or copyright, and contemporary controversies such as regulation of the

Internet or the World Wide Web. All submissions will be blind reviewed and there will be one or more panels composed of competitively selected papers. Refer to "HOW TO SUBMIT PAPERS AND PANEL/PROGRAM PROPOSALS" at the beginning of the call. *Also see "Convention Paper Distribution Center," "Poster Sessions," and "Special Note" at the beginning of the call.*

Gay and Lesbian Concerns Caucus and the Gay/Lesbian/Bisexual /Transgender Communication Studies Division

Elizabeth Whitney, Communication Dept, Univ of Utah, Salt Lake City, UT 84112; office 801-581-6888; melismo@earthlink.net
Copies: 4
Deadline: February 1, 2000
Specify student papers: no
Specify debut papers: no
Maximum length: 25 pages

The Caucus and Division invite submissions of papers and panel proposals addressing (1) advocacy, professional networking, and mentoring to gay men, lesbians, and bisexuals in the field of communication, and (2) lesbian, gay male, bisexual, and queer studies and scholarship in the field of communication. No e-mail submissions will be accepted. Refer to "HOW TO SUBMIT PAPERS AND PANEL/PROGRAM PROPOSALS" at the beginning of the call. *Also see "Convention Paper Distribution Center," "Poster Sessions," and "Special Note" at the beginning of the call.*

Group Communication Division

Joann Keyton, Dept of Communication, Univ of Memphis, TCA 143, Memphis, TN 38152-6522; office 901-678-3185; fax 901-678-4331; jkeyton@memphis.edu
Copies: 5
Deadline: February 1, 2000
Specify student papers: yes
Specify debut papers: no
Maximum length: 30 pages excluding title page, references, figures and tables

The Group Communication Division invites submission of papers, competitive papers, thematic panels, and proposals for other types of programs (including poster sessions) that focus on group communication theory, research, pedagogy, facilitation, and other applications/practices. The Division is committed to encouraging scholarly inquiry into group communication across many different types of groups and contexts (e.g., task/decision-making, occupational, social, educational, familial, health, recreational, and political/civic groups) using many different methods (e.g., quantitative, qualitative, and rhetorical; naturalistic and laboratory). Papers authored solely by students should indicate "student" in the upper-right corner of the cover page, so they can be considered for the best student paper award. Papers suitable for poster sessions should indicate this on the cover page. We are especially interested in interactive thematic panels/programs (e.g., dialogues, round table discussions, etc.). No e-mail or faxed submissions accepted. Please include a stamped, self addressed envelope to facilitate notification of receipt of submission. Refer to "HOW TO SUBMIT PAPERS AND PANEL/PROGRAM PROPOSALS" at the beginning of the call. *Also see "Convention Paper Distribution Center," "Poster Sessions," and "Special Note" at the beginning of the call.*

Health Communication Division

Alicia Marshall, Dept of Speech Communication, MS #4234, Boulton Hall, Texas A&M Univ, College Station, TX 77843-4234; office 409-845-5500; aamarsh@aca.tamu.edu
Copies: 5
Deadline: February 15, 2000
Specify student papers: yes
Specify debut papers: no
Maximum length: 25 pages including references

The Health Communication Division invites the submission of completed papers or program proposals that focus on theory, research, and/or practice of health communication. All papers and program proposals will be submitted to competitive, blind review. All submissions should include a 100-200 word press release and the author/title page of papers or the participant/presentation information for panel proposals must be e-mailed in addition to a hard copy that is submitted with the paper/panel proposal. Refer to "HOW TO SUBMIT PAPERS AND PANEL/PROGRAM PROPOSALS" at the beginning of the call. *Also see "Convention Paper Distribution Center," "Poster Sessions," and "Special Note" at the beginning of the call.*

Human Communication and Technology Commission

Clark Germann, Metropolitan State College at Denver, Campus Box 35, P.O. Box 173362, Denver, CO 80217-3362; office 303-556-3453; fax 303-556-8135; germannc@mscd.edu
Copies: 4
Deadline: February 1, 2000
Specify student papers: yes
Specify debut papers: no
Maximum length: article length

The Commission invites panels and papers on topics that support the examination of theory and application of contemporary communication technology as related to human communication studies, pedagogy, and other functions. The Commission is especially interested in Human Communication and Technology as related to areas of rhetoric, ethics, intellectual property rights, teaching and learning, security, accessibility, accountability, globalism, distance education, training and development, and other topics. Please indicate if program proposals or papers are particularly appropriate for co-sponsorship. Refer to "HOW TO SUBMIT PAPERS AND PANEL/PROGRAM PROPOSALS" at the beginning of the call. *Also see "Convention Paper Distribution Center," "Poster Sessions," and "Special Note" at the beginning of the call.*

Instructional Development Division

Scott A. Meyers, Dept of Communication Studies, Creighton Univ, Omaha, NE 68102; office 402-280-2530; fax 402-280-2143; scotia@creighton.edu
Copies: 5
Deadline: February 2, 2000
Specify student papers: yes
Specify debut papers: yes
Maximum length: article length

The Division sponsors competitively-selected papers and thematic programs. Papers submitted for the competitive programs should address theory or research relevant to instruction and learning, communication education, and communication in instructional contexts. Reviews of literature, essays and suggestions for application of theory and research are also appropriate. The Division provides a $50 award to the top student-authored paper. To be considered for the award all authors must be students and the word "Student" must be in the upper right hand corner of the title page. The papers will be evaluated by a panel of judges, and those selected will be critiqued by a respondent at the presentation. Proposals for programs or workshops will be selected on the basis of appropriateness to instructional development, significance of the topic and interest to people in a variety of instructional settings. Proposals for programs should include a statement of commitment by each participant. Please indicate if program proposals or papers are particularly appropriate for a poster session or co-sponsorship. Refer to "HOW TO SUBMIT PAPERS AND PANEL/PROGRAM PROPOSALS" at the beginning of the call. *Also see "Convention Paper Distribution Center," "Poster Sessions," and "Special Note" at the beginning of the call.*

International Forensics Association

Barbara Baron, Speech Dept, LAH 310, Brookdale Community College, Newman Springs Rd, Lincroft, NJ 07738; office 732-224-2211; bbaron@brookdale.cc.nj.us
Copies: 3
Deadline: February 15, 2000
Specify student papers: yes
Specify debut papers: no

The Association invites submissions for papers or program proposals relating to forensics, debate, performance studies or rhetorical issues, especially from a cross-cultural or international perspective. Refer to "HOW TO SUBMIT PAPERS AND PANEL/PROGRAM PROPOSALS" at the beginning of the call. *Also see "Convention Paper Distribution Center,"*

"Poster Sessions," and "Special Note" at the beginning of the call.

International and Intercultural Communication Division

T. Todd Imahori, c/o Dept of Speech and Communication Studies, San Francisco State Univ, 1600 Holloway Ave, San Francisco, CA 94132-1722; FOR DIRECT MAILING: Dept of Foreign Languages, Seinan Gakuin Univ, 6-2-92 Nishijin, Sawara-ku, Fukuoka, 814-8511 JAPAN; office +81-092-841-1311 x2561; fax +81-092-823-2506; imahori@seinan-gu.ac.jp
Copies: 5
Deadline: February 1, 2000
Specify student papers: yes
Specify debut papers: no

The Division invites submissions for contributed papers, student papers, and thematic panels in international, intercultural, and/or cultural communication. Co-sponsored panels and non-paper formats will also be considered. E-mail submissions are encouraged. Send e-mail clearly titled as "IICD Submission." For submissions with complex figures/tables, hard copies should be sent. For international mailing allow one week for delivery via airmail. Refer to "HOW TO SUBMIT PAPERS AND PANEL/PROGRAM PROPOSALS" at the beginning of the call. *Also see "Convention Paper Distribution Center," "Poster Sessions," and "Special Note" at the beginning of the call.*

Interpersonal Communication Division

Judee Burgoon, Dept of Communication, Univ of Arizona, Tucson, AZ 85721; office 520-621-5818; fax 520-621-5504; judee@u.arizona.edu
Copies: 5
Deadline: February 1, 2000
Specify student papers: yes
Specify debut papers: yes
Maximum length: 25 pages excluding tables, references, and appendices

The Division invites completed papers and panel proposals related to interpersonal communication antecedents, processes, and outcomes. Papers should include a 100-150 word abstract, and all information identifying authorship should be removed from four of the five copies. Panel proposals appropriate for co-sponsorship by multiple NCA units and which address the conference theme of the Engaged Discipline are also encouraged. Panel proposals should include a 250-500 word description of their purpose and contents, a complete listing of the presenters and titles of their presentations, and identification of the relevant divisions/commissions/caucuses to whom the panel is aimed. Refer to "HOW TO SUBMIT PAPERS AND PANEL/PROGRAM PROPOSALS" at the beginning of the call. *Also see "Convention Paper Distribution Center," "Poster Sessions," and "Special Note" at the beginning of the call.*

Intrapersonal Communication and Social Cognition Division

Ron Tamborini, Michigan State Univ, Dept of Communication, East Lansing, MI 48824; office 517-355-0178; tamborini@pilot.msu.edu
Copies: 4
Deadline: February 15, 2000
Specify student papers: yes
Maximum length: 25 pages excluding tables and figures

The Division seeks papers and panel/program proposals concerning the cognitive and affective processing of communication. Submissions may be theoretical, methodological or empirical in nature. Research on how message encoding or decoding is influenced by information processing, attention, emotion, or belief systems is encouraged, regardless of the setting in which it occurs. Works that investigate the processing of communication in face-to-face (e.g., relational, group, or organizational) or mediated (e.g., mass or new technologies) contexts are welcome. Relevant topics include, but are not limited to, social influence, social perception, imagined interaction, and inner speech. Program Chair/Moderator should not be a paper presenter or respondent on the program. Refer to "HOW TO SUBMIT PAPERS AND PANEL/PROGRAM PROPOSALS" at the beginning of the call. *Also see "Convention Paper Distribution Center," "Poster Sessions," and "Special Note" at the beginning of the call.*

Kenneth Burke Society

Bryan Crable, Dept of Communication, Villanova Univ, 800 Lancaster Ave, Villanova, PA
19085-1699; office 610-519-4750
Copies: 4
Deadline: February 1, 2000
Specify student papers: yes
Specify debut papers: yes
Maximum length: 15 pages

The Kenneth Burke Society welcomes papers and program proposals that (1) interpret or
address Burke's theoretical and critical approaches, (2) apply Burkean concepts to a
communication event, be it rhetorical, mass-mediated, interpersonal, etc., (3) synthesize
Burkean ideas with other lines of scholarship, or (4) develop aspects of Burkean scholarship in
new directions. Papers will be evaluated competitively, with a "Best Student Paper" and "Best
Paper" award. As well, a "Top Four Competitive Papers" panel will be announced. A 100-word
abstract should be included with each copy of the paper. Program proposals are especially
encouraged. They should be tightly organized around themes, such as "Burke and Marxism" or
"Reading Rhetoric From Permanence and Change." Those interested in program submissions
are encouraged to seek out appropriate co-panelists through the Burke-L, H-Rhetor, or
CRTNET list servers. Refer to "HOW TO SUBMIT PAPERS AND PANEL/PROGRAM
PROPOSALS" at the beginning of the call. *Also see "Convention Paper Distribution Center,"
"Poster Sessions," and "Special Note" at the beginning of the call.*

Korean American Communication Association

E.J. Min, Dept of Communications, Rhode Island College, Providence, RI 02908; office
401-456-8270; fax 401-456-8379; emin@grog.ric.edu
Copies: 5
Deadline: February 15, 2000
Specify student papers: yes
Specify debut papers: no
Maximum length: 25 pages excluding tables and references

KACA invites papers and panel proposals that address theoretical, methodological, and
application issues in Korean and/or Korean American communication research. Papers and
panels developing theory, practice, field research and case studies relating to the themes are
especially encouraged. Papers that deal with intra/intercultural relations, comparative studies,
issues or identification and gender, interpersonal, organizational, media, and new
communication technologies are invited. Refer to "HOW TO SUBMIT PAPERS AND
PANEL/PROGRAM PROPOSALS" at the beginning of the call. *Also see "Convention Paper
Distribution Center," "Poster Sessions," and "Special Note" at the beginning of the call.*

La Raza Caucus

Jennifer L. Willis-Rivera, Dept of Speech Communication, Southern Illinois Univ,
Carbondale, IL 62901-6605; office 618-453-1882; fax 618-453-2812; jwillis@siu.edu
Copies: 5
Deadline: February 15, 2000
Specify student papers: yes
Specify debut papers: yes

The La Raza Caucus invites program proposals and papers exploring Chicano/Latino culture
and communication. Of special interest are explorations linking the conference theme with the
Chicana/o and Latina/o community, as well as those addressing praxis and community activism.
Refer to "HOW TO SUBMIT PAPERS AND PANEL/PROGRAM PROPOSALS" at the beginning
of the call. *Also see "Convention Paper Distribution Center," "Poster Sessions," and "Special
Note" at the beginning of the call.*

Lambda Pi Eta

Frances Broderick, Communications Dept, College of Mount Saint Vincent, 6301 Riverdale
Ave, Riverdale, NY 10471; office 718-405-3453; fax 718-405-3346; fbrod@aol.com
Copies: 6
Deadline: February 1, 2000

Specify student papers: yes
Specify debut papers: no

Lambda Pi Eta, the national communication honor society for undergraduates, invites outstanding papers authored by undergraduate students in all areas of communication scholarship which focus on the speech communication discipline. Papers may be co-authored, but all contributors must be undergraduate students at the time the paper is written. Only completed papers will be accepted. All student papers will be considered for presentation at the convention. However, only papers submitted by members of Lambda Pi Eta will be considered for the Stephen A. Smith Award. Refer to "HOW TO SUBMIT PAPERS AND PANEL/PROGRAM PROPOSALS" at the beginning of the call. *Also see "Convention Paper Distribution Center," "Poster Sessions," and "Special Note" at the beginning of the call.*

Language and Social Interaction Division

Madeline M. Maxwell, Dept of Speech Communication, Univ of Texas, Austin, Austin, TX 78712; office 512-471-1954; fax 512-471-3504; mmaxwell@utxvms.cc.utexas.edu
Copies: 5
Deadline: February 1, 2000
Specify student papers: yes
Specify debut papers: no

The Language and Social Interaction Division solicits competitive papers and panel proposals concerning the utilization of speech, language, or gesture in human communication including studies of discourse processes, face-to-face interaction, communication competence, speech act theory, cognitive processing, and conversation analytic, ethnographic, ethnomethodological, and sociolinguistic work. Paper abstracts will be accepted, but completed papers are preferred. Papers which are authored solely by students who have not completed the Ph.D. are eligible for a student award and should be identified by writing "Student" in the upper right corner of the title page. Refer to "HOW TO SUBMIT PAPERS AND PANEL/PROGRAM PROPOSALS" at the beginning of the call. *Also see "Convention Paper Distribution Center," "Poster Sessions," and "Special Note" at the beginning of the call.*

Latina/Latino Communication Studies Division

Michelle A. Holling, Institute for Human Communication, California State Univ Monterey Bay, 100 Campus Center, Building 2, Seaside, CA 93955-8001; office 831-582-3889
Copies: 4
Deadline: February 15, 2000
Specify student papers: yes
Specify debut papers: yes

The Division invites program proposals and papers exploring Latina/Latino, Chicana/Chicano, and Hispanic culture and communication scholarship. Of special interest are explorations linking the interconnections between culture, ethnicity, gender, sexuality, and communication processes. Proposals for thematic panels and papers should include a 100-150 word abstract for each presentation. The Division confers "Top Paper" awards. Refer to "HOW TO SUBMIT PAPERS AND PANEL/PROGRAM PROPOSALS" at the beginning of the call. *Also see "Convention Paper Distribution Center," "Poster Sessions," and "Special Note" at the beginning of the call.*

Mass Communication Division

***Papers*: Shing-Ling S. Chen, 257 CAC, Dept of Communication Studies, Univ of Northern Iowa, Cedar Falls, IA 50614-0357; office 319-273-6021; chens@cobra.uni.edu**
***Panel proposals*: Mary Beth Oliver, 210 Carnegie Bldg, College of Communications, Penn State University, University Park, PA 16802; office 814-863-5552; mbo@psu.edu**
Copies: 5
Deadline: February 1, 2000
Specify student papers: yes
Specify debut papers: no
Maximum length: 25 pages

The Division invites competitive papers and thematic panel proposals for program sessions addressing theory, research, or methodological issues in mass communication. Papers will be evaluated anonymously by the Division Research Committee and those selected will be critiqued by a respondent. Student papers should be prominently marked "Student" on both the title page *and* first page of the text. Late requests or papers exceeding the specified length will not be accommodated. Refer to "HOW TO SUBMIT PAPERS AND PANEL/PROGRAM PROPOSALS" at the beginning of the call. *Also see "Convention Paper Distribution Center," "Poster Sessions," and "Special Note" at the beginning of the call.*

National Federation Interscholastic Speech and Debate Association

Treva Dayton, NFISDA, 11724 NW Plaza Circle, Kansas City, MO 64153; office 816-464-5400; fax 816-464-5571; tkdayton@nfhsmail.org
Copies: 4
Deadline: February 15, 2000
Specify student papers: yes
Specify debut papers: no

The National Federation Interscholastic Speech and Debate Association invites submission of program ideas, individual papers, completed programs, and other special activity proposals in the general area of speech and debate practice, theory, or pedagogy. The NFISDA is also interested in speech communication education in and out of the classroom. Individuals who are not otherwise participating in NFISDA programs are encouraged to volunteer to serve as program chairs and/or respondents. Preference will be given to programs featuring participants from the high school community. Refer to "HOW TO SUBMIT PAPERS AND PANEL/PROGRAM PROPOSALS" at the beginning of the call. *Also see "Convention Paper Distribution Center," "Poster Sessions," and "Special Note" at the beginning of the call.*

National Forensic Association

Clark D. Olson, Dept of Communication, Box 871205, Arizona State Univ, Tempe, AZ 85287-1025; office 602-965-3825; fax 602-965-4291; clark.olson@asu.edu
Copies: 3
Deadline: February 15, 2000
Specify student papers: yes
Specify debut papers: yes

The National Forensic Association invites individual papers and program proposals relating to forensics theory, practice and/or pedagogy, including Lincoln/Douglas debate. Panels which embody the convention theme will be of particular interest. Refer to "HOW TO SUBMIT PAPERS AND PANEL/PROGRAM PROPOSALS" at the beginning of the call. *Also see "Convention Paper Distribution Center," "Poster Sessions," and "Special Note" at the beginning of the call.*

Organizational Communication Division

Ted Zorn, Dept of Management Communication, Univ of Waikato, Private Bag 3105, Hamilton, New Zealand; office 647-838-4776; fax 647-838-4358; tzorn@waikato.ac.nz
Copies: 5
Deadline: February 1, 2000
Specify student papers: yes
Specify debut papers: no
Maximum length: 30 pages excluding title page, abstract, references, tables, and figures

The Division invites competitive papers and panel proposals on the theory, research, and teaching of organizational communication. The Division embraces critical, empirical and interpretive approaches to research. Competitive papers must be written to conceal the authors' identity and institution. If papers have multiple authors, the name of the most likely presenter of the paper should be circled. Also note on this page if you are willing to present the paper in a poster session. Papers should include a 50-75 word abstract and a list of important keywords characterizing the paper. Papers should strictly not exceed 30 typed, double-spaced pages. Program proposals should include a 200-word abstract plus a statement that each participant agrees to attend. Refer to "HOW TO SUBMIT PAPERS AND PANEL/PROGRAM PROPOSALS" at the beginning of the call. *Also see "Convention Paper Distribution Center," "Poster Sessions," and "Special Note" at the beginning of the call.*

Peace and Conflict Communication Commission

Bruce C. McKinney, School of Speech Communication, James Madison Univ, Harrisonburg, VA 22807; office 703-528-6228
Copies: 4
Deadline: February 15, 2000
Specify student papers: no
Specify debut papers: no
Maximum length: 20 pages

The Peace and Conflict Communication Commission invites papers, panel proposals, performances, film and video screenings of new work, interactive sessions, and other programs exploring peace communication. Of special interest are proposals concerned with empirical research into strategies for peace communication, peace education, peace and conflict communication criticism, and conflict mediation and negotiation. Particularly welcome are programs and papers that reflect the interdisciplinary nature of peace and conflict communication studies and/or that shed light on the domains of peace communication inquiry and instruction. Submitters should indicate their willingness to have their work scheduled as a poster session. Refer to "HOW TO SUBMIT PAPERS AND PANEL/PROGRAM PROPOSALS" at the beginning of the call. *Also see "Convention Paper Distribution Center," "Poster Sessions," and "Special Note" at the beginning of the call.*

Performance Studies Division

John D. Anderson, Emerson College, 100 Beacon St, Boston, MA 02116; office 617-824-6746; janderson@emerson.edu or henryjames@aol.com
Copies: 7
Deadline: February 1, 2000
Specify student papers: yes
Specify debut papers: yes
Maximum length: 20 pages

The Performance Studies Division invites proposals for competitive papers, programs, thematic panels, interactive sessions, and special presentations that explore topics in performance theory and practice. Proposals that feature discussion and innovative structures are encouraged. All proposals should anticipate strict limitations on presentation time (in general, 10-15 minutes per paper) to allow for sufficient response. Single copies of program proposals may be submitted but must include the required information. E-mail and fax submissions should be followed by hard copy. Refer to "HOW TO SUBMIT PAPERS AND PANEL/PROGRAM PROPOSALS" at the beginning of the call. *Also see "Convention Paper Distribution Center," "Poster Sessions," and "Special Note" at the beginning of the call.*

Phi Rho Pi

Cynthia Dewar, City College of San Francisco, 50 Phelan Ave, S132, San Francisco, CA 94112; office 415-239-3101; fax 415-239-3919; cdewar@ccsf.cc.ca.us
Copies: 3
Deadline: February 15, 2000
Specify student papers: no
Specify debut papers: no

Phi Rho Pi invites submissions of thematic panels, individual papers, and CRAFT (Coaching, Running, and Administering Forensics Tips) programs relating to any aspect of forensic activity. Ideas are welcome from any and all levels of educational forensic activity (i.e., high school, community college, university). All areas of forensics—debate, interpretation, platform, limited preparation, and interpretative theater—are encouraged. CRAFT programs should include (1) a short description of the coaching/administering strategy for forensics (2-3 pages); (2) a copy of any handouts or supplemental material that will be used; (3) the name, address, and phone number of the author(s). The concept of CRAFT grew out of the GIFTS Series. Coaching/administering ideas should be capable of presentation in 10 minutes. Submissions presume a commitment to attend the convention. All submissions will be competitively selected. Refer to "HOW TO SUBMIT PAPERS AND PANEL/PROGRAM PROPOSALS" at the beginning of the call. *Also see "Convention Paper Distribution Center," "Poster Sessions," and "Special Note" at the beginning of the call.*

Pi Kappa Delta

Joel Hefling, Dept of Communication Studies and Theatre, South Dakota State Univ, Box 2218, Brookings, SD 57007-1197; office 605-688-4390; fax 605-688-6511; heflingj@ur.sdstate.edu
Copies: 3
Deadline: February 15, 2000
Specify student papers: yes
Specify debut papers: no

Pi Kappa Delta is calling for program proposals and papers in the areas of forensics theory, practice or pedagogy. Submissions which are suitable for poster sessions should be so identified. Proposal submissions presume a commitment to attend the 2000 NCA convention. All submissions will be competitively selected. Refer to "HOW TO SUBMIT PAPERS AND PANEL/PROGRAM PROPOSALS" at the beginning of the call. *Also see "Convention Paper Distribution Center," "Poster Sessions," and "Special Note" at the beginning of the call.*

Political Communication Division

Michael Pfau, School of Journalism and Mass Communication, 5016 Vilas Hall, Univ of Wisconsin, Madison, Madison, WI 53706; office 608-262-0334; fax 608-262-1361; mwpfau@facstaff.wisc.edu
Copies: 4
Deadline: February 15, 2000
Specify student papers: yes
Specify debut papers: yes

The Division invites competitive papers and thematic panel proposals. Submissions should explore theoretical and/or critical issues related to the study of political communication. The Division accepts both original research and analytic essays. All methodologies are welcome. Thematic panel proposals should include a statement indicating all panelists have agreed to participate in the program. Refer to "HOW TO SUBMIT PAPERS AND PANEL/PROGRAM PROPOSALS" at the beginning of the call. *Also see "Convention Paper Distribution Center," "Poster Sessions," and "Special Note" at the beginning of the call.*

Public Address Division

Richard J. Jensen, Hank Greenspun School of Communication, 4505 Maryland Parkway, Box 455007, Univ of Nevada, Las Vegas, Las Vegas, NV 89154-5007; office 702-895-4491; rjensen@nevada.edu
Copies: 5
Deadline: February 1, 2000
Specify student papers: yes
Specify debut papers: yes

The Division invites submissions for "Contributed Papers in Public Address," "Debut Papers in Public Address," and thematic panels. Essays should be capable of presentation in 15 minutes. The Debut Program is for scholars who have not published in an NCA journal or appeared on an NCA program. No e-mailed or faxed proposals will be accepted. Refer to "HOW TO SUBMIT PAPERS AND PANEL/PROGRAM PROPOSALS" at the beginning of the call. *Also see "Convention Paper Distribution Center," "Poster Sessions," and "Special Note" at the beginning of the call.*

Public Relations Division

Charles Lubbers, School of Journalism and Mass Communication, 104 Kedzie Hall, Kansas State Univ, Manhattan, KS 66506-1500; office 913-532-6890; lubbers@ksu.edu
Copies: 4
Deadline: February 15, 2000
Specify student papers: yes
Specify debut papers: yes

The Division invites submissions of theoretical, methodological or empirical papers and program proposals. Student and Debut papers will be given special consideration. Refer to "HOW TO SUBMIT PAPERS AND PANEL/PROGRAM PROPOSALS" at the beginning of the call. *Also see "Convention Paper Distribution Center," "Poster Sessions," and "Special Note" at the beginning of the call.*

Religious Communication Association

Copies: 3
Deadline: February 15, 2000

The RCA invites program proposals and competitive papers concerned with communication and religion. Refer to "HOW TO SUBMIT PAPERS AND PANEL/PROGRAM PROPOSALS" at the beginning of the call. Send copies of each paper or program to the appropriate division:

Theory: **Steven Kaminski, 229 Piney Mountain Road, Greenville, SC 29609; office 864-242-9936**
Curriculum & Instruction: **Thomas Kuster, Bethany Lutheran College, LH207C, Mankato, MN 56001; office 507-386-5336**
Interpersonal and Organizational: **Gordon L. Forward, Point Loma Nazarene Univ, 3900 Lomaland Dr, San Diego, CA 92106; office 619-440-4482**
Public Address: **Bohn Lattin, Communication Studies, Univ of Portland, 5000 N Willamette, Portland, OR 97203; office 503-282-7352**
Performance Studies: **Edwin Hollatz, Wheaton College, 501 E College Ave., Wheaton, IL 60187; 630-752-5093**
Mass Media and Mass Forum: **Gregory Spencer, Westmont College, 955 LaPaz, Santa Barbara, CA 93108-1023, office 805-565-6195**
Gender and Cultural Studies: **Marcia Everett, Malone College, 515 25th Street NW, Canton, OH 44709; office 330-471-8335**

The overall planner for the association is: Kenneth Chase, Dept of Communication, Wheaton College, Wheaton, IL 60187; office 630-752-5261. RCA would also like to request nominations for three awards granted annually: the outstanding dissertation award, the outstanding book award and the outstanding article in religious communication completed during the previous academic year (through June 30, 1999). Nominations for the three awards must be accompanied by four copies of the work nominated and a cover letter stating why the work is deserving of recognition. Nominations are due by August 31, 2000 and may be sent to Kim Phipps, Messiah College, Grantham, PA 17027; office 717-691-6013. *Also see "Convention Paper Distribution Center," "Poster Sessions," and "Special Note" at the beginning of the call.*

Rhetorical and Communication Theory Division

Dale Brashers, Dept of Speech Communication, 702 S Wright St, 244 Lincoln Hall, Univ of Illinois, Urbana, IL 61801; office 217-333-2683; dbrashers@uiuc.edu
Copies: 5
Deadline: February 15, 2000
Specify student papers: yes
Specify debut papers: yes
Maximum length: 4-6 single spaced pages excluding title page

The Division invites thematic proposals for programs as well as individual papers. The Nichols-Ehninger Award will be given to the top-ranked student paper presented on the Division's programs during the 2000 convention. To be considered for this award, the paper must be marked "Student Authored" on the cover page (if multiple-authored, all authors must be students). The Division also wishes to receive nominations for a Distinguished Scholar Award, and for a New Investigator Award. Nominees for the latter should be no more than eight years from receipt of their Ph.D. Submissions via e-mail or fax will not be accepted. Refer to "HOW TO SUBMIT PAPERS AND PANEL/PROGRAM PROPOSALS" at the beginning of the call. *Also see "Convention Paper Distribution Center," "Poster Sessions," and "Special Note" at the beginning of the call.*

Semiotics and Communication Commission

Jacqueline M. Martinez, Communication Dept, 1366 LAEB, Room 2114, Purdue Univ, West Lafayette, IN 49707-1366; office 765-494-7547; fax 765-496-1394; martinez@purdue.edu
Copies: 5
Deadline: February 15, 2000
Specify student papers: yes

Specify debut papers: no

The Commission invites completed papers, detailed abstracts and panel proposals that (1) develop semiotic theory; (2) appraise and/or apply the work of a major theorist; (3) offer insight on gender, race, ethnicity, class, sexuality, disability or other issues of social concern; (4) critically analyze a cultural text or artifact; (5) examine the interdisciplinary contributions of semiotics, and (6) address how alternative forms of communicating originate. Student papers are welcome. Detailed abstracts should include a bibliography as well as a title page. Refer to "HOW TO SUBMIT PAPERS AND PANEL/PROGRAM PROPOSALS" at the beginning of the call. *Also see "Convention Paper Distribution Center," "Poster Sessions," and "Special Note" at the beginning of the call.*

Senior College and University Section

Theodore F. Sheckels, Professor of English and Communication, Randolph-Macon College, Ashland, VA 23005; office 804-752-7288; tsheckel@rmc.edu
Copies: 4
Deadline: February 15, 2000
Specify student papers: yes
Specify debut papers: yes

The Section presents programs and papers that cut across the traditional sub-disciplinary concerns represented in the divisions. The Section takes special interest in programs relevant to smaller institutions. Program planners seek programs and papers concerned with curriculum development, professional awareness, student advising, effective teaching, the role of speech communication departments on campus and in the community, and other concerns not directly addressed in the divisions of the NCA. In particular, the session solicits competitive research papers resulting from the collaborative efforts of small college teachers and their students (includes independent study papers). Refer to "HOW TO SUBMIT PAPERS AND PANEL/PROGRAM PROPOSALS" at the beginning of the call. *Also see "Convention Paper Distribution Center," "Poster Sessions," and "Special Note" at the beginning of the call..*

Spiritual Communication Commission

Carol Morgan, 9590 Copper Creek Court, Miamisburg, OH 45342; office 937-229-2380
Copies: 2
Deadline: February 15, 2000
Specify student papers: yes
Specify debut papers: yes

The Spiritual Communication Commission invites papers and program proposals on any aspect of communication and spirituality including theory, practice, performance, history, or pedagogy. Papers and programs may consider spirituality from any of a wide range of perspectives—Western, Eastern, African, or Native; theistic or non-theistic; associated with any religion or with no formal religion; traditional or alternative. Refer to "HOW TO SUBMIT PAPERS AND PANEL/PROGRAM PROPOSALS" at the beginning of the call. *Also see "Convention Paper Distribution Center," "Poster Sessions," and "Special Note" at the beginning of the call.*

States Advisory Council

Jerry Buley, Dept of Communication, Arizona State Univ, P.O. Box 871205, Tempe, AZ 85287-1205; jerry.buley@asu.edu
Copies: 3
Deadline: February 15, 2000
Specify student papers: no
Specify debut papers: no

The States Advisory council invites program proposals and papers related to the goals, roles, activities, initiatives, innovations, issues, or agenda of state associations in communication/theatre. Presentations should fit a 12-15 minute time slot per paper or discussant. Refer to "HOW TO SUBMIT PAPERS AND PANEL/PROGRAM PROPOSALS" at the beginning of the call. *Also see "Convention Paper Distribution Center," "Poster Sessions," and "Special Note" at the beginning of the call.*

Student Section

Jennifer S. Czarnik, 434 Sell Hall, Campus Box 4480, Normal, IL, 61790-4480; 309-438-7308; jsczarn@vs6000.cmp.ilstu.edu
Copies: 5
Deadline: February 1, 2000
Specify student papers: yes
Specify debut papers: yes
Maximum length: 25 pages excluding title page, references, tables and figures

The Student Section invites graduate and undergraduate students to submit competitive papers, panels, and other programs having general interest to the field of communication studies. Papers, panels, and programs submitted to the Student Section may be theoretical, methodological, empirical, or rhetorical in nature. Only finished papers will be accepted for review. The top three competitive papers will each receive a $50 award. Alternate formats and/or topics directly related to the convention theme, student issues, or the communication field are especially welcome. Anyone listed on a paper or program proposal must be able to attend the 2000 convention. Refer to "HOW TO SUBMIT PAPERS AND PANEL/PROGRAM PROPOSALS" at the beginning of the call. *Also see "Convention Paper Distribution Center," "Poster Sessions," and "Special Note" at the beginning of the call.*

Theatre Division

Sharon Ammen, Performing and Visual Arts, St. Mary-of-the-Woods College, St. Mary-of-the-Woods, IN 47803; office 812-535-5286; fax 812-535-5127; sammen@gte.net
Copies: 3
Deadline: February 15, 2000
Specify student papers: yes
Specify debut papers: no

The Theatre Division invites submissions for the following: program proposals; Student and Contributing papers; and workshops in the broad areas of history, criticism, acting, directing, pedagogy, performance theory and text, staging, and literature. Performances, performance presentations, and short courses in all areas of theatrical practice are also welcome. Papers for the Student and Contributing panels will be competitively selected from those submitted. The Student Scholar Panel is for scholars who have not published in any NCA journal or appeared as part of any NCA sponsored convention program. An award will be presented to the Outstanding Student paper. Papers should be designed for a 15-20 minute presentation (NOT including time for formal response and/or discussion). Refer to "HOW TO SUBMIT PAPERS AND PANEL/PROGRAM PROPOSALS" at the beginning of the call. *Also see "Convention Paper Distribution Center," "Poster Sessions," and "Special Note" at the beginning of the call.*

Training and Development Commission

Joseph Cardot, Communication Dept, Abilene Christian Univ, Box 28156, Abilene, TX 79699; office 915-674-2136; fax 915-674-6966; joe.cardot@communication.acu.edu
Copies: 4
Deadline: February 6, 2000
Specify student papers: yes
Specify debut papers: no

The Training and Development Commission invites submission of panels and papers on training and development fostering learning and performance that address the challenges faced by speech communication educators who work or plan to work as professionals in the corporate world. The Commission is especially interested in conflict resolution, presentations, interviewing, coaching and counseling, leadership, gender, diversity, corporate change, executive management, and technology management, etc. . . Programs may be of an invited or competitive nature and submitted papers may be reports of training programs, styles, techniques, research, and/or grant partnerships with corporate organizations involving training practices. Refer to "HOW TO SUBMIT PAPERS AND PANEL/PROGRAM PROPOSALS" at the beginning of the call. *Also see "Convention Paper Distribution Center," "Poster Sessions," and "Special Note" at the beginning of the call.*

Visual Communication Commission

Sheree Josephson, Dept of Communication, Weber State Univ, 1605 University Circle, Ogden, UT 84408-1605; office 801-626-6164; fax 810-626-7975; sjosephson@weber.edu
Copies: 3
Deadline: February 15, 2000
Specify student papers: no
Specify debut papers: no

The Commission invites competitive papers, panel proposals, and poster sessions that advance theory, research, and instructional development in visual communication. The focus of papers and presentations should be on how visual symbol systems, visual imagery, or visual presentations function to construct and produce meaning. Papers may address a broad spectrum of methodology and application including visual literacy and cognition, media effects, visual/verbal languages, narrative, visual images and culture/ethnography, documentary photography, architecture and design, propaganda images, and visual aspects of political campaigns. Panels and papers that reflect the conference theme or include off-site activities related to visual communication are encouraged. Refer to "HOW TO SUBMIT PAPERS AND PANEL/PROGRAM PROPOSALS" at the beginning of the call. *Also see "Convention Paper Distribution Center," "Poster Sessions," and "Special Note" at the beginning of the call.*

Women's Caucus

Roseann Mandiuk, Dept of Speech Communication, Southwest Texas State Univ, San Marcos, TX 78666-4616; office 512-245-3136; fax 512-245-3138; rm07@academia.swt.edu
Copies: 4
Deadline: February 1, 2000
Specify student papers: no
Specify debut papers: no
Maximum length: panel proposals only

The Women's Caucus invites program proposals (no papers please) that address its mission, which is to advocate for women's improved status, voice, and opportunities in the discipline. In keeping with the spirit of its mission, the Caucus invites innovative formats which encourage wide participation and involvement. Especially welcome are programs with participants who are students, recent graduates and/or scholars who have not previously presented on a Caucus-sponsored program. Program proposals should include a rationale, detailed description, identification of all participants, and a statement committing all proposed participants to attend if the proposal is accepted. Identify potential co-sponsors, if any. Please be certain that no participants have agreed to serve on more than one Caucus program. Refer to "HOW TO SUBMIT PAPERS AND PANEL/PROGRAM PROPOSALS" at the beginning of the call. *Also see "Convention Paper Distribution Center," "Poster Sessions," and "Special Note" at the beginning of the call.*

NCA POLICY ON THE USE OF AUDIO-VISUAL EQUIPMENT

AT CONFERENCES AND CONVENTIONS

It is the NCA policy to provide reasonable A/V support of presentations at its annual convention and at its conferences. NCA recognizes that such support is essential to some presentations and greatly enhances the effectiveness of others. The number of requests for A/V support has risen steadily in recent years and is likely to continue to increase, in terms of both the amount and the type of equipment that is needed.

To help control the costs of equipment rental and to provide the best possible support of presenters, NCA has established the following guidelines regarding A/V support at its convention and conferences.

1.   **Request before the published deadline**. The NCA Convention Manager and the Meeting Coordinator attempt to schedule programs with similar equipment needs into the same room in order to make maximum use of the rental. Therefore, it is critical that A/V support requests be submitted before the published deadline. The deadline is ordinarily the same as the deadline for program proposals. No A/V equipment will be provided to a program that fails to meet published deadlines.

2.   **Keep requests to a minimum**. It is tempting to request one of everything, just in case it is needed. Presenters and planners are asked to carefully screen requests and to submit only those that are essential to the program. As a general rule, the more sophisticated the equipment the more it costs to rent. Presenters and planners are asked to keep their requests as simple as possible. A chalkboard can substitute for a poster pad or overhead, etc . . .

3.   **Expensive equipment will not be supplied**. NCA will normally approve requests for the following equipment: chalkboard, easel, flip chart, audiocassette player/recorder, overhead projector, slide projector, VCR. NCA will NOT normally approve requests for expensive equipment such as: PC's, camcorders, laser pointers, satellite links, teleconference equipment, LCD panels/projectors, and video data projectors.

4.   **Short Courses**. Short courses have a fee that is based on an assumption of a minimum standard of copying for handouts and a minimum level of A/V equipment. The base short course fee is established to offset the costs of operating all the short courses. Requests for non-traditional A/V will likely result in increases to the fees.

5.   **Media Forums**. NCA's Media Forum programs are designed to facilitate discussion and presentation of programs related to leading edge research and technology. Therefore, Media Forums have priority when A/V resources are allocated and non-standard equipment is requested.

6.   **Personal equipment is discouraged**. Contracts for A/V equipment is negotiated by NCA. In many cases the hotel provides A/V services and have policies that prohibit use of personal equipment. Neither NCA or the hotel can be responsible for the security of personal equipment.

7.   **On-site rentals**. Individuals may elect to rent equipment at the convention of conference at their own expense. Most hotels have an on-site A/V department. Such equipment may not be charged to the Association.

8.   **NCA responsibility**. The A/V contract is negotiated by the NCA National Office. Any questions regarding the A/V equipment should be directed to the convention manager.

TEXAS TECH
UNIVERSITY

COMMUNICATION STUDIES

Programs leading to the B.A. and M.A.

The Department of Communication Studies at Texas Tech University is the best investment available today for serious students of communication. You will receive leading edge instruction by a supportive faculty distinguished for excellent teaching and research productivity. You will enjoy superb facilities in an attractive setting within a mid-sized, prosperous, and accessible city. You will be enchanted by the culture and climate of the Southwest. Teaching and research assistantships, fellowships, and scholarships are available for the qualified student.

The Faculty

John Bliese, (Ph.D., Kansas)
Karla Jensen, (Ph.D., Kansas)
Brian McGee, (Ph.D., Ohio State)
Deborah McGee, (Ph.D., Ohio State)
Melanie Neal, (M.A., Texas Tech)
Bolanle Olaniran, (Ph.D., Oklahoma)

David Roach, (Ed.D., Texas Tech)
Robert Stewart, (Ed.D., West Virginia)
Trent Webb, (M.A., S.W.TX. State)
David Williams, (Ph.D., Ohio)
Robert Whitbred, (Ph.D., Illinois)

For more information, contact:

Dr. David Roach, Chair
Department of Communication Studies
Texas Tech University
Box 43083
Lubbock, Texas 79409-3083

Fax # (806) 742-1025
**Web page address:
http://www.ttu.edu/~coms
Phone # (806) 742-3911

UNIVERSITY OF WASHINGTON

DEPARTMENT OF SPEECH COMMUNICATION

Degree Programs leading to the B.A., M.A., and Ph.D.

- Interpersonal and relational communication
- Communication and new technologies
- Aesthetics of spoken discourse
- Philosophy of communication
- Communication in teaching and learning
- Rhetoric of science
- Cultural communication
- Intercultural cooperation and mediation
- Freedom of speech
- Political communication
- Small group processes
- Constructions of gender and race
- Nonverbal communication
- Argumentation
- Ethnography of communication
- Rhetorical theory and communication
- Communication education
- Public discourse

LEAH CECCARELLI   JODY D. NYQUIST   RAKA SHOME
LISA COUTU   MALCOLM R. PARKS   ANN Q. STATON
JOHN GASTIL   GERRY PHILIPSEN   JOHN STEWART
VALERIE MANUSOV   ROBERT M. POST   BARBARA WARNICK

for more information contact:

Barbara Warnick
  Department Chair, or
John Stewart
  Graduate Program Coordinator
(206) 543 - 4860

Department of
Rhetoric and Communication
University of Washington
Box 353415
Seattle, WA 98195-3415

Index of Program Sponsors

Affirmative Action and Intercaucus Committee, 1646

African American Communication & Culture Commission, 1121, 1234, 1321, 1334, 1421, 1521, 1621, 2121, 2130, 2221, 2421, 2521, 2621, 2628, 2721, 3121, 3221, 3421, 3424, 3433, 3521, 3621, 3633, 4124, 4328

American Alliance for Theatre and Education, 1226

American Association for Rhetoric of Science & Technology, 0125, 1466, 1566, 1632, 2166, 2266, 2466, 2566, 2666, 3166, 3266, 3466, 3566, 3666, 4143, 4243

American Forensic Association, 1153, 1653, 2153, 2434, 2753, 3653, 4153

American Society for the History of Rhetoric, 0178, 1144, 1272, 1372, 1472, 2171, 2271, 2471, 2671, 2734, 3271, 3471, 3571, 3671, 4244

American Studies Commission, 1164, 1364, 1564, 2164, 2464, 2546, 2664, 3164, 3234, 3464, 3664, 4144, 4264

Applied Communication Division, 1128, 1228, 1238, 1328, 2141, 2228, 2538, 2722, 3129, 3229, 3439, 3529, 4226

Argumentation and Forensics Division, 1232, 1332, 1432, 2231, 2326, 2643, 3132, 3531, 3632, 4132, 4232, 4332

Asian Pacific American Communication Studies Division, 1359, 1659, 2133, 2529, 2759, 3429, 3659

Asian/Pacific American Caucus, 1359, 1659, 2633, 2759, 3429, 3659

Association for Chinese Communication Studies, 1370, 1570, 1631, 2170, 2470, 2670, 3170, 3570, 3670

Association for Communication Administration, 0114, 1131, 1331, 1431, 2125, 2431, 2541, 2641, 3125, 3431, 3629

Association for Rhetoric & Communication in Southern Africa, 3239

Basic Course Division, 0107, 1149, 1249, 1449, 1549, 1649, 2149, 2249, 2430, 2449, 2530, 2549, 2649, 2749, 3149, 3249, 3449, 3549, 3649, 4149, 4249

Black Caucus, 0114, 1122, 1624, 2234, 2324, 2628, 3136, 3224, 3424, 3524, 3633, 4124, 4224

Caucus on Disability Issues, 1155, 1455, 1629, 2255, 2455, 2655, 3427, 3655

Central States Communication Association, 1630, 2622

Challenging Boundaries Series, 1214, 1314, 1414, 1514, 1614, 2214, 2321, 2414, 2514, 2578, 2614, 2714, 3114, 3214, 3414, 3514, 3614, 4216

Chinese Communication Association, 2168, 2468, 2668

Commission on American Parliamentary Practice, 1365, 3647

Commission on Communication Assessment, 1456, 1556, 2131, 2656, 2736, 3128, 3307, 3656

Commission on Communication in the Future, 1239, 1553, 2235, 2453, 2553, 3253, 3453, 3546, 4235, 4335

Communication Apprehension & Avoidance Commission, 1255, 1655, 2126, 2233, 2555, 3155, 3233, 3455, 3555

Communication Ethics Commission, 1457, 2132, 2257, 2315, 2319, 2537, 2730, 3657, 4357

Communication Needs of Students at Risk Commission, 1130, 2247, 2630, 3430, 4330

Communication and Aging Commission, 1151, 1551, 2451, 2651, 2746, 3651

Communication and Law Commission, 1166, 1266, 2167, 2267, 2428, 2567, 2667, 3267, 3467, 3567, 3667

Community College Section, 1357, 1557, 2028, 2137, 2436, 2557, 2733, 3028, 3326, 3438, 3538, 4257

Council on Ph.D. Programs, 2178

Critical and Cultural Studies Division, 1108, 1135, 1208, 1308, 1408, 1508, 1535, 1608, 2108, 2134, 2208, 2408, 2508, 2608, 2708, 3108, 3133, 3208, 3216, 3408, 3508, 3631, 4108, 4116, 4208, 4308

Cross Examination Debate Association, 1172, 1572, 1627, 1672, 2129, 2172, 2272, 2472, 2572, 2672, 3172, 3272, 3472, 3572, 3635, 3672, 4321

Delta Sigma Rho-Tau Kappa Alpha, 2146, 3247

Eastern Communication Association, 0746, 2230

Educational Policies Board, 1426, 2535, 2742, 3314, 3646, 4326

Elementary & Secondary Education Section, 2114, 2256, 2632, 2756, 3143, 3642

Emeritus/Retired Members Section, 1357, 2157, 3156, 3557

Environmental Communication Commission, 1453, 2127, 2253, 2427, 2653, 3032, 3553, 4353

Ethnic and Racial Diversity Committee, 2246

Ethnography Division, 0178, 1136, 1163, 1206, 1263, 1333, 1363, 1434, 1463, 1563, 1663, 2163, 2263, 2463, 2511, 2563, 2663, 2732, 2763, 3163, 3263, 3463, 3563, 3663, 4163, 4263, 4363

Experiential Learning in Communication Commission, 0106, 1169, 1269, 1369, 1433, 1569, 1643, 2046, 2169, 2238, 2269, 2322, 2469, 2669, 3135, 4316

Family Communication Division, 0121, 1118, 1126, 1315, 1318, 1418, 1518, 1533, 1618, 2118, 2218, 2314, 2418, 2518, 2618, 3435, 3628, 4128, 4130, 4228, 4238, 4344

Feminist and Women Studies Division, 1123, 1223, 1323, 1423, 1523, 1527, 1623, 2123, 2223, 2307, 2423, 2523, 2533, 2623, 2723, 3123, 3223, 3235, 3423, 3521, 3523, 3535, 3623, 4123, 4135, 4223, 4323

Freedom of Expression Commission, 1129, 1229, 1329, 1429, 1660, 2531, 2631, 3432, 3658, 4160, 4260, 4360

GIFTS Series, 2412

Gay & Lesbian Concerns Caucus, 0114, 1529, 2724, 3226

Gay/Lesbian Transgender Communication Studies Division, 1355, 1555, 1628, 2155, 2534, 2755, 3255, 3316, 3434, 4255, 4355

Group Communication Division, 1115, 1215, 1354, 1428, 1528, 1615, 2215, 2445, 2515, 2619, 3310, 3616

Health Communication Division, 1137, 1227, 1337, 1345, 1437, 1537, 1607, 2136, 2433, 2435, 2627, 2718, 3436, 3437, 3627, 4127, 4227, 4327

Human Communication and Technology Commission, 0115, 1107, 1507, 1639, 2107, 2207, 2243, 2407, 2507, 2607, 2707, 3131, 3207, 3324, 3407, 3507, 3607, 4139

Instructional Development Division, 1154, 1254, 1454, 1554, 1654, 2154, 2226, 2254, 2454, 2554, 2626, 2754, 3137, 3154, 3212, 3254, 3319, 3554, 3654, 4154, 4254, 4354

International & Intercultural Communication Division, 1116, 1133, 1216, 1233, 1316, 1416, 1516, 2116, 2216, 2316, 2416, 2516, 2553, 2616, 2716, 3116, 3127, 3227, 3416, 3516, 4231, 4331

International Forensic Association, 1526, 2547, 2647

International Listening Association, 1326

Interpersonal Communication Division, 1343, 1443, 1543, 2143, 2243, 2445, 2543, 2743, 3119, 3219, 3310, 3443, 3543, 3643, 4130, 4230, 4338, 4339

Intrapersonal Communication/Social Cognition Commission, 1356, 1656, 2156, 2638, 2738, 3146, 3256, 3456

Kenneth Burke Society, NCA Branch, 1265, 1565, 1665, 2165, 2265, 2565, 2665, 3165, 3265, 3465, 3565, 3630, 4325

Korean American Communication Association, 3539, 3639

La Raza Caucus, 1661, 2227, 2761, 3230, 3461, 4261

Lambda Pi Eta, 1157, 1257, 2457, 2525, 3257

Language and Social Interaction Division, 0116, 1407, 1436, 1536, 1636, 2128, 2236, 2308, 2437, 2637, 2737, 3140, 3240, 3440, 3540, 3640, 3643, 4134, 4234, 4334

Latina/Latino Communication Studies Division, 1361, 2227, 2456, 2661, 2761, 3230, 3561, 3661, 4261, 4361

Mass Communication Division, 1114, 1237, 1306, 1406, 1506, 1578, 1606, 2138, 2206, 2438, 2506, 2606, 2727, 3106, 3206, 3406, 3506, 3606, 4138

Media Forum Series, 1238, 1338, 1438, 1538, 2140, 2240, 2440, 2540, 2640, 2740, 3141, 3241, 3441, 3541, 3641

NCA 1999 Nominating Committee, 0815, 2815

NCA 2000 Convention Planners Committee, 0724, 4125

NCA 2000 Nominating Committee, 4225

NCA Committee on Committees, 0946

NCA First Vice President, 1336, 2115, 2125, 2415, 2615, 2715, 3125, 3315, 3515, 3615

NCA Legislative Council, 0418, 3418, 4118

NCA Resolutions Committee, 1231

NCA Second Vice President, 0123

National Communication Association, 0713, 1404, 1513, 1677, 1712, 1811, 2432, 2478, 2532, 2978, 3711, 3811

National Educational Debate Association, 2232

National Federation Interscholastic Speech & Debate Association, 1344, 1444, 2654, 3147, 3454

National Forensic Association, 1635, 2273, 2573, 3173, 3273, 3530, 3673

Organizational Communication Division, 1139, 1245, 1339, 1445, 1539, 1545, 1645, 2124, 2224, 2245, 2545, 2644, 2645, 2745, 3139, 3145, 3237, 3245, 3445, 3545, 3645, 4136, 4236, 4336

Peace and Conflict Communication Commission, 1170, 1270, 1470, 1670, 2270, 2570, 2636, 2735, 3171, 3270, 3447, 3547, 3638

Performance Studies Division, 1110, 1210, 1310, 1327, 1410, 1427, 1510, 1610, 2111, 2211, 2311, 2411, 2527, 2611, 2711, 2911, 3110, 3210, 3410, 3510, 3610, 4110, 4210, 4310

Phi Rho Pi, 2173, 2229, 2473, 2673, 3473, 3612

Pi Kappa Delta, 1046, 1469, 1669, 2047, 2569, 3169, 3173, 3269, 3569, 3634

Political Communication Division, 1134, 1145, 1222, 1322, 1422, 1522, 2122, 2222, 2422, 2522, 2539, 2639, 2739, 3122, 3222, 3422, 3522, 3537, 3622, 4122, 4222, 4322

Poster Session, 1201, 2201, 3201

Public Address Division, 1119, 1219, 1319, 1419, 1519, 1619, 2119, 2219, 2419, 2429, 2536, 2635, 2719, 3107, 3419, 3519, 3619, 4119, 4219, 4319

Public Relations Division, 0108, 1141, 1241, 1243, 1341, 1441, 1541, 1641, 2144, 2241, 2315, 2426, 2441, 2744, 3244, 3444, 3533, 3637, 4241, 4341

Publications Board, 1347, 1546, 3626

Religious Communication Association, 1162, 1262, 1362, 1462, 1534, 1562, 1662, 2162, 2262, 2462, 2562, 2629, 2662, 2762, 3142, 3162, 3262, 3462, 3534, 3636, 3662, 4162, 4233, 4262, 4333

Research Board, 1532, 1626, 2323

Rhetorical and Communication Theory Division, 1152, 1244, 1252, 1352, 1452, 1552, 1652, 2152, 2157, 2252, 2452, 2552, 2652, 2729, 2752, 3138, 3152, 3252, 3452, 3552, 3652, 4152, 4252, 4352

Roundtable Series, 2556, 2741, 3412, 3556

Seminar Series, 0132, 0133, 0134, 0135, 0137, 0138, 0139, 0140, 0141, 0142, 0143, 0144, 0153, 0154, 0155

Semiotics and Communication Commission, 1264, 1464, 1664, 2264, 2564, 2747, 3238, 3264, 3564, 3665, 4164

Senior College & University Section, 1142, 1235, 1242, 1342, 1442, 1542, 1633, 1640, 2142, 2242, 2306, 2442, 2542, 2642, 2726, 3157, 3308, 3608, 4142, 4242, 4342

Short Courses, 1158, 1159, 1160, 1161, 1458, 1459, 1460, 1461, 2158, 2159, 2160, 2161, 2458, 2459, 2460, 2461, 3158, 3159, 3160, 3161, 3458, 3459

Society for the Study of Symbolic Interaction, 1657, 2544, 2757, 3246, 4157

Southern States Communication Association, 1647, 2446, 2646

Spiritual Communication Commission, 1451, 2244, 2526, 2751, 3251, 3526, 4151

Spotlight on Scholarship, 1439, 2327, 3126, 3306

States Advisory Council, 2406, 2532, 2657, 2706, 3232

Student Section, 1125, 1225, 1325, 1425, 1525, 1625, 2135, 2443, 2528, 2612, 3228, 3625

Table Talk Series, 1230, 1330, 1430, 1530, 2237, 2328, 2424, 2524, 2728, 3321, 3323, 4129, 4329

Teachers on Teaching, 1351, 1634, 2151, 3151, 3451

Theatre Division, 1124, 1143, 1224, 1324, 1424, 1524, 1616, 1910, 2174, 2274, 2474, 2574, 2674, 2731, 3130, 3174, 3215, 3274, 3474, 3574, 3624, 3674, 3912, 4115, 4215, 4315

Training and Development Division, 0115, 1340, 1440, 1540, 1642, 2112, 2139, 2239, 2439, 3144, 3242, 3324, 4140, 4240

Virginia Association of Communication Arts and Sciences, 1346

Visual Communication Commission, 1335, 1435, 1638, 2268, 2658, 2758, 3134, 3231, 3442, 3542, 3644, 4121

Western States Communication Association, 0859

Women's Caucus, 0114, 1251, 1527, 1651, 2324, 2444, 2551, 2725, 3236, 3428, 3544, 4351

World Communication Association, 2447

Index of Participants

Aakhus, Mark A., 0115, 2514, 3131
Abar, Edwin J., 1142, 1569, 2046, 3253
Abbey, Cecilia L., 1455
Achten, Greg, 3472
Adamko, Christine, 2201
Adams, Catherine Michele, 4308
Adams, Katherine L., 0859, 3236
Adams Trujillo, Mary, 1122
Adelman, Mara B., 1314, 2722
Aden, Roger C., 3414
Adkins, Mark E., 0115
Adler, Ronald B., 1158
Afifi, Tanya, 2314
Afifi, Walid A., 2445, 2543, 3219, 3443
Agnew, Lois P., 2671
Aguayo, Angela J., 2725, 4223
Ah Yun, Kimo, 3473
Ahern, R. Kirkland, 3456
Airne, David, 1608, 2133
Aitken, Joan E., 0143, 1239, 2707, 3158
Akindes, Fay Y., 2663
Akita, Kimkio, 2551
Al-Najran, Talal, 2206
Al-Obaidi, Jabbar A., 3122
Albert, David, 4322
Albert, Rosita D., 1339
Albrecht-Crane, Christa, 1535
Alcock, Elizabeth R., 1541
Aleman, Carlos G., 2761
Aleman, Melissa W., 0178, 1551
Alexander, Alison, 1160, 1331, 2125, 2541, 2641, 3125
Alexander, Bob E., 2672
Alexander, Bryant K., 1555, 4330
Alexander, Dennis C., 0859
Alexander, Stewart C., 1115, 1607, 3540
Algan, Ece, 3516
Alkidas, Laurette, 4235
Allen, Brenda J., 1223, 1339, 2130, 2628, 3136, 3306, 3633
Allen, Gary, 2173
Allen, Jerry L., 0746, 1655, 2230, 2555, 3233
Allen, Lini, 1638, 2658, 3251
Allen, Mike, 1245, 3621, 4338
Allen, Myria W., 3139
Allen, Terre H., 3254, 3324
Allman, Joyce L., 1235
Alston, Arion, 1201
Althouse, Matthew T., 4352

Altman, Hilary R., 3614
Alvaro, Eusebio M., 1345, 1506
Alwood, Edward M., 2155
Amason, Patricia, 3129
Ames, Carole, 1640
Ames, Ina R., 0418, 1542, 1633, 2642, 2726, 3418, 4118, 4225, 4342
Ammen, Sharon, 0724, 1124, 1224, 1424, 2174, 2731, 3130, 4125
Amoroso, Henry C., 1239
Amos, Rikki D., 1654, 2718
Amster, Peter, 2911
Andersen, Janis F., 1431
Andersen, Kenneth E., 2319, 4242
Andersen, Peter A., 0859
Andersen, Robin, 3542
Anderson, Carolyn M., 1115, 1539, 2215, 2619, 3437
Anderson, Darla, 1365
Anderson, Isolde G., 4262
Anderson, Jeffrey F., 1201, 2239
Anderson, Joel David, 2531
Anderson, John D., 0724, 1410, 2527, 3255, 4125
Anderson, Karen A., 1254
Anderson, Lisa, 4164
Anderson, Mary, 4262
Anderson, Monica F., 0418, 0815, 1231, 2174, 2731, 2815, 3130, 3418, 4118, 4315
Anderson, Nancy L., 0178
Anderson, Patrick W., 3410
Anderson, Robert, 3430
Anderson, Shawny, 2664, 4144
Anderson, Traci L., 3201
Andrews, David L., 1508
Andrews, James R., 0141
Anson, Chris, 1244
Anthony, M. Susan, 1124, 2274
Anton, Corey, 1265, 2462, 3152, 3665
Apker, Julie A., 2718
Applbaum, Ronald L., 2328, 2541, 2641
Applegate, James L., 0123, 0418, 0946, 1231, 1513, 2125, 3314, 3418, 4118, 4127
Appleyard, Jane E., 1437
Araujo, Alice R., 1222
Arduini, Tony L., 1451
Arliss, Laurie, 0121
Armada, Bernard J., 1421, 1538, 3201

Armon, Charissa, 3274
Arneson, Pat, 2322, 2537, 2656
Arnett, Ronald C., 0133, 1149, 2570, 2745
Arnold, Lorin B., 4228
Arntson, Paul, 1443
Arquette, Toby J., 2718
Arthos, John, 3452
Artz, B. Lee, 2722
Arungwa, Joy, 2616
Asante, Molefi K., 1121, 3306, 4328
Asen, Robert B., 3252, 4119, 4352
Ashcraft, Karen L., 1223, 1339
Ashley Crawford, Brett, 1201
Atkin, Charles K., 1543
Atkins-Sayre, Wendy L., 2725
Atkinson, Ann J., 2758
Atkinson, Carol A., 3316
Atkinson, Walter L., 2534
Attias, Bernardo, 1208, 2108, 3216
Aune, James A., 0418, 1231, 1352, 2157,
    2729, 3418, 4118, 4225, 4336
Aune, Krystyna S., 2156, 2418, 3643
Aust, Charles F., 2138, 3546
Austin, Deborah A., 4351
Austin, Gayle M., 3110
Avanzino, Susan, 3654
Avdeyeva, Tatyana, 2745, 4136
Avery, Robert K., 2431, 2728, 3431
Avis, Teri J., 2557
Avtgis, Theodore A., 1543, 2201
Aylor, Brooks, 2412, 2539, 3622
Ayotte, Kevin J., 1572, 3164, 3508, 3632
Ayres, Joe, 1546, 2233, 3155, 3555, 3626
Ayres-Sonandre, Debbie M., 1255, 2126,
    3155
Babcock, Amanda, 2636
Babrow, Austin S., 2435, 4127
Bach, Betsy W., 2226, 2541, 2626, 4254
Backlund, Philip M., 3307, 3514, 3656,
    4241
Backus, Dencil K., 1235, 3323
Bacue, Aaron E., 2445
Baesler, E. James, 4262
Baglia, William Jay, 2118
Bahk, C. Mo, 3206
Bailey, Courtney W., 1523
Bailey, Steven, 2565, 3406, 4363
Baker, Barbara L., 1527, 2533, 2725, 3664
Baker, Jennifer L., 1533
Baker, Mary Alice, 3622
Bakkar, Ammar A., 2122
Balas, Glenda R., 1306, 2664
Baldner, Cathryn A., 1427
Balfantz, Gary L., 3674
Ballard, Dawna I., 1615, 3621
Ballard-Reisch, Deborah S., 2518, 2618,
    4130, 4226
Balmert, Michael E., 2169
Balsamo, Anne, 2423
Balter-Reitz, Susan J., 1229
Balthrop, Bill, 0114, 1160, 2431, 2541
Banks, Anna, 2757

Banks, Mary, 1643
Banks, Stephen P., 2757
Bantz, Charles R., 0114, 0418, 3418, 4118
Banwart, Mary C., 1201, 1545
Barbato, Carole A., 2215, 3319
Barberich, Michael W., 3464
Bardhan, Nilanjana, 1441, 2201, 3238,
    3506
Barfield, II, Rufus L., 2619
Baringer, Doreen K., 2154, 2718
Barnes, Jessica, 3533
Barnes, Judith A., 2657
Barnes, Sue, 0724, 1230, 2453, 2658, 3128,
    3231, 3546, 4125, 4335
Barnes-Kloth, Rhonda, 4353
Barnett, Jennifer, 1257
Barnett Gibson, Kimberly D., 3423
Barnhurst, Kevin G., 2606
Baron, Barbara S., 1526, 2273, 2547, 2647
Barr, Sherrey L., 3201
Barraclough, Robert A., 2201, 2226, 2626
Barrera Valdivia, Pedro, 3461
Barrett, Janice M., 1541, 4129
Barry, Ann Marie, 2162
Barry, Lisa R., 0138, 1451, 3138, 3523
Bartanen, Michael, 1046, 2047, 3634
Barton, Matthew H., 2123, 2219
Barwind, Jack A., 1564
Basso, Joseph, 3242
Bates, Benjamin R., 2672
Bates, M. Todd, 1352
Bauer, Michael H., 3169
Baughman, Linda, 1337
Baum, Karie Leigh, 3643
Bauman, Richard, 2711, 3652
Bauschard, Stefan A., 1344, 2654
Baxter, Leslie A., 0859
Baxter, Nathan A., 2262
Baym, Geoffrey, 1306
Baysinger, Che L., 2724, 3226
Bazerman, Charles, 2152
Beach, Wayne A., 1436, 1636, 3640, 4234,
    4344
Beadle, Mary E., 2442
Beall, Melissa L., 0107, 0418, 1239, 2430,
    2530, 2649, 3158, 3418, 3672, 4118,
    4149, 4254
Beard, David, 1552
Beasley, Myron M., 1321, 3163, 3421, 4255
Beatty, Michael J., 0418, 1546, 2237, 3233,
    3418, 3626, 4118
Bechler, Curt, 2441, 2754
Beck, Christina S., 1537, 2128, 2236
Becker, Becky K., 1363, 2574
Becker, Catherine B., 2563
Becker, Jennifer A., 4128
Beckett, Shawn, 4154
Bedner, Nelle, 4354
Beebe, Steven A., 1149, 2541, 3514
Beery, Stacie A., 2549
Beherns, Bridget M., 2457
Behnke, Ralph R., 3233, 3455, 3555

Beigle, Jennifer E., 1518
Beisecker, Thomas D., 1166
Belicka, Lisa A., 3666
Beliveau, Ralph J., 3138
Bell, Elizabeth E., 3223
Bell, Katrina E., 1624, 3163, 4351
Bellamy, Robert V., 2506, 3206
Belling, Matthew W., 3522
Bello, Richard S., 3256
Bellon, Joseph G., 2719
Benjamin, James, 3222
Benkendorf, Ray R., 2665
Bennedetti, Lisa, 3612
Bennett, Beth S., 3571
Bennett, Melody, 1359
Bennett, Milton J., 1456
Bennington, Ashley J., 1228
Benoit, William L., 2422, 3622, 4232, 4352
Benoit-Barne, Chantal, 4232
Benson, Thomas W., 1325, 2246, 2323
Bentley, Sheila C., 1326
Benton, Carol L., 0418, 1529, 1628, 3316, 3418, 4118, 4225, 4355
Berens, Eileen M., 1269
Berger, Charles R., 3206, 3310
Berger, Jason, 4341
Berger, Leigh, 2463
Bergman, Teresa G., 1663, 4121
Berkeley, Anne R., 4115
Berkowitz, Judith M., 3436
Berkowitz, Sandra J., 1123
Berland, Jody, 1208
Berman, Scott J., 1201
Bernat, Elizabeth R., 3137, 3412, 3614
Bernstein, Arla G., 2539
Bernum, Belinda A., 3649
Berry, Catherine, 4310
Berry, Elvera B., 1665, 2662, 3630
Berry, Michael R., 1172, 1344
Berry, S. Torriano, 1334
Berryman-Fink, Cynthia, 3514
Bertelsen, Dale A., 2524
Berube, David M., 2654, 4321
Bethea, Lisa Sparks, 3651
Betz, Brian R., 4357
Bevan, Jennifer, 3443
Bicak, Peter J., 2652
Biesecker, Barbara A., 0418, 0815, 1123, 1231, 2815, 3216, 3418, 4118
Biesecker-Mast, Susan L., 1135, 1623
Bile, Jeffrey T., 2472
Billings, Andrew C., 2438, 2521, 4355
Bineham, Jeff L., 3134
Binsfield, Doug, 4332
Bippus, Amy M., 2418, 4130
Bird, Chad, 4262
Birdsell, David S., 2422
Birkholt, Marty J., 3569
Black, Cheryl, 1201
Blackburn, Catherine M., 1526, 2547, 2647, 3214
Blackstone, Barbara, 1643

Blair, Carole, 1347, 1546, 2323, 2540, 2608, 3552
Blake, Cecil A., 1121, 3306, 4124
Blaney, Joseph R., 1362, 3462
Blankenship, Jane, 2615
Blauner, Bob, 2108
Blicke, Gerhald, 2643
Blivess, Steven N., 2273, 3207
Blocker, Jane M., 2411
Blomberg, Dianne L., 0724, 2507, 4125
Blomstrom, Sally, 1615
Bloom, Vincent L., 3455
Bloomberg, Dianne L., 3131
Blotkamp, Cecelia M., 3143, 3642
Blue, Janet, 2716
Boase, Paul H., 1364, 1677, 3156
Bochin, Hal W., 1526
Bochner, Arthur P., 0121, 1657, 2463, 2757, 3246
Bodary, David L., 1357, 2028, 2733, 3028
Bodenman, Janet R., 3529
Bodensteiner, Keri A., 4219
Boehler, Tony, 2201
Boggs, Cathy, 3645
Bogos, Fran P., 2114
Bohan, Robert C., 0724, 2028, 2733, 3028, 4125
Bohlmann, Rachel, 2578
Boileau, Don M., 1365, 2541, 2641, 3629, 4129
Boisseau, Robin, 2274
Bollis-Pecci, Tamara S., 0114, 1418, 2118, 2518
Bolls, Paul D., 2506
Bonaguro, Ellen W., 3427
Bond, Wayne S., 3128
Bonin, Andy, 2169
Bonito, Joseph A., 3140, 3643
Book, Cassandra L., 1640, 3431
Booth-Butterfield, Melanie, 0746, 2230, 2447, 2718, 3430
Booth-Butterfield, Steven, 0418, 3418, 4118
Bor, Aaron, 3654
Borchers, Timothy A., 2165, 3454
Borda, Jennifer L., 2723
Borden, Sandra L., 2537
Bordwell, Marilyn E., 1563, 2531
Boren, Robert R., 2139, 4140
Borisoff, Deborah, 0746, 2230, 2424, 2728, 3529, 4323
Bormann, Ernest G., 2135, 3557
Borzi, Mark G., 4226
Bosco, Beatrice, 3912
Boster, Franklin J., 1615, 3407, 4230
Bostrom, Robert N., 1326, 2738
Bourland-Davis, Pamela G., 1141, 4341
Bourne, Jay G., 3438
Bowdre, Karen M., 2240
Bowers, Detine, 2419
Bowers, Peggy, 1457
Bowers, Jr, A. A., 3308

Bowman, Michael S., 0418, 0815, 1231, 1410, 2527, 2815, 3418, 3610, 4118
Bowman, Ruth L., 2611, 3610
Boyd, Joshua, 2441
Boylan, K. C., 2673, 3473, 3612, 4257
Bozik, Mary E., 1554, 1639, 2256, 3319, 3654
Bracci, Sharon L., 0724, 1457, 2132, 2315, 2730, 3442, 4125
Bradford, Lisa, 2116, 3621, 4338
Bradley, Sabrina, 3421
Bradshaw, Jessica, 4262
Braithwaite, Charles A., 2263, 2437, 3137
Braithwaite, Dawn O., 0106, 0121, 0859, 1315, 1443, 4254
Brand, Jeffrey D., 1232, 2657, 3667
Brandon, James M., 2174
Brant, Curtis, 3645
Brashers, Dale E., 0724, 1137, 1428, 1607, 2515, 2718, 2729, 4125, 4252
Bratich, Jack, 2134, 2208
Brazeal, LeAnn M., 2249, 4232
Brenders, David A., 3135
Breshears, David F., 1153, 1572
Bresnahan, Mary Jiang I., 2516, 4134
Brewer, Edward C., 1229
Brigance, Linda C., 1519
Brisby, Nathan, 1201
Brito, Robert B., 1565
Britten, R. Scott, 3622
Britts, Melissa, 3667
Broadfoot, Kirsten J., 1263
Brock, Bernard L., 1565, 3557, 4325
Brockett, Mary A., 3462
Broda-Bahm, Kenneth T., 2172
Broderick, Frances M., 2457
Bromley, Patricia, 4238
Brommel, Bernard J., 1118
Bronson Brierly, Allen, 4322
Brookes, Gregory N., 1333
Brookey, Robert A., 1355, 4244
Brookins, B. Jordan, 3424
Brooks, Dwight E., 2121, 2240, 2721
Brooks, Robert F., 3654
Broome, Benjamin J., 1133, 2735
Brooten, Lisa B., 3516
Brouwer, Daniel C., 3252, 3422
Brow, Jessica N., 2528
Brown, Claire L., 1642
Brown, Donnel A., 1128
Brown, Linda C., 2137, 3326, 3642
Brown, Mary L., 1414
Brown, Richard Harvey, 2252
Brown, Robert E., 4341
Brown, Robert S., 1319
Brown, Rockell A., 4224
Brown, Sonja M., 1234, 3121
Brown, Tiffany, 1521
Brown, Timothy J., 1614, 2421
Brown, William J., 4262
Brown Zahn, Susan, 2469
Brown-Owens, Kristin A., 3664

Brown-White, Shauntae R., 2221
Browne, Donald R., 1129
Browne, Stephen H., 1419, 2119, 3466
Brownell, Judi, 1530
Browning, Larry D., 0106, 3643
Bruess, Carol J., 1414, 2460, 3212, 3435, 4154
Brumley-Shelton, Angela F., 4163
Brummett, Barry, 2665
Bruning, Jonathan H., 2658
Brunson, Deborah A., 3214
Bryant, Jennings, 0121, 1331, 1553, 2506
Bsumek, Peter K., 2466
Buchanan, Martha, 2531
Buchanan, Merry C., 1537, 2763, 3540
Buckner, Jasaun, 1257
Buckrop, Jacquelyn J., 0724, 2149, 2430, 2530, 3149, 3549, 4125, 4139
Buehler, Daniel O., 2127
Buell, Cindy, 2442
Buerkel, Rick A., 1126, 1249, 2206, 2518, 3628
Buerkel-Rothfuss, Nancy, 0107, 0121, 0418, 1249, 1315, 1533, 2206, 2430, 2530, 3418, 4118, 4225
Buescher, Derek T., 2108, 3506
Buley, Jerry L., 2406, 2706, 3232
Buller, David B., 1626
Bullis, Connie A., 2645
Bulusu, Aparna S., 1154, 1316, 1454
Bunzli, James, 1201
Burbank, Carol, 3215
Burd, Gene, 3201, 3414
Burgas, Nancy, 3545
Burgess, Jennifer, 1201
Burggraf Torppa, Cynthia, 0418, 0815, 1126, 1269, 2815, 3418, 3628, 4118
Burgoon, Judee K., 0418, 1347, 1546, 1626, 2323, 3119, 3219, 3310, 3418, 3626, 4118
Burgoon, Michael, 1345
Burianova, Eva, 2616
Burk, Nanci M., 3249, 4140, 4330
Burk, Tamara L., 1346, 2142, 2256, 2406, 2656, 2706, 4142
Burke, Barbara R., 2546
Burke, Charlotte G., 1434, 3563
Burke, David C., 1224
Burke, Ken, 2268, 3442
Burkett, Jennifer S., 2718
Burkhart, Thomas, 2201
Burleson, Brant R., 1532, 2178, 2445, 3237, 3310
Burnett, Ann K., 2267, 2573, 3267
Burnett, Kathleen M., 3654
Burnett, Nicholas F., 1229
Burnette, Ann E., 2567
Burnette, Mark W., 3174
Burow Flak, Elizabeth, 3215
Burrell, Nancy A., 1245
Burt, Amy S., 3428, 3674
Burtis, Trudy E., 4316

Busselle, Rick, 3206
Butler, Allison T., 3542
Butler, John R., 2755, 3255
Butler-Ellis, Jennifer, 4238
Buttny, Richard, 0116, 0724, 1564, 2128, 2637, 4125
Buzzanell, Patrice M., 1223, 3545, 4327
Byers, Lori A., 1414, 1614, 2460, 4154
Byers, Peggy Y., 3267, 4139
Bylund, Carma L., 2738, 3437, 3614
Byrd, Marquita L., 3429
Bystrom, Dianne G., 1145, 2222, 2539
Cabrer, Francisco, 3461
Cabrera, Jose E., 3664
Cady, Kathryn A., 2201, 3671
Cagle, John A., 2228
Cahn, Dudley D., 1239, 2707, 3607
Cai, Bei, 4329
Caillouet, Larry M., 2254
Calafell, Bernadette M., 3235, 3661
Calcagno, Claire S., 2535
Calder, Charles, 3239
Caliendo, Guillermo G., 2755
Callahan, L. Clark, 2639
Callison, Marybeth G., 1430, 1549
Calloway-Thomas, Carolyn, 2246, 2307, 2444, 2742, 3221, 3314, 3646
Camacho, Melissa, 4123
Cameron, Charles, 3114
Cameron, Kenzie A., 3407, 4230, 4327
Campbell, John A., 2162, 2322, 2471, 2666, 3466, 4119
Campbell, Karlyn K., 2307, 2471
Campbell, Rose G., 2435
Campbell, Shannon B., 2721
Campos, Kristina, 2472
Campton, Carl, 2556
Canary, Daniel J., 4338
Cannon, Patrick O., 1139
Cantor, Joanne R., 4138
Cantrill, James G., 2127, 2427, 3032
Cantu, Rosalinda, 2618, 2715
Cape Jr., Robert W., 1272, 1372, 3471
Capo, Kay Ellen, 1110, 1510
Capwell-Burns, Amy E., 1151, 2223
Carbaugh, Donal A., 0116, 2263, 2316
Carcasson, Martin, 4222
Cardillo, Linda W., 2718
Cardot, Joseph J., 0724, 1556, 1642, 3144, 4125, 4162
Carey, Colleen M., 0418, 2528, 2612, 3418, 4118, 4225
Cargile, Aaron C., 1316
Carilli, Theresa M., 1201, 1338, 3428
Carleton, Jill M., 1219
Carley, Cindy, 3326
Carlin, Diana B., 0418, 1145, 2422, 3418, 4118, 4225
Carlin, Phyllis, 1136, 1427
Carlin, Scott, 1427
Carlone, David A., 3245, 4357
Carlson, A. Cheree, 1123, 4223

Carpenter, Harrison, 2166
Carpenter, Katheryn E., 1533
Carpenter, Peter, 2911
Carpenter, Ronald H., 4122
Carr, Robert, 4235
Carrell, Lori J., 2154
Carrier, Rebecca A., 1406, 2206
Carrillo Rowe, Aimee M., 2123, 2408, 2661, 3561, 4361
Carroll, Craig E., 2124
Carson, Christy L., 3543
Carter, C. C., 1625
Carver, Cynthia R., 2573
Carver, M. Heather, 1310, 3223, 3537
Carver, Mary M., 4219
Case, Gretchen A., 2111, 4110
Casey, Mary K., 4338
Caskey, Douglas L., 2174
Cassidy, Margaret, 1230
Castor, Theresa R., 2321
Caswell, Erika, 4264
Catchings, Billy W., 1529, 2644, 3255
Cates, Carl M., 0114, 2262, 2406
Catt, Isaac E., 0114, 1264, 1664, 4164
Caudill, Sally A., 2739
Caughlin, John P., 1315, 2243, 3119
Cavenaugh, Gregory L., 4110
Cavin, Margaret, 3270
Cawyer, Carol S., 2454, 3449
Ceccarelli, Leah M., 3466
Cegala, Donald J., 0418, 1345, 3418, 3627, 4118, 4225
Chadha, Kalyani, 1659
Chadwick, Scott A., 1107, 1433, 3447, 3547, 4139
Champion, Victoria L., 1441
Chan, Kara KW, 3663
Chan-Olmsted, Sylvia, 3506
Chandler, Robert C., 1556, 2762
Chandran, Gayathri, 2551
Chang, Angela, 1631
Chang, Briankle G., 1439, 1659, 2529, 2633
Chang, Changfu, 2170
Chang, Hui-Ching, 2616, 2716, 4329
Chang, Mao-Chen, 3165
Chang, Yu-Li, 2551
Chanslor, Mike D., 1522
Chantrill, Patricia A., 1241
Chapin, John R., 2201, 3654
Chapman, Suzanne W., 1651, 2740
Chapman, Virginia L., 2232, 3169
Charland, Maurice, 3152
Charles-Williamson, Cherylann, 3433
Charlesworth, Dacia, 1169, 3157, 3253
Charron, Lori J., 1639, 3407
Charron, Michael J., 1639, 3142
Chase, Kenneth R., 2629, 3636
Chatham-Carpenter, April, 2649
Chatmon, Charmetra, 2221
Chawla, Devika, 1318, 2169
Check, Terence P., 2127, 2427, 3032

Chen, Guo-Ming, 1170, 1216
Chen, Ling, 2716, 3570, 4329
Chen, Shing-Ling S., 1136, 1237, 2161, 2544, 3246
Chen, Tai Ping, 2270
Chen, Victoria, 2564
Cheney, George E., 1339, 2322, 3245
Cheng, Chung Ying, 1570
Cheng, Joyce, 3659
Cheng, Pei-Chi, 3429
Cherry, Eileen C., 1324
Cherry, Lynn, 2644, 3245
Chesebro, James W., 0418, 0746, 1546, 2230, 2524, 3418, 3626, 4118, 4326
Chesebro, Joseph L., 2254, 3201
Cheshier, David M., 2652
Chesley Gammon, Jessica, 1257
Chetro-Szivos, John, 1214, 1440, 3201
Chew, Martha I., 1618, 3561, 4261
Chilberg, Joseph C., 3251
Chisolm, Marla, 2137
Chitgopekar, Anu S., 2133
Chory, Rebecca M., 1125, 2235, 2433, 3201
Christ, William G., 0114, 0946, 1331, 3307, 3656
Christensen, Christian, 2416
Christians, Clifford G., 1457
Christiansen, Adrienne E., 2739
Chryslee, Gail J., 1553, 3231, 3442
Chua, Briana, 2636
Chuang, Rueyling, 1216, 1631, 2470, 3116, 3429
Chudzik, Joanne, 3625
Chung, Jensen, 1170, 2168
Church, Russell T., 1627, 2129, 3635
Chvasta, Marcy R., 1210
Cissna, Kenneth N., 1443, 1647, 2646
Citarella, Ralph, 1406
Claas, Steven A., 2666
Clair, Robin P., 1339, 1463, 1539, 2563
Clapp, Derek C., 1254, 2443
Clark, Bonnie L., 1557, 2657, 2740, 3531, 4232
Clark, Deborah J., 3464, 4361
Clark, E. Culpepper, 0114
Clark, Norman E., 2201
Clark, Ruth Anne, 0418, 3418, 4118
Clark, Ryan Elizabeth, 2457
Clasen, Patricia R. W., 4354
Clayman, Steven E., 1536
Cline, Jeffrey D., 2718
Clinkscales, Marcia J., 3433, 4236
Cloud, Dana L., 1308, 3126, 3423, 4216
Cmiel, Kenneth, 2752
Coakley, Carolyn G., 1326
Coates, Ryan, 1521
Coburn-Engquist, Jennifer L., 1608, 2507
Cockett, Lynn, 3523
Cody, Michael J., 1227, 3607
Coffey, Mary, 4308
Coffman, Stephen L., 2442
Colby, Stacia, 1257

Cole, Kara, 1449
Cole, Mark, 2116
Cole, Robert A., 3152
Cole, Tim D., 3135
Coleman, Bud, 3510
Coleman, Colleen A., 3459
Coleman, Landon, 3434
Collie, Susan J., 4332
Collier, Linda M., 4321
Collier, Mary Jane, 0114, 1133, 1252, 1546, 3626
Collins, Catherine A., 0114
Collins, Mary E., 0418, 1647, 2646, 3418, 4118, 4162, 4262
Collins, Paul, 0115
Colvert, Audra L., 1455, 2242
Comella, Lynn, 2723
Compton, Josh, 3614
Comstock, Jamie, 2418, 2554
Conaway, Roger N., 1458
Condit, Celeste M., 2178, 2307
Coney, Dawn, 1440
Conlee, Connie J., 0859, 1404
Connell, Sara, 1337
Connolly, Maureen, 1264
Conquergood, Dwight, 3410
Constantinides, Helen, 3166, 3566
Content, Robert L., 1236
Contractor, Noshir S., 1578, 2124, 2245, 2545
Conville, Richard L., 0123, 1161, 1443
Coogan, David, 3166
Cook, Jeff S., 1533, 2273
Cook, Susan L., 2607
Cook-Mucci, Wendy, 1225
Cooks, Leda M., 1216, 2661, 2761, 3116, 3561, 3661, 4361
Coombs, W. Timothy, 0108, 1556, 2241, 2744
Coonfield, Gordon, 1535
Cooper, Erica F., 3621
Cooper, Martha D., 1457, 4129
Cooper, Pamela J., 1554, 1610
Cooper, Stephen D., 2141
Cooper Chen, Anne, 2551
Coopman, Stephanie, 2107, 2446
Copeland, Gary A., 1647, 2646
Corbin, Susan D., 4134
Corcoran, Joe, 2673, 3473
Cordeiro, Tania, 2606
Cordova, Nathaniel I., 0724, 2227, 2456, 3230, 4125, 4261, 4325
Corey, Frederick C., 2563, 3316, 4255
Corman, Steven R., 1615, 3445
Corte, Denise, 2274
Corum, Daniel H., 1229
Cos, Grant C., 1134, 1421
Costain, Gene, 1308
Costigan, James T., 1578
Costley, Mary A., 3664
Cotter, Melissa, 2565
Coulter, Benjamin B., 1462, 1653

Countryman, John C., 1143, 2174, 4115
Courtright, Jeffrey L., 2144, 2201, 2441, 3142, 4260
Courtright, John A., 2431, 3319
Cox, J. Robert, 4216
Cox, Stephen A., 1255, 1549
Crable, Bryan, 1265, 2462, 2565, 3465, 3630
Craig, Robert T., 3452, 3614
Craig, Tom, 1264, 4164
Crano, William D., 3456
Crawford, James G., 2255, 2614
Crawford, Lyall, 2162, 2468
Crawford, Mikiko L., 3201, 3319
Crawley, Rex L., 3163, 3412
Creasman, Paul, 1201
Crenshaw, Carrie, 1223
Crider, Janel A., 2463, 2645
Crisson, Roberta L., 1524, 2474, 4115
Critchfield, Andrew, 2234
Crocker-Lakness, James W., 1451, 2526
Croft, Sharon E., 1163
Cronen, Vernon E., 1440
Cronin, Michael W., 2158
Cronje, Ruth J., 2666
Cronn-Mills, Daniel D., 0418, 1232, 1329, 2146, 2231, 2573, 3132, 3247, 3418, 4118, 4225
Cronn-Mills, Kirstin J., 1329, 2146, 3132, 3247
Crowley Rooks, Sheri, 2116
Crume, Alice L., 1251, 1328, 2607, 2763
Cruz, Michael G., 1354, 1615
Cuklanz, Lisa M., 1623, 3644
Cummings, Kevin J., 1660, 4232
Cummings, Melbourne S., 0815, 1121, 1621, 2246, 2541, 2628, 2815, 3521
Cunningham, Audrey J., 3438
Cupach, William R., 3543
Curtin-Alwardt, Nancy J., 3157
Cusmano, Susan, 2449
Cutler, Mary, 3215
Cypher, Joy M., 2655, 3465
Cyphert, Dale, 4252
Czerwinski, Anne Marie, 3251, 4151
Czubaroff, Jeanine L., 3652
Dace, Karen L., 1339, 2234
Dahlberg, John S., 1434, 1663
Dahlquist, Daniel, 3674
Daigle, Lisa, 2249, 2412
Dailey, Sheron J., 1427
Dainton, Marianne, 1343, 1518, 2518
Dalesio, John V., 2718
Dalmaso, Alice, 4263
Daly, John A., 0418, 0946, 1634, 2246, 2736, 3308, 3418, 4118
Dance, Frank E. X., 2607, 3131
Dangerfield, Celnisha, 1521
Daniel, Arlie V., 1630, 2622
Daniel, Jack L., 0418, 1121, 1518, 2130, 3418, 3633, 4118, 4328
Daniels, Ted, 3114

Danielson, Ken, 1128
Danielson, Mary Ann, 1328, 1549, 1645
Dannels, Deanna P., 1244, 2736
Dantas, Gustavo, 1437
Danuser, Barbara A., 3212
Darling, Ann L., 2454, 2736
Darsey, James, 0418, 1419, 2471, 2755, 3126, 3418, 4118
Dartey, Doris Y., 1122, 1624, 4351
Darwin, Thomas J., 4243
Dates, Jannette L., 1160, 1331, 3121
Dauber, Cori E., 3632
Daugherty, Terry, 2235
Daughton, Suzanne M., 0418, 0815, 2429, 2536, 2815, 3418, 4118
Davidson, Drew, 1107
Davilla, Roberta A., 0121, 1126, 1518, 2649, 3212, 3628
Davis, Christopher E., 2718
Davis, Cochece, 3219
Davis, Julie, 4219
Davis, Lillian, 0106
Davis, Michael, 3166
Davis, Olga I., 1621, 2324, 3306
Davis, Shannon R., 1352, 2539
Davis, Tracy, 2611
Davis, Wade S., 0418, 0815, 2201, 2412, 2528, 2815, 3228, 3418, 3671, 4118
Davison, Veronica, 2240
Dawes-Kaylor, Pamela A., 2444
Dawson, Ashley, 3408
Day, Kenneth D., 1406, 2168, 4129
Dayton, Treva, 3147, 3454
Dearing, James W., 2627
Deatherage, Scott, 1672
Deaton, Gary D., 3438
DeCaro, Peter A., 2668
DeChaine, D. Robert, 2464
Decker, Warren D., 3572
Decui, Andreea, 2666
Dee, Juliet L., 1229, 1660, 2631, 3432
Deem, Melissa D., 2307, 2440, 3408
Deetz, Stanley A., 2264, 2644
DeFrancisco, Victoria L., 2468
DeHaan, Kathleen A., 3165, 3245
DeHart, Jean L., 2326
Deifell, David C., 3522, 3623
Delgado, Fernando P., 1361, 2715, 3661
Delicath, John W., 1453, 4353
DellaNoce, Dorothy J., 3638
Deluca, Kevin M., 1453, 2315, 2552
DeMaria, Katherine J., 4243
Deming, Caren J., 2440
Demo, Anne T., 2219, 2552
Denman, Sarah N., 1431
Denton, Robert E., 3422
Depew, David J., 2566
Depoe, Stephen P., 1453, 1564, 2653, 4353
Derbyshire, Lynne, 1219, 2119
Derme, Christine, 2143
Derryberry, Bob R., 2569
DeSantis, Alan D., 1356

Descutner, David, 2164, 2614
DeSwarte Gifford, Carolyn, 2578
deTurck, Mark A., 2143
DeVito, Joseph, 3126
Dewar, Cynthia E., 2173, 2229, 2473, 2673, 3473, 3612
DeWine, Sue, 1238, 1340, 2238, 2741, 3412, 3545
Di Chiro, Giovanna, 1453
Diaz, Angeli R., 1663, 3264
Dick, Margaret K., 4144
Dickmeyer, Linda B., 2573, 3554
Dickmeyer, Scott G., 1232, 2573
Dickson, Fran, 0121, 1126, 1315, 1418, 2518, 3628
Dicochea, Perlita R., 1108
Diehl, Heath A., 2574
Diers, Audra, 3569
Diggs, Rhunette C., 0121, 1518, 2621, 3221
Dillard, Courtney L., 3171, 3422, 4216
Dillard, James P., 3310
Dillard, Scott E., 2724, 3226, 3674, 4255, 4328
Dillon, Michael, 1241
Dimitriadis, Gregory J., 2721
Disbrow, Lynn M., 0107, 2028, 2557, 3028, 3326
Dixon, Lynda D., 1151, 1527, 2123, 2533, 3437, 3535, 4162
Dixon, Travis L., 2138
Djurovic, Angela Z., 3542
Dobbs, Linda K., 2718
Dobkin, Milton, 1677
Dock, Marcy, 1126, 3628
Dodd, Carley H., 3144
Doherty, Taylore, 3174
Dolan, Jef, 0106, 1369, 1513
Dolan, Jill, 2311
Domenici, Kathy L., 3423
Donald, Ralph R., 1569, 2642, 4342
Dong, Qingwen, 1406, 2168
Donmoyer, Deidra D., 3523
Donnerstein, Ed, 4138
Donovan, Barna, 3654
Dorgan, Kelly A., 1234, 1537, 3253
Dorries, Bruce R., 2455
Dorsey, Laura K., 1343, 3433, 3521
Dorsey, Leroy G., 3619
Dostal Neff, Bonita, 1243, 1341, 1541, 2744, 3244
Doswell, Chontrese, 3424
Dougherty, Debbie S., 1328, 1645
Dow, Bonnie J., 1219, 2440, 2536, 4144
Dowlin, Sheryl L., 2570
Downes, Edward J., 3537, 4129
Downey, Sharon D., 2140, 4223
Doxtader, Erik, 3210
Doyle, Mary Agnes, 1110, 1410
Drake, Laura E., 1615
Dreibelbis, Gary C., 2173
Drenth, Amy S., 1318
Drew, Robert S., 1107, 1563, 1663, 2757

Drew, Shirley K., 3563
Droge, David, 0123, 3314, 4119
Drucker, Susan J., 1129, 1564, 2728, 3323, 4360
Drummond, Kent G., 0418, 2128, 3140, 3418, 4118, 4225
Drushel, Bruce E., 4160
Drzewiecka, Jolanta A., 1516, 3227, 4116
Du, Tai, 4128
Dubiel, Richard M., 2132, 2315, 2730, 4357
Duck, Steve, 2314
Dudash, Elizabeth, 1172
Dudczak, Craig A., 4129
Duffy, Bernard K., 4122
Dufresne, Jean M., 2165
Duggan, Ashley P., 1315
Dukes, Janice L., 1124, 1424
Dunbar, Kelly P., 3653
Dunbar, Nancy R., 2656
Duncan, Randy, 3644
Duncan, Sarah, 3556
Duncan, Veronica J., 2130, 2421, 3306, 3633, 4328
Duncanson, Tom, 1660
Dunkelberger, Kathryn, 1257
Dunn, Daniel M., 1338
Dunn, Deborah S., 2162, 3607
Dupree, April, 4121
Duquette Smith, Cynthia, 4319
Duran, Robert L., 0746, 2230
Durbin, Teresa E., 3215
Dutcher, James, 1444
Dutwin, David J., 1606, 3456, 3622
Dwyer, Karen K., 2233, 2459
Dybvig, Kristin C., 1672
Dyer, Shannon S., 1656, 2272, 3267, 3614, 4262
Eadie, William F., 0418, 1443, 2707, 3418, 4118
Earl, Noel, 3173
Earnest, William J., 2155
Eastin, Matthew, 1661, 2235
Eastman, Susan T., 2438, 2506
Eberly, Rosa A., 4152
Eblen, Anna L., 3171, 3447, 3547
Eckles, Gary W., 1346
Eckloff, Maurine C., 0115, 1540, 1642, 2112, 2407
Eckstein, Nancy J., 1162, 1315, 2412
Edelman, Samuel M., 0154, 2216
Edelmayer, Kathleen M., 1329
Edley, Paige P., 1523, 3535
Edmonds, Mike L., 2146, 3247
Edmunds, Robert F., 1456, 2131
Edwards, Chad, 1254
Edwards, Janis L., 2658, 2740, 3231, 3422
Edwards, Jason, 1522
Edwards, Patricia A., 2233
Edwards, Paul C., 1110, 1610, 2911
Edwards, Renee, 3256
Edwards, Richard E., 3454

Egbert, Nichole L., 1345, 2156
Eguchi, Mariko, 2716
Ehrenhaus, Peter C., 3234
Ehret, Donald M., 2436
Ehrlich, Larry G., 3672
Eicher-Catt, Deborah L., 1264, 2564, 2747
Eicholtz, Mary M., 3240, 3412
Eidenmuller, Michael E., 2262
Einhorn, Lois J., 2526, 4151
Eisenberg, Anne F., 1519
Eisenhour, Jerry, 4215
Eisner, Sharon, 1310
Ekachai, Daradirek, 2744
Ekachai, Gee, 1233
Ellingson, Laura L., 2163, 2723, 4327
Elliott, Cindi, 4151
Elliott, R. Rennae, 1122, 1624, 2412
Ellis, Ann, 1143
Ellis, Beth H., 2523, 4323
Ellis, Carolyn S., 0418, 1333, 2563, 2732,
    3263, 3418, 4118, 4157, 4225, 4310
Ellis, Donald G., 2308, 4252
Ellis, Joyce, 4351
Ellis, Kathleen S., 2554, 3145, 4331
Ellis, Timothy J., 4357
Elmer, Gregory, 1208
Elmes-Crahall, Jane, 1364
Elson, Omowale T., 3521
Emel, Susan R., 1649
Emery, Daniel L., 3228, 3571
Emmers-Sommer, Tara M., 4338
Emmert, Philip, 1530
Enderle, Amy, 1149
Endo, Hiromi, 4262
Endres, Thomas G., 2657
Endress, Valerie A., 2565, 3222, 4225
Engen, David E., 2754
Engleberg, Isa N., 1357, 1426
English, Patricia J., 2201
Engstrand, Kristin C., 3561
Enos, Richard, 1272, 2734
Erbert, Larry A., 3543
Erney, Jackie, 1141
Etherton, Mark, 3173
Ettema, James S., 3106
Evans, Adeline L., 2621
Evans, Anna M., 2621
Evans, Karen C., 3447, 3547
Everett, Marcia K., 1462
Ezzell, Martha, 2306
Faber-McAlister, Joan, 1651
Fabj, Valeria, 0140, 2115, 3165
Facciponti, Laura, 1524, 1616, 2174
Faherty, Patrick, 4215
Fahs, Michael L., 1642, 2239, 3242
Fairhurst, Gail T., 2245, 2644
Fairly, Michael, 4334
Falato, Wendy L., 2445
FalerSweany, Margaret L., 2166
Falkowski, Kristan, 1549, 3257
Fall, Joseph P., 1141
Fall, Lisa, 1141, 1641

Farah, Laila A., 3428
Farrar, William J., 2619
Farrell, James M., 1419
Farrell, Kathleen, 2443, 4336
Farrell, Mike, 1201
Farrell, Thomas B., 1552, 3614
Farrugia, Rebekah, 1323
Fassett, Deanna L., 1130, 2763
Faulkner, Sandra L., 2543
Faux, William V., 1660
Feeley, Thomas H., 2143, 3129, 4230
Feeney, Gregory J., 2118
Feezel, Jerry D., 1554
Feinstein, Marjorie C., 1369
Fenske, Mindy E., 1410, 4110
Ferguson, Mary Ann, 3436
Ferguson, Paul, 1310
Ferris, James, 1646, 2255
Ferris, Julie E., 2201, 3671, 4135
Ferris, Pixy, 1230
Fillippeli, Susan E., 3667
Finch, Cynthia, 2233
Fine, Elizabeth C., 1510, 2711
Fine, Gary Alan, 1657
Fine, Marlene G., 4129, 4323
Fink, Joel, 3434
Finnegan, Cara A., 2552, 2664
Fischbach, Robert M., 1429
Fischer, Christine M., 1245
Fish, Virginia E., 2229
Fishbein, Martin, 1437, 3542
Fisher, Celeste A., 2121
Fisher, Michael A., 3172
Fisher, Jr., William P., 3439
Fishman, Donald, 0139, 1129, 1365, 2415,
    3432, 3647, 4341
Fitch, Fred E., 1162
Fitch, Kristine L., 0116, 0418, 0815, 2128,
    2263, 2316, 2815, 3418, 3625, 4118
Fitch-Hauser, Margaret, 1530
Fitzgerald, Pam, 3673
Flanagin, Andrew J., 2207, 3645
Flanigan, Jolane, 2201
Fletcher, James, 1431
Fleuriet, Cathy A., 0418, 0815, 1231, 1426,
    2249, 2815, 3418, 4118
Flint, Lyle J., 2228, 2538, 4139
Fliotsos, Anne, 2274
Flora, Jeanne K., 2518, 3119
Flores, Lisa A., 1108, 1646, 2116, 3623,
    4108, 4223
Floyd, Kory, 0418, 2743, 3418, 4118, 4355
Flynn, Thomas R., 1206, 1429, 2144, 3432
Foeman, Anita K., 1269, 2424
Folger, Joseph, 3638
Folsom, Ed, 2752
Folwell, Annette L., 3651, 4127
Fong, Mary, 0724, 1516, 1631, 2136, 2529,
    2633, 4125
Fontenot, Jolie C., 3445
Foote, Joe S., 1160, 1342
Forbes, Diane A., 3521, 4236

Ford, Sherry G., 3456
Ford, Wendy Z., 1314, 2238
Ford-Ahmed, Trevellya, 1321, 3238, 4351
Forster, Barbara, 1428
Fortier, Sandra M., 1328
Fortney, Shirley D., 1655, 3154
Forward, Gordon L., 1445, 1662, 4262
Foss, Karen A., 3423, 4135
Foss, Sonja K., 2472, 3423
Foster, Daniel, 3265
Foster, Ellisa J., 1139
Foster-Kuehn, Myrna, 1235, 1470
Fournier, Michelle E., 2453
Foust, Christina R., 1432, 2219, 3132
Fowles, Jeb, 4138
Fox, Susan A., 2651, 2746, 3427
Fraleigh, Douglas M., 1229
Frame, Melissa J., 1455, 2163, 3606
Frana, Adrian W., 2756
Franey, Kimberly J., 2718
Frank, David A., 3170
Frank, Jennifer, 2241
Frank, Robert E., 2326, 4232
Frank, Robert L., 3531
Frank, Volker, 1428, 2207
Frankel, C. David, 3215
Franklin, April I., 3537
Frappier, Glen, 3572
Fraser, Benson P., 1118
Frederick, Mark, 1128
Frederick, Tracy R., 1669
Freeley, Austin J., 3557
Freeman, Heather, 4230
Frentz, Thomas S., 2140
Freshley, Dwight, 1677
Frey, Lawrence R., 0418, 0815, 1215, 1428,
    1528, 1630, 2215, 2321, 2622, 2722,
    2815, 3229, 3418, 3616, 4118, 4263
Friedenberg, Robert V., 3419
Friedlander, Jennifer, 1335, 3133
Friedrich, Gustav W., 2454, 4326
Friesen, Clark W., 2149
Friesen, Melissa, 3174
Fritch, John E., 2753
Frobish, Todd S., 3207, 3571, 4354
Froemling, Kristin K., 2122, 3201
Frymier, Ann B., 1654, 2226, 2424, 2554,
    2626
Fudge, Kelly J., 4228
Fugate, Amy L., 2229
Fujimoto, Etsuko, 2116
Fuller, Linda K., 1336
Fuller, Rex M., 1270, 1470
Fuller, Steve, 2466
Fuller, Jr., James W., 2152
Fulton, Carol, 1433
Funayama, Izumi, 2437, 3416
Fung, Heidi, 3240
Fuoss, Kirk W., 1610, 2611
Fursich, Elfriede, 1608, 2408, 3122
Fuss-Reineck, Marilyn E., 1639
Gabrich, Chrys, 2306, 2542, 2657

Gailiun, Michelle, 1607
Gaines, Elliot I., 1464, 2747, 3238
Gajjala, Radhika, 1154, 1206, 1306, 3266,
    3535
Galati, Frank, 2911
Galician, Mary-Lou, 3141
Gallagher, Chrissy L., 1429
Gallagher, Dennis, 2607
Gallagher, Victoria J., 1244
Galloway, Ryan W., 1653
Galloway, Terry, 1410, 3510
Galvin, Kathleen M., 0121, 1533
Gamble, Michael W., 3321
Gamble, Teri S., 3321
Ganakos, Joseph M., 3212
Ganas, Monica C., 3162
Ganer, Patricia M., 2434
Ganesan, Puvana, 2735
Ganesh, Shiv, 3463, 4136
Gao, Zhihong, 2168
Gaonkar, Dilip P., 2208, 3519 3652
Gareis, John W., 1364
Garlough, Christine L., 2133
Garner, Thurmon, 2221, 4328
Gass, Robert H., 1459
Gates, Denise, 3524
Gates, Kelly A., 1466
Gaudino, James L., 0418, 0946, 1404, 1513,
    1646, 2178, 2525, 2541, 2641, 3418,
    4118
Gaut, Deborah R., 3212
Gayle, Barbara M., 1551
Geel, Justin, 1201
Gehrke, Pat J., 1572
Geiser, Michael, 3614
Geist, Patricia, 0178, 1263, 1333, 2163,
    3139, 3263
Gellis, Mark D., 1142
Gemin, Joseph V., 1664, 2464
Gentry, Jeffery J., 1669
Gentzkow, Melissa B., 1662
George, Joan A., 2163
George, Lisa N., 2718
Gerber, Matthew G., 3653
Gerding, Kristi, 3269
Gerken, Jill K., 2114
German, Kathleen M., 3142, 4260
Germann, Clark, 0115, 1540, 1642, 2207,
    2407, 3131, 3324
Germano, Michael C., 2201
Gernant, Renea B., 3569
Gershon, Richard A., 1233
Gibson, Dirk C., 1641, 2127, 2469, 3567,
    4261
Gibson, Melissa K., 2238, 2439, 3412
Gilbert, Helene, 2714
Gilbert, Joanne R., 1327, 2111
Gilchrist, James A., 2439
Giles, Howard, 2451, 2651
Giles, Steven M., 2118
Gillespie, Marie, 2414

Gillespie, Patti P., 1124, 2174, 2615, 2731, 3130, 4315
Gillespie, S. Renee, 2255, 2751
Gillespie, Thom, 2322
Gillespie, William L., 1341
Gillotti, Cathy M., 4127
Gingrich-Philbrook, Craig S., 1410, 3210
Ginosar, Tamar, 3201
Giorgio, Grace A., 3523, 4363
Girton, Matthew K., 1541
Glaser, Hollis F., 2253
Glaser, Peter A., 2112, 2556, 3412
Glaser, Susan R., 2112, 2556, 3412
Glenn, Cathy, 2149, 4208
Glenn, Phillip J., 1636, 2236, 3440, 4344
Glenn, Robert J., 3438
Glickman, Andrew, 2407
Glover, Sarah J., 4263
Gobetz, Robert H., 1406, 3537
Godbold, Linda C., 1227
Godes, Bridget, 3653
Goins-Phillips, Terilyn, 1340
Gojdycz, Tania K., 2201, 2718
Golden, Alfred, 1442
Golden, Annis G., 1206
Golden, Kathleen M., 4263
Goldman, Derek, 2911, 4210
Goldsmith, Daena J., 1137
Goldzwig, Steven R., 2419, 2522
Golish, Tamara, 0107, 1315
Golombisky, Kimberly D., 3123
Gomez, Adelina M., 3139
Gonzalez, Alberto, 1339, 2246, 2670, 2715, 3266
Gonzalez, M. Cristina, 1263, 1463, 2751, 3263, 3461, 3563
Gonzalez-Pinto, Raul E., 1507, 2663
Good, Tim, 4215
Goodall, H.L. (Bud), 0178, 1139, 1263, 3263
Goodier, Bethany C., 1139, 4336
Gooding, Andrew J., 3464
Goodnight, G. Thomas, 0418, 1152, 3164, 3418, 4118
Goodnight, Lisa J., 0107, 3649
Goodnight, Lynn, 0418, 0815, 1444, 2632, 2815, 3418, 4118
Goodwin, Jean, 1152, 1272, 1372, 2578, 3658
Gorcyca, Diane A., 2144
Gordeyeva, Yulia, 4226
Gordon, Dexter B., 2221, 3108
Gordon, Ronald D., 3526
Gorsevski, Ellen W., 1638, 2639
Goshorn, Frederick K., 4353
Gossett, Loril M., 3201
Gottshall, Cynthia M., 2642
Gouran, Dennis S., 2515
Govang, Don C., 1434, 3172
Gozzi, Raymond, 3453, 4335
Grady, Dennis P., 2618, 3316
Graff, Richard J., 2671

Graham, David N., 1201
Graham, Elizabeth E., 1654, 3319
Grandpre, Joseph R., 1345
Grant, Charles H., 3437
Grant, Jo Anna, 3651, 4127
Grapsy, Ronald P., 1154
Gratson, Scott D., 2518
Grau, Irene, 3553
Graves, Darci L., 3201
Graves, Michael P., 4233
Gray, Pamela L., 1249, 1449
Gray, Paul H., 1310, 2111
Gray, Roberta L., 2321, 2651
Gray Briggs, Abigail, 2412
Greeley, Lynne, 3624
Green, Cable T., 2206
Green, Ruth L., 2524
Greenberg, Bradley S., 1661, 3206
Greene, John O., 3310
Greene, Mandi, 4262
Greene, Ronald, 1135, 3408, 3631
Greenstreet, Robert, 1669, 2657
Greer, Norman S., 2256
Gregg, Andrea R., 1355
Gregg, Richard B., 3315
Gregory, Jeffrey E., 2232
Grice, George L., 2158
Gricenko Wells, Ludmilla, 3201
Griffin, Cindy L., 2472, 3423
Griggs, John W., 3538
Grimes, Diane S., 1339, 1645, 3563
Grimes, William T., 2567
Grindstaff, Davin A., 1608, 2155
Gring, Mark A., 1162
Gronbeck, Bruce E., 1519, 1657, 3138, 3422
Grooms, Linda D., 3262
Groot, Melissa, 3201
Grosche, Bianca, 0107
Gross, Alan G., 1632, 2252, 3566, 4244
Gross, Brian, 2208
Gross, Daniel D., 1144, 3251
Gross, Larry, 3126
Gross, Michael A., 1445, 3645
Grossberg, Lawrence, 1337, 2423, 3133, 3208, 3410, 3508
Grube, Jean, 4227
Gruber, Diane, 2464, 2546
Guerrero, Andre Sebastian, 1406
Guerrero, Laura K., 2738, 3443, 3543, 3645
Gullickson-Tolman, Elizabeth, 3157, 3544
Gumpert, Gary, 1129, 1564, 1677, 2728, 3557, 4360
Gunderson, Kathryn M., 2758
Gundlach, Dean P., 2673
Gunkel, David J., 2207
Gunn, Joshua, 1552
Gura, Timothy, 2111, 3316
Gurien, Robin A., 2142, 4142
Gutin, Myra G., 1159
Guzley, Ruth M., 3654
Haas, Stephen M., 2718, 3119

Hack, Konrad W., 1662
Hacker, Mary Kathleen, 1235
Hackman, Michael Z., 2458, 4331
Haefner, Margaret J., 0418, 1578, 2438, 2727, 3418, 4118, 4225
Hafen, Susan, 1245, 2763, 3116
Haffey, Deborah B., 2232
Hagan, Martha A., 0178, 1434
Hahn, Dan F., 3222
Hahn, Laura K., 2468
Hale, Jerold L., 1626, 2143
Halkowski, Tim R., 1436
Hall, Alice E., 1435
Hall, Barbara I., 0724, 2406, 2706, 3232, 4125
Hall, Blaine M., 1332
Hall, Bradford J., 1416
Hall, Christian A., 2718
Hall, G. Jon, 2161, 2544, 3672, 4322
Hall, John R., 1345
Hall, Jon, 1201
Hall, Peter M., 1657
Hall, Wynton C., 3107
Haller, Beth A., 0724, 1629, 2455, 4125
Hallsten, Jodi L., 1255
Halone, Kelby K., 1326, 1656, 2141, 3445, 4316
Halpin, Marcy L., 1572, 3632
Halualani, Rona T., 1108, 3227, 3663, 4116
Hamel, Stephanie A., 1245
Hamera, Judith A., 0418, 1546, 3210, 3418, 3626, 4118
Hamilton, Heidi E., 1519, 3164
Hamilton, Jennifer J., 4353
Hamilton, Margaret, 3566, 4143
Hamilton, Mark A., 2643, 2738, 3146, 3256, 3436
Hamlet, Janice D., 2324, 4351
Hammer, Mitchell R., 1456, 3171
Hammerback, John C., 2446, 2715
Hammerstrom, Erik, 2256
Hammond, Scott C., 2168
Hample, Dale, 3310
Handy Bosma, Juanita E., 2437
Hank, Heather M., 2245
Hanna, Michael S., 1149
Hansen, Alan D., 2437, 3406
Hansen, Andrew C., 2635
Hansen, Hans Vilhelm, 1152
Hansen-Horn, Tricia L., 1541, 4252
Hanson, Jarice, 1160
Hanson, Reeze L., 2046, 2557
Hanson, Trudy L., 1426, 1527, 2533, 2623, 3321
Haratonik, Peter L., 1230
Harden Fritz, Janie M., 1149, 2306, 2645, 2745
Haridakis, Paul M., 3567
Hariman, Robert, 0418, 0815, 1231, 2252, 2608, 2729, 2815, 3418, 4118
Harney, Diane M., 2201
Harold, Christine L., 3152

Harper, Anneliese M., 0418, 3418, 4118
Harper, Nancy L., 0114, 1330
Harper, Vernon, 3136, 4224
Harpine, William D., 1319, 3471, 4232
Harrington, Dana, 1144
Harrington, Nancy G., 2118
Harris, Alan C., 1664, 2128, 2747
Harris, Heather E., 3224, 3433
Harris, Lisa A., 1421
Harris, Lowell, 1522
Harris, Nikita Y., 2234, 3433
Harris, Tina M., 1234, 2240, 2562, 2618, 3121, 3221, 3459
Harris, Virgie N., 0724, 1121, 2130, 3633, 4125, 4328
Harris, William R., 3271
Harris-Jenkinson, Patty, 4257
Harrison, Frank, 3432
Harrison, Teresa M., 2707, 4322
Harsin, Jayson, 2219
Hart, Bradford A., 1449
Hart, Joy L., 1351
Hart, Roderick P., 1319, 2323
Hart, Zachary P., 2645, 2745
Harter, Lynn M., 0107, 3134, 3229, 4354
Hartman, Rosanne L., 1251
Hartnett, Stephen J., 1164
Harvey, Vickie L., 2542
Hasian, Marouf, 1319, 1452, 2408, 2667, 3234
Haskins, Ekaterina V., 2271, 2565, 3565, 4336
Haslett, Beth J., 0121
Haspel, Kathleen C., 1407, 2737, 3523
Hatfield, Katherine L., 3269
Hatfield, Susan R., 1456, 3656
Haun, Martha J., 3647
Hauser, Gerard A., 2452, 3452, 4208
Havens, Timothy, 2721
Hawkins, Katherine, 0114, 0418, 0815, 0946, 1527, 2533, 2815, 3321, 3418, 4118, 4129
Hay, Ellen A., 0724, 2131, 4125
Hay, James, 1508
Hayden, Bradley, 3556
Hayes, Cecelia, 1143
Haynes, Janice, 1214, 4123
Haynes, Julia A., 1619
Haynes, W. Lance, 1230, 2665, 3630
Hayward, Pamela A., 1242
Hazen, Michael D., 2266, 3108, 3670
Hazleton, Vincent, 1556
Heald, Gary R., 1541
Healy, Eric Franklin, 3165
Hearit, Keith M., 2441
Hearne, Tina K., 3233
Heath, Robert L., 2241, 3244
Heaton, Daniel W., 1163, 1555, 1910
Hefferin, Deborah, 0418, 1647, 2646, 3143, 3418, 4118
Hefling, Joel L., 1046, 1469, 2047, 2569, 3569, 3634, 4332

Hegde, Radha S., 1231, 1527, 2327, 2423, 2533
Heidel, Bethany, 1242
Heineman, John R., 0418, 0724, 1529, 2247, 2724, 3143, 3226, 3316, 3418, 4118, 4125
Heinemann, Robert L., 3608
Heisel, Alan D., 2643, 2718, 3201
Heisey, D. Ray, 1170, 1570, 2168, 2270, 2670
Heisey, Ian S., 2270
Heisler, Jennifer M., 2218, 2549, 4238
Heiteen, Jan, 2756
Held, Rebecca M., 3664
Hellbusch, Susan E., 3569
Heller, Lisa K., 2572
Helsel, Christine R., 3656
Hemenway, Paul T.M., 1346
Hemmer, Jr., Joseph J., 3201
Hemphill, Michael R., 0114
Henderson, Bill, 3672
Henderson, Bruce, 1524
Hendrix, Katherine G., 1154, 1454, 2324, 4354
Hendry, Judith E., 2253, 2427, 2653, 3032
Henningsen, David D., 1354, 1615
Henry, David, 1131
Henry, Jessica M., 2242
Henry, Tommy, 3147
Heo, Chul, 3441
Herbeck, Dale A., 2631, 3432, 3658, 4360
Herbert, Sharnine S., 2721, 3424
Heritage, John C., 1536, 3437, 3640, 4234, 4344
Hermann, Marc, 3553
Herndon, Sandra L., 1454, 1623, 3453
Herold, Kelly P., 1629, 2455, 3427
Herrick, James A., 2662
Hess, Jon A., 1149, 3657
Hester, Janet, 1255
Hetherington, Laurel T., 2139, 3544, 4140
Hetzel, Marilyn A., 1124, 1616, 2174, 3474
Heuett, Brian L., 2126, 2233
Hewitt, Stephani, 1551
Hickman, Mark S., 1635, 3173
Hicks, Darrin K., 1408, 3408
Hicks, Deborah, 1333
Hicks, Michon, 2628
Hickson, Mark, 2323
Hiebner, Glynis C., 1545, 1641, 4139
Hiebsch, Gary C., 2262
Hildebrant, Jill, 4110
Hill, Arlene, 3274
Hill, Patricia S., 2562, 3221
Hill, Randall T., 2311
Hilliard, D. Nebi, 1555
Hillis, Mark, 4262
Hinchcliff-Pelias, Mary, 2247, 2630
Hinck, Edward A., 1449, 3269, 3673
Hinck, Shelly, 0106, 2169, 3673
Hindman, M'Liss, 2173, 2229
Hines, Stephen C., 2718, 4127

Hirokawa, Randy Y., 1354, 1625, 2178, 3237
Hirst, Russell K., 2662
Ho, Evelyn Y., 3240
Ho, Philip C., 4355
Hoar, Nancy J., 1569, 2453, 3453
Hobbs, Jeffrey D., 1556, 2472
Hobbs, Jodee, 2472
Hobgood, Linda B., 4142
Hodgson Jr., Robert, 1534
Hoeksema, Thomas B., 1155
Hoerl, Kristen E., 1523
Hoey, Sharon A., 3165
Hoffman, David C., 3565
Hoffman, Mary F., 1223, 1329, 1462
Hoffmann, Janet M., 2201
Hoffner, Cynthia A., 2531, 2727, 3606
Hogan, J. Michael, 1119
Hogg, Mary C., 2256, 3656, 4149
Hohauser-Thatcher, Melissa, 1363
Hohmann, Hanns J., 1152, 2671
Holbert, R. Lance, 1506, 3256
Holden, Jessica, 2457
Holderman, Lisa B., 2438
Holladay, Sherry J., 0724, 2651, 2746, 3651, 4125
Hollatz, Edwin A., 3662
Holling, Michelle A., 1108, 2227, 2623, 3230, 4261
Hollingshead, Andrea B., 1115
Holloway, Madison, 1440
Holloway, Rachel L., 2241
Hollwitz, John C., 3529
Holm, Todd T., 1469, 3412
Holman Jones, Stacy L., 2511, 2732, 4310
Holmes, Karen L., 3531
Holt, Sandra W., 3214
Holt-Day, Janna L., 3326
Honeycutt, James M., 1161, 3456
Hongmei, Gao, 2168
Hoover, Judith, 2447, 4219
Hopf, Tim S., 2233
Hopkins, Christiana M., 2436
HopKins, Mary Frances, 0815, 1410, 2815
Hopkins, Sonya, 1357, 1414
Horne, Janet S., 2422
Horner, William T., 3537
Hornik, Robert, 2538
Horrigan, Joan E., 1365, 3647
Horvath, Cary W., 2149
Horwitz, Linda D., 3419
Hosman, Lawrence A., 1647, 2228, 2646
Hostetler, Michael J., 1119, 3419
Hostetter, Robert D., 1324, 1510
Houck, Davis W., 2171
Houde, Lincoln J., 1201
Houston, Marsha, 0114, 1621, 2130, 2324, 2508, 3633
Houston, Renee, 1545
Houts, Renate M., 1315
Howard, John, 1151
Howard, Leigh Anne, 1163

Howard, Loretta, 3621
Howard, Undraye, 3621
Howell, Valerie, 1454, 2243
Howley, Kevin, 1107
Hsu, Chia-Fang, 3455
Hu, Allison D., 3455
Huang, Lin-Mei, 1216
Huang, Ren-He, 2138
Huang, Shaorong, 1370, 2670, 3170
Hubbard, Robert J., 1201
Hubbell, Anne P., 1545, 3545
Huber, Stefanie, 3553
Hubler, Mike T., 1566
Huffman, Karla J., 2149
Hugenberg, Barbara S., 4149
Hugenberg, Lawrence W., 1426, 1546,
    3149, 3549, 3626, 4149
Hughes, Holly, 2211, 2311
Hughes, Kelly M., 3612
Hughes, Patrick C., 2518
Hughes, Sherick A., 1270, 3108
Hulbert-Johnson, Ruth A., 0123, 2131, 3307
Hullett, Craig R., 2549, 2743, 3256
Hummert, Mary Lee, 2451, 2746
Hunt, Marilyn D., 2444, 2644
Hunt, Stephen K., 2247, 2630, 3132
Hunter, Christopher D., 3432, 4360
Hurley, Mary E., 1464
Huss, Jennifer M., 1462, 2408
Husson, William, 4322
Huston, Ted L., 1315
Hwang, John C., 2470
Hyde, Michael J., 0133, 1472, 2153, 2462
Hynes, Thomas J., 2326
Ibrahim DeVries, Basma, 1639, 2239
Ifert, Danette E., 1655, 2154, 3154
Ige, Dorothy W., 0418, 3418, 4118
Ijams, Karen A., 3643
Imahori, Todd, 0724, 1359, 2416, 2633,
    3127, 3429, 3659, 4125
Inch, Edward S., 2569
Infante, Dominic A., 2538
Inge, Dorothy W., 4241
Inman, Karen, 0106
Irizarry, Cynthia A., 3445
Isa, Masako, 4331
Isaacson, Frederick W., 1440, 2201, 2469
Isgro, Kirsten, 1514
Itaba, Yoshihisa, 4231
Iverson, Joel O., 1608
Ivie, Robert L., 1610, 2178, 2752, 3315
Ivy, Diana K., 1527, 2533, 2623, 2725, 3236
Iwakuma, Miho, 1455
Iwata, Chris, 4257
Jablonski, Carol J., 1562, 2119, 2536
Jabro, Ann D., 2306, 2427, 3032
Jackaway, Gwenyth L., 4138
Jackson, Andrea H., 4224
Jackson, David B., 2141
Jackson, Michele H., 1115, 2514
Jackson, Robert N., 4249

Jackson, Ronald L., 0114, 0418, 1521, 2130,
    2628, 3136, 3221, 3306, 3418, 3633,
    4118, 4236
Jackson, Sally A., 2178, 2514
Jackson, Shannon P., 2611
Jacobson, Ron L., 1230
Jaffe, Clella I., 1542
Jain, Nemi C., 1133, 2735
James, Anita C., 3412
James, Navita C., 2240, 2606
James-Hughes, Jacqueline, 3524
Jameson, Jessica K., 3270
Jamieson, Kathleen, 1712, 3542
Janas, Michael J., 2326, 4119
Jandt, Fred E., 3126
Janssen, Volker, 3553
Japp, Debra K., 2739, 3134
Japp, Phyllis M., 2165, 2739, 3134
Jarman, Jeffrey W., 1672, 3451
Jarmon, Leslie H., 2269
Jarvis, Sharon E., 1422, 4322
Jasinski, James, 1652, 3234, 3552
Jasko, Susan A., 0418, 1235, 3128, 3323,
    3418, 4118, 4129
Jassem, Harvey, 1129
Javidi, Akbar, 2112
Jazayeri, Alexia S., 1516, 2735
Jefferson, Bonnie S., 0139, 1365
Jenckes, Norma, 1143
Jenkins, Keith B., 2159, 3214
Jenks, Elaine B., 2255, 4163, 4327
Jennings, Dave, 2439
Jennings, William P., 2639
Jensen, Arthur D., 1564
Jensen, Joli K., 2606, 2752
Jensen, Karla K., 1254, 1649, 2154, 2218
Jensen, Richard J., 0724, 2429, 2715, 4125
Jensen, Scott L., 1046, 2047, 2231, 2569,
    3172, 3634
Jia, Wenshan, 1416, 1570, 2553, 2670
Jianbin, Jin, 2170
Johannesen, Richard L., 3657
Johns, Becky L., 2629, 3636, 4162
Johnson, Amy J., 2243, 4238
Johnson, Brenda L., 1437
Johnson, Craig E., 1442, 1542, 2458, 4331
Johnson, Deryl B., 0418, 1224, 1324, 1524,
    2174, 2474, 2731, 3130, 3418, 4118,
    4225, 4315
Johnson, E. Patrick, 1163, 1555, 1621, 2311
Johnson, Fern L., 0114, 3321
Johnson, Karen, 2455
Johnson, Mary C., 1125
Johnson, Michael, 1242
Johnson, Orin G., 1154, 1454, 3649
Johnson, Scott D., 2619, 2754
Johnson, Thomas J., 2122
Johnson-Jones, Joni M., 2135
Johnstone, Christopher, 1451, 2271, 2734
Jones, Billie J., 3264
Jones, Charlotte M., 2128, 2269, 2433,
    3440

Jones, Davina A., 2562, 3221
Jones, DeWitt, 2232
Jones, Holly, 2621
Jones, Janna, 2464, 3464
Jones, Jennifer L., 3612
Jones, John M., 4219
Jones, Joni L., 1621, 2527, 3223, 4110
Jones, Kevin T., 3162
Jones, Mark J., 1237, 4123
Jones, Stacy H., 2757
Jones, Steve, 1208, 1578, 2544, 3266
Jones, Susanne, 1315, 1625, 2156, 2738, 3456
Jones-Corley, Jennifer, 1549, 2749
Joraanstad, Mark, 3538
Joraanstad, Pamela J., 3538
Jordan, Amy B., 1114
Jordan, John W., 2443
Jordan-Jackson, Felicia F., 0418, 2130, 3418, 3633, 4118
Jorgensen-Earp, Cheryl R., 0418, 2119, 3418, 4118
Jorgenson, Jane E., 2618, 3145
Joseph, Lori J., 2718
Joseph, Roy, 2652, 4222
Josephson, Sheree, 1553, 3231
Jovanovic-Mattson, Spoma, 1670, 2257, 2455
Joyce, Teddi, 3544
Judd, Ben, 2555
Jung, Colette S., 3464, 4323
Jung, Eura, 3539
Junker, Kirk W., 2466
Kaakinen, Joanna M., 1551
Kahl, Mary L., 0138, 0418, 2429, 2635, 3222, 3418, 4118, 4225
Kahlenberg, Susan, 2438
Kahn Egan, Seth, 3138
Kahn-Egan, Chrys, 1201, 3138
Kaid, Lynda Lee, 1145, 2222, 2639
Kakita, Hideki, 4231
Kalbfleisch, Pamela J., 0114, 1647, 2646
Kallan, Richard A., 2415
Kamalipour, Yahya R., 1233, 4331
Kaminski, Steven H., 1162
Kamrath, Christopher, 3408, 3519
Kanata, Tamie, 2735, 4331
Kandath, Krishna P., 1237, 2107, 3655, 4163
Kane, Ryan E., 1669
Kane, Thomas, 2153, 3164
Kanengieter, Marla R., 1638, 3134, 3231, 4121
Kang, Jong G., 3539, 3639
Kang, Mee-Eun, 3639
Kang, Seok, 3606
Kanter, Jodi, 2111
Kapoor, Priya, 1507
Kapoor, Suraj P., 2716
Kappler, Barbara J., 1316, 1416, 2201
Karmon, Carolyn L., 1614, 2460
Karns, Vicki L., 1332, 1635, 3273, 3530
Karpanty-Yantis, Rachel E., 2454

Kasch, Chris R., 4127
Kasle, Sydne E., 3526
Kasprzyk, Danuta, 1437
Kassing, Jeffrey W., 2538, 2644, 3145
Katz, Elihu, 3106
Katz, Steven B., 3564
Kauffeld, Fred J., 1152
Kavoori, Anandam P., 1439, 1659
Kawamura, Lisa M., 3473
Kay, Ruth E., 2632, 3454
Kaye, Barbara K., 2122
Kazanskaya, Natliya V., 1541
Kazoleas, Dean C., 1556
Kearney, Patricia, 2237, 3324
Keaten, James A., 2233, 2424, 2555
Keehner, Mary F., 1164, 2655, 3463
Keeler, John D., 1262
Keeling, Brittany, 1201
Keeshan Nadler, Marjorie, 2254, 3629, 4154
Kellar-Guenther, Yvonne B., 3435
Kelley, Colleen E. (CA), 1643
Kelley, Colleen E. (PA), 2570
Kelley, Venita A., 2324
Kelly, Douglas, 2644
Kelly, Lynne, 2233, 2424
Kelly, Tressa M., 3623
Kelly, William, 2116
Kelso, Kari C., 3267
Keltner, John (Sam), 1677
Kelty, Mark J., 1143
Kendall, Kathleen E., 3222
Kendig, Daun G., 3110
Kendrick, Eric, 2249
Kennan, Bill, 1556
Kennedy, Kimberly A., 1362, 1407
Kennerly, Rebecca M., 4110
Kenny, Wade R., 1265, 2265, 2462, 4325
Kenski, Henry C., 2539
Kenski, Kate M., 1437, 1606, 2539
Kent, Drew, 1610
Kent, Michael L., 1641, 2441, 3465, 3533
Kern, Montague, 0418, 0815, 1145, 1231, 2815, 3418, 4118
Kernisky, Debra A., 1241, 2201
Kersten, Kevin, 2162
Ketrow, Sandra M., 2515
Keyser, Michelle, 3564
Keyton, Joann, 0418, 0724, 1231, 1354, 1456, 1528, 2215, 2461, 3129, 3229, 3418, 3616, 4118, 4125, 4225
Kicenski, Karyl K., 2108
Kiewra, Kenneth A., 3254
Kilmer, Heather L., 1343
Kim, Geisun, 2241
Kim, Joohoan, 3122, 3639
Kim, Kyong L., 3264, 3539
Kim, Min-Sun, 3659
Kim, Shin-Dong, 3639
Kim, Taehyun, 3639
Kim, Yang-Soo, 3539
Kim, Young Yun, 2316
Kimsey, William D., 1270, 1470

Kincaid, Amie D., 4135
Kindred, Jeannette W., 1461
King, Andrew A., 0418, 1546, 3418, 3626, 4118
King, Christy L., 4162
King, Cynthia E., 1641, 3444
King, Larry J., 3622
King, Randall E., 1662
King, Samantha, 1508
King, Stephen A., 2221
Kinloch, Valerie, 4235
Kinnard, Mary E., 3224
Kinney, Bradford L., 1364
Kinney, Jennifer M., 1151
Kinney, Terry A., 3270
Kinsella, William J., 4143
Kinser, Amber E., 1206, 3463
Kirby, Erika L., 2745
Kirch, Michael W., 3273, 4315
Kirkpatrick, Lois, 1241
Kirkwood, William G., 3529
Kirschner, Tony L., 1408, 4308
Kistenberg, Cindy J., 1327, 3255
Kitron, Uriel, 1336
Kiwanuka-Tondo, James, 3436
Kiyomiya, Toru, 3201
Kleeman, Kole, 1430
Kleiman, Howard M., 4160
Klein, Craig A., 2446
Kleine, Michael, 1460, 2244
Klien, Stephen A., 3522, 4129
Klimowicz, Stan, 1251
Kline, Brian D., 0107
Kline, Susan L., 2637, 2737
Klinger, Geoffrey D., 1266
Klinger, Mark R., 1506
Klope, David C., 3462
Klorer, Kimberly A., 3143, 3642
Kloss, Joseph A., 4263
Klumpp, James F., 2315, 2665, 2753, 4325
Kluver, Randy, 1370, 1631, 2553, 3170
Klvana, Tomas P., 1522, 1660
Klyukanov, Igor E., 3564
Klyukovski, Andrew A., 1201, 2249, 3622
Knapp, David D., 1237
Knapp, Mark L., 0106, 0418, 0815, 1160, 1331, 1626, 2178, 2541, 2641, 2815, 3418, 3643, 4118
Knight, Richard A., 1526
Knobloch, Leanne K., 3443
Knutson, Roxann L., 2672
Koch, Nicola, 1201
Koch, Stephen C., 2172, 3272
Koch, Warren G., 3526
Koehler, Carol, 2112, 3132
Koerber, Amy, 1566
Koermer, Chas D., 3645
Koester, Jolene, 1131, 2316
Kohl, Virginia, 2630, 4336
Koite, Kaori, 1623
Kolb, Judith A., 1201
Komnenic, Ljiljana, 2419

Konick, Steven, 1336
Konsky, Catherine W., 2716
Koponen, Angela, 1638, 3251
Kosaka, Takashi, 2133, 3429
Kosberg, Roberta L., 1543
Koshikawa, Fusako, 2555
Kostecki, Eleanor M., 2238, 2439
Kotarba, Joseph, 3246
Kotlowski, Joseph John, 2268
Kottenstette, David T., 3474
Koven, Michele E. J., 3240
Kowalczyk, Laura, 2531
Kozicki, Kim M., 3655
Kraidy, Marwan M., 1507, 2663, 3127, 3238, 3516
Kraig, Robert A., 1119, 2719
Kramer, Eric M., 2637
Kramer, Esther A., 3641
Kramer, Michael R., 3265
Kramer, Michael W., 2224, 2645
Krampien, Penny L., 1633, 2542, 2726
Kray, Susan, 0154
Krcmar, Marina B., 1506
Kreisher, Robert D., 1139
Krendl, Kathy A., 2178, 3431
Kreps, Gary L., 1238, 1336, 2431, 2728, 3323, 3427
Krider, Diane S., 4316
Krikorian, Dean H., 2235
Krips, Henry P., 1335, 2266, 3133
Krizek, Robert L., 1263, 2645, 4129
Krone, Kathleen J., 0418, 0815, 1645, 2124, 2224, 2644, 2815, 3418, 4118
Kruckeberg, Dean A., 2144, 2315, 3244
Krupar, Karen R., 0115, 1540, 2046, 2407, 3131, 3324
Kubey, Robert W., 4264
Kuhn, Timothy R., 3445, 3645, 4136
Kully, Robert D., 1330, 1677, 2157
Kulp, Cailin, 4130
Kumar, Deepa, 1308, 2208, 4216
Kurz, Linda S., 2112
Kuster, Thomas A., 2229
Kuswa, Kevin D., 1153, 1425, 2614
Lackey, Tisha L., 2638
Lacour, Chante, 2241
Lacroix, Celeste C., 2164
Laffoon, E. Anne, 2115
LaFrance, Betty H., 1543, 2543
Lahman, Mary P., 2542
Lain, Brian, 1572, 3228, 3523, 4153
Laine-Timmerman, Linda E., 1139
Lakey, Paul N., 2516, 2616, 3144, 4162
Laliker, Melanie K., 2143
Lamar, O. Sylvia, 2621
Lambert, Bruce L., 1137, 2136
Lamoureux, Edward Lee, 2629, 3453, 3636
Lamoureux, Elizabeth R., 1433
Lampl, Linda L., 1206
Landman, Margaret, 3667
Landreth-Etherton, Virginia B., 3173
Lane, Derek R., 2749

Lane, Gina E., 1627, 2129, 2753, 3635
Lane, Shelley D., 2714
Lane-Johnson, Liz, 1323
Langan, Emily J., 2243, 3625
Lange, Jonathan I., 3553
Langellier, Kristin M., 1510, 4328
Langford, Catherine L., 3107
Langsdorf, Lenore, 1252, 1472
Langseth, Kristina M., 1414
Lanicek, Tracey Q., 1119, 1522
Lannutti, Pamela J., 4327
LaPidus, Jules, 3125
Large, Gerry, 4215
Larson, Gary W., 3615
Larson, Gregory, 4357
Larson, Mary S., 0418, 0815, 1231, 2727, 2815, 3418, 4118
Latham, Angela J., 3624
Lattin, Bohn D., 1262, 2762, 3462
Lauer, Ilon M., 3271
Lauman, Robyn, 1225
Lavey, Martha, 2911
LaWare, Margaret R., 1244, 1514, 2115
Lawrence, Betty Jane, 0107
Lawrence, Samuel G., 2737, 3540
Lawson, Harold, 3569
Lawson, John, 1444
Layng, Jacqueline M., 3253
Lazili, Paula, 2538
Lazu, Malia, 3165
Le Poire, Beth A., 0418, 1315, 1443, 1626, 2743, 3418, 4118, 4238
Lea, Carolyn, 1623
Leach, Joan, 0125, 1632, 2566, 3666
LeBaron, Curtis D., 1636
Lechtreck, Bob, 2673
Lederman, Linda C., 0114, 1330, 3201
Lee, Andrew Ann, 2221
Lee, Christine, 2270
Lee, Jaesub, 3145
Lee, Jaihyun, 3539
Lee, Jong-Hwa, 2708
Lee, Josephine W., 3443
Lee, Karen King, 3462
Lee, Lin-Lee, 2668, 3123
Lee, Moon Jeong, 1356, 3436
Lee, Oh-Hyeon, 3539, 4108
Lee, Ronald E., 3462
Lee, Wenshu, 0418, 0815, 1527, 2456, 2533, 2708, 2815, 3116, 3418, 4116, 4118
Leeds-Hurwitz, Wendy, 2321, 2564, 4334
Leeman, Richard W., 2578, 4119
LeFevre, Andrienne, 2567
Leff, Michael, 0418, 1532, 1626, 2178, 2322, 2415, 3125, 3418, 3619, 4118
Lefkowitz, Eva L., 2314
Leibowitz, Kenneth, 2136
Leichty, Greg, 1241, 1441, 2426, 3637
Leininger, Joan E., 0418, 1357, 1646, 1677, 3156, 3418, 4118, 4225

Leland, Chris M., 0418, 0815, 2231, 2815, 3418, 4118
Lempert, Lora, 2523
Lengel, Laura B., 1507, 2553, 2616, 3416
Lenning, Alisha A., 1525
LeNoir, Nina M., 4215
Lent, John A., 2616
Leonard, Jessica S., 1230
Leonard, Mary Kate, 2218
Lerner, Gene H., 1536
Leroux, Neil R., 1562
Lerstrom, Alan C., 0418, 0815, 1342, 1633, 2542, 2726, 2815, 3418, 3608, 4118
Leslie, Andrew W., 2153
Leslie, Kristen B., 1137, 2156
LeVan, Michael T., 1130
Levasseur, David G., 2167, 3465
Levin, Shirlee A., 0123
Levina, Marina, 1437
Levine, Elana H., 1663
Levine, Kenneth J., 2538, 3436, 4160
Lewandowski, Eileen M., 3438
Lewis, Laurie K., 1245, 3545
Lewis, Todd V., 3534
Lewis, William F., 1452
Li, Huihui, 3264
Li, Shuang, 1170
Li, Shupeng, 2668
Liang, Beatrice, 2651
Liang, Chung-hui, 3240
Liang, Xuelun, 1359
Licklider, Barb, 1433
Lieberman, Jerome, 4336
Liebes, Tamar, 2414
Lillie, Janet M., 3545
Limon, M. Sean, 2543
Lin, Wei-Kuo, 1506
Lin Classon, Hsiu-chen, 1224
Lind, Rebecca A., 1578, 2438, 2727, 4264
Linder, Richard, 2239
Lindmark, Joyce, 2415
Lindrum, David, 1332
Lindsay, Samm, 2123
Lindvall, Terrence R., 1534, 2662
Linkugel, Wilmer A., 4219
Linney, John P., 4353
Linz, Daniel G., 2138
Lippert, Lance R., 2247, 2630
Lipton, Mark, 1664, 2155
Litke, Rebecca A., 0107
Littlefield, Robert S., 1046, 2047, 3634
Litvin, Joel P., 2642
Liu, Dejun, 2170, 2668, 3670
Liu, Huichuan, 3253
Liu, Lu, 1570
Liu, Shuang, 4136
Lockford, Lesa, 1427, 3110
Lockridge, Rebecca B., 3231
Lodge, Mary Jo, 3174
Loftis, Scott A., 1449
Logan, Christie A., 1130, 3474
Lollar, Karen L., 1107, 2207, 3131, 3652

Lombardo, Amy J., 4353
Long, Beverly W., 1310, 2111, 2615
Long, Kathleen M., 0746, 1655, 2230, 3154
Long, Kathy L., 2526
Long, Lynette M., 3652
Long, Shawn D., 3621
Lont, Cynthia M., 1323
Lopez de Miranda, Alexandre, 2257, 2443, 4357
Louden, Allan, 2153, 2326
Louis, Ross, 4110, 4210
Lovaas, Karen E., 4355
Love, Don E., 3155
Lowe, Leah, 1610
Lowery-Hart, Russell D., 1414, 2460, 3673, 4154
Lowrie, Sue E., 2272, 2472, 2572
Lowry, Ann, 1328
Lowry, Dennis T., 2668
Lu, Shuming, 2670, 3170, 3570
Lu, Xing (Lucy), 1370, 3170, 4129, 4329
Lubbers, Charles A., 0724, 1243, 2144, 2426, 2669, 3244, 3444, 3637, 4125
Lucaites, John L., 2552, 2729, 3234
Lucas, Mary, 2439
Lucas, Stephen E., 2635, 3419
Lucchetti, Anne E., 2218
Lucus, Mark, 2173
Lulofs, Roxane, 2412, 3162
Lum, Casey M. K., 0418, 1631, 3127, 3227, 3418, 4118, 4225
Lumsden, Donald L., 1269, 2541
Lumsden, Gay, 1269
Lundy, James C., 0724, 1201, 1464, 2747, 3564, 3665, 4125
Lustig, Myron W., 0859
Lynch, John, 2755
Lynch, Terese, 3638
Lyne, John, 2566
Lyons, Meg S., 2718
Ma, Ringo, 1170, 2170, 4329
Mabry, Edward A., 1215
MacBride, Francine R., 2618
Macchi, Adam, 1118
MacDoniels, Joseph W., 2442
MacDougall, Robert C., 1356
MacGeorge, Erina L., 2445
Machiorlatti, Jennifer A., 3641
Macke, Frank J., 1264, 3665
Mackey-Kallis, Susan B., 1265, 1451
MacLennan, Janet, 1340
MacLennan, Jennifer M., 2507
Macoubrie, Jane, 1354, 2619
Maday, Renee, 2637
Madsen, John A., 1243
Madura, Dawn, 2135
Maguire, Kathryn C., 1356, 2243
Mahaffey, Jerome D., 1352, 2219, 3406
Mahan-Hays, Sarah E., 1665, 2664
Maines, David R., 1657
Makau, Josina M., 1457, 2472
Makoul, Gregory, 3515

Malik, Saadia Ali, 2551
Malin, Brenton J., 1125, 3441
Malley, Carlene, 3606
Mallin, Irwin A., 1452
Mandavilli, Anupama, 2116
Mandelbaum, Jenny S., 1636
Mandeville, Mary Y., 0115, 0724, 1540, 2407, 3131, 4125
Mandziuk, Roseann M., 0724, 1527, 2201, 2533, 2725, 3123, 4125, 4129
Maney, Sharon L., 2522
Mangrum, Faye G., 4334
Manigault, Omerosa, 3407
Manning, Killian E., 2111
Manning, Laura M., 2535
Manning, Linda D., 2518, 4228
Manolescu, Beth I., 2671
Manusov, Valerie L., 2516
Mares, Marie-Louise, 1114
Marin, Noemi C., 0134
Marinelli, Terese M., 1345
Markham, Annette N., 2757
Markham Shaw, Charla L., 1327
Marrow-Ferguson, Sherilyn R., 1418, 4238
Marsh, Pamela S., 1406
Marshall, Alicia A., 0724, 1227, 1661, 3627, 4125
Marshall, Brenda D., 1442
Marshall, Kristin L., 1633, 2542, 2726
Marsowicz, Anthony, 2755
Martin, Annette, 1363
Martin, Donald R., 0106, 2046, 2469, 3135
Martin, Glen, 4262
Martin, Judith N., 2316
Martin, L. John, 1370
Martin, Matthew M., 1115, 1539, 2643, 3154
Martin, Phil A., 3173
Martinez, Jacqueline M., 2747, 3564, 4164
Martinez, Melissa, 3414
Martinez Pollack, Tessa, 3538
Martinson, Jay R., 1162, 1242
Martinson, Jeanette, 1242
Maruyama, Masazumi, 3416
Marvin, Carolyn A., 3106
Masterson, John T., 0114
Mastro, Dana E., 1661, 2235
Mastrolia, Barbara A., 4241
Mastronardi, Maria, 1337, 4144
Matabane, Paula W., 1334
Matei, Sorin, 3201
Matelski, Marilyn J., 3122, 4360
Mater, Marie A., 3553
Mathies, Sam C., 1442
Mathison, Maureen A., 2736
Matlon, Ronald J., 2667
Matsumoto, Gordon T., 2511
Matsumoto, Shigeru, 4231
Matthews, Donna, 0418, 3418, 4118
Matthews, Gray, 1421, 1652, 3201
Mattiello, Jill N., 2718
Mattina, Anne F., 0138, 1123, 2723

Mattingley, Barbara C., 1418
Mattrey, Michelle J., 1525, 4338
Mattson, Marifran, 1463, 1537, 3627
Matula, Theodore, 2201, 2412
Matyash, Olga, 4226
Mavor, Carol, 2411
Maxfield, Andrew M., 2435
Maxwell, Madeline M., 0724, 2128, 2636, 4125
Maxwell, Richard M., 1233
May, Steven K., 3245, 3563
Maynard Farinola, Wendy Jo, 2207
Mayo, Adrienne Jene, 3421
Mays, Helena R., 3538
Maze, William A., 3201
Mazzarella, Sharon R., 2551
McAdoo, Laura, 1161
McAlister, Joan, 1135
McAllister, Matthew P., 2640, 3406
McBride, Brian, 1153
McBride, Karin E., 1318
McBride, M. Chad, 1656
McCabe-Juhnke, John E., 2569
McCain, Thomas A., 2206, 2728, 3431
McCaleb, Chris, 3274
McCall, Jill, 4128
McCalla, Melissa, 2468
McCann, Jennifer, 4227
McCarthy, Cameron R., 2134
McCarthy, Robert, 3519
McCartney, Brian, 3274
McCartney, Jessica, 3274
McChesney, Robert, 1308
McClanahan, Andrea M., 4128
McClish, Glen A., 4152
McCloskey, Deirdre N., 2152
McClure, Leola, 1345
McComas, Katherine A., 2127
McCorkle, Suzanne, 0114, 0418, 2623, 3122, 3418, 4118
McCormick, Ray, 3162
McCoy, Ken W., 4215
McCroskey, James C., 1347, 1546, 1654, 2154, 2237, 2643, 4326
McCroskey, Linda L., 1201
McDaniel, James P., 1452, 2652
McDermott, Virginia M., 1137
McDonald, Becky A., 0418, 2164, 2241, 2426, 2744, 3418, 3637, 4118, 4225
McDonald, Kelly M., 1672, 3451
McDonald, Trevy A., 2121, 4351
McDorman, Todd F., 0724, 2428, 3567, 4125, 4352
McDowell, Earl E., 2538
McElreath, Mark P., 3444
McEvoy, Patricia J., 2567
McEwen, Janet S., 2638
McFarland, S. Diane, 1251, 3427
McGarrity, Matthew K., 1119
McGee, Brian R., 1231, 2231, 2672
McGee, Daniel, 3164, 3632
McGee, Michael C., 2265

McGlone, Libby A., 2436
McGregor, Annie, 3215
McGuire, Michael, 1451
McHale, John P., 1201, 1522, 4352
McHenry, Keith E., 3121
McIlwain, Charlton, 3108
McIntush, Holly G., 3107
McKenney, Janet K., 0418, 0815, 2815, 3418, 4118
McKenzie, Nelya J., 2446
McKeon Lillie, Janet K., 1661
McKerrow, Raymie E., 0418, 0946, 1513, 1712, 2508, 2706, 3418, 3711, 3811, 4118
McKevitt, Felicity, 4322
McKinney, Bruce C., 0724, 1270, 1470, 2424, 3447, 3547, 4125
McKinney, Mitchell S., 1145, 4322
McKinney, William J., 1169, 3253
McKinnon, Lori M., 1422, 3537
McKissick, Heather M., 1107, 2407
McKown, Robert J., 2719
McLaughlin, Kelly C., 2723
McMahan, David T., 3435, 4149
McManus, Robert M., 1262
McMillan, Jill J., 2322
McMullian, Britton, 3667
McNeilis, Kelly S., 3627
McOmber, James B., 2122, 4143
McPhail, Mark L., 3127, 3227
McPhee, Robert D., 0132
Meadows-Hogan, Suzanne, 2435
Means Coleman, Robin R., 2121, 3121
Mechling, Elizabeth W., 4319
Mechling, Jay, 4319
Medford, Gail S., 1616, 2174, 2474, 3624
Medhurst, Martin J., 3107
Medoff, Norman J., 1578
Medved, Caryn E., 2745, 3545, 4238
Meeske, Milan D., 0114
Mehmen, Karmen, 1136
Meiners, Eric B., 1539, 3456
Meisenbach, Rebecca J., 2441
Meister, Mark, 2427, 3032, 3134, 4319
Mejias, Ulises A., 1107
Meldrum, Helen M., 2136
Melkote, Srinivas R., 1359
Mello, W. Bradford, 1236, 2412
Melton, Matthew, 3262, 4333
Mendelson, Michael, 2515
Mendible, Myra, 2456
Mendoza, S. Lily, 1516, 2663, 3563, 4116
Menzel, Kent E., 2154, 3254
Mercieca, Jennifer R., 2762, 4352
Merrill, Lisa, 2611
Merriman, Tim, 3674
Merritt, Bishetta D., 1334, 3424
Messman, Susan J., 1549, 2445
Messner, Beth A., 2164, 4139
Mester, Cathy S., 2570
Metts, Charles R., 2268
Metts, Sandra, 1630, 2622, 4254

Metz, J. M., 3615, 4335
Metzler, Bruce, 2232
Meussling, G. Vonne, 3244
Meyer, Gary S., 4227
Meyer, Janet R., 2738, 3146, 3310, 3456
Meyer, Marcy E., 4323
Meyers, Renee A., 1245, 1428, 1528, 2515
Michaels Hollander, Erica, 3430
Michal-Johnson, Paula, 2655
Michel, Neil, 2540
Mickunas, Algis, 2264, 3665
Miczo, Nathan, 2543
Mifsud, Mari Lee, 0178, 1272, 1372, 2171, 2754, 3271
Mikesell, Rebecca L., 2218
Miklaucic, Shawn, 1508, 2134
Milburn, Trudy A., 1451
Miles, Susan C., 1225
Millar, Dan P., 1641, 2144, 2201
Millay, Bradford M., 4227
Millen, Jonathan H., 2406
Miller, Brett A., 1362, 3614
Miller, Carolyn R., 1144, 1244
Miller, Claude H., 1345, 2156
Miller, Jackson B., 1169
Miller, Jeffrey A., 3644
Miller, Jerry L., 1469, 1635, 2146, 2539, 3247
Miller, John J., 4325
Miller, Joseph B., 1342
Miller, Katherine I., 2718, 3645
Miller, Lynn C., 1510, 4157
Miller, Maggie Z., 1333, 2163
Miller, Michelle A., 1126, 1263, 2118, 2314, 2511, 3628, 4230
Miller, Pamela C., 1542, 1633, 2142, 2726
Miller, Patrick, 3128
Miller, Peggy J., 3240
Miller, Rita M., 2758
Miller, Shane A., 3132
Miller, Toby, 1508, 3408
Miller, Vernon D., 2645, 2745
Millette, Diane M., 3201
Millhous, Lisa M., 1528
Mills, Melanie B., 0178, 4163
Mills, Ryan D., 3507
Millsap, Susan P., 2569
Minch, Kevin M., 3471, 4160
Mindel, Francine M., 1430
Mineo, Paul J., 2643, 2738
Minielli, Maureen C., 1230, 3522, 4335
Mink, Bernadette, 3622
Mino, Mary, 2524
Miraglia Lindsay, Gwen, 3143
Mitchell, Gordon R., 1172, 1466, 2566, 3632
Mitchell, Innes W. R., 1222
Mitchell, Joseph, 2524
Mitchell, Karen S., 4240
Mitchell, Nancy E., 3462
Mitchell, W.J. T., 2552
Mitnick, Andrea D., 1306

Mitra, Ananda, 2759
Miyahara, Akira, 3659
Mladenka, Jennifer D., 3233
Modaff, Daniel P., 2269, 3440
Modaff, Lawrence M., 2269
Moemeka, Andrew A., 2414, 4124
Moffitt, Kimberly R., 3136, 3424
Mohr, Cynthia D., 3206
Mohsen, Raed A., 3430
Mohundro, Sarah L., 1357
Molden, Dan T., 1646, 3429
Monahan, Diane M., 3237
Monfils, Barbara S., 3535
Monge, Peter R., 2545
Mongeau, Ann Marie, 2201
Mongeau, Paul A., 0418, 0815, 2543, 2815, 3119, 3219, 3418, 4118
Mongia, Radhika, 3208
Monroe, Bethanie, 3174
Montalbano-Phelps, Lori, 4241
Montano, Daniel, 1437
Montgomery, Barbara M., 0114
Montgomery, Carol, 1369
Moon, Dreama G., 1108, 1527, 2223, 2316, 2533, 3321
Moore, Cindy, 2169
Moore, Linda L., 0418, 3418, 4118
Moore, Meredith A., 2541
Moore, Michael R., 2326
Moore, Nina-Jo, 0114, 3272
Moorti, Sujata, 2723
Moreau, Michelle, 1638, 3442
Morello, John T., 2422, 3308
Morgan, Carol A., 0724, 2526, 4125
Morgan, Eric L., 1214
Morgan, Jayne M., 2124
Morgan, Susan E., 1656, 3256
Morimoto Yoshida, Yuko, 2416
Morin, Aysel, 1315
Morley, Donald D., 3139
Morman, Mark T., 2435
Morr, Mary Clair, 1315, 3119
Morreale, Sherwyn P., 0123, 0418, 1157, 2237, 2319, 2525, 3143, 3314, 3418, 4118
Morrill, Joshua H., 1615
Morris, Charles E., 3126, 3466, 3619
Morris, Heather, 1406
Morris, Melinda M., 1537
Morris, Richard, 0418, 0815, 1231, 2815, 3127, 3418, 4118
Morris, Scott B., 2206
Morris, Stanley, 1429, 3432
Morrison, Carlos D., 1521, 2130, 2628, 3136, 3633
Morrison, Kelly, 1543, 4238
Morrow, Terence S., 1266, 3467
Mortensen, C. David, 3160
Mortenson, Steven T., 2445
Morton-Brown, Marla A., 1210
Moss, Christina L., 2173, 2231, 3531

Mottet, Timothy P., 2226, 2554, 2626, 3154, 3554
Mughazy, Mustafa, 2437
Muir, Clive, 1314
Muir, Janette K., 0746, 2230, 2740
Muir, Star A., 3630
Muldrew, Benjamin, 2619
Mullen, Lawrence J., 3206
Muller, Heidi L., 1652, 3140
Mumby, Dennis K., 1339, 2245
Mummert, Jack, 2173
Mund, Matthew D., 1242
Mundy, Frank, 1616
Munoz, Jose, 2411
Munshaw, Joe A., 1362
Muppidi, Sundeep R., 1359
Murfield, Loren O., 1118, 3142, 3462
Murphy, Alexandra G., 1139, 1445, 3135
Murphy, B. Keith, 1332, 3531
Murphy, Bren O., 1228, 2722
Murphy, Janet L., 4322
Murphy, John M., 1134, 3552
Murphy, Patrick D., 1507
Murphy, Sally K., 1239
Murphy, Tracy L., 2201
Murray, Jeffrey W., 1457, 2257, 3565
Murray-Johnson, Lisa M., 2435, 4134
Musambira, George W., 3629
Myers, Eddie, 1430, 3173
Myers, Scott A., 0724, 1549, 1618, 2201, 2226, 2626, 3154, 3449, 4125
Myrick, Roger K., 4355
Nabi, Robin L., 1606, 2538, 3256, 3542
Nadjar, Ann, 1347
Nadler, Lawrence, 3629
Nainby, Keith E., 1619
Najor, Michele A., 3444
Nakagawa, Gordon W., 1659, 2759
Nakanishi, Masayuki, 3543
Nakayama, Thomas K., 0137, 0815, 1525, 1646, 2327, 2508, 2815, 4116
Nalley, Sara L., 4115
Nance, Teresa A., 1269, 2621, 3221
Narang Sawhney, Deepak, 2108
Nash, John, 2272
Natalle, Elizabeth J., 1228
Natharius, David, 0106, 3141, 3236
Nebashi, Reiko, 2516
Neer, Michael R., 3132
Neidig, Judith L., 1137, 2718
Nelson, Elizabeth J., 0418, 3418, 4118
Nelson, Jeffrey, 1355
Nelson, Jenny, 2444
Nelson, John S., 1451
Nelson, Katherine L., 2618, 4130
Nelson, Mark, 2673
Nelson, Mark D., 2249, 3549
Nelson, Patricia S., 2406
Nelson, Paul E., 0418, 2328, 2649, 3418, 4118
Nelson, Richard A., 1231
Nelson, Sam, 4321

Nero, Charles I., 2324
Neuleib, Robert D., 2756
Neumann, David R., 2159
Newell, Jay, 2235
Newman, Marc T., 1262, 3534, 4233
Newman, Robert P., 3315
Newman, Sara J., 4244
Ng, Debbie, 1137
Nicholson, John H., 0114, 2418
Nicotera, Anne M., 0418, 1645, 3418, 3621, 4118, 4236
Niles, Lyndrey A., 2178, 3224
Nimocks, Mittie J. A., 0114, 2112, 4238
Nir, Lilach, 1606
Nishino, Yoshimi, 1336
Nitcavic, Richard G., 4139
Nitz, Michael E., 3553
Nix, Chris L., 1351, 3137, 4134
Nix, James, 1343
Noels, Kimberly A., 2651
Noggle, Gary A., 2537, 2639, 3159
Nolle, Vicki L., 1225
North, Christine L., 4227
Northup, Brent, 2132, 2269, 2730, 3657
Norton, Hanna, 2121
Norton, Heather, 3169
Novek, Eleanor M., 3507
Nudd, Donna M., 1410, 1610, 2311
Nussbaum, Jon F., 1455, 1551, 4127
Nwoso, Peter, 2421, 4124
Nyquist, Jody D., 2535
O'Brien, Carrie, 1125
O'Brien, Jill L., 3135
O'Brien Hallstein, D. Lynn, 1646, 2536, 2725
O'Connell, Brian M., 1429, 3432
O'Connor, Margaret, 1310
O'Connor, Marybeth, 1338
O'Connor, Penny, 2649
O'Donnell, Brett M., 1172
O'Donnell, Timothy M., 1466, 1632, 2266
O'Geary, James S., 3537
O'Hair, H. Dan, 0815, 1443, 1546, 2815, 3626, 4127
O'Hara, Michael M., 3215, 3624
O'Keefe, Barbara J., 2545
O'Keefe, Daniel J., 2143
O'Keefe, Virginia P., 2632, 3143, 3642
O'Mara, Joan, 2555
O'Mara, John, 2555
O'Rourke, Sean, 0141, 0815, 1647, 2646, 2815
O'Shaughnessy, Meghan, 2457
O'Sullivan, Patrick B., 2107, 2607
Obotetukudo, Solomon W., 1442, 3421
Obregon, Rafael, 1343, 3661
Odendahl, Jules A., 2211
Odom, Minuen A., 1625
Oetzel, John G., 1618, 3616
Ofulue, Nneka I., 2562
Ohashi, Rie, 2516
Ohland, Christopher J., 3625

Okabe, Roichi, 1116, 3659
Okigbo, Charles C., 4124
Okoli, Emeka J., 3262
Okuda, Hiroku, 1116
Olaniran, Bolanle A., 1107, 1541, 1655
Oldham, Jessica, 1257
Oliver, Mary Beth, 0724, 2138, 2727, 4125
Olsher, David, 2236
Olson, Clark D., 2273, 2547, 2647, 3530
Olson, Kathryn M., 2115, 2419
Olson, Lester C., 3623
Olson, Loreen N., 1315, 1623
Olson, Marisa S., 3138
Olson, Mark J.V., 2111
Olson, Scott R., 2414, 4139
Omolodun, Olateju S., 1410
Ono, Kent A., 0724, 1439, 2108, 2456,
    3108, 3506, 3631, 4125
Onoda, Natsu, 2911
Onwumechili, Chukwuka A., 2616, 3416
Opffer, Elenie E., 1670
Oppliger, Patrice A., 2138
Orban, Donald K., 1649
Orbe, Mark P., 1122, 2234, 2521, 3524,
    4236
Orrego, Victoria, 2435
Orthmann, Lee, 3257
Osborn, Michael M., 2322
Osterman, Heather M., 1533
Ostrenko, Margaret Z., 3651
Ott, Jennifer, 1333
Over, William, 2553
Owen, A. Susan, 1131, 2440, 3234, 3615
Pace, Roger C., 2249
Packer, Jeremy, 1408, 2134, 4308
Packman, Hollie, 1556
Padilla, Mariposa, 1641
Page, Deborah, 3245
Pagel, Sonya K., 3564
Pagen, Michele A., 1224, 1616, 2174, 2731,
    3130, 3215
Paine, Richard E., 3273
Palczewski, Catherine H., 0140, 1123, 2115,
    3653, 4123
Palenchar, Michael J., 2241
Palmer, Akilah, 1521
Palmer, David L., 2658
Palmeri, Tony J., 1565, 2665
Palmgreen, Philip C., 1656
Panetta, Edward M., 2326, 4122
Pardo, Miri, 2526
Parenio, Sue, 4129
Parisi, Barbara, 2174, 2574, 4115
Park, Hee Sun, 1416
Park-Fuller, Linda M., 3110
Parker, Lea J., 1229, 2453
Parker, Richard A., 1229, 3253, 3546
Parker, Robyn E., 1565
Parker, Sara J., 2236
Parr, N. Carlotta, 1340
Parrella, Gilda C., 3638
Parrett, Danette R., 4263

Parrish-Sprowl, John, 2414, 3323, 4226
Parrott, Roxanne, 0418, 0815, 1231, 1345,
    2627, 2815, 3253, 3418, 3627, 4118
Parry-Giles, Shawn J., 1619, 2119
Parry-Giles, Trevor, 2119
Partain, David, 3144
Partlow, Sarah T., 2572
Parton, Sabrena R., 1201
Pascarell, Rose, 3236
Pasha, Nilofer H., 1506
Pastorek, Angela, 2531
Patel, Dhaval S., 2435, 2549
Patterson, Brian R., 1551, 2201
Patterson, James D., 2245
Patterson-Pratt, Julie R., 1143, 1616, 2174,
    2474, 2731, 3130, 3274
Patton, Gregory H., 0106, 2112, 3135
Pauley, Garth E., 2421
Pauley, John L., 2262, 2629, 3636
Pauley, Kathi L., 1435
Pauli, Carol, 2412
Paulson, Jon W., 3419
Pavlich, Margaret E.M., 1241
Pawlowski, Donna R., 1549, 1618, 3529,
    4228
Payne, Holly J., 2254
Payne, J. Gregory, 1134, 2431
Payne, Kay E., 2254
Paynor, Margaret, 1157, 2457
Paystrup, Patricia, 2253
Peacock, Susi, 3416
Pearce, Kimber C., 2762
Pearce, W. Barnett, 2722
Pearson, Judy C., 0114, 0418, 1431, 2151,
    2328, 2447, 2742, 3418, 3646, 4118
Pearson, Kyra L., 2201, 3519, 3623
Pearson, Michael V., 1269
Pecchioni, Loretta L., 1656, 3651, 4127
Peck, Nan J., 1346
Pecora, Norma, 2551
Pedersen, Isabel, 1201
Pednekar-Magal, Vandana, 1359
Peeples, Jennifer A., 2253
Pelias, Ronald J., 3110
Pendell, Sue D., 0418, 3418, 4118
Penington, Barbara A., 2412
Pennington, Dorthy, 3221
Pennock-Delgado, Kristie, 3664
Perea, Elizabeth, 4363
Perez, Frank G., 4261
Perger, Ronald A., 1628, 4355
Perkins, Terry M., 0107, 1549
Perlich, John R., 2242, 3273
Perrigo, Eileen M., 0106, 2046, 2469, 2669
Perry, Ben J., 1343
Perry, Danielle, 3533
Perry, Krin B., 1226
Perry, Lisa A., 3467
Perry, Stephen D., 1201, 3606
Perse, Elizabeth M., 2438, 2506, 3319
Persi, Nina C., 2107, 4154
Perucci, Anthony T., 3410, 4108

Petefish, Amanda, 1224
Peters, Kelly J., 4332
Petersen, Debra L., 2739
Peterson, Eric E., 1210, 3463
Peterson, Jennifer L., 1115, 1137, 1607, 3612, 4227
Peterson, Tarla R., 2751
Peterson, Valerie V., 3565
Peticolas, Alison P., 1670, 2257
Petrello, Rolland C., 3612
Petronio, Sandra, 0121, 0859, 1315, 4254
Pezzullo, Phaedra C., 1453, 4216, 4353
Pfafman, Tessa M., 1237
Pfau, Michael, 0724, 1145, 1506, 1606, 2422, 3256, 4125
Pfau, Michael W., 2719
Philipsen, Gerry F., 0116, 2263, 3240
Phillips, Ed, 2139, 4140
Phillips, Julie D., 1638, 2655, 3465
Phillips, Kendall R., 4208
Phillips, Penny A., 1563
Phillips-Gott, Patricia C., 2421, 3621
Phipps, Kim S., 2629, 3462, 3636
Picart, Caroline Joan S., 1435
Pici, frances anne, 4315
Pickering, Barbara A., 3653
Pickett, James R., 2266
Pierce, Camisha, 3430
Pierce, Dann L., 3462
Piercy, Karen R., 1432, 1635, 4132
Pietri, Myrna, 0418, 2227, 2661, 2761, 3230, 3418, 4118, 4225
Piland, Jamey A., 3236
Pilotta, Joseph, 2264
Pineau, Elyse L., 1327, 1510, 4149
Pineda, Richard D., 1565, 1653, 2272
Pitzer, Nathan, 1325
Pixy, Sharmila, 1456
Planalp, Sally, 0418, 3119, 3219, 3418, 4118, 4225
Plax, Timothy G., 3324
Plec, Emily J., 1537, 2123
Pledger, Linda M., 1460, 2244
Ploeger-Tsoulos, Joanna S., 2566
Plotkin, Richard S., 2531
Plummer, Evelyn J., 3214
Pober, Peter M., 3316
Pohl, Gayle M., 1341, 1541
Poirot, Kristan, 1525
Pokora, Rachel, 1245
Polacheck, Lori A., 2173
Polcar, Leah E., 3140, 4252
Polk, Kent J., 1422
Pollitt, Brent K., 3455
Pollock, Della, 2411, 2527
Pollock, John C., 1406
Pollock, Mark A., 2722, 3552
Pomerantz, Anita M., 0116, 1436, 4234, 4344
Pomper, Markus, 3540

Poole, Marshall S., 0418, 0815, 1115, 1231, 1428, 1528, 2514, 2815, 3418, 4118, 4225
Poole Martinez, Stephanie, 2463
Poorani, Ali A., 1539
Popovich, Deidre L., 4238
Porhola, Maili, 2201
Porter, Jeanne L., 1624, 4351
Porter, Sharon B., 1230
Posner, Jeanne S., 0114, 1646, 3316
Post, Douglas M., 1345
Post, Robert M., 4315
Potee, Nanette, 2201
Potts, M. Lee, 3474
Potts, T. G., 4352
Poulakos, John, 2171, 3671
Poulakos, Takis, 2171
Poulos, Chris N., 1252, 1407
Poulsen, Susan B., 4228
Pounds, Keith C., 1130, 3655
Powell, Kimberly A., 2326
Power, Christopher, 2749
Powers, John H., 2553, 2716
Powers, William G., 3155
Poyner, Barry C., 0141, 3647, 4162
Prather, Danna E., 1651, 2528, 2612, 3228, 3523, 4121
Pratt, Cornelius B., 2414, 4341
Pratt, Steven B., 2763
Preisinger, Catherine, 1257
Preiss, Ray W., 2638
Prescott, Margaret E., 4238
Press, Andrea, 4363
Pribyl, Charles B., 2555
Price, Joseph M., 1166
Prisco, Gabrielle, 1223
Prividera, Laura C., 1151
Proctor, Russell F., 1158, 2754
Projansky, Sarah, 2440
Propp, Kathleen M., 1238
Prosser, Michael H., 1570, 2553
Prusank, Diane T., 1618
Przybylo, Jeff F., 2242, 3612
Ptacek, Karen M., 2638
Puchot, Raymond C., 1557, 1646, 2137, 2227, 3230, 3612
Puckett, Anita, 2711
Pudlinski, Christopher J., 2141
Pulaski, Michelle M., 3206
Purdy, Michael W., 1530
Pym, Anne, 1451
Quainoo, Vanessa W., 4351
Querido, Ernesto, 4321
Query, Jim L., 2722, 3129, 3229, 3427
Quianthy, Richard L., 2131, 2656, 3232, 3307
Quigley, Brooke, 0114
Quinn, Laura, 2207
Rabe, Benjamin J., 3625
Rademacher, Lee M., 3649
Ragan, Sandra L., 1238, 1537, 1636, 2308, 3436, 4134, 4227

Rakova, Vanda, 1335, 3133
Ralston, Steven M., 3529
Ram, Anjali, 2223, 2663, 3116
Ramirez, Artemio, 2743
Ramirez Berg, Charles, 1361
Ramos, Lori C., 1201
Rampal, Kuldip, 1233
Rampoldi-Hnilo, Lynn A., 1661, 3206
Ramsey, Michele E., 2635
Ramsey, Ramsey Eric, 2644
Rancer, Andrew S., 1543, 2643
Randall, Neil F., 1201
Randels, Kathy, 3410
Rangel, Nicolas, 4222
Rankin, Caroline T., 1343
Ranney, Frances J., 4235
Ranta, Richard R., 0114, 1404, 1647, 2541,
    2646
Rao, Anand, 1172, 2266, 2466, 3553
Rao, Nagesh, 1316, 3227, 3515
Rapp, Michael D., 3555
Rascon, Luz Elvia, 3461
Rasmussen, Karen, 4223
Rathbun, Renton, 3662
Ratliff, Gerald Lee, 1142, 1616, 2174, 2474,
    2574, 3608, 4215
Ratliffe, Sharon A., 2447, 2615, 4242
Ratzan, Scott C., 3439
Rawe, Jennifer, 3653
Rawlins, Brad L., 2446
Rawlins, William K., 1463, 1657
Ray, Angela G., 1364, 3471
Ray, Eileen B., 1337, 2523
Ray, George B., 2523, 4228
Real, Kevin J., 1115, 1227
Record, Angela R., 1423
Reding, Stephanie M., 3123
Redmond, Mark V., 3514
Redmond, Patti A., 4257
Reed, Edwin A., 3606
Reed, Jackie, 1443
Reed, James W., 3538
Reed, Lori K., 1337, 1423
Reed, William R., 2638
Reel, Bradley W., 1557
Reffue, John D., 1557, 2557
Rehling, Diana L., 3134, 4228
Reich, Nina M., 1464, 2725, 4223
Reichert, Tom, 1506, 3256
Reid, Ronald F., 2157
Reid-Martinez, Kathaleen, 3262
Ren, Li, 3227
Renegar, Valerie R., 2272, 2572
Rentschler, Carrie, 1408
Reppert, James E., 3438
Retzinger, Jean P., 0724, 2427, 3032, 4125
Reynolds, J. Lynn, 3201
Reynolds, Rodney A., 3319, 4262
Rhea, Jill, 1614
Rhee, Jieun, 1464
Rhodes, Jack L., 1526
Ribeau, Sidney A., 2246, 2328

Ricciotti, Lisa A., 2531
Rice, Donald E., 1342
Rice, Jody, 2173
Rice, Jonah L., 2229
Richards, Gale L., 3156
Richardson, Brian K., 1245, 3643
Richardson, Laurel, 2757, 4157, 4310
Richardson, Randolph, 1332, 2173, 2231,
    2326, 3531
Richmond, Virginia P., 1655, 2444
Richter, Christopher J., 2264
Riddle, Bruce L., 1115, 1539, 2215
Riffe, Nancy A., 1223
Rigdon, Jennifer L., 1169
Riggins, Jana M., 3454
Rigsby, Enrique D., 1421
Riley, Doris, 4333
Riley, Robin, 4233
Ringer, R. Jeffrey, 0135
Rintamaki, Lance, 3540, 4363
Riordan, Ellen, 1423
Ritchie, David, 1131
Ritsma, Natasha, 2134
Ritter, Kurt, 4222
Ritz, Brenda K., 2638
Roach, K. David, 1655, 3154, 3449
Robbins, Jean, 3616
Roberto, Anthony J., 1543
Roberts, Charles, 1326, 1530
Roberts, Felicia, 1436, 1537
Roberts, Kellie W., 1232, 2146, 2326, 3247
Roberts, Laura R., 2743
Roberts, Mary M., 1554
Robertson, Craig, 1508, 2134, 4308
Robertson, Rissa, 3606
Robertson, Terry A., 2135, 2539, 3201
Robichaud, Daniel, 3564
Robinson, Jeffrey D., 1436, 1536, 3440
Robinson, Rena Y., 0418, 3418, 4118
Robinson, William L., 3149
Rocca, Kelly A., 2538, 3154
Rock, Robert C., 3439
Rockler, Naomi R., 4264
Rockwell, Steven C., 1553
Rodgers, R. Pierre, 0418, 1421, 3418, 4118
Rodino, Michelle L., 1466, 3266, 4336
Rodino, Virginia T., 1441, 2315
Rodrigues, Pravin A., 2529, 2633, 3429
Rodriguez, America, 1361
Rodriguez-Gilman, Eldra, 2160
Roe, Kim, 1332
Roe, Rick, 1332
Roebuck, Erick J., 3534
Rogan, Randall, 3171, 3270, 3447, 3547
Rogers, Everett M., 3515
Rogers, Jack E., 3172
Rogers, L. Edna, 0121, 1626
Rogers-Pascual, Maria, 2661
Roghaar, Lisa A., 2418
Rohlfing, Mary E., 3544
Rollins, Joel D., 1153, 1344, 1672, 2654
Rolls, Judith A., 1340

Roloff, Karen M., 0106, 0724, 1369, 2046, 2160, 4125
Roloff, Leland, 1110, 1310
Romanelli, David M., 3572
Romanowski, William D., 1362, 4333
Roome, Dorothy M., 3239
Roos, Nancy N., 1364
Roper, Shannon L., 1230
Ropp, Cyd C., 4243
Rosado, Teresa M., 2167, 2428, 2567, 3467
Rose, Heidi M., 1327, 3264
Rose, Nancy Oft, 0418, 3418, 4118
Rosen, Eric, 2311, 2911
Rosenoir, Derrick, 1318, 2169
Roskos-Ewoldsen, Beverly, 1506
Roskos-Ewoldsen, David R., 1506, 2443
Ross, Peter G., 3406, 4316
Ross, Roseanna G., 0106
Ross, Shawna, 3673
Ross, Susan M., 2623, 4152
Ross, Susan Mallon, 1429, 1564, 3658
Rosser, Jane, 1359
Rossow, Marshel D., 1336
Rost Goulen, Nancy, 4316
Rosteck, Thomas, 3552
Rothenbuhler, Eric W., 3106
Rothman Bradley, Korey, 1201
Rothwell, William J, 1201
Rountree, J. Clarke, 2446
Routsong, Tracy, 4332
Roux, James C., 2201
Rowan, Katherine E., 2433
Rowe, Carol, 1365
Rowett, Kelly, 4110
Rowland, Robert C., 1222, 3451
Roy, Jody M., 3522, 3619
Rubin, Alan M., 1506
Rubin, Janet E., 1226
Rudd, Andrew E., 1514
Ruddick, Thomas E., 2028, 2174, 2733, 3028
Rufo, Kenneth A., 3152
Rumbough, Timothy B., 2122, 2412
Rushing, Janice H., 2140
Russell, Jane A., 2718
Russo, Tracy C., 1433, 2444, 3145, 3607
Rust, Joseph H., 1557
Rutherford, Denney G., 1539
Rutledge, Lewis E., 1662
Rutter, Jon D., 1164, 1425
Ryan, Daniel J., 3265
Ryan, Halford R., 3530
Ryan, Melanie J., 1406
Ryan, Stephen M., 1116
Rybacki, Donald J., 3444
Rybacki, Karyn C., 3444
Ryden, Patricia A., 4264
Sabee, Christina M., 2272, 3554, 3614
Sabetta, Thomas J., 0418, 2028, 2733, 3028, 3418, 4118, 4225
Sage, Diana M., 2207
Sahlstein, Erin M., 2243, 3435, 4134, 4338

Sakamoto, Masahiro, 2555
Salazar, James B., 1164
Salazar, Philippe J., 3239
Salinas, Christopher D., 1565, 1653, 3139
Sallot, Lynne M., 2241
Salmon, Charles T., 2433
Salo, Colleen, 2438
Saltmarsh, John, 0123, 3314
Samp, Jennifer A., 1231
Sampedro Blanco, Victor Federico, 2606
Samra, Rise J., 1243, 4341
Samter, Wendy, 2445
Sandel, Todd L., 1352, 3240
Sanders, Gerald H., 1677, 2157, 2434, 3156, 3557
Sanders, Omari, 2525
Sanders, Robert E., 0116, 2308, 3140
Sanderson, Cami M., 1469
Sandine, Brian, 1245, 3445
Sandmann, Warren G., 1229, 2631, 4129
Sani, M. H., 3524
Sargent, Jack E., 1315
Sargent, Margaret M., 3540
Sargent, Stephanie L., 1356, 3606
Sarkela, Sandra J., 2758
Sartorius Kraidy, Ute, 3516
Sasina, Kathryn, 3201
Sasseen, Marianne, 2714
Sattell, Susan S., 1210, 1665
Saunders, Vickey, 1334
Sauter, Kevin O., 2739
Savage, Ann M., 1323
Sawyer, Chris R., 0724, 2126, 3233, 3455, 3555, 4125
Sawyer, J. Kanan, 1606
Schaefer-Faix, Noreen M., 1170, 2201
Schaller, Kristi A., 1430, 2249, 3549
Scharrer, Erica, 1251
Schegloff, Emanual, 1536
Schely Newman, Esther, 3663
Schenone-Stevens, M. Carla, 1235, 2201, 2412
Schiappa, Edward, 1552, 2152, 2734
Schickel, Kristy, 2241
Schliesman, Terence S., 3555
Schliessmann, Michael R., 3471
Schmidt, Jacqueline, 1342, 2442, 2642
Schmidt, Lainen, 2241
Schmidt, Wallace V., 1458
Schmitt, Julie, 3174
Schmitt, Kelly L., 1114
Schmitz, Joseph, 3266
Schneider, Cory A., 2636
Schneider, Priscilla A., 1643, 2412
Schneider, Rebecca, 2411
Schneider, Stacy, 2531
Schnell, James A., 1660, 2149, 3241, 3430, 3670
Schnoor, Larry, 1232, 1432, 1635, 2573, 2657, 3273, 3530
Schnurer, Maxwell, 1572, 4153
Scholl, Juliann C., 2443

Schonfeldt-Aultman, Scott M., 2456, 3239
Schrader, David C., 1540
Schrag, Calvin L., 2462
Schreiber, Lisa M., 2123, 2521, 4230
Schriver, Kristina L., 1610, 2172, 3473
Schrodt, Paul, 1625, 2638
Schroeder, Anthony B., 3242
Schroeder, Lisa M., 1506
Schroeder, Stephen P., 3612
Schroll, Chris, 3506
Schueler, Judy, 3439
Schuessler, Joel, 1639
Schuetz, Janice E., 2667
Schultz, David P., 3207
Schultz, Jennifer, 1242
Schultz, Pamela D., 2537
Schultze, Quentin J., 1262
Schwartz, Karola M., 4322
Schwartzman, Roy J., 1344, 1451, 2322, 2654, 3128, 3308, 4129, 4321
Schwarz, Edward A., 1649, 2137
Schweers, Kathryn, 3642
Scott, Andrea T., 3643
Scott, Catherine, 3416
Scott, Craig R., 1428, 1615, 2124, 2207, 3555
Scott, Cynthia, 3257
Scott, Erika Rae, 3257
Scott, Karla D., 2324
Scott, Maria M., 2142
Scott, Ronald B., 3121, 3221
Scott, Sherry B., 3433
Scott, Tamara, 3424
Scovell, Paul E., 1404, 2228, 2570
Scult, Allen M., 1472, 2252
Scuorzo, Dawn, 1406
Secklin, Pam L., 4163
Seeger, Matthew W., 1546, 2132, 2319, 2537, 2631, 2730, 3626
Seelig, Michelle I., 4121
Sefcovic, Enid, 1422
Sefton, Lori A., 2139, 4140
Segaard, Matthew W., 4143
Segrin, Chris, 2518, 3119
Seibert, Stacy, 3612
Seibold, David R., 0418, 1615, 2556, 2619, 3237, 3418, 4118
Seifert, Angie, 3625
Seiler, William J., 0107, 2749, 3137, 3649
Seiter, John S., 1459
Selby, Gary S., 1562
Self, Lois S., 0114, 1623
Selfridge, Melanie J., 2621
Sellnow, Deanna D., 0107, 1161, 2430, 2530
Sellnow, Timothy L., 0106, 1161, 2657
Semati, M. Mehdi, 1233, 1535
Sen, Ruma J., 2708
Senecah, Susan L., 2427, 3032, 4353
Sequeira, Debra-Lynn, 1462, 2162
Serro-Boim, Anastacia D., 2322, 4129
Settle, Peter L., 1157

Sewell, Edward, 2740
Sewell, Jessica, 1408
Seymour, Ruth A., 3524
Shachar, Orly, 1523
Shaffer, Dusty, 3667
Shailor, Jonathan G., 2564
Shanahan, William E., 4153
Shaner, Jaye L., 1551, 2746
Shapiro, Alan J., 3610
Shapiro, Brian S., 1425
Shapiro, Elayne J., 1551
Sharf, Barbara F., 1333, 2544
Shaw, Charla L., 2446
Shaw, Marilyn M., 2449
Shea, B. Christine, 2623, 4136
Sheckels, Theodore F., 0724, 1145, 1319, 1633, 2142, 2442, 2539, 2726, 4125, 4322
Shedletsky, Leonard J., 0143, 1239, 2707, 3158
Sheehan, Megan A., 3206
Sheffield, William T., 3572
Shefner-Rogers, Corinne, 3515
Shelley, Deborah B., 3155
Shelton, Michael W., 2749
Shemwell, Lisa D., 3173
Shen, Jinguo, 2170
Shepard, Carolyn A., 1315
Shepherd, Gregory J., 1223, 3106
Shepler, Sherry R., 3108, 3452, 4325
Sherblom, John C., 2707, 3407, 3616
Sherry, John L., 2237
Shields, Donald C., 1242
Shields, Ronald E., 0418, 1110, 1610, 2174, 2527, 3418, 4115, 4118, 4225
Shih, Joy Christina, 3655
Shim, Doobo, 3639
Shimpach, Shawn, 3519
Shires, V. Jeffrey, 0142, 1362
Shirono, Itsuo, 3458
Shissias, Anthony, 3257
Shockley-Zalabak, Pamela S., 1539, 2224, 3145
Shoemaker, Deanna B., 4310
Shome, Raka, 2327, 2408, 2508, 3535, 3631
Shomesh, Michael, 3257
Shotter, John, 2321
Shouse, Eric, 4108
Shubin, Tim, 1201
Shue, Laura L., 1614, 2164, 2460
Shugart, Helene A., 2608, 3223
Shuler, Sherianne, 1223
Shumate, Michelle, 1556
Shuter, Robert, 1133, 1215, 2415
Shyles, Leonard, 3506
Sias, Patricia M., 1445, 2224, 2745
Siddall, Ralph W., 3265
Siddens, Paul J., 2630
Siegel, Paul, 2531
Sievert, Andrew, 3606
Sigman, Stuart J., 2737, 4334

Signer, Jordana M. K., 3145
Signorielli, Nancy, 2438
Silberg, Kelsey, 2531
Silk, Kami J., 4327
Sillars, Malcolm O., 0859
Siltanen, Susan A., 1647, 2646
Silva, Michelle, 1335
Silva, Vesta T., 1651
Silvestri, Vito N., 1134
Simerly, Greggory D., 1627, 2129, 3169, 3635
Simonds, Cheri J., 3449, 3549, 4249
Simons, Herbert W., 1466, 2265
Simonson, Peter D., 2752, 3106
Simpson, Jennifer L., 1670
Simpson, Timothy A., 2216
Sims, Anntarie L., 2130, 2521, 3136, 3633
Singh, Mukhbir, 3238
Singhal, Arvind, 1343, 2627, 3227, 3661
Singleton, Loy A., 1553
Sinha Roy, Ishita, 2223
Sintay, G. Scott, 1354
Sisco, John I., 0114
Sisson, Richard K., 3434
Sitaram, K. S., 2553
Siuyi Wong, Wendy, 3644
Skarphol Kaml, Shannon, 1652, 2658, 3456
Skiles, Christopher J., 2201, 2761, 3271, 3542
Skourup, Jan, 2112
Skow, Lisa M., 2736
Slack, Jennifer D., 1208, 1535
Slagell, Amy R., 0107, 1219, 2578, 2749
Slagle, Ray A., 0418, 0815, 1231, 1628, 2242, 2534, 2815, 3126, 3418, 4118
Slayden, David, 1322
Sloat, James M., 1128
Sloop, John M., 0137, 2429, 3615
Smit, Christopher R., 1155
Smith, Craig A., 1647, 2522, 2646
Smith, Craig R., 2531, 2762, 3107
Smith, Daniel L., 1432, 1635, 3273, 3530
Smith, David H., 2722
Smith, Guy, 2745
Smith, John W., 1629
Smith, Karen A., 3249
Smith, Kim, 1449
Smith, Matthew, 4315
Smith, Matthew J., 2107, 2238, 3137
Smith, Michael F., 2201, 3270, 3447, 3547
Smith, Rachel, 4361
Smith, Ralph R., 1628, 2155, 3126, 3522
Smith, Robert M., 0114, 1554, 2406, 3232, 3656
Smith, Roger W., 0724, 1642, 2507, 4125
Smith, Ross, 1672
Smith, Sandi W., 1543
Smith, Sherri, 0114, 2324
Smith, Stephen A., 2415, 3658
Smith, Tia L., 1321
Smitter, Roger, 3608
Smyres, Kerrie M., 1625, 3123

Smythe, Mary J., 3629
Snee, Brian J., 3464, 3522
Snider, A. C., 4321
Snider, Kevin J. G., 2524
Snively, Morris E., 0418, 2256, 2632, 3143, 3418, 4118, 4225
Snow, Brian C., 3253
Snowden, Monique L., 1115, 1545
Snyder, Leslie B., 3436
Sobnosky, Matthew J., 2115
Socha, Thomas J., 0121, 0418, 1126, 1231, 1518, 1647, 2218, 2646, 3418, 3628, 4118, 4225
Soderlund, Gretchen, 3508
Sohl, Laura L., 2449, 2649
Solomon, Denise H., 0724, 3219, 3443, 4125
Sommer, Steven M., 1328
Somrak, Theresa M., 3439
Song, Jong-Gil, 2739
Sopory, Pradeep, 2738, 3540
Sotirin, Patricia J., 1434, 1535, 3663, 4323
Sotomayor, Olga A., 1619
Soukup, Charles E., 1315, 3407
Soukup, Paul A., 1230, 1534, 2669
Soule, Kari P., 3655
Souza, Tasha J., 2321, 2454
Sowards, Stacey K., 2272
Sowder, Fred, 3436
Spangle, Michael L., 2433, 3161
Spangler, Matthew J., 1310
Spann, Thomas, 2642, 4342
Spano, Shawn, 2321
Sparaco, Lisa A., 1406
Speakman, Shanna R., 2549
Spemizza, Denise, 2112
Spicer, Greg, 1135, 3666
Spiecker, Shelley C., 2167, 2267
Spielvogel, J. Christian, 4108
Spiker, Chance, 2638
Spiker, Julia A., 2639
Spirek, Melissa M., 1154
Spitler, John, 3667
Spitzberg, Brian H., 4254
Sprague, Jo, 0815, 1130, 2535, 2815, 4326
Sprague, Rhonda J., 2218, 4238
Springston, Jeff K., 0418, 0815, 1441, 2426, 2744, 2815, 3244, 3418, 3637, 4118, 4227
Sprinkle, Matthew B., 2156
Spry, Tami L., 0178, 1427, 3110
Squires, Catherine R., 2121
Sriussadaporn-Charoenngam, Nongluck, 2216
St. Clair, Diane, 3144
Stabile, Carol, 3266, 3508
Stacks, Don W., 0114, 1141
Stafford, Laura L., 1343, 2518
Stage, Christina W., 1463, 2511
Staley, Constance, 4331
Stallard, Merrie Jo, 1166, 2167, 2267
Stallworth, Virginia, 3616

Stamp, Glen H., 2418, 3540, 3643, 4128
Standerfer, Christy C., 2244, 2751
Starke-Meyerring, Doreen, 1566, 3566
Starosta, William J., 1133, 1216, 2516, 3521
Staske, Shirley A., 1126, 3628, 4134, 4344
Stavitsky, Alan, 3431
Steen, Susan, 2116
Stefani, Lisa A., 3458
Stein, Sarah R., 3541
Steinberg, David L., 2172, 3272, 3572
Steiner, Linda C., 2223
Steiner, Mark Allan, 1262, 2262
Steinfatt, Thomas M., 0155, 2553
Step, Mary M., 3606
Stephen, Timothy D., 2707, 4322
Stephens, Ronald J., 3306
Stephenson, Michael T., 1356, 1656
Stepp, Pamela L., 1228
Sterk, Helen M., 1128, 1327, 2562
Stern, Carol S., 1524
Stern, Christi, 2457
Sterne, Jonathan E., 1208, 3508
Sterns, Patrick L., 1234
Stevens, Monte, 3572
Stevenson, Ron, 1653
Stewart, Alan D., 1323
Stewart, Charles J., 2522
Stewart, John R., 2321
Stewart, Lea P., 1330, 3201
Stewart, Patricia J., 3262
Stewart, Robert A., 2262
Stewart, Stacey, 2274
Steyn, Melissa E., 3239, 4116
Stivers, Tanya, 2236, 3140, 3437
Stockton, Robert L., 0724, 2632, 4125
Stoda, Mark J., 1266
Stohl, Cynthia, 0418, 1215, 2224, 2545,
    2745, 3418, 4118, 4225
Stoll, Edwina L., 2657
Stone, Barbara, 1344, 2654
Stone, Jason, 2672
Stoner, Matt, 3607
Stormer, Nathan E., 2608, 3463
Stout, Karen R., 2645
Strader, Sara E., 3233
Strain, Lega K., 3233
Strain, Robert L., 1222
Strange, Lisa S., 1219
Strate, Lance A., 1230, 2607, 3323, 3453,
    4335
Strauman, Elena C., 2163, 2723, 4327
Strawn, Dudley, 1456
Streb, Matthew J., 1365
Street, Jessica, 3319
Street, Nancy L., 3122
Streiff, Jean A., 0418, 2114, 2632, 3418,
    4118
Strine, Mary S., 1410, 3216
Strine III, Harry C., 2547, 2647
Striphas, Theodore G., 1208, 3408
Strom, William O., 1162
Stroman, Carolyn A., 1334, 3121, 4224

Strother-Jordan, Karen E., 1122, 1624, 4351
Stuart Wilber, Daniel, 3663
Stuckey, Janice R., 2249
Stuckey, Mary E., 4222
Stucky, Nathan P., 1610, 2711
Stutman, Randall K., 2556
Subervi, Federico, 1361
Suchy, Patricia H., 4210
Sugimoto, Naomi, 1116, 4331
Sullivan, Charlotte A., 1428
Sullivan, Dale L., 1272, 1372, 2166, 2271,
    2662
Sullivan, Katherine, 2674
Sullivan, Lea Anne, 1423
Sullivan, Maggie M., 3157, 3249
Sullivan, Patricia A., 2419, 2522
Sullivan, Robert G., 2271
Sullivan, Sheila J., 1251
Sun, Jung-kuang, 3570
Sun, Zhenbin, 3570
Sung, Jenny Moon, 2156
Sunwolf, 0724, 1238, 1428, 2267, 3229,
    4125
Suopis, Cynthia A., 1214, 2637
Supriya, K. E., 2123, 2327
Surges Tatum, Donna, 3307, 3439
Susskind, Alex M., 1539
Sussman, Gerald, 1566, 2616, 3414
Sutton, David L., 3667
Sutton, Jane, 2171
Suzuki, Shinobu, 1539, 2516
Suzuki, Takeshi, 1116
Swanson, David L., 2178
Swanson, Don R., 1642, 2112, 3242
Swaroop, Sunwill, 3174
Swart, Karen, 1551
Swarts, Valerie R., 1201
Swift, Christopher N., 1552
Sypher, Howard E., 1239, 2178, 3158, 3607
Taddiken, Tawnya, 3625
Taft-Kaufman, Jill, 1201, 3110
Tallman, Amy, 1242
Tallmon, James M., 1272, 1372, 2471
Tamborini, Ron C., 0724, 2138, 2235, 3146,
    3256, 4125
Tanchisak, Krisda, 1654
Tanno, Dolores V., 1133, 1463, 2715
Tappa, Jill Nicole, 3257
Tardy, Charles H., 2116
Tardy, Rebecca W., 1343
Tate, Tara, 1625, 2572, 3672
Taylor, Anita, 0114, 1239, 2615, 3123, 3236
Taylor, Bryan C., 1339, 1563, 1670, 2127,
    2653, 2729, 3216
Taylor, Donald S., 4124
Taylor, James R., 2124, 3665
Taylor, Jeff, 3269
Taylor, Jenny A., 2743
Taylor, Juandalynn L., 1361, 2521, 3663
Taylor, Karen M., 1466, 2566
Taylor, Kelly S., 1910
Taylor, Maureen, 1441, 1641, 3533

Taylor, Orlando L., 0418, 0946, 1513, 2125, 2328, 2525, 2628, 3125, 3418, 3711, 4118

Teas Gill, Virginia, 1436

Teboul, J. C. Bruno, 3135

Tedesco, John C., 2222, 3537

Telnarova, Zdenka, 2616

Tepper, Samuel R., 2167

Terlip, Laura A., 1541, 4240

Terrill, Robert E., 1435, 2219, 2635

Terry, Suzanne, 2638

Tessmann, Renee, 4230

Teubner, Gillian, 4260

Tevelow, Amos A., 2208, 3571

Teven, Jason J., 2254

Tew, Michael A., 1635

Tewksbury, David, 2206

Thackaberry, Jennifer, 1545, 1652

Thames, Richard H., 1665, 2265, 3630

Thebus, Jessica, 2911

Thierstein, Joel, 1233

Thilborger, Chad S., 1618

Thimons, Edward D., 2435

Thirakanont, Anucha, 1233

Thomas, Cathy L., 3173

Thomas, David A., 2152, 4333

Thomas, Debyii S., 3224

Thomas, Douglas E., 0418, 3418, 3631, 4118, 4225

Thomas, Jim, 2544

Thomas, Robert, 1607

Thomas-Maddox, Candice E., 1414, 1654, 2226, 2626, 3319, 3654, 4154, 4238

Thomason, W. Ray, 1231

Thompson, Carol L., 0114, 1460, 2244, 2751

Thompson, Frank M., 2146, 3247

Thompson, Gary L., 1438

Thompson, Jennifer A., 1252

Thompson, Kathy, 1530

Thompson, Marceline E., 1454, 2244, 2314, 2751

Thompson, Robert I., 4151

Thompson, Teresa L., 1345, 4127

Thompson Issac, Jennifer, 1414

Thornock, Ronna M., 2407

Thorpe, Judith M., 1306

Thweatt, Katherine S., 3554

Tice, Elizabeth T., 1461

Tiemens, Robert K., 2178

Tieu, Trung T., 1529, 2724, 3226, 4255

Tiff, Natasha, 4128

Tillmann-Healy, Lisa M., 2543

Tillson, Lou D., 1331, 2444

Tilton, Amy M., 0724, 1125, 2528, 3107, 4125

Timmerman, C. Erik, 2207, 2507, 3129

Timmerman, David M., 2171, 2734

Timmerman, Lindsay M., 2418, 3435, 3543, 4338

Ting-Toomey, Stella, 1618

Tisdale, Julie, 2435

Titsworth, Brian S., 0107, 2630, 3137, 3254, 4254, 4354

Toale, Mary C., 2201, 2718

Tobin, Leesa E., 1159

Todd, Timothy S., 1255, 1549, 3430

Tofanelli, Jennifer L, 1201

Toland, Nasha, 3625

Toles-Patkin, Terri, 3145

Tolhuizen, James H., 4241

Tomasovic, Susan Kay, 2474, 3257

Tomlinson, James E., 2122

Tompkins, Paula S., 2319, 2534

Tompson, George, 1215

Tonn, Mari Boor, 0815, 1419, 2471, 2565, 2815

Torn, Jon Leon, 1619, 2271, 3421

Torrens, Kathleen M., 2652

Torres, Shawn A., 2708

Totland, Steve, 2911

Tovares, Raul, 2761

Townes, Shawn, 1321, 2444, 3163

Towns, Jim, 3622

Townsend, Tiffany, 2314

Townsley, Nikki C., 2645, 3139, 3201, 4123

Tracy, Karen, 0116, 1652, 2308

Tracy, Sarah J., 1645, 2463, 3237

Trapani, William C., 3228, 4153

Traudt, Paul J., 2506

Trautman, Todd C., 2172, 3537

Treadaway, Glenda J., 1627, 2129, 2326, 3635

Treichler, Paula A., 2423

Tremblay, Wilfred, 3253

Trent, Judith S., 0114, 2178, 2246, 2615

Trethewey, Angela C., 1339

Triece, Mary E., 3623, 4323

Trimarco, Allison, 3912

Trinastich, Christine E., 2201, 3643

Troester, Rod L., 2570

Trost, Melanie R., 3443

Troup, Calvin L., 1149, 1241

Trowbridge, Kevin S., 1107, 2243

Truch, Nina J., 2523

Trujillo, Mary, 4262

Trujillo, Nick L., 0178, 2263, 2732, 3263

Trumbo, Craig W., 2127

Tryboski, Julie, 3619

Tsai, Chi-Feng, 1107

Tsfati, Yariv, 1237, 1437

Tsutsui, Kumiko, 2216

Tucker, Diana L., 2528, 2612, 3249, 3544, 4121

Tucker, Terrance, 4210

Tuefel, Kenneth, 3515

Tuleja, Elizabeth A., 1201

Tuman, Joseph S., 1229, 3432

Tumas-Serna, Jane, 2264, 2747, 3264

Turman, Paul D., 0107, 1315, 3201

Turner, Jeanine W., 1607, 4227

Turner, Kathleen J., 0153, 1562, 2536

Turner, Lynn H., 0121, 0418, 0724, 1126, 1404, 3151, 3418, 3628, 4118, 4125

Turner, Paaige K., 1645, 2645, 4163
Turner, Scott, 1640
Turow, Joseph G., 1114
Turpin, Paul, 2152
Tusing, Kyle J., 2143
Tyson, Cornelius B., 2201
Tyus, Jeffrey L., 3163
Ulmer, Robert R., 0107
Underberg, Larry R., 2232, 3169
Usui, Naoto, 4231
Vaca Cortes, Jesus, 3461
Valde, Kathleen S., 3139
Valdes Caraveo, Rosario, 3461
Valdivia, Angharad N., 1423
Valdivia-Sutherland, Cynthia, 3473
Valencic, Kristin M., 2643, 3233
Valente, Tom, 2627
Valentine, Kristin B., 1427, 2511, 3235
Van Deman, Felicia B., 3235
Van Horn, Tasha L., 1639, 4242
Van Mersbergen, Audrey M., 2734
Van Rheenen, Dwayne D., 1128
Van Zant, Rita L., 2421
Vancil, David L., 1365
Vande Berg, Leah R., 0859, 2440
Vanderford, Marsha L., 1345, 2722, 3627
Vandeventer, Dee, 1341
Vangelisti, Anita L., 0121, 1532, 1618, 2314, 2518, 3119, 4130
Vankevich, Ned, 3114, 3452
Varallo, Sharon M., 2468
Vargo, Susan S., 1340
Varner, Teri L., 1363, 2234, 4310
Vartabedian, Robert A., 1526
Vasby Anderson, Karrin, 1123
Vatz, Richard E., 0144, 2157, 2214, 2433, 3222
Vavrus, Mary D., 0724, 2546, 4125, 4144, 4264
Velu, Sanjanthi, 1359
Verdell, Kim L., 2121, 2721
Verkruyse, Peter A., 1562
Vickery, Micheal R., 3507
Vigil, Tammy R., 4219
Villarruel, Francisco, 1543
Vincent, Renee, 1143, 2174, 3574
Violanti, Michelle T., 0724, 1527, 2141, 2533, 2623, 2722, 3229, 4125
Violette, Jayne L., 2412
Vivian, Bradford J., 3466
Vivion, Michael J., 3556
Vogl-Bauer, Sally M., 2538
Voight, Phillip A., 1355, 1628, 3467
Von Haeften, Ina, 1437
Vonburg, Ron, 3671
Vondrasek, Deanna, 1157
Voss, Deborah J., 2266, 3666
Voth, Ben D., 4260
Voytuk, Jim, 3125
Vrchota, Denise Ann, 1433, 2469, 3514
Vrooman, Steven S., 1325, 1608, 2763
Vukovich, Daniel, 3208

Wachtel, Tara, 1428
Waggenspack, Beth M., 0138, 3149, 4249
Waggoner, Catherine E., 3223
Wagner, Andrea T., 3510
Wagner, Thomas R., 2412
Wahl, Shawn T., 1254
Wainwright, Anthony J., 3207
Waisbord, Silvio, 2414
Waldeck, Jennifer H., 3237, 3324, 3645
Waldhart, Enid S., 2444, 2749
Waldron, Vincent R., 1231, 2435, 2644, 3310
Walker, Cynthia W., 2201
Walker, Felicia R., 1257
Walker, James R., 2206, 2506
Walker, Kandi L., 0114, 1126, 1418, 2118, 2518, 3628
Walker, Kasey L., 1215, 2245
Walker, Robyn C., 2135
Walker, Susan R., 3254
Wallace, James D., 1642, 2407, 3407
Wallace, Samuel P., 3149
Waller, Dennis R., 1442
Walls, Celeste M., 2619
Walsh, Susan, 1523
Walstrom, Mary K., 1607
Walters-Kramer, Lori A., 1514
Walton, Justin D., 2739
Walzer, Arthur E., 1144, 1272, 1372, 4244
Wander, Philip C., 1425, 2508, 2708
Wang, Hong, 2716, 3670
Wang, Jianglong, 2470
Wang, Mei-ling, 1370, 2136, 3570
Wang, Minmin, 3170, 4329
Wang, Pei, 3670
Wang, Shujen, 0815, 1439, 1659, 2759, 2815
Wanzer, Melissa B., 1654, 4154
Waples, David A., 4263
Ward, Allan L., 1460, 2244
Ward, Annalee R., 4233
Ward, Richard L., 1435, 3442
Wardrope, William J., 2239
Warnick, Barbara, 2178, 2516, 2671
Warren, John T., 1130, 1210
Warren, Kiesha T., 2234, 2521
Warren, Michael S., 2155
Warren Isenhart, Myra, 3161
Wartella, Ellen A., 1114, 1431, 2423, 2541, 2606, 4138
Wasser, Frederick, 1308
Watson, David R., 2241
Watson, Nessim J., 1142, 2614
Watt, Danette M., 2223
Watts, Eric K., 0724, 2130, 2721, 3136, 3633, 4125
Way, John, 3166
Weaver, James B., 1356, 3606
Webb, Dorothy, 4115
Webb, Lynne M., 0114, 0121, 1651, 2725
Webb Craft, Sondra, 2649
Weber, David E., 1252, 2607

Weber, Dawn, 1318
Weber, E. Sue, 1469, 1523
Weber, Keith, 3254
Weeks Simanski, Julie, 2412
Weger, Harry W., 4252
Weibel, John, 3671
Weigel, Beth A., 2507
Weigel, Daniel J., 2518, 2618, 4130
Weiler, Michael, 4122
Weinberg, Lee S., 2157, 2433
Weiner, Judith L., 3443
Weintraub, Sara C., 0418, 1154, 2226, 2626, 3212, 3418, 4118, 4225
Weiss, Denise, 1553
Weiss, Robert O., 2146, 3169, 3247, 3308
Welker, Linda S., 3110
Wells, Charles W., 1425
Wells, Scott D., 2639, 2739, 3201
Wells, Susan, 4208
Wendel, Nicole A., 2564, 4163
Wendt, Ronald F., 0178, 0724, 1563, 2322, 2732, 4125, 4208
Wendt, Ted A., 2322
Wenzlaff, Sue L., 1172, 1444
Werner, Teresa A., 1252, 1407
Wertheimer, Molly M., 0138, 1159
Wesley, Gina C., 2156, 3146
West, Daniel A., 3569
West, Lee, 2637, 3221
West, Richard L., 0418, 0815, 1231, 2151, 2226, 2535, 2626, 2742, 2815, 3151, 3418, 3646, 4118, 4354
Westerfelhaus, Robert G., 1343, 1563, 3240, 3661
Whalen, Henry, 2714
Whaley, Bryan B., 4127
Wharton, George C., 1542, 2442, 2642, 3546, 4342
Whedbee, Karen E., 1272
Wheeler, Gretchen E., 2229, 2473, 2753
Wheeler, Shannon, 1242
Wheeless, Lawrence R., 2638
Whillock, David E., 1322
Whillock, Rita Kirk, 1322
Whitchurch, Gail G., 0121
White, Dennis, 1322, 3172
White, Leah E., 2649, 3672, 4316
White, Mark B., 0946, 1421, 1646, 2130, 2246, 3633
White, Zachary M., 1664
Whitecap, Valerie A., 2114
Whitfield, Toni S., 2669, 3212
Whitmore, Brent A., 1665
Whitney, Elizabeth J., 0724, 1555, 1628, 3428, 4125, 4355
Whitt, Deborah L., 1118
Whitt, Ronald E., 1118
Whittemore, Joel T., 4222
Wickelgren, Bruce F., 2649, 3672, 4332
Wiebel, Jon, 3164
Wieder, D. Lawrence, 0116, 3640, 4334
Wiethoff, Carolyn M., 1355, 1445, 2412

Wightman, Carol, 1232
Wignall, Dennis L., 2607, 3324, 3407, 3546
Wildermuth, Sue M., 2453, 3270, 3507, 3649
Wiley, Stephen B., 2408
Wilkes-Carilli, Michelle, 2139, 4140
Wilkins, Amanda M., 2472
Willard, Barbara E., 1519
Willard, Charles A., 1351
Wille-Peterson, Jennifer L., 3627
Willets, Nancy J., 0418, 3418, 4118
Williams, Angie M., 2746
Williams, Christine, 3174
Williams, David C., 3315
Williams, David E., 1541, 2672
Williams, James, 3174
Williams, Jim B., 2574
Williams, Ken, 1107, 2107
Williams, Kimberly, 3430
Williams, L. Glen, 1649
Williams, Mary Lynn M., 1354, 1615
Williams, Mary Rose, 4235
Williams, Sheryl L., 3201
Williams, Susanne L., 2165, 2247, 3430
Williamson, L. Keith, 2749
Willihnganz, Shirley C., 1351
Willis-Rivera, Jennifer L., 0724, 2227, 3230, 4125
Wills, Caitlin M., 2253
Wills, Maggie A., 3526
Wilson, Amanda M., 4128
Wilson, Barbara J., 1114
Wilson, Gary B., 1316, 2668, 3416
Wilson, Georgia, 3667
Wilson, Paula J., 3222
Wilson, Steven R., 3310
Winbush, Ray, 1121
Winchatz, Michaela R., 0116, 2437
Windes, Russel R., 2534
Windt, Theodore O., 3315
Winebrenner, Terrence C., 2673
Winegarden, Alan D., 3142
Wingard, Leah, 2737
Winkler, Carol K., 2326, 2719, 3315
Winn, J. Emmett, 3406
Winn, Laura L., 2118
Wise, J. Macgregor, 1208, 1535
Wiss, Kathryn A., 2758
Withers, Lesley A., 3206
Witherspoon, Patricia, 1228, 2431
Witmer, Diane F., 1441, 2162, 2463, 3131, 3407, 3607
Witte, Kim, 2435
Wolf, Stacy E., 3510
Wolff, Karen M., 1428, 2243
Wolford, Lisa, 1616, 2311
Wolniewicz, Rebecca A., 3249
Wolski, Stacy L., 3256
Wolvin, Andrew D., 1326, 1530, 1634, 2742, 3646, 4326
Wong, Jean, 2437
Wong, Norman C. H., 3455, 3643

Wong, Wendy, 4108
Wong (Lau), Kathleen, 0418, 1659, 2133, 2529, 2759, 3418, 3659, 4116, 4118, 4225
Wongprasert, Tanichya K., 2126, 2555
Wood, Andrew F., 2107, 2464, 3531
Wood, Jennifer F., 1234, 2562, 3459
Wood, Jennifer K., 2306
Wood, Julia T., 0106, 1223, 2322, 2523, 4254
Wood, Roy V., 0133, 2415
Woodard, Emory H., 1114
Woods, Alicia, 3144
Woodward, Gary C., 3422
Woodyard, Jeffrey L., 1122, 2130, 2521, 2669, 3524, 3633
Woodyard, Kerith, 3272
Wooldridge, Deborah J., 3435
Woolsey, Mark J., 2673
Workman, Thomas A., 0724, 1227, 1330, 1432, 2165, 2231, 3116, 3531, 4125, 4132
Worley, David W., 1629, 2201, 2256, 2630, 4149
Worth, David S., 1206
Worthington, Debra L., 1166, 2167, 2267, 2428
Worthy, Shawn, 1440, 2507
Wotring, C. Edward, 3654
Wrench, Jason S., 1355
Wright, Kevin T., 1115, 2228, 2443, 2651
Wright, Mark H., 2214
Wright, Trina J., 1122, 2234
Wulff, Donald H., 2535
Wynn, Dianna R., 3407
Wzontek, Joanne, 1341
Xiao, Xiaosui, 1216
Yamazaki, Jane W., 2416, 2667, 4123
Yambor, Marjorie Lynne, 3506
Yammine, Pascal R., 2545
Yan, Wenjie, 2168
Yang, Fang-Chih, 3208
Yang, Hwei-Jen, 1142
Yaross Lee, Judith, 1164
Yastremski, David A., 2114, 3143
Yates, Guy P., 2753, 3273
Yeh, Becky, 2470
Yelsma, Paul L., 1418, 2618
Yep, Gust A., 0155, 0418, 0815, 1231, 1336, 2456, 2815, 3418, 4118, 4127, 4355
Yerby, Janet, 1318, 1449
Yi, Jung-Soo, 1516

Yin, Jing, 1416
Yoder, Donald D., 3149, 3549, 4249
Yoder, Joshua, 2270
Yokochi, Yumiko, 1416
Yook, Eunkyong L., 2555, 3539, 3639
Yoshimura, Stephen M., 3443
Young, Cory L., 2623, 3316
Young, Jennifer L., 4319
Young, Marilyn J., 3315
Young, Melissa J., 1656
Younger, Jan Joseph, 2740
Yousman, Bill, 3108
Yu, Hong-Sik, 1325
Yu, Xuejian, 4136
Yu, Yanmin, 2170, 3570
Yulis, Spiro G., 1157, 1406, 2525
Yum, Young-Ok, 3539
Yungbluth, Stephen, 2118
Zaeske, Susan M., 1419, 2429
Zaguidoulline, Marat, 2518
Zajacz, Rita, 1266
Zak, David, 3434
Zakel, Lori E., 0418, 1426, 2412, 2656, 2742, 3418, 3646, 4118
Zamanou-Erickson, Sonia, 1225, 2112
Zarefsky, David, 1160, 2326, 2719
Zaug, Pamela J., 1445, 2735
Zeidler, Tom, 3273, 4132
Zeigler, James, 3673
Zeilinski, Marian, 1201
Zelizer, Barbie, 2268
Zhang, Jianying, 3227
Zhang, Mei, 2670
Zhao, Yong, 1640
Zhong, Mei, 2201, 3670
Zickmund, Susan, 1472, 2718, 3657, 4319
Ziegelmueller, George W., 2753
Zilkha, Katerine A., 2636
Zillmann, Dolf, 1356
Zimmer, Eric A., 3542
Zimmerman, Mary, 2911
Zimmerman, Miriam L., 1542
Zindler, Debra, 1245
Zizik, Catherine H., 1526
Zlotkowski, Edward, 0123, 2125, 2669, 3314
Zompetti, Joseph P., 1153, 1344, 1572, 4153
Zorn, Theodore E., 0724, 1215, 2124, 2224, 2763, 3245, 4125
Zubric, Stephen J., 1506, 3256
Zuckerman, Cynthia E., 2435
Zulick, Margaret D., 2153

1999 DIRECTORY OF EXHIBITORS

Chicago Hilton & Towers

Thursday, November 4, 9:00 a.m. - 5:00 p.m.
Friday, November 5, 9:00 a.m. - 5:00 p.m.
Saturday, November 6, 9:00 a.m. - 4:00 p.m.

Exhibitor	Booth
Addison Wesley Longman	501
Allyn & Bacon	311-312
Association for Education in Journalism and Mass Communication	214
Basic Books	415
Bedford/St. Martin's	409-411
Burgess Publishing	508
Central States Communication Association	217
Communication Associates	215
C-SPAN	408
Eastern Communication Association	217
Educational Video Group	403
Greenhaven Press, Inc.	202
Greenwood Publishing Group	205
Guilford Publications	310
Hampton Press, Inc.	213
Harcourt College Publishers	203
Houghton Mifflin Company	404
International Communication Association	216
JAI/Ablex	506
Kendall/Hunt Publishing Company	313-316
Lambda Pi Eta	217
Lawrence Erlbaum Associates	413-414
Mack Printing Group	206
Mayfield Publishing	401-402
McGraw-Hill	502-503
Michigan State University Press	212
National Communication Association	207-209
Oxford University Press	507
Pearson Custom Publishing	416
Peter Lang Publishing	505
Rowman & Littlefield Publishers, Inc.	210
Roxbury Publishing Company	301
Sage Publications, Inc.	405-407
Southern Illinois University Press	204
Southern States Communication Association	217
State University of New York Press	412
Strata Publishing, Inc.	304
Taylor and Francis	504
University of Alabama Press	201
University of Chicago Press	302
University of South Carolina Press	303
University Press of America	211
Wadsworth Publishing	305-308
Waveland Press, Inc.	309
Western States Communication Association	217
Westview Press	415

Index Of Advertisers

PROGRAM ADVERTISERS

Advertiser	Page
Allyn & Bacon	394-395
Arizona State University	358
Basic Books	396
Bedford/St. Martin's	398-401
California State University, Northridge	130
Cleveland State University	130
Cornell University	392
Duquesne University	Inside back cover
Emerson College	397
Georgia State University	402
Greenwood Publishing Group	429
Guilford Publications	403
Hampton Press, Inc	404
Houghton Mifflin	405
Ithaca College	406
Kendall/Hunt Publishing Company	407
Kutztown University	222
Longman	408
Mayfield Publishing	410-411
McGraw Hill	409
Ohio University	412
Peter Lang Publishing	413
Rollins College	414
Rowman & Littlefield Publishers	415
Roxbury Publishing Company	416
Rutgers University	417
Southern Illinois University Press	418
State University of New York Press	222
Strata Publishing, Inc.	430
Texas Tech University	354
University of Alabama Press	420-421
University of Chicago Press	419
University of Illinois	Inside front cover
University of Maryland	422
University of Oklahoma	423
University of South Carolina Press	424
University of Southern California	425
University of Washington	354
Wadsworth Publishing Company	426-427
Waveland Press, Inc.	Back cover
Westview Press	428

Index

Innovations in Communication

NEW FROM ALLYN & BACON FOR 2000

Beebe & Beebe
PUBLIC SPEAKING:
An Audience-Centered Approach,
Fourth Edition

This text serves as a foundation in speechmaking as it guides students through every step of the process and narrows the gap between the classroom and the real world. Its distinctive and popular *audience-centered approach* emphasizes the importance of analyzing and considering the audience at every point along the way. This approach helps students to be constantly aware of and learn to adapt to the cultural, co-cultural, gender, and experiential diversity of their audiences. Numerous examples, excerpts, and sample speeches support the instruction, while recap boxes and end-of-chapter activities reinforce and extend the lessons of the text.

FEATURES

* Technology Advantage
  * New cutting-edge information about technology and public speaking, including the Speaker's Home-page, expanded coverage of electronic searches and databases, key guidelines on evaluating websites, and more!
  * Companion website *www.abacon.com/beebe* features links to related Internet sites and updates to links in the text, the *Virtual Classroom* bulletin board for students and instructors, speechmaking exercises and tips, and an online study guide.
* New material in Chapter 2 provides concrete sugges-tions for overcoming speech anxiety.
* A full chapter on ethics and Ethical Questions at the end of each chapter introduce students to ethical and free speech issues, as well as plagiarism and tolerance.

Bookstore Order #: 0-205-29559-2

SPEECH COMMUNICATION

DiSanza & Legge
BUSINESS AND
PROFESSIONAL COMMUNICATION:
Plans, Process, and Performance
Bookstore Order #: 0-205-29585-1

Frey, Botan & Kreps
INVESTIGATING COMMUNICATION:
An Introduction to Research Methods,
Second Edition
Bookstore Order #: 0-205-19826-0

Fujishin
THE NATURAL SPEAKER,
Third Edition
Bookstore Order #: 0-205-29575-4

Knapp & Vangelisti
INTERPERSONAL COMMUNICATION
AND HUMAN RELATIONS,
Fourth Edition
Bookstore Order #: 0-205-29573-8

Lulofs & Cahn
CONFLICT: From Theory to Action,
Second Edition
Bookstore Order #: 0-205-29030-2

Peterson
COMMUNICATING IN ORGANIZATIONS:
A Casebook, Second Edition
Bookstore Order #: 0-205-29589-4

Renz & Greg
EFFECTIVE SMALL GROUP COMMUNICATION
IN THEORY AND PRACTICE
Bookstore Order #: 0-205-28201-6

Richmond & McCroskey
NONVERBAL BEHAVIOR IN
INTERPERSONAL RELATIONS,
Fourth Edition
Bookstore Order #: 0-205-29577-0

Rybacki & Rybacki
ADVOCACY AND OPPOSITION:
An Introduction to Argumentation,
Fourth Edition
Bookstore Order #: 0-205-29583-5

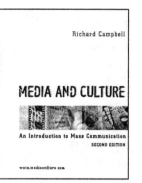
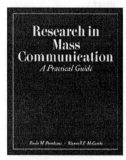

Available Now!

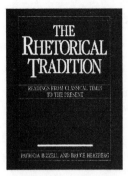

1990/CLOTH/1282 PAGES

THE RHETORICAL TRADITION
Readings from Classical Times
to the Present
Patricia Bizzell, _College of the Holy Cross_
Bruce Herzberg, _Bentley College_

This award-winning volume is the first comprehensive anthology of primary texts covering the history of rhetorical theory. 56 selections from 44 important figures provide a thorough survey from classical antiquity through the modern period. Substantial chapter introductions and headnotes for each period and selection provide social and intellectual context as well as a general grounding in the history of rhetorical theory.

New—Coming This Fall!

DECEMBER 1999
SPIRAL-BOUND
240 PAGES

A POCKET STYLE MANUAL
Third Edition
Diana Hacker, _Prince George's Community College_

Adopted at more than 1,300 schools across the country in more than 20 different academic departments, this inexpensive, quick reference to the essentials of research and writing in print and online is now revised and updated to be even more useful for students in all disciplines. Examples are drawn from a variety of disciplines to help students apply their writing skills to all types of assignments. A special ESL section addresses common trouble spots for nonnative speakers.

Already adopted at over 1,300 schools

DECEMBER 1999
SPIRAL-BOUND
240 PAGES

ONLINE!
A Reference Guide to Using Internet Sources
2000 Edition
Andrew Harnack and **Eugene Kleppinger**,
both of _Eastern Kentucky University_

The best-selling pocket guide to using Internet sources — now in a new edition — includes FAQs from students about using the Internet, a new chapter on distance learning, a new chapter on troubleshooting common Internet research problems, and more on evaluating electronic sources than is found in any other book.

BEDFORD/ST. MARTIN'S

1–800–446–8923 ■ www.bedfordstmartins.com

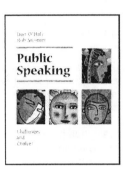

Innovative Texts for Communications

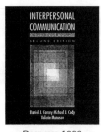

ANNOUNCING A NEW DOCTORAL PROGRAM IN

COMMUNICATION STUDIES

Georgia State University, located in the heart of Atlanta, is pleased to announce the creation of a new doctoral program in communication, commencing with the Fall 2000 semester. Our goal is to prepare students to integrate communication theory and research, whether they work in the university classroom or the communication industry boardroom.

DEGREE TRACKS

Studies in Public Communication
Students will study how new media technologies are transforming cultural persuasive practices. Coursework in mass communication, public argument, communication subcultures, political communication, new media, social movements, and international communication.

Studies in the Moving Image
Students will explore the transformation of the visual and performing arts in the digital age. Coursework in digital media studies, film theory, communication technology, interactive media, and performance studies.

GRADUATE FACULTY

Joseph Anderson (Iowa), *Film & Cognition*
Gayle Austin (CUNY) *Feminism / Performance Theory*
Jack Boozer (Emory) *Film Genres, Screenwriting*
David Cheshier (Iowa) *Public Argument, Rhetoric*
James Darsey (Wisconsin) *Rhetoric, Social Movements*
William Evans (Temple) *Discourse & New Media*
Shirlene Holmes (SIU) *African-American Performance*
Darin Klein (Pennsylvania) *Audience Research, Political Communication*
Greg Lisby (Tennessee) *Communication Law*
Marian Meyers (Iowa) *Media Studies, Feminism / Cultural Studies*
Ray Miller (Oregon) *Theater, Dance*
Lawrence Rifkind (Florida State) *Gender & Communication*
Mary Ann Romski (Kansas) *Language Development*
Sheldon Schiffer (USC) *Interactive Media*
Jaye Shaner (Kansas) *Communication Research, Communication & Aging*
Greg Smith (Wisconsin) *New Media Theory*
Sujatha Sosale (Minnesota) *International Communication, Mass Communication Theory*
Leonard Teel (GSU) *International Communication, Media History*
Frank Tomasulo (UCLA) *Film Theory, Politics & Film*
Carol Winkler, CHAIR (Maryland) *Public Argument, Visual Communication*

CONTACT

Director of Graduate Studies
Department of Communication
University Plaza
Georgia State University
Atlanta, Georgia 30303
404 / 651-3200

Visit the Department's Web Page
http://www.gsu.edu/~wwwcom/comm.html

Full Assistantship Support Available

Georgia State University, a unit of the Univ. System of Ga., is an equal opportunity educational institution and is an equal opportunity / affirmative action employer.

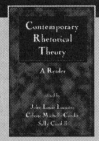

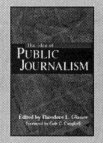

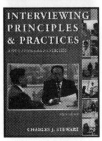

── Other new titles from Mayfield Publishing ──

Now Available!

Intercultural Communication in Contexts, Second Edition
by Judith N. Martin and Thomas K. Nakayama

This text addresses the core issues and concerns of intercultural communication by integrating three different perspectives: the social psychological, the interpretive, and the critical. A corresponding reader by the same authors is also available.

Coming Soon!

Communicating about Health: Current Issues and Perspectives
by Athena du Pré

This text outlines the research and theory of health communication and offers practical advice and examples to students.

Also from Mayfield...

▶ **Introduction to Mass Communication:** Media Literacy and Culture
  Stanley J. Baran

▶ **Readings in Mass Communication:** Media Literacy and Culture
  Kimberly Massey

▶ **Public Speaking in a Diverse Society,** Second Edition
  Patricia Kearney and Timothy G. Plax

▶ **Fundamentals of Communication,** Second Edition
  Melvin L. DeFleur, Patricia Kearney, and Timothy G. Plax

▶ **Group Communication:** Process and Analysis
  Joann Keyton

▶ **Perspectives on Family Communication**
  Lynn H. Turner and Richard West

▶ **Interviewing:** Speaking, Listening, and Learning for Professional Life
  Rob Anderson and George M. Killenberg

▶ **Nonverbal Communication:** Forms and Functions
  Peter A. Andersen

▶ **The World Wide Web:** A Mass Communication Perspective
  Barbara K. Kaye and Norman J. Medoff

Celebrate with Mayfield Publishing! Stop by our booth for an invitation to our party Friday night.

 Mayfield Publishing Company • 1280 Villa Street, Mountain View, CA 94041 (800) 433-1279 • www.mayfieldpub.com

OHIO UNIVERSITY

SCHOOL OF Interpersonal Communication

Set in the foothills of the Appalachian Mountains, Ohio University is the oldest university in the Northwest Territory and has one of the most prestigious graduate communication programs in the country. Established in 1960, the Ph.D. program in Interpersonal Communication was the second doctoral program created at OHIO.

Students in the program come from across the country and around the globe. Currently, there are 60 students in the program with representatives from China, Malaysia, Indonesia, Thailand, Japan, India, Korea, Canada, and Russia. Approximately 70 percent of the students receive financial awards.

The School offers degree programs leading to the B.S., M.A., or Ph.D., specializing in **organizational communication, rhetorical studies, communication theory,** and **interpersonal communication.** Programs incorporate both applied and theoretical approaches.

phone: 740.593.4825
e-mail: http://cscwww.cats.ohiou.edu/~incodept/

FACULTY

Roger Aden—Rhetorical Studies & Popular Culture
Christina Beck—Interpersonal & Health Communication
Charles Carson—Instructional Communication
Tom Daniels—Organizational Communication
Cedric Dawkins—Organizational Communication
David Descutner—Rhetorical Studies & Philosophy of
 Communication
Sue DeWine—Organizational Communication
Ted Foster—Persuasion
Elizabeth Graham—Interpersonal Communication
Claudia Hale—Interpersonal Communication & Mediation
Anita James—Organizational Communication
Margaret Killough—Health & Legal Communication
Judith Yaross Lee—Rhetorical Studies & American Studies
Raymie McKerrow—Rhetorical Studies
Jerry Miller—Political Communication
Daniel Modaff—Organizational Communication
Paul Nelson—Interpersonal Communication
Michael Papa—Organizational Communication
Wendy Papa—Organizational Communication
Nagesh Rao—Health & Intercultural Communication
Timothy Simpson—Intercultural Communication
Arvind Singhal—Interpersonal & Organizational Communication
J.W. Smith—Rhetoric, Public Address & Campaign Communication
Candice Thomas-Maddox—Interpersonal & Cross Cultural
 Communication
Ray Wagner—Rhetorical Studies

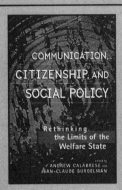

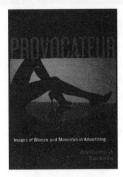

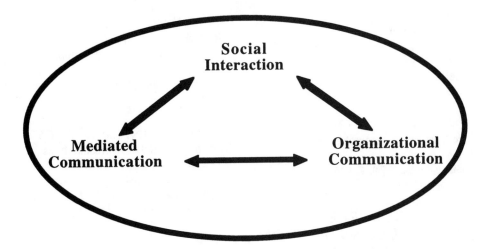

STUDIES IN RHETORIC AND COMMUNICATION

E. Culpepper Clark, Raymie E. McKerrow, and David Zarefsky, Series Editors

Addressing Postmodernity
Kenneth Burke, Rhetoric, and a Theory of Social Change

BARBARA A. BIESECKER

"Biesecker reveals Burke's energy and originality and her own talent in bringing understanding and significance to his theories. . . . An important source for rhetoricians, philosophers, and sociologists, this book will become a classic interpretation of Kenneth Burke's works."—*CHOICE*

144 pages   ISBN 0-8173-0874-1 $29.95 cloth

Lift Every Voice
African American Oratory, 1787–1900

EDITED BY PHILIP S. FONER AND ROBERT JAMES BRANHAM

"This collection testifies to the ongoing struggle against racial injustice, inequality, and prejudice, while the speeches themselves discredit assertions of black inferiority and white supremacy. Essential and enlightening reading for all Americans."—*Library Journal*

912 pages   ISBN 0-8173-0906-3 $24.95 paper

OF RELATED INTEREST

Voices in the Wilderness
Public Discourse and the Paradox of Puritan Rhetoric

PATRICIA ROBERTS-MILLER

"This book examines what has gone wrong with public discourse and deliberation in the United States using the American Puritans as a case study that informs our understanding of current practice."—Gregory Clark

Brigham Young University

240 pages   ISBN 0-8173-0939-X $34.95s cloth

Alabama NEW from   **THE UNIVERSITY OF ALABAMA PRESS**
Orders (773) 568–1550 • Fax orders (773) 660–2235
or (800) 621–8476 • www.uapress.ua.edu

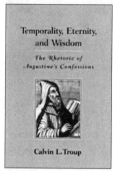 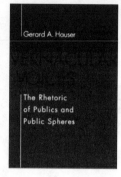  

COMMUNICATION

Speech Communication

**The Challenge of
Effective Speaking**
Eleventh Edition
Rudolph F. Verderber
0-534-56250-7

**Communication in
Our Lives**
Second Edition
Julia T. Wood
0-534-56070-9

**Communication Theories
in Action: An Introduction**
Second Edition
Julia T. Wood
0-534-51627-0

**Case Studies in Interpersonal
Communication:
Processes and Problems**
Dawn O. Braithwaite
and Julia T. Wood, Editors
0-534-56538-7

**Relational Communication:
Continuity and Change in
Personal Relationships**
Second Edition
Julia T. Wood
0-534-56160-8

Interpersonal Communication
Fourth Edition
Sarah Trenholm and Arthur Jensen
0-534-56151-9

**Intercultural Communication:
A Reader**
Ninth Edition
Larry A. Samovar
and Richard E. Porter
0-534-56241-8

**Argumentation and Debate:
Critical Thinking for Reasoned
Decision Making**
Tenth Edition
Austin J. Freeley
and David L. Steinberg
0-534-56115-2

**Communicating in Groups and
Teams: Sharing Leadership**
Third Edition
Gay Lumsden and Donald Lumsden
0-534-56232-9

**Communication Research:
Strategies and Sources**
Fifth Edition
Rebecca B. Rubin, Alan M. Rubin, and
Linda J. Piele
0-534-56169-1

Voice and Articulation
Fourth Edition
Kenneth C. Crannell
0-534-52354-4

Ask us about **Infotrac® College Edition!**

THE CUTTING EDGE OF COMMUNICATION

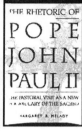

20% CONVENTION ATTENDEE DISCOUNT

20% CONVENTION ATTENDEE DISCOUNT

Theodore Parker
Orator of Superior Ideas
By David B. Chesebrough
Foreword by Mark A. Noll
Greenwood Press • 1999 • 0-313-30873-X • $65.00

The Public Journalism Movement in America
Evangelists in the Newsroom
By Don H. Corrigan
Praeger Publishers • 1999 • 240 pages
0-275-95781-0 • $59.95

Political Communication in America
Third Edition
By Robert E. Denton, Jr. and Gary C. Woodward
Praeger Paperback • 1998 • 328 pages
0-275-95783-7 • $22.95

Helen Keller, Public Speaker
Sightless But Seen, Deaf But Heard
By Lois J. Einhorn
Great American Orators, No. 23
Greenwood Press • 1998 • 184 pages
0-313-28643-4 • $55.00

Corporate Advocacy
Rhetoric in the Information Age
Edited by Judith D. Hoover
1998 PRide Award-Best Book in Public Relations,
National Communication Association Division of
Public Relations
Quorum Books • 1997 • 272 pages
1-56720-066-4 • $65.00

> For complete book and order information
> visit our webpage at www.greenwood.com

Communication Patterns in the Presidential Primaries
A Twentieth-Century Perspective
By Kathleen E. Kendall
(Praeger Series in Political Communication)
Praeger Publishers • 1999 • 0-275-94070-5 • $55.00E

Women and Mass Communications in the 1990's
An International, Annotated Bibliography
Compiled by John A. Lent
Greenwood Press • 1999 • 464 pages
0-313-30209-X • $79.50

Principal Photography
Interviews with Feature Film Cinematographers
By Vincent LoBrutto
Praeger Paperback • 1999 • 264 pages
0-275-94955-9 • $22.95

The Rhetoric of Pope John Paul II
The Pastoral Visit As a New Vocabulary of the Sacred
By Margaret B. Melady
Praeger Publishers • 1999 • 272 pages
0-275-96298-9 • $65.00

Campaign Strategies and Message Design
A Practitioner's Guide from Start to Finish
By Mary Anne Moffitt
Praeger Paperback • 1999 • 224 pages
0-275-96470-1 • $22.95

GPG GREENWOOD PUBLISHING GROUP INC
88 Post Road West • P.O. Box 5007 • Westport, CT 06881-5007
Telephone (203) 226-3571 • Office FAX (203) 222-1502

PLACE YOUR ORDER TOLL-FREE, 24 HOURS-A-DAY: 1-800-225-5800   AD99